Perspectives

on the United Arab Emirates

Perspectives

on the United Arab Emirates

Foreword
Clovis Maksoud

Editors
Edmund Ghareeb
Ibrahim Al Abed

Published by Trident Press Ltd
Text copyright ©1997: contributing authors/Trident Press Ltd.
Layout and design © Trident Press

Editors: Edmund Ghareeb, Ibrahim Al Abed
Editorial consultant: Peter Hellyer
Editorial assistant: Gabrielle Warnock
Production editor: Paula Vine

Published with the cooperation of the Higher Committee for the UAE Silver Jubilee and
the Ministry of Information and Culture, PO Box 17, Abu Dhabi, United Arab Emirates.
Tel: (9712) 453000; Fax: (9712) 450458. E-mail: mininfex@emirates.net.ae

The views expressed by the contributing authors are entirely their own and do not
necessarily reflect the opinions of the publishers or the UAE Government.

British Library Cataloguing in Publication Data
A CIP catalogue record for this book is available from the British Library

Editor's note:

*Transliteration of Arabic names needs some explanation. Since this is a multi-disciplinarian,
non-specialist text strict accuracy, especially as regards the use of the ayn and hamza, has
given way to general usage. In addition, proper names which have become institutionalized
in a certain form remain that way. This approach did not necessarily meet the requirements
of all contributors but aesthetics and common usage won out in the end.*

Trident Press Ltd, Standbrook House, 2- 5 Old Bond Street, London, WIX 3 TB
Tel: 0171 491 8770 Fax: 0171 491 8664 E-mail: tridentp@iol.ie

ISBN 1-900724-04-9

Contents

Foreword

Clovis Maksoud

My association with the United Arab Emirates goes back to the year 1976 when the late Seif Ghobash, then Minister of State for Foreign Affairs, invited me to address the newly established Institute for Diplomacy. The federation was five years old and already in the throes of development and social reconstruction.

The oil wealth augured challenge to the leadership, namely how to allocate resources and ensure a wide inclusion in the evolving welfare system introduced by Sheikh Zayed, the President of the UAE, and his associates in the burgeoning federation. Since then, I have had the opportunity to visit the Emirates and witness the steady progress, as well as the role the UAE was assuming within its Arab patrimony and in regional and international affairs.

Let me spell out what is accepted as genuinely meaningful to the Arabs as the federation continues to be a paradigm to be emulated at a moment in their history when division and acrimony tends to frustrate much of their legitimate aspirations and rights.

The concept of the federation was implemented in order to reconcile the urge for unity and the objective reality of varied conditions and historic experiences. In this respect the particularities of each of the constituent entities were factored into the legal framework of its Arab national identity. In other words, while uniformity of purpose was ascertained, the rigorous and overbearing constraints of conformity was avoided. A unity of diversity ensured the legitimacy of the new unifying structures and the unique socio-historical contribution of each of the emirates that formed this vibrant federation. These emirates asserted their Arab identity as justification for their unity and this entailed on the part of the UAE's leadership a deliberated involvement in affairs as they relate to a vision of a common Arab destiny. This explains why, for example, the UAE sought to professionalize its national commitments. The diplomatic institute was one of the means to train emerging cadres to communicate UAE's commitments and to ensure the maturing sense of national responsibility. This dual function was necessitated to service the UAE's policies pertaining to the Arab national purpose, the need for an enlightened Islamic solidarity, a dynamic presence in the Non-Aligned movement and a significant and persuasive role in the United Nations. Let me explain:

What is the Arab national purpose which the UAE seeks to serve? While the objective of Arab unity at this historical juncture is far-fetched, the UAE's policy is to act as a catalyst for coordination among Arab states, a conciliator of differences, a mediator of disputes, a provider of assistance for development and enhancement of political cohesion, a facilitator of institution building, an anchor for much of Arab talent, a home for the uprooted, a healer of many wounds inflicted on Palestinian Lebanese and a provider of generous contributions to learning centres and cultural undertakings. Among the latest endeavours was the innovative initiative on Jerusalem in November 1995 to bring into focus the future of this tormented and occupied city, to raise universal consciousness on its predicament and to accelerate awareness of the international responsibilities for its deliverance.

When the Iraqi regime invaded Kuwait the UAE was steadfast in its support for Arab legitimacy. Sharing strong feelings of disdain for President Hussein's behaviour, it never allowed its legitimate opposition to Iraq's invasion and policies to derail its deep and integral association with the people of Iraq.

The presence of many Arabs from several states to partake in the building of the institutional infrastructure, as well as in the overall social fabric, made a deep impression on the Arab conscience and wove a wide sense of appreciation of the wisdom associated normally with the attitudes and policies of the UAE.

Sheikh Zayed, is like all his citizens, deeply religious. To the UAE, Islam not only defines individual relations with his or her creator it is, in addition, an enriching spiritual experience, a moral code for sensible behaviour and enlightened existence. Islam, in this respect, eschews violence, abhors reckless fanaticism and disclaims excessive zealotry. It is this understanding of Islam that explains the UAE's openness and hospitality, its tolerance of diversity, its willingness to interact while at the same time conserving its tradition, its propensity to access while in the meantime preserving and protecting its defining constraints. From this optic the UAE has been in the vanguard of promoting Islamic solidarity, empowering Muslims throughout the world and strongly bringing to the forefront Islam's authenticity and its universal relevance and values. This explains UAE's role in the Organization of Islamic Conference and the strong bonds that the UAE has with various Muslim countries and societies.

Herein lies one of UAE's problems with Iran's claim to the three islets, a dispute in which both the UAE and lately Iran are hoping for a peaceful resolution. For many generations, trade and commerce, were and continue to be, a growing determinant of social and cultural relations between Iran and the UAE, especially with the vital Emirate of Dubai. When the federation was formed these relationships remained intact while Iran experienced a major transformation after its revolution in 1979. While Iraq and Iran were engaged in a violent and a vengeful role, the UAE was eager to advocate the need for conciliation among Muslim states. Notwithstanding its natural identification with Arab Iraq, the UAE never allowed any contradiction between the Arab national identity to diminish its responsibility to contribute and enhance Islamic solidarity.

Iraq's regime's invasion of Kuwait in August 1990 jolted the entire Arab nation and inflicted a most painful wound on the concept of Arab nationalism, in the same manner that conflict between Muslim states tended to debilitate Islamic solidarity. Painstakingly, the UAE continued to pursue a healing policy with both constituencies to which it proudly belongs and is eager to serve. Sheikh Zayed's personal role in the pursuit of bringing to both the Arab and Muslim worlds, and within each, a sensible balance in attitudes and policies has been significant. This translates that anger with Iraq's government's behaviour should never evolve into support for measures that hurt the Iraqi people and dismember the Iraqi state. By the same token the UAE's genuine grievance and complaint of Iran's hegemonic policies should not obscure the bonds of the common spiritual experience, the degree of cultural affinity and the vision of a shared neighbourhood. This perception of commonality has prevented the endemic disputes of the three islets from derailing the constancy of the vision.

The UAE is, as a result of the oil boom, considered a wealthy state. Within the Emirates there are inevitable economic discrepancies. The thrust of the federation's development policy is characterized by the urge to optimize complementarity among the seven federated emirates while enabling each to sustain its respective individuality. Herein lies the roots of the UAE's sense of responsibility within and towards the poorer countries and societies. It is this awareness of responsibility that made the UAE play a pivotal role in development projects and a variety of assistance and philanthropic programmes. As the UAE's President Sheikh Zayed pioneered the movement to support educational and cultural programmes at national and international levels many successful entrepreneurs followed his example and initiated creative projects in several fields. Besides the Zayed Foundation, mention should be made of one of the best private collection of books, documents and original texts in the entire Arab and Muslim worlds founded by Juma Al Majid in Dubai. In addition to Al Majid's private collection and library, the many benefactors throughout the Emirates of cultural prizes, festivals and the majestic Cultural Foundation in Abu Dhabi where lectures, seminars, exhibitions, concerts and symposia are held and where participants from all over the Arab world and Global South countries are drawn, give the Emirates' citizens and residents exposure to diverse cultural experiences making them more appreciative of their own roots and heritage, and diminishing any insular disposition.

True, the UAE's generosity was spontaneous, however there were instances of minor breaches of trust from those who, misreading hospitality for vulnerability, sought to exploit and abuse their welcome. This led the UAE to channel its assistance into institutional frameworks and project-oriented programmes which enabled it to clearly uncover the sycophant and rediscover the authentic. This meant that elementary goodness became less prone to being taken advantage of, rendering this goodness a valuable advantage for the state and its society within the Emirates itself and for the world to which the UAE belongs.

The 'world' of the UAE is not confined to its basic Arab identity, the Islamic constituency and the Global South - formerly Non-Aligned, but also the international community represented by the United Nations. True all independent states belong to the UN, true also that most of the UN members contribute to its deliberations and budget; true finally that many are recipients of UN agencies' advice and assistance, but there are some states that are actively engaged in promoting and pursuing the values enshrined in its Charter.

When I served at the UN during the 1980s as the Arab League's representative, I was witness and privy to the United Arab Emirates' role as a conciliator within the Arab group and as a dynamic activist when the UAE became a member of the UN's Security Council.

Here again the 'sensible centre' which characterized its position and policies within the region were amplified in the positions it took and policies it adopted both in the General Assembly and in the Security Council. The UAE's special role in enhancing the status of the Palestinians, diplomatically, economically and legally, was among the factors that made the momentum of support for the Palestinian cause in the UN so impressive. On a personal note, I can testify that the UAE's mission to the UN was consistently in the vanguard of mobilizing our Arab group. Its legal Counsel, the late Burhan Hammad, was mandated by the Chief of UAE's Mission at the UN to be always at the disposal of all the Arab members. For the record, Burhan, a Palestinian, indicated to us that in the UAE mission to the UN, he felt at home serving his homeland's cause from the diplomatic vantage he occupied. This 'feeling at home' is shared by the thousands of Arab citizens living, working, building, teaching, trading and investing in the United Arab Emirates. The building boom in the various cities of the Emirates testifies to the mettle of Arab engineering and architecture. Schools that are run by Lebanese, Palestinians and Egyptians are models of excellence preparing the children of the UAE to reinforce and improve the emerging University system.

The 'feeling at home' is deeply felt in the welcoming climate that the media enjoys in the UAE. It is here that all the branches of the media express and articulate the deeply felt thoughts of the Arab people and their aspirations. Suffice to mention the editorials of *Al-Khaleej*, published in Sharjah, the Satellite TV of Dubai, the educational TV of Sharjah, the widespread Arab and international news of *Al-Ittihad* and Abu Dhabi TV, and many radio programmes and journals dealing with women's issues, environment and social change. In this field of information and communication, an example of Arab intellectual community exists and performs.

English papers published by many of the Arab publishing houses service the interests of the guest communities, especially those from the countries of the Indian sub-continent. They serve a dual purpose - keeping them abreast of developments in their countries of origin and of those developments in their county of residence. In many ways they constitute a bridge by which understanding is forged between the Gulf states, the Arab states and the vital and important subcontinent in Asia. And if a spillover touches their citizens, whether business, professional, or diplomats from the West, it would be beneficial for all concerned that Arab opinions expressed in these media outlets are understood.

On the twenty-fifth anniversary of the foundation of the United Arab Emirates, in 1996, one celebrated the 'sensible centre', the steadfastness of commitment to the rights and hopes of the entire Arab patrimony, the enlightened expression of its Islamic experience and devotion, the steadiness of its reconciliation of tradition with the imperative of modernization, the subtle dignity of its international relations and the collective wisdom of a leadership that forged the federation of the United Arab Emirates just over 25 years ago.

Introduction

Edmund Ghareeb

Following the withdrawal of the British from the Arabian Gulf, a prominent Middle East specialist predicted that the region was likely to face 'great upheaval', as a result of which 'existing boundaries and traditional regimes' could not be expected to survive. He also predicted that 'there is no realistic possibility of the present Gulf rulers coming together of their own accord in any political grouping worth talking about'.

The Arab side of the Gulf to which this seasoned observer referred has witnessed great upheaval. The region as a whole has experienced the Dhofar rebellion, the Iranian Revolution, the Iraq-Iran War, the Yemeni War, and the Iraq invasion of Kuwait. Most significant of all is the impact of the Arab-Israeli conflict and its consequences.

But the United Arab Emirates (UAE) has emerged as one of the few successful ventures in Arab unity. At the time of its establishment in 1971, many foreign observers doubted the ability of the UAE to survive for even a few months, let alone a few decades, and predicted that it would go the way of the ill-fated Federation of Arab Emirates of the South which was formed in 1967. The UAE has defied this grim prediction. The federation has not merely endured as the longest surviving pan-Arab union, but has experienced one of the most remarkable, rapid, and dramatic socio-economic periods of development in the history of the region.

On the eve of its establishment, the UAE had very few institutional infrastructures upon which a federal state could build. All federal ministries had to be constructed from the ground up. The foreign ministry started with the minister and a staff of three. The problem was further complicated by the lack of experienced and skilled personnel. As late as the 1950s, the Emirates had only one school, and by 1971 the number of local college graduates scarcely numbered a hundred. The country lacked adequate roads, medical services, electricity and sewage facilities. Banking, transportation and communication facilities and services were almost non-existent.

Today, the UAE may be considered one of the fastest growing economies in the region, with a highly developed modern infrastructure that ranges from the largest man made port to a system of communications linking every part of the country to the region and the world. Four lane highways unite all corners of the state, while six international airports provide easy access to the rest of the world, putting an end to the isolation long experienced under British control. Modernization and urbanization have brought about dramatic changes in thinking and political outlook which have greatly contributed to the consolidation of its political system.

Prior to the discovery of oil, few outside the region had heard of the Emirates and of the other Gulf countries. Yet its location at the centre of the world's great trade routes between Asia, Africa and Europe and its central position in the Gulf gave it strategic importance. This strategic importance is partly due to the legacy of the region's ancient history as a trading centre which goes back to the fourth millennium BC; but in modern history the Portuguese, Dutch, French, and finally British traders vied with each other to deal with established Arab traders for control of the lucrative sea trade routes with India and the Far East.

For the British, the lower Gulf was a vital link for communications and trade, while serving as a centre for control of the routes to India. However local rulers and traders who had been engaged in active privateering (often called piracy by the British) challenged Britain's attempt to maintain dominance in the region, in a movement which expressed local resentment against British economic interference and military intervention. Prior to the nineteenth century, the Qawasim fleet, which was composed of over 700 large and small ships, transported goods and people between Gulf ports, India and East Africa, challenged the British entry into the Gulf. This led to a period of on-going confrontations. The people of the region, whose economy before oil depended on pearling, fishing, and agriculture, relied extensively on trade. The British, using gunboat diplomacy, responded to the local challenge by destroying the al-Qawasim fleet and the fort at Ras al-Khaimah. To maintain its dominance in the region and to gain local cooperation, Britain opposed outside intervention and entered into a series of maritime agreements with the rulers. These agreements referred to the lands of Arab rulers as the Trucial coast. While the British presence curbed local rivalries, it caused the isolation of the region for the next 150 years and established British pre-eminence in the area.

Following the discovery of oil in the 1950s and its increased value in the 1970s, the Arab Gulf countries entered into a period of economic prosperity which enhanced their political position and independence. In 1968, owing to mounting economic difficulties at home and growing anti-colonial sentiments in the Arab World, Britain announced the intention of withdrawing its military presence from the area east of the Suez by 1971. Its withdrawal from India, and the Suez debacle in 1956, had already weakened its position in the Middle East. As Britain's attempt to create an elaborate defence scheme linking Kenya, Bahrain, Sharjah and Singapore ended in failure, it decided to give up its protectorate over Kuwait in 1961, retaining control only of the Trucial States, Qatar and Bahrain. In 1967 Britain withdrew from Aden. The next three years were characterized by much political manoeuvring illustrating the interplay of local and regional forces.

In 1968, Sheikh Zayed of Abu Dhabi and Sheikh Rashid of Dubai agreed to merge their states and called on the rulers of Sharjah, Ajman, Umm al-Qaiwain, Fujairah, and Ras al-Khaimah, as well as Qatar and Bahrain to unite. The two leaders, Sheikh Zayed and Sheikh Rashid, were motivated not only by the British decision to withdraw, but also by the Gulf situation and the Arab regional environment. The threat of radical movements in Oman and in South Arabia were a matter of concern, as their wealth and small size might invite external interference. Historic territorial and dynastic rifts between Bahrain and Qatar prevented them from joining the union. Instead each opted for independence. In July 1971, six of the seven remaining emirates decided to unite, and the United Arab Emirates was officially inaugurated on 2 December 1971. Ras al-Khaimah joined the union in February 1972.

From its inception the union faced serious internal and external challenges. Tribalism, internal tribal rivalries and conflicts, immense sudden wealth, and rapid social change threatened its stability from within while externally, being born into a turbulent and uneasy regional environment, it was faced with hostile and reluctant neighbours, as well as with territorial and security problems. The question was raised as to how this pluralistic system would work, and whether it could survive.

Saudi Arabia, which had close ties with Qatar and Bahrain, had favoured a union of the nine states. Moreover, it had a territorial dispute with Abu Dhabi. It therefore refused to recognize the declared Union. Two days before the establishment of the UAE, Iran, which had territorial designs and political ambitions to play the role of a regional superpower, moved to occupy the Greater and Lesser Tunbs belonging to Ras al-Khaimah. It also had made claims on Sharjah's island of Abu Musa. To the south and east, the Sultanate of Oman was facing a serious insurgency led by the leftist Dhofar Liberation Front. Owing to all these circumstances, the leaders of the UAE decided to establish ties and seek the acceptance and support of the larger Arab world and beyond. These moves formed the basis of the UAE's Arab and foreign policy which has generally remained constant over the years.

Despite predictions to the contrary, the UAE did not collapse. Instead it has grown stronger and more unified over the past 25 years. The factors pushing for unity and integration have been greater than the forces of divisiveness and disintegration. The country has succeeded in overcoming complex internal problems and rivalries and while some internal disagreements remain, they no longer pose a threat to stability.

The continued success of this experiment is due to a number of factors: one of these is the invaluable role played by the founding fathers, led by Sheikh Zayed, his fellow rulers, and a handful of highly talented and dedicated advisors who helped to set the Emirates on a course characterized by moderation and realism. They played a major role in drawing up the Provisional Constitution and in laying the foundations for a modernized state.

The founding fathers were aware that the Union was small in size and in population, and that its new found oil wealth made it vulnerable to outside threats. They realized that they would have to depend on their own elements of strategy. Aware of the difficulty of trying to unite disparate and, at times, competing interests too quickly, the rulers pursued a policy described by the late Professor Enver Koury as 'functionalism'. This process began by integrating under the federal umbrella the least controversial areas such as communications and social services. These were measures likely to promote a common national bond and identity, and to enhance the role of the central authorities and institutions. In addition, there existed a core unit headed by a leader with a strategic Unionist mission. The federated states are linked together by their common social structure, their geographic contiguities, and by their political and social characteristics. The majority of people share an Arab, Muslim and tribal heritage as well as similar social and economic goals. The federation, benefiting from the homogenous cultural and social nature of society, has grown stronger. The combination of all these factors has led to a gradual acceptance of the Union, even by those who had doubts about it. Furthermore, a new generation has grown up which knows only the federation and its institutions and symbols.

The effectiveness and expansion of federal institutions and responsibilities, particularly those which touch the lives of the citizens of the country, contributes to a sense of common identity and greater national cohesion. The UAE's abundant oil wealth, which has been the driving engine of the country's social and economic modernization, has served to reconcile rivalries and to cement relations between competing interests. Recognizing that oil is a depletable commodity, the UAE has been diligently pursuing a policy of economic diversification. The progress in fields such as housing, health education, communication and transportation has helped to weld the country into a firmly linked whole, while the very idea of the Union has become a living and irreversible reality to a populace affected by modernization and urbanization.

The commitment of the rulers of the wealthier states to the concept of unity, along with their willingness to share the benefits of oil wealth with the poorer states, has further strengthened the political system. The UAE's tolerance, liberality and openness to its Arab neighbours has also strengthened its regional position. The inherited territorial disputes with Saudi Arabia and Oman have been resolved peacefully and replaced with a policy of bilateral cooperation and coordination through the Gulf Corporation Council (GCC). These two countries are among the UAE's closest allies and largest trading partners. To avoid tensions, good neighbourliness has been given priority over self-interest. The UAE's unresolved territorial dispute with Iran has not been allowed to overshadow ties, and the search for a peaceful solution to the conflict continues unabated.

Another factor which has contributed greatly to the survival of the Union is the recognition that there are no viable alternatives. The cost of going it alone in such a regional environment is too high. The desire to work together has been reinforced by the turbulent events witnessed in the region from the Arab-Israeli Wars, the Iranian Revolution, the Afghan War, the Iraq-Iran War, the Gulf War and the Yemen War. The violent upheavals, fragmentation and political dislocations experienced by some countries in the area have only served to encourage the people of the UAE to hold fast to their unity in order to avoid similar tragedies.

Economic liberalism, laissez-faire economics and the UAE's role as an important international trading centre have further strengthened this role. The founding of the GCC has induced the UAE to change many of its laws and regulations in order to be able to deal with the requirements of the GCC on a state to state level. The nature of the federal system, while frustrating at times, usually allows for diverse processes and viewpoints. This has led to a more tolerant and open atmosphere which has greatly contributed to the success of the union's federal experiment.

The UAE is living in a turbulent area and could not possibly be immune to the regional environment. Consequently, policies aimed at achieving domestic prosperity and friendly ties with the countries of the region and the world have been diligently pursued. These policies have both strengthened internal stability and enhanced the UAE's regional role. Internally, the UAE has continued to consolidate and enhance the role of the Federal Government and to eliminate differences among its emirates. However, the saturation of the labour market with foreign workers poses a challenge to the country's social stability and security. The Federal Government is constantly seeking ways to reduce dependence on foreign labour and to check illegal immigration. Adopted since independence, its economic system has been consolidated. Policies on taxation, employment, free health care and education, and large investments in the infrastructure have helped to create the right environment for economic growth.

In recent years a number of studies have been written on the Gulf countries by academics, journalists, businessmen and travellers. Most of these studies have focused on the larger countries such as Iran, Iraq, Saudi Arabia and, more recently, on Kuwait. Other states of the same region have not received the attention they deserve. Only a small number of scholarly books have been published on the UAE and most of these works are now either dated or out of print. For this reason we felt that an up-to-date country survey was needed. It is hoped that this work, written by a number of prominent academics and specialists, will provide both an historical and geographical background and an account of socio-economic developments and foreign policy in the UAE, thus filling a gap in information on one of the most successful new countries to have emerged since the Second World War.

In his preface, Clovis Maksoud brings to the forefront the view of an Arab scholar-diplomat who has closely observed the working of the UAE since its early days. He outlines this evolution and its meaning to the Arab region and to the wider Islamic world.

The physical transformation of the UAE's landscape through the aeons is unfolded in the chapter by Kenneth Glennie who describes the geological history of the country's dramatic mountains; its salt-dome islands, several of which are associated with important gas and oil fields; as well as the process of sedimentation which formed the sand dunes and salt flats, especially the effects of high-latitude glaciation and melting which alternately dried out and flooded the Arabian Gulf.

Pursuing a different but complementary area of study, Daniel Potts examines the archaeology and history of the UAE in the period ranging from 7000 BC to 676 AD. Potts traces the artefactual, architectural, faunal and botanical record of settlement, highlighting local developments and important relationships with neighbouring areas such as India, Iran, Bahrain and Mesopotamia.

Geoffrey King continues with an account of the history and related archaeology of the UAE during the Islamic period. He examines the conditions of the region and its cultural and political framework at the time of the rise of Islam, including the evidence of the recently excavated monastery at Sir Bani Yas. Particular use is made of the Arabic source material and the evidence of recent fieldwork in Abu Dhabi, Ras al Khaimah and other emirates during the time of the Prophet and the first Caliphs.

Frauke Heard-Bey provides two inter-related chapters: the first focuses on the role of tribalism in UAE society, discussing the dispersal of different tribal groups, their specialization in certain economic activities, and their adaptation to the environment through the development of ways to exploit its meagre resources whether in the mountains, on the coast or in the desert.

Frauke Heard-Bey's second chapter carries the historical account through to the post-imperial period. After the First World War the British consolidated their position in the Gulf, leading to new agreements with the rulers and to a heightened British role. In examining the period following the Second World War, the author argues that the UN-inspired spirit, coinciding with the exploration and eventual production of oil, led to modest British development efforts which proved helpful during initial phases of the federation's formation.

Indicating that the establishment of the Union did not occur in a vacuum, Ibrahim Al Abed traces the early federation and cooperation proposals among the smaller Gulf states back to 1937. He shows how those proposals and other efforts stirred much interest and debate among the people and the rulers and how they paved the way for the establishment of the UAE in 1971. He provides an in-depth historical background to the formation, consummation and emergence of the UAE, concentrating particularly on the federal system and the powers given to it under the Constitution. Al Abed argues that the federation has become a way of life.

Malcolm Peck discusses both the circumstances under which the UAE was formed and the institutions of the federation. He argues that the 1971 Constitution blends the Western presidential and parliamentary systems with little apparent connection to the tribal system and traditional modes of decision-making such as *shura* and *ijma* which have, nevertheless, helped to shape the role of the new institutions.

The UAE's role in the United Nations and its relationship with the World Trade Organization and other international organizations is the focus of Jenab Tutunji's contribution. The UAE's ties with the Gulf Cooperation Council, the Arab League and OPEC are analysed in terms of its relationship with the UN and the relationship of each of those bodies with the others; the perspective adopted is based on the structure of national interests and the obstacles to collective action.

William Rugh's chapter provides a well structured overview of the basic components which make up the UAE's foreign policy. The role of Sheikh Zayed bin Sultan Al Nahyan and his style of leadership in guiding the country's foreign policy since its inception is discussed in depth. In addition, a number of specific foreign policy cases of the UAE over the past 25 years are analysed, as is the UAE's relations with other Gulf states, Iran, Iraq and other countries.

The dispute with Iran over the three islands, the Greater and Lesser Tunbs and Abu Musa, and its legal dimensions is discussed by Mohamed Al Roken. He lists Iran's historic and legal arguments to justify its takeover of the islands and points out that these arguments are legally weak and that the use of force to occupy the islands is illegitimate. Recently, the UN Secretary General offered his good offices should the two parties seek mediation, and the UAE has offered to bring the issue before the International Court of Justice. This suggestion has been rejected by Iran. Al Roken warns against any attempt at internationalizing the dispute because the consequences would bring about tensions that would prevail all over the Gulf.

Mohamed Shihab's chapter enumerates and analyses the factors which have led to rapid socio-economic transformation within the UAE over the past 25 years, producing an income level comparable to that of industrialized countries. An abundance of natural resources in oil and gas provided the revenues for the state to grow in an unconventional manner. A 'once-for-all' strategy of social and economic infrastructural development rapidly took place, leading to significant advancements in education and health, in agriculture, to industrialization, increased employment, urbanization, a transformation of domestic demand and production, and a burgeoning of foreign trade.

Mouza Ghubash's chapter explores a number of relevant and significant themes on social development in the UAE and raises important issues surrounding the role tradition plays in development. Her exploration on the relationship between social institutions and tribalism presents unusual and little known facts about this topic.

Ali Al Sadik's chapter provides an in-depth analysis of the economy of the UAE and its evolution since independence. The author provides useful statistics such as the rate of growth of the GDP with and without the oil sector's contribution. He also deals with challenges facing the country such as the high percentage of expatriates in the labour force and the need for further economic diversification.

The history and development of the UAE's oil and gas industry and its relations with OPEC and with the international oil and gas companies are analysed by Philip Barnes. In its pursuit of a consistent and innovative policy of determining and fully exploiting its energy resources, the UAE has been able to expand its production capabilities and maximize the value of its oil on the international market. This forward looking policy is unlikely to change according to Barnes. He further argues that the plans for the oil and gas industry will allow the country to continue to move forward on solid economic grounds.

Evolution of The Emirates' Land Surface: an Introduction

Kenneth W. Glennie

Introduction

With the exception of the Omani territory in the north-eastern Ru'us al Jibal (Musandam Peninsula) and north-central Oman Mountains, the United Arab Emirates (UAE) occupies a broad strip of land flanking the southern shores of the Arabian Gulf between the Qatar Peninsula and the Gulf of Oman. Much of that land consists of relatively low-lying rolling dunes and interdune areas forming the north-eastern limit of the Rub' al-Khali (Empty Quarter of Saudi Arabia), which reach 150 m above sea level in the region to the north of Al-Liwa. In the northern emirates, the dunes extend up to the Oman Mountains. To the south-east, however, the eastern limit of the dunes coincides approximately with the Oman border, where they overlie the *deflated* (wind eroded) surface of sub-horizontal fluvial sediments that had earlier been transported westward from the mountains (Fig. 1).

   A general lack of rainfall ensures that most of Arabia is a desert. Summer temperatures can approach 50°C on the Gulf coast of the Emirates, where relative humidity averages between 50 and 60 per cent. Inland, however, temperatures can exceed 50°C and relative humidity be less than 20 per cent (United Arab Emirates University). Over the western lowlands of the Emirates, annual rainfall is mostly less than 40 mm. In Al-Ain the mean annual rainfall is 96 mm and yet the potential yearly evaporation is over 3000 mm (*op.cit.* Plate 44). With a high rate of evaporation and an annual rainfall over the Oman Mountains that rarely reaches 200 mm, this highland area, which has elevations within the Emirates of over 1500 m, must also be classified as desert; its desert status is emphasized by its surface of almost continuous barren rock and a sparse vegetation confined mostly to the floors of wadis.

   With the exception of the south-western Ru'us al-Jibal, the rocks exposed within the mountains of the Emirates differ markedly from those that contain deeply buried oil and gas fields in the west and beneath the southern Gulf. Also, the extensive plains of fluvial sediments that flank the mountains are evidence of a former, much wetter, climate than is indicated by the younger dune sands and salt-covered sabkhas that overlie their extremities. The history of deposition and deformation of these rock units, the much more recent evidence of rapid changes in climate from very humid to hyper-arid, together with the geological processes that culminated in today's desert surface, form the topic of the following pages.

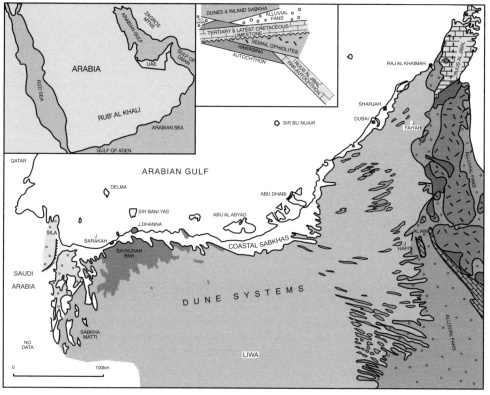

Fig. 1. Simplified geological map of the United Arab Emirates. Inset diagram indicates some of the complex geometrical relationships between rock units of the mountains and flanking areas. See also Table 1.

Mountain and Subsurface Geological Framework

The subsurface

The oldest exposed rocks underlie the whole of the Emirates except the Oman Mountains and immediate flank areas; they are seen at only two localities on the mainland, Jabal Ali south-west of Dubai and Jabal Dhanna in the western part of Abu Dhabi, but also occur on several offshore islands (e.g. Sir Bani Yas, Sir Bu Nuair; Fig. 1). These *jabals* and islands are dome-shaped at the surface and are cored by Hormuz Salt (named after similar salt on Hormuz Island in the Straits of Hormuz). The salt was deposited almost 600 million years ago on the floor of an almost enclosed sea when evaporation resulted in its water becoming super-saturated with respect to *halite* (common salt) (see also Glennie 1987: Fig. 12a). About 20 million years before the present (20 *Ma BP*), the Red Sea was also floored by salt in a similar way. Salt can flow and, unlike the sedimentary rocks that overlie it, cannot be compacted with increased depth of burial. For this reason, the salt is now less dense than most of its overburden and, using any vertical weakness, penetrates upward *(diapirism)* through the overlying rock sequence to form *salt domes* at the surface. In the south-eastern Gulf, the source of the diapiric Hormuz salt now lies at a depth of some 10 km (Beydoun 1991). *Hydrocarbon source rocks* of similar age occur in Oman, and may be present in the Gulf area, but because of deep burial must long since have generated their oil and gas. Several of the offshore salt domes are associated with the occurrence of oil and gas where *reservoir rocks* have been deformed by the rising salt to create a *trap* (e.g. Umm Shaif, Zakum).

Arabia, as part of the megacontinent *Gondwana,* was located south of the Equator throughout the Palaeozoic era (Table 1). Initially it was geometrically 'up-side-down' (Fig. 2) relative to the poles as Gondwana moved south across the south pole (and came up the other side the 'right-way up') under the influence of *plate-tectonic* processes (see below). Because Arabia's southern traverse was undertaken largely in temperate latitudes, most of the Palaeozoic rocks comprise sandstones and shales, a small exposure of which occurs in Jabal Rann, south-west of Dibba. Hydrocarbon source rocks of Silurian age are known in both Oman and Saudi Arabia, and might be viable for the generation of oil also in western Abu Dhabi.

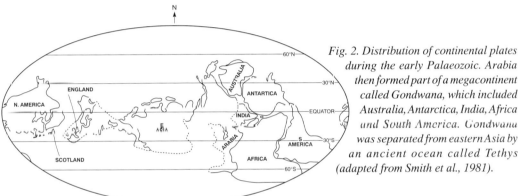

Fig. 2. Distribution of continental plates during the early Palaeozoic. Arabia then formed part of a megacontinent called Gondwana, which included Australia, Antarctica, India, Africa and South America. Gondwana was separated from eastern Asia by an ancient ocean called Tethys (adapted from Smith et al., 1981).

In complete contrast, between the Late Permian (about 260 Ma BP) and Late Miocene (part of Neogene on Table 1; about 5-10 Ma BP), Arabia slowly drifted northwards across the Tropics, where warm, shallow, tropical seas were ideal for the growth of corals and other shallow-marine creatures with calcareous shells; their accumulation after death led to the formation of varieties of *limestone.* Depending partly on a water depth that varied with time, the sea floor was intermittently covered by a variety of rocks that included organic-rich muds, mostly of Jurassic and Cretaceous age, but also some Triassic formations, which later became the source of hydrocarbons (oil and gas) now stored in porous carbonate rocks (limestones and *dolomites)* (see Table 1). Reservoir rocks range in age from the Late Permian (Khuff Formation) to the Jurassic, where the Arab reservoirs are important, and Cretaceous (Shuaiba, Mauddud and Mishrif), to the Lower Tertiary (Pabdeh Formation). Seals, preventing the relatively buoyant hydrocarbons from escaping to the sea floor, cap the reservoirs. The best of these are *evaporites* such as *gypsum* and *anhydrite* inter-bedded with the different Arab reservoir horizons, or the overlying latest Jurassic Hith Formation (Al Silwadi et al. 1996). These seals were probably deposited on extensive coastal sabkhas similar to those now found along the shore and on the offshore islands of Abu Dhabi (Alsharhan & Whittle 1995).

For source rocks to become *mature* and give up their oil, they need to be buried to a depth where the temperature approaches that of boiling water (about 3 km, depending on the local *temperature gradient* through the underlying rock sequence). At a depth of around 4 km, it starts to become mature for gas production but post-mature for the generation of oil, and by

AGE Ma	PERIOD	PLATFORM AREA ① — GROUP	PLATFORM AREA — FORMATION	MUSANDAM PENINSULA ② (PARAUTOCHTHONOUS)	OMAN MOUNTAINS ③ (ALLOCHTHONOUS)
2	CENOZOIC — QUATERNARY / NEOGENE	FARS / PABDEH		ERODED/ NOT DEPOSITED	
65	PALEOGENE		PABDEH (G)		SEMAIL NAPPE
145	MESOZOIC — CRETACEOUS	ARUMA / WASIA / THAMAMA (G)	LAFFAN (S) / MISHRIF (O) / MAUDDUD (O) / SHUAIBA (S/O)	MUSANDAM	HAWASINA: SUMEINI / HAMRAT DURU / AL ARIDH / KAWR / UMAR
208	JURASSIC	SAHTAN (S)	ARAB (O) / DIYAB (S) / ARAEJ (O) / MARRAT (O)	ELPHINSTONE	
251	TRIASSIC	AKHDAR (H)	JILH (S) / KHUFF (G)	RUUS AL JIBAL	
300	PERMIAN			THRUST OVER ARUMA & HAWASINA	
360	CARBONIFEROUS	MAJOR HIATUS			
410	PALAEOZOIC — DEVONIAN				
440	SILURIAN				
500	ORDOVICIAN	?			
590	CAMBRIAN	HORMUZ SALT			
700	PRECAMBRIAN	?			
800		CRYSTALLINE BASEMENT FIRST FORMED AROUND 950 Ma B.P.			

NOTES:

1. Autochthonous rock units - Geological groups in L.H. column. R.H. column lists some important source rocks (S) and oil- (O) & gas- (G) bearing formations. Note Basal Cambrian Hormuz Salt.

2. Parautochthonous rocks of Musandam Peninsula are similar to those of the platform area but have been thrust short distance over Aruma and Hawasina covering deeper platform rocks, probably at end of Paleogene.

3. South of the Musandam Peninsula, the Hawasina comprises an imbricate sequence of continental slope (Sumeini) and ocean floor sediments (Hamrat Duru to Umar groups). They are overlain by the Semail Nappe comprising former oceanic crust. Obduction of both Hawasina & Semail took place during time span of deposition of the Aruma Group on the Arabian Platform.

⟵ indicates sense of thrusting

HSG = Hajar Supergroup

Table 1. Rock units of the United Arab Emirates. A simplified outline emphasising differences between the Oman Mountains and subsurface of the desert plains. Some important oil and gas horizons within the autochthonous Hajar Super Group of the Arabian Platform are shown (R= reservoir rock; S= source rock and C= cap rock or seal). Note that the Hawasina and Semail nappes were obducted onto the Arabian continental margin during the late Cretaceous.

6 km, the temperature is so high (around 180°C) that even gas generation ceases (post-mature for gas). Newly generated oil is squeezed out of its source bed and migrates (usually upward) into a porous reservoir rock (e.g. sandstone, dolomite). The oil or gas can be retained in the reservoir rock only if it is kept in by an impervious *cap rock* or *seal,* and the reservoir/seal couplet forms a trap. Structural deformation of the reservoir/seal couplets, to form traps, can occur in a variety of ways; these can include fault movement at basement level, which affects all overlying rocks, differential compaction of underlying sands and shales and, most prominently in the southern Gulf area, diapiric uplift of the Eo-Cambrian Hormuz salt and

its sideways withdrawal from the deep salt horizon to feed that diapirism (Fig. 3). A simple outline of the maturation and migration of hydrocarbons from source rock to reservoir and trap is given in Glennie (1995). For a general discussion of Arabian petroleum geology, see Beydoun (1991) and more specifically for the Emirates, Alsharhan (1989).

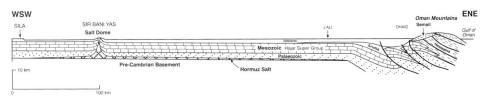

Fig. 3. Schematic W-E geological cross-section through the United Arab Emirates. Deformation leading to the creation of hydrocarbon traps within the Hajar Super Group resulted from movements associated with basement faults and the Hormuz salt (small diapir at J. Ali not shown) generally too small to show at scale of section. The nappes of the Oman Mountains were obducted when the eastern margin of Arabia and adjacent ocean floor attempted to underthrust oceanic crust now represented by the Semail Nappe.

The Oman Mountains

The origin of the subsurface rocks that underlie the greater part of the Emirates has been told in relatively simple terms, but that of the Mountains is much more complex and its interpretation is not without controversy (Robertson and Searle 1990: Glennie 1995). Its presentation thus requires more space.

The creation of the Oman Mountains is closely connected with the plate-tectonic processes mentioned above. This hypothesis is based on two observations:

- The continents are composed of relatively thick (20-70 km), light and buoyant crust (*continental crust*), while the oceans are floored by a thinner (4-10 km), denser crust (*oceanic crust*); both 'float' on a slightly plastic *mantle* that is capable of flowing as a slow-moving convection current under the influence of radioactive heat generated in the core of the Earth.
- New oceanic crust is created from molten *magma* filling tension gashes within existing crust and extruded as lava on the ocean floor at *mid-ocean ridges,* while a similar amount of older crust is carried back down into the Earth's mantle at arcuate oceanic trenches (*subduction zones*); thus the Earth's circumference remains more or less constant as the continents and adjacent oceanic crust move away from the 'spreading' oceanic ridges and converge elsewhere at subduction trenches.

Perhaps the clearest example of the above processes is seen today on either side of the Americas. In the Atlantic Ocean, depending on location, the Americas have been moving away from Europe and Africa at an average rate of about 5 cm a year for the past 60 to 100 million years (60-100 Ma) or more, the axis of spreading being the submarine Mid Atlantic Ridge; while at the western margin of South America, oceanic crust of the Pacific Plate is being *subducted* beneath the Andes (see e.g. Glennie 1992; 1995).

For much of the Palaeozoic era, Gondwana was separated from Asia by a major ocean known as Tethys (Fig. 2). In the Late Permian, some 260 or 270 Ma BP, a continental block comprising Anatolia, Central Iran, Helmand (south Afghanistan) and perhaps Tibet, separated from the Arabian-Indian margin of Gondwana to form a *microcontinent* (Glennie 1995:

Fig. 16). The intervening area became floored by a relatively narrow spreading ocean called Neo-Tethys 1 (sequentially, there were two), which probably was rather like the modern Red Sea. Although there are some doubts about the oceanic nature of its underlying crust (it may have been 'thinned' and volcanically ruptured continental crust (Béchennec et al. 1988, 1990)), Neo-Tethys 1 seems to have had a spreading life of probably less than 50 Ma, for, in the Late Triassic, the newly formed microcontinent was itself split into two by a new axis of spreading and the creation of another ocean (Neo-Tethys 2: Fig. 4) that was to exist for over 100 Ma. Neo-Tethys 1 ceased to spread from then on. The southward narrowing microcontinent between the two oceanic areas, Neo-Tethys 1 and 2, comprised Anatolia, the Sirjan-Sanandaj zone of Iran (Glennie et al. 1990; Glennie 1995), and possibly a number of mountain-size 'fragments' of shallow-marine limestone and marble within the Hawasina Series referred to as 'Exotics' (Al-Aridh and Kawr groups of Table 1); exotic because these whitish marbles look out of place in their surroundings of the much darker rocks of the adjacent *Semail Nappe* (former oceanic crust) and the deep-water sediments (limestone and red-brown *chert;* see below) of the *Hawasina Series.*

The Hawasina comprises sequences that vary in thickness from about 1000 to 200 m and range in age from the Triassic (locally Late Permian) to the mid Cretaceous. The thinner and, more particularly, the uppermost parts of the sequences are commonly distorted and tightly folded. Furthermore, a large part, or even the total sequence, is commonly repeated in an imbricate fashion (like a row of books on a shelf, all leaning in one direction) as they partly overlie each other. A simplified picture of sedimentation on the ocean floor can be deduced by reconstructing the imbricate pile back into their original positions relative to each other (Glennie et al. 1973, 1974).

When Neo-Tethys 1 formed, its floor was covered with sediments derived from the edge of the Arabian continental shelf; at the continental shelf edge, shallow-marine organisms, including calcareous grasses, thrived in well-oxygenated waters, and shells or, in the case of the grasses, lime mud, accumulated when they died. The shells were partly fragmented by wave action and also by burrowing organisms. The whole formed a metastable mass of sediment that could be dislodged by the shock of an earthquake or even a violent storm. Such dislodged sediment would slide down the continental slope and develop into a relatively high-velocity flow called a *turbidity current,* which finally deposited its entrained sediment over the lower *continental rise* and *abyssal plain* of the ocean as a bed called a *turbidite.* Turbidity currents have been recorded in modern environments at speeds of up to 70 km/hour (Holmes 1978), and their momentum carries them far across the abyssal plain.

At depths greater than some 3000 to 4000 m, calcium carbonate is unstable. The fine calcareous muds that settle out from suspension in the oceanic waters are especially susceptible to replacement by silica to form reddish brown cherts (a rock rather like flint), which are characterized by the siliceous framework of very small unicellular creatures called radiolaria (i.e. they form radiolarian cherts). Turbidites and radiolarian cherts make up much of the Hawasina sedimentary sequence. The volumetrically greater calcareous turbidites dominated deposition closest to the Arabian continental shelf edge, while the much thinner red cherts were in the deepest water farthest from the shelf edge (Glennie et al. 1973, 1974; Glennie 1995).

In complete contrast to the turbidites and cherts, the 'Exotics' form large blocks of white shallow-marine limestone, commonly recrystallized to marble (a process that destroyed many

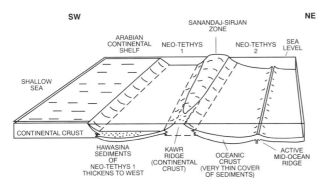

Fig. 4. Block diagram to illustrate the spatial relationships between the Arabian continental margin, Neo-Tethys 1 and 2, and the intervening Sirjan-Sanandaj-Kawr microcontinent during the Jurassic and Early Cretaceous.

of the fossils that may have been present initially). The 'Exotics' seem to have been derived from the far side of Neo-Tethys 1 relative to the Arabian continental margin (Kawr Ridge on Fig. 4). Most 'Exotics' are underlain by an association of a red siltstone and *pillow lavas* formed by extrusion of lava at the sea floor. At Jabal Rann, south-west of Dibba, however, 'exotic' limestone overlies Ordovician sandstone, which indicates the presence of continental crust. These observations suggest that the 'Exotics' probably formed as the outcome of continental break-up and the creation of a new intervening ocean. The largest known 'Exotic' in the Mountains is Jabal Kawr, in Oman, which is almost 1000 m thick and over 25 km across.

The Anatolia-Sirjan-Sanandaj microcontinent that separated Neo-Tethys 1 and 2 narrowed southward (Fig. 4), and along much of the Oman coastline of Arabia was probably represented by little more than the 'Exotic' Limestones (Kawr Ridge). As the Kawr Ridge had little or no exposure above sea level, it generated no sediment by erosion other than carbonate fragments; thus this part of Neo-Tethys 2 was deprived of sediment other than a rain of the finest clay-size particles settling out of suspension in the oceanic waters and eventually forming radiolarian chert (Umar Group, Table 1).

Sedimentation in the relatively narrow Neo-Tethys 1 took place from the Late Permian to the mid Cretaceous, and, in Neo-Tethys 2, from the Late Triassic until the mid Cretaceous. As Neo-Tethys 2 continued to widen, so the Africa-Arabian and adjoined South American portions of Gondwana moved to the west or south-west away from the Neo-Tethyan axis of spreading. Sometime during the later Early Cretaceous, however, Africa and South America began to separate to create the intervening South Atlantic Ocean (Glennie et al. 1990; Glennie 1995). South America continued to move to the west, but Afro-Arabia had to reverse its sense of motion and move away from the South Atlantic spreading axis. With Neo-Tethys 2 continuing to spread, very strong compressional stresses soon developed. These were relieved by the creation of an easterly-dipping trench down which the oceanic crust of first the western part of Neo-Tethys 2 and then Neo-Tethys 1 was subducted. During that process, the sediments covering the floor of both Neo-Tethys 1 and 2 were scraped off the down-going oceanic plate to form the *accretionary wedge* of imbricate sequences of the Hawasina mentioned above (Glennie et al. 1990; Glennie 1995).

Subduction zones are of two types (see Fig. 6 in Glennie 1995):

• Andean Type: oceanic crust at the eastern edge of the Pacific Plate is currently being subducted beneath the Andes mountain range. As the sedimentary cover is scraped off the down-going oceanic crust, the Andes are elevated a little more. The uppermost sediments being subducted are considerably younger than the overlying rocks of the Andes Mountains; moisture associated with the descending plate lowers the melting point of rock and causes volcanic activity (together with the intrusion at depth of granite) in the overlying Andes.

• Ocean-ocean subduction: the oceanic crust of Neo-Tethys 2, when initially subducted, was possibly up to 100 Ma old and had therefore had enough time since its formation at a spreading ridge to cool down. The old and cold crust was relatively dense, and preferred to descend steeply rather than at a gentle angle; this, in turn, caused the axis of bending to roll back away from the subduction trench, thereby creating crustal tension in a geological structure that had developed initially because of crustal compression. Crustal tension inevitably leads to volcanic activity and the creation of new oceanic crust; this new oceanic crust became the Semail Nappe of the Oman Mountains (see Lippard et al. 1986).

Because the new axis of spreading developed behind the subduction trench, the newly created oceanic crust is said to have resulted from *back-arc spreading*. It is noteworthy here that the newly formed oceanic crust was younger than most of the ocean-floor sediments that were being subducted nearby.

Subduction of the oceanic crust and the growth of an *accretionary wedge* of ocean-floor sediments beneath the future Semail Nappe began some 110 Ma BP (Lippard et al. 1986). The difficulty of trying to 'swallow' the thick 'exotic limestones' down the subduction trench can be imagined from the amount of recrystallization and fracturing that affected the limestones; they were sheared from their mixed continental and ocean-margin substrate. When, later, the even thicker continent margin of Arabia reached the subduction trench, it could neither be sheared off nor 'swallowed'; it became jammed within the upper part of the subduction zone, and subduction ground to a halt.

The South Atlantic Ocean continued to widen, however, and the back-arc spreading axis just east of the subduction trench was still active. Compressional stresses built up until another subduction trench formed further to the east. In the Oman Mountains, the Late Cretaceous timing of nappe emplacement (*obduction*) can be dated by the fossil content of the Aruma Group sediments (Table 1) being deposited adjacent to the nappes being emplaced. In the Inner Makran of Iran, the presence of volcanic bombs in slightly younger Late Cretaceous marine sediments indicates that a new subduction process had already been in progress there for a few million years (Glennie et al. 1990). The Makran subduction trench is still active today, and has built an accretionary wedge of marine sediments that extends to the present southern coastline of Iran east of the Straits of Hormuz.

When the new subduction trench formed in Iran, compressive stresses in the Oman Mountains sector were removed, allowing the leading edge of the Arabian continent to rise isostatically (like a piece of wood being released under water), causing the separation of what now became the Semail Nappe from its formerly contiguous oceanic crust of back-arc type. This uplift caused the accretionary wedge of Hawasina sediments, together with the Semail Nappe, to slide a little further onto the essentially immovable *autochthonous* continental shelf sequence, the whole process being known as *obduction*. At this time (end Cretaceous), the Hawasina and Semail did not form a high mountain range, but rather an island chain, the flanks of which were covered by Early Cenozoic shallow-marine limestones that extended westward across the rest of the Emirates.

Uplift into the present mountain range did not begin until about the end of the Paleogene or early Neogene, possibly as a result of continental collision between Arabia and Iran associated with the opening of the Red Sea and perhaps of other plate movements including that of India. As part of this event, the highland area of Ru'us al-Jibal (Fig. 1) was pushed westward slightly and compressed along a series of reverse faults, and now at the mountain edge locally overrides Paleogene strata in the subsurface (Fig. 3); other examples of the structural style can be found in Boote et al. (1990) and Dunne et al. (1990). This compression is clearly expressed by the steep western flank of the coastal mountain just north of Sha'm. East of Ras al-Khaimah, in the Hagil *Window* just north of the exit of Wadi Bih, the shallow-marine rocks of the Ru'us al-Jibal and Elphinstone groups can be seen to overlie units of the Hawasina with a thrust contact. The amount of horizontal over-thrusting is believed to have been no more than a few kilometres.

The surface of Jabal Hafit, just south of Al-Ain, consists of Lower Cenozoic limestones and marls that have now been deformed into a sharp, steeply flanked anticline whose axis plunges to both north and south. The time of its deformation is believed to have coincided with uplift of the Oman mountains, possibly by reactivation of one of the underlying thrust planes within the Hawasina. Further north, Jabal Faiyah forms a similar structure that has been dissected sufficiently to expose underlying rocks of the Semail Nappe. Cenozoic rocks are also exposed along the mountain edge to the east and north-east of Jabal Hafit (e.g. Jabal Qamar).

Along the coast of Oman in the vicinity of Muscat, and to the south-east almost as far as Sur, are a number of elevated horizontal wave-cut terraces, up to 150 m above present sea level, which indicate that the Oman Mountains have continued to rise during the past few million years or so. A similar terrace in the northern Emirates has been cut into the western edge of the southern Ru'us al-Jibal, south of the exit of Wadi Bih (due east of Ras al-Khaimah). In contrast, the northern extremity of the Oman Mountains is being depressed below sea level as its offshore continuation across the Straits of Hormuz is subducted beneath the Makran coast. According to Vita Finzi (1979), the northern tip of the Musandam Peninsula is subsiding at the very rapid rate of about 6 mm per year.

The rate of horizontal closure between Arabia and Asia is not known. That it continues to do so, even if relatively slowly, is attested by the many violent earthquakes experienced in Iran as the outer edge of the Arabian Plate (north-east edge of the Zagros Mountains) grinds against the adjacent Sanandaj-Sirjan zone; geologists have aptly named this earthquake-prone contact the Crush Zone.

Miocene Terrestrial Sediments of Western Abu Dhabi

At the time of continental collision between Arabia and Asia during the early Miocene (early Neogene), shallow-marine sedimentation was replaced by terrestrial conditions over much of the Gulf region. In western Abu Dhabi, the Shuwaihat Formation comprises deformed evaporitic sediments that are replaced upwards by dune sands which, like those of today, were deposited under the influence of a northern (*shamal*) wind; the sands are riddled with the moulds of plant roots (Glennie and Evamy 1968), which indicate the former proximity of the water table at fairly shallow depth. Among other places, such sediments are exposed on Shuwaihat island, at Jabal Dhanna and south of Sila (Fig. 1).

With an erosional interval representing several million years, the dune sands are overlain by fluvial gravels and sands of the Baynunah Formation (Fig. 1), which contain a wide variety of vertebrate fossils of both terrestrial and aquatic types: crocodile, turtle, hippopotamus, an early type of elephant, buffalo and ostrich, as well as smaller mammals (Whybrow and Hill, in press). The change from arid dune and sabkha to the more humid conditions needed for the hippopotamus and crocodile to thrive requires a considerable change in climate, a change that seems to have taken place repeatedly during the past million years or so. The erosional time gap between the Suwaihat and Baynunah formations is possibly the result of a considerable fall (100 m?) in global sea level when Antarctica used that volume of water to form its thick cover of ice.

Quaternary Sediments of the Emirates

The influence of high latitude glaciations on Arabian deserts

During the past million years or more, one event has repeatedly affected global climate, including that of tropical deserts. With a cyclicity of around 100 ka, the whole of Scandinavia and the northern half of North America, including Greenland, suffered a repeated slow build-up of an ice cover up to two or three kilometres thick, which then melted very rapidly (Shackleton 1987; Boulton 1993); because global temperatures were lower during glaciations, many highland areas became the sites of mountain glaciers, whereas the ice cap over Antarctica, which had been a permanent feature of the southern hemisphere from at least the Miocene onward, only expanded and contracted in size.

Apart from lowering global temperatures, these glaciations affected climate in two other ways:

• Because the ice caps became the centres of very large areas of high atmospheric pressure, all other air-pressure belts around the globe were squeezed towards the low-pressure equatorial area. With isobars much closer together than is the case today, global winds will have been much stronger and more persistent than any we now experience.
• So much water went into building the ice caps that global sea level at the last glacial maximum, about 20 ka BP, was some 120 or 130 m lower than today's. Since the floor of the Arabian Gulf is everywhere less than 120 m deep, during glacial maxima the exposed floor of the Gulf would have been the site of sand dunes migrating southward and across the Emirates into the Rub' al Khali under the influence of the northern (shamal) wind; the only sign of water in the Gulf area would have been in the combined Tigris-Euphrates river, which derived its water from the wetter Anatolian highlands and reached the open sea south of the Straits of Hormuz.

The high-latitude glaciations took some 80 to 100 ka to reach their maximum extent, and then melted within little more than 10 ka to produce a global sea level similar to the present one by about 6 ka BP; thus sea level rose at an average rate of about 1 cm per year but possibly exceeded 4 cm/year for short periods (Boulton 1993). This flooding is thought to have been the origin of the biblical story of 'Noah's Flood', perhaps around 9 ka BP. Noah is thought to have lived in an area now covered by the Arabian Gulf. Over the almost flat floor of the Gulf, any continuous rise in sea level would have been noticed by the people living there. Noah's family possibly lived in the drier environment of a gentle rise to escape the effects of a rainfall that was considerably higher than any experienced today. As sea level rose in the Gulf, Noah's slightly elevated pasturage would have been cut off from the mainland and then be seen to shrink in area, leading to the need for a boat or barge if he and his family and flocks were to survive the encroaching sea; necessity is the mother of invention.

Many desert areas, including much of the Sahara, had a higher rainfall between about 10 and 6 ka BP. This induced the growth of much more vegetation, which fed abundant game, leading to the term 'Climatic Optimum'; since then, most topical deserts have become more arid again (e.g. Petit-Maire 1994).

Flooding of the Gulf had a profound effect on the Emirates. Instead of sand dunes migrating freely into the area from the north, the supply of wind-driven sand was progressively cut off by the increasing extent of sea water. The wind continued to blow, however, so that in areas close to the expanding sea, sand was deflated (removed by wind action) down to the level of the water table, which was rising in concert with the rising sea level. The resulting moist surface developed into sabkhas, which are described later.

Fluvial sediments

When there is sufficient rainfall, fluvial gravels and sands are transported down the mountain sides and across the valley floors within the mountains; today, such rainwater reaches the sea about once in every ten years in the northern Emirates, but south of Jabal Faiyah it always dissipates within the sand dunes that block the lower reaches of the wadis and never reaches the sea.

West of the mountains is a broad sheet of fluvial sands and gravels that spread for a considerable distance beneath the present cover of dune sands. In south-east Oman, the same spread of *alluvial fans* reaches as much as 200 km south of the mountains; in the north, they extend beneath the floor of the Arabian Gulf. The time of deposition of some of the younger gravels now exposed in incised wadi banks have been dated at around 30,000 and 70,000 thousand years before present (30 and 70 ka BP), while others, in Wadi Dhaid for instance, coincided with the Climatic Optimum (Sanlaville 1992). The fans have been subjected to repeated deflation, however, and near-surface sediment has been dated at over 400 ka, while the degree of alteration of some ophiolite-rich fluvial sediment suggests deposition up to a million or more years ago. The extent of these sediments and the size of the pebbles and boulders found in them, indicate that at the time of their deposition there was much more rainfall over the area than is experienced today. The surfaces of such alluvial fans are exposed between some of the large linear dunes of the eastern emirates (Fig. 1).

Quaternary fluvial sediments are rarely exposed between the dune cover of most of the western emirates. Along the western side of Sabkha Matti, however, at the western limit of Abu Dhabi, another sequence of fluvial gravels is exposed at the surface. The attitude of the bedding laminae indicates that there, an ancient river flowed towards the north or north-east. The types of rock (e.g. limestone, volcanic lava) represented by the pebble content of the gravels point, in this case, to a source in the south-western highlands of Saudi Arabia. The time of their deposition has been dated at over 200 ka BP (Goodall 1995), which obviously was another period of higher rainfall than now.

Sabkhas

Sabkhas are flat areas of sand, silt or clay that are covered by a crust of salt (halite) for at least a part of the year. *Coastal sabkhas* are flooded by the sea during storm and spring high tides, whereas the inland variety has no direct marine influence but derives its moisture from rare rainfall and the proximity of the water table at shallow depth, within *capillary reach* of the surface.

Coastal sabkhas and lagoons

As already mentioned above, coastal sabkhas formed when the supply of wind-driven sand from the north was cut off during the post-Glacial flooding of the Gulf and deflation removed dry sand down to the level of the water table. Water evaporates from the damp surface, especially during the hot summer months, which becomes saturated with halite (common salt) that crystallizes to form a hard crust. Beneath the surface, calcium sulphate also becomes concentrated and forms a mush of gypsum crystals about 50 cm below the surface. At ground temperatures greater than about 42°C, the water of crystallization is driven from the gypsum crystal lattice to create anhydrite. Shinn (1983) has many illustrations of sabkhas in the emirates and other areas of the Gulf.

Perhaps the most characteristic feature of a coastal sabkha is a widespread mat of thin, black, algae. Most of the time, this *algal mat* is dry, and commonly cracked and curled up at the edges like flakes of mud in a dried-out pond. During high spring tides, however, or when storm winds drive sea water over the almost horizontal sabkha surface, the algae springs to life and regenerates into a slimy, wrinkly, rubbery layer. The slimy surface traps fine calcareous particles carried over the surface by the waves, and when it cracks and curls, wind-blown sand and silt can be trapped beneath its edges; with time, the sabkha again acquires a crust of halite.

When halite crystallizes, it prefers to do so by growing horizontally rather than by increasing its thickness vertically. A space problem ensues, which is resolved by the salt sheets over-thrusting each other if thin, or by forming polygons (ideally hexagons) as it grows thicker.

Coastal sabkhas cover the surfaces of most of the extensive system of low islands south-west and just to the north-east of Abu Dhabi island. Along the coast of especially Umm al-Qaiwain and Ras al-Khaimah, however, the development of longshore bars has resulted in the creation of a series of shallow lagoons, which have tidally formed deltas at their mouths (Glennie 1970, Figs 98-100). Wave action builds the longshore bars into beaches, from which sands (mostly the wave-broken remains of shells and carbonate skeletons of sea grasses) are blown into the lagoon behind. In addition, as small carbonate-shelled creatures die, they leave their shells on the lagoon floor, which becomes shallower and eventually builds up to, or even above, normal high-tide level, and then acquires its own cover of coastal sabkha including a mat of black algae. North of Ras al-Khaimah town, the longshore bars formed the sites of small fishing communities, which progressively moved seaward as each site became separated from the sea by the next bar to extend northward.

Inland sabkhas

Inland sabkhas differ from the coastal variety in having no direct marine influence on their development. Their supply of water comes from rare rainfall and the presence of a water table within capillary reach of the surface; a balance is achieved between evaporation and deflation at the surface and the supply of water from below which can trap wind-blown sediment, both being affected seasonally. Algae may be present, but extensive algal mats are not well developed; like coastal sabkhas, gypsum crystals form a layer below the surface.

Within the Emirates, extensive inland sabkhas are found in three areas: at the landward margins of the coastal sabkhas beyond the reach of storm tides and extending into some adjacent interdune areas; in the large broad interdune areas between the huge dunes of Al-Liwa; and in Sabkha Matti, a low lying area in the far west of Abu Dhabi, about 60 km across and extending south from the coast for almost 150 km, much of it being within Saudi Arabia. The surface of Sabkha Matti is still no more than 40 m above sea level some 100 km south of the coast.

In the Liwa, several small flat-topped hills (mesas) are capped by a gypsum-cemented layer indicative of former sabkha conditions. Lightly cemented dune sand, whose bedding attitudes indicate sand transport towards the south south-east (the same as today) is exposed in the flanks of these mesas; similar dune sands can be seen in pits dug below the gypsum-cemented surface of the interdune sabkhas, which are at an elevation of some 80 to 90 m above sea level. The time of deposition of the dune sands has been dated as 12 ka (in pits) and 40 and 141 ka BP in the mesas, thereby indicating that both dune and sabkha-producing conditions have been repeated in the area; the younger dune sands were preserved by the rise in the level of the water table during the melting of the last high-latitude ice caps. In Sabkha Matti, the deflated relics of former dunes surrounded by damp sabkha indicate that, prior to the last rise in the level of the water table, this area also was the site of dunes migrating southward away from the present Arabian Gulf. Both the Sabkha Matti and Liwa sabkhas are products of the present high water table, which is associated with the current interglacial high sea level. During glaciations, sabkhas occurred in neither inland nor current coastal areas.

The sabkha is a dangerous place and chances should never be taken with one, its salt-encrusted surface often looking deceptively firm. Beneath the thin crust of the coastal sabkha the algal mat and underlying mush of gypsum crystals and clay-size carbonate has little bearing strength. Unwary humans are likely to break through the surface and sink to their knees, especially if the crust is new, while narrow-tyred vehicles can become a total loss. Inland sabkhas are little safer. A bedouin tribesman in search of fresh pastures after rain, is likely to test the feasibility of crossing a suspect surface by sending first sheep and goats in the care of young light-weight children, followed in turn by himself with the heavier camels, and then his wife driving a laden Toyota Landcruiser pickup truck.

Sand dunes

Away from the Oman Mountains and the Abu Dhabi coastline, the surface of the Emirates is dominated by the presence of sand dunes. *Dunes* migrate in the direction of the sand-transporting wind. With a *linear dune,* this is achieved by the movement of sand along the dune flanks and deposition (causing elongation) at its down-wind end; if the up-wind supply of sand ceases for any reason (e.g. flooding of the Gulf), that end of the dune 'shrivels' and the dune shortens as sand is removed and not replaced. The same principle applies to *transverse dunes,* but because their long axes are at right angles to the wind, sand is transported over the top of the dune to its leeward side (where it forms an *avalanche slope* with a maximum inclination of 34°) rather than around its flanks. Where the supply of sand is limited, crescent-shaped *barchans* are formed; here, in addition to the movement of sand over its crest to the avalanche slope, sand is also readily transported along the dune flanks, which are drawn out into the long 'horns' that point down wind. On a much smaller scale, the axes of *ripples* are always at right angles to the wind that formed them, so their distribution gives an indication of the pattern of wind flow over and around the dune.

Across central Abu Dhabi, a broad belt of large, partly eroded (deflated) north-west to south-east trending linear dunes skirt the north-east margin of the Liwa, and lose their linear character as the Oman border is approached; this is re-established where the dunes overlie the alluvial fans that flank the Oman Mountains (Fig. 1). To the north of Jabal Hafit, the dune axes swing towards the north-east as the mountains are approached (Besler, 1982). These variable trends are thought to outline the fairly constant direction of dune-forming winds at, or shortly after, the peak of the last glaciation; since that time, the outlines of the dunes have been modified but the basic plan is still recognizable. Fitting into the same wind pattern are the giant *barchanoid* dunes (up to 150 m above the interdune sabkhas) of the Liwa. The axes of these dunes are also transverse to the dune-forming wind, which blew towards the south south-east. Travelling further to the west, the modern (and perhaps also the ancient) winds blow increasingly towards the south, eventually to veer south-westward across the central Rub' al-Khali towards the mountains of Yemen. This semi-circular pattern is typical of what are known as *trade wind deserts* (following the same sort of path as the trade winds sought by sailing ships heading westward to the Americas) such as the Sahara or, in the southern hemisphere, the Australian desert.

The broad pattern of large dunes outlined above has been modified by the effects of changing sea level in the Gulf. When sea level rose at the end of the last glaciation, the supply of aeolian sand from the north was stopped. Although the wind still blew, its direction was out of equilibrium with the geometry of the existing dunes, so their shape became modified; these modifying winds apparently were not so strong as formerly, so the new resulting dune forms were smaller than the pre-existing large dunes. This can be seen by the belt of small transverse dunes that drape the northern and north-eastern margins of the Liwa.

Over the course of recent history, the trade winds have not been so constant in direction as one might imagine. Today's strongest sand-transporting wind (the northern shamal) at Abu Dhabi airport has shifted about 30° to the north relative to its Glacial equivalent, and the winds are more variable than they used to be. This variability is indicated by small west-east trending linear dunes that cross the interdune areas of the Awir oasis in southern Dubai, for instance, and other similar areas further north; it is also indicated south-west of Jabal Hafit by star-shaped peaks on some of the large linear dunes, which form when winds blow in more than one direction. Today's more variable dune pattern is thought to be a product of a wind system that is weaker than it was in Glacial time.

Every time the Arabian Gulf was flooded by the sea, shallow-marine organisms flourished and eventually died, many leaving the evidence of their former existence on the sea floor in the form of calcareous shells. When the Gulf floor was exposed to the wind during sub-Polar glaciations, the smaller of these shells were transported southward to the Emirates where they formed carbonate dunes. Similar dunes near the coast of north-western India are known as 'miliolite' after their content of miliolid foraminifera, and the same name has been applied in south-eastern Arabia. Inland from the coast, miliolite is widely exposed, in many cases within the core of, or adjacent to, modern dunes (e.g. draping exposures of the Baynunah Formation in western Abu Dhabi, along the Al-Liwa road between Silmiya and Hameem, or the Abu Dhabi - Al-Ain road south-east of Bani Yas). Along the Hameem road, two sequences of miliolite are separated by evidence of a wetter climate; the lower sequence has a depositional age of 99 ka BP and the upper of 64 ka BP, times when the sea surface was about 25 and 80 m, respectively, below the present level of the Arabian Gulf. A study of the bedding attitudes of the miliolite indicates variations in wind direction similar to those deduced for the modern dunes (Glennie 1994).

It is clear that the dune systems of the Emirates have been controlled not only by global shifts in wind direction, but also by glacially controlled changes in exposure of the Gulf floor, which in turn have controlled the distribution of both coastal and inland sabkhas. Those dunes and sabkhas are still reacting to today's climate and associated wind directions.

Brief History of the Quaternary in the Emirates

The early Quaternary history of the Emirates is very poorly known. The limited evidence from sparsely dated alluvial fans suggests that it was probably a time of much higher rainfall than now. By about a million years ago, or perhaps as late as half a million years BP, near-polar glaciations led, in the Gulf area, to cyclic repetitions of lower sea level and stronger winds that caused sand dunes to migrate southward, with the warmer interglacials giving higher rainfall and less active dunes. For the past 5000 years, we seem to have been heading slowly in the direction of increased aridity associated in the long term (80,000 years later?) with another full glaciation in high-latitude areas.

Conclusions

By extrapolation from elsewhere, the history of the Emirates and adjacent areas of Arabia over the past 600 million years or so seems to have been mostly one of relative stability. Following tropical shallow-marine conditions of sedimentation in the late Precambrian, the area was largely terrestrial during much of the succeeding Palaeozoic time span. Deep erosion preceded the Permian separation of a microcontinent from the eastern margin of Arabia; the following marine transgression was associated with the successive creation of Neo-Tethys 1 and 2. Throughout most of the Mesozoic era, the Emirates was the site of shallow-marine sedimentation except in the two branches of Neo-Tethys, where deep-marine deposition took place. This situation was brought to an end by closure of Neo-Tethys 1 and 2, and the obduction of deep-oceanic sediments and a slice of newly formed back-arc oceanic crust onto the Arabian continental margin to form an island arc. The succeeding shallow-marine limestone deposition was terminated in the east when the Oman Mountains began to be uplifted into a high range some 30 Ma BP, but stable conditions of sedimentation continued over the bulk of the Emirates until major glaciations began to induce lower global sea levels perhaps some two to five million years ago and created the present land surface. Near-polar glaciations have controlled sea level in the Arabian Gulf for at least the last 500,000 years, thereby also controlling the supply of dune sand from the north or the cutting off of that supply, with the resulting widespread deflation and creation of sabkhas.

Glossary of Geological Terms

abyssal plain: the almost horizontal floor of an ocean between the continental slope and mid-ocean ridge, commonly found at depths in excess of 4000m.

accretionary wedge: a wedge of sedimentary rocks that were scraped off the surface of a down-going plate during subduction.

aeolianite: a consolidated sedimentary rock formed of wind-deposited sand; commonly but not necessarily rich in carbonate grains.

algal mat: a sheet of rubbery algae that covers the coastal sabkha surface after flooding.

allochthonous: term implying derivation or transport from elsewhere; the Hawasina and Semail are allochthonous because they did not originate where now found.

alluvial fan: a fan-like spread of fluvial distributary channels, commonly at the junction of mountain and plain; fans coalesce along the length of the Oman Mountains.

anhydrite: an evaporite mineral composed of calcium sulphate, $CaSO_4$, found in some sedimentary rocks. Often derived from *gypsum* by losing its *water of crystallization.*

autochthonous: a term implying an origin where now found, i.e. not transported from elsewhere. Noun: "autochthon".

avalanche slope: also known as **slip-face.** The slope that forms when wind-blown sand from the windward side of a dune passes into the calm air of the leeward side. The sand will start to slip if further deposition would result in the maximum angle of repose for dry sand of 34° to be exceeded.

back-arc: the arcuate area 'behind' the hanging wall of a subduction zone; it may be subjected to either compression or extension.

back-arc spreading: the process of creating new oceanic crust in the back-arc area behind a subduction trench.

barchan: see **dune.**

barchanoid dunes: see **dune.**

BP: abbreviation of Before Present, often given in ka, thousands (k) of years (a).

capillary: resembling a hair; of very small bore. If a tube of very small bore is immersed in water, the water will rise up within the tube as a result of capillary attraction.

cap rock / seal: an impervious rock (seal) overlying a fluid-bearing reservoir.

carbonate: general term for calcium and magnesium carbonates (limestones and dolomites).

carbonate-compensation depth: the depth below which most carbonate particles become unstable and slowly dissolve.

chert: beds of finely crystalline deep-water silica.

Climatic Optimum: the state of an ideal climate; inferred for existing desert regions to have had sufficient annual rainfall to render the area an ideal place for man to live. Such conditions are thought to have prevailed over much of the Saharan and Arabian deserts between about 9000 and 6500 years ago.

continental crust: the lighter (less dense) of the two main types of the Earth's crust, which forms most land masses but may extend below shallow seas.

continental shelf: that part of the sea floor between the coast and the marked change in slope at the shelf edge, whose depth averages about 120m. Continental shelves vary in width from a few kilometres to over 1000 km.

continental slope & rise: the two form the slope (upper part, to perhaps 1500m) of the ocean floor between the continental shelf edge and the abyssal plain at depths of about 4000m or more.

convection current: the transfer of heat from one part of a fluid or gas to another by flow of the fluid or gas from the hotter parts to the colder. A fluid will rise if heated from below because, through expansion, it becomes less dense than the cold.

deflation: the blowing away of dry fine-grained rock material (sand and dust), by the wind. A form of aeolian erosion at work chiefly in deserts.

diapir, diapirism: salt (halite) is less dense than most other rocks and is easily deformed. When buried at depth, salt is more buoyant than overlying rocks; it may then withdraw sideways to create a vertical bulge (salt pillow) that deforms overlying strata into anticlines and, by breaking through them, create salt domes and even salt walls. This process is known as diapirism; the product of diapirism is a diapir.

dolomite: a calcium-magnesian limestone, commonly formed by alteration of shallow-marine limestone.

dune: accumulation of wind-blown sand that possesses one or more slipfaces. Its size is dependent on the availability of sand and the ability of the wind to carry sand to the top without removing it again. The finest sand grains are usually found at the crest. There are several types of dune but only those common in eastern Arabia are described here.

> *barchan:* crescent-shaped sand dune, which migrates downwind in the direction of its horns. It has a gentle windward slope and a slipface on its lee slope. Barchans sometimes unite laterally to form rather irregular *barchanoid dunes.*
>
> *barchanoid dunes:* cross between a *barchan* and a *transverse dune.*

linear dune: dune whose long axis is parallel to the prevailing dune-forming wind; it grows by extending downwind. Avalanche slopes, where present, are almost parallel to the axis of the dune and can face towards either flank. May occur as a swarm of parallel dunes as in the Rub al Khali or the Wahiba.

megadune: any large dune whose height exceeds about 60 m and has a crestal spacing of about 500 m or more. Most are thought to have formed during the last major glaciation.

star dune: a roughly star-shaped pyramidal dune with three or more radiating arms with slip faces. Thought to form where seasonal winds are strongly oblique to each other. May result also by modification of older transverse or longitudinal dunes.

transverse dune: a dune whose long axis is at right angles to the prevailing dune-forming wind. Likely to break up into barchanoid and then barchan dunes if the supply of sand is not maintained.

evaporites: minerals, mostly anhydrite, gypsum or halite (common salt), that are typically formed in areas where the rate of evaporation exceeds that of rainfall or fluvial influx (i.e. in desert areas)

Gondwana: an ancient mega-continent named after the Gond tribe of northern India. Comprised Antarctica, Australia, India, Afro-Arabia and South America. It began to split up into its modern components in the later Mesozoic.

gypsum: an *evaporite* mineral, Calcium Sulphate ($CaSO_4. 2H_2O$), typically found just below the surface of coastal and inland sabkhas. Alters to *anhydrite* when it loses its *water of crystallization.*

Hawasina: an imbricate wedge of sediments of Mid Permian to mid Cretaceous age that were deposited over the floor of Neo-Tethys 1.

hydrocarbons: any organic compound comprising carbon and hydrogen, usually refers to oil and gas.

ka: abbreviation for thousands (**k**) of years (**a**)

limestone: calcium carbonate ($CaCO_3$), mostly of biogenic origin, and largely formed in shallow seas.

linear dune: see **dune**

Ma: abbreviation for millions (**M**) of years (**a**).

magma: molten rock when still within the Earth's crust or Mantle.

mantle: the part of the Earth, nearly 3000 km thick, that underlies crust of both continental and oceanic type.

maturation, maturity: the process of 'ripening' a source rock to the state where it generates oil or gas; the state of a source rock with respect to its ability to generate oil or gas. Considered to range from immature, before any oil or gas has been generated, through mature to post-mature, when no additional oil or gas can be generated from it.

megadune: see **dune**

mesa: a mesa is a flat-topped plateau bounded on at least three sides by steep, commonly cliffed slopes. The bedding is normally horizontal. A **butte** is a very small mesa. Both are found in the Miocene strata of western Abu Dhabi.

microcontinent: a sub-continent or continental sliver calved from a major continental plate by processes of crustal separation and spreading.

mid-ocean ridge: a (mostly) submarine ridge that transects an oceanic area and is a locus of generation of new oceanic crust.

migration: the passage of a newly generated oil or gas out of a source rock (primary migration), and its movement via rock conduits to other locations, including hydrocarbon traps (secondary migration).

nappe: a large sheet-like rock unit that has been tectonically emplaced (thrust) over a dominantly sub-horizontal or low-angle floor (e.g. Semail Nappe of Oman Mountains); at the contact, older rocks overlie younger rocks, which is the reverse of what happens during deposition of normal sedimentary sequences.

nappe emplacement (obduction): the placing of a nappe above another (usually autochthonous) rock unit without implying whether this relationship was the result of over-thrusting or underthrusting.

Neo-Tethys: that part of the ancient ocean Tethys formed when the Sirjan-Sanandaz microcontinent separated from the eastern (Arabian) margin of Gondwana.

obduction: the process by which former oceanic crust or a wedge of oceanic sediments comes to lie upon crust of continental type.

oceanic crust: the type of crust that characteristically underlies the Earth's oceans; it is denser than continental crust.

ophiolite: obducted oceanic crust, now separated from previously contiguous crust of oceanic type.

parautochthonous: a rock unit that is not quite autochthonous, and has undergone some (thrust) transport; e.g. the Ru'us al Jibal rock units.

pillow lava: the pillow-like masses of rock that form when magma is extruded below water and chilled rapidly.

plate: one of the major areas of the Earth's crust, normally comprising continental and contiguous oceanic crust.

plate tectonics: the processes by which the Earth's crustal plates are formed and interact with each other.

porosity: the pore spaces within a rock; in oil fields, these pores are filled with oil or gas.

reservoir, reservoir rock: any rock that can contain moveable fluids in its pore spaces.

ripple: a surface undulation , generally of unconsolidated sand, whose wavelength depends on wind strength and is constant with time. The ripple axis is always transverse to the wind. The coarsest grains are found at the crest. The ripple height depends on the range of grain sizes present and the wind strength.

sabkha: a flat area of clay, silt or sand, commonly with crusts of salt. Subdivided into:

    1) *coastal sabkha:* a coastal flat at or just above the level of normal high tide. Its sediments consist of sand, silt or clay and its surface is often covered with a salt crust formed by the evaporation of water drawn to the surface by capillary action or from occasional marine inundations. The coastal sabkha is characterized by the presence of algal mats and the occurrence of gypsum and anhydrite within its sediment. It is subject to *deflation* down to the water table.

    2) *inland sabkha:* a flat area of clay, silt or sand, commonly with saline encrustations, that is typical of desert areas of inland drainage and some interdune areas. Their salts may be formed by evaporation of surface water, or of water drawn to the surface from the water table by capillary action.

salt dome: a dome-shaped structure caused by the upward penetration of a circular plug of salt, commonly 1-2 km in diameter, through overlying strata; the plug may also give strata through which it fails to penetrate a domal shape.

Semail Nappe: the name given to the huge ophiolite nappe of the Oman Mountains.

Semail ophiolite: the huge ophiolite slab of the Oman Mountains typically comprising peridotites and harzburgites, partly serpentinized, gabbros and basaltic pillow lavas.

shamal: Arabic word for north: applied to north or northwest wind that blows down the Arabian Gulf and clockwise across the Rub al Khali.

star dune: see **Dune.**

source rock: a rock rich in organic matter which, if heated sufficiently, will generate oil or gas.

subduction: the process at a plate margin of crustal consumption down a subduction zone.

subduction zone: a sloping linear zone down which crust and overlying sediment of mostly oceanic type passes into the mantle beneath the edge of another plate, commonly but not exclusively of continental type.

temperature gradient: the change in temperature measured over a given distance; usually measured in °C/km. Often used to calculate depth at which source rocks become mature.

thrust: a reverse fault or slide plane, on which older rocks have been emplaced over younger ones.

thrust sheet: a sheet of rock that has been tectonically emplaced over a younger rock sequence, the two units commonly being separated by a relatively low-angle thrust plane: a nappe.

Trade Wind Desert: a term sometimes applied to those deserts in subtropical land areas that are crossed by the *trade winds*.

transverse dune: see **Dune.**

trap: any deformation (fold, fault, wedge-out) of a reservoir rock/seal couplet that can cause hydrocarbons to be trapped as they migrate from their source rocks.

turbidite: the sedimentary deposit that settles out from a turbidity current; its sediment is commonly graded from coarse at the base to fine at the top..

turbidity current: high velocity current of relatively dense turbid sediment and water that occasionally flows across the floor of some ocean basins from a site usually high on the adjacent continental slope.

wadi: desert watercourse, dry except after rain.

water of crystallisation: the water present in hydrated compounds such as gypsum ($CaSO_4.2H_2O$). If the temperature of the gypsum crystal is raised above about 42°C, either by deep burial or by near-surface heating in a desert, it loses its water of crystallisation ($2H_2O$) and becomes the anhydrous mineral *anhydrite*.

window: an area where erosion has cut down through a thrust plane to expose the underlying rocks: e.g. Hagil Window in the south-west Ru'us al Jibal.

Bibliography

Alsharhan, A. S. 'Petroleum Geology of the United Arab Emirates', *Journal of Petroleum Geology*, 12(3) (1989) pp 253-88.

Alsharhan, A. S. & Whittle, G. L. 'Carbonate-Evaporite sequences of the Late Jurassic, southern and south-western Arabian Gulf', *American Association Petroleum Geologists Bulletin* , 79 (11) (1995) pp 1608-30.

Al-Silwadi, M. S. Kirkham, A. Simmons, M. D. & Twombley, B. N. 'New insights into regional correlation and sedimentology, Arab formation (Upper Jurassic), offshore Abu Dhabi', *GeoArabia* , 1(1) (1996) pp 6-27.

Béchennec, J. Le Métour, J. Rabu, D. Villey, M. and Beurrier, M. 'The Hawasina Basin: a fragment of a starved passive continental margin, thrust over the Arabian Platform during obduction of the Semail Nappe', *Tectonophysics*, 151 (1988) pp 323-42.

Béchennec, F. Le Metour, J. Rabu, D. Bourdillon-de-Grissac, Ch.Wever, P. de. Beurrier, M. & Villey, M. 'The Hawasina Nappes: stratigraphy, palaeogeography and structural evolution of a fragment of the south-Tethyan passive continental margin' in A.H.F. Robertson, M.P. Searle, & A.C. Ries, (eds), *The Geology & Tectonics of the Oman* Region, Geological Society Special Publication 49 (1990) pp 213-23.

Besler, H. 'The north-eastern Rub' al Khali within the borders of the United Arab Emirates', *Zeitschrift für Geomorphologie,* N.F. 26(4) (1982) pp 495-504.

Beydoun, Z. R. 'Arabian Plate Hydrocarbon Geology and Potential - a plate tectonic approach', *AAPG Studies in Geology* , 33 (1991) pp 1-77.

Boote, D. R. D. Mou, D. & Waite, R.I. 'Structural evolution of the Suneinah Foreland, Central Oman Mountains' in A.H.F. Robertson, M.P. Searle, & A.C. Reis (eds), *The Geology & Tectonics of the Oman Region,* Geological Society Special Publication 49 (1990) pp 397-418.

Boulton, G.S. 'Ice Ages and Climatic Change' in P. McL. D. Duff (ed), *Holmes' Principles of Physical Geology* (4th ed) London, Chapman & Hall (1993) pp 439-69.

Dunne, L. A. Manoogian, P.R. & Pierini, D. F. 'Structural style and domains of the Northern Oman Mountains (Oman and United Arab Emirates)' in A.F. Robertson et al. (eds), *The Geology & Tectonics of the Oman Region,* Geological Society Special Publication 49 (1990) pp 375-86.

Glennie, K.W. and Evamy, B.D. 'Dikaka: plants and plant-root structures associated with aeolian sand' *Palaeogeography, Palaeoclimatol., Palaeoecol.,* 4 (1968) pp 77-87.

Glennie, K. W. *Desert Sedimentary Environments.*, Developments in Sedimentology 14, Amsterdam, Elsevier (1970).

Glennie, K. W. 'Desert Sedimentary Environments, present and past - a summary', *Sedimentary Geology* , 50 (1/3) (1987) pp 135-65.

Glennie, K. W. 'Plate Tectonics & the Oman Mountains', *Tribulus* , 2(2) (1992) pp 11-21.

Glennie, K. W. 'Wind Action and Desert Landscapes' in P.McL.D Duff (ed), *Holmes' Principles of Physical Geology* (4th ed) London, Chapman & Hall (1993) pp 470 504.

Glennie, K. W. 'Quaternary dunes of SE Arabia and Permian (Rothegend) dunes of NW Europe: some comparisons', *Zeitblad Geol. Paläontol.* Teil 1. 11/12 (1994) pp 1199- 1215.

Glennie, K. W. *The Geology of the Oman Mountains. an outline of their origin,* Beaconsfield, Scientific Press (1995).

Glennie, K. W. Boeuf, M.G.A. Hughes Clarke, M.W. Moody-Stuart, M. Pilaar, W.F.H. & Reinhardt, B.M. 'Late Cretaceous nappes in the Oman Mountains and their geologic evolution', *American Association Petroleum Geologists Bulletin* , 57(1)(1973) pp 5-27.

Glennie, K. W. Boeuf, M. G. A. Hughes Clarke, M. W. Moody-Stuart, M. Pilaar, W. F. H. & Reinhardt, B. M. *Geology of the Oman Mountains,* Verhandelingen Koninklijk Nederlands Geologisch Mijnbouwkundig Genootschap, 31 (1974).

Glennie, K. W. Hughes Clarke, M. W. Boeuf, M. G. A. Pilaar, W. F. H. & Reinhardt, B. B. 'Inter-relationship of Makran-Oman Mountains belts of convergence' in A. H. F.Robertson, M. P. Searle, & A. C. Reis (eds), *The Geology & Tectonics of the Oman Region,* Geological Society Special Publication 49 (1990) pp 773-86.

Goodall, T. M. *The geology and geomorphology of the Sabkhat Matti region (United Arab Emirates): a modern analogue for ancient desert sediments from north-west Europe,* PhD thesis, University of Aberdeen (1995).

Holmes, A. *Principles of Physical Geology* (3rd ed) Van Nostrand Reinhold. (1978).

Lippard, S. J. Shelton, A.W. & Gass, I.G. *The Ophiolite of Northern Oman.* Geological Society Memoir 11 (1986).

Petit-Maire, N. 'Natural variability of the Asian, Indian and African monsoons over the last 130 ka.' in Desbois, M & Désalmand (eds) *Global Precipitation and Climate Change,* NATO ASI Series Vol 126, Berlin, Springer-Verlag (1994) pp 3-26.

Robertson, A.F.H. & Searle, M.P. 'The northern Oman Tethyan continental margin: stratigraphy, structure, concepts and controversies' in A.H.F. Robertson, M. P. Searle, & A. C. Ries (eds), *The Geology & Tectonics of the Oman Region.* Geological Society Special Publication 49 (1990) pp 3-25.

Sanlaville, P. 'Changements climatiques dans la péninsule Arabique durant le Pléistocène supérieur et l'Holocène' *Paléorient,* 18 (1992) pp 5-26.

Shackleton, N. J. 'Oxygen isotopes, ice volume and sea level', *Quaternary Science Review* , 6 (1987) pp 183-190.

Shinn, E. A. 'Tidal Flat Environment' in Scholle, P. A., Bebout, D. G. & Moore, C. H. (eds) 1983 *Carbonate Depositional Environments.*, American Association Petroleum Geologists Memoir 33 (1983) pp 171-210.

Smith, A. G. Hurley, A. M. & Briden, J. C. *Phanerozoic Palaeocontinental World Maps.* Cambridge University Press (1981).

United Arab Emirates University, *The National Atlas of the United Arab Emirates,* Al-Ain (1993).

Vita Finzi, C. 'Rates of Holocene folding in the coastal Zagros near Bandar Abbass, Iran', *Nature* , 278 (1979) pp 632-4.

Whybrow, P. J. & Hill, A. (in press) *Fossil Vertebrates in Arabia,* Yale University Press.

Before the Emirates:
An Archaeological and Historical Account
of Developments in the Region c. 5000 BC to 676 AD

Daniel T. Potts

Introduction

In the short space of 40 years the territory of the former Trucial States and modern United Arab Emirates (UAE) has gone from being a blank on the archaeological map of Western Asia to being one of the most intensively studied regions in the entire area. The present chapter seeks to synthesize the data currently available which shed light on the lifeways, industries and foreign relations of the earliest inhabitants of the UAE.

Climate and Environment

Within the confines of a relatively narrow area, the UAE straddles five different topographic zones. Moving from west to east, these are (1) the sandy Gulf coast and its intermittent sabkha; (2) the desert foreland; (3) the gravel plains of the interior; (4) the al-Hajar mountain range; and (5) the eastern mountain piedmont and coastal plain which represents the northern extension of the Batinah of Oman. Each of these zones is characterized by a wide range of exploitable natural resources (Table 1) capable of sustaining human groups practising a variety of different subsistence strategies, such as hunting, horticulture, agriculture and pastoralism. Tables 2-6 summarize the chronological distribution of those terrestrial faunal, avifaunal, floral, marine, and molluscan species which we know to have been exploited in antiquity, based on the study of faunal and botanical remains from excavated archaeological sites in the UAE. Unfortunately, at the time of writing the number of sites from which the inventories of faunal and botanical remains have been published remains minimal. Many more archaeological excavations (Fig. 1) have taken place which have yielded biological remains that have not yet been published. Nevertheless, a range of sites with a published floral and faunal record already exists which extends from the late prehistoric era of the fifth/fourth millennium BC to the first few centuries AD, and these leave us in no doubt that the pre-Islamic inhabitants of the region exploited a very wide range of plants, animals, fish and shellfish. So far from being an inhospitable desert, the land and waters of the modern UAE presented its ancient inhabitants with an enormous variety of exploitable, economically important resources.

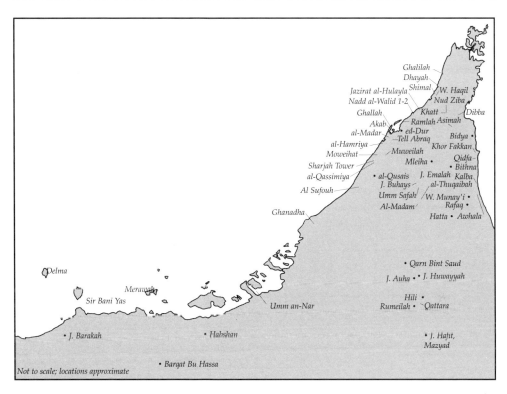

Fig. 1. Map of the UAE, showing the approximate locations of the archaeological sites mentioned in the text.

Table 1. Environments and resources of significance in the past found in the UAE

Resource Category	Gulf Coast	Desert	Interior Piedmont	Mountains	Eastern Piedmont
Faunal	fish shellfish dugong cormorant marine turtles	small mammals gazelle camel	camel	small mammals freshwater fish	fish shellfish marine turtles crabs
Floral	mangrove fodder plants fuel plants medicinal plants	fodder plants fuel plants medicinal plants timber	cultivars fodder plants fuel plants medicinal plants	timber cultivars fodder plants fuel plants medicinal plants	grazing plants timber fodder plants
Mineral	sandstone beach rock lime pearls shell	sandstone	well-drained soils	limestone igneous rock copper iron soft-stones	igneous rock limestone shell
Water	brackish	brackish	abundant	abundant	abundant
Resource Utilization	fishing pearling limited gardening pastoralism	pastoralism oasis horticulture	agriculture horticulture pastoralism	horticulture pastoralism hunting	horticulture pastoralism fishing

Table 2. Mammalian fauna attested on archaeological sites in the UAE

Species	Late Prehistoric	Umm an-Nar	Wadi Suq	Iron Age	Mleiha/ed-Dur
Mammal (wild)					
Rodentia		Tell Abraq[1]	Tell Abraq	Tell Abraq	Mleiha[2]
rat (*Rattus rattus*)					ed-Dur[3]
mouse (*Mus musculus*)					ed-Dur
Rueppell's fox (*Vulpes rueppelis*)					ed-Dur
Arabian red fox (*Vulpes vulpes*)					ed-Dur
fox (*Vulpes* sp.)			Tell Abraq	Tell Abraq	Mleiha
gazelle (*Gazella subgutturosa*)		Tell Abraq Umm an-Nar[4]	Tell Abraq	Tell Abraq	
gazelle indet. (*Gazella gazella* ssp.)	Akab[5]	Tell Abraq	Tell Abraq	Tell Abraq	ed-Dur Mleiha
bottlenose dolphin (*Tursiops truncarus*)					
dolphin indet. (*Delphinus* sp.)		Umm an-Nar	Tell Abraq	Tell Abraq	ed-Dur
dugong (*Dugong dugon*)	Akab	Tell Abraq Umm an-Nar?	Tell Abraq	Tell Abraq	ed-Dur
rorqual (*Balaenoptera*)		Umm an-Nar			
Arabian oryx (*Oryx leucoryx*)		Tell Abraq Umm an-Nar	Tell Abraq	Tell Abraq	ed-Dur
African oryx (*Oryx beisa*)		Umm an-Nar			
camel (*Camelus dromedarius*)		Tell Abraq Umm an-Nar	Tell Abraq		
deer (*Dama mesopotamica*)					ed-Dur
Mammal (domestic)					
Zebu (*Bos indicus*)		Tell Abraq? Umm an-Nar	Tell Abraq	Tell Abraq	
taurine cattle (*Bos taurus*)		Tell Abraq?			ed-Dur Mleiha
sheep (*Ovis aries*)		Tell Abraq Umm an-Nar	Tell Abraq	Tell Abraq	ed-Dur Mleiha
goat (*Capra hircus*)		Tell Abraq Umm an-Nar	Tell Abraq	Tell Abraq	ed-Dur Mleiha
canid indet.			Tell Abraq	Tell Abraq	Mleiha
dog (*Canis familiaris*)					ed-Dur
donkey (*Equus*)					Mleiha
equid indet.		Tell Abraq	Tell Abraq	Tell Abraq	ed-Dur
dromedary camel (*Camelus dromedarius*)			Tell Abraq		ed-Dur Mleiha
Bactrian camel (*Camelus ferus* f. *bactriana*)					ed-Dur

[1] Stephan, in press.
[2] Gautier 1992.
[3] Van Neer and Gautier 1993.
[4] Hoch 1979, 1995.
[5] Prieur and Guerin 1991.

Table 3. Reptiles and birds attested on archaeological sites in the UAE

Species	Late Prehistoric	Umm an-Nar	Wadi Suq	Iron Age	Mleiha/ed-Dur
Reptile (wild)					
green turtle (*Chelonia mydas*)	Akab[1]	Tell Abraq[2] Umm an-Nar	Tell Abraq?	Tell Abraq?	ed-Dur[3]
Bird (wild)					
Socotra Cormorant (*Phalacrocorax nigrogularis*)		Tell Abraq Umm an-Nar[4]	Tell Abraq	Tell Abraq	ed-Dur Mleiha[5]
ostrich (*Struthio camelus*)		Tell Abraq			Mleiha
snake bird (*Anhinga rufa*)		Umm an-Nar			
duck (*Anas querquedula*)		Umm an-Nar			
flamingo (*Phoenicopterus* aff. *ruber*)		Umm an-Nar			
giant heron? (*Ardea bennuides*)		Umm an-Nar			
bird unident.			Tell Abraq	Tell Abraq	
Bird (domestic)					
chicken (*Gallus gallus* f. *domestica*)					ed-Dur

[1] Prieur and Guerin 1991.
[2] Stephan, in press.
[3] Van Neer and Gautier 1993.
[4] Hoch 1979, 1995.
[5] Gautier 1992.

Table 4. Fish attested on archaeological sites in the UAE

Species	Late Prehistoric	Umm an-Nar	Wadi Suq	Iron Age	Mleiha/ed-Dur
Fish (marine)					
Carcharhinidae					
requiem shark (*Carcharhinus* sp.)					ed-Dur[1]
Sphyrnidae					
hammerhead shark (*Sphyrna* sp.)					ed-Dur
shark indet.		Umm an-Nar[2]			ed-Dur
Pristidae					
sawfish (*Pristis* sp.)		Umm an-Nar			ed-Dur
Dasyatidae (Trygonidae)					
stingray (*Dasyatis?*)		Umm an-Nar			ed-Dur
Clupeidae					
herring (*Clupeidae* indet.)					ed-Dur
Chanidae					
milkfish (*Chanos chanos*)					ed-Dur
Ariidae					
sea catfish (*Arius thalassinus*)					ed-Dur
Belonidae					
needlefish (*Tylosurus crocodilus*)					ed-Dur
Platycephalidae					
flathead (*Platycephalus indicus*)					ed-Dur
Serranidae					
sea bass/grouper (*Epinephelus* sp.)					ed-Dur
Carangidae					
jacks and pompanos					ed-Dur
(*Scomberoides* sp.)					
(*Seriola* sp.)					
(*Megalaspis cordyla*)					
(*Carangoides chrysophrys*)					
(*Carangoides* sp.)					
(*Caranx* sp.)					
(*Gnathodon speciosus*)					
(*Alectis indicus*)					
(*Ulua mentalis*)					
Carangidae indet.					
Lutjanidae					
snapper (*Lutjanus* sp.)					ed-Dur
Gerreidae					
mojarra (*Gerres* sp.)					ed-Dur
Haemulidae					
grunt (*Pomadasys* sp.)					ed-Dur
Lethrinidae					
emperor (*Lethrinus* sp.)	al-Madar?[3]				ed-Dur
Sparidae					
porgie					ed-Dur
(*Crenidens crenidens*)					ed-Dur
(*Acanthopagrus berda*)					ed-Dur
(*Acanthopagrus latus*)					ed-Dur
(*Rhabdosargus sarba*)					ed-Dur
(*Rhabdosargus* sp.)					Mleiha
(*Argyrops spinifer*)					ed-Dur
Sparidae indet.	al-Madar?				ed-Dur
Ephippidae					
spadefish (*Platax* sp.)					ed-Dur
Mugilidae					
mullet (*Mugilidae* indet.)					ed-Dur
					Mleiha
Sphyraenidae					
barracuda (*Sphyraena* sp.)					ed-Dur
Scaridae					
parrotfish (*Scarus* sp.)					ed-Dur
Siganidae					
rabbitfish (*Siganus* sp.)					ed-Dur
Scombridae					
bonito/tuna (*Euthynnus affinis*)					ed-Dur
					Mleiha
tuna (*Thunnus* sp.)					ed-Dur
					Mleiha
Scombridae indet.					ed-Dur
Tetraodontidae					
puffer (Tetraodontidae indet.)					ed-Dur
fish indet. (still under study)		Tell Abraq[4]	Tell Abraq	Tell Abraq	
Fish (freshwater)					
Cyprinidae					
barbel (*Barbus* sp.)					ed-Dur
Crustaceans					
crab et al. (still under study)	al-Madar	Tell Abraq	Tell Abraq	Tell Abraq	ed-Dur
					Mleiha

[1] Van Neer and Gautier 1993.
[2] Hoch 1979, 1995.
[3] Uerpmann and Uerpmann, in press.
[4] Stephan, in press.

Table 5. Plants and cultivars attested on archaeological sites in the UAE

Species	Late Prehistoric	Umm an-Nar	Wadi Suq	Iron Age	Mleiha/ed-Dur
Flora (wild)					
mangrove (*Avicennia marina*)			Tell Abraq?		
extinct mangrove (*Rhizophora* type)			Tell Abraq?		
Christ's thorn (*Ziziphus spina-christi*)			Tell Abraq?		Mleiha[1]
		Hili 8[2]			
tamarisk (*Tamarix* sp.)			Tell Abraq?		
oat (*Avena* sp.)		Hili 8			
Flora (domestic)					
wheat (*Triticum* sp.)		Umm an-Nar[3]			Mleiha
emmer wheat (*Triticum dicoccum*)		Hili 8			
bread wheat (*Triticum aestivum*)		Tell Abraq[4]	Tell Abraq		
		Hili 8			
barley (*Hordeum* sp.)		Umm an-Nar			Mleiha
2-row hulled barley (*Hordeum distichon*)		Hili 8			
6-row hulled barley (*Hordeum vulgare*)		Tell Abraq	Tell Abraq	Tell Abraq	
		Hili 8			
6-row naked barley (*H. vulgare* var. *nudum*)		Hili 8			
date-palm (*Phoenix dactylifera*)		Tell Abraq	Tell Abraq		ed-Dur
		Hili 8		Muweilah[5]	
melon (*Cucumis* sp.)		Hili 8			

[1] Coubray 1988.
[2] Cleuziou and Costantini 1980, Cleuziou 1989, Potts 1994b.
[3] Willcox 1995.
[4] Willcox and Tengberg 1995.
[5] P. Magee, pers. comm.

Most of the flora and fauna utilized by the pre-Islamic population of the region is still to be found in the area. This fact is not an unequivocal indication that no climatic change has taken place since the prehistoric past, but it is certainly an indication that the changes which have taken place have been minor rather than major ones. At the height of the Flandrian Transgression, c. 4000 BC, sea-level in the Arabian Gulf reached its peak around half a metre higher than it is today, and until c. 3000 BC a more humid environment prevailed, largely as a result of wind systems which were weaker than those at present, 'permitting convection-induced thunder storms in coastal and mountainous areas' (Glennie et al. 1994: p 3). After 3000 BC today's arid regime set in and although there have been minor adjustments in climate since that time, it is safe to say that the basic pattern observable in the region today has prevailed for the past five millennia.

The Arabian Bifacial Tradition (c. 5000-3100 BC)

During the last glacial maximum (from c. 68,000 to 8,000 BC), winds were so strong in the desert regions of the globe that they 'probably blew at sand-transporting speeds for much of each glacial winter' in eastern Arabia causing 'severe dessication, even at reduced air temperatures, producing conditions that were probably too severe for man to tolerate' (Glennie et al. 1994: pp 2-3). This fact, perhaps more than any other, helps to explain the absence of Pleistocene hominid occupation and Middle and Upper Palaeolithic stone tool industries in the UAE. The only exception to this yet identified may come from a site at Jabal Barakah in the Western Region of Abu Dhabi where a radial core was recovered from the surface which resembles early European and African material (McBrearty 1993).

Table 6. Molluscan fauna attested on archaeological sites in the UAE

Species	Late Prehistoric	Umm an-Nar	Wadi Suq	Iron Age	Mleiha/ed-Dur
Marine molluscs					
Bivalves					
Alectryonella plicatula					Mleiha[1]
Amiantis umbonella		Tell Abraq[2]	Tell Abraq Shimal[3]	Tell Abraq	
Anadara sp.					Mleiha
Anadara antiquata			Shimal		
Anadara ehrenbergeri	al-Madar[4]			Tell Abraq Awhala[5]	Mleiha
Anadara uropigimelana					Mleiha
Anodontia edentula					Mleiha
Asaphis deflorata			Tell Abraq	Tell Abraq	Mleiha
Asaphis violascens			Shimal		
Balanus sp.				Tell Abraq	
Barbatia fusca				Tell Abraq	Mleiha
Barbatia helblingii			Shimal		
Barbatia sp.	al-Madar				ed-Dur[6]
Callista erycina	Akab[7]	Tell Abraq	Tell Abraq Shimal	Tell Abraq Awhala	Mleiha
Cardita sp.					ed-Dur
Certhidea cingulata		Tell Abraq			ed-Dur
Chama sp.					Mleiha
Chlamys ruschenbergerii		Tell Abraq	Tell Abraq Shimal		Mleiha
Circe corrugata			Shimal		Mleiha
Circenita callipyga			Shimal	Tell Abraq	Mleiha
Decatopecten plica					Mleiha
Glycymeris sp.					ed-Dur Mleiha
Glycymeris lividus		Tell Abraq			Mleiha
Glycymeris maskatensis		Tell Abraq	Tell Abraq Shimal	Tell Abraq	Mleiha
Isognomon tegumen			Shimal		
Laevicardium papyraceum					Mleiha
Mactra lilacea					Mleiha
Marcia sp.			Shimal	Awhala	Mleiha
Marcia hiantina	Akab al-Madar	Tell Abraq	Tell Abraq Shimal	Tell Abraq Muweilah[8]	ed-Dur Mleiha
Marcia opima				Tell Abraq	
Modiolus phillipinarum					ed-Dur
Periglypta puerpera					Mleiha
Pinctada sp.		Tell Abraq?	Tell Abraq	Tell Abraq Awhala	ed-Dur Mleiha
Pinctada margaritifera		Tell Abraq	Tell Abraq Shimal	Tell Abraq Muweilah	Mleiha
Pinctada radiata	al-Madar		Tell Abraq Shimal Tell Abraq	Muweilah	ed-Dur Mleiha
Pinna sp.					
Pteria marmorata					Mleiha
Saccostrea cucullata	Akab Hamriyah[9] al-Madar	Tell Abraq	Tell Abraq Shimal	Tell Abraq Awhala Muweilah	ed-Dur Mleiha
Sanguinolaria cumingiana			Tell Abraq		
Solen sp.					Mleiha
Spondylus sp.			Tell Abraq	Tell Abraq	ed-Dur Mleiha
Spondylus ?*exilis*			Shimal		
Spondylus gaederopus					Mleiha
Sunetta effosa					Mleiha
Tivela damaoïdes					Mleiha
Trachycardium sp.					Mleiha
Trachycardium lacunosum			Tell Abraq Shimal	Tell Abraq	ed-Dur Mleiha
Turitella sp.					ed-Dur
Venus verrucosa					Mleiha
Marine molluscs					
Gastropods					
Architectonia perspectiva			Tell Abraq?		
Babylonia spirata					Mleiha
Bullia sp.					Mleiha
Bullia tranquebarica				Tell Abraq	
Bursa sp.?					Mleiha
Bythinia sp.					Mleiha
Cerithium sp.					Mleiha
Cerithium caeruleum					Mleiha
Cerithidea cingulata		Tell Abraq	Shimal	Tell Abraq	ed-Dur
Charonia sp.?					Mleiha
Conus sp.			Tell Abraq		Mleiha
Conus betulinus					Mleiha
Conus striatus					Mleiha

Table 6. Molluscan fauna attested on archaeological sites in the UAE (Continued)

Species	Late Prehistoric	Umm an-Nar	Wadi Suq	Iron Age	Mleiha/ed-Dur
Conus textile					ed-Dur
Cronia konkanensis			Shimal		Mleiha
Cuma lacera		Tell Abraq?	Tell Abraq?		
Cymatium sp.					Mleiha
Cypraea sp.			Tell Abraq		ed-Dur
					Mleiha
Cypraea arabica			Tell Abraq		Mleiha
Cypraea clandestina				Awhala	
Cypraea gracilis					ed-Dur
Cypraea grayana				Awhala	
Cypraea aff. *lentiginosa*					Mleiha
Cypraea turdus		Tell Abraq	Tell Abraq		ed-Dur
			Shimal		Mleiha
Engina mendicaria					ed-Dur
Ficus subintermedia		Tell Abraq	Tell Abraq?	Tell Abraq	Mleiha
		Jabal al-Emalah[10]	Shimal		
		Al Sufouh[11]			
Fusinus arabicus					ed-Dur
Lunella coronatus			Shimal		
Monilea obscura			Shimal		Mleiha
Murex (Hexaplex) kuesterianus	Akab	Tell Abraq	Tell Abraq	Tell Abraq	ed-Dur
	Hamriyah			Muweilah	Mleiha
	al-Madar				
Murex scolopax				Tell Abraq	
Nassarius arcularius plicatus		Tell Abraq			
Nassarius coronatus					Mleiha
Nassarius sp.			Shimal		
Nerita sp.					Mleiha
Nerita albicilla					Mleiha
Neverita sp.?					Mleiha
Neverita didyma			Tell Abraq	Tell Abraq	Mleiha
Oliva bulbosa		Tell Abraq	Shimal	Tell Abraq	ed-Dur
					Mleiha
Patella sp.					ed-Dur
Phalium faurotis					Mleiha
Phasianella solida			Shimal		
Phasienella variegata					Mleiha
Planaxis sulcatus					Mleiha
Polinices tumidus					Mleiha
Polinices sp.			Shimal		
Rapana bulbosa					Mleiha
Siratus kuesterianus			Shimal		
Strombus decorus persicus			Tell Abraq	Tell Abraq	ed-Dur
			Shimal		Mleiha
Terebralia palustris	Akab	Tell Abraq	Tell Abraq	Tell Abraq	ed-Dur
	Hamriyah		Shimal	Awhala	Mleiha
	al-Madar			Muweilah	
Thais mutabilis?					Mleiha
Thais savignyi			Shimal		
Tonna sp			Shimal		Mleiha
Tonna dolium					Mleiha
Tonna luteostoma?					Mleiha
Trochus erythraeus		Tell Abraq	Tell Abraq?		Mleiha
			Shimal		
Turbo coronatus	al-Madar	Tell Abraq	Tell Abraq	Tell Abraq	Mleiha
Turbo radiatus					Mleiha
Turritella sp.					ed-Dur
					Mleiha
Turritella cochlea					Mleiha
Turritella torulosa					Mleiha
Umbonium vestiarium			Shimal		
Vermetes sulcatus					ed-Dur
Scaphopods					
Dentalium octangulatum		Al-Sufouh	Shimal		Mleiha
		Jabal al-Emalah			
Freshwater molluscs					
Melanoides tuberculata					ed-Dur

[1] Prieur 1989, 1994.
[2] Prieur 1990.
[3] Glover 1991.
[4] Uerpmann and Uerpmann, in press.
[5] E. Thompson, pers. comm.
[6] Van Neer and Gautier 1993.
[7] Prieur and Guerin 1991.
[8] E. Thompson, pers. comm.
[9] Jasim 1996.
[10] Benton and Potts, in press.
[11] Benton 1996.

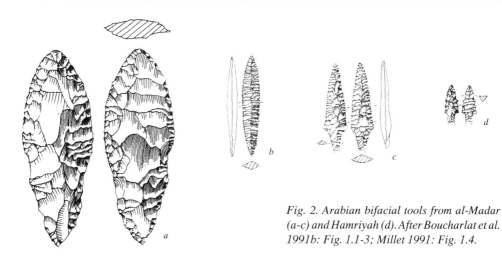

*Fig. 2. Arabian bifacial tools from al-Madar
(a-c) and Hamriyah (d). After Boucharlat et al.
1991b: Fig. 1.1-3; Millet 1991: Fig. 1.4.*

The last glaciation collapsed around 10,000 years ago, and the slightly moister conditions which ensued from c. 8000 to 3000 BC have often been described as a Climatic Optimum (Glennie et al. 1994: p 3). It was during this period that the first securely dated human settlements in the region appeared. Finely pressure flaked, bifacial stone tools (Fig. 2) belonging to what has been called the 'Arabian bifacial tradition' have been found on a large number of sites in a wide range of environmental zones throughout the Emirates. The most important of these are listed in Table 7. Tanged points, foliates, blades, knives, drills and other tools attest to the diversity of the tool-kit of the region's first inhabitants. Affinities with material from the Eastern Province of Saudi Arabia, Qatar and Bahrain are obvious, suggesting that the entire region may have formed a single cultural province at this time.

Table 7. Principal late prehistoric sites in the UAE

Location	Site	Literature
Jazirat al-Hamra	Nadd al-Walid 1-2	Gebel 1988; Glover et al. 1990; Uerpmann 1992
Ras al-Khaimah	Wadi Haqil	deCardi 1985
Khatt	Kh 92, 117-119, 135	de Cardi et al. 1994
Umm al-Qaiwain	al-Madar	Cauvin & Calley 1984; Boucharlat et al. 1991b; Haerinck 1994b Uerpmann & Uerpmann n.d.
	Ramlah	Uerpmann & Uerpmann n.d.
	Akab	Prieur & Guerin 1991; Boucharlat et al. 1991a
	Tell Abraq	Potts 1991a
Sharjah	al-Hamriya	Cauvin & Calley 1984; Minzoni Déroche 1985a; Haerinck 1991a; Millet 1991; Boucharlat et al. 1991a; Haerinck 1994b; Jasim 1996
	al-Qassimiya	Minzoni Déroche 1985a; Calley & Santoni 1986; Millet 1988; Boucharlat et al. 1991a
	Sharjah Tower	Millet 1988
Mleiha/	P15, 18-19,	Minzoni Déroche 1985b; Millet 1989
Jabal Faiyah	21-22, 28 Jabal al-Emalah	unpubl.
Jabal Buhays	Jabal Buhays	S. Jasim, H.-P. and M. Uerpmann, pers. comm.
Al Madam	Al-Madam	Gebel 1988
Qarn Bint Saud	Qarn Bint Saud	Gebel 1988
Al-Ain	Jabal Huwayyah	Copeland & Bergne 1976; Gebel et al. 1989
	Jabal Auha	Gebel 1988
	Mazyad	Gebel 1988; Gebel et al. 1989
	Hili 8	Inizan and Tisier 1980
Western Province	Barqat Bu Hassa	Gebel 1988
	Habshan	Gebel 1988
	Jabal Barakah?	McBrearty 1993
Abu Dhabi	Dalma	Hellyer 1993, Flavin and Shepherd 1994
islands	Merawah	'Neolithic flints...'

In other respects these areas also show shared traits. Painted pottery of Ubaid-type, imported from Mesopotamia, has been found on many of the coastal sites in the UAE, eastern Saudi Arabia, Qatar, Bahrain and the islands of Kuwait, revealing the existence of contacts between these regions and the peoples of southern Iraq in the fifth millennium BC. Petrographic analysis, moreover, has confirmed that some (and most probably all) of the pottery found on the Arabian bifacial sites in eastern Saudi Arabia was imported from Mesopotamia itself, and the likelihood that such was the case in respect to the material found on sites in the UAE is equally strong (Méry 1994: p 398). Be that as it may, it is important to underscore the fact that this introduction of pottery into the region did not lead immediately to the birth of a local ceramic industry, something which did not appear until the third millennium BC.

Contact with areas to the north may also help account for the introduction of domesticates such as sheep, goat and cattle, the wild forerunners of which were never at home in south-eastern Arabia (Uerpmann and Uerpmann n.d.). All of these domesticates have been found on Arabian bifacial sites in eastern Saudi Arabia and they are present at Ras al-Hamra 6 in Oman by the fifth millennium as well. Thus, it is likely that they were being herded on sites in the UAE by this time. As the stone tool industry found throughout eastern Arabia which precedes the bifacial tradition - known as Qatar B (but absent in the UAE) - shows clear affinities to the pre-pottery Neolithic industry of the Levant, it has been suggested that this may have been the ultimate source of both the people and the herd animals which eventually populated eastern Arabia during the earlier portion of the mid-Holocene Climatic Optimum, beginning c. 5000 BC.

The fact that the tool kit of the earliest inhabitants of the region contained numerous projectile points should not lead us to conclude prematurely that they were primarily hunters. Rather, Uerpmann and Uerpmann (n.d.) have stressed that herders will maximize their own flocks' secondary products - such as milk, fleece and hair - by preserving their animals and hunting to provide any meat desired. Thus, the Arabian bifacial sites may be those of herders who supplemented their diet by hunting, rather than hunters who kept a few domestic animals.

Whether or not these groups were fully sedentary is unknown. A transhumant pattern of occupation along the coasts in the winter, when fishing and shellfish gathering would have been the main pursuits, and summer residence in the interior, when pastoralism and, eventually, horticulture, were practised, is entirely feasible and well-attested elsewhere in south-eastern Arabia (Lancaster and Lancaster 1992: p 345), if as yet unproven for the prehistoric UAE. Certainly this would account for the fact that coastal sites, which usually contain some areas of shell midden formation, are generally not very deep, whereas interior sites generally have little if any stratification. It would also account for the uniformity in the tool-kit evidenced in both the coast and the interior of the UAE.

As yet we know little about the people who inhabited the territory of the UAE at this time. Burials in an Arabian bifacial site along the coast of the Umm al-Qaiwain lagoon have been excavated but not yet published (C.S. Phillips, pers. comm). At Jabal Buhays, S. Jasim of the Sharjah Department of Antiquities has begun the excavation of an important collective burial just beneath the surface at the base of the *jabal*. This is being continued by H.-P. and M. Uerpmann and is certain to produce important results, particularly as the site is aceramic, shows evidence of tools attributable to the Arabian bifacial tradition, and contains exclusively cremated skeletal remains.

The Late Fourth and Early Third Millennium (c. 3100-2500 BC)

At the end of the fourth millennium, c. 3100-3000 BC, a major suite of innovations appeared in the material culture inventory of the region. For the first time collective burials in the form of above-ground tombs (Fig. 3) built of unworked stone appear at two sites in the UAE, Jabal Hafit (including Mazyad) and Jabal al-Emalah. Named after the site where they were first discovered, these 'Hafit'-type tombs are completely without precedent in the local archaeological sequence. What is more, a number of them have yielded small, biconical ceramic vessels, many so badly preserved as to have lost their original surfaces, but some on which a panel of painted, geometric decoration in black can still be seen (Potts 1986a). Not only are these vessels (Fig. 3) superficially reminiscent of so-called 'Jamdat Nasr' pottery from southern Mesopotamia, but analyses of examples from both Jabal Hafit (Méry 1991: p 72) and Jabal al-Emalah (unpubl.) have confirmed that this material was imported, some of it from the type site Jamdat Nasr in south-central Iraq.

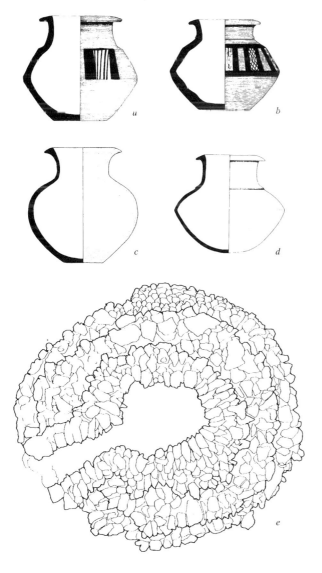

Because of the fact that most of the Hafit tombs in the UAE were robbed in antiquity little data is available on their occupants (but cf. Højgaard 1985), and it is difficult to get a good idea of just how many people were normally buried within them. More than one is probably all that can be said at the moment, but, given the restricted size of their keyhole-

Fig. 3. Selected examples of Jamdat Nasr-type pottery (a-d) from Hafit-type tombs at Jabal Hafit excavated by the Danish expedition and a plan of one of the tombs (6.4 m. in diameter) excavated by the French mission (e). After Frifelt 1971: Figs. 12A, 17A, 22B and 22A; and Cleuziou et al. 1978: Pl. 15.

45

like, interior chambers, it cannot have been greater than perhaps a dozen or so. Around the keyhole a large area of mounded, unworked rock was heaped up, sometimes with a discernible 'bench' encircling the exterior. Whereas the tombs at Jabal Hafit range in size from an estimated 7 to 11 m in diameter (Frifelt 1971: p 377), the Jabal al-Emalah examples are approximately 11 to 12 m across (Benton and Potts 1994). In addition to their pottery, other imported finds of note include a class of roughly square, bone or ivory beads with two diagonal perforations. These find identical parallels in Iran at Susa, Tepe Hissar and Tepe Yahya and in Mesopotamia at Uruk, always in contexts dating to c. 3000 BC (Frifelt 1980: Pl. XVa; Potts 1993a: p 183 for full refs.).

To date the settlements of the population buried in the Hafit tombs of south-eastern Arabia (examples are also found further south in Oman) have yet to be discovered. Although it has been argued by S. Cleuziou that the occupation of the settlement at Hili 8 in Al-Ain began c. 3100 BC there are good grounds for questioning this early date. Thus, it is striking that the two radiocarbon determinations on which this contention is based (MC-2266 and 2267) are roughly 500 years earlier than the next earliest date from the site and, moreover, both of these early dates derive from samples of wood charcoal (Potts n.d.a). As experience has shown at other sites, radiocarbon determinations run on charcoal are often anomalously early because the wood in question was old by the time it was burned. Thus, for example, a ship's timber or architectural beam may have been used initially, re-cycled several times, and finally burned as fuel hundreds of years after its initial employment, unlike dates, fruit pips, matting, and other organic materials which have a much more finite lifespan. If we discount Hili 8 as a settlement which may have existed in tandem with the period in which the graves on the slopes of Jabal Hafit were built, we are left with no settlements with which to pair these important funerary monuments.

The question naturally arises why and how the contact which transmitted the Jamdat Nasr vessels from Mesopotamia to the Oman peninsula was organized. In most discussions of this phenomenon an economic motivation is ascribed to the Mesopotamian bearers of the Jamdat Nasr-type ceramics and beads which have appeared at Jabal Hafit and Jabal al-Emalah. What resources they may have been in search of is unknown, but it is generally admitted that copper from the al-Hajar mountains is a likely candidate. Certainly small pins and awls of copper have been found in Hafit burials (Frifelt 1971), but it cannot always be assumed that these date to the original period in which these tombs were used, and at both Jabal Hafit and Jabal al-Emalah we have ample evidence for the later re-use of the tombs during the third, second and first millennia BC and, at the latter site, as late as the fifth or sixth century AD (see below). More relevant, perhaps, is the fact that the earliest proto-cuneiform texts from Uruk in southern Mesopotamia which date to c. 3400-3000 BC - the so-called 'Archaic Texts' - already contain references to 'Dilmun' copper. Dilmun was later identified with mainland eastern Saudi Arabia and Bahrain, but as there is no copper in either of these areas it has usually been assumed that the copper in question must have come from further afield. On analogy with the situation in the late third and second millennia BC the copper source most often invoked is that which stretches from Fujairah in the north (Hassan and al-Sulaimi 1979) to lower Oman in the south. Thus, although there is no proof as yet, it has generally been assumed that the motivation behind the Jamdat Nasr-period contact between the UAE and southern Mesopotamia was the incipient trade in copper.

The Mid- to Late Third Millennium (c. 2500-2000 BC)

The agricultural settlement of south-eastern Arabia was predicated upon the domestication of the date-palm (*Phoenix dactylifera*). Without the date-palm, the shade necessary for the growth of other, less hardy cultivars, including cereals, vegetables and fruits, was lacking. Once the bustan-type of garden came into existence, watered by wells which tapped the relatively abundant and shallow lenses of sweet water found throughout much of the UAE, the basis was laid for the development of the kind of oasis living which is so characteristic of the wadi settlements of the region. Herd animals, such as sheep, goat and cattle, of course played a part in the development of a full oasis economy, but no single species was so critical in this process as the date-palm.

The earliest agricultural villages of the UAE were thus agriculturally based, and perhaps, in order to safeguard their investment in land, water and natural resources, the inhabitants of those villages felt compelled to construct imposing fortifications. These buildings appear for the first time in the middle of the third millennium and are an architectural *leit fossil* of the so-called 'Umm an-Nar' period (c. 2500-2000 BC). Like their later descendants at sites such as Nizwa in Oman, the fortress-towers of south-eastern Arabia took the form of raised, circular platforms consisting of massive crosswalls and intervening hollows filled with gravel, the entirety of which supported a surface raised up off the ground (by as much as 8 m) with a still higher, outer wall for defence. Undoubtedly small buildings stood upon these raised platforms as well. Every example excavated to date is also distinguished by the presence of a well in the centre of the building, and it may be justifiably asked whether or not the entire fortress is not a 'lock' placed upon the precious water supply of the village in which the fortress was located.

In the UAE, examples of such Umm an-Nar fortress-towers have been excavated at Hili 1 (Fig. 4), Hili 8 (Cleuziou 1989), Bidya (Al Tikriti 1989), Tell Abraq (Potts 1990a, 1991a, 1993b, 1995a) and Kalba (C.S. Phillips, pers. comm). Whereas most of these range in size between 16 and 25 m in diameter, the tower at Tell Abraq, at 40 m in diameter, is by far the largest yet uncovered. The social and political implications of these towers is intriguing. There is no longer any doubt that, by the late third millennium BC, the Oman peninsula was identified in Mesopotamian cuneiform sources as **Magan** (Sumerian) or *Makkan*

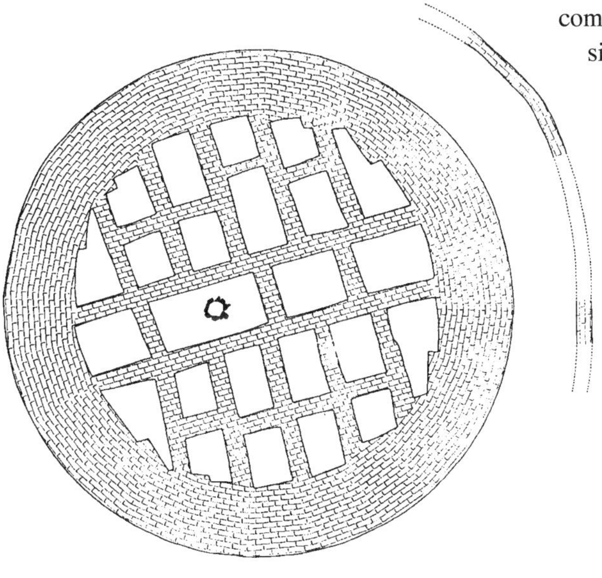

Fig. 4. The Umm an-Nar-period fortress-tower of Hili 1, 24 m. in diameter. After Frifelt 1975: Fig. 3.

(Akkadian). In addition to safeguarding the agricultural settlements in their environs, the towers of the Umm an-Nar period may also have been the power centres for the 'lords of Magan' against whom several of the Old Akkadian emperors, including Manishtusu and Naram-Sin, campaigned in the twenty-third century BC (Potts 1986b, n.d. b). Manishtusu's allusion to campaigning against no fewer than 32 'lords of Magan' implies a decentralized political landscape at the time, and one can well imagine a situation in which petty sheikhs, each in control of a certain amount of territory centred around a primary settlement (such as Tell Abraq, Bidya, Hili, etc.) dominated by a fortress-tower, banded together to repulse the Akkadian invasion of Magan. It should also be noted that unfortified settlements of a more ephemeral nature have also been discovered, particularly along the Gulf coast (e.g. at Ghanadha, see Al Tikriti 1985; Al Sufouh, see Benton 1996; at ed-Dur, see Boucharlat et al. 1988: pp 2-3; and Umm an-Nar, Frifelt 1991).

In general, the dead of the Umm an-Nar period were buried in circular, stone tombs faced with finely-masoned ashlar blocks, although rectangular chambers, perhaps for secondary reburial of bone from circular tombs which had become full, are also known (Haerinck 1990-91). Examples of Umm an-Nar circular tombs were first encountered by a Danish expedition on the island of Umm an-Nar in Abu Dhabi in 1958 (Frifelt 1991). Thus it was that the island gave its name to the period of which these tombs are characteristic. Umm an-Nar-type tombs range in size from c. 4 to 14 m in diameter. Internally, the structures have a variable configuration of crosswalls which may either be free-

Fig. 5. The Umm an-Nar-type tomb at Al Sufouh, 6 m. in diameter. After Benton 1996.

standing, bounded on each end by a passage leading from one half of the tomb to the other, or joined to the external tomb wall, dividing the interior of the tomb into two halves without access to each other. By 1995, examples of Umm an-Nar tombs (Fig. 5) had been excavated in both coastal and inland Abu Dhabi (Umm an-Nar island, Hili area), Dubai (Al Sufouh and Hatta), Ajman (Moweihat), Umm al-Qaiwain (Tell Abraq), and Ras al-Khaimah (Shimal, Wadi Munay'i). The better-preserved examples show that literally hundreds of individuals were buried in these tombs along with a wide range of grave furniture, including soft-stone bowls; fine and domestic black-on-red ceramics (Fig. 6) of local manufacture (Frifelt 1990); incised grey and painted black-on-grey pottery (Fig. 6) from south-eastern Iran or Baluchistan (Cleuziou and Vogt 1985); copper-bronze weaponry (daggers, spearheads; cf. Pedersen and Buchwald 1991, on Umm an-Nar-period metallurgy); personal items of jewellery such as bracelets and necklaces incorporating thousands of beads, a significant proportion of which are Harappan paste micro-beads from the Indus Valley; and other exotic items such as ivory combs (Potts 1993d), gypsum lamps (Potts 1995a), and linen (Reade and Potts 1993).

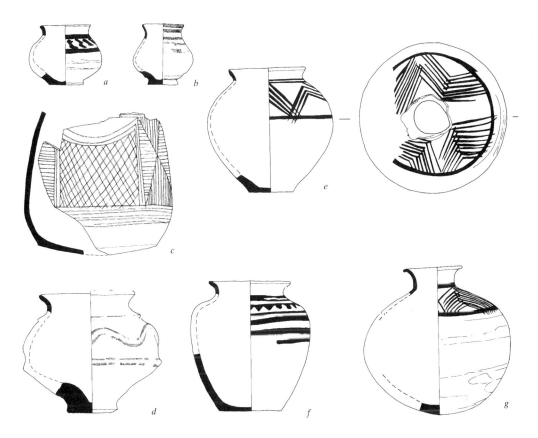

Fig. 6. A selection of Umm an-Nar-period pottery from the tomb at Al Sufouh, including black-on-grey (a-b), incised grey (c), fine tan with raised meandering ridge (d), and fine black-on-orange (e-g). After Benton 1996.

Like their Hafit counterparts, many Umm an-Nar-period tombs were robbed in antiquity, but those excavated at Umm an-Nar, Hili North (Tomb A), Tell Abraq, Shimal, Moweihat and al-Sufouh have yielded substantial quantities of human skeletal remains which are beginnng to provide important evidence on the diet and health of the late third millennium population of the Oman peninsula. Furthermore, they reveal that all age grades, from foetal infants to elderly adults, were interred together in these tombs. One of the most intriguing questions concerns the relationship between the individuals buried in the different chambers of a tomb. Recent analyses of the epigenetic traits on teeth (cf. Højgaard 1980) from three of the tombs excavated by the Danish expedition on Umm an-Nar indeed supports the idea that the individuals buried within a single tomb were genetically related, probably representing members of closely inter-married families (Alt, Vach, Frifelt and Kunter 1995).

Palaeopathological inferences can also be drawn from an analysis of Umm an-Nar-period skeletal remains. At Tell Abraq, for example, A. Goodman and D. Martin have studied some 6442 analysable post-cranial elements from the western half of the tomb, in addition to hundreds of disarticulated teeth. Some of the preliminary conclusions of their work may be summarized as follows:

Periostitis and osteomyelitis, both of which result from non-specific infections such as staph and strep, are found on roughly half of the tibia recovered. Signs of trauma in the form of healed and unhealed lesions (mainly on the hands, ribs, and forearms) and osteochondritis dessicans (lesions which develop in response to trauma to joint systems) were detected on roughly 5% of all skeletal elements. Osteoarthritis was found in a significant proportion of the adult population. Fluorosis (exaggerated bone formation at muscle and ligament attachments) and anemia of unknown origin leading to perotic hyperostosis (thickening of the cranium) were also found. Turning to the dental evidence, fluorosis is suggested by dental mottling in a large portion of the dental finds. Attrition was extremely severe, as was caries in certain individuals, and enamel hypoplasisas (severe enamel growth disruption due to infection) were common among children. (Potts 1993b: p 121).

Perhaps most surprising in the tomb at Tell Abraq was the discovery, amongst otherwise disarticulated bone, of a unique, fully articulated female aged c. 20. 'Abnormal upward curvature of the spine of about 30° beyond normal, early osteoarthritis changes in the right knee and ankle, a mild deformity of the left foot and mild changes in the right foot' suggest that 'the female was sedentary, overused her right leg and had a neuromuscular imbalance of the lower left leg. It further suggests the individual suffered from a neurological disease of several years' duration which led to partial crippling' ('At Tell Abraq...' 1994). After considerable consultation with a wide range of specialists, D. Martin has confirmed that poliomyelitis is the most likely diagnosis, making this the earliest recorded instance of polio ever confirmed in the archaeological record anywhere in the world.

Mention was made above of contact between late third millennium Magan and the Old Akkadian empire. Not only are these connections attested to in cuneiform sources, but complementary archaeological evidence exists in the form of large, buffware storage jars from Umm an-Nar island (Fig. 7), confirmed by analysis to be Mesopotamian (Mynors 1982), and a seal-impressed jar fragment of Syrian provenance (Amiet 1975, 1985). This material indicates the transport of a liquid, perhaps oil, from Mesopotamia to Umm an-Nar island at this time. Contacts were also maintained in other directions as well. The incised grey and painted black-on-grey wares from numerous Umm an-Nar tombs were manufactured in southern Iran and/or Baluchistan (Blackman et al. 1989). Settlements such as Tell Abraq, Hili 8, and Asimah (in

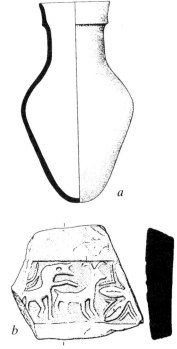

Fig. 7. An Early Dynastic III-type, Mesopotamian storage jar from Grave 1 (a) and a cylinder seal-impressed sherd (b) from the settlement on Umm an-Nar. After Frifelt 1991: Fig. 86 and 1995: Fig. 255.

Fig. 8. The ivory comb from the late Umm an-Nar-period tomb at Tell Abraq.

Ras al-Khaimah) have yielded diagnostic examples of black-washed, finely levigated, thick micaceous orange ware which comes from the Indus Valley (Cleuziou 1992: p 97; Potts 1994c: p 617 and Fig. 53.3). These certainly represent fragments of storage jars, suggesting that something was being exported from the Harappan world to the Gulf in bulk. It has recently been posited that a milk-product, perhaps a sort of cheese, was the commodity in question (Gouin 1990: pp 48-49). The presence of diagnostically Harappan etched carnelian beads, as well as thousands of paste micro-beads, and cubical chert weights with identical parallels at all of the major Harappan sites, and small objects of ivory, also implies contact with the Indus Valley in the late third millennium Finally, a unique ivory comb (Fig. 8) from the tomb at Tell Abraq can be reliably identified on the basis of its particular floral decoration as an import from Bactria (northern Afghanistan/southern Uzbekistan) (Potts 1993d).

Excavations at Asimah in the interior of Ras al-Khaimah have revealed the existence of stone alignments consisting of raised platforms and subterranean graves which, on the basis of their associated finds, also date to the Umm an-Nar period (Vogt 1994a: pp 101ff). These monuments, which have been compared with the triliths and alignments of southern and western Arabia, suggest that a degree of cultural diversity existed in late third millennium south-eastern Arabia which has yet to be adequately investigated.

The Early and Middle Second Millennium (c. 2000-1200 BC)

For many years it was thought that a major discontinuity occurred in the archaeological sequence of the Oman peninsula at the end of the third millennium This was speculatively linked to disruptions in the Indus Valley, where the Mature Harappan period came to an end and the Post-Harappan or Late Harappan era began. In the Indus Valley these changes were long attributed to the Aryan invasion, but this explanation has fallen out of favour with most scholars and remains purely conjectural. The absence of direct references to Magan in Mesopotamian cuneiform sources after the Ur III period (2100-2000 BC) also led scholars to speculate that the alleged Aryan invasion may have caused further disruptions, via a sort of cultural 'ripple effect', in south-eastern Arabia. The settlement record of the region seemed to evaporate, leaving very few sites occupied on anything like a full-time basis, and making it difficult to find the habitations of the many individuals buried in the collective, second millennium tombs of the sort first found at Shimal, but known by the name 'Wadi Suq' after a site in Oman first investigated by Karen Frifelt (Frifelt 1975: pp 377-378). Finally, the notion that the camel (*Camelus dromedarius*) was domesticated sometime in the second millennium gave rise to theories of a reversion to full-time nomadism after the Umm an-Nar period, leading some scholars to view the 'Wadi Suq period' (c. 2000-1300 BC) as a cultural 'dark age' in the region (cf. the discussion in Potts 1993c: pp 427-435).

It remains true today that the absolute number of early second millennium settlements in the UAE and Oman is not great, but on those which have been investigated, such as Tell Abraq, and from the surface indications at a site like Nud Ziba in Ras al-Khaimah (Kennet and Velde 1995), some population centres continued to be inhabited on a full-time basis and show no signs of a cultural 'decline'. At Tell Abraq, for example, the large fortress-tower of the Umm an-Nar period continued in use down to the middle of the second millennium, with modifications to the outer walls and the construction of new buildings in the interior. Apart from these architectural modifications, there is a major change detectable in the diet of the site's inhabitants, with marine resources (fish and shellfish) becoming more important than they had been in the late third millennium and accounting for about 50 per cent of all dietary requirements (Potts 1995a: p 96). A similar swing from the exploitation of terrestrial fauna (sheep, goat, cattle) to marine resources has also been observed at Shimal as one moves from the earlier to the later second millennium (Grupe and Schutkowski 1989). However, domesticated camel is not attested until the Iron Age and Wadi Suq camel 'nomadism' cannot be invoked as an explanation for the changes in material culture - particularly in the ceramic repertoire - which characterize the period. Moreover, both Tell Abraq and Nud Ziba (Kennet and Velde 1995) provide examples of ceramics which are clearly transitional between Umm an-Nar and classic Wadi Suq types, suggesting that the change from one period to the next was evolutionary rather than revolutionary.

The later Wadi Suq levels at Tell Abraq are paralleled by the occupation of the settlement at Shimal in Ras al-Khaimah, where an area of habitation at the base of the al-Hajar mountains, and within sight of an ancient mangrove lagoon, was located (Vogt and Franke-Vogt 1985; Velde 1990, 1991, 1992). Shimal, and the nearby sites of Ghalilah and Dhayah are, however, better known for the many collective tombs of the Wadi Suq period located there. These belong to a number of different formal types. All are constructed of unworked boulders and *wadi* pebbles, often of massive size. Unlike their Umm an-Nar counterparts, which were round, the Wadi Suq tombs were generally oval. The simplest 'Shimal' type is an elongated oval enclosure which can be up to 30 m long and roughly 2 m wide (e.g. in the case of Bidya 1; see Al Tikriti 1989: 102ff) with an entrance in one of the long sides. The 'Ghalilah' type is constructed like a broad oval with a central, freestanding wall in the interior. This is used to support the capstones, the ends of which rest on the upper surface of the outer and inner walls. Finally, the 'Khatt' type resembles a Shimal-type tomb with an entrance at one end which is enclosed by an outer wall, thus consisting of two burial spaces, the interior chamber of the 'Shimal'-type structure and a corridor running around its perimeter (Potts 1990b/I: Fig. 28). At Asimah, in the interior of Ras al-Khaimah, a number of graves with second millennium finds (e.g. As 13) have been excavated which represent a type previously unattested in the region (Vogt 1994a: p 41). These are notable by virtue of their oval shape, marked by a stone

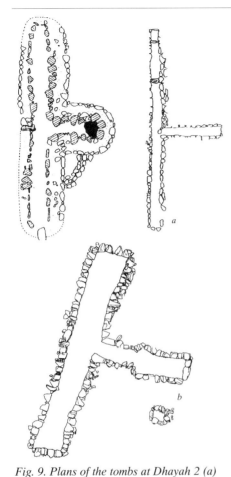

Fig. 9. Plans of the tombs at Dhayah 2 (a) and Bithna (b). After Kästner 1990: Abb. 4, and Corboud 1990: Fig. 4.

Fig. 10. Socketed spearheads of the Wadi Suq period from Dhayah 2 (a-b), and cairn 2 at Jabal Hafit (e). After Kästner 1990: Abb. 6; Vogt and Franke-Vogt 1987: Fig. 21.5-6; and Cleuziou et al. 1979: Pl. 16.1.

wall on the surface, which encloses a subterranean burial chamber, not unlike the original Wadi Suq graves investigated by Frifelt in the 1970s. Many Wadi Suq-period tombs have also recently been excavated at Jabal Buhays, south of Mleiha in the interior of Sharjah, and at Khor Fakkan, on the east coast of the country (S. Jasim, pers. comm).

Subterranean, horse-shoe-shaped tombs in the Wadi al-Qawr of southern Ras al-Khaimah (Phillips 1987) and the Qidfa oasis of Fujairah (unpublished but on display in the Fujairah Museum) must also be dated to the Wadi Suq period. Although previously attributed to the Iron Age (e.g. Potts 1990b/I: p 364), it is now clear from the finds made at Qidfa that the original construction and use of these tombs dates to the second millennium, and that the classic Iron Age material found within them represents the secondary reuse of these structures at a much later date. Subterranean, T-shaped tombs (Fig. 9), such as those excavated at Dhayah (Kästner 1990, 1991) and Bithna (Corboud 1990; Corboud et al. 1996) also date to the Wadi Suq period. Finally, individual inhumation graves dug into the *sabkha* at al-Qusais (Taha 1982-1983), a suburb to the east of Dubai, include many of Wadi Suq date.

The Wadi Suq period is notable for the explosion in metallurgy witnessed at this time. Although often robbed in antiquity, some Wadi Suq tombs, such as the horseshoe-shaped structure at Qidfa, have yielded literally hundreds of weapons and vessels. Where the Umm an-Nar period was characterized

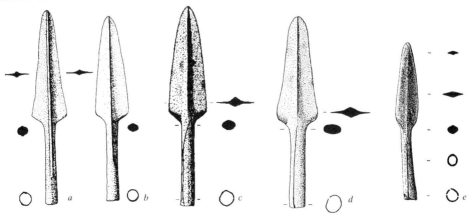

by daggers and spears, the Wadi Suq period witnessed the introduction of the long sword, the bow and arrow, and a new, light type of socketed spearhead (Fig. 10). These innovations in weaponry are surely significant for our understanding of Wadi Suq-period society. The long swords of Qidfa, al-Qusais, Qarn Bint Saud Grave 3 (Lombard 1979: Pl. LI.1-4; Vogt 1985: Taf. 122.1-4) and Qattara (Lombard 1979: Pl. LI.5-6) are double-edged weapons with a raised, central midrib and a concave butt-end marked by rivet holes for the attachment of a separate hilt. The double cutting-edge implies that these were thrusting weapons, and the lack of a well-attached hilt means that they would have been poor devices for slashing. Judging by the light weight of Wadi Suq socketed spearheads, it can be suggested that they were to be used on throwing spears. A comparison with the cuneiform evidence from third millennium Ebla, in Syria, shows that many of the Wadi Suq spearheads are within the weight range of the light throwing spears used there (63.2-79 g.), whereas none of them attain the weight of the heavier points mounted on thrusting lances which were used by foot soldiers at Ebla and weighed approximately 237-474 g. each (Waetzoldt 1990: p 2). The appearance of these weapons, along with hundreds of cast bronze, lanceolate arrowheads with a raised, flattened midrib, suggest an evolution in the technology of warfare during the second millennium unprecedented in the earlier archaeological record of the region.

Fig. 11. Wadi Suq-period soft-stone vessels from Shimal tomb 6 (a-e). After de Cardi 1988: Fig. 12.

In the late third millennium an industry arose in the manufacture of soft-stone vessels - generally bowls, beakers and compartmented boxes - decorated with dotted-circles made using a bow drill. During the Wadi Suq period the numbers of soft-stone vessels deposited in tombs increased vastly and new shapes, along with the addition of incised diagonal and horizontal lines in clusters (Fig. 11), allow us to easily separate the later soft-stone vessels from their third millennium forerunners (Häser 1988, 1990a, 1990b).

The continuities visible in settlement at a site like Tell Abraq - in metallurgical technology; in the manufacture of stone vessels, and in the ceramic industry - all point to the obvious conclusion that the Umm an-Nar/Wadi Suq divide, however real archaeologically, was not a complete rupture. We have little evidence of the people themselves from this era, largely because of the poor state of preservation of most of the skeletal remains excavated to date, and the lack of publication of such important complexes as Qidfa and Qattara. The skeletal material from the tombs at Shimal was highly fragmentary (Wells 1984, 1985; Schutkowski and Herrmann 1985) but studies of the teeth have shown that the population there showed low rates of molar attrition, suggestive of a low 'intake of dried fish, more efficient grain grinding or sieving, or less grain intake' which may reflect a diet heavily dependent on fresh fish and shellfish; low rates of caries, suggesting 'that fermentable carbohydrates [e.g. dates] did not play a large role' in the diet; high rates of calculus formation, associated with other dental pathologies, such as caries-induced abscessing, which 'most probably reflect different dietary constituents, food preparation techniques, or levels of oral hygiene' vis-à-vis other populations in the region; and moderate to severe ante-mortem tooth loss, 'possibly due to inflammation of the periodontium caused by extensive calculus' (Littleton and Frøhlich 1993: pp 440-444).

Some indication of an accumulation of wealth during the Wadi Suq period is provided by an interesting class of gold and electrum plaques in the form of two animals, standing back to back, often with their tails curled up in a spiral. Examples (Fig. 12) are now known from Dhayah (Kästner 1990: Taf. 40, 1991: Fig. 6a), Qattarah (Potts, 1990b/I: Pl. IX), and Bidya (Al Tikriti 1989: Pls. 74A, 95B). Some of that wealth may have been accumulated through long-distance trade in copper, a commodity for which Dilmun (modern Bahrain) became famous as a retailer to the southern Mesopotamian market city of Ur in the early second millennium. The discovery at Tell Abraq of over 600 sherds of Barbar red-ridged pottery, now shown to be compositionally identical to the pottery from the settlement at Saar on Bahrain (Grave et al. 1976b), points to the clear existence of contacts in that direction. Moreover, both Tell Abraq (Potts 1994c) and Shimal (de Cardi 1988: Fig. 11) have Post-Harappan pottery in early second millennium contexts which reflect the ongoing existence of contacts with the Indus Valley at this time.

Fig. 12. Wadi Suq-period gold and/or electrum animal plaques from Bidya (a) and Qattara (b-d). After al-Tikriti 1989: Pl. 74.

55

From the Late Second to the Late First Millennium (c. 1200-300 BC)

Two innovations occurred in the late second millennium which were to revolutionize the economies of south-eastern Arabia. The domestication of the camel, attested by the end of the second millennium at Tell Abraq (Stephan n.d.), opened up new possibilities for land transport, while the discovery of the principles of using sub-surface water channels for the transportation of water from aquifers to gardens - so-called *falaj* irrigation - made possible the extensive irrigation of gardens and agricultural plots which resulted in a veritable explosion of settlement across the Oman peninsula (Potts 1990b/I: pp 390-392).

In conformity with usage elsewhere in Western Asia, particularly Iran, the period from c. 1200 to 300 BC has traditionally been referred to as the 'Iron Age'. No term could be less appropriate, however, for in south-eastern Arabia iron was not used until the following period (see below). Nevertheless, it is convenient to term this era the Iron Age, particularly when referring to comparable sites and finds from other areas, such as Baluchistan, Iran, and Mesopotamia. Based on the evidence from Tell Abraq, the Iron Age sequence in the UAE can be divided into three sub-periods,

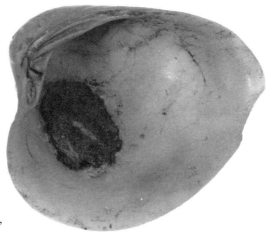

Fig. 13. Half of a bivalve (Marcia) shell from an early Iron Age (Iron I) context at Tell Abraq containing atacamite, a cuprous pigment widely used as eye-makeup in antiquity.

labelled Iron I (1200-1000 BC), II (1000-600 BC) and III (600-300 BC) (Magee 1995). With the exception of a tomb at Asimah (As 100) which contains Iron I material (Vogt 1994a: pp 81ff), all of the evidence for early Iron Age occupation comes from the Gulf coast sites of Shimal, Tell Abraq, and a series of shell middens at al-Hamriyah in Sharjah. Fish and shellfish continued to be important in the diet of the Iron I inhabitants, although domesticated sheep, goat and cattle were kept, and gazelle, oryx, dugong, turtle and cormorant were exploited as well (Stephan n.d.; Magee 1995: p 269). Domesticated wheat and barley were cultivated at this time (Willcox and Tengberg 1995), and the date-palm remained as important as ever. The ceramics of the Iron I period show clear signs of continuity with the latest Wadi Suq material, and are in general very coarse, grit-tempered, handmade wares, often in large, open bowl and vat-like shapes (Potts 1990a: pp 103-109). Half of a bivalve shell (*Marcia hiantina*) from an Iron I context at the site was found by x-ray powder diffraction analysis to contain atacamite (Fig. 13), a cuprous pigment widely used in the ancient world as eye make-up (Thomas and Potts 1996).

The Iron II period is the 'classic' Iron Age in the UAE and is attested at a number of extensively excavated sites with substantial mudbrick architecture such as Rumeilah, Bint Saud, Hili 2, Hili 14 and Hili 17 in the Al-Ain area; al-Thuqaibah and Umm Safah on the al-Madam plain;

and Muweilah in the sandy desertic area near the Sharjah International Airport. Many other sites, both graves and settlements, have been located, and it is estimated that at least 150 sites of this period have been documented in the UAE and neighbouring Oman. The explosion in settlement at this time is generally attributed to the invention of *falaj* irrigation technology, and cultivation using the hoe may be inferred from the recovery of a bronze hoe-blade at Rumeilah (Boucharlat and Lombard 1985: Pl. 72.7; Weisgerber 1988: Pl. 161; Potts 1994a).

It is interesting to note that the Iron II period also witnessed the appearance of fortified strongholds, such as Hili 14 in Al-Ain (Boucharlat and Lombard 1989), Husn Madhab in Fujairah (Hellyer 1993b), Jabal Buhays north of al-Madam (Boucharlat 1992), and Rafaq in the Wadi al-Qawr. The purpose of these fortresses, it may be argued, was to safeguard the agricultural settlements associated with them, particularly their precious *aflaj*, and the concentration of power in such centres is an important social and political phenomenon. A cuneiform inscription from Nineveh in Assyria speaks of the existence of at least one 'king' in the Oman peninsula at this time, an individual named Pade, king of Qade, who lived at Is-ki-e (modern Izki in Oman) and sent tribute to the Assyrian emperor Assurbanipal in or around 640 BC (Potts 1990b/I: p 393).

Political and economic control by central bodies may also be implied by the appearance at this time of a tradition of stamp seal manufacture, evidenced at a number of sites including Rumeilah (Boucharlat and Lombard 1985: Pl. 66.5-9), Muweilah (unpubl.), Tell Abraq (Potts 1991a: Fig. 135) and Bint Saud (Stevens 1992). Contacts with foreign regions are suggested by a soft-stone pendant from Tell Abraq (Potts 1991a: Figs. 136-137) which shows a figure reminiscent of the Neo-Assyrian and Neo-Babylonian depictions of the *lamashtu* demoness, an evil spirit who spread disease, and it is most probable that such pendants were worn to protect their owners from sickness. Some indication of how such foreign contacts were effected is given by another pendant from Tell Abraq which shows the only Iron Age depiction of a boat in the Oman peninsula (Potts 1991a: Figs. 142-143). In this case the boat appears to be a square-sterned vessel with a sharp bow and triangular sail (Potts 1995b: p 564). The sail is obviously similar to the Arab lateen sail, otherwise unattested in the region until the Sasanian period and absent in the Mediterranean until c. 900 AD. The Tell Abraq pendant is thus the earliest depiction of a lateen sail yet discovered.

The third and final sub-period of the Iron Age, Iron III, is not very well known, although occupation is attested at half a dozen settlements including Tell Abraq, Shimal, Rumeilah, Hili 17, Hili 2, Nud Ziba and al-Thuqaibah (Magee 1995: p 345), as well as graves in the Wadi al-Qawr (unpubl., in the Ras al-Khaimah Museum) and Dibba oasis (unpubl., in the Fujairah Museum). The appearance of previously unattested shapes in so-called 'Burnished Maroon Slipped Ware' is significant, for this material, almost certainly imported from Iran, finds close parallels at a number of Iranian sites, including Baba Jan, Godin Tepe, Nad-i Ali, Dahan-i Gulaiman, Tal-i Zohak, and Pasargadae, in contexts dating to between the sixth and fourth centuries BC (Magee 1995: pp 182-183). When combined with the literary and epigraphic record of Achaemenid control over the satrapy of Maka (cf. *Makkan*, **Magan**), the conclusion becomes inescapable that the sudden appearance in the UAE of ceramics paralleled in Achaemenid contexts in Iran is a reflection of the fact that the area was at this time part of the Persian satrapy of Maka (Potts 1990b/I: 394ff; de Blois 1989). In spite of the fact that messengers from Maka, some of whom are referred to as 'Arabs', are attested in the Persepolis Fortification

Texts (PF 1545, 2050; PFa 17, 29) in the year 505/4 BC, as are rations for the satrap of Maka (PF 679-680) in the years 495/4 and 500/499 BC (Potts 1990b/I: pp 395-397), we still have no idea where the Persian capital of the satrapy may have been located. A contingent from Maka formed part of Xerxes' army at Doriscus in 480 BC (Herodotus, *Hist.* 7.68), and we can get some impression of how they looked from the depictions of Mačiya (inhabitants of Maka) on several Achaemenid monuments, the clearest of which is found on the grave of Darius II at Persepolis (Potts 1985: Fig. 1a). There the Mačiya (Fig. 14) is shown wearing only a short kilt, with a sword slung over his shoulder by a strap. The crescentic pommel of the sword hilt is interesting, and recalls the many Iron Age short swords found at sites in the UAE such as al-Qusais (Fig. 14), Qidfa, Jabal Buhays and Rumeilah (Lombard 1981; Weisgerber 1988).

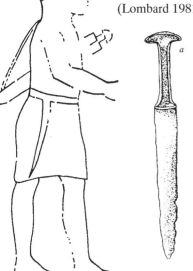
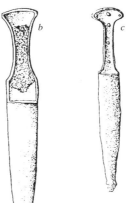

Fig. 14. Examples of Iron Age short swords from al-Qusais (a-e) and a depiction of a Mačiya, or native of Maka, from the base of the throne of Darius II on his grave relief at Persepolis. After Lombard 1985: Fig. 107.374-378 and Potts 1985: Fig. 1a.

The Mleiha (Late Pre-Islamic A-B) period (c. 300-0 BC)

The dissolution of the Persian Empire must have impacted on south-eastern Arabia, for, with the defeat and death of Darius III, Maka was no longer a Persian satrapy. On the other hand, Alexander the Great's conquests never touched the Arabian side of the Gulf and, while he inherited much of what had formerly been the Achaemenid empire, the famous 'last plans' of the Macedonian conqueror, which included an invasion of Arabia, never advanced beyond the stage of initial reconnaissance (Potts, 1990b/II: pp 1-22). Thus, by the third century BC south-eastern Arabia was free of foreign political influence, and it is in this context that the developments of the subsequent centuries must be viewed, for none of Alexander's Seleucid successors was able to establish any sort of Greek dominance in the region either.

How significant these trends were for the local population is difficult to assess. Certainly we can see evidence of continuity as well as change in the local ceramic repertoire, enough to be certain that the basic industry and the people who made and used the wares remained the same. But our evidence is severely restricted and, with the exception of Mleiha, a sprawling settlement on the gravel plain south of Dhayd in the interior of Sharjah which extends over an area several square kilometres in extent (Boucharlat 1987-1988, 1989; Boucharlat and Mouton 1991, 1993), we have no other settlements which can be attributed to this time horizon. On the basis of their excavations, French archaeologists working at Mleiha have divided the sequence into four sub-periods, viz. Mleiha I (Iron Age), II (300-150 BC), IIIA (150-0 BC), and IIIB (0-200 AD). For the purposes of this chapter we shall consider Mleiha II and IIIA together, as these correspond to the interval between the end of the Iron Age and the appearance of a different cultural phenomenon best represented further north at ed-Dur on the coast of Umm al-Qaiwain (see below).

The occupation of Mleiha represented the continuation of human occupation, in an optimally watered and well-drained area, which had begun in the late prehistoric era (cf. Table 7). The earliest, post-Iron Age settlement probably consisted of *barastis* or *'arish*, palm-frond houses, eminently suited to the hot climate of the Oman peninsula. The dead, however, were buried in more substantial structures, mudbrick cists surmounted by a solid tower of brick, capped by crenellated stone ornaments. These structures, which have no antecedents in the region, recall the funerary towers of Palmyra, Qaryat al-Fau, and the early periods at Petra (Boucharlat and Mouton 1993: p 281).

Both settlement and graves have yielded quantities of ceramics, some of it of obviously local manufacture, carrying on and modifying the norms established during the Iron Age, and some of it foreign. This includes glazed pottery, perhaps produced in south-western Iran or southern Iraq; red and black wares readily identifiable as coming from the north-east Arabian mainland or adjacent islands of Bahrain or Failaka; and even Greek pottery, imported from the Aegean or Mediterranean. In addition to Greek black-glazed sherds identical to finds from the Athenian Agora, more than half a dozen stamped Rhodian amphora handle fragments (Fig. 15) provide precious clues to the absolute chronology of Mleiha. The named and generally datable Rhodian amphora manufacturers attested at Mleiha include *Iasonos* (early second century BC), *P(ana)mo(u) Ant(ig)onou* (late 3rd/early 2nd cent. BC), and *EpiAriotuvos/Theomoaori(os)/ou* (200-175 BC) (Mouton 1992: p 48).

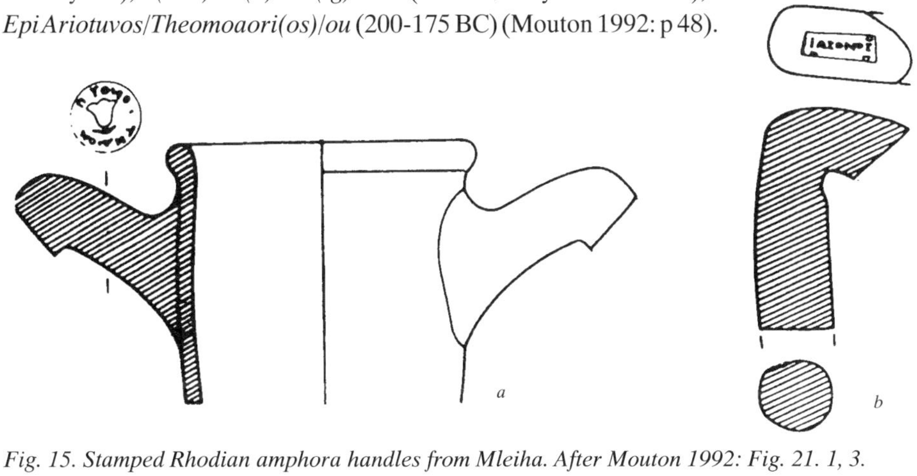

Fig. 15. Stamped Rhodian amphora handles from Mleiha. After Mouton 1992: Fig. 21. 1, 3.

Engraved bronze bowls and beehive-shaped, alabaster vessels from Mleiha II contexts recall examples from South Arabia (Potts 1990b/II: Fig. 18; Boucharlat and Mouton 1993: Fig. 6), a fact which is important in connection with the recovery of several items (stone stelae, bronze bowls) inscribed in South Arabian characters (Fig. 16). By themselves, these inscriptions

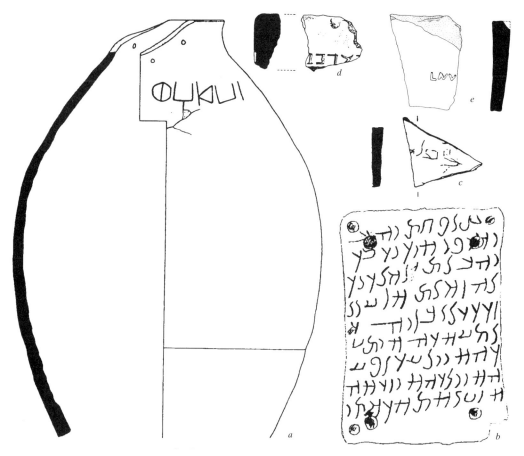

Fig. 16. Examples of inscribed material in South Arabian (a), Aramaic (b-d) and Latin (e) from Mleiha (a-b) and ed-Dur (c-e). After Mouton 1992: Fig. 148 and Teixidor 1992: Fig. 2.

do not necessarily imply contact with South Arabia, for the simple fact that the South Arabian script was also used in north-eastern Arabia to write the so-called Hasaitic inscriptions (Potts 1990b/II: 69-85), many of which begin with the same formula as the Mleiha funerary stele, *nafs/wqbr*, i.e. 'memorial and tomb (of)...' (cf. the discussion in Müller 1978: p 150; Potts 1990b/II: p 268, n. 11). Moreover, alabaster vessels like those found at Mleiha, although of undoubted South Arabian manufacture, have also been discovered at sites like Thaj in north-eastern Saudi Arabia. Several coins found on the surface of the site are, however, unequivocally South Arabian (Sedov 1995). The question of South Arabian contact and cultural influence is an important one, particularly in view of the legend of the Azd migration out of Yemen and its contribution to the later tribal configuration of Oman.

One of the cultural innovations which characterizes the late pre-Islamic era is the appearance of iron for the first time in the archaeological record of south-eastern Arabia. Alongside utilitarian items such as nails, long swords and arrowheads (Mouton 1990) were used. Whether or not they were manufactured locally is another matter, but in addition to the existence of iron-bearing zones near Jabals Faiyah, Emalah and Buhays, south of Mleiha, the site itself has surface scatters of iron slag (Ploquin and Orzechowski 1994: pp 26ff) suggesting that secondary refining and casting were carried out there. Why iron was not adopted earlier is a mystery. Certainly the abundance of copper sources in the al-Hajar mountains, and the ancient tradition of copper metallurgy may have been a factor contributing to a lack of interest in iron. It has also been suggested that the Seleucid political presence in the Gulf region acted as a catalyst by way of introducing new types of armour and weaponry, made of iron, to peoples previously accustomed to the use only of copper-bronze (Lombard 1989: p 37).

The ed-Dur (Late Pre-Islamic C) Period (c. 0-200 AD)

By the first century AD we have reached a period for which considerably more literary documentation exists, albeit of a difficult nature to use. The Roman writer Pliny the Younger (23/24-79 AD) completed his *Natural History* in 77 AD and, to judge from his account of the peoples and places of south-eastern Arabia (*Nat. Hist.* VI.32. pp 149-152), combined with the second century AD testimony of Cl. Ptolemy's map of Arabia (Fig. 17), the area of the UAE

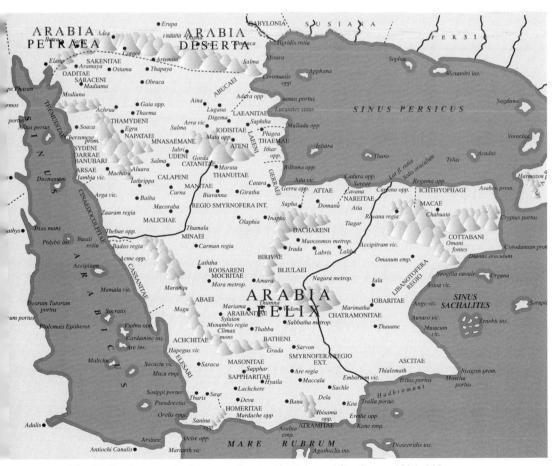

Fig. 17. Southeastern Arabia according to Cl. Ptolemy. After Groom 1994: 200.

61

was full of settlements, tribes, and physical features, the names of which he recorded for us. Fixing the locations of these, and linking them with archaeological sites, has proven difficult, but it has been argued that 'the town of Omana, which previous writers have made out to be a famous port of Carmania (Pliny, *Nat. Hist.* VI.32. pp 149) [Kerman province in Iran]' may be identified with the large, nearly 4 km sq. settlement of ed-Dur in Umm al-Qaiwain (Potts 1988, 1990b/II: pp 306ff; Groom 1994, 1995). The same site is, moreover, mentioned (§ 36) at about the same time in the anonymous *Periplus of the Erythraean Sea*, an important text which documents the maritime trade between Alexandria in Egypt and Barygaza in India. Certainly the archaeological remains of ed-Dur leave us in no doubt that the site was the most important coastal settlement in the lower Gulf during the first centuries AD.

Located opposite what is today a sheltered branch of the Umm al-Qaiwain lagoon, ed-Dur extends for well over 1 km in a north-east/south-west direction, and is in places up to 1 km wide. Within this vast area is a dispersed collection of private houses, graves, a fort, and a temple, along with extensive sherd scatters without associated standing architecture which probably represent areas of former *barasti* habitation. Originally investigated in the early 1970s by an Iraqi expedition, ed-Dur was the object of a collaborative expedition from four European universities between 1987 and 1994 (Boucharlat et al. 1988, 1989; Haerinck 1991b, 1992, 1993, 1994a, 1994d; Haerinck et al. 1992, 1993).

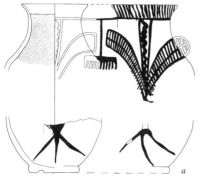

Fig. 18. Examples of early (a) and late (b) Namord ware from ed-Dur. After Potts in press c.

Most of the architecture at the site is built of beach rock (Ar. *farush*), a calcareous concretion which forms offshore in shallow tidal areas and can be easily broken into slabs for use as building material. Large houses, some with numerous rooms and round corner towers, have been excavated as well as small, one-room dwellings. The use of alabaster for windowpanes is important and marks the earliest archaeological attestation of alabaster for this purpose in the Arabian Peninsula (Potts 1996). Graves may be either simple subterranean cists for individual inhumations, or large, semi-subterranean collective tombs consisting of a subterranean chamber reached via a stairway from the surface, surmounted by a barrel vault. In general terms the more elaborate graves resemble Parthian tombs at Assur in northern Mesopotamia.

The ceramics from the site are dominated by glazed wares, almost certainly of Parthian manufacture and imported either from southern Mesopotamia or south-western Iran. Fine black-on-orange painted 'Namord' ware (Fig. 18), imported from south-eastern Iran or Baluchistan, indicates contacts across the Straits of Hormuz (Potts n.d. c), while rare sherds of Indian Red Polished Ware point to ties with the Indian sub-continent. As the *Periplus* indicates, during the mid-first century AD Omana was the most important port in the lower Gulf, and was twinned with the port of Apologos at the head of the Gulf, a site perhaps located somewhere near modern Basra and one of the main maritime outlets for the kingdom of Characene (Potts 1988). While traffic down the Red Sea and across the Indian Ocean provided one

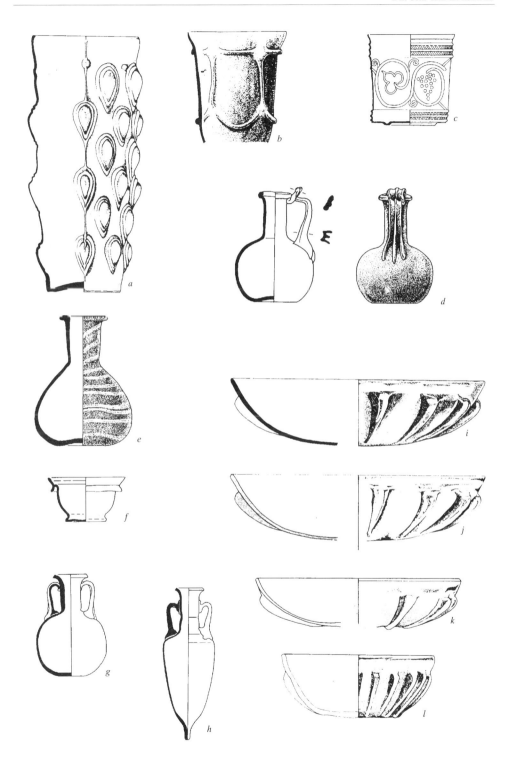

Fig. 19. A selection of Roman glass from ed-Dur. After Potts in press d.

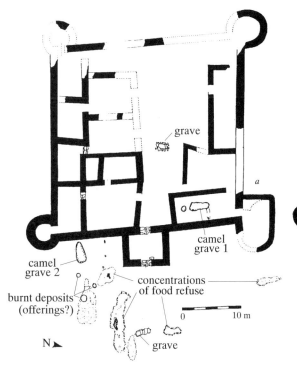

grave

camel grave 1

camel grave 2

concentrations of food refuse

burnt deposits (offerings?)

N

grave

0   10 m

a

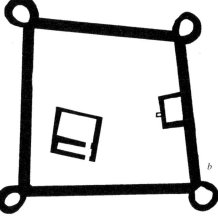

b

Fig. 20. The Area F building complex (a) and the fort (b) at ed-Dur. After Mouton 1992: Figs. 150 and 55.

means for the Roman acquisition of exotica from India and the east, overland caravan traffic between Palmyra in Syria and the cities of Vologesias, Seleucia and Spasinou Charax in Iraq, followed by seaborne travel down the 'Characene corridor' to Omana and on to India provided an alternative route (Potts n.d. d). The latter mechanism may well have been responsible for the diffusion of quantities of Roman glass to ed-Dur (Fig. 19), most of which dates to the first century AD (e.g. pillar-moulded bowls); at least one western Roman amphora (Papadopoulos 1994); and a handful of Characene coins dating to the reigns of Attambelos II (44/45 AD), Attambelos IV (58/59 AD) and Attambelos VI (104/105 AD) (Potts 1988: pp 141-142). The single Roman coin from ed-Dur, an undated PONTIF MAXIM issue of Tiberius (Howgego and Potts 1992) may have reached the site in the same manner.

The concentration of political power which one may presume to have existed in an emporium like ed-Dur was undoubtedly centred on the fort (Fig. 20) excavated in 1973 by the Iraqi expedition. Measuring roughly 20 m on a side, and with four circular corner towers each 4 m in diameter, the fort is built of beach-rock and shows affinities to contemporary Parthian fortifications in Mesopotamia. South of the fort is an important temple, excavated by the Belgian expedition, which was a simple, one-room, square structure, roughly 8 m on a side, of beach-rock faced with finely worked gypsum plaster imitating ashlar masonry. An incense burner from the temple, inscribed in Aramaic with the name Shams, suggests that this was a shrine dedicated to the pan-Semitic solar deity.

While ed-Dur was the prime settlement of this period on the Gulf coast, Mleiha was certainly the leading centre in the interior. One of the most important discoveries made in recent excavations at the site was a square fort with square corner towers in Area CW, the main outer wall of which was 55 m long, attributable to Mleiha IIIB (0-200 AD) (Benoist et al. 1994: p 12). Associated with the fort, moreover, was a stone mould (Fig. 21) for the production of coins (Boucharlat and Drieux 1991), and as the right to strike coinage was generally a royal

Fig. 21. A coin mould
from Mleiha. After
Boucharlat and
Drieux 1991: Fig. 2.

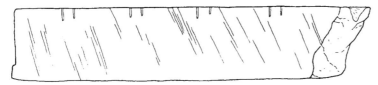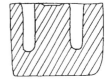

prerogative in the ancient world, it is likely that the Mleiha fort represents the power centre of the polity centred on the site. The coins minted at Mleiha - hundreds of which have been discovered at both ed-Dur and Mleiha (Potts 1991b, 1994d; Haerinck 1994c; Grave et al. 1996a) - were modelled on the coinage of Alexander. They show a debased head of Heracles wearing the pelt of the Nemean lion on the obverse, and a seated figure, based on that of Zeus, on the reverse. Whereas the original Greek models had the name ALEXANDER clearly written in Greek on the reverse, the Mleiha/ed-Dur coins (Figs. 22-23) bear a legend in angular, lapidary-style Aramaic which can be read as 'Abi'el, son/daughter of *bgln/tmyln/tlmyl/tym..*' (Potts 1994d: p 43). However the patronymic should be read, the name Abi'el is always clear, and as this must be the monarch who originally minted coins of this type, we can safely conclude that Abi'el was an important ruler in this region during the late pre-Islamic era.

The situation is complicated, however, by the fact that variant, prototypical issues with the name Abi'el have been found in a hoard on Bahrain datable to the second century BC. Thus, the later Mleiha issues from the first century AD may have repeated the name of an important political figure in the region long after that individual had died, just as the many Asiatic issues which were based on those of Alexander repeated the name of the Macedonian king over and over again, even centuries after his lifetime. Until this issue can be resolved it is wisest not to assume that the fort at Mleiha represents the stronghold of the eponymous Abi'el. That Aramaic was the language of the populations of Mleiha and ed-Dur at this time is, however, confirmed not only by its use on coinage, but also by the discovery of other inscribed objects, such as a unique bronze plaque from Mleiha (Teixidor 1992) and several short lapidary inscriptions at ed-Dur (Haerinck et al. 1991: p 36).

Fig. 22. A silver tetradrachm of Abi'el (Class S2)
from Mleiha; weight 14.68 g., diameter 2.70 cm.
After Potts 1994d: 45, no. 183.

Fig. 23. A silver tetradrachm of Abi'el (Class XLVI)
from Mleiha; weight 16.02 g., diameter 2.20 cm.
After Potts 1994d: 66, no. 338.

The End of the pre-Islamic Era (c. 240-635 AD)

Although the extent of the political influence of the Parthians in south-eastern Arabia has long been debated, there is little doubt that their Sasanian successors swiftly imposed their will on the inhabitants of the region shortly after coming to power. According to the *Karnamak-i Artachsher-i Papakan*, the 'Book of Deeds' recounting the exploits of Ardashir (224-240), founder of the Sasanian state, *mĕvnyg'n* or natives of Mazun (the name given to Maka in Middle Iranian, Syriac, Armenian and Arabic sources; see de Blois 1989) fought against Ardashir early in his career. Later Arab sources, such as al-Dinawari (c. 895) and the anonymous *Nihayatu'l-irab fi ahbari'l-furs wa'l-'arab* (c. 1000-1050), contend that Ardashir campaigned in Oman. Certainly the great Ka'aba of Zoroaster inscription at Naqsh-i Rustam near Persepolis lists MZWN, i.e. Mazun, as the twenty-seventh land in the empire of Shapur I (240-270 AD), Ardashir's son (Gignoux 1971: p 92-93; Potts 1990b/II: p 329).

Archaeologically, however, there is little concrete evidence of Sasanian presence in the UAE. The few coins recovered on the Gulf coast include a pair of badly preserved bronzes of Ardashir and Shapur II (309-379) from Ghallah, an island in the lagoon of Umm al-Qaiwain, as well as a silver coin of the latter king from Tell Abraq (Potts and Cribb 1995: pp 129-130). In Fujairah, a small hoard of 18 silver coins was discovered which included issues of two late Sasanian monarchs, Hormizd IV (579-590) and Khusrau II (590-628) (Hellyer 1995).

The absence of Sasanian material should not be interpreted as a sign that there was no settlement in the region at this time. The latest occupation at Tell Abraq can be dated to this period by the Shapur II coin found in 1993 in a context close to the surface (Potts and Cribb 1995: p 130). Area F at ed-Dur, a large, multi-roomed house with corner towers, represents the most extensively excavated complex of this date found so far (Lecomte 1993). It is well-dated by the numerous examples of Sasanian glass found there, all of which find close parallels at sites in Mesopotamia. Further up the coast, at Jazirat al-Hulayla, late pre-Islamic ceramics and structures have also been found (Kennet 1994: Figs. 9-11; T. Sasaki, pers. comm). In the interior, several intrusive burials with iron weaponry (spear, sword, pike) dug into the prehistoric tombs at Jabal al-Emalah can be attributed to the very end of the pre-Islamic period. A fragmentary individual buried with an iron sword in Tomb I has produced a corrected radiocarbon date of 455-583 AD, while a fully articulated individual buried with an iron-tipped spear from Tomb III has been dated to 513-624 AD.

A third burial at Jabal al-Emalah with iron accoutrements was that of a camel in its own, oval grave ringed by stones. Camel burials are a phenomenon well-attested in the late pre-Islamic era throughout the Arabian peninsula (Vogt 1994b), and elsewhere in the UAE they are known at both ed-Dur (Lecomte 1993) and Mleiha (S. Jasim and H.-P. Uerpmann, pers. comm). Yet it would be wrong to suggest that the religious climate of the era was dominated either by Arab paganism (viz. camel burial) or Zoroastrianism (viz. Sasanian influence). Nestorian Christianity was a decidedly important component of the religious milieu at this time as well.

In 424 Yohannon, bishop of Mazun, attended an important synod at Markabta de Tayyae in Iraq, where the Nestorian church proclaimed its independence from Antioch (Potts 1990b/II: p 333). This is the first concrete evidence of Nestorian Christianity in south-eastern Arabia, although the *Vita Ionae*, an account of the life of a monk named Jonah who lived in the time

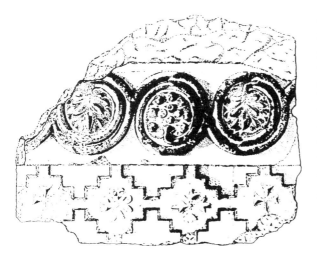

Fig. 24. A stucco fragment from a Nestorian building on Sir Bani Yas. After King and Hellyer 1994: 6

of the *catholicus* Barb'ashmin (343-346), says that Jonah built a monastery 'on the borders of the black island', a locale which some Nestorian scholars have sought amongst the islands between Qatar and Oman. In this connection it is obvious to consider the islands off the coast of Abu Dhabi as a likely site for Jonah's monastery. The recent discovery on the island of Sir Bani Yas (Hellyer 1993a; King and Hellyer 1994) of a monastery and church, complete with carved stucco ornamentation including a cross (Fig. 24), is of enormous interest in this respect.

The literary testimony of Nestorian Christianity in the region does not resume until 544, perhaps due to a temporary loss of control over the area by the Sasanians and their Lakhmid vassals at the hands of the Kinda of central Arabia (Potts 1990b/II: pp 334-335). Be that as it may, in 544 David, bishop of Mazun, attended the Nestorian synod of Mar Aba I, and in 576 Samuel attended the synod of Mar Ezechiel. Mazun is included in an important Armenian list of the provinces of the Sasanian empire compiled late in the Sasanian period, and it is certain that the region was under Sasanian control at the time of the Islamic conversion.

Two majors towns of the period are mentioned in literary sources, Tuwwam and Dibba. Both towns were taxed by the Al Julanda, clients of the Sasanians who reported to the Persian *marzban* (military governor) at al-Rustaq in Oman (Potts 1990b/II: p 337). Tuwwam, although identifiable with the region of Buraimi (Wilkinson 1964: p 344), is invisible archaeologically, for no late pre-Islamic remains contemporary with the period of Sasanian governance have been unearthed there. Dibba, of course, is still the name of a major port and oasis settlement on the east coast of the UAE which is today divided between Oman, Fujairah and Sharjah. Although the archaeology of Dibba in the late pre-Islamic era is yet to be investigated, the literary record is more ample.

In his *al-Muhabbar*, Ibn Habib called Dibba 'one of the two ports of the Arabs; merchants from Sind, India, China, people of the East and West came to it' (Shoufani 1972: p 156). At this time Dibba paid a tithe to Al Julanda b. Al Mustakbir on the occasion of a fair held each year for five nights beginning on the first day of Rajab. The commercial importance of Dibba at this time explains why Jaifar, one of the Al Julanda addressed by the Prophet in a letter carried by Abu Zayd and 'Amr b. Al 'As in the year 630 (AH 8), sent a messenger to Dibba exhorting its inhabitants to convert to Islam (Ross 1874: pp 118-119). Just a few years later, however, Dibba became the base of Laqit b. Malik, the leader of the *al-Riddah* or apostasizing movement, and the crushing of that movement by the armies of Abu Bakr (Shoufani 1972: p 8) created one of the largest and most important historical sites in the UAE, a vast cemetery said to contain upwards of 10,000 slain rebels (Potts 1990b/II: p 345) on the outskirts of Dibba.

Christianity in Mazun certainly survived some decades after the Muslim conversion, for Stephen, bishop of Mazun, attended a synod in Mesopotamia in 676. The apostasy of the Christian community, however, was rife in this period, a fact amply documented by a series of letters sent by the Nestorian catholicos Isho'yahb III to Simeon of Rev-Ardashir in Iran, complaining about the conversions of 'your people in Mazun' (Potts 1990b/II: p 346). The subsequent absence of any more bishops from Mazun at the synods of the Nestorian church is an indication that Christianity probably did not survive in south-eastern Arabia much beyond the seventh century.

Conclusion

It is scarcely possible to draw a simple conclusion from the rich archaeological and historical record of the pre-Islamic past of the UAE, but several observations suggest themselves nonetheless. Quite clearly, archaeological research during the past decade has proceeded at a pace scarcely imaginable even 20 years ago, and there has been a veritable explosion of knowledge as the bibliography appended here attests. Archaeological museums have appeared all over the country which display the impressive finds of numerous excavations. The modern inhabitants of the UAE have an archaeological and historical past which should make them the envy of many of their neighbours, and dispel once and for all the notion that this region was peripheral in antiquity. Had it been peripheral, why would a series of Old Akkadian, Achaemenid, or Sasanian emperors have expended so much energy on campaigning in the area? The lack of a local written record comparable to the cuneiform archives of Mesopotamia or the hieroglyphs of Egypt must never blind us to the fact that, in antiquity, the region of the UAE was a strategic, well-resourced, important part of the cultural mosaic of ancient Western Asia. With the continued good will of the rulers of the seven emirates it is to be hoped that archaeological research in the UAE continues to make advances at the pace set by a committed body of scholars from a variety of nations during the past ten years. Let us hope, also, that their ranks are swelled by the addition of more indigenous scholars from the UAE itself.

Bibliography

Abbreviations

AAE   Arabian Archaeology & Epigraphy
AUAE   Archaeology in the United Arab Emirates
PSAS   Proceedings of the Seminar for Arabian Studies

Alt, K.W., Vach, W., Frifelt, K. and Kunter, M. 'Familienanalyse in kupferzeitlichen Kollektivgräbern aus Umm an-Nar; Abu Dhabi', AAE, 6 (1995) pp 65-80.

Al Tikriti, W.Y. 'The archaeological investigations on Ghanadha island 1982-1984: Further evidence for the coastal Umm an-Nar culture', AUAE, 4 (1985) pp 9-19.

Al Tikriti, W.Y. 'The excavations at Bidya, Fujairah: the 3rd and 2nd millennia BC culture', AUAE, 5 (1989) pp 101-114.

Amiet, P. 'A cylinder seal impression found at Umm an-Nar', East and West, 25 (1975) pp 425-426.

Amiet, P. 'Quelques témoins des contacts de Suse avec les pays du Levant au IIIe et IIe millénaires', in J.-M. Durand and J.-R. Kupper (eds), Miscellanea Babylonica: Mélanges offerts à Maurice Birot, Paris, Editions Recherche sur les Civilisations (1985) pp 9-12.

'At Tell Abraq - the earliest recorded find of polio', The University of Sydney - Research, Sydney, External Relations Division (1994) p 20.

Benoist, A., Mokaddem, K. and Mouton, M. 'Excavations at Mleiha site: The 1993 and 1994 seasons', in Mouton, M. (ed), *Archaeological Surveys and Excavations in the Sharjah Emirate, 1993 and 1994: A Seventh Interim Report*, Lyon, Maison de l'Orient (1994) pp 11-19.

Benton, J.N. *Excavations at Al Sufouh: A third millennium site in the Emirate of Dubai, United Arab Emirates*, Turnhout, *Abiel* 1 (1996).

Benton, J.N. and Potts, D.T. *Jabal al-Emalah 1993/4*, Sydney, unpubl.

Blackman, M.J., Méry, S. and Wright, R.P. 'Production and exchange of ceramics on the Oman peninsula from the perspective of Hili', *Journal of Field Archaeology*, 16 (1989) pp 61-77.

Boucharlat, R. 'Entre la Méditerranée et l'Inde: Établissements du Golfe Persique à l'époque Gréco-Romaine', *Bulletin de la Société Française d'Archéologie Classique*, 21 (1987-1988) pp 214-220.

Boucharlat, R. 'Documents arabes provenant des sites "hellénistiques" de la péninsule d'Oman', in T. Fahd (ed), *L'Arabie préislamique et son environnement historique et culturel*, Leiden, Univ. des sciences humaines de Strasbourg, Travaux du Centre de Recherche sur le Proche-Orient et la Grèce antique 10, (1989) pp 109-126.

Boucharlat, R. 'Note on an Iron Age hill settlement in the Jabal Buhais', in Boucharlat, R. (ed), *Archaeological Surveys and Excavations in the Sharjah Emirate, 1990 and 1992: A Sixth Interim Report*, Lyon, Maison de l'Orient (1992) p 19.

Boucharlat, R., Dalongeville, R., Hesse, A., and Millet, M. 'Occupation humaine et environnement au 5e et au 4e millénaire sur la côte Sharjah-Umm al-Qaiwain (U.A.E.)', *AAE*, 2 (1991a) pp 93-106.

Boucharlat, R. and Drieux, M. 'A note on coins and a coin mold from Mleiha, Emirate of Sharjah, U.A.E.', in Potts, D.T. *The Pre-Islamic Coinage of Eastern Arabia*, Copenhagen, Carsten Niebuhr Institute Publications 14, (1991b) pp 110-117.

Boucharlat, R., Haerinck, E., Lecomte, O., Potts, D.T., and Stevens, K.G. 'The European archaeological expedition to ed-Dur, Umm al-Qaiwayn (U.A.E.): An interim report on the 1987 and 1988 seasons', *Mesopotamia*, 24 (1989) pp 5-72.

Boucharlat, R., Haerinck, E., Phillips, C.S. and Potts, D.T. 'Archaeological reconnaissance at ed-Dur, Umm al-Qaiwain, U.A.E.', *Akkadica*, 58 (1988) pp 1-26.

Boucharlat, R., Haerinck, E., Phillips, C.S. and Potts, D.T. 'Note on an Ubaid-pottery site in the Emirate of Umm al-Qaiwain', *AAE*, 2 (1991b) pp 65-71.

Boucharlat, R. and Lombard, P. 'The oasis of Al Ain in the Iron Age: Excavations at Rumeilah 1981-1983, Survey at Hili 14', *AUAE*, 4 (1985) pp 44-73.

Boucharlat, R. and Mouton, M. 'Cultural change in the Oman peninsula during the late 1st millennium BC as seen from Mleiha, Sharjah Emirate (U.A.E.)', *PSAS*, 21 (1991) pp 23-33.

Boucharlat, R. and Mouton, M. 'Importations occidentales et influence de l'hellénisme dans la péninsule d'Oman', in A. Invernizzi and J.-F. Salles (eds), *Arabia Antiqua: Hellenistic centres around Arabia*, Rome, Serie Orientale Roma LXX.2 (1993) pp 275-289.

Calley, S. and Santoni, M.-A. 'Sounding at the prehistoric site al-Qassimiya', in R. Boucharlat (ed), *Archaeological Surveys and Excavations in the Sharjah Emirate, 1986: A Third Preliminary Report*, Lyon, Maison de l'Orient, (1986) pp 13-15.

Cauvin, M.-C. and Calley, S. 'Preliminary report on lithic material' in R. Boucharlat (ed), *Survey in Sharjah Emirate, U.A.E. on behalf of the Department of Culture, Sharjah: First Report (1984)*, Lyon, Maison de l'Orient, (1984) pp 17-20.

Cleuziou, S. 'Excavations at Hili 8: a preliminary report on the 4th to 7th campaigns', *AUAE*, 5 (1989) pp 61-88.

Cleuziou, S. 'The Oman peninsula and the Indus civilization: A reassessment', *Man and Environment*, 17/2 (1992) pp 93-103.

Cleuziou, S. and Costantini, L. 'Premiers éléments sur l'agriculture protohistorique de l'Arabie orientale', *Paléorient*, 6 (1980) pp 245-251.

Cleuziou, S., Pottier, M.-H. and Salles, J.-F. 'French archaeological mission, 1st campaign, December 1976/February 1977', *AUAE*, 1 (1978) pp 8-53.

Cleuziou, S. and Vogt, B. 'Tomb A at Hili North (United Arab Emirates) and its material connections to southeast Iran and the Greater Indus Valley', in J. Schotsmans and M. Taddei (eds), *South Asian Archaeology 1983*, Naples, Istituto Universitario Orientale, Dipartimento di Studi Asiatici, Series Minor XXIII, (1985) pp 249-277.

Copeland, L. and Bergne, P. 'Flint artifacts from the Buraimi area, Eastern Arabia, and their relations with the Near Eastern post-Paleolithic', *PSAS*, 6 (1976) pp 40-61.

Corboud, P. 'Compte-rendu de la campagne 1989 du Survey Archéologique du Fujairah (U.A.E.)', *The Arabian Gulf Gazetteer*, 1 (1990) pp 18-19.

Corboud, P., Castella, A.-C., Hapka, R. and im Obersteg, P. *Les tombes protohistoriques de Bithnah (Fujairah, Émirats Arabes Unis)*, Mainz, Terra Archaeologica 1 (1996).

Coubray, S. 'Preliminary remarks about the 1988 paleobotanical sampling in the Sharjah Emirate', in R. Boucharlat (ed), *Archaeological Surveys and Excavations in the Sharjah Emirate, 1988: A Fourth Preliminary Report*, Lyon, Maison de l'Orient, (1988) pp 74-75.

de Blois, F. 'Maka and Mazun', *Studia Iranica*, 18 (1989) pp 157-167.

de Cardi, B. 'Further archaeological survey in Ras al-Khaimah, U.A.E., 1977', *Oriens Antiquus*, 24 (1985) pp 163-240.

de Cardi, B. 'The grave goods from Shimal tomb 6 in Ras al-Khaimah, U.A.E.', in D.T. Potts (ed) *Araby the Blest*, Copenhagen, Carsten Niebuhr Institute Publications 7, (1988) pp 45-72.

de Cardi, B., Kennet, D. and Stocks, R.L. 'Five thousand years of settlement at Khatt, UAE', *PSAS*, 24 (1994) pp 35-80.

Flavin, K. and Shepherd, 'Fishing in the Gulf: Preliminary investigations at an Ubaid site, Dalma (UAE)', *PSAS*, 24 (1994) pp 115-134.

Frifelt, K. 'Jamdat Nasr fund fra Oman (Jamdat Nasr graves in the Oman)', *Kuml* (1971) pp 355-383.

Frifelt, K. 'On prehistoric settlement and chronology of the Oman peninsula', *East and West*, 25 (1975) pp 359-424.

Frifelt, K. '"Jemdet Nasr graves" on the Oman peninsula', in B. Alster (ed), *Death in Mesopotamia*, Copenhagen, Akademisk Forlag, (1980) pp 273-279.

Frifelt, K. 'A third millennium kiln from the Oman peninsula', *AAE*, 1 (1990) pp 4-15.

Frifelt, K. *The Island of Umm an-Nar, Vol. 1, Third Millennium Graves*, Aarhus, Jutland Archaeological Society Publications 26/1, (1991).

Frifelt, K. *The Island of Umm an-Nar, Vol. 2, The Third Millennium Settlement*, Aarhus, Jutland Archaeological Society Publications 26/2, (1995).

Gautier, A. 'Preliminary report on the fauna of Mleiha', in R. Boucharlat (ed), *Archaeological Surveys and Excavations in the Sharjah Emirate, 1990 and 1992: A Sixth Interim Report*, Lyon, Maison de l'Orient (1992) pp 56-57.

Gebel, H.-G. *Südostarabien. Prähistorische Besiedlung/Southeast Arabia. Prehistoric Settlements*, Wiesbaden, Tübinger Atlas des Vorderen Orients B I 8.3 (1988).

Gebel, H.-G, Hannss, C., Liebau A. and Raehle, W. 'The late Quaternary environments of 'Ain al-Faidha/Al-'Ain, Abu Dhabi Emirate', *AUAE*, 5 (1989) pp 9-48.

Gignoux, P. 'La liste des provinces de l'Eran dans les inscriptions de Sabuhr et de Kirdir', *Acta Antiqua*, 19 (1971), pp 83-94.

Glennie, K.W., Pugh, J.M., and Goodall, T.M. 'Late Quaternary Arabian desert models of Permian Rotliegend reservoirs', *Exploration Bulletin*, 274 (1994/3) pp 1-19.

Glover, E. 'The molluscan fauna from Shimal, Ras al-Khaimah, United Arab Emirates', in K. Schippmann, A. Herling and J.-F. Salles (eds), *Golf-Archäologie: Mesopotamien, Iran, Kuwait, Bahrain, Vereinigte Arabische Emirate und Oman*, Buch am Erlbach, Internationale Archäologie 6 (1991) pp 205-220.

Glover, E., Glover, I. and Vita-Finzi, C. 'First-order ^{14}C dating of marine molluscs in archaeology', *Antiquity*, 64 (1990) pp 562-567.

Gouin, P. 'Râpes, jarres et faisselles: la production et l'exportation des produits laitiers dans l'Indus du 3e millénaire', *Paléorient*, 16/2 (1993) pp 37-54.

Grave, P., Bird, R. and Potts, D.T. 'A trial PIXE/PIGME analysis of Pre-Islamic Arabian coinage', *AAE*, 7 (1996a) pp 75-81.

Grave, P., Potts, D.T., Yassi, N., Reade, W., and Bailey, G. 'Elemental characterisation of Barbar ceramics from Tell Abraq', *AAE*, 7 (1996b) pp 177-187.

Groom, N. 'Oman and the Emirates in Ptolemy's map', *AAE*, 5 (1994) pp 198-214.

Groom, N. 'The *Periplus*, Pliny and Arabia', *AAE*, 6 (1995) pp 180-195.

Grupe, G. and Schutkowski, H. 'Dietary shift during the 2nd millennium BC in prehistoric Shimal, Oman peninsula', *Paléorient*, 15 (1989) pp 77-84.

Haerinck, E. 'The rectangular Umm an-Nar-period grave at Mowaihat (Emirate of Ajman, United Arab Emirates)', *Gentse bidragen tot de kunstgeschiedenis en oudheidkunde*, 29 (1990-91) pp 1-30.

Haerinck, E. 'Heading for the Straits of Hormuz, an 'Ubaid site in the Emirate of Ajman (U.A.E.)', *Arabian Archaeology and Epigraphy*, 2 (1991a) pp 84-90.

Haerinck, E. 'Excavations at ed-Dur (Umm al-Qaiwain, U.A.E.) - Preliminary report on the second Belgian season (1988)', *AAE*, 2 (1991b) pp 31-60.

Haerinck, E. 'Excavations at ed-Dur (Umm al-Qaiwain, U.A.E.) - Preliminary report on the fourth Belgian season (1988)', *AAE*, 3 (1992) pp 190-208.

Haerinck, E. 'Excavations at ed-Dur (Umm al-Qaiwain, U.A.E.) - Preliminary report on the fifth Belgian season (1991)', *AAE*, 4 (1993) pp 210-225.

Haerinck, E. 'Excavations at ed-Dur (Umm al-Qaiwain, U.A.E.) - Preliminary report on the sixth Belgian season (1992)', *AAE*, 5 (1994a) pp 184-197.

Haerinck, E. 'More prehistoric finds from the United Arab Emirates', AAE, 5 (1994b) pp 153-147.

Haerinck, E. 'Héraclès dans l'iconographie des monnaies arabes pré-islamiques d'Arabie du Sud-est?', *Akkadica*, 89-90 (1994c) pp 9-13.

Haerinck, E. 'Un service à boire décoré: A propos d'iconographie arabique préislamique', in H. Gasche, M. Tanret, C. Janssen and A. Degraeve (eds), *Cinquante-deux reflexions sur le Proche-Orient Ancien offertes en hommage à Leon de Meyer*, Louvain, Peeters, (1994d) pp 401-426.

Haerinck, E., Metdepenninghen, C. and Stevens, K.G. 'Excavations at ed-Dur (Umm al-Qaiwain, U.A.E.) - Preliminary report on the second Belgian season (1988)', *AAE*, 2 (1991) pp 31-60.

Haerinck, E., Metdepenninghen, C. and Stevens, K.G. 'Excavations at ed-Dur (Umm al-Qaiwain, U.A.E.) - Preliminary report on the third Belgian season (1989)', *AAE*, 3 (1992) pp 44-60.

Haerinck, E., Phillips, C.S., Potts, D.T. and Stevens, K.G. 'Ed-Dur, Umm al-Qaiwain (U.A.E.)', in U. Finkbeiner (ed), *Materialien zur Archäologie der Seleukiden- und Partherzeit im südlichen Babylonien und im Golfgebiet*, Tübingen, Wasmuth, (1993) pp 183-193.

Häser, J. *Steingefäße des 2. vorchristlichen Jahrtausends im Gebiet des Arabischen/Persischen Golfes: Typologie der Gefäße und Deckel aus Serpentinit, Chlorit, Steatit und verwandten Steinarten*, Berlin, Free University, unpubl. M.A. thesis (1988).

Häser, J. 'Soft-stone vessels of the 2nd millennium BC in the Gulf region', *PSAS*, 20 (1990a) pp 43-54.

Häser, J. 'Soft-stone vessels from Shimal and Dhayah (Ras al-Khaimah, U.A.E.)', in F.M. Andraschko and W.-R. Teegen (eds), *Gedenkschrift für Jürgen Driehaus*, Mainz, Von Zabern, (1990b) pp 347-355.

Hassan, M.A. and al-Sulaimi, J.S. 'Copper mineralization in the northern part of Oman mountains near Al Fujairah, United Arab Emirates', *Economic Geology*, 74 (1979) pp 919-946.

Hellyer, P. 'New discoveries on Dalma and Sir Bani Yas', *Tribulus*, 3/2 (1993a) p 16.

Hellyer, P. 'Iron Age Fort in Fujairah', *Tribulus*, 3/2 (1993b) p. 17.

Hellyer, P. 'Safavid and Sassanian coins in Fujairah', *Tribulus*, 5/1 (1995) p 25.

Hoch, E. 'Reflections on prehistoric life at Umm an-Nar (Trucial Oman) based on faunal remains from the third millennium BC.' in M. Taddei (ed), *South Asian Archaeology 1977*. Naples, Istituto Universitario Orientale Seminario di Studi Asiatici Series Minor 6 (1979) pp 589-638.

Hoch, E. 'Animal bones from the Umm an-Nar settlement', in K. Frifelt, *The Island of Umm an-Nar Vol. 2. The Third Millennium Settlement*, Aarhus, Jutland Archaeological Society Publications 36/2 (1995) pp 249-256.

Højgaard, K. 'Dentition on Umm an-Nar (Trucial Oman), 2500 BC', *Scandinavian Journal of Dental Research*, 88 (1980) pp 355-364.

Højgaard, K. 'SEM (scanning electron microscope) examination of teeth from the third millennium BC excavated in Wadi Jizzi and Hafit', in J. Schotsmans and M. Taddei (eds), *South Asian Archaeology 1983*, Naples, Istituto Universitario Orientale, Dipartimento di Studi Asiatici, Series Minor XXIII, (1985) pp 151-156.

Howgego, C. and Potts, D.T. 'Greek and Roman coins from eastern Arabia', *AAE*, 3 (1992) pp 183-189.

Inizan, M.-L. and Tixier, J. 'Industrie lithique taillée de Hili 8', *AUAE*, 2-3 (1980) p 72.

Jasim, S.A. 'An Ubaid site in the Emirate of Sharjah (U.A.E.)', *Arabian Archaeology and Epigraphy*, 7 (1996) pp 1-12.

Kästner, J.-M. 'Vorbericht über zwei untersuchte Kollektivgräber in Dhayah (Ras al-Khaimah, U.A.E.)', in F M Andraschko and W.-R. Teegen (eds), *Gedenkschrift für Jürgen Driehaus*, Mainz, Von Zabern, (1990) pp 339-346.

Kästner, J.-M. 'Some preliminary remarks concerning two recently excavated tombs in Dhayah/Ras al-Khaimah', in K. Schippmann, A. Herling and J.-F. Salles (eds), *Golf-Archaologie: Mesopotamien, Iran, Kuwait, Bahrain, Vereinigte Arabische Emirate und Oman*, Buch am Erlbach, Internationale Archäologie 6 (1991) pp 233-244.

Kennet, D. 'Jazirat al-Hulayla - early Julfar', *Journal of the Royal Asiatic Society*, 4 (1994) pp 163-212.

Kennet, D. and Velde, C. 'Third and early second-millennium occupation at Nud Ziba, Khatt (U.A.E.)', *AAE*, 6 (1995) pp 81-99.

King, G.R.D. and Hellyer, P. 'A Pre-Islamic Christian site on Sir Bani Yas', *Tribulus*, 4/2 (1994) pp 5-7.

Lancaster, W. and F. 'Tribe, community and the concept of access to resources: Territorial behaviour in southeast Ja'alan', in M.J. Asimov and A. Rao (eds), *Mobility and territoriality: Social and spatial boundaries among foragers, fishers, pastoralists and peripatetics*, Providence/Oxford, Berg Publishers (1992) pp 343-363.

Lecomte, O. 'Ed-Dur, les occupations des 3e et 4e s. ap. J.-C.: Contexte des trouvailles et matériel diagnostique', in U. Finkbeiner (ed), *Materialien zur Archäologie der Seleukiden- und Partherzeit im südlichen Babylonien und im Golfgebiet*, Tübingen, Wasmuth (1993) pp 195-217.

Littleton, J. and Frøhlich, B. 'Fish-eaters and farmers: Dental pathology in the Arabian Gulf', *American Journal of Physical Anthropology*, 92 (1993) pp 427-447.

Lombard, P. *Aspects culturels de la péninsule d'Oman au début du 1e millénaire av. J.C.*, Paris, University of Paris 1, unpubl. M.A. thesis (1979).

Lombard, P. 'Poignards en bronze de la péninsule d'Oman au Ier millénaire: Un problème d'influences iraniennes de l'Âge du Fer', *Iranica Antiqua*, 16 (1981) pp 87-93.

Lombard, P. *L'Arabie orientale à l'Âge du Fer*, Paris, Univ. of Paris 1, unpubl. PhD thesis (1985).

Lombard, P. 'Âges du Fer sans fer: Le cas de la péninsule d'Oman au Ier millénaire avant J.-C.', in T. Fahd (ed), *L'Arabie préislamique et son environnement historique et culturel*, Leiden, Travaux du Centre de Recherche sur le Proche-Orient et la Grèce Antiques de l'Université des Sciences Humaines de Strasbourg 10 (1989) pp 25-37.

Magee, P. *Cultural change, variability and settlement in southeastern Arabia from 1400 to 250 BC: The view from Tell Abraq*, Sydney, The University of Sydney, unpubl. PhD thesis (1995).

McBrearty, S. 'Lithic artifacts from Abu Dhabi's Western Region', *Tribulus*, 3/1 (1993) pp 13-14.

Méry, S. 'Origine et production des récipients de terre cuite dans la péninsule d'Oman à l'Âge du Bronze', *Paléorient*, 17 (1991) pp 51-78.

Méry, S. 'La céramique, témoin de la dynamique culturelle en Arabie durant la Protohistoire', in *Terre cuite et société: La céramique, document technique, économique, culturel*, Juan-les-Pins, Editions APDCA (1994) pp 395-406.

Millet, M. 'The lithic industry, 1988 report', in R. Boucharlat (ed), *Archaeological Surveys and Excavations in the Sharjah Emirate, 1988: A Fourth Preliminary Report*, Lyon, Maison de l'Orient (1988) pp 19-28.

Millet, M. 'Archaeological soundings', in R. Boucharlat (ed), *Archaeological Surveys and Excavations in the Sharjah Emirate, 1989: A Fifth Preliminary Report*, Lyon, Maison de l'Orient (1989) pp 22-27.

Millet, M. 'Comments on the lithic material from an 'Ubaid site in the Emirate of Ajman (U.A.E.)', *AAE*, 2 (1991) pp 91-92.

Minzoni Déroche, A. 'The prehistoric periods: the artefacts', in R. Boucharlat (ed), *Second Archaeological Survey in the Sharjah Emirate, 1985: A Preliminary Report*, Lyon, Maison de l'Orient (1985a) pp 21-26.

Minzoni Déroche, A. 'Survey on prehistoric sites', in R. Boucharlat (ed), *Second Archaeological Survey in the Sharjah Emirate, 1985: A Preliminary Report*, Lyon, Maison de l'Orient (1985b) pp 53-61.

Mouton, M. 'Les pointes de flèches en fer des sites préislamiques de Mleiha et ed-Dur, E.A.U.', *AAE*, 1 (1990) pp 88-103.

Mouton, M. *La péninsule d'Oman de la fin de l'Âge du fer au début de la période sassanide (250 av.-350 ap. J.-C.)*, Paris, Univ. of Paris 1, unpubl. PhD thesis (1992).

Müller, W.W. 'Ein Grabmonument aus Nağran als Zeugnis für das Frühnordarabische', *Neue Ephemeris für semitische Epigraphik*, 3 (1978) pp 149-157.

Mynors, H.S. 'An examination of Mesopotamian ceramics using petrographic and neutron activation analysis', in A. Aspinal and S.E. Warren (eds), *The proceedings of the 22nd symposium of archaeometry*, Bradford, Schools of Physics and Archaeological Sciences (1983) pp 377-387.

'Neolithic flints from Merawah', *Tribulus*, 3/1 (1993) p 20.

Papadopoulos, J.K. 'A Western Mediterranean amphora fragment from ed-Dur', *AAE*, 5 (1994) pp 276-279.

Pedersen, C.H. and Buchwald, V.F. 'An examination of metal objects from Tell Abraq, U.A.E.', *AAE*, 2 (1991) pp 1-9.

Phillips, C.S. *Wadi Al Qawr, Fashgha 1. The excavation of a prehistoric burial structure in Ras Al Khaimah, U.A.E., 1986*, Edinburgh, Dept. of Archaeology, Univ. of Edinburgh Project Paper No. 7 (1987).

Ploquin, A. and Orzechowski, S. 'Palaeo-metallurgy at Mleiha: Preliminary notes', in Mouton, M. (ed), *Archaeological Surveys and Excavations in the Sharjah Emirate, 1993 and 1994: A Seventh Interim Report*, Lyon, Maison de l'Orient (1994) pp 25-32.

Potts, D.T. 'From Qadê to Mazûn: Four notes on Oman, c. 700 BC to 700 AD', *Journal of Oman Studies*, 8/1 (1985) pp 81-95.

Potts, D.T. 'Eastern Arabia and the Oman peninsula during the late fourth and early third millennium BC', in U. Finkbeiner and W. Röllig (eds), *Ğamdat Naṣr: Period or Regional Style?*, Wiesbaden, Ludwig Reichert (1986a) pp 121-170.

Potts, D.T. 'The booty of Magan', *Oriens Antiquus*, 25 (1986b) pp 271-285.

Potts, D.T. 'Arabia and the kingdom of Characene', in D.T. Potts (ed) *Araby the Blest*, Copenhagen, Carsten Niebuhr Institute Publications 7 (1988) pp 137-167.

Potts, D.T. *A prehistoric mound in the Emirate of Umm al-Qaiwain: Excavations at Tell Abraq in 1989*, Copenhagen, Munksgaard (1990a).

Potts, D.T. *The Arabian Gulf in Antiquity*, I and II, Oxford, Clarendon Press (1990b).

Potts, D.T. *Further excavations at Tell Abraq: The 1990 season*, Copenhagen, Munksgaard (1991a).

Potts, D.T. *The Pre-Islamic Coinage of Eastern Arabia*, Copenhagen, Carsten Niebuhr Institute Publications 14 (1991b).

Potts, D.T. 'The late prehistoric, protohistoric, and early historic periods in Eastern Arabia (ca. 5000-1200 BC)', *Journal of World Prehistory*, 7 (1993a) pp 121-162.

Potts, D.T. 'Four seasons of excavation at Tell Abraq (1989-1993)', *PSAS*, 24 (1993b) pp 117-126.

Potts, D.T. 'Rethinking some aspects of trade in the Arabian Gulf', *World Archaeology*, 24 (1993c) pp 423-440.

Potts, D.T. 'A new Bactrian find from southeastern Arabia', *Antiquity*, 67 (1993d) pp 591-596.

Potts, D.T. 'Contributions to the agrarian history of eastern Arabia I. Implements and cultivation techniques', *AAE*, 5 (1994a) pp 158-168.

Potts, D.T. 'Contributions to the agrarian history of Eastern Arabia II. The cultivars', *AAE*, 5 (1994b) pp 236-275.

Potts, D.T. 'South and Central Asian Elements at Tell Abraq (Emirate of Umm al-Qaiwain, United Arab Emirates), c. 2200 BC - 300 AD', in A. Parpola and P. Koskikallio (eds), *South Asian Archaeology 1993*, vol. II. Helsinki, Annales Academiae Scientiarum Fennicae Ser. B-271 (1994c) pp 615-628.

Potts, D.T. *Supplement to the Pre-Islamic Coinage of Eastern Arabia* (Copenhagen, Carsten Niebuhr Institute Publications 16 (1994d).

Potts, D.T. 'Eine frühe Stadt in Magan: Ausgrabungen in Tell Abraq', *Das Altertum*, 41 (1995a) pp 83-98.

Potts, D.T. 'Watercraft of the Lower Sea', in R. Dittmann, U. Finkbeiner and H. Hauptmann (eds), *Beiträge zur Kulturgeschichte Vorderasiens: Festschrift für Rainer M. Boehmer*, Mainz, Von Zabern (1995b) pp 559-571.

Potts, D.T. 'The diffusion of light by translucent media in antiquity: Apropos two alabaster windowpane fragments from ed-Dur (United Arab Emirates)', *Antiquity*, 70 (1996) pp 182-188.

Potts, D.T. 'Re-writing the late prehistory of southeastern Arabia: A reply to Jocelyn Orchard', *Iraq*, in press a.

Potts, D.T. '**en**, **lugal** and **ensi** in early historic Magan', *Journal of Cuneiform Studies*, in press b.

Potts, D.T. 'Namord ware in southeastern Arabia', in press c.

Potts, D.T. 'The Roman relationship with the *Persicus sinus* from the rise of Spasinou Charax (127 BC) to the reign of Shapur II (309-379 AD)', in S. Alcock (ed), *The Early Roman Empire in the East*, Oxford, Oxbow, in press d.

Potts, D.T. and Cribb, J. 'Sasanian and Arab-Sasanian coins from eastern Arabia', *Iranica Antiqua*, 30 (1995) pp 123-137.

Prieur, A. 'Notes on the Malacofauna', in R. Boucharlat (ed), *Archaeological Surveys and Excavations in the Sharjah Emirate, 1989: A Fifth Preliminary Report*, Lyon, Maison de l'Orient (1989) pp 28-31.

Prieur, A. 'Etude faunistique et aspects anthropiques du site de Tell Abraq', in Potts, D.T., *A prehistoric mound in the Emirate of Umm al-Qaiwain, U.A.E.: Excavations at Tell Abraq in 1989*, Copenhagen, Munksgaard (1990) pp 141-151.

Prieur, A. 'Molluscs from Mleiha' in M. Mouton (ed), *Archaeological Surveys and Excavations in the Sharjah Emirate, 1993 and 1994: A Seventh Interim Report*, Lyon, Maison de l'Orient (1994) pp 33-38.

Prieur, A. and Guerin, C. 'Découverte d'un site préhistorique d'abattage de dugongs à Umm al-Qaiwain (Emirats Arabes Unis)', *A. A. E.*, 2 (1991) pp 72-83.

Reade, W.J. and Potts, D.T. 'New evidence for late third millennium linen from Tell Abraq, Umm al-Qaiwain, U.A.E.', *Paléorient*, 19 (1993) pp 99-106.

Ross, E.C. 'Annals of 'Omán, from early times to the year 1728 AD from an Arabic ms. by Sheykh Sirha'n bin Sa'id bin Sirha'n bin Muhammad, of the Benú 'Alí tribe of 'Oman', *Journal of the Asiatic Society of Bengal*, 43 (1874) pp 111-196.

Schutkowski, H. and Herrmann, B. 'Anthropological report on human remains from the cemetery at Shimal', in Vogt, B. and Franke-Vogt, U. *Shimal 1985/1986: Excavations of the German Archaeological Mission in Ras al-Khaimah, U.A.E., A Preliminary Report*, Berlin, Berliner Beiträge zum Vorderen Orient 8 (1987) pp 55-65.

Sedov, A. 'Two South Arabian coins from Mleiha', *AAE*, 6 (1995) pp 61-64.

Shoufani, E. *Al-Riddah and the Muslim conquest of Arabia*, Toronto, Univ. of Toronto Press (1972).

Stephan, E. 'Preliminary report of the faunal remains of the first two seasons of Tell Abraq/Umm al Quwain/United Arab Emirates' in H. Buitenhuis and H.-P. Uerpmann (eds), *Archaeozoology of the Near East II*, Leiden, Universal Book Services, in press.

Stevens, K.-G. 'Four "Iron Age" stamp seals from Qarn bint Sa'ud (Abu Dhabi Emirate - U.A.E.)', *AAE*, 3 (1992) pp 173-176.

Taha, M. 'The archaeology of the Arabian Gulf during the first millennium BC', *Al-Rafidan*, 3-4 (1982-1983) pp 75-87.

Teixidor, J. 'Une inscription araméenne provenant de l'Émirat de Sharjah (Émirats Arabes Unis)', *Comptes rendus de l'Académie des Inscriptions & Belles-Lettres* (1992) pp 695-707.

Thomas, R. and Potts, D.T. 'Atacamite pigment at Tell Abraq in the early Iron Age', *AAE*, 7 (1996) pp 13-16.

Uerpmann, H.-P. and M. 'Ubaid pottery in the eastern Gulf - new evidence from Umm al-Quwain (U.A.E.), *AAE*, 7 (1996) pp 125-139.

Uerpmann, M. 'Structuring the Late Stone Age of Southeastern Arabia', *AAE*, 3 (1992) pp 65-109.

Van Neer, W. and Gautier, A. 'Preliminary report on the faunal remains from the coastal site of ed-Dur, 1st-4th century AD, Umm al-Quwain, United Arab Emirates' in H. Buitenhuis and A.T. Clason (eds), *Archaeozoology of the Near East, Proceedings of the first international symposium on the archaeozoology of southwestern Asia and adjacent areas*, Leiden, Universal Books Services (1993) pp 110-118.

Velde, C. 'Preliminary remarks on the settlement pottery in Shimal (Ras al-Khaimah, U.A.E.)', in F.M. Andraschko and W.-R. Teegen (eds), *Gedenkschrift für Jürgen Driehaus*, Mainz, Von Zabern (1990) pp 357-378.

Velde, C. 'Preliminary remarks on the settlement pottery in Shimal', in K. Schippmann, A. Herling and J.-F. Salles (eds), *Golf-Archäologie: Mesopotamien, Iran, Kuwait, Bahrain, Vereinigte Arabische Emirate und Oman*, Buch am Erlbach, Internationale Archäologie 6 (1991) pp 265-288.

Velde, C. *Die spätbronzezeitliche und früheisenzeitliche Siedlung und ihre Kermaik in Shimal/Ras al Khaimah (Vereinigte Arabische Emirate)*, Göttingen, Georg-August University, unpubl. M.A. thesis (1992).

Vogt, B. *Zur Chronologie und Entwicklung der Gräber des späten 4.-2.Jtsd.v.Chr. auf der Halbinsel Oman: Zusammenfassung, Analyse und Würdigung publizierter wie auch unveröffentlichter Grabungsergebnisse*, Göttingen, Georg-August University, unpubl. PhD thesis (1985).

Vogt, B. *Asimah: An account of a two months rescue excavation in the mountains of Ras al-Khaimah, United Arab Emirates*, Dubai, Shell Markets Middle East (1994a).

Vogt, B. 'Death, resurrection and the camel', in N. Nebes (ed), *Arabia Felix: Beiträge zur Sprache und Kultur des vorislamischen Arabien, Festschrift Walter W. Müller zum 60. Geburtstag*, Wiesbaden, Harrassowitz (1994b) pp 279-290.

Vogt, B. and Franke-Vogt, U. *Shimal 1985/1986: Excavations of the German Archaeological Mission in Ras al-Khaimah, U.A.E., A Preliminary Report*, Berlin, Berliner Beiträge zum Vorderen Orient 8 (1987).

Waetzoldt, H. 'Zur Bewaffnung des Heeres von Ebla', *Oriens Antiquus*, 29 (1990) pp 1-38.

Weisgerber, G. 'Oman: A bronze-producing centre during the 1st half of the 1st millennium BC', in J.E. Curtis (ed), *Bronzeworking centres of Western Asia c. 1000-539 BC*, London, Kegan Paul International (1988) pp 285-295.

Wells, C. 'Appendix 1. Human bone', in Donaldson, P. 'Prehistoric tombs of Ras al-Khaimah', *Oriens Antiquus*, 23 (1984) pp 213-218, 277-280.

Wells, C. 'Human bone', in Donaldson, P. 'Prehistoric tombs of Ras al-Khaimah', *Oriens Antiquus*, 24 (1985) pp 87-88.

Wilkinson, J.C. 'A sketch of the historical geography of the Trucial Oman down to the beginning of the sixteenth century', *The Geographical Journal*, 130 (1964) pp 337-349.

Willcox, G. 'Some plant impressions from Umm an-Nar island' in K. Frifelt, *The Island of Umm an-Nar Vol. 2. The Third Millennium Settlement*, Aarhus, Jutland Archaeological Society Publications 36/2 (1995) pp 257-259.

Willcox, G. and Tengberg, M. 'Preliminary report on the archaeobotanical investigations at Tell Abraq with special attention to chaff impressions in mud brick', *AAE*, 6 (1995) pp 129-138.

The History of UAE: The Eve of Islam and the Islamic Period

Geoffrey R. King

Introduction

The Islamic archaeology of the United Arab Emirates (UAE) has been investigated in a sustained manner only in the past few years. However, there is now a growing body of material that complements the historical sources and although there are still many gaps, nevertheless archaeology has given concrete form to periods hitherto mere blanks in the country's history. The historical sources are quite well known and often cited, but the archaeological record provides a different depth of picture, showing the existence of an architectural tradition and also a degree of social and economic structure that is not immediately apparent from the scattered literary sources.

The environment is such that for much of the UAE, standing monuments rarely, if ever, long survive above ground, given their fragile building materials. For the Islamic period, as for earlier times, archaeological excavation is the only means to retrieve the history of the UAE. Recent concentration on the archaeology of the last 2000 years has produced very interesting results, bringing the country into the historical framework of the Near East as a whole.

The Landscape and the Islamic Geographers

The processes whereby the UAE landscape was exploited in the past are being gradually understood for the Islamic period as well as for ancient times. Beginning in the far west, the coastal region of Abu Dhabi and the interior is a harsh area with a deep coastal band of salt flats (sabkha) that lies between the sea and the sands of the Empty Quarter. The coast is extremely hard to travel along because of the sabkha, and after rain it is virtually impassable. Furthermore, the shore is often so shallow and befouled by shoals that it is difficult for boats under sail to navigate. For the Islamic period, settlement on the shore is rare west of Abu Dhabi up to the Qatar border, but there is a growing body of evidence to show that there was often activity on the offshore islands, whether seasonal or permanent. East of Abu Dhabi, however, ports are more frequent. By the sixteenth century, many of the place names known today on the coast had already emerged. However, in earlier times, it is only Julfar (in Ras al-Khaimah) and Dibba (in Fujairah and Sharjah) which are readily recognizable.

Beyond the sabkha, much of western part of the UAE is arid sand desert. By the Islamic period, the ancient river system of the Sabkha Matti had long since ceased to flow. However, the inland oases at Liwa and at Al-'Ain were always fertile and supported date plantations, and their production always served as a major element of the local economy.

In the east and north, the sands and plains give way to the high mountains of Jabal Hajar, part of the range that runs from Jabal Akhdar in the Sultanate of Oman through to Ru'us Jibal and Ras Musandam, the high promontory that overlooks the Straits of Hormuz. Rainfall is heavier here and this is reflected in the far greater fertility that characterizes Ras al-Khaimah, Fujairah and the parts of the emirates of Sharjah and Dubai that lie in this region. For later Islamic times (*i.e.* fourteenth to fifteeenth century and later) the greatest concentration of settlement was in the northern highlands and coast of the modern UAE and it is reasonable to suppose that this was true in earlier times as well, although the point has yet to be demonstrated archaeologically in a comprehensive manner.

Although Dibba, Julfar and Tuwwam (Al-'Ain, al-Buraimi) among modern UAE towns are mentioned in the Arabic sources from the arrival of Islam onwards, it is not until the ninth century that additional names begin to be recorded. Ibn Khurradadhbih (Ibn Khurradadhbih: p 111), a former official of the Abbasid postal service, writing in *ca* 885-6, provides a series of itineraries that reflects the official record of the main routes through the Islamic world in his period. He describes a coastal route from the 'Uman Peninsula to Makkah, mentioning Farak, 'Awkalan, Habat(?), and then al-Shihr, a port of the south coast of Yemen. It is unclear where the first three places were located although it seems that they must be sought along the Batinah coast of Fujairah and the Sultanate of Oman or in Dhofar and Mahra. Elsewhere (p 113), Ibn Khurradadhbih mentions the towns of Bahrain: it must be recalled that Bahrain to the medieval Arab geographers means not only the island but the mainland opposite and its hinterland. He refers to al-Khatt, al-Qatif, al-Aara and Hajar, all apparently in Saudi Arabia today. The next place name is al-Faruq, and then Bainunah. The location of al-Faruq is unclear but Bainunah is located in the Western Region of the Emirate of Abu Dhabi.

Ibn Khurradadhbih also cites a verse by the famous eighth century poet of the Umayyad period, Al Nabigha, who refers to the wild cows of Bainunah. It is worth noting that the fertile northern emirates of the UAE have numbers of humped back cows that are indigenous to the country. Furthermore, uniquely in Arabia, there is a tradition of bull-fighting in Fujairah emirate where bulls are pitched against each other (Hellyer 1990: pp 50-54). Although this custom has been associated with the Portuguese inheritance of the UAE, local sources suggest that it is far more ancient: the verse by Al Nabigha, cited by Ibn Khurradadhbih, implies that this may be correct.

Al Maqdisi in the tenth century describes the citadels (*qasaba*) of 'Uman', which included Suhar; Nizwa; al-Sirr; Danak; Dibba; Salut or Salub; Julfar; Samad; and Lasya Milh (Al Maqdisi, *Ahsan*: pp 70-71). Elsewhere, he mentions Khasab in Musandam. He then mentions other east Arabian towns - al-Ahsa' (al-Hasa'); Sabun; al-Zarqa'; al-Uwal; al-'Uqayr; and al-Yamama (today apparently all in Saudi Arabia or Bahrain). His itinerary generally runs from east to west: Suhar and Nizwa are now in the Sultanate of Oman; Dibba, as we have seen, is in Fujairah and Sharjah territory, while Julfar is in Ras al-Khaimah and all are easy to place on the modern map. There follows Lasya Milh and Samad, and the next place Al Maqdisi mentions (al-Ahsa') is in Saudi Arabia today, whereas Samad and Lasya Milh seem to be in the UAE.

Abu'l-Faraj Qudama (pp 151-2) writing between 932 and 948 gives an itinerary from 'Uman to Basra, recording a place between them called al-Sabkha. It was apparently in the UAE, as the next places mentioned in the itinerary are Qatar and al-'Uqair (now in Saudi Arabia). Al-Sabkha was also known to Al Idrisi (Al Idrisi 1972: ii: p 162; trans. Jaubert 1836: i: p 157), writing in 1154 in Sicily for the Norman king, Roger II. He refers to an itinerary from Suhar, to Damar, Masqat, al-Jabal and Julfar. Al-Jabal must refer to the Jabal Hajar mountain range. After Julfar, Al Idrisi, like Qudama, says that the traveller sailed to Bahrain via the port of (al-) Sabkha. Al-Sabkha remains unidentified but it could be identical with Al Maqdisi's Lasya Milh, given the suggestion of salt in the latter's name. The name Sabkha is vague and generalized and could be anywhere on the salt-flats (sabkha) that run along the UAE coast westwards from Umm al-Qaiwain to Abu Dhabi emirate. Both Lasya Milh and Sabkha are located west of Julfar, but could be associated with any of the ports in the salt flats, but whether a predecessor of Umm al-Qaiwain, Ajman, Sharjah or Dubai is impossible to determine. Sharjah may be associated with Ptolemy's Sarkoepolis and Lasya Milh and/or Sabkha (Potts 1992: ii: pp 319-320). Al-Jumayra near Dubai was certainly settled in the ninth century as current excavations suggest, and would be a persuasive candidate for identification with al-Sabkha and Lasya Milh.

Al Idrisi is very specific about the UAE. He should be treated with some caution as his work, produced in Palermo, was based on reports, although these reports seem to be based on direct observation. Along with the text is his famous map which appears in a number of manuscripts of his work and is one of the most significant documents for Arabian geography since the second century AD map of Claudius Ptolemy. His mapping and account of the coast of the UAE is extremely informative, only superseded by Portuguese mapping and descriptions of the sixteenth and seventeenth centuries.

Al Idrisi knew the western waters of UAE as the Sea of Qatar and described the islands there briefly but accurately as desert islands which were frequented only by sea birds and land birds. These shed guano which would be collected and transported to al-Basra where it would fetch a high price. It would be used on the farms and gardens to manure vines and dates at al-Basra itself and elsewhere. Al Idrisi's report is remarkable in its accuracy. The colonies of seabirds on the offshore islands of western Abu Dhabi are vast, and islands favoured by them are indeed deep in their guano. The island of Kardhal, north of Ghagha' in western Abu Dhabi, is an example, inhabited today by thousands of cormorants, but there are many other nesting sites.

Al Idrisi also mentions the pearl beds although he associates them with Suhar, Damar, Muscat and with al-Jabal (*i.e* Musandam) and Julfar. However, he says nothing of the far more extensive group of pearl-beds that lie in the western waters of the UAE coast. Although important in Al Idrisi's day as in all periods, the informants of Al Idrisi were probably more aware of the harbours whose fleets fished for pearls than the location of the pearl beds themselves. We have to wait for the Venetian jeweller, Gasparo Balbi, before the western pearl beds come into historical view, although there can be little doubt that their exploitation is very ancient and was merely unnoticed by the geographers of the medieval period.

Yaqut, writing in *ca* 1225, recorded an itinerary (*Mu'jam*: i: p 507) which ran from al-Bahrain in al-Khatt, to al-Qatif, al-Ara, Hajar, Bainunah, al-Zara, Jawatha, al-Sabur and al-Ghaba. This is curious as Bainunah is displaced far to the north, but the itinerary's sequence seems confused. Elsewhere (i: p 802), he refers to Bainunah as a place between 'Uman and al-Bahrayn, which fits better with the true geography of eastern Arabia. He also speaks of

Tuwwam (Al-'Ain) having its own citadel (*qasaba*) and that in his day, the principal citadel of 'Uman was Suhar.

Yaqut (*Mu'jam*: ii: p 104; also ii: p 63) also knew Julfar as Jullafar or Jurrafar which he describes as a town in 'Uman with many sheep and which produced cheese and *samn* which was carried to the surrounding country.

The Venetian state jeweller Gasparo Balbi in 1580 made a visit to the territory of the UAE to examine the pearling industry and is most instructive for the record that he made of the name-places along the coast from al-Qatif to the Gulf of 'Uman. He is the first to show the antiquity of many place names in use today and yet not recorded by the Arab geographers and historians. Like Al Idrisi, he knows the sea off the coast as the Sea of Qatar and mentions the following places now in UAE territory (Balbi in Slot 1993: pp 36 ff): Daas (Das), Emegorcenon (Qarnain), Anzevi (Arzanah), Zerecho (Zirkuh), Delmephialmas (Delma), Sirbeniast (Sir Bani Yas), Aldane (Dhanna), Cherizan (identified as Khawr Qirqishan, just off the island Abu Dhabi (Slot 1993: p 38), Dibei (Dubai), Sarba (Sharjah), Agimen (Ajman), Emegivien (Umm al-Qaiwain), Rasalchime (Ras al-Khaimah), Sircorcor (Khawr al-Quwayr), Debe (Dibba) Chorf (Khawr Fakkan) and Chelb (Kalba). All of these are identifications which have been reasonably proposed by Slot.

When the Portuguese under Albuquerque arrived in the area, they noted Julfar among the coastal towns as a place with a fleet, while Duarte Barbosa in the sixteenth century noted that the Julfar people were merchants and navigators. Pedro Teixera speaks of boats from Bahrain and Julfar going each summer to the pearl fisheries further up the Gulf. He also mentions local pearl fisheries off Julfar. As recent archaeology in western Abu Dhabi increasingly shows, there was a great deal of activity in the area of the pearl beds and this was not only marked in later Islamic times but probably sustained communities of pearl fishers at a far earlier date as well.

The UAE on the Eve of Islam

On the eve of Islam, the eastern coast of Arabia was ruled by a variety of powers. In the north-east, the Bani Lakhm Arab kings of al-Hira (now in Iraq) had very recently faded (*ca* 611). One of the main tribes in eastern Arabia was 'Abd Al Qays and in the south-east, the tribe of Azd was beginning to dominate much of 'Uman, challenging the foothold of the forces of the powerful Sasanian Empire which ruled Iraq, Iran and parts of Central Asia and Sind. The Sasanian and Byzantine Empires (the latter with its capital at Constantinople) together constituted the two great powers of the period. Their mutually destructive warfare in the sixth and early seventh century forms the background to the rise of Islam, the new faith which was soon to overwhelm the Sasanians completely and greatly to truncate the Byzantine state.

The Sasanians were a presence on both sides of the Gulf, having established their power on the Arabian coast in the fourth century AD. The position of their governors was maintained by strongholds on or near the Arabian coasts, such as Rustaq and Demetsjerd at Suhar, names attested by the early Islamic sources. Both are in the Sultanate of Oman today. So far there is no clear archaeological evidence of the Sasanian presence in the UAE, but there is a growing body of information suggesting settlement in various parts of the UAE in the centuries preceding the coming of Islam.

The Sasanian presence in south-eastern Arabia has recently been discussed by Potts (1992: pp 328-340; see also: Piacentini 1985: pp 57-77; Wilkinson 1973: 40-51). In the course of the wars with the Byzantines, the Sasanians extended their authority westwards and in 570 they appointed a governor in Yemen, which they were able to do because of their hold on south-eastern Arabia. It was only with the coming of Islam in the seventh century that Sasanian power was swept away from both 'Uman and Yemen forever.

However, before Islam, the Sasanians in 'Uman were already increasingly threatened by the local Azdi tribal forces under the Al Julanda kings. The balance swung in favour of the local Arabs when the Al Julanda joined with the Muslims from al-Madinah, and the Sasanian outposts were overwhelmed and their forces expelled in 630. The Sasanians had suffered defeat at the hands of the Byzantine emperor the previous year and the success of the Muslims and the Al Julanda in south-eastern Arabia presaged the subsequent defeats of the Sasanians at the hands of the Muslims in Iran over the next 20 years.

Little is known of the pre-Islamic history of south-eastern Arabian tribes which were to take so important a role in the expulsion of the Sasanians. The Azd, led by Al Julanda, had originated in Yemen, but there were non-Azd tribes as well. Their territory encompassed both the modern UAE and the Sultanate of Oman. The non-Azd tribes collectively were known in later times as Nizar.

A branch of Azd was found at Dibba on the Batinah coast of the UAE, where the Al 'Atik branch of the tribe dominated. Another branch, Huddan, resided along the modern UAE coast between Ra's Musandam and Qatar, while Humaym were at Nizwa. Elements of the Azd were already on the islands of the Gulf on both the Arabian and the Iranian side before the rise of Islam. Of the little that is known of the pre-Islamic Azd, it is clear that they were seamen, merchants and fishermen. At the time of the coming of the Islam, the tribes seem to have been pagan. Hisham ibn Al Kalbi (*Kitab al-Asnam*: p 54) says that the Azd, along with the northern Arabian tribes of Tayyi' and Al Quda'a, worshipped an idol called Bajir or Bajar. However, there is growing evidence of Christianity in the Gulf (including the UAE) before Islam, and this suggests a religious picture that was more complex. Local traditions current in the UAE that certain tribes including Manasir were Christian before the coming of Islam thus may well have some foundation.

At the time of the coming of Islam, the leadership of the Arabs of south-eastern Arabia was a matter of dispute. The Al Julanda ruling house of the Azd, led by two brothers, Jaifar and 'Abd (or 'Abbad), and centred on the Batinah coast at Suhar, were in conflict with the Al 'Atik tribe of Azd who lived in the interior of the country. The latter were led by Laqit b. Malik Al 'Atiki, who seems to have lived at Dibba.

According to Ibn Habib, however, Dibba was also sometimes under the control of the Al Julanda, for on the last day of the Muslim month of *Rajab*, they would administer an annual fair there, one of the great markets of pre-Islamic Arabia (Potts 1992: p 339). Ibn Habib records that Dibba was one of the two ports used by the Arabs (Suhar being the other). Merchants would come from Sind, India and China for this fair and if not an exaggeration, it suggests a broad Indian Ocean trade before Islam, although one is cautious in accepting that merchants from China arrived at this early date.

Although Dibba is mentioned in the Arabic sources as an important place, it does not seem to offer much archaeological evidence so far to indicate its character on the eve of

Islam or in the early Islamic period. However, future research may amend this view (de Cardi 1971: p 257).

While some places well known to the Arabic sources have not produced correspondingly informative archaeology for this period, archaeological research in recent years in the UAE has produced a far more complex and fuller picture of life in the country. Indeed, as with so much of the history of the country, it will eventually prove to be archaeological evidence rather than literary material that is the main source of information for long periods of its history. The dating evidence for the late pre-Islamic and early Islamic site is generally based on ceramics, much of it imported and reflecting commercial connections in the Gulf region.

The settlements identified so far vary markedly in character. At the Straits of Hormuz is Jazirat al-Ghanam, off the great headland of Musandam, now in the northern enclave of the Sultanate of Oman. A site there is attributed to the early fourth century on the basis of ceramic evidence. The site includes rectangular structural remains near to the sea and it has been associated with the Sasanian presence (de Cardi 1973: pp 305-310; de Cardi 1975: pp 24-26). Of far less certain identification is a site in Fujairah emirate, a well-constructed *falaj* in the Wadi Safad, which locally is said to be Sasanian, but although it is certainly ancient, its dating has yet to be confirmed.

Other sites of similar antiquity have begun to be identified in the northern emirate of Ras al Khaimah. Recent field work at Jazirat al-Hulayla off the coast at Rams and inland at Khatt has provided evidence of settlement in the Sasanian/early Islamic period (Kennet and King 1994: pp 167-169; de Cardi et al. 1994: pp 54-58). Al-Hulayla and Khatt are very different to each other. Al-Hulayla is a low sandy barrier island close to the Ras al-Khaimah coast, forming the side of a coastal creek, Khawr al-Khuwair, opposite the town of Rams. The archae-ological evidence at al-Hulayla is largely in the form of ceramic scatters, with no early structural remains surviving above the surface. These remains have either eroded or the settlement was one of *'arish* huts which have left no surface trace. The role of al-Hulayla as a harbour is underlined by the safe anchorage of Khawr al-Khuwair.

Khatt is a very different site, situated inland at the foot of the hills on the borders of the emirates of Ras al-Khaimah and Fujairah. Here there are several archaeological tells of great antiquity amidst farmland and groves of trees, in an area well supplied with water. Recent investigations at Khatt have shown that occupation of this fertile site goes back to the Stone Age, and there are other burials of fourth to third millennium BC. In the course of survey, ceramics were noted that indicate settlement in the first five centuries of the first millennium AD period and the late Sasanian/early Islamic period. In contrast to the site of Mleiha further south in Sharjah emirate or al-Dur in Umm al-Qaiwain, settlement at Khatt continued on into the Islamic period and the site deserves further investigation. The site of Kush also seems to be related to the same periods and Derek Kennet's current investigations should assist in clarifying matters there.

The settlements at the Hellenistic sites of al-Dur (Umm al-Qaiwain), excavated by an international team and al-Mleiha (Sharjah), excavated by a French team, do not appear to outlast the fourth century AD although there are links in terms of ceramics with sites of the early centuries AD further west in Abu Dhabi. As they had faded before the coming of Islam, an unanswered question arises as to their relationship with the settlement pattern that emerges on the eve of Islam and in the early Islamic period.

It is probably impossible now to assess the archaeological significance of the sites of Umm al-Qaiwain, Ajman, Sharjah and Dubai in this early period, but to the west of Dubai, the important site of al-Jumayra goes back to the Sasanian and the Umayyad periods according to its first excavator (Baramki 1975). It is also increasingly clear that it had an active life in the early Islamic period with ceramics of the classic glazed wares of the early Abbasid period represented among the finds. Until the present excavations at al-Jumayra led by Dr Husain Al Qandil of Dubai Museum are published, it would be premature to estimate the origins and longevity of this important site.

As in much earlier times, the plentiful water resources of Al-'Ain and al-Buraimi, the Tuwwam of the Arab geographers and historians, made the great inland oasis an important place in the early Islamic period and its numerous *falaj* systems show the longevity of organized settlement and cultivation there. The oasis is repeatedly mentioned in the context of events of the early Islamic period, but published archaeological accounts for the area on the eve of Islam or in the Islamic period generally are rare. A French team working in 1976 at Al-'Ain when the area was far less disturbed by development than today seems only to have found later Islamic material, dated to after the sixteenth century (Cleuziou 1976-7: p 10).

Only recently has activity from the early centuries AD to the early Islamic period been recognized through archaeological work on the coast of Abu Dhabi. To the east of Abu Dhabi, a ceramic scatter found on the mainland at Ras Bilyaryar is dated to the centuries immediately preceding Islam. As for Abu Dhabi island itself, there is no information as it had been heavily built over before archaeological investigation took place, and we know nothing of the centuries before Islam or the early Islamic period in this district.

On the offshore islands of the UAE a series of sites has been identified in recent years. A survey by a French team in 1979 on the island of Delma, near the town of the same name, noted a major building attributed to a Sasanian/early Islamic date, although it has since vanished (Harter, Cleuziou *et al.* 1979: pp 10-15). Ceramics of the fifth to eighth century date were recovered from a site on the outskirts of Delma during the 1992 season of the Abu Dhabi Islands Archaeological Survey and given its plentiful water supplies in the past, it seems very likely that Delma was a place of some regional importance before the rise of Islam and also in the Islamic period itself, to judge by Cleuziou's observations and our own.

Further west, on other offshore islands of Abu Dhabi emirate, a number of sites of the immediately pre-Islamic centuries have been recognized in the course of archaeological survey since 1993. Finds on the island of Yasat al-'Ulya' included third to fourth century AD ceramics and a small representation of Early Islamic ceramics. A significant site of similar date was found on the neighbouring island of Yasat al-Sufla', with remains of buildings indicated by low mounds that represent the traces of collapsed architecture. Sites of the same date are located on the island of Ufsayya and on the mainland opposite. Yet another site of some size was found on the island of Ghagha', one of a small group of islands in the westernmost waters of the UAE. Like the other sites of the area, that on Ghagha' island was of third to fourth century date. Later Islamic structures were built over the site, although much remained to indicate the extent of the earlier occupation and its importance.

The most remarkable discovery on the Abu Dhabi islands for this period immediately preceding Islam has been made at al-Khawr on the island of Sir Bani Yas, off the coast at

Courtyard house north of the church at al-Khawr, Sir Bani Yas, Abu Dhabi Emirate (1995).

Jabal Dhanna. The landscape of the island has been changed by landfilling and extensive tree planting in recent years, but at al-Khawr on the eastern side of the island, a group of sites was identified in 1992 which was dated to about the sixth century AD, and included several courtyard houses and a large occupation mound which is now recognized as a Nestorian monastery and church.

The structures so far exposed were reduced to their lower wall courses, but they were all remarkably well preserved with a fine plaster finish on the internal wall surfaces and floors. The monastery consists of a rectangular enclosure with chambers surrounding a central courtyard. The church stands in its centre at the highest point. In the course of the excavation numerous pieces of fine decorative plaster were recovered, decorated with relief motifs of grape leaves, grape clusters and Christian crosses of the same character as other Nestorian crosses found at sites of similar date elsewhere in the Gulf at Faylaka' (Kuwait), al-Jubail (Saudi Arabia), and at al-Kharg island (Iran).

The church is on an east-west axis, measuring at least 14 m east to west and it has three aisles. When abandoned it collapsed with the east wall falling onto its own decorative plaster, thus protecting and preserving a large amount of the decoration that covered the building on the exterior and possibly on the interior. The original design seems to have consisted of string courses decorated with grape clusters, vine leaves and crosses that ran in bands across the exterior of the building.

The presence of Nestorian churches in eastern Arabia conforms with the Arab textual accounts of Christianity in the east of the Peninsula at the time of the coming of Islam. The Bani Lakhm Arab kings of al-Hira in south-west Iraq were Nestorian Christians and their role was that of maintaining a buffer state for the Sasanians in their conflicts with the Byzantines and their allies in the desert. Other Arab tribes were also Christian, including Bani Taghlib and the north Arabian and Syrian tribes of Ghassan, Kalb and Judham, while Christianity was also well established in Yemen before Islam.

The ecclesiastical arrangements of the Nestorian church in eastern Arabia are reasonably well understood. The Nestorian province of Bet Qatraye included Bahrain and its opposite coast, al-Hasa' and Qatar, and also a number of bishoprics. Further to the east was Bet Mazunaye, which encompassed the modern Sultanate of Oman and the territory of the UAE. Its centre was Suhar and several of its bishops are known. As we have seen, for the Arab geographers, all of south-eastern Arabia, including the territory of the UAE, was known as 'Uman, and the Syriac term of Mazunaye likewise signifies this same broad geographical concept. It therefore seems reasonable to assign much of the UAE to the territory of Bet Mazunaye rather than to Bet Qatraye. However, the location of the boundary between Bet Qatraye and Bet Mazunaye is unclear and Sir Bani Yas is very close to wherever this boundary may have been. It is therefore difficult at present to be sure to which ecclesiastical division the al-Khawr monastery at Sir Bani Yas belonged.

The Syriac sources speak of the foundation of monasteries in the Gulf as early as the fourth century AD. The presence of a monastery on at least one Gulf island is specifically mentioned. Furthermore, in 676, bishops of the Nestorian church attended a council at Darin on the island of Tarut off the Saudi Arabian coast; the bishops met there after visiting unspecified islands, presumably to visit other clergy residing on these islands. This sounds very much like a reference to Sir Bani Yas or Kharg. Whether true or not, it is to this world of pre-Islamic Gulf Christianity and Christian Arab communities that the Sir Bani Yas monastery belongs.

Christianity persisted side by side with Islam in eastern Arabia for several decades but eventually it seems to have faded, supplanted by the dominant new faith of Islam. It seems to have simply eroded away, perhaps because of conversion to Islam and buildings like that on Sir Bani Yas would have been abandoned and would have deteriorated until they finally collapsed.

The Islamic Period

The sources

The sources for the history of the UAE in this period are either the Arabic historians and geographers of the Abbasid period or they are later compilations based on these works. For the very early years of Islam, these sources are quite informative and deal with certain incidents at length. The period after the Prophet Muhammad's death in AD 632 is also well documented under the Rightly Guided Caliphs and their Umayyad and Abbasid successors, when the region is the scene of a number of events, mostly military in character. However, while some episodes are recorded in detail, silence tends to prevail for much of the time.

With the post-Mongol period there is some limited information from numismatics, a source which may eventually make a greater contribution when the later Islamic coin series from the area are better understood. However, it is only with the onset of European travel in the area and military intervention, starting with the Portuguese, that sources become detailed and relatively plentiful.

After the fourteenth century the evidence is far better archaeologically, especially for Julfar, the key site for the UAE as a whole. From about this date and thereafter, there are numerous sites throughout the UAE, especially on the coast, that reflect activity in the Late Islamic period (roughly the fourteenth/fifteenth century down to recent times). Many of these sites seem to be associated with the pearl trade and with fishing, but others are in agricultural areas, especially in the north.

The period of the Prophet Muhammad and the first caliphs

The territory that now constitutes the UAE emerges quite clearly into view in the earliest years of Islam in the context of the Prophet Muhammad's invitation to the people to convert to the new faith of Islam. The area also figures prominently in the events of the *Riddah* (Apostasy) wars of 632-634. Knowledge of the Prophet's message seems to have seeped into south-eastern Arabia, as well as to al-Hasa' and Bahrain in eastern Arabia before large scale conversion and acquiescence to the new faith occurred.

As we have seen, by the time of the first contacts between south-eastern Arabia with the Islamic community at al-Madinah, the Sasanian state had begun to decline and weaken in the course of the long wars with the Byzantines, and the Azd were putting pressure on the Sasanian outposts along the coast. In 630, the Prophet Muhammad sent as a missionary to the Azd a Companion, Abu Zayd Al Ansari from the Madinan tribe of Khazraj, who was responsible for gathering pages of the Qur'an during the Prophet's lifetime. He then also sent a newly converted member of Quraysh, 'Amr b. Al 'As. According to a late source, there had been contacts with 'Uman even earlier, with an individual called Mazin b. Ghadubah being the first from south-eastern Arabia to accept Islam when he went to the Prophet at al-Madinah and converted there (Sirhan *Annals:* p 9).

'Amr arrived bearing a letter from the Prophet and passed through Tuwwam (Al-'Ain/al-Buraimi) before continuing to the Batinah coast to present the letter to the Sasanian governor who rejected the Prophet's message. 'Amr, now joined with Abu Zayd, then went to the Al Julanda kings of the Azd, either near Sohar at Demetsjerd, a palace built by the Sasanians, or at Nizwa, and presented the Prophet's letter to 'Abd who recognized the importance of the matter when he broke the letter's seal. Reading it, he passed it on to his brother Jaifar. They agreed on its significance and said that they needed to consider the matter at length. A council of the Azd was called and it was decided that they should all convert to Islam. This was agreed by all their kin who accepted the Prophet's message and consented to pay the Qur'anic *zakat.* Jaifar then sent messages to invite all the people in 'Uman to submit to Islam. Among others, he sent messages to Dibba, and to the furthest flung parts of 'Uman to the north, by which the territory of the UAE is probably intended (Sirhan *Annals:* p 9-10).

The conversion of the Al Julanda and the Azd to Islam now became tied to hostility between the Azd and the Sasanian government. The Sasanians maintained their rejection of Islam and, led by the Al Julanda princes, the Azd attacked them, killing Maskan, the Sasanian administrator, and besieging the rest of their forces in the fort of Demsetjerd where they finally surrendered. The defeated Sasanians agreed to evacuate the country and to relinquish all their gold, silver and property.

With the Persians expelled, 'Amr b. Al 'As continued to administer 'Uman until the Prophet's death in 632 and the succession of Abu Bakr as the first Caliph. The Julanda prince 'Abd went to al-Madinah where he was received with pleasure by the newly appointed Caliph who praised the conversion of the people and wrote to them to compliment them. The point at which this happened is unclear, however, for at the death of the Prophet, the great uprising known as the *Riddah* (or Apostasy) wars broke out against Islamic rule in much of Arabia. Central Arabia followed a false prophet, Musaylima, while in the east and south, rebellions took place all the way from Bahrain to 'Uman, Mahra and Yemen. The famous Muslim general Khalid b. Al Walid was sent to al-Yamama in central Arabia by the Caliph to put down Musaylima and while Khalid suppressed this threat, other commanders were sent into eastern Arabia. 'Ala' Al Hadrami was sent to reduce the apostates of Bahrain (the eastern coast of Arabia and the island of the same name) while Hudhaifa b. Mihsan Al Ghalfani, of the Yemeni Himyarites, and Arfaja Al Bariqi, a member of Azd, were sent to suppress apostates in south-eastern and southern Arabia.

Abu Bakr ordered Hudhaifa to march on 'Uman, where he was to be supported by Arfaja, and to advance with all speed. In 'Uman, they were to support the Muslims, reinforcing 'Abd and Jaifar, the Al Julanda leaders against their opponents among dissident Azd elements. The expedition was then to continue into Mahra on the southern coast, where Arfaja would command. They were reinforced by 'Ikrima b. Abi Jahl, who had been engaged in the campaigns in central Arabia against Musaylima with Khalid b. Al Walid. After suppressing the apostates in 'Uman and Mahra, the Caliph ordered that the Muslim forces should continue through the Hadramawt to Yemen, there to join up with Al Muhajir b. Abi Umayya.

The Caliph's plan of campaign responded to the nature of Arabian communications through south-eastern Arabia that are reflected in later itineraries recorded by the Islamic geographers. Because of the great natural obstacle of the Empty Quarter sand sea, the Muslim forces were forced to march from al-Madinah and central Arabia in a great circuit along the north side of the sands and then through territory that today lies in the UAE, to reach the 'Uman Peninsula before turning south-west and west to southern Arabia. Repeatedly in the Islamic period, we see evidence in itineraries that caravans and armies would cross the territory of the emirates and circumvent the sands to reach the Batinah and the interior of 'Uman.

The nature of the landscape ensures that any large force moving through the area by land must march west of the soft sabkha salt-flats when the weather is wet in winter and spring and east of the deep sands of the Empty Quarter. Access to the wells at Tuwwam (Al-'Ain, al-Buraimi) is essential in such a march until the more plentiful water sources of the Jabal Hajar and Jabal Akhdar are reached. Thereafter, it is possible to cross the mountains to the Batinah coast on the Gulf of 'Uman and its access to the Indian Ocean. It was apparently awareness of the nature of the landscape and the water resources that dictated Abu Bakr's plan of campaign against the apostate forces in the south-east of the peninsula.

In 'Uman, the leader of the apostasy was Laqit b. Malik Al Azdi, known as 'the one with the crown' (Dhu'l-Taj), whom we already encounter as a figure of some importance in pre-Islamic times as a rival of the Al Julanda rulers of the country (Al Tabari 1993: pp 151-155; Al Baladhuri 1916: p 117). With the death of the Prophet Muhammad, Laqit had rebelled and had worsted the forces of the Muslim Julanda leaders. Al Tabari says that 'Abd and Jaifar were forced to seek refuge in the mountains and the islands of the sea while Laqit dominated the rest of the country. The mountains must mean Jabal Hajar and Jabal Akhdar that form a great spine that runs from the Sultanate of Oman through the northern territories of the UAE up to the Straits of Hormuz at Musandam. The islands mentioned are presumably those off the shore of the emirates and where Azd are known to have spread before Islam. Fleeing to these more remote areas, the Al Julanda leadership awaited reinforcements from al-Madinah.

The combined force of the Madinan army, led by Hudhaifa and supported by Arfaja and 'Ikrima, reached a place called Rijam which was close to 'Uman. This place is identified by Miles with Tuwwam, i.e., Al-'Ain, al-Buraimi (Miles 1966: p 36). Using this as a base, the Madinan forces made contact with 'Abd and Jaifar who then met them at Suhar on the coast of the Batinah. The Muslim forces, including those from south-eastern Arabia and from al-Madinah, now set about fragmenting the apostates, writing to the chiefs of tribes that had supported Laqit. The first to be approached was the leader of the Banu Judayd, who decided to abandon Laqit. After thus weakening the apostates, the Muslim army advanced to meet Laqit at his base at Dibba. Dibba is described by Al Tabari as a great market and *misr* or town, and as we have seen, Ibn Habib confirms the extent of its trading network. According to F. Donner it was sometimes the capital of 'Uman. He also notes that it had been garrisoned by the Sasanians before Islam (Donner 1993: p 153, note 964).

A battle broke out between the two sides at Dibba, apparently somewhere in the plain just inland from the present coastal town, judging by the location of the graveyard which is still pointed out as the burial place of the Companions of the Prophet who fell there. Laqit placed their women and children behind his position to harden the resolve of his men and make them fight more fiercely in their anxiety to protect their families. Initially, Laqit prevailed but the Muslims were reinforced by the other tribes, including members of 'Abd Al Qays and elements from Bani Najiya of the Quda'a who had settled in 'Uman before Islam. Thus strengthened, the Muslims prevailed and Laqit's followers fled, leaving many dead. According to Al Tabari, 10,000 died although numbers are often exaggerated in the texts, and may merely indicate 'a large number'.

The victorious Muslims proceeded to loot the market at Dibba. The captives seized were sent to Abu Bakr with one fifth of the booty, which included the enemy's flocks and 'Arfaja led the prisoners to al-Madinah. Hudhaifa remained in south-eastern Arabia where Abu Bakr appointed him Governor, an office which he held after the death of the Caliph in 634. He calmed the situation with the tribes, and all of the Azd returned to Islam while 'Ikrima marched on with his forces from al-Madinah and those whom he had recruited from the people of 'Uman. They pursued the apostates into Mahra on the south coast of Arabia before marching to Shihr in Yemen. Al Tabari describes ' Ikrima's army as including people from the seacoast and from the islands (Al Tabari 1993: pp 156-157), as well as from Najd and the incense country. It is tempting to see the Gulf islands indicated in this reference.

The invasion of Iran

In *ca* 637 according to Al Tabari, the Governor of the province of Bahrayn, 'Uthman b. Abi Al 'As, was ordered by 'Umar b. Al Khattab, the second Caliph, to make an attempt to invade the coast of Sasanian Iran. The Muslim forces were 3000 strong and consisted of forces from Azd, 'Abd Al Qays, Najiya and Rasib. They set out by sea from Julfar and sailed across the Gulf to the island of Ibn Kawan (Qays) where they encountered the Sasanian Governor of the island whom they defeated (Al Tabari 1993: I: p 2698). They then continued to invade the coast of Fars and the Iranian interior. It is not clear exactly what Julfar was at this stage, but it is evident enough that it had a port. Given that the site known as Julfar that lies just north of Ras al-Khaimah city is dated post-fourteenth century, it is tempting to suggest that Julfar was elsewhere and could be associated with Jazirat al-Hulayla further north on the coast or another site. It is possible that the name Julfar moved around the coast over time when anchorages changed as the creeks silted and sand-bars off-shore built up.

The Umayyad period

With the death of the third Caliph 'Uthman b. 'Affan in 656, the Caliphate fell into contention between the fourth Caliph, 'Ali b. Abi Talib, and the Umayyad Governor of Syria, Mu'awiya b. Abi Sufian. When the Umayyads come to power as Caliphs in 661, the people of 'Uman remained aloof and remained outside Umayyad rule. It was not until some time towards 705 that Al Hajjaj b. Yusuf Al Thaqifi, the powerful Governor of the eastern Islamic world under the Caliph 'Abd Al Malik, launched an attack on south-eastern Arabia to bring it under Umayyad control. Until this time it had remained under the Julanda rulers, descended from the leaders who had converted to Islam in the time of the Prophet Muhammad.

To end south-eastern Arabia's autonomy, the Umayyads sent a fleet and army that marched by land to 'Uman (Sirhan *Annals:* pp 10-11; Ibn Razik 1871: pp 2-5). The fleet landed at Julfar which served as a naval base for the expedition in the course of the campaign. The first Umayyad forces were defeated by the Azd and the Umayyad general Qasim b. Shi'wa was killed. Faced with this reverse, Al Hajjaj then dispatched another army under Qasim's brother, Muja'a, with 40,000 men to 'Uman. This force was divided so that the horses and camels travelled by land while the rest of the force went with a fleet by sea. The land force must have crossed the UAE to reach the rendezvous but there is no indication as to the route they followed. Given the dangers of the shallow coastal waters and the difficulties of the sabkha, it seems impossible that the army and the fleet could have maintained visual contact with each other as they travelled through what is now the UAE.

The Umayyad land force was defeated by the Azd at a water source some days from a place called Bushir or Balqa'a which has been identified by Badger with al-Falj mentioned by Al Idrisi (p 153) and placed near to Julfar (Ibn Razik 1871: p 3, note 2). However, this is far from certain. Given the passage of the Umayyad army through the territory of the modern UAE, and the role in the campaign of Julfar as the landing place for their fleet, it is not at all unlikely that the Umayyad army was defeated by the Azd as they advanced to their rendezvous point at Julfar.

The defeated Umayyad land army fled, but the sea-borne force landed at a place recorded as al-Bunana. This could be Bainunah in Abu Dhabi emirate but it would have been little advantage for the Umayyads to land so far west and it seems likely that another source (Ibn Razik 1871: p 4) is more accurate, recording the landing place with different orthography as al-Yunaniya of Julfar. This suggests that al-Yunaniya was part of a broader district called Julfar, and thus should be located in the present emirate of Ras al-Khaimah.

When the Umayyad fleet landed at Julfar an individual from Tuwwam (Al-'Ain, Buraimi) came to them and told them that dispute had arisen among the Azd after they had defeated the Umayyad land army. The Umayyad sea-borne forces assembled at Julfar under Muja'a were greater than the Azdi force that remained in the area under Sa'id b. 'Abbad (or 'Abd?), the brother of the 'Uman leader, Sulaiman Al Julanda. Faced with superior force, Sa'id retreated by night into the mountains and the Umayyads pursued him and besieged him.

Meanwhile, the Umayyad fleet, consisting of 300 vessels, sailed around the Straits of Hormuz to anchor at Masqat harbour. The Julanda leader, Sulaiman, managed to burn more than 50 of the Umayyads' boats, while the rest escaped. He then attacked the main Umayyad army under Muja'a and put them to flight. Muja'a retreated with his remaining ships and returned to Julfar where he based himself while he wrote to Al Hajjaj, the Umayyad Governor of the East, based in Iraq, requesting reinforcements. In response, Al Hajjaj sent Muja'a a new army consisting of 5000 cavalry from Syria who marched by land to Julfar. Thus strengthened, the Umayyads overcame the resistance of the Julanda and the Azd of 'Uman. In the aftermath of the victory, the Umayyads appointed Sayf b. Al Hani Al Hamdani as Governor of 'Uman. The Julanda fled to the land of the Zanj - east Africa - and only re-emerged as a power in south-eastern Arabia later in the Umayyad period. The south-east Arabian sea trading connection that must have existed in pre-Islamic times probably prompted the Julanda flight to the Zanj and the episode presages connections with Africa in later Islamic times.

The Abbasid period

When the Abbasid Caliphs seized power from the Umayyads in 750, they soon turned their attention to 'Uman to put down the revival of Azdi and Julanda independence which seems to have affected not only the mainland of south-eastern Arabia but the islands of the Gulf as well. The Abbasid Caliph Al Saffah sent an army to 'Uman, led by Shiban b. 'Abd Al 'Aziz Al Yashkuri, to ensure the allegiance of Julanda b. Mas'ud, the Azdi leader. The Abbasid fleet sailed from al-Basra to Ibn Kawan island on the east side of the Gulf and then sailed on to 'Uman, although the harbour that they used is not mentioned. However, Shiban was killed in the fighting that ensued with the Azd. Even before this, the Caliph had decided to send a new commander, Khazim b. Khuzaima, to help confront the Azd. When Khazim arrived, he found Shiban dead. He sought the allegiance of the people of the country to the Abbasids, but they refused and in the fighting that followed, the Abbasid forces killed the leaders of Julanda and 10,000 of their supporters according to Al Tabari. This final battle took place at Julfar, which was probably the port used by the Abbasids as it had been for the Umayyads before them (Al Tabari, *Ta'rikh*, tertia series, i: pp 78-79; Ibn Razik:pp 7-8; Sirhan *Annals*: pp 121-122).

According to Al Tabari, during the fighting, Khizam burnt the houses of the Julanda's followers using naphtha. When they saw their houses burning, they fled from their prepared positions to protect their families and the Abbasid army fell upon them and slaughtered them. There is a long tradition of using wood and reed for housing in the Gulf. As early as the Ubaid period we find post holes suggesting the presence of huts and the archaeological and literary evidence shows that similar huts were still in use as late as the nineteenth and early twentieth centuries, usually called *barasti* by Europeans but more correctly known as *'arish*. The episode of the burnt huts suggests that a substantial number of the houses of Julfar were indeed *'arish* in 751-2. This is the first literary information describing structures at Julfar and, given the impression of the common housing of the past in the area, it is extremely plausible that the houses were of wood.

The most destructive intervention occurred when the Abbasid Caliph Al Mu'tadid came to the throne in 892. The Abbasid Governor of Iraq and the Gulf, Muhammad b. Nur, approached him with a plan to support anti-Ibadhi forces (or anti-Julanda forces) in south-eastern Arabia with the intention of obliterating the Ibadhis and their Julanda leadership, bringing the country back under the direct rule of the 'Abbasid Caliphate (Miles 1966: pp 77-84; Ibn Razik 1871: pp 22-25; Sirhan: pp 21-23).

A large Abbasid force set out, including members of the north Arabian tribe of Al Tay'. The force consisted of 25,000 men, including 3500 armoured cavalry. With stores and equipment sent with the fleet to land at Julfar, the rest of the army, under Muhammad b. Nur, marched through eastern Arabia by land to secure Julfar from landward. They would have followed the routes through the western parts of the UAE to reach the northern emirates just as the forces of the Caliph Abu Bakr and the Umayyads had done in earlier times. With his naval base at Julfar secured to ensure communications with al-Basra, Muhammad b. Nur marched inland to Tuwwam (Al-'Ain, al-Buraimi), before crossing the highlands to advance on Nizwa. The strength of the Abbasid army was such that the people of south-eastern Arabia could not resist. Some fled to Shiraz and al-Basra, while others went to Hormuz. At this stage, Nizwa was the main town of 'Uman and of the Azd and it was seized by Muhammad b. Nur and the local forces were routed. After a brief uprising, Muhammad b. Nur was driven back and worsted at Dibba but recovered and set about ravaging the country, wrecking much of south-eastern Arabia. Muhammad b. Nur's assaults included killing and torture of the people, the breaking up of the infrastructure and filling of the *falaj* and the burning of books. It is possible that the violence visited on the country by Muhammad b. Nur will eventually be recognized in the archaeaological record, although this is only a cautiously advanced hypothesis.

While Muhammad b. Nur was engaged in ravaging 'Uman, apparently laying the country low for decades to follow, there was general disruption in many parts of the Abbasid Caliphate including the Gulf. By the end of the ninth century the Abbasids were greatly diminished, controlled by their Turkish military commanders and prone to lose control of distant provinces to local governors. Control of parts of the Gulf was lost in the course of the great Zanj rebellion in southern Iraq, a revolt that was once represented as a slave uprising but has also been described as a conflict over the control of Gulf trade. The Zanj sacked al-Basra in 871 and remained a threat thereafter. Not long after, the massively disruptive Qaramita state arose in eastern and northern Arabia, based in al-Hasa' and Bahrain. This sectarian group raided over the whole of Arabia, attacking the south-east, destroying the security of the pilgrim road from Iraq to the Hijaz, raiding into Syria in the north and to Yemen in the south, and sacking al-Basra in 923. In 930 they carried out the great sacrilege of attacking the pilgrimage in Makkah and seizing the Black Stone from the Ka'ba, bearing it off to eastern Arabia.

These disruptions affected south-eastern Arabia but have yet to be assessed in their consequences for settlement in the UAE in this period. On the opposite side of the Gulf, events during the course of the tenth century were also grave for the great regional trading centre of Siraf which had flourished from the Sasanian period until its destruction by massive earthquakes in 977, after which it declined. As its commercial dominance faded and other centres supplanted it, the Siraf merchants scattered as far as the Red Sea and Africa. Beneficiaries of the decline of Siraf included Suhar in 'Uman whose heyday as a trading and agricultural centre appears to have occurred in the tenth century, a direct consequence of the decline of Siraf and a change in the trading pattern. As Siraf fell from its previous eminence, Qays island also grew in prominence.

Matters on the UAE side of the coast in this period are far from clear. It seems that Julfar retained its eminence as a port, but archaeological evidence of the nature of the country in this period is scanty or entirely absent so far. The implication of the literary texts is that certain places persisted as important regionally and where literary evidence exists for the period from the tenth to the twelfth century and thereafter, the implication is that there was some level of continuity at certain UAE sites, especially at Dibba and Julfar.

The tenth century evidence for the settlement of the UAE is largely based on literary sources as the archaeological material is so slight at present, although this may well change in the future. It seems that some places continued settled, with pottery at al-Jumayra in Dubai, in Wadi Haqil just east of Ras al-Khaimah, at Jazirat al-Hulayla and at al-Khatt showing at least activity on and near the UAE coast in this period, whatever the level of destruction in the interior of 'Uman around Nizwa. According to Al Hamdani there was a great *hisn* or fortress of the Bani Riyam in 'Uman, (Al Hamdani 1884: I: p 52) but he does not say where it was. However, Miles associates Riyam with al-Buraimi/Al-'Ain (Tuwwam) and it is tempting to equate the *hisn* with Al-'Ain. In this context, it is interesting to note that Yaqut in *ca* 1225 also speaks of a citadel or fortress (*qasaba*) at Tuwwam as we have seen above.

It seems that the instability of the late ninth century in south-eastern Arabia continued into the tenth century. In 930, immediately after his assault on Makkah, the Qaramita leader Abu Tahir sent his forces from al-Ahsa' in eastern Arabia to attack 'Uman and in varying degrees they remained a force in the country down to 965. In that year, in the power vacuum that followed Qaramita withdrawal, the Buwayhid Mu'izz Al Dawla, Emir of Kirman, invaded south-eastern Arabia, joining the Buwayhid Emir Adud Al Dawla of Iraq in Siraf before landing their combined force with their fleet at Julfar and bringing the country under their control. When their position was threatened they undertook a further invasion in 972 and Adud Al Dawla took south-eastern Arabia under his direct rule. The Buwayhids remained a power in the country until some time before 1053 when their authority waned on the eve of the destruction of the Buwayhid state in Iraq and Iran by the Seljuk Turks in 1055.

The Great Seljuk Sultans based themselves at Isfahan and they also reinstated the Abbasid Caliphate in Baghdad, establishing a Sunni revival across much of the Islamic world in their westward advance from Central Asia. In south-eastern Arabia their presence is scantily recorded, but Ibn Al Mujawir mentions a Seljuk prince of Kirman who also held 'Uman and this may have remained true until the fall of the Seljuk dynasties in 1186.

The thirteenth century and later Islamic period

The entire complexion of the political framework of the Middle East was transformed with the vastly destructive Mongol invasions initiated by Genghiz Khan in the thirteenth century. These culminated in the sack of Baghdad in 1258 and the murder of the Caliph. This brought the line of continuous successors to the Abbasid Caliphate to an end for the first time since they had established their rule in 750. In the aftermath of the Mongol invasions, a series of new regimes emerged, among them the Turkish Kara Katayans of Kirman who dominated the south-east of Arabia from 1224 until 1364, and the princes of Hormuz who moved to the island of the same name in 1300. The rulers of Hormuz still dominated the lower Gulf when the Portuguese arrived on the scene in the later fifteenth century. The princes of Hormuz continued as a regional power, in conjunction with the Portuguese, until the Safavid Shah Abbas brought their rule to an end along with that of the Portuguese in 1622. The coinage struck by the Hormuz princes at Jarun (Old Hormuz) was circulated in considerable quantities at Julfar in the fourteenth to seventeenth century period.

Excavations at Julfar (1991). In the centre of the picture is the excavation of the five successive mosques carried out by the British team. Beyond is the area excavated by the French team.

For the period from the fourteenth century to the late Islamic period, when south-eastern Arabia was affected by these broader political events, archaeological evidence abounds in the UAE. While sites all along the coasts and in the interior of the UAE bear witness to settlement in this period, almost always based on ceramic evidence, it is at the excavated Islamic port site at Julfar in Ras al-Khaimah that the period comes most clearly to light. Excavations there have shown that the site currently known as Julfar, the immediate predecessor of the city of Ras al-Khaimah, dates from the fourteenth century, when a hut settlement was established on a sand bar which had only recently emerged from the sea.

The Julfar of the early Islamic period seems almost certainly to have shifted from its original site to be succeeded by this fourteenth century Julfar. It is possible that the original Julfar of early Islamic times was at al-Hulayla to the north where pre-Islamic and earlier Islamic ceramics have been found. It is hinted by Al Idrisi that by the twelfth century, sand-bars or siltation were a noticeable feature affecting navigation in the Julfar area and it may be that the harbour of the earlier Julfar silted up and it was found necessary to move to a new site, the fourteenth century Julfar, just outside Ras al-Khaimah city. This Julfar is the site mentioned throughout the Portuguese period in the Gulf when the town enjoyed great prosperity as the regional trading entrepôt. Its commercial network is reflected in the quantities of Chinese, Vietnamese and Thai ceramics recovered in excavation, along with Indian glass bangles and Iranian pottery.

The Julfar of this later period had a commercial prominence which made it the relative equivalent of modern Dubai as a trading centre. Duarte Barbosa (Barbosa 1918: i: pp 73-74) in 1517 describes the local merchants as being wholesale dealers, persons of worth and great navigators. When the Portuguese arrived, Julfar was under the jurisdiction of the King of Hormuz who benefited from its commerce and its pearling fleet (Dalboquerque 1875: I: p 246). In the early sixteenth century the Portuguese came to dominate the Indian Ocean trade with their string of forts from Hormuz to Goa, Malacca and Macao, and this sixteenth to seventeenth century period brought a great expansion to Julfar. The centre of the town was in the walled area known as al-Mataf which has recently been excavated by an international team of archaeologists.

During this period, Julfar transformed from a place with huts to a town of much larger sand-brick houses and in the area excavated by the Japanese team, a grid-like pattern of streets was found between the sand-brick houses. In the central area of al-Mataf, the small sand-brick mosque of early date underwent a series of reconstructions as the congregation increased, leading to the need for larger mosques. As a result, a sequence of five mosques were built one above the other all on the same site with ever increasing dimensions and dating from *ca* the fourteenth century through to the sixteenth or seventeenth century.

Maps of the coast of Arabia in the Atlas of Lazaro Luis, dated 1563, show a number of fortresses that the Portuguese built including that at Julfar where a pronounced inlet is also marked, probably relating to a silted creek which once formed the harbour. The silting of the harbour may account for the decline of Julfar that occurred in the seventeenth century and the rise of its southern neighbour, Ras al-Khaimah, some time after the expulsion of the Portuguese by the local Arabs in the seventeenth century. As we have seen, Ras al-Khaimah was known to Gasparo Balbi in 1580, and also to the local Arab navigator Ibn Majid in the latter half of the fifteenth century, while Duarte Barbosa in 1617 also refers to it.

By the eighteenth century, Ras al-Khaimah was associated with the rise of its Al Qassimi sheikhs who still rule the emirate of Ras al-Khaimah. The fortress of the town was built by the Al Qassimi and now is the National Museum of Ras al-Khaimah. Sondages by J. Hansman suggested to him that the site of the fort had served as a camp during the military occupation of south-eastern Arabia by the Afsharid Turkman Ruler of Iran, Nadir Shah, between 1737 and 1749. Hansman suggested that a number of sites around Ras al-Khaimah were already Nadir Shah's camps. This is more doubtful, although the fortress at Khatt, inland from Ras al-Khaimah, seems to have been used by Nadir Shah's forces.

Further north along the coast is a ruinous fortress at al-Dayi', on the summit of a steep slope below the mountains. It is near to the harbour of Rams on Khawr al-Khuwayir. Al Dayi' played a role along with Ras al-Khaimah in the fighting with the British expeditionary forces of 1809 and 1819. Inland there are yet other fortifications of the later Islamic period, including the Qasr Za'ba overlooking Shimal, and a whole system of towers that reflect the defensive needs of Ras al-Khaimah in the eighteenth and nineteenth centuries.

Such fortifications are not confined to the north. All along the coasts and in the hinterland of the UAE are fortresses that are associated with the main towns and relate to the later Islamic period. Portuguese fortresses like that at Khawr Fakkan, Kalba and Julfar are known from maps like those of Lazaro Luis, but there are a number of major later Islamic forts of local origin including those at Fujairah, Umm al-Qaiwain, Ajman, Dubai and Abu Dhabi. Inland at Al-'Ain the present fortifications recall the fact that there was a fort at Tuwwam, the early Islamic predecessor of Al-'Ain/al-Buraimi, in the tenth to twelfth centuries as we have seen.

Further west, remains of a fortress have been identified at Mantiqat al-Sirra near Madinat Zayed in western Abu Dhabi (Czastka and Hellyer 1994: pp 9-12). This fortress has been associated with events in around the year 1633 when forces of the first Ya'aruba imam of 'Uman, Nasir b. Murshid, came into conflict with tribal opponents, including members of Bani Yas, at the fort of al-Dhafra in the sandy area that formed the border of al-Dhafra 'on the confines of Oman'. It has been suggested that this textual reference to a fort at al-Dhafra refers to the Mantiqat al-Sirra fortress. The presence of the Bani Yas in this episode, taken with Balbi's reference to the island of Sir Bani Yas (Sirbeniast) in 1580, shows the longevity of the presence of the Bani Yas rulers of Abu Dhabi in the region.

Apart from military architecture, there is no shortage of evidence of settlement elsewhere for this later period in the UAE, and it is only really useful to spotlight areas where recent work has specifically noted this ubiquitous material. The later Islamic period is so widely distributed that material is found in virtually all settlement areas, distinguished usually by the Julfar-type later Islamic ceramics. Some, but probably not all, of these ceramics come from Wadi Haqil, near Shimal (Ras al-Khaimah) where some of the numerous kilns have been excavated by R. Stocks. Surface surveys by the Abu Dhabi Islands Archaeological Survey have also identified extensive occupation during the late Islamic period on islands off the coast of Abu Dhabi, which excavations on Balghelam, north-east of Abu Dhabi, suggest may, in fact, relate to the sixteenth or seventeenth centuries onwards.

In Fujairah there are numerous later Islamic sites and a brief survey in Wadi Safad, north of Fujairah city, in 1994 produced results typical of the Batinah area and the highland valleys and foothills. Along the course of the Wadi there were numerous examples of houses and a fortress overlooking the agricultural land along the valley floor, all sites belonging to perhaps the past 300 to 500 years although this dating is very approximate. Other valleys in the region are likely to have similar settlements of the same age. On the high peaks between Fujairah, Ras al-Khaimah and Musandam are also numerous farmsteads which are currently in use but many of which are of some age (Dostal 1983).

Not far to the north on the coast of Fujairah is the remarkable four domed mosque at al-Bidiyya whose design is unique in the UAE and which also belongs to the general framework of the later Islamic period. However, while other older mosques are known elsewhere in the UAE - at Julfar, al-Falayya, Jazirat al-Hamra' and Delma - the mosque at al-Bidiyya is related to a very different architectural tradition. It hints at mosques in Yemen, especially on the Red Sea coast, but it could also suggest Indian connections.

In the course of restoration of the traditional houses in the Khawr area of Sharjah, foundations of older buildings were exposed in recent years which probably related to the later Islamic period and Sharjah's past as a trading harbour. As to the wind tower houses of Dubai, although not old, they preserve a Gulf architectural tradition of antiquity. However, as with all such traditional building, their coral and plaster construction materials are so fragile that no architecture of this type lasts more than a century or two, and monuments on the coasts tend not to survive. Similarly, clay structures in the interior often have a relatively short life and it is only in the stone building regions of the highlands that structures survive for longer. Thus the extant architecture of Dubai, and the few other examples that remain in the UAE, especially at Sharjah, Jazirat al-Hamra in Ras al-Khaimah and on the island of Delma in Abu Dhabi, should be regarded not only as rare survivors of traditional building, but as an echo of a longer architectural tradition. This extant architecture may help recreate some idea of the lost buildings of Gulf towns of the past. To this extent, the surviving mosques of Delma and its Muraykhi Pearl House, the houses, mosque and fort of Jazirat al-Hamra', and the remains of the architecture of Sharjah and Dubai or the mosque at al-Bidiyya in Fujairah give some idea of the possible appearance of the lost buildings of Julfar and other Gulf towns. These extant traditional buildings are thus archaeological artefacts as well as monuments of national heritage.

In recent years, the extent of later Islamic period settlement has become clearer in the little known area west of Abu Dhabi city. As we have seen, Delma preserves a number of later Islamic traditional buildings and the numbers of graveyards around the town and early

The Muraykhi pearl merchant's house at Delma during restoration (1994).

foundations that emerged in the course of restoring the Muraykhi mosque in the old town all point to an extensive settlement in later Islamic times. Delma was a great centre for pearling and the early twentieth century accounts of Indian merchants involved in the trade there may well reflect connections based on the exploitation of the pearl-beds that have gone on for centuries.

At Marawah, there are three villages which are associated with the same later Islamic period and again mosques and graveyards reflect activity in this period. The same picture emerges still further west, on a number of islands, including Sir Bani Yas where two villages have been noted and where the remains of a pearling camp were found on one of the beaches. This camp had Chinese ceramics as did a nomad campsite on the north side of the island, an interesting indication of the ramifications of the Far Eastern trade inside the Gulf in the fourteenth to sixteenth century.

Finally, again in the far west of Abu Dhabi emirate, in the heart of the pearling area, are the islands Humr, Ghagha', Ufsayyah and the Yasats, where numerous middens with pearl oyster shells indicate the vigour of the industry, while late Islamic ceramics and, in particular, late Islamic graveyards indicate the degree of population and settlement of these islands in this period. Today the sites are deserted but this is probably only a result of the decline of the pearling industry in the present century. In the past, the pearl beds were the basis of settlement, whether seasonal or permanent, on these islands, and here and elsewhere the growing body of archaeological information points to this later Islamic period as one of the most active in the history of the country.

Bibliography

Al Baladhuri, *The Origins of the Islamic State*, trans. into Eng. from the Arabic, P.K. Hitti, New York (1916).

Baramki, D.C. 'An Ancient Caravan Station in Dubai', *Illustrated London News*, 2903 (1975)).

Barbosa, D. 'The Book of Duarte Barbosa' (trans. M.L. Dames), *Hakluyt Society* I (1918).

Boxer, C.R. (ed) *Commentaries of Ruy Freyre de Andrada*, London (1930).

de Cardi, B. and Doe, B. 'Archaeological Survey in the Northern Trucial States', *East and West* , 21 (1971) nos 3-4, pp 225-276.

de Cardi, B. with sections by Vita-Finzi C. and Coles, A. 'Archaeological Survey in Northern Oman, 1972', *East and West* , 25 (1972) pp 9-75.

de Cardi, B. 'A Sasanian Outpost in northern Oman', *Antiquity* , xlvi no 184 (1973) pp 305-310.

de Cardi, B., Kennet, D. and Stocks, R.L. 'Five thousand years of settlement at Khatt, UAE', *Proceedings of the Seminar for Arabian Studies* , 24 (1994) pp 35-114.

Cleuziou, S. 'Mission Archéologique Francaise. 1ère Campagne, Decembre 1976/Fevrier 1977', *Archéologie aux*

Emirats Arabes Unis. Archaeology in the United Arab Emirates, Al-'Ayn (1976-1977).

Costa, P.M. (ed) *Musandam*, London (1991).

Czastka, J. and Hellyer, P. 'An archaeological survey of the Mantakha As'sirra area in Abu Dhabi's Western Region', *Tribulus*, Vol. 4.1 (April 1994) pp 9-12.

Dalboquerque, A. 'The Commentaries of the Great Afonso Dalboquerque' I (trans. W. de G. Birch), *Hakluyt Society* LIII (1875).

Dostal, W. *The Traditional Architecture of Ras al-Khaimah (North)*, Wiesbaden (1983).

Al Hamdani, *Geographie der Arabischen Halbinsel* M.H. Muller (ed), Leiden (1884).

Hansman, J. *Julfar. An Arabian Port*, London (1985).

Hardy-Guilbert, C. 'Julfar, cité portuaire du Golfe arabo-persique à la periode islamique', *Archéologie islamique* II (1991) pp 162-203.

Harter, G., Cleuziou, S., Laffont, J.P., Nockin J. and Toussaint, R. *Emirat d'Abu Dhabi. Propositions pour Dalma* , (Sept.-Oct. 1979) pp 10-15.

Hellyer, P. *Fujairah. An Arabian Jewel*, Dubai (1990).

Hisham ibn Al Kalbi, *the Book of Idols,* Princeton (1952).

Ibn Khurradadhbih, *Kitab al-Masalik wa'l-Mamalik et excerpta e Kitab al-Kharadj*, ed. and trans. into French from the Arabic by M.J. de Goeje, Leyden (1967).

Al Idrisi, *Opus Geographicum*, ed. A. Bombaci, U. Rizzitano, R. Rubinacci, L. Veccia Vaglieri, Naples, Rome (1972).

Al Idrisi, .trans. into French from the Arabic, P.-A. Jaubert, *La Geographie d'Edrisi*, Paris (1836).

Kennet D. and King, G.R.D. 'Jazirat al-Hulayla----early Julfar', *JRAS* (1994) 3rd series, vol. 4, part 2, pp 163-212.

Kennet, D. and Connolly, D. *The Towers of Ra's al-Khaimah,* London (1995)

King, G.R.D. 'Excavations of the British team at Julfar, Ras al-Khaimah, United Arab Emirates: Interim Report on the first season (1989)', *Proceedings of the Seminar for Arabian Studies* , 20 (1990) pp 79-93.

King, G.R.D. 'Excavations of the British team at Julfar, Ras al-Khaimah, United Arab Emirates: Interim Report on the second season (1990)', *Proceedings of the Seminar for Arabian Studies* , 21 (1991) pp 123-134.

King, G.R.D. 'Excavations of the British team at Julfar, Ras al-Khaimah, United Arab Emirates: Interim Report on the third season', *Proceedings of the Seminar for Arabian Studies* , 22 (1992) pp 47-54.

King, G.R.D. 'Nizwa', EI².

    'Musandam', EI².

'Ra's al-Khayma', EI² .

King, G.R.D., Dunlop, D., Elders, J., Garfi, S., Stephenson A. and Tonghini,C. 'A Report on the Abu Dhabi Islands Archaeological Survey (1993-4)', *Proceedings of the Seminar for Arabian Studies* , 25 (1995) pp 63-74.

Lorimer, J.G. *Gazetteer of the Persian Gulf, 'Oman, and Central Arabia*, Calcutta (1908).

Al Maqdisi, *Kitab Ahsan al-Taqasim fi ma'rifatal-iqlim*, (ed), M.J. de Goeje, Leyden (1967).

Miles, S.B. *The Countries and Tribes of the Persian Gulf*, London (1966).

Piacentini, V. 'Ardashir I Papakar and the wars against the Arabs. Working hypothesis on the Sasanian hold of the Gulf', PSAS, 15 (1985) pp 57-77.

Potts, D.T. *The Arabian Gulf in Antiquity* Oxford, 2 vols (1992).

Qudama (Abu'l-Faraj) in Ibn Khurradadhbih, *Kitab al-Masalik wa'l-Mamalik et excerpta e Kitab al-Kharadj*, ed. and trans. into French from the Arabic by M.J. de Goeje, Leyden (1967).

Salil ibn Razik, *History of the Imams and Seyyids of 'Omân*, ed and trans. into Eng. from the Arabic by G.P. Badger, London (1871).

Sasaki T. and Sasaki, H. 'Japanese excavations at Julfar---1988, 1989, 1990 and 1991 seasons', *Proceedings of the Seminar for Arabian Studies* XXII (1992) pp 105-120.

Simpson, St. J. *Aspects of the archaeology of the Sasanian Period in Mesopotamia*, D. Phil. thesis, Oxford (1992).

Sirhan ibn Sa'id ibn Sirhan, *Annals of Oman: History of Oman from 1728 to 1883*, Cambridge (1984)

Slot, B.J. *The Arabs of the Gulf 1602-1784*, Leidschendam (1993).

Al Tabari, *Ta'rikh*, M.J. de Goeje (ed), Leiden (1881-5).

Al Tabari, *The History of Al Tabari*, trans. into English from the Arabic and annotated by F. Donner, x. 'The Conquest of Arabia', NY 1993.

Whitcomb, D.S. 'The Archaeology of Oman: a preliminary discussion of the Islamic Periods', *Journal of Oman Studies,* I (1975) pp 123-157

Wilkinson, J.C. 'Arab-Persian land relationships in late Sasanid Oman', *Proceedings of the Seminar for Arabian Studies*, 3 (1973) pp 40-51.

Wilkinson, J.C. 'The Julanda of Oman', *Journal of Oman Studies,* I (1975) pp. 97-108.

Wilson, A.T. *The Persian Gulf*, London (1959) p 3.

Yaqut, *Mu'jam al-Buldan*, F. Wuestenfeld (ed), Leipzig (1866-69).

---

[1]   The Arab geographers use the broad geographical term 'Uman to describe the territory encompassed by the United Arab Emirates and the Sultanate of Oman ('Uman). The term is used here and throughout this account in its broad geographical sense here rather than in reference to the modern political boundaries.

The Beginning of the Post-Imperial Era for the Trucial States from World War I to the 1960s

Frauke Heard-Bey

The UAE never was a colony, but its forerunner, the 'Trucial States',[1] was increasingly absorbed into the British orbit by a system of agreements which successive British Governments, first in Delhi and then in London, deemed necessary in order to best pursue their particular objectives of the day.

The First World War was like lightning and thunder bursting forth from the storm clouds which European imperialistic ambitions had fomented. This was not the time for letting the privileged position, which Britain had acquired on the Arab side of the Gulf,[2] slip from her hands. Rather, in order to consolidate her hold, it was necessary to be prepared to support the war effort in the Middle East, regardless of whether or not the Gulf became a war zone. During the period before the War, the German plan to nominate Kuwait as a terminus for the proposed Baghdad Railway was perceived as part of an increasing threat to the British position of hegemony in the Gulf. This justified enhancing and elaborating the set of treaties, in which the rulers of the then six Trucial States - like other Arab rulers in the area - had agreed in 1892 to 'on no account enter into any agreement or correspondence with any Power other than the British Government'.[3]

Another important objective was to prevent arms from reaching sensitive areas such as Afghanistan or Baluchistan on the fringe of the British Empire. The countries in the entire region were all closely watched, and eventually treaties were made in November 1902 in which the rulers agreed to 'absolutely prohibit the importation of arms for sale...or the exportation therefrom'.[4] In 1911 it was agreed that concessions for pearling, sponge fishing and related economic activities should not be granted except with the permission of the British Political Resident for the Gulf in Bushire.[5] This undertaking had the additional benefit for the local population that no outsiders were permitted to exploit the resources, which were a significant part of their livelihood. Practical benefits for the far-flung Empire, such as way-leaves for telegraph lines or the demarcation of shipping lanes by buoys and lighthouses, were secured as the need arose. Thus a *cordon sanitaire* was thrown around the Arab states of the Gulf, which in the event meant, for the British at least, a well covered flank when Turkey, aided by Germany, engaged in hostilities in southern Iraq in 1916.

After the defeat of the main rivals within the Gulf region, Turkey, Germany and Russia, the previous British political and strategic considerations of the nineteenth century - with the desired effect of denying the littoral states of the Gulf contacts with other European powers - gave way to the pursuit of economic goals. During the War it had become evident that access to oil resources had become of prime importance. Finds in Persia and Iraq had already indicated that the entire region could be rich in oil. Therefore, Britain wanted to ensure that in the areas where she had already secured political influence, no other nation would pip her at the post if and when a race for oil concessions were to ensue. Between February and May of 1922 the rulers of the Trucial States gave an undertaking that if the search for oil commenced in their territories they would not grant 'any concession in this connection to any one except to the person appointed by the High British Government'.[6] Similar agreements had already been signed in 1913/14 by Kuwait and Bahrain, whereas British diplomatic efforts never achieved the same level of influence with Ibn Saud the new Ruler of Central Arabia.[7]

However, for more than a decade British oil companies were unable to take advantage of this privileged position in the Trucial States, because they were committing their capital and resources to the areas where oil had already been found, Persia and Iraq. Oil was then also discovered in Bahrain in 1932, and there were good prospects for discovery in Kuwait and the Al-Hasa area - all in American-owned concessions. The London-based multinational consortium, which had been restructured after the First World War to exploit the known deposits in Iraq, the Iraq Petroleum Company Ltd (IPC),[8] secured a concession in Qatar in 1935 with the help of the British Government. In the same year IPC formed a subsidiary called Petroleum Concessions Ltd (PCL) in order to secure oil concessions on the Trucial Coast and in Oman and to exclude American companies in these areas.

PCL's negotiations with the individual rulers proved to be tough and protracted and on numerous occasions required intervention by the British Political Agent in Bahrain as the long arm of the British Government. The first of these concessions was signed in 1937 by the Ruler of Dubai; the last to sign was the newly independent Ruler of Fujairah in 1952.[9] The Trucial States had so far been perceived by the British primarily as a string of settlements dominated by the rulers of the coastal city states. From the early 1930s onwards, British policy towards the Trucial States became much more intrusive in preparation for the operation of oil company personnel in the uncharted hinterland. The way in which the rulers dealt with domestic matters was now more closely monitored and, on occasions, severely censored, and the British authorities took an interest in inter-tribal strife and the increasing number of territorial disputes in the hinterland. The frequency, not only of the letters, which were sent to the rulers via the Residency Agent in Sharjah, but also of the visits of one or another of the warships stationed in the Gulf increased, carrying the Political Agent from Bahrain or Kuwait or even the Political Resident from Bushire - depending on the urgency and importance of the matter. The Senior Naval Officer in the Gulf, and even the captains of the ships, were also empowered to conduct political negotiations.

As communications between Britain and its Indian Empire developed to include air travel, and when landing facilities on the Iranian side of the Gulf were withdrawn, the Trucial States were considered as essential staging posts first for military and, later, for civilian planes. The British needed to be successful in negotiating agreements for runways, refueling facilities and emergency landing strips for their seaplanes and aircraft.[10] Since 1932 there were overnight facilities at a purpose-built fortress near a landing strip in Sharjah for the crew and passengers of (British) Imperial Airways. The strategically placed facilities for air communications, in particular at Sharjah, played an important role during the Second World War, and were secured by constant monitoring of developments in the area through copious exchanges of letters and frequent visits from the Agent in Sharjah, and the British personnel in Bahrain, Bushire, India and London. The oil concessions remained dormant due to the shortage of men, money and steel during the Second World War and for several years thereafter.[11]

In all matters of communication with the British Government, the sole addressees in every state were the rulers. Since the early nineteenth century the status of an incumbent ruler had usually been much enhanced by the importance which the 'High Government' placed on a 'Trucial Ruler' to the exclusion of a tribal sheikh in the interior.[12] But since the end of the second decade of the twentieth century, when the decline of the pearling industry spelled great economic hardship for the region, the population in these states, lead by the merchants, strongly resented the fact that all the potentially lucrative arrangements and concessions, for which the British Government or foreign companies made payments, were agreed exclusively with the rulers. This further enhanced an already existing regional trend to xenophobia and encouraged alienation between the rulers and their people.

After the War the search for oil began in earnest in 1950, when the first drilling rig was erected on the coast of Abu Dhabi. But many dry holes were drilled in several locations of the Trucial States and its adjacent sea bed before oil was struck in commercial quantities off-shore from Abu Dhabi in 1959 and on-shore in the desert of the same state in 1960. Export facilities were built and shipments began in 1962 and 1963 respectively. The influx of foreign personnel working for the oil companies and, eventually, an ever increasing number of men with the many construction and service companies, made it imperative that their safety was guaranteed while they were working in remote locations. In response to these requirements a British officered local force was established in 1951, the 'Trucial Oman Scouts'. A host of regulations were enacted to ensure their security, to define their legal status in the country as well as to cover many other issues. The Political Agency, staffed by British officials since 1949, was moved from Sharjah to Dubai in 1954, and a new Political Agency was opened for Abu Dhabi in 1957. Legal arrangements for British protected people were made in so called 'Orders in Council', decided upon in London. The British-made immigration rules were implemented by the Political Agencies. Thus, British involvement on a daily basis became very much more obvious, but because it coincided with a period of perceptible economic improvement, at least for those people who obtained employment with one of the companies, this was probably less resented than when the oil companies first arrived before the War.

As for the British Government's approach to this region within the slowly disintegrating empire, the changes which were sweeping the global political scene in the post-war era also made their mark here. The plight of people in developing countries was being discussed in the United Nations. Britain, too, became morally obliged to care for the population of this region which was under her domination and from which she had over time benefited so much more than she had been required to care for. Once the necessity to become active in the development of the Trucial States had become widely accepted, several efforts were initiated. The Foreign Office profited from the fact that a number of its members, who came to serve in the Gulf, had already been involved in development in the Sudan Civil Service. They and others were prepared to implement this new approach to the British imperial role - to help to improve the living standards of the people, and to prepare the area of the Trucial States for the changes which were to be expected if oil was found there. The world economic recession of the 1930s, the decline of the pearling industry, and the impact of the Second World War had combined to reduce the Trucial Coast to poverty. The finances which the British Government was prepared to commit to this task were very limited, but a number of dedicated civil servants, engineers, military personnel and other specialists managed to have an impact in several fields and laid the groundwork for the road to recovery.

The rulers of the seven Trucial States were brought together in the 'Trucial States Council', which met regularly and decided upon the priorities for the 'Trucial States Development Office'.[13] Modest beginnings in health care, road building, agricultural extension work, vocational training, statistics and surveys of water and soil resources were made in the 1950s. Such efforts accelerated and brought visible results in the 1960s, when Abu Dhabi began to pay the lion's share for these development projects. This leading role, which was taken by Abu Dhabi, already pointed the way forward to the foundation of the Federation of the United Arab Emirates in 1971, an independent state which benefited from the oil-wealth of her member states.

With this event the British Political Agency, which had been perceived by many in the country to be the hub of influence and power, was transformed into the British Embassy[14] - one among a fast growing number of diplomatic missions in the country, thus symbolically marking the end of the imperial era in the Gulf.

[1]   This was the name given to the area (with the exception of Bahrain and Qatar) under the sovereignty of the rulers who had signed the 'General Treaty' with the representative of the East India Company in 1820.

[2]   The supervision of developments on the Arab side of the Gulf was coordinated by the British Political Resident in Bushire; from 1823 a 'Native Agent' was sent to Sharjah to maintain a channel of communication with this Coast.

[3]   C.U. Aitchison, *A Collection of Treaties, Engagements and Sanads Relating to India and Neighbouring Countries*, Delhi, Government of India (1933) p 256.

[4]   *Ibid.*, p 257.

[5]   *Ibid.*, p 263

[6]   *Ibid.*, p 261

[7]   See G. Troeller, *The Birth of Saudi Arabia. Britain and the Rise of the House of Sa'ud*, London, Frank Cass (1976) pp 34ff.

[8]   The shareholding at the time was: 23.75 per cent each BP, Shell, Companie Francaise des Petroles (later Total), and Near East Development Corporation (half Mobil and half Standard Oil Co. of New Jersey) and 5 per cent Mr. Gulbenkian's Participations and Explorations (Partex).

[9]   See for details F. Heard-Bey, *From Trucial States to United Arab Emirates. A Society in Transition,* London, Longman (1982) pp 296f.

[10]   See R.S. Zahlan, *The Origins of the United Arab Emirates,* New York, St. Martin's Press (1978) pp 98ff.

[11]   A team of geologists had visited some parts of the hinterland in 1936 and some seismic investigations had followed in 1946.

[12]   For instance, the decision as to who should be the Ruler in Kalba in the 1930s was entirely a British one, as was the later decision to reincorporate Kalba into the state of Sharjah in 1951 after a series of struggles over succession.

[13]   See also for the following Heard-Bey, *op. cit.,* pp 319ff.

[14]   The Agent in Abu Dhabi became the Ambassador to the UAE, while the Agent in Dubai became a Consul General.

The Historical Background and Constitutional Basis to the Federation

Ibrahim Al Abed*

Introduction

The United Arab Emirates was established as a federal state on 2 December 1971, as a result of two distinct, but related, events. One was the signature by the Government of the United Kingdom and the rulers of the seven emirates (formerly known as the Trucial States or Trucial Oman) of separate instruments bringing to an end the treaty relationship that had existed between them since the early nineteenth century. The other was the agreement between rulers of six of the emirates, Abu Dhabi, Dubai, Sharjah, Ajman, Umm al-Qaiwain and Fujairah, the previous July, to establish a federation to be known as the United Arab Emirates simultaneously with the ending of the treaty relationship with Britain. The seventh emirate, Ras al-Khaimah, formally acceded to the new federation on 10 February 1972.

The decision to establish the federation followed the gradual evolving of a consensus that their small population, their small size, (only Abu Dhabi being larger than 1500 square miles), and their poverty (only Abu Dhabi and Dubai being oil producers) did not permit them each independently, or in smaller groupings, to establish a viable, independent, political and constitutional entity. This is not to mention those objective factors, whether cultural, religious and social, which the various emirates hold in common.

In January 1968, the Government of the United Kingdom had indicated its intention of bringing to an end its treaty relations with the Trucial States, and with two other Gulf sheikhdoms, Bahrain and Qatar, by the end of 1971. During the nearly four years between that British declaration and the establishment of the United Arab Emirates, the ruling families in the seven emirates, along with those of Bahrain and Qatar, together with their advisers, engaged in a lengthy series of meetings and negotiations on the appropriate political and constitutional structure to be adopted upon British withdrawal.

These negotiations were initially based upon a search for a nine state federation, including Bahrain and Qatar, and also involved the neighbouring independent Arabian Gulf states of Kuwait and Saudi Arabia, who acted, individually and together, as conciliators and mediators, and, on occasion, as supporters of one or other of the nine intending partners in the federation. The Government of the United Kingdom supported the efforts to create a federation and played an important role in the process that led to its eventual establishment.

* The author wishes to thank Peter Hellyer for his helpful comments on this chapter.

The creation of the United Arab Emirates in 1971 was the result of the consultations and negotiations in the period since January 1968. The concept of creating some form of constitutional structure linking together the emirates of the Arabian Gulf, while, at the same time, retaining key elements of their individual identities can, however, be traced back over several decades. An examination of that process is of relevance in analysing the dynamics of the politics of the federation.

The First Proposal for Inter-emirate Cooperation

The first proposal that can be traced for the creation of some kind of association between the sheikhdoms of Bahrain, Qatar and the Trucial States, together with Kuwait, surfaced during 1937, and was put forward by representatives of the colonial power, the United Kingdom. It subsequently created considerable local debate, both within and outwith the ruling families.

At that period, Britain was in treaty relations with all of the nine states as well as Kuwait, under the terms of which, inter alia, their rulers could not engage in independent relations with foreign powers, and were obliged to accept the advice of Britain in certain defined areas.

The British presence was centred on the office of the Political Resident, Persian Gulf (PRPG) in Bahrain, although there were other officers and Political Agents in several other states. The PRPG reported to the Government of India, then responsible for British interests on the western littoral of the Arabian Gulf, (with the exception of the recently emerged Kingdom of Saudi Arabia), while the latter communicated with the Imperial Cabinet in London through the India Office.

The British proposal was presented to the rulers of the states during the course of 1937 (Hamaidan 1967: pp 231-232). According to an interview in the magazine *Al Bahrain* in June 1939 by a member of the ruling Al Maktoum family of Dubai, Sheikh Mana bin Hashar Al Maktoum, it included the following points:

• The establishment of a unified educational system, with a central administrative headquarters in Bahrain, and also a unified postal service.
• The creation of a common nationality, with the abolition of the necessity of passports for travel between the member emirates.
• The unification of the judiciary and legislative systems.

The proposal was also said to include the unification of ground and naval forces under a central command and administration. A federation council was proposed, with each emirate 'to send a representative according to an approved system' while indirect taxation could be levied to raise money for federal expenses. According to Sheikh Mana 'the advice and assistance of Great Britain is to be sought in implementing the project, due to its special relations with these parties, and for being the Arab's ally in more than one part of the world.'

According to another report (*Al Bahrain*, 6.1939), the creation of an assembly was also proposed, with representatives from each emirate, either to be appointed by the ruler or to be elected by the population, having the power to propose financial regulations and to ratify draft legislation put forward by the Federation Council.

The British proposal came at a time when the PRPG and other British officials were deeply involved in negotiations designed to win oil exploration concessions in the Trucial States for the British-controlled Iraq Petroleum Company (IPC). These negotiations were by no means always smooth and easy, and as a result, relations between Britain and the rulers were not always cordial. Indeed, some rulers were clearly opposed to any proposal which could lead to a greater degree of British involvement in their emirates. Perceived, by the British at least, as being one of the more difficult rulers was Sheikh Shakhbut bin Sultan Al Nahyan of Abu Dhabi.

By 1938, the Government of the United Kingdom was pre-occupied with the looming Second World War, which broke out in Europe the next year, and little energy was expended on promotion of the Gulf federation proposal. The contents of the proposal, however, became widely known throughout the states involved, and provoked considerable political discussion, some of which was reflected in local journals. Abdullah Al Zayed, owner of the magazine *Al Bahrain*, made use of his columns to promote the concept of greater integration. In June 1939, in the front page interview with Sheikh Mana Al Maktoum cited above, he commented: 'We pray that the aspirations of Sheikh Mana (for a federation) are realized, so that we can see this plan going beyond the area of thinking towards action'. He then added:

> *We are confident that Their Excellencies Sheikh Sultan bin Saqr* (Al Qassimi)*, the Emir of Sharjah, and Sheikh Shakhbut bin Sultan* (Al Nahyan)*, the Emir of Abu Dhabi, welcome the plan. We also believe that His Excellency Sheikh Sultan bin Salem* (Al Qassimi)*, the Emir of Ras al-Khaimah, does not see otherwise. There will be no need to seek the acceptance of His Excellency Sheikh Ahmed Al Jaber* (Al Sabah, of Kuwait)*, who was the first to think about it* (the concept of greater co-operation)*, and has spent much time working for its sake.*

Although no action was taken, either by Britain or by the rulers, to implement the proposal, reports in *Al Bahrain* over the course of the next five years indicated that discussion of the topic continued. On 22 August 1939, for example, the magazine reported: 'We have learned that the Emirs of the Gulf have convened their Councils to discuss (the idea of a federation) and they are happy and keen on their endeavour.'

In the same issue, *Al Bahrain* published an article described as a summary of reports in other press, including *Arab Association* and *Arab Newsletter*. It reported that:

> *The general belief in the Arab Emirates overlooking the Gulf is one calling for the need for its citizens to be brought closer together so that they may preserve their national identity. These Emirates have carried out 'national propaganda,'* (contacts) *in this respect that is soon expected to bear fruit.*
> *The ruling Emirs have started to view closeness between the Emirates as a factor of* (common strength)*, as long as each Emir maintains his own independence in his own state.*

The report again summarized the outlines of the proposal, with more detail on some points. On the unification of posts and telegraphs, for example, it said that fees and salaries should also be defined, and that a single administrative system should be created 'on the basis of the percentage of each emirate in the revenues'. On the creation of a joint military force, it said that the proposal suggested that:

> *each military unit in each Emirate has its autonomous unit, but* (should be) *linked with the units of the other Emirates in an alliance under one general command and staff. According to the rules of this alliance, the units can participate in defensive and offensive*

manoeuvres in any part within the border of the federation. Each Emirate will have to spend on its military units according to decisions by the General Command. The rules will apply to the ground, naval and air forces.

On the proposed Federal Assembly or Council, the magazine said that it was to be established with representatives from each emirate, chosen 'either by appointment or election, or both, taking into consideration the population of each Emirate'. It added that the Council: 'will have to study all laws and regulations issued by the Judicial Council before endorsing them. Each Emirate has to show absolute subjugation, and is responsible for implementing these laws.'

Kuwait, Bahrain, Qatar, Abu Dhabi, Dubai and Sharjah were said to be involved in the plans. *Al Bahrain*, however, added 'the Emirates which are expected to merge are over twenty, and those which have been mentioned are only the larger among them'.

At the time, the British, through the PRPG, also recognized the separate identity of Ras al-Khaimah, Ajman and Umm al-Qaiwain, as well as Kalba, which had been granted recognition in the mid-1930s and was reintegrated into Sharjah in 1951. The emirate of Fujairah, officially recognized in 1952, was also seeking a British acknowledgement of its separate status. The other 'emirates' considered by the *Al Bahrain* editor were not identified, but may well have included some of the near-autonomous inland tribes or small coastal villages like Hirah in Sharjah, which had earlier unsuccessfully sought independent status. 'Considering Britain's position towards this plan,' the paper wrote, 'it is obvious that it does not propose it, but has not opposed it or obstructed it, if it has been brought to its attention.'

In a subsequent issue of the magazine on 28 September 1939, *Al Bahrain* reproduced a letter it said had come from 'a senior (official) on the Omani Coast (i.e. the Trucial States), who asked not to be named and who swore he was ready to exert his influence, and money and blood for the sake of the (federation of emirates) if need be.' The letter, the identity of whose author has not been determined, said in part that the topic of a possible federation of emirates:

has become the main theme for discussions in councils (majalis) *and clubs, and the focus of thinking among those interested in the future of the Arabs in this part of their nation. We do not know what share* (of attention) *it took in Kuwait, Bahrain and Qatar, although the newspapers which have dwelt on the subject have confirmed the great interest of the inhabitants there.*

The federation of the Emirates is beneficial not only for the Emirates. Its main benefit is for the Emirs themselves, because in order to have such unity, there should be a Federation Council, and a constitution, that guarantees the status of the Emirs, and defines a way of succession to the thrones, as well as preventing any aggression from one party against another, from within and from without, as well as against internal revolts. They (the Emirs) *would be involved in building their countries for the prosperity of their peoples, and in education of their youth.*

The correspondent from the Trucial States went on to refine further some of the suggestions already made on the powers and structure of the federation. These included a proposal that each emirate should be 'called to elect representatives, one to each 4000 inhabitants. The representatives will be from the Emirs or from the people'. He added that he had no objection to either Kuwait or Bahrain as a base for the Council, but added that he personally preferred Bahrain, because it was an island and in the geographical centre of the region.

Considering the fact that all the Emirates have special links with Britain, and that no possible danger to the area's Arabism and existence can arise from this relationship, the Emirates will have to seek assistance from this country (Britain) *in a way that will ensure the growth and steadfastness of the federation.*

Finally, the correspondent said that the duties of the federation should include 'the task of working towards cementing the links and alliances with neighbouring Arab countries, particularly the Kingdoms of Saudi Arabia and Iraq.' 'Now', he concluded, 'is it not time to take the first step, and for the Emirs to call each other together for a preparatory meeting to discuss this subject?'

The emirs, however, made no attempt to do so, while the PRPG, with his masters in Bombay and London pre-occupied by the Second World War, took no initiatives on the subject. Abdullah Al Zayed, the campaigning editor of *Al Bahrain*, continued to promote the concept of greater inter-emirate co-operation, and to suggest that there was a degree of support from members of the ruling families. On 7 August 1941, the paper reported a statement by Sheikh Sultan bin Saqr Al Qassimi of Sharjah, said to have been made during a visit to the paper, as follows:

I pray to God that the Arab Emirs in the Gulf succeed in uniting and in eliminating the causes for differences and discord (between them). *May He direct them towards forging a unity that brings them together, and puts away hatred.*

On 11 September 1941, Abdullah Al Zayed reported a visit to his office by Sheikh Humaid bin Muhammad bin Salem Al Qassimi, nephew and son-in-law of the Ruler of Ras al-Khaimah, and commented:

It is a delight to be able to mention that all the Emirs and dignitaries we have been able to meet from the Coast of Oman (Trucial Oman) *expect and support the idea that the Arab Emirates on the Gulf unite in an alliance that would make of them one country, as it is one nation, provided that each Emir maintains the right to run his own internal affairs as he does now.*

Al Zayed's continual campaigning and prompting, however, achieved little. Nearly three years later, on 23 March 1944, he wrote an editorial entitled 'Will the Gulf be one state?' It said, in part:

Over and over again, we have written about this subject, which is of particular concern to us. The editor of this newspaper has personally ascertained the views of many Emirs and Sheikhs in the Gulf. He is also confident that Great Britain has no objection to this project, if the sheikhs of the Emirates should express their desire for a Federation. It is even probable that it will take an initiative in giving assistance.
We repeat here what we have often said, that the Federation of Arab Emirates in the Gulf does not mean that any Emir will cede his throne, or lose any of his influence or income. On the contrary, the wars between the Emirates will end, to be replaced by lasting peace and stability.

It is now our hope that the Emirs will convene a conference amongst themselves to complete discussion of the subject, as they have already (discussed it) *individually.*

The proposal during the 1930s for the creation of some form of greater inter-emirate co-operation in the Gulf came to naught, despite evidence that, at least as individuals, some of the emirs supported it. Moreover, the involvement of Britain in the Second World War pre-occupied the colonial power, while in the years immediately after the War, Britain was primarily concerned at a regional level with her impending withdrawal from India and, to a lesser extent, the impact that would have upon her interests in the Arabian Gulf.

The concept, however, was the first concrete formula to be put forward for a form of regional co-operation between the emirates, and was, moreover, a formula that incorporated all of the basic elements that were to compose the basic structure of succeeding plans and proposals. These included the concept that any viable federal structure should acknowledge the separate identity and authority within his emirate of each sheikh, with particular relation to the armed forces and his authority over his own subjects, even if the latter were members of any Federal Council or Assembly. Also included was the concept that any such entity to be established should have a form of collective leadership in which the individual sheikhs should all participate, as well as some form of popular representation, either through selection or election. Significantly, there was also a recognition that at least a tacit approval for any such structure should be sought from the largest Arab states in the region, Saudi Arabia and Iraq. Indeed, some of the emirs were reported to have visited Riyadh to discuss the 1937 idea with the Saudi monarch, Abdul Aziz Al Saud, and to seek his blessings.

The Trucial States Council

The Political Resident, Persian Gulf, and his political superiors, had taken no action to promote the 1937 proposal, but in 1952, in the aftermath of her withdrawal from the Indian sub-continent, Britain took a new initiative which was confined to the Trucial Coast.

At the time, there were seven states or emirates that were recognized as having independent identities, all of which were in treaty relations with the United Kingdom. These were Abu Dhabi, Dubai, Sharjah, Ras al-Khaimah, Umm al-Qaiwain, Ajman and Fujairah. In the same year, Fujairah had at last succeeded in winning from Britain the recognition as a separate entity for which it had been struggling intermittently for almost a century, while in the previous year Kalba, just south of Fujairah, had been re-absorbed into the Emirate of Sharjah, following the extinction of the adult male line of the local branch of the ruling Al Qassimi family of Sharjah.

The British initiative took the form of the creation of the Trucial States Council, an informal body composed of the sheikhs of the seven emirates and chaired by the British Political Agent in the Trucial States, resident in Dubai. The Council was designed primarily as an informal gathering, with no charter, written code or regulations, and its members were given to understand that it was to act as a consultative institution. Its intended purpose during its bi-annual meetings was to discuss matters of common concern and to prepare recommendations for the Political Agent (Fenelon 1973: p 39). Under the terms of the treaties regulating the British relationship with the emirates, the sheikhs were obliged in certain fields, moreover, to act upon the advice of the PRPG or the Political Agent. During the subsequent years, covering nearly two decades, discussions in the Council centred upon matters of economic development, on services of general interest, such as education, health, traffic control and the control of locusts and on other items, of concern also to the British, such as the total abolition of the smuggling and sale of slaves, citizenship and travel documents (Hawley 1971: pp 25-27).

In 1958, six years after it was established, and in the wake of major changes in the Arab world such as the republican revolution in Iraq and the tri-partite action by Britain, France and Israel against Egypt, the Council, at the prompting of the Political Agent, established three sub-committees, for agriculture, education and public health. In 1964, another major committee, entitled the Deliberative Committee, was established, with the tasks of undertaking preliminary work on the agendas to be placed before the meetings of the Council itself, of deciding upon the priorities for projects and of drafting recommendations for the Council. The Committee had two members from each of the Trucial States and met approximately every two months (Hawley 1971: p 25). In 1965, the British Political Agent vacated the chair of the Council, and the member sheikhs then elected a Chairman from amongst their own number, to serve for a one year term. The first so to be elected was the Ruler of Ras al-Khaimah, Sheikh Saqr bin Muhammad Al Qassimi (Al-Azminah Al-Arabiyyah no. 84, 15.10.1980: pp 6-7).

During the course of 1965, the administrative structure associated with the Council was further developed, with the creation of the Development Office and the Development Fund. These were given the task of co-ordinating the modest development projects in the seven emirates until the Fund was dissolved, after the formation of the Federation of the UAE, in early 1972. Its duties were then transferred to the institutions of the new state (ibid.). The activities of the Fund were financed by the British, who in 1965 increased the budget for the Council's Five Year Plan from £350,000 to £1,000,000, and also made an annual appropriation of a further £200,000 for current development expenditure. Much to the delight of the British, who believed that some of the oil revenues enjoyed by Abu Dhabi, which had begun production in 1962, should be spent in the poorer emirates, when Sheikh Zayed bin Sultan Al Nahyan became Ruler of Abu Dhabi on 6 August 1966 he immediately made a grant of a further £500,000 to the Development Fund, with subsequent substantial grants in 1967 and 1968, by which time he was the largest contributor. Other funds came from Kuwait, which was also providing assistance to the emerging educational sector (Fenelon 1973: pp 39-40).

The purpose of this chapter being to examine the gradual progress of the Trucial States towards the formation of the federation, the achievements of the Trucial States Council need not be analysed in detail. It is apparent, however, that the Council was a joint venture that pointed the way towards a federation, and that its formation, and its acceptance by the rulers, implied a recognition of the essential unity, or at least common interest, of the seven Trucial States.

The Council served as a forum for discussion and exchange of views between the rulers, initially under the watchful eye of the British Political Agent. It also provided a framework for co-operation and for the adoption of a certain degree of collective responsibility for common problems that permitted each individual ruler to operate at a level broader than that of his own individual tribe or sheikhdom. As a result, this first concrete experiment in inter-emirate collaboration played an important function in helping to reduce the degree of competition between the rulers and, at the same time, giving them experience in collaborating for mutual benefit.

The Bi-partite Union

In January 1968, the British Government informed the rulers of the Trucial States, and of Qatar and Bahrain, that they intended to bring the treaty relationship between them and Britain to an end by the close of 1971, as part of a process of British withdrawal from East of Suez. The British decision meant, in effect, that the Trucial States were to be granted independence, a development that not only took the rulers by surprise, since they had been informed only a couple of months before that such a withdrawal would not take place, but was also one that was by no means universally welcomed. Indeed, the first reaction of several was to ask the British to stay.

One of the immediate results of the British decision was the additional impetus given to the already expanding co-operation between the rulers within the framework of the Trucial States Council. Looking further ahead, however, Sheikh Zayed of Abu Dhabi promptly recognized the need for discussion with his fellows on the nature of any future relationship.

On 18 February 1968, only a few weeks after the British had informed the rulers of their decision to withdraw, the rulers of the two largest and wealthiest emirates, Sheikh Zayed of Abu Dhabi and Sheikh Rashid bin Saeed Al Maktoum of Dubai, met at As-Sameeh, close to their mutual border. The original purpose of the meeting was to discuss and to settle a disagreement over onshore and offshore borders, this being resolved quickly by a cession of territory by Abu Dhabi to Dubai, including the site of today's Port of Jebel Ali. As both rulers may have suspected, the offshore areas involved in the cession of territory were later discovered to contain substantial oil reserves.

Although both rulers had not abandoned the hope of persuading the British to reverse their decision, they also discussed the likely prospects for the region should withdrawal take place. In order to prepare for such an eventuality, they agreed that they would create a two-emirate union which others would be invited to join. The terms of the agreement provided for foreign affairs, defence, security, immigration and social affairs to be union responsibilities, with each emirate retaining responsibility for judicial and other internal affairs (*Rozal Yousif,* 2.8.1971). Article 4 of the Abu Dhabi - Dubai Agreement invited the rulers of the other five Trucial States to discuss the agreement, and to adhere to it. The rulers of Qatar and Bahrain were also invited to confer with the rulers of the Trucial States in order to discuss the future of the region as a whole, with a view to seeing whether a common stance could be adopted between the nine separate political units (*ibid.*).

This agreement was short-lived, for the rulers of the other Trucial States, along with those of Qatar and Bahrain, signified their immediate acceptance of the offer to join the new union. On 25 February 1968, the nine rulers met in Dubai, signing an agreement on 27 February to establish the 'Federation of the Arab Emirates'. This agreement was to come into effect on 30 March 1968 (Al Rayyes 1973: p 75). The agreement stipulated that the purpose of the federation was:

> *to cement ties between them* (the members) *in all fields, to co-ordinate plans for their development and prosperity, to reinforce the respect of each one of them for the independence and sovereignty of the others, to unify their foreign policies and representation, and its higher policy in international, political, defence, economic, cultural and other matters.*

It further stipulated that the highest body, the Supreme Council, (comprising the nine rulers) 'shall be responsible for issuing the necessary federal laws and that it is the supreme authority in deciding on issues of reference, and shall take its decisions by a unanimous vote.' The Chairmanship of the Council was to be 'rotated annually among its members,' with the Chairman representing the federation 'internally and before foreign states'.

Under the terms of the Dubai Agreement, executive authority was delegated to a Federal Council which was to act as an executive arm of the Supreme Council. Article 8 of the agreement, however, made it clear that the Federal Council:

would carry out its functions to strengthen the collective defence of their countries, with a view to safeguarding their security, safety and mutual interests in such matters as to ensure the fulfilment of their aspirations and realize the hopes of the greater Arab homeland.

The second chapter of the Agreement defined the top federal, political and executive authorities and the financial structure of the federation, while the third dealt with defence, justice and the site of the capital of the federation. Ultimate political authority was vested in the Supreme Council. This body was assigned the task of drawing up:

a permanent and comprehensive charter for the Federation, and the formulation of its overall policies on international, political, defence, economic, cultural and other affairs that are in accordance with the aims of the Federation.

There was a notable lack of precision on matters of defence, justice and the capital. Article 12 provided that:

The contracting Emirates shall co-operate in strengthening their military capabilities in accordance with the right of legitimate defence, both individual and collective, of their existence, and their common duty to repel any armed aggression to which any one of them may be subjected. The Emirates shall also co-operate, according to their resources and needs, in developing their individual or collective means of defence to meet their obligation.

Article 13, on justice, called for the establishment of a Supreme Court, and for its formation, organization and functions to be defined by law, while the relationship between the Supreme Council and the Federal Council was clarified by Article 10, which stated that 'decisions of the Federal Council shall not be deemed final unless approved by the Supreme Council'. The permanent headquarters of the federation was left to be determined by the Supreme Council at a later stage. Finances were covered, in general terms, in Article 6, which said that: 'the general budget of the Federation shall be issued by a decision from the Supreme Council. The law shall fix the budget revenues and the share to be paid by each member Emirate'.

The agreement also stated that local affairs were to remain within the jurisdiction of each member emirate, with precise details to be determined by the Supreme Council at a later date.

The agreement between the nine rulers to form the Federation of Arab Emirates was made at speed, and, in consequence, the terms of the charter agreed upon were loosely worded in legal terms and thus subject to differing interpretations. Although the Supreme Council was to meet on four occasions over the subsequent 18 months, it was unable to reach lasting agreement on any point, except that the federation itself was not viable.

The Failure of the Federation of Arab Emirates

A detailed examination of the various deliberations between leaders of the emirates and of the contacts that took place between them is outside the purview of this chapter. The underlying obstacles that gave rise to the differences between the nine members are, however, of importance in understanding the reasons for its eventual collapse, effectively from the date of the last meeting of the Supreme Council, on 21 October 1969.

One obstacle of considerable importance was inherent in the Charter of the Federation itself. Although the new entity was named the 'Federation of Arab Emirates,' the Charter itself stipulated that its purpose was, in part, 'to reinforce the respect of each one of them for the independence and sovereignty of the others' (*ibid.*).

The agreement, as mentioned earlier, required the Supreme Council to take decisions only on the basis of unanimity, and single rulers could, and often did, prevent such unanimity being reached. Moreover, the agreement was silent on questions relating to the organization and composition of the Federal Council, including the manner in which its members were to be selected. This again, according to one observer, 'handicapped the process of implementation as the Supreme Council was not able to reach an agreement on these matters '(*Al-Azminah*, 26. 11. 1980: pp 6-7). The agreement also lacked precision on questions such as the sources of federal revenues and the contribution to be made by each emirate to the federal budget, while an examination of the deliberations of Supreme Council meetings indicates that the Council also failed to reach agreement on these two points (*ibid.*). In addition, there was no clear indication in the agreement as to whether or not the member emirates had consented to the establishment of a joint defence force. As a result, some rulers supported the unification of the various military and para-military forces, while others insisted on maintaining their own independent armed units (*ibid.*).

Rivalry over the respective status of the rulers and their emirates was also clear during the life of the Supreme Council, with competition for leadership and for positions. This was particularly evident between Bahrain and Qatar, neither of which had participated in the work of the Trucial States Council that had brought the other seven emirates, and their rulers, closer together in the previous decade and a half. Both eventually decided to withdraw from efforts to create a viable federation, and became separately independent, on 14 August 1971 and 1 September 1971 respectively, although by that stage the Federation of Arab Emirates itself had long since ceased to exist.

The competition between the two, however, permitted Abu Dhabi to emerge as a mediator. Though with a smaller population than Bahrain, and at a lower level of development than either Dubai or Qatar, Abu Dhabi was largest of the nine emirates in terms of size. It was also the wealthiest, with its rapidly expanding oil production far outstripping not only that of Bahrain and Qatar, but also that of Dubai (which did not commence exports until 1968), the only other oil producer in the Trucial States. This, coupled with the generosity of Abu Dhabi's Sheikh Zayed towards the other emirates, helped to make him the person most likely to be acceptable to his colleagues as leader of the federation of the seven Trucial States that was to emerge after the collapse of the federation of nine.

Qatar and Bahrain also disagreed over the site of the proposed federal capital. At the fourth and final Supreme Council meeting it was agreed that Abu Dhabi should be the temporary capital, with a permanent site to be built later between Abu Dhabi and Dubai. When a year later the deputy rulers met in Abu Dhabi to attempt to revive the moribund federation, the question of the capital was again raised and Bahrain withdrew its previous acceptance, rendering the agreement on Abu Dhabi null and void.

Subsequently the federation of the Trucial States that became the United Arab Emirates adopted the same compromise in its provisional constitution in 1971, naming Abu Dhabi as temporary capital pending construction of a permanent capital, to be named Al-Karamah, on the Abu Dhabi-Dubai border. Both Dubai and Ras al-Khaimah raised the question of a permanent capital on a number of occasions during the 1970s, demanding that it should be built. The Abu Dhabi Ruler and UAE President, Sheikh Zayed, however, embarked on a process of turning Abu Dhabi into a *de facto* capital. Only financial considerations, plus the rapid creation of established facts in terms of construction on the ground, led the two emirates to drop their demand after 1979. It was to take a further 17 years, until May 1996, before the Supreme Council of the UAE, adopting the Provisional Constitution as permanent, finally endorsed Abu Dhabi as the permanent capital.

Another major point of contention between members of the Supreme Council of the Federation of Arab Emirates was the method to be followed in determining the composition of the proposed Federal Council or Parliament. Bahrain, with the largest population, proposed a ratio based on population. Qatar and the others, with much smaller populations, refused (Heard-Bey 1984: p 359). Subsequently, at the October 1969 Supreme Council meeting, Bahrain agreed to the principle of equal representation, with four members from each emirate. At the October 1970 meeting of deputy rulers, however, it retracted its previous agreement, and again demanded a form of proportional representation (*Al-Azminah* no. 95, 14. 1. 1981: pp 6-7). The opposition of the remaining eight deputy rulers led Bahrain's representative to announce his intention of refraining from taking any further part in subsequent discussions 'before ensuring that the Constitution ensures the rights of the people of the Union, particularly in so far as the representation of the people in the Union Council is concerned.' (*ibid.*)

A further unresolved point was the question of voting within the Supreme Council itself. The 1968 Dubai Agreement had originally called for unanimity. The draft constitution subsequently prepared stipulated that decisions on 'substantial' matters should be taken by unanimous vote, but that decisions on other, less important, matters should be taken on the basis of a simple majority. Bahrain rejected this for reasons related to its opposition to other related articles, while when the subject was raised at the deputy rulers' meeting in Abu Dhabi in October 1970, there were several differing viewpoints (*ibid.*).

Following the collapse of the deputy rulers' meeting in October 1970, it became clear by early 1971 that Bahrain and Qatar had chosen to follow an independent course, and the rulers of the seven Trucial States were obliged to re-consider their plans to deal with the approaching British withdrawal, not least because any remaining hopes that the Conservative Government, elected in June 1970, would reverse the decision to withdraw taken by its Labour predecessor had finally been dashed. The British Government, too, was eager to ensure that a viable structure of government would exist upon its departure, not least because of the collapse in 1967 of the superficially similar South Arabian Federation. The British Government had sponsored the federation in the area that became independent as the People's Republic of Southern Yemen, with a Marxist Government that in 1971 was actively supporting subversion of the existing order both in Oman and in the Trucial States. Equally keen to have a satisfactory agreement worked out, again partly because of the fear of a spread of the virus of revolution from South Yemen, were the Governments of the other Arabian Gulf states, Kuwait and Saudi Arabia, both of whom had been actively engaged in promoting the federation of nine concept.

The Bahraini and Qatari decisions represented, at one level, a terminal blow to the embryo federal structure, because both emirates had a substantially higher level of education, and, hence, more qualified local personnel. At the same time, however, their departure, which left Abu Dhabi and Dubai far outweighing their five colleagues in terms of area, population and wealth, made it easier for the Trucial States to move towards agreement amongst themselves.

On 10 July 1971, the seven Trucial States rulers met in Dubai. Eight days later, six of them announced the formation of the United Arab Emirates. Ras al-Khaimah declined to join, although not ruling out the possibility of doing so in the future.The discussions leading to the creation of the Federation of the UAE, which centred, in part, on amendments being proposed to the draft Constitution for the Federation of Arab Emirates, indicated that substantial differences existed.

The rulers of the small five, excluding Abu Dhabi and Dubai, proposed three key amendments. As far as a federal capital was concerned, they suggested that the plan to build a new capital between Abu Dhabi and Dubai should be abandoned and that, instead, a headquarters for the new Federal Government should be built somewhere between Dubai and Sharjah, saying that the funds for a new capital would be better spent on development schemes in the emirates that were not oil producers. The five further stressed that there should be full equality between the seven in all respects, including the composition of a national assembly and the voting process within the Supreme Council (Heard-Bey 1984: p359). Neither Abu Dhabi nor Dubai were prepared to accept these points, the last of which, in particular, was in direct contradiction to the powers they themselves sought.

On the second day of the meeting, four of the five withdrew their support for the proposals they had put forward the day before. Only Sheikh Saqr bin Muhammad Al Qassimi, Ruler of Ras al-Khaimah, continued to press them. In the subsequent days of talks, the remaining six rulers agreed to adopt a revised version of the draft Constitution for the defunct Federation of Arab Emirates, the key difference being that decisions by the Supreme Council of Rulers were to be taken by a majority vote, but both Abu Dhabi and Dubai had to be part of the majority. Abu Dhabi was approved as provisional capital.

Sheikh Zayed of Abu Dhabi was elected as the first President of the United Arab Emirates, while Sheikh Rashid of Dubai was elected Vice-President, both terms to run for five years from 2 December 1971, the date on which the treaties with Britain were to come to an end, and to be renewable.

The national assembly, which was given the name of Federal National Council, was to be comprised of 34 members, eight each from Abu Dhabi and Dubai, six from Sharjah, and four each for the three smaller emirates of Ajman, Umm al-Qaiwain and Fujairah. Six places were to be allocated to Ras al-Khaimah, should it eventually decide to join the federation. It was also agreed that the Constitution should have a provisional status for five years, after which it was to be replaced by a permanent Constitution.

Examination of the Provisional Constitution makes it clear that the views of Abu Dhabi and Dubai carried the day, with the four smaller, and poorer, emirates feeling themselves obliged to accept the demands of their more powerful neighbours. They were encouraged to do so by scarcely veiled suggestions being made by advisers to the Abu Dhabi and Dubai rulers that the two had already reached agreement on a contingency plan to press ahead with a bi-partite federation should the others fail to accede to their terms. The smaller emirates were also encouraged to join, however, by the pledge from Sheikh Zayed of Abu Dhabi that his emirate's oil resources would be used for the benefit of all of the federation's members. 'Abu Dhabi's oil and all its resources and potential are at the service of all the Emirates,'(Heard-Bey 1984: p 349). The rulers already had the evidence of Sheikh Zayed's generosity before them, Abu Dhabi having been the largest single contributor to the Trucial States Development Fund since 1968, as noted earlier.

In the discussions leading up to the agreement, as during the previous attempt to create the Federation of Arab Emirates, neighbouring states and the British played an important role. While Kuwait proffered advice and assistance as a mediator, Saudi Arabia made it clear that it would not recognize any federation unless it obtained a satisfactory answer to its territorial claims on Abu Dhabi. The Shah of Iran, for his part, having agreed in 1970 to drop his claim to Bahrain following the results of a test of opinion supervised by the United Nations, made it clear that there could be no possibility of him accepting the formation of a federation among the Trucial States unless he obtained the islands of Greater and Lesser Tunb, belonging to Ras al-Khaimah, and Abu Musa, belonging to Sharjah.

The British were left with the sometimes difficult task of cajoling and encouraging the rulers of the emirates to proceed to agreement. With the collapse of efforts to create the Federation of Arab Emirates, the rapid approach of the self-created deadline of December 1971 for a final British withdrawal from the Gulf meant that British policy was, at times, a mixture both of carrot and stick. This was particularly true where the smaller emirates were concerned, whose rulers continued to show a reluctance to accept the inevitability of a British departure until almost the date of the actual establishment of the United Arab Emirates.

When intransigence threatened to complicate future acceptance of the federation by Iran, British tactics echoed past imperial attitudes. Thus Sharjah's Ruler was informed that he must make an agreement with Iran on sharing authority on Abu Musa, while the Ruler of Ras al-Khaimah, who completely rejected the suggestion that he should cede the Tunbs, found simply that Iran was given to understand by Britain that it would not oppose a military seizure of the islands, particularly if this could take place just before Britain formally relinquished its authority.

At the end of November 1971, with the establishment of the UAE a matter of days away, Sharjah signed a Memorandum of Understanding with Iran on the sharing of authority over Abu Musa without either of the two parties relinquishing its claims of sovereignty. This was followed by a night attack by Iranian forces on the Tunbs, during which a number of Ras al-Khaimah policemen were killed. The Iranian occupation has continued to complicate relations between the UAE and Iran throughout the course of the subsequent 25 years.

Ras al-Khaimah's application for membership of the Federation was accepted unconditionally on 10 February 1972, without any changes in the Provisional Constitution.

The Federal System

The new state which came into existence on 2 December 1971 had its basis in the Provisional Constitution. Adopted by the rulers on behalf of their emirates, it represented a consensus on the form of the state which they agreed to establish, and on the concessions that they agreed to make with relation to a surrender of part of their sovereign powers to the new federal bodies. (In July 1996 the Supreme Council of the Federation decided unanimously to drop the word 'Provisional'. The Constitution thus became permanent.) It represented, therefore, an expression of the political status quo at the end of the 1960s in the southern Arabian Gulf, including Qatar and Bahrain, in the light of the impending British withdrawal. Both Qatar and Bahrain had taken part in the earlier negotiations that preceded the formation of the UAE, when the Federation of Arab Emirates, grouping all nine emirates, was under discussion. Indeed, one observer has suggested that had they not been involved in the early stages of the negotiations, 'many compromises which now form part of the constitution would have been settled very differently'. The relationship between Qatar and Bahrain was marked by strong rivalry and competition, encouraging both to introduce a variety of legal formulations into the draft of the Constitution which they believed would either safeguard their own position, or counter the position or influence of the other.

The preamble of the Constitution stipulates that the rulers of the emirates agreed to the Constitution for the sake of, among other matters:

> *Desiring also to lay the foundation for federal rule in the coming years on a sound basis, corresponding to the realities and the capacities of the Emirates at the present time, enabling the Union, so far as possible, freely to achieve its goals, sustaining the identity of its members providing that this is not inconsistent with those goals and preparing the people of the Union at the same time for a dignified and free constitutional life, and progressing by steps towards a comprehensive, representative, democratic regime in an Islamic and Arab society free from fear and anxiety.*

The Supreme Council

The Supreme Council of the Federation (FSC) is the federation's highest authority, and is composed of the rulers or of those designated to represent them. According to the Constitution, the Supreme Council has exclusive executive powers, powers of ratification, and legislative powers. The executive powers lie in the following spheres:

- Acceptance of a new member of the federation. Such acceptance should be unanimous (Article 1).
- Election of the President and the Vice-President from among its members.
- Formulation of the general state policy, in all matters conferred by the Constitution upon the federation, and consideration of all matters that could help to achieve the objectives of the federation, and the common interests of its members (Article 47, clause 1).
- Maintaining supreme control over the affairs of the federation (Article 47, clause 7).
- Drafting its own Rules and Procedures Bill, in which the Council may define those matters to be considered procedural (Article 48).

The Supreme Council also enjoys limited, but decisive, powers of ratification in the following, on which initial decisions may be taken by the individual emirates, the President or the Council of Ministers:

* Approval of any decision taken by two or more emirates on some form of merger.
* Article 143 of the Constitution stipulates that 'any emirate shall have the right to request the assistance of the Armed Forces or the Security Forces of the Union in order to maintain security and order within its territories whenever it is exposed to danger. Such a request shall be submitted immediately to the Supreme Council of the Union for decision.' (While the President and the Council of Ministers may collectively take immediate action if the Supreme Council is not in session, they are obliged to call the Supreme Council into immediate session in order to sanction the move.)
* The Council has the power to endorse or reject any administrative agreements that may be concluded between individual emirates and neighbouring countries.
* It approves the resignation or dismissal of the Prime Minister, upon recommendation from the President.
* It endorses declaration of defensive war upon a proposal from the President.
* It has the power to endorse any decrees from the Council of Ministers on the appointment, resignation and dismissal of judges of the Supreme Court.
* It endorses international treaties and agreements concluded by the Council of Ministers.
* It approves any declaration of martial law by the President provided it has the approval of the Council of Ministers.

The Supreme Council also has an absolute legislative prerogative, retaining the final say on federal legislation. According to the Constitution, the Council of Ministers may propose legislation, which, after discussion in the Federal National Council, is then submitted to the Supreme Council for approval or rejection. The Supreme Council may thus issue any law, with or without consent of the Council of Ministers and the Federal National Council. In view of the dual roles of Supreme Council members as rulers as well as members of the highest federal body, the Council may, according to the Constitution, delegate some of its powers while it is not in session to the President and the Council of Ministers jointly. However:

The ratification of international treaties and agreements, enforcement and lifting of martial law, declaration of war, and the appointment of the President and judges of the Supreme Council under no circumstances can be delegated. (Article 115)

An important aspect of the Supreme Council's structure is the fact that although each member emirate has a single vote, the votes are not themselves of equal significance. On substantive issues, such as those related to general policy, ratification of agreements, treaties and draft laws, appointment of the Prime Minister, declaration of war, or the imposition of martial law, a majority decision may be taken, but the representatives on the Council of Abu Dhabi and Dubai must be counted among the majority. The principle of a simple majority applies only to procedural matters.

The Supreme Council is, therefore, the supreme authority of the state holding the ultimate strings of executive and legislative powers, whether exclusively or in nominal partnership with other federal organs. The fact that it is composed of the rulers of the emirates, or their delegated representatives, adds to its powers, since it was the rulers (or their predecessors) who agreed voluntarily to establish the state. The Council, therefore, reflects the independent status of each emirate, while each member derives his legitimacy from his status as a ruler rather than from being a Council member.

Constitutionally, the Supreme Council is a form of collective leadership. The special powers allocated to the rulers of Abu Dhabi and Dubai give them additional weight in the Council, and hence in the federation as a whole, a recognition of the fact that they are the two largest emirates in terms of population, area and resources. This represents a force for a consensus among Council members, since Abu Dhabi and Dubai can determine whether or not a decision is taken on non-procedural matters.

The President

The President and Vice-President are elected by the Supreme Council for a term of five years, which may be renewed, under the terms of Articles 51 and 52 of the Provisional Constitution. In the absence of the President, the Vice-President assumes his responsibilities. The President is accorded a wide range of legislative and executive powers under the terms of the Constitution, that can be divided into three categories:

• Powers derived from his position as President, discharged by him alone.
• Powers exercised either through the Supreme Council or through the Council of Ministers.
• Powers exercised through the Council of Ministers.

As chief executive of the state, the President also enjoys other powers that include, inter alia, the right to convene and preside over meetings of the Supreme Council. He may also, if the need arises, call a joint meeting of the Supreme Council and the Council of Ministers in his capacity as Commander-in-Chief of the Armed Forces. The stipulation in the Constitution that the President represents the Union externally and internally provides him with real authority in the direction of foreign policy.

The President is also entrusted with signing laws, decrees and decisions sanctioned by the Supreme Council and with supervising implementation through the Council of Ministers, under the terms of Article 54, clause 4.8. Presidential powers include the ratification of treaties and international agreements after approval by both the Supreme Council and the Council of Ministers (Article 47, clause 4, 96, 115, 140, 146) and the declaration of defensive war and of martial law. The President also has the power to nominate the Prime Minister, accept his resignation and terminate his appointment and to appoint the President and members of the Federal Supreme Court, although the latter two must be approved by the Supreme Council.

Under that category of power exercised through the Council of Ministers, the President is responsible for supervising the execution of all federal laws, decrees and decisions, through the Council of Ministers as a whole, and through its members (Article 60). He also appoints all senior officials, both military and civilian, after such appointments are approved by the Council of Ministers.

The President has additional significant powers exercised together with the Supreme Council and the Council of Ministers. He may overrule the rejection by the Federal National Council of draft legislation, or may delete any amendments introduced into such legislation, and may then promulgate it after its ratification by the Supreme Council (Article 110, clause 3 A).

Together with the Council of Ministers, the President also has the power, should the need arise between meetings of the Supreme Council:

to promulgate the necessary laws in the form of decrees which shall have the force of law. Such decree-laws must be referred to the Supreme Council within a week. If they are approved, they shall have the force of law, and the Federal National Council shall be notified at its next meeting. (Article 113)

Legislative powers of the President also include the authority to promulgate decrees, together with the Council of Ministers, provided that these shall not pertain to ratification of international agreements or treaties, or to declaration or lifting of martial law, or to declaration of a defensive war, or to appointment of the President and judges of the Supreme Court (Article 115).

The Council of Ministers

The Constitution describes the Council of Ministers as 'The Executive authority of the Union,' and states that it is responsible, under the control of the President and the Supreme Council, 'for carrying out all the internal and external affairs entrusted to the Union' (Article 60).

The Council of Ministers is, in particular, charged with the following functions:

- Following up the implementation of the general policy of the Union, both internally and externally.
- Initiating draft federal laws, and submitting them to the Federal National Council prior to submission to the President and the Supreme Council for ratification and promulgation.
- Issuing regulations necessary for the implementation of federal legislation.
- Supervising implementation of Union laws, decrees, decisions and regulations by all concerned authorities whether in the Union as a whole, or in the individual emirates (Article 60, clauses 1, 2, 5, 6).

It is not, however, entrusted with the task of formulating the general policy of the federation, but only with the responsibility of following up the implementation of policy laid down by the Supreme Council.

Ministers are officially nominated by the Prime Minister. In practice, an unofficial quota distributes the number of portfolios, and the portfolios themselves, among the individual emirates, rendering the Ministers dependent, partially, upon the ruler who nominates them.

The Federal National Council

The Federal National Council is essentially consultative, although it is a legislative organ in terms of forms and procedures. It comprises 40 members, distributed according to a fixed pattern. Abu Dhabi and Dubai have eight seats each, Sharjah and Ras al-Khaimah have six seats each, and Ajman, Fujairah and Umm al-Qaiwain have four seats each (Article 68). Members from each emirate are chosen by their ruler who is free under the terms of the Constitution to choose how to select them and to renew their term, which lasts for two years. Since the inception of the UAE, members have been nominated. However, Article 77 of the Constitution states that a member of the FNC represents the people of the federation as a whole, and not those of his emirate.

The FNC has no ability to propose legislation, this falling within the jurisdiction of the Council of Ministers (Articles 60 and 100). It may only produce recommendations and observations on draft legislation referred to it by the Council of Ministers. The FNC may, however, discuss the draft legislation, and approve, amend or reject it before the Council of Ministers presents it to the President and the Supreme Council. If amendments are suggested by the Federal National Council, the draft legislation, as amended, may be referred back to the FNC by the President. If the Federal National Council continues to uphold such amendments, contrary to the wishes of the Supreme Council, the President may promulgate the legislation after it has been ratified by the Supreme Council (Article 92).

The Federal National Council is empowered to 'discuss any general subject pertaining to the affairs of the Union, unless the Council of Ministers informs the FNC that such discussion is contrary to the highest interests of the Union' (Article 92). The Federal National Council may question Ministers or the Prime Minister on matters within their jurisdiction (Article 93). It may not, however, call for a vote of confidence either in the Council of Ministers as a whole, or in any of its members, since they, individually and collectively, are responsible to the President and the Supreme Council (Article 64).

The Federal judiciary

A further component of the federal system is the judiciary, of which the highest authority is the Supreme Court, which is entrusted with the following functions:

- It may adjudicate in disputes between member emirates, or between one or more emirates and the Federal Government, 'whenever such disputes are submitted to the Court upon the request of any of the interested parties' (Article 99, clause 1).
- It has the power to examine the constitutionality of federal laws, if contested by any emirate, and also the constitutionality of any legislation promulgated by one of the emirates.
- It may interpret the provisions of the Constitution upon request from the federal or an emirate Government.

The Court's interpretations or judgements are final and are binding upon all parties (Article 99).

Relationship between the legislature and the executive

The Constitution clearly favours the executive rather than the legislature.

The executive, in the persons of the President and other individual members of the Supreme Council, appoint the members of the legislature, the Federal National Council, while the President has the power both to postpone its meetings and to dissolve it. Either the President or the Council of Ministers may initiate legislation, and may veto any amendments put forward by the FNC. Furthermore, under Article 110, clause 4, the Constitution gives the executive power to issue legislation when the FNC is not in session, provided the FNC is notified when next in session. When the Supreme Council is in recess, the Constitution gives the President and the Council of Ministers the authority jointly to issue federal decrees equivalent to federal law, whenever urgent need arises. Thus power ultimately resides with the executive and the legislature participates in decision making only in a consultative capacity.

The Basic Features of the Federation

The formation of the UAE represented a voluntary cession of powers by the rulers of the individual emirates to the new state. This decision was clearly spelt out in the Provisional Constitution, which stated, inter alia, their 'desire to establish an independent and sovereign federal state'. Article 1 of the Constitution depicted the United Arab Emirates as a 'federal state'. Article 6 emphasized that 'the people of the Federation are one people' and they therefore enjoy, according to Article 8, 'one nationality'. To underline the supremacy of the new state over the emirates, the Constitution granted to the federation exclusive jurisdiction over foreign affairs and the declaration of war, as explained above.

The five federal bodies, the Supreme Council of Rulers, the office of the President, the Cabinet, the Federal National Council and the Federal Judiciary, began operating before mature local authorities had been created. They had, furthermore, the constitutional power, under Articles 60 and 125 of the Constitution, to implement policies, and to exercise jurisdiction directly, without any interference from a local authority.

Paragraph 1 of Article 60 allotted to the Cabinet 'the duty of following up the implementation of the general policy of the federation, both internally and externally'. Paragraph 6 of the same Article stipulates that the Council of Ministers may 'supervise the implementation of the laws, decrees, regulations, and decisions through all relevant parties in the Federation of the Emirates'.

Article 125 commits the governments of each emirate to take all necessary measures 'to ensure the implementation of the laws promulgated by the federation and the international treaties and agreements it concludes, and to issue the necessary local laws, regulations, decisions, and orders to put this into effect'. The same article bestows on the federal bodies 'the power to supervise the implementation by the local Governments of the federal laws, decisions, international agreements and treaties, and the federal justice verdicts'. The administrative and judicial authorities in the individual emirates are also called upon 'to offer all possible assistance to the Federal authority in this respect'.

While the Constitution emphasizes the individual entity of each member emirate, making the Supreme Council more of a body for the emirates and their rulers than for the people of the federation, at another level it clearly lays down in Article 151 its supremacy, and that of any federal law, decree or decision over those promulgated by individual emirates. Article 99 also gives additional weight to federal legislation, stipulating that the Supreme Court may examine: 'the constitutionality of legislations promulgated by one of the Emirates, if they are challenged by one of the Emirates on the grounds of violation of the Constitution of the Union or the Union laws'. However, the Constitution imposes no restriction upon any emirate that may wish to withdraw from the federation.

Although the Constitution enumerates the legislative and executive powers of the federation, it also stipulates that all residual powers fall within the jurisdiction of the individual emirates, thus recognizing their status with relation to the federal institutions. The separation of powers between the federation and its constituent emirates is, thus, of considerable importance. While Article 2 of the Constitution stipulates that: 'the Union shall exercise sovereignty in matters assigned to it, in accordance with this Constitution, over all territory and territorial waters laying within the international boundaries of the individual Emirates', Article 3 emphasizes that: 'the member Emirates shall exercise sovereignty over their own territories and territorial waters in all matters which are not within the jurisdiction of the Union as assigned in this Constitution'.

The Manifestations of Unity in the Constitution

The Constitution charges federal authorities with virtually all the functions of a unitary state. The Federal Government has thereby been given exclusive legislative and executive jurisdiction in foreign affairs, along with a virtual monopoly over the conclusion of treaties and implementation of international agreements.

Two restrictions with relation to foreign affairs were specified. The first, in Article 124, said that:

Before the conclusion of any treaty or international agreement which may affect the states of any of the Emirates, the competent Union authorities shall consult this Emirate in advance. In the event of a dispute, the matter shall be referred to the Supreme Court for a ruling.

The second, in Article 123, stipulates that individual emirates:

may conclude limited agreements of a local and administrative nature with the neighbouring states or regions, save that such agreements must not be inconsistent with the interests of the Union, or with Union Laws, and provided that the Supreme Council of the Union is informed in advance. If the Council objects to the conclusion of such agreements, it shall be obligatory to suspend the matter until the Union Court has ruled on that objection as early as possible.

Such exceptions do not in themselves bestow an autonomous identity upon the emirates at an international level, since the prerogatives specified are also restricted in several ways, while they are within the rules of the Constitution, and are not absolute rights as with wholly sovereign states.

Internally, the federation, according to the Constitution, was also to have exclusive legislative and executive powers over a wide range of functions. Article 120 lists 19 subjects for which the federal authorities have the sole responsibility, both in legislation and in implementation of laws, regulations and orders pertaining to these matters. Some are directly linked to the nature of the federation, while others represent a surrendering of authority by individual emirates.

The first category includes matters related to the federal armed forces and to defence and security of the federation against all threats, internal or external. The list also includes the following: order in the federal capital (when built); federal employees and the judiciary; federal finances, taxes, royalties and general loans; construction and maintenance of roads deemed to be major highways; federal property; the national census, nationality and immigration; and federal information.

The second category of powers assigned to the federation includes matters that touch upon, and are related to, the sovereignty of each emirate, but which have been transferred by the rulers to the federal authorities. Two types of powers are incorporated in this category. The first gives federal authorities exclusive legislative jurisdiction over communications, social services and economic matters. The second type allows the sharing of authority between federal and local authorities, whereby the first legislates, and the second uses, the powers under such legislation to issue the necessary regulations to ensure implementation. The areas covered are enumerated in Article 121 of the Constitution, and include labour relations and social security; estates ownership and expropriation for public interests; extradition of criminals; banks; insurance; the protection of animal and agricultural resources; major legislation; courts; protection of copyrights; publications; importation of weapons and ammunition unless for the use of the armed and security forces of any emirate; other aviation matters not within the domain of the Union's executive prerogatives; defining territorial waters and regulating navigation.

The third major formal aspect of unity is the existence of a federal executive authority, whose jurisdiction covers all emirates. This authority implements general policy of the federation, executes federal laws and administers public utilities and services.

Even where individual emirates are assigned power to implement certain matters (Article 121), the Council of Ministers is given authority to supervise implementation of federal laws, whether undertaken by federal or by local authorities.

The Constitution also incorporates other matters within the jurisdiction of the federation. These include the declaration of martial law (Article 146), the elimination of taxes and internal tariffs (Article 11), allocations from the federal budget to finance and implement projects in individual emirates (Article 132), the formation of unified armed forces, and the right to form federal security forces (Article 138).

The existence of a federal judicial authority, including the Federal Supreme Court, is a further feature of the unifying powers incorporated in the Constitution. Article 125 obliges individual member emirates to implement the rulings of the federal courts.

The Jurisdiction of the Individual Emirates

The Constitution states that 'all matters not specifically stipulated as falling within federal jurisdiction are to be considered within the domain of the member Emirates' (Article 116). Thus while the rulers of the emirates decided voluntarily to form a federation, and to surrender to it some of their sovereign prerogatives, they retained, at the same time, aspects of sovereignty on an emirate level. In effect, they kept authority sufficient to ensure that a ruler continues to be the absolute authority within his emirate, and that the emirate itself maintains the essential ingredients of government. The Constitution states in Article 3 that 'member Emirates shall exercise sovereignty over their own territories and territorial waters in all matters that are not within the jurisdiction of the Union'. Residual sovereignty is further identified in Article 10, which states that the federation would seek to safeguard its own independence, sovereignty, security and stability, while taking into account the fact that each emirate should respect the sovereignty of the others in their own internal affairs, within the framework of the Constitution.

In foreign affairs, sovereignty of the individual emirates is more strictly limited. They may, according to Article 123, make 'limited agreements of a purely local administrative nature' with neighbouring states, within the confines of the interests and laws of the federation, provided that the Supreme Council is given prior notice. The second clause of the article, however, gives each emirate the right 'to retain their membership in the Organization of Petroleum Exporting Countries, OPEC, and the Organization of Arab Petroleum Exporting Countries, OAPEC, or to join them,' whereby such emirates would have (albeit limited) independent international personae. No emirates have, in fact, chosen to exercise this option. The same article also recognized 'treaties or agreements concluded by member emirates with states or international organizations' without specifying any such agreements or their nature. At the same time, Article 124 required federal authorities to consult in advance with any individual emirate 'prior to the conclusion of any international agreement or treaty that might affect the status of such Emirate'. The article thus underlines the right of the member emirates at least to be consulted.

Internally, the individual emirates have retained more authority. They, and their rulers, are the ultimate sources of authority, while federal bodies enjoy specific powers granted by these sources.

At the time that the rulers of the emirates created the federation, in July 1971, they did not enjoy full political independence, then still being in treaty relations with the United Kingdom. Thus the powers granted to the federal bodies did not, in effect, diminish the powers they were accustomed to practise and they preserved the bulk of the functions they considered essential to maintain their own authority. Furthermore, the voluntary surrender of powers, or of part of their powers, by the rulers did not preclude their ability, collectively or individually, at any time, to reverse their previous decision.

The traditional status of each ruler within his emirate gave him the power to block the local implementation of any federal law or decision considered to be unacceptable, or incompatible with his own interests. Each emirate may legislate on affairs within its own borders, provided that such legislation is not in contradiction with the Constitution. Each emirate also specifically has the power to undertake the execution of federal law dealing with local matters.

Article 104 of the Constitution gives each emirate the authority to establish or maintain its own judicial organs, to deal with matters outside the jurisdiction of the federal judicial authorities. In addition, the Constitution also spells out other rights for member emirates that underline their retention of powers, the most important of which are related to the ownership of natural resources and the right to establish special armed forces. Article 23 states 'the natural resources and wealth in each emirate shall be considered to be the public property of the emirate,' and not the federation. Article 142 adds that the member emirates also 'shall have the right to set up local armed forces ready and equipped to join the defence machinery of the Union, to defend the Union against any armed aggression if the need arises'.

Other indications of the independence of the member emirates can be found in Articles 5 and 118 of the Constitution. Article 5 gives them the right to retain their own flags. Article 118 stipulates that:

two or more Emirates may, after obtaining the approval of the Supreme Council, agglomerate in a political or administrative unit, or unify all or part of their public services or establish a single or joint administration to run any such service.

The Constitution lacks clarity on the funds to be made available for financing of the federal budget. Article 127 says that member emirates 'shall contribute a specified proportion of their annual revenues to cover the annual general budget expenditure of the Union'. The Constitution does not, however, settle jurisdiction over the collection of, or contribution of, such funds, leaving the financing of the federal budget to be decided on the basis of agreement between all or a number of member emirates. Thus the ability of federal authorities to perform the tasks allocated to them is affected by the budget contributions of individual emirates.

In summary, the power structure in the UAE favours the member emirates rather than the federal authorities, for the following reasons. Firstly, the Constitution, while enumerating the matters within the jurisdiction of the federation itself, left those of the member emirates undefined, covering all matters not specifically assigned to the federal authorities. The emirates are the source of authority, and the federation merely a means for the devolution of part of the authority.

Secondly, the legislative jurisdiction of federal authorities is restricted, in matters that are not federal by nature, to a limited number of subjects, such as communications, education, health, currency and electricity supply. Moreover, the legislative prerogatives bestowed on the federal authorities in accordance with Article 121 of the Constitution are not, in themselves, exclusive. Article 149 gives the member emirates a share of such authority:

As an exception to the provisions of Article 121 of this Constitution, the Emirate may promulgate legislation necessary for the regulation of the matters set out in the said Article, without violation of Article 151 of this Constitution.

Article 149, therefore, conflicts with Article 121, since it permits individual emirates to promulgate legislation even on matters specifically allocated to the federation. The reservation thus spelt out at the end of Article 149 can, however, operate as a balancing factor if the federal authorities decide to challenge any moves by individual emirates that they consider contrary to the provisions of federal laws and decisions. There is a clear duplication of authority in some areas of powers allocated to the federation and to the emirates. In the words of one jurist:

Article 120 gives the Federation the exclusive legislative and executive authority on foreign affairs, while Article 121 gives it sole legislative jurisdiction, without executive powers, on the definition of territorial waters and on navigation on the high seas.

Furthermore, within the federation all legislative powers reside ultimately in the Supreme Council and, hence, the rulers. No federal legislation can be promulgated without approval by at least five of the seven rulers, including those of Abu Dhabi and Dubai. As a result, the local authorities of the emirates, and considerations related to them, are predominant in the sphere of legislation

Thirdly, executive authority also resides ultimately in the Supreme Council. In addition, the executive powers of federal institutions are restricted to particular and specified matters. The local authorities are entrusted not only with the execution of their own laws and regulations, but also with that of laws and regulations where jurisdiction is shared with the federal authorities, although the latter retain the formal right of supervision. The manner in which the Constitution refers to financing of the federal budget adds to the limitations on the extent of federal executive authority. No such limitations in financial affairs are placed upon individual emirates.

Fourthly, the judicial system laid down in the Constitution neither changes nor limits the status of local emirate judicial authorities. It simply adds a new level of courts, headed by the Supreme Court, which has specific functions. It also permits each emirate, if it so chooses, to merge its own system with the federal system.

Conclusion

Looking back 25 years, the federation is a fact of life. The political elite in the UAE has taken its time to ponder on the various approaches to form the federation. The fact that the Constitution was ratified and declared permanent in May 1996 means that the temporary nature of the situation has been removed.

There is still room for amendment in the Constitution and a committee formed by the Supreme Council is currently working on a report to be submitted by May 1997. It is widely expected that this committee will come out with proposals which will reinforce the federation, eliminating some of the grey areas in the division of powers between the federal and the local authority towards increasing the powers of the federal agencies and strengthening the Federal National Council by giving it a greater share in the political process, especially in terms of the right to propose laws.

The general feeling is that the new Constitution will provide the legal translation of the practices which have been taking place during the course of the past 25 years. If we look back 25 years, the actual experience has shown that certain steps have been taken to increase the jurisdiction of some of the federal agencies, such as Dubai putting its Courts under the umbrella of the federal judicial system. At the same time, there has been a tendency to create some new local departments, for example Sharjah Television and Ajman Television. These are not in conflict with the Constitution: rather, they are in total conformity and are part of the natural growth of bureaucracy, stemming from a real need. It should be noted that all television stations operate within the framework of the Constitution and the resolution taken by the Supreme Council in 1976, and are under the political supervision of the federal Ministry of Information and Culture and the federal laws and regulations governing media in the country.

It is healthy to have continuous dialogue and discussions. Even in the late 1970s, when the discussions led at certain points to critical moments, the dynamics of the political process was able to resolve the various contradictory views and reach a mutually agreeable settlement.

Bibliography

Ali Hamaidain, *Lavenir Politique des Principantes Petrolieres du Golfe Persique*, these, Paris (1967).
Al Rayyes, R.N. *The Conflict of Oasis and Oil: The Problems of Arabian Gulf, 1968-1971*, (Arabic), Beirut, Al-Nahar Press Services, (1973).
Al-Azmineh Al Arabiyyah.
Anthony, J.K. *Arab States of the Lower Gulf: People, Politics, Petroleum,* Washington D.C., Middle East Institute (1975).
Fenelon, K.G. *The United Arab Emirates; An Economic and Social Survey*, London, Longman (1973).
Hawley, D.*The Trucial States,* London, George Allen & Unwin (1971).
Heard-Bey, F. *From Trucial States to United Arab Emirates : A Society in Transition*, London, Longman, (1984).

Formation and Evolution of The Federation and its Institutions

Malcolm C. Peck*

Introduction

The Trucial States, which in 1971 became the Federation of the United Arab Emirates, did not struggle for complete independence nor even seek it; it was thrust upon them. When the British Government made the decision to withdraw protection from these states it was done without warning, compelled by the then ruling Labour Party's 1968 decision to relinquish the United Kingdom's security responsibilities east of Suez. Thus the rulers of these states, who had grown comfortable in their reliance on British political, diplomatic, and military power in an uncertain and dangerous part of the world, were faced for the first time with the prospect of determining and securing their own destinies. Because this eventuality had not been seriously contemplated and because the British Government had taken only a slight interest in the affairs of these states apart from their strategic importance along the imperial route of communications to India, and then only recently, there had been little preparation for independence and its challenges.

The Confused Prologue to Federation

Despite a widespread perception that the United Arab Emirates and the other small Gulf Arab states are artificial creations of the British, the UAE in fact reflects in its political form and dynamics a deliberate lack of British involvement in the Trucial States' internal affairs until a late date, leaving tribal loyalties and structures largely unaffected. The effect of British intervention through the series of treaties implemented between 1820 and 1892 was to freeze the principal power relationships of tribal groupings. Thus, the Al Qawasim family and the Bani Yas tribal confederation which controlled what are now the northern emirates and the emirate of Abu Dhabi, respectively, were confirmed as the dominant elements within the Trucial States. The Bani Yas eventually gained the upper hand in their rivalry with the Al Qawasim, largely because the latter's naval power had been eclipsed by the British and because the Bani Yas were a broad, land-based confederation. What is

The author wishes to acknowledge the kindness of Dr John Duke Anthony and Dr F. Gregory Gause III who made helpful suggestions in the preparation of this chapter.

indisputable is that the initial British military intervention in the southern Gulf had the effect of altering the power relationship between the two rival groupings. More importantly, by dealing with the Trucial States as a unit, the British gave some sense of natural coherence to the grouping of the several sheikhdoms signatory to the 1820 treaty and later engagements. For a considerable period of time they were obliged to cooperate in various common, if limited, treaty obligations.

Nevertheless, it is fair to describe the fundamental British attitude towards the Trucial States as one of 'benign neglect,' at least until very late in the long period of British protection.[1] Only concern for control over oil exploration concessions, the development of imperial air routes, the exigencies of the Second World War, and the threats posed by the Soviet Union and Arab radicalism led to a significant upgrading of Britain's own political representation in the Trucial States and to some significant involvement in their social, economic, and political development. One manifestation of this was the creation of the Trucial States Council in 1952 which brought together the rulers of the seven sheikhdoms for periodic meetings (usually twice a year) to discuss issues of common interest.[2] This was done initially with the British Political Agent, the senior representative of the British Government in the Trucial States, presiding. Later the chairmanship passed from one ruler to another on a rotating basis. The principal benefit conferred by the council was to provide a systematic means of regular communication amongst the rulers for the first time. The Council and the Trucial States Development Office (which later carried out modest development projects) provided, during their brief existence, the basis for core institutions of the future independent union. Nevertheless, when the Labour Government reached its January 1968 decision to withdraw British protection from the Trucial States, for domestic economic reasons having nothing to do with the sheikhdoms themselves, there had been little tutelary preparation for the new phase.

The time period allotted to the rulers of the Trucial States to prepare for the withdrawal of protection and federation was brief, and was imposed with little, if any, warning. Moreover, a lengthy list of other negative factors seemed to militate against the success of whatever state or states might emerge when British withdrawal was effected. A consideration of these factors and how they were overcome is instructive in seeking an understanding both of how the UAE was born and why it has endured.[3] It is true that in 1971 the UAE adapted major governmental institutions from the Trucial States Council (the model for the Supreme Council of Rulers), the Trucial States Development Council (from which the Abu Dhabi Fund for Economic Development evolved), and the Trucial Oman Scouts (core of the federal armed forces). Moreover, one of the seven sheikhdoms, Dubai, had experienced a 'reform movement' as early as 1938, when members of the merchant oligarchy and a branch of the Al Maktoum opposed to the ruler, forced on him administrative reforms, some of which endured.[4] Nevertheless, the whole governing structure of the new federal state had to be devised and constructed in a short time with few relevant precedents and traditions to draw upon.

Another essential item of independent statehood was largely lacking: settled borders. The very concept of exact territorial borders was alien to a tribal society where a sheikh's dominion over people and control over various resources such as water and pasturage, as well as the extent of a tribe's *dar* or range, which waxed and waned according to circumstances, were what mattered. It was not until petroleum exploration concessions were let that the need for precise territorial definitions of authority was seriously felt. The British made some efforts to promote agreements on boundary lines, notably those of the redoubtable Julian Walker whose careful research on relevant factors in the Trucial States helped obtain agreement to a significant amount of boundary-drawing. Nevertheless, when the decision to withdraw from the Gulf was made, all the Gulf Arab states had extensive borders in dispute. This was true of Bahrain and Qatar, which have engaged in territorial disputes since the latter threw off Al Khalifa rule in the nineteenth century, and of the Trucial States where boundary definition was only partial and deep-seated rivalries absorbed the individual sheikhdoms. These included, most significantly, the border dispute between Abu Dhabi and Dubai which had erupted into warfare in 1948, and the several border disputes of Sharjah and its neighbours. The Abu Dhabi - Dubai rivalry was of particular importance, because those two states would dominate any federation among the Trucial States by virtue of their size and wealth. The success of that federation would presuppose their ability to work together.

A further, critical uncertainty was the fundamental question of which states would come together as a federation. This was generally posed as a matter of whether it would be the seven Trucial States plus Bahrain and Qatar, or the former grouping alone. The uncertainty, however, extended to the question of whether all of the seven would unite. This unsettled issue of who would be in or out continued to vex the process of the establishment of the federation until the British withdrawal; in the case of one emirate, Ras al-Khaimah, it carried even beyond that point.

Yet another deeply troubling issue which these states faced on the eve of their independence was the claims of powerful neighbours to some or all of their territory. Announcement of the British intention to withdraw from the Gulf brought renewed claims from the Shah's Government of Iran to the island of Bahrain. Iran also claimed the lower Gulf islands of Abu Musa and the Tunbs, recognized by the British as belonging to two of the Trucial States, Sharjah and Ras al-Khaimah, respectively. The other major claimant was Saudi Arabia which had long asserted claims to a large part of Abu Dhabi's territory and saw in British withdrawal an opportunity to redress what it considered an injustice perpetrated and sustained by the British.

Iran and Saudi Arabia presented conventional threats of territorial claims. The new state of South Yemen had emerged in 1967, when its leaders overthrew the Federation of South Arabia which the British had created on the eve of their withdrawal from Aden Colony and its hinterland. This state represented a new and different kind of threat when, in 1969, it came under radical Marxist leadership. South Yemen was a radical revolutionary state whose goal was the overthrow of all the traditional regimes in the region. During the time established for British withdrawal from the Gulf, South Yemen had begun actively to assist a radical leftist organization already in active rebellion against the Sultan's Government in Oman. Its name, Popular Front for the Liberation of Oman and the Arab Gulf (in other permutations the organization was known as Popular Front for the Liberation of the Occupied Arab Gulf and Popular Front for the Liberation of Oman), suggested clearly its intent. While the circum-stances of pre-independence Aden and the Gulf sheikhdoms were very different in many respects, there was widespread fear that something like what had occurred in South Arabia could occur in the Gulf.

Finally, the rapid evolution towards federation was complicated, if not jeopardized, by British vacillation after the decision to withdraw from the Gulf had been taken and announced. Indeed, there was considerable uncertainty in the Labour Government of Harold Wilson even before the decision was taken. By May 1967 the Government was seriously considering withdrawal from the Gulf; on 18 November 1967 the devaluation of the British pound seemed to confirm that policy; yet in the same month, just two months before Wilson announced withdrawal, the Foreign Office issued an assurance that the British military presence would be maintained in the Gulf region. Following the 16 January 1968 announcement, withdrawal remained the policy until it was thrown in doubt by the election victory in June 1970 of the Conservatives. The Government of Edward Heath temporized until 1 March 1971, nine months short of the date projected for withdrawal, before finally affirming that policy.[5]

The factors, then, that militated against the emergence of a successful federation of seven or nine Gulf Arab states were considerable. Informed observers were doubtful of the chances of any such grouping.[6] Interestingly and perhaps decisively, several of these seemingly negative factors had the paradoxical effect of working to the advantage of the future federation.

Britain's unexpected decision to withdraw from the Gulf was a rude shock to rulers who had contemplated development of their oil wealth under the continuing aegis of British-assured security. But it had the effect of concentrating their attention on the creation of a federation more forcefully than if they had enjoyed a more leisurely approach to those issues. The anomaly of British-protected states in the Middle East would almost certainly have come to an end soon, particularly after the termination of Kuwait's similar protected status in 1961 and the recent withdrawal from Aden and South Arabia. Moreover, further insulation from the challenges of an unprotected existence would arguably have made the eventual transition more complicated and difficult.

In the minds of many observers, a federation of nine was preferable to one of seven, since all the states involved were mini-states with tiny populations and few significant natural resources other than oil and gas. Indeed, Kuwait and Saudi Arabia urged this fully inclusive approach to federation. That it failed, however, was almost certainly an advantage for the Trucial States. The lower Gulf states had reason to fear that Bahrain would try to dominate such a federation, drawing on its much more advanced state administration, greater political sophistication, and a population then larger than that of the other states of the lower Gulf. Further, such a federation would have been riven by the long-standing enmity of Bahrain and Qatar, especially as those two states were closely aligned with Abu Dhabi and Dubai, respectively. The natural ties and habits of community were generally stronger amongst and between the seven Trucial States than in the larger grouping, reinforcing the case for the smaller federation on the basis of geographic contiguity. (Bahrain as an island is physically separated from all its neighbours, though attached now to Saudi Arabia by a causeway. Abu Dhabi's territory adjoined that of Qatar but their population centres were separated by several hundred miles of roadless desert and Saudi Arabia had already strongly indicated its determination to alter its borders with Abu Dhabi to include establishing a Saudi corridor to the Gulf south and east of the Qatari peninsula, an arrangement which was in fact negotiated in 1974.)

At the same time, the meetings of rulers and other representatives from Bahrain and Qatar as well as from the Trucial States between 1968 and 1970 to discuss the possibility of federation were useful in fully exploring the issues that had to be faced. These meetings were, in effect, a kind of intense, practical seminar whose utility was enhanced by the inclusion of the additional interlocutors. Moreover, as one astute scholar has observed, the UAE reaped a very specific and enduring benefit from this exercise. In adopting, with suitable modifications, the constitution which had been drawn up for the projected federation of nine, it gained for its own use a document which had been carefully crafted to accommodate the concerns and interests of all the states in the anticipated wider grouping. Thus the Constitution of the UAE was from the outset an effective source of flexibility and creative ambiguity in coping with the challenges of a federal union.[7]

The collapse of the Federation of South Arabia and the subsequent emergence of a radical leftist government in Aden, whose goal of overthrowing the Arabian Peninsula's traditional regimes seemed within reach as the rebellion which it was assisting gained ground in Oman, appeared to be a negative and distinctly threatening development affecting the birth of the UAE. In fact it served a highly useful purpose by offering a clear signal to the leaders of the new state that economic and social issues had to be seriously addressed to avoid the possibility of discontent and political radicalization in their own populations.

Sheikh Zayed bin Sultan Al Nahyan, the driving force behind creation of the UAE, had become Ruler of Abu Dhabi in 1966. From the start Zayed was motivated by the conviction that it would be politically fatal not to use to its fullest advantage the rapidly growing wealth from oil production to promote the development of both Abu Dhabi and the poorer Trucial States. The escalating rebellion in neighbouring Oman, in large part a consequence of the ruler Sultan Said's parsimony and the leftward lurch of Marxist South Yemen, confirmed his belief that an improved life for the people of the area was important in securing their continuing support for traditional, conservative, hereditary government. In the years just after he had become Ruler of Abu Dhabi, Zayed provided the great bulk of the funds dispensed by the Trucial States Development Fund; after the establishment of the UAE and with the growth of oil revenues he continued to do so on an increased scale.

Thus, early on, Zayed established with the whole Trucial States population the kind of compact that the other Arabian Peninsula oil producers had reached with theirs, whereby rapid economic development and widespread sharing of the wealth would be exchanged for continued acceptance of hereditary, patriarchal rule without political challenge. In the months just before the UAE became independent, he created the 'Abu Dhabi Fund for Arab Economic Development', later called 'Abu Dhabi Development Fund' to provide aid to other Arab and, eventually, non-Arab countries. This helped to dampen some regional threats as when the UAE and Kuwait used foreign aid to encourage South Yemen to end its aggression against Oman and enter into negotiations which eventually led, in September 1982, to a border settlement and the establishment of diplomatic relations between those two states.

Movement towards creation of a federation among the Trucial States was also accelerated and reinforced by a pattern of various deficiencies among the seven which convinced them that none could go it alone. Ajman, Fujairah, Ras al-Khaimah and Umm al-Qaiwain all had tiny populations and lacked both significant hinterlands and wealth. Sharjah had prospects of moderate wealth but otherwise shared the deficiencies of the above. All these had divided territories, except for Umm al-Qaiwain, forming a confused patchwork of enclaves and exclaves, while all but Sharjah lacked the modern bureaucratic structures that would be required to manage successfully a modernizing state, unitary or federated. Dubai had considerable wealth, both from its long mercantile career and incipient oil production, and possessed a lean but efficient state administration. It too, however, lacked territorial depth, while Abu Dhabi possessed over 80 per cent of the territory and the lion's share of the hydrocarbon wealth, but had only recently begun to develop the administrative structure which a wealthy, independent state would require. Although Ras al-Khaimah briefly delayed joining the UAE, it never seriously contemplated existence outside the federation. In a dangerous neighbourhood all the Trucial States realized that if they did not remain together the chances were very high of their being toppled separately. Thus, whatever real differences and rivalries existed, the seven sheikhdoms were drawn together by the strong sense of a shared fate.

A further very great advantage was that the rulers of the seven states could conduct all their discussions and negotiations between 1968 and 1971 in comparative privacy and were able to take action on fundamental issues with virtually no reference to the great majority of their subjects. The process was elite-driven, quintessentially top-down. So long as the rulers maintained the support of their extended families, clans and tribes, they could act freely. Thus, it was possible for key decisions to be taken and implemented quickly without fear of domestic challenge. Had the rulers not been able to move towards federation in this way, it is hard to imagine that the process could have been completed successfully in the brief time allotted to them. This was particularly so as that interval (not quite four years) was further diminished by the lengthy false start towards a federation of nine and by the confusion resulting from the British Conservative Government's vacillation on the question of withdrawal.

Formation of the United Arab Emirates

What was undoubtedly of greatest importance in ensuring the UAE's birth and survival was Sheikh Zayed's commitment of his state's resources and his own leadership to the success of the enterprise. Like the Prussian-led German empire, which 100 years earlier Otto von Bismarck had brought into being, the UAE was built around a preponderant state whose leader had a forceful personality and considerable leadership skills. Despite Abu Dhabi's wealth and size, however, only intelligent and energetic exploitation of those assets could assure the birth and survival of the UAE.

It was Sheikh Zayed who began the process of moving towards a federation which would ensure the Trucial States' survival and security and when, at a late hour, the prospects for federation were in serious jeopardy it was he who rescued them. Following Harold Wilson's 16 January 1968 announcement of British withdrawal from east of Suez, including the Gulf, Zayed went almost immediately to Dubai to discuss with that state's ruler, Sheikh Rashid bin Saeed Al Maktoum, an appropriate reaction. On 18 February 1968 they concluded and announced agreement on a federation between them, urged the other five Trucial States to join, and invited Bahrain and Qatar to discuss the future of the region with them. When, three and a half years later, no federation had emerged with British withdrawal close at hand, Zayed again seized the nettle and engaged Rashid and the other Trucial States rulers in the decisive discussions which determined the essential nature of the UAE.

The last phase of the period leading up to the creation of the UAE began on 1 March 1971 when, following British envoy Sir William Luce's third mission to the Gulf to help determine the British course of action, the Conservative Government finally determined on the withdrawal of military forces from the Gulf by the end of December 1971. As Bahrain and Qatar subsequently moved towards independence on their own, Zayed felt the need to act with dispatch.

On 1 July 1971 he established Abu Dhabi's first cabinet as well as a consultative assembly to provide, with the help of advisers and civil servants from other Arab countries, an institutional structure for that state should it be compelled to stand by itself after British withdrawal. Zayed took this action because he feared that the go-it-alone course of Qatar, to which Dubai was closely aligned, might lead the latter to reconsider becoming part of a federation.[8] At the same time he hoped that by dramatically taking the initiative he could induce Dubai and the other Trucial States to unite with Abu Dhabi. Thus, at his urging, the seven rulers met in Dubai on 10 July in their capacity as members of the Trucial States Council to consider the issue of federation and, on 18 July, formation of the UAE was announced. To achieve a workable union, Zayed first had to come to terms with his powerful Trucial States rival, Sheikh Rashid.

Despite the dominant role of Zayed and Abu Dhabi, the parentage of the new federation was decidedly mixed, with the interaction of two contrasting personalities who represented very different constituencies and interests shaping the birth and development of the UAE. The rivalry was deep-seated, dating to the 1833 defection of the Al Bu Falasah subsection of the Bani Yas in Abu Dhabi to establish a separate sheikhdom in Dubai. The latter became a cosmopolitan, outward-looking mercantile city-state, while Abu Dhabi remained a traditional tribal federation. The personalities of the two rulers perfectly reflected the character of their sheikhdoms. Zayed was a forceful tribal leader who embodied the bedouin qualities of courage and magnanimity. He was strongly committed to a truly integrated union of the seven Trucial States and prepared to use his own state's resources generously to secure that end. Rashid was a merchant prince whose pragmatic vision embraced primarily his own state and its prosperity. He was disdainful of less sophisticated neighbours and chary of committing his own state's resources to a larger enterprise. But his careful calculations persuaded him of the practical necessity of creating a political federation with the other sheikhdoms when British protection was withdrawn.

In their negotiations, Rashid's shrewd bargaining skills and Zayed's readiness to be magnanimous to ensure the success of the new union led the latter to make numerous concessions to the former, almost to the point of bestowing political parity on Dubai. Despite their pronounced disparity in size, wealth, and military power, Zayed agreed that Dubai would share with Abu Dhabi the right of veto in the federation's most important governing body, the Supreme Council; and that any substantive issue decided by the Federal Government must have the support of Dubai as well as Abu Dhabi. Rashid insisted on an equal number of votes in the Federal National Council, the UAE's federal advisory body, and secured senior positions for his three sons in the Federal Government. He himself served as Vice-President. With these far-reaching concessions Zayed secured Rashid's commitment to support the federation, though not his support for Zayed's concept of a closely integrated union. For the rest of his life Rashid consistently supported the Federal Government's essential authority. He would not, however, yield more autonomy than was absolutely necessary.

The Constitution and the Institutions of the Federal Government

The Constitution adopted on 18 July 1971 for the UAE was, as earlier observed, an adaptation of the document drafted for the projected union of nine. Its hallmark was its provisional ambiguity, designed to gain the approval of states and rulers with differing views of the federation into which they were entering. (The Constitution was made permanent only in 1996.) This, in part, explains its length (151 articles) and the seeming contradiction between some of its stated principles and goals.

The language of the Constitution's preamble suggests that it is meant to be seen as a document charting an evolutionary course towards a new kind of government. Thus, it commits the union to progress 'towards a complete representative democratic rule' but precedes that with the observation that federal rule must be established 'in harmony with the Amirates' existing conditions and potential,' clearly indicating that traditional social and cultural norms would shape the new state's evolution. Another interesting juxtaposition of modern, secular values with traditional values occurs in the articles dealing with religion. Like the constitutions of most other Arab countries, Islam is recognized as the official religion of the union (Article 7). At the same time, the 'freedom to exercise religious worship shall be guaranteed... provided it does not disturb public peace or violate public morals' (Article 32), and discrimination between citizens or inequality before the law on the basis of religion is explicitly rejected (Article 25).

The Constitution combines both blueprints for Western, representative institutions and formulas for preserving political power as exercised by traditional, patriarchal, elites. Thus, the pattern of governmental authority that was established betrays a marked contrast of both provenance and stated goals. The Federal Supreme Council - sometimes referred to as the Supreme Council of the Union - represents the union's highest political authority and has both executive and legislative powers. It sets the general policy of the UAE, elects the president and vice-president, ratifies federal laws and international treaties, and prepares the federal budget. Each ruler has a single vote and procedural matters are determined by a simple majority vote, but substantive issues require the concurrence of both Abu Dhabi and Dubai, reflecting the formula worked out between Zayed and Rashid, thus giving veto power to each. This explicit apportionment of political power represents a departure from traditional norms which emphasize decision-making by consensus (*ijma'*).[9] At the same time, membership in the Supreme Council is established on the wholly traditional basis of leadership of the tribes or tribal federations that dominate each emirate, thus giving institutional form to paternalistic, authoritarian rule. The substantial role of the president also reflects something of the society's patriarchal norms. He convenes and presides over the Supreme Council's meetings, represents the UAE in its foreign relations, oversees the implementation of federal laws and decrees, can commute judicially imposed sentences, and must approve the execution of any death penalty. With the Supreme Council's approval he appoints the prime minister and, in consultation with the latter, appoints federal ministers. With the concurrence of the federal cabinet, or Council of Ministers, he appoints senior government officials.

The Council of Ministers also combines executive and legislative functions, but may be regarded as the real seat of legislative authority. Most laws are initiated in the council and it establishes regulations necessary for the implementation of federal laws. It also prepares the federal budget and supervises implementation of federal laws and decrees, Supreme Court decisions, and international treaties. Currently the Council of Ministers comprises 21 members, of whom 10 are from ruling families. The balance are chosen as much for their positions in the emirates' elites, typically from merchant families close to the rulers, as for their technical and professional abilities. Thus, in the Council of Ministers, the most important government institution in which the politics of balance and inclusion are played out, that process is effectively limited to the members of ruling families, close commoner allies, and a handful of technocrats.

The Federal National Council (FNC) in its formal structure appears to approximate most closely a federal legislature. In spite of the fact that the Constitution devotes no fewer than 26 articles to describing the structure, functions, and prerogatives of the council, its powers are only advisory and it has, therefore, little capacity to affect the political process. Although the Constitution grants the council the power to approve, amend, or reject draft laws (Article 89), it makes clear that the Supreme Council can ratify and the president issue a law regardless of the FNC's action (Article 110). The FNC has 40 members with its seats allotted according to a weighted formula which gives Abu Dhabi and Dubai eight each, Sharjah and Ras al-Khaimah six apiece, and the remaining emirates of Ajman, Fujairah and Umm al-Qaiwain four each. It meets for annual sessions of not less than six months and members serve two-year terms, indefinitely renewable. The FNC was viewed at its creation as a means for promoting a stronger sense of community at the federal level and, presumably to that end, leaves open the possibility of popular election of its members. In practice, however, because each ruler has continued to select trusted supporters from the various emirate elites, the body does not represent the people of the UAE in a meaningful way.[10] Its deliberations can produce thoughtful critiques of draft legislation and it can and does raise issues of broad public concern through the questioning of ministers. Yet, in its essential nature, the FNC resembles more closely a traditional consultative *diwan* or *majlis* than a modern representative body.

The Constitution establishes a federal judiciary whose highest authority is the Supreme Court (sometimes referred to as the Higher Federal Court) and which also includes Courts of First Instance. The Supreme Court, whose president and member judges are appointed by the UAE President with the approval of the Federal Supreme Council, can rule on the constitutionality of federal laws, interpret the provisions of the Constitution, deal with inter-emirate disputes or contentions between individual emirates and the Federal Government, and serves as the nation's final court of appeal. The Courts of First Instance have jurisdiction over administrative, commercial and civil disputes between individuals and the Federal Government, as well as criminal and civil cases occurring in the federal capital (Article 102). The way in which the federal judiciary is defined, as in the cases of the other institutions of the Federal Government, reflects an attempt to embody both modern, Western norms of justice in the UAE and those of traditional Arab-Islamic society. On the one hand the Constitution defines all citizens as equal before the law, explicitly forbidding discrimination on the basis of religion and social status (Article 25) and it establishes that those accused of breaking the law are to be considered innocent until proven guilty (Article 28). On the other hand all judicial matters not delegated to the federal courts are left to local judicial bodies in the individual emirates (Article 104). This means that local justice is dispensed under the close supervision of the local ruler in traditional fashion. Moreover, a recent decree has given authority in nearly all criminal cases to *shari'a* courts (Muslim religious courts) rather than to civil courts.[11] At the federal level, however, the judiciary is the one branch of government which, as one scholar has noted, really represents the ideal of an integrated state.[12]

The Federation Secured

After an accelerated gestation period and anxious birth, the UAE's federal authority faced several potentially serious challenges in its infancy. In February 1972 the Ruler of Sharjah, Sheikh Khalid bin Muhammad Al Qassimi, was assassinated by a cousin who had previously been removed by the British as ruler. The Federal Government intervened to thwart the coup attempt and installed as the new ruler Sheikh Sultan bin Muhammad, who had been UAE minister of education. This affirmed the primacy of federal authority over that of the Al Qassimi tribe which traditionally would have selected the new ruler. Later in the same year Sharjah and Fujairah clashed with loss of life over a small disputed parcel of territory. Once again the Federal Government successfully intervened to assert its authority and impose order.

These and other successful assertions of federal power, combined with the 1974 Abu Dhabi-Saudi Arabia border agreement and the crushing of the rebellion in Oman's Dhofar Province in 1975, had removed doubts about the UAE's ability to survive within the first few years of its existence. Moreover, in keeping with Sheikh Zayed's concern for making tangible benefits available to the federation's populations, the UAE launched major programmes of physical and social infrastructure. In a very short time, modern highways joined all the population centres of the country (at independence, Abu Dhabi Town and Dubai, separated by over 100 km of desert, were linked by dhow or four-wheel drive vehicles) and rapid construction of large scale housing projects and schools proceeded throughout the UAE. These were all visible and compelling evidence, most dramatic in the poorer emirates, of the benefits conferred by the Federal Government and helped to consolidate its legitimacy and support early on.

There remained, however, the question of whether the union would take the form of a centralized state, with the seven emirates closely integrated under the Federal Government, or would pursue a gradualist approach towards greater federal power with each emirate retaining its essential autonomy. Sheikh Zayed, as we have seen, embodied the former concept of the federal role and Sheikh Rashid the latter. While Rashid did not hesitate to support Zayed in the assertion of federal authority to thwart the 1972 coup attempt in Sharjah, he was, from the beginning, steadfast in opposing any significant enhancement of federal power or corresponding diminution in the exercise of emiral autonomy. The starkly opposed visions of the two leading political figures of the UAE on a fundamental issue of the nation's political structure and dynamics precipitated a series of what may be described as constitutional crises.

In 1976 Rashid and some other rulers, in opposition to Zayed, refused to accept a strengthening of the Federal Government and Zayed threatened not to serve another term as UAE President. He was induced to reconsider when general agreement was reached on unification of defence and security forces while the matter of adopting a permanent constitution (called for in the document itself after five years) was simply deferred. This compromise accord also left open the important issues of whether oil resources should be owned and immigration policy determined by the Federal Government. Full integration of the defence and security forces was not finally achieved for nearly 20 years. The 1976 crisis established a pattern whereby every five years the president would be continued in office and the Constitution would remain provisional while basic questions concerning federal and local powers were essentially deferred. It was in early 1979, however, that the most serious such crisis arose when, in part because of the threats to regional stability perceived in the Iranian revolution and the imminent Israeli-Egyptian treaty, the Federal National Council and the Council of Ministers urged the Supreme Council to adopt plans to make the UAE stronger and more cohesive.

Through the spring of 1979, the matter continued to be debated. After a series of meetings and deliberations, most of which were in public (in the press and in the streets through demonstrations), Rashid agreed to become Prime Minister (as well as Vice-President), implying greater support for federal authority but, again, with no meaningful movement towards the more integrated union that Zayed desired. The ongoing dispute between the unionists (*wahdawis*) and the federalists (*ittihadis*) will continue, rooted in the deliberately ambiguous compromises of the Constitution and not susceptible of obvious solution because of the veto power which Zayed felt compelled to yield to Dubai to win that emirate's adherence to the union. While the Constitution is flexible in its interpretation of federal and local powers, it is inflexible in terms of the process by which it can be amended.[13] A *modus vivendi* based on the adherence to the Constitution has prevailed since Sheikh Rashid assumed the role of the Prime Minister.

Although the rulers on the Supreme Council have not reached any consensus on the creation of a stronger union through amendment of the Constitution, there has been some strengthening of federal authority. Shortly after the creation of the UAE, greater consolidation of federal powers was achieved when Abu Dhabi merged its cabinet with that of the Federal Government and Sharjah and Fujairah combined key departments of their governments with the corresponding federal departments. In the area of external security, the 1976 agreement gave at least formal expression to a federal UAE defence force, though real progress towards the goal was slow. Further, there has been a diminution in the tendency of individual emirates to exploit their constitutional rights to pursue limited, independent foreign policies. No emirate has exercised its right to separate membership in the Organization of Petroleum Exporting Countries (OPEC) or, with the exception, briefly, of Dubai, the Organization of Arab Oil Exporting Countries (OAPEC) and Abu Dhabi has extended its OPEC membership to the whole federation. While Dubai and Sharjah caused some embarrassment to the Federal Government by following different courses of action towards Iran during the Iran-Iraq War, the experience of the Gulf War and the continuing intractability of the UAE dispute with Iran over Abu Musa and the Tunbs seems to have helped to forge a more unified position towards the region and its dangers. Finally, in the twenty-fifth anniversary year of the UAE, 1996, both the capital and the Constitution lost their provisional nature. The Constitution's call for the creation of a new capital midway between Abu Dhabi City and Dubai has yielded to practical reality, with Abu Dhabi now recognized as the permanent capital, and the Constitution at last ratified as a permanent document. This provides appropriate symbolism at the country's quarter century mark in its suggestion of the federation's permanence.

While the *wahdawi-ittihadi* debate remains unresolved, there is much to suggest that the UAE will endure as the one really successful example of political union in the Arab world. (The Yemen Arab Republic, or North Yemen, merged with the Peoples' Democratic Republic of Yemen, or South Yemen, in 1990, but was maintained only by the North's military defeat of the South's attempt to secede in 1994.) The extent of the UAE's oil wealth is such that a high standard of living can be sustained for a long time, acting as an effective emollient for any political disaffection. Despite Iranian occupation of the lower Gulf islands claimed by the UAE, the country now enjoys much greater regional security than it did during its first two decades of existence. Inter-emirate border disputes have been largely resolved and rivalries, particularly that of Abu Dhabi and Dubai, have acquired a friendly character and appear unlikely to provoke really major disputes.

Key to the federation's survival and stability has been the continued strength and vitality of tradition, combined with continuity in the institutions of government. The federal institutions created by the Constitution, despite their modern form, have operated in accordance with well established norms of traditional exercise of political authority. Both legislative and executive powers remain firmly in the hands of a hereditary elite whose legitimacy derives from effective family and tribal leadership, reinforced by the wealth at its disposal. Equally important, the system as it has evolved has preserved key traditional institutions themselves. Thus, by well-established custom, rulers and other members of ruling families hold *majlises* or councils where subjects are invited to present petitions or raise issues. This mechanism and the inspection tours that bring Zayed and other UAE leaders close to their subjects provide means of personal communications between ruled and rulers which, despite the rapid growth and urbanization of the population, remain effective.

Moreover, together with the gradual consolidation and strengthening of federal authority noted above, there has been a noteworthy development of local government. Abu Dhabi has retained and extended its own central governing authority, established before independence, the Executive Council, under Sheikh Khalifa bin Zayed, the Abu Dhabi Crown Prince. Under this council, an Eastern and Western Region operate to make government more manageable in the largest and most populous of the emirates, together with a Consultative Council, parallel to the Federal National Council, and appointed municipal governments in the two large cities of Abu Dhabi and Al-Ain. Roughly similar local governments, varying greatly in size and complexity with the size and wealth of the emirate in question, have been developed in each emirate. They deal with a range of local issues such as water and electricity supply and public works, as well as with external affairs, such as trade, in which the Constitution permits them significant independence. Paralleling this has been the development of municipal authorities in the other emirates, all of which, except Fujairah and Ras al-Khaimah, are overwhelmingly urban. With its two enclaves on the east (Gulf of Oman) coast, Sharjah has devolved considerable authority to the governing authorities of Khor Fakkan and Kalba.

Without question the most important factor in sustaining the UAE for 25 years and endowing it with its present strength and stability has been Sheikh Zayed's leadership, as notable for its longevity as for its effectiveness. From 1946 to 1966, as the representative in Al-Ain of his brother Shakhbut, Zayed displayed special talents for securing and maintaining the loyalty of the tribes and gained a reputation, especially in his management of the local irrigation systems, for dedicated stewardship of the state's resources and their utilization for the people's benefit. As Ruler of the whole emirate from 1966, Zayed combined these capabilities with the mastery of genealogical politics, the key to successful governance of a patriarchal state, by carefully distributing both incomes and positions of authority among the branches of the ruling Al Nahyan family. Within the fairly narrow confines of the traditional system he has practised the politics of inclusion, ensuring the support of the *ulema* or religious scholars who apply the *sharia*, as well as tribal elements and leading commoner families. Zayed naturally projects the bedouin qualities important to establishing legitimacy in the eyes of his followers. Thus he displays generosity in personal and official behaviour and, in stark contrast to the ruling family of neighbouring Saudi Arabia, evidences an almost austere lifestyle. A central factor in securing Zayed's legitimacy as Ruler of Abu Dhabi and the UAE is his solicitude for Islamic education and institutions and his own unostentatious but sincere Islamic piety. His view of Islam emphasizes a flexible pragmatism which contrasts with the strident, confrontational nature of views expressed elsewhere in the Arab world and has helped to prevent the development of Islamic extremism in the UAE.

What is perhaps most striking about Zayed is his ability to embody and help sustain a system of traditional social, cultural, and political values while intuitively understanding and effectively dealing with the modern world which has thrust itself upon Abu Dhabi and the UAE. But if his leadership credentials have to do with flexibility and broadmindedness, they derive equally from his ability and determination to champion the causes of those for whom he bears responsibility. He has established his credentials as a nationalist, first in defending and advancing the interests of Abu Dhabi then those of the UAE. Thus Zayed has made the Iranian actions against the islands of Abu Musa and the Tunbs, long claimed by Sharjah and Ras al-Khaimah, fully a UAE question. Indeed, at the international level he has acquired something of the character of an Arab elder statesman, especially through his efforts to mediate the Iran-Iraq war, but also with regard to South Yemen and Oman and North Africa as well. All this has added to his stature as a father figure enjoying great admiration and affection throughout the UAE. Seldom if ever has an individual been so identified with the birth and development of a new country.

For so long as Zayed remains President of the UAE the country's survival and stability seem assured. He is, however, nearly 80, though in good health, which gives some urgency to the matter of what may happen after his passing. This and related questions loom when one looks beyond the first quarter century of the UAE.

What Lies Ahead?

Twenty-five years on, one could offer a compelling argument that the UAE can continue indefinitely on a secure and stable course without changing the institutions of government as they are today. In an astonishingly brief time it has made the transition from one of the world's poorest states to one of the wealthiest, securing the benefits of that wealth to all its citizens. There is no appreciable discontent or call for change and the people enjoy a considerable degree of freedom, with none of the repression that is all too common elsewhere in the Middle East. A pragmatic balance has been struck in the authority wielded by federal and local institutions of government which might well be the envy of devolutionary Republicans in Washington, DC. A modern, or at least modernized, state has been established on a solid foundation of traditional values and habits of governance.

It is interesting, in this regard, to reflect that even before the UAE and its sister Gulf Arab states had emerged from British protection, the conventional wisdom among most scholars and other analysts had consigned them to an early demise as feeble anachronisms while the secular, military-based, Arab socialist regimes of the day were hailed as the models of the future. The traditional, tribal, patriarchal states have endured and prospered while the careers of the bold new experiments of the 1950s and 1960s have fared less well. Moreover, in part due to Zayed's astute foreign aid diplomacy, the region is far less threatening than before.

Indeed, with the defeat of Iraq in the Gulf War and the demise of the Soviet Union, the current regional and international environments are probably more favourable than at any time since the birth of the UAE. What might cloud this picture and suggest that the evolution of the federation's governing institutions is not or should not be considered complete?

The 1995 yearbook of the UAE proclaims that 'it is possible for the country to move forward with the mechanics of a modern administrative structure while, at the same time, ensuring that the best of the traditions of the past are maintained, adapted and preserved.'[14] It is difficult, however, to believe that such a neat dichotomy can be maintained indefinitely. The forces of modernization and change cannot be easily segregated and contained and will undoubtedly exercise progressively an impact on the political institutions of the country. Although, as noted above, there is no significant popular call for political change, a growing sentiment for democracy, or at least for increased political participation, may be found among the elites of the UAE and other Arab states, given voice by intellectuals, businessmen, and others.[15] The international arena, following the Gulf war of 1991 and the collapse of the Soviet Union together with the unchallenged global role of the United States, appeared to favour strongly the adoption of more democratic governments. Even if this impulse continues to wax and wane, it remains a force of consequence. Perhaps more important is that the educated elite of the UAE, which favours greater political participation, is growing.[16]

At the same time, there are, as many scholars have noted, significant obstacles to the introduction of democracy, not only in states with traditional, autocratic forms of government, but in the Arab world generally. In a country like the UAE, where most wealth has been generated through activities of the state, no strong middle class such as brought about the rise of democracy in the West has emerged. A civil society of associative linkages among citizens is only present in embryonic form. Even more fundamentally, it has been pointed out that democracy is not something which political leaders can bestow. It must emerge from a political culture and, in that regard, one is led to ponder that in an Islam-based society the source of legitimacy for political rule is God's command, not the accountability of rulers to the ruled.[17]

The dilemma, then, is how to manage an evolution from what one wag described as 'shu'ocracy' to democracy. Without attempting an answer, it may be suggested that it will be hard if not impossible to compensate for the loss of Zayed's leadership when he departs the scene unless strong federal government institutions, buttressed by wide popular support, are in place. Several kinds of domestic crises can be imagined, among them a pronounced decline in oil income, a challenge by one or several emirates to federal authority, or the impact of political turmoil in a neighbouring state. It may be wondered if the UAE could have weathered the 1972 coup attempt in Sharjah had not leaders of Zayed's and Rashid's stature been present to use their prestige in asserting federal authority. It could also be questioned whether the fallout from the 1987 coup attempt in Sharjah could have been contained without Zayed's dominating presence. Zayed's commanding personal authority was a key factor in seeing the country through a long period of menacing external threat.

With the selection of the president in the hands of the seven rulers, the process is really an exercise in traditional *shura* (consultation) and *ijma'* (consensus) among tribal leaders. When the leader (who has until now dominated the UAE and been the only real choice for president) has passed from the scene, there will be no obvious criteria, apart from Abu Dhabi's size and wealth, to determine the selection of his successor.

Zayed has been progressively relinquishing presidential duties to his Crown Prince, Sheikh Khalifa, particularly in the domestic sphere, so that he will have had a considerable apprenticeship before his expected assumption of the presidential mantle. Khalifa has been handling state affairs especially in the absence of the President and sharing in the decision-making inner circle in all matters of the state for almost two decades. He represented his father at the Arab summit in Cairo in June 1996, marking the first time since becoming UAE President in 1971 that Zayed had not attended an Arab summit.[18] Khalifa may prove to be a capable successor to his father as UAE President. What is certain is that however able he and subsequent leaders of the country may be, they cannot hope to enjoy anything like Zayed's stature. It has been the country's singular good fortune to have had as its principal architect and sole leader in its first 25 years of independence someone who could personify the state and serve as a father figure to all its people. In part, however, that has also contributed to the difficulty of creating or even seriously contemplating the creation of strong, popularly based political institutions for the future.

The era in the lower Gulf which produced and shaped Zayed has passed. His like will not be seen again in the UAE or elsewhere. In an uncertain future, without a dominant personality to embody the nation and speak for its people, the old autocratic, tribal order, whatever its virtues, is likely to find it increasingly difficult to cope with future challenges.

[1] This description is used in Peter J.Vine, et al., *Yearbook of the United Arab Emirates* 1995, London, Planet Publishing Ltd, (1995) p 23.

[2] British motivation in creating the council may have been a mix of highminded and more cynical impulses. For an instance of the latter interpretation, viewing the council as a scheme to consolidate British rule by reliance on political power indirectly wielded through the rulers, see A.O. Taryam, *The Establishment of the United Arab Emirates 1950-85,* London, Croom Helm (1987) p 16.

[3] Good narratives of the events analysed below can be found in Frauke Heard-Bey, *From Trucial States to United Arab Emirates: A Society in Transition,* London and New York, Longman (1982) pp 336-69; Ali Mohammed Khalifah, *The United Arab Emirates: Unity in Fragmentation,* Boulder, Colorado, Westview Press and London, Croom Helm (1979) pp 19-35; and A.O. Taryam, *op. cit.,* pp 64-196.

[4] On the reform movement in Dubai see Rosemarie Said Zahlan, *The Origins of the United Arab Emirates. A Political and Social History of the Trucial States,* London, The Macmillan Press Ltd (1978) pp 150-61.

[5] See Heard-Bey, *op. cit.,* pp 336-7 and 360.

[6] See for example David Holden, *Farewell to Arabia,* New York, Walker and Company (1966) p 159.

[7] See Heard-Bey, *op. cit.,* p 371.

[8] On this point see Heard-Bey *op. cit.,* p 362.

[9] Khalifa, *op. cit.,* pp 34-35.

[10] See Heard-Bey *op. cit.,* p 375 and Muhammad Saleh Al Musfir, *The United Arab Emirates: An Assessment of Federalism in a Developing Polity*, Ph.D dissertation submitted to the State University of New York at Binghamton (1984) p 112.

[11] Alfred B. Prados, with the assistance of Ross Kaplan, *United Arab Emirates: Background and U.S. Relations,* CRS Report for Congress, Washington, DC: The Library of Congress (19 June 1995) p 3.

[12] Al Musfir, *op. cit.,* p 134.

[13] Al Musfir, *op. cit.,* pp 104-5.

[14] Vine, et al., *op. cit.,* p 23.

[15] For a thoughtful commentary on this phenomenon, especially in the UAE, see Jamal Al Suweidi, 'Arab and Western Conception of Democracy,' in David Garnham and Mark Tessler (eds), *Democracy, War, and Peace in the Middle East,* Bloomington and Indianapolis: Indiana University Press (1995) pp 83-4.

[16] See *ibid.,* p 108 on the attitudes of students at the UAE National University at Al-Ain.

[17] See *ibid.,* pp 85 and 88.

[18] 'Sheikh Zayed Will Not Attend the Summit and He Designates the Heir Apparent to Represent the Emirates,' *Al-Hayat,* 18 June 1996.

Bibliography

Anthony, J.D.*The Arab States of the Lower Gulf: People, Politics, Petroleum,* Washington, DC, The Middle East Institute (1975).

Fenelon, K.G. *The United Arab Emirates: An Economic and Social Survey*, London, Longman (1973).

Gause, F. G. III *Oil Monarchies: Domestic and Security Challenges in the Arab Gulf States*, New York, Council on Foreign Relations Press (1994).

Holden, D.*Farewell to Arabia,* New York, Walker & Company (1966) p 159.

Hooglund, Eric and Toth Anthony 'United Arab Emirates,' in Helen Chapin Metz (ed), *Persian Gulf States: Country Studies*, Washington, DC Federal Research Division, Library of Congress (1994) pp 199-249.

Heard-Bey, Frauke *From Trucial States to United Arab Emirates: A Society in Transition*, London and New York, Longman (1982).

Ibrahim, S. E. 'Democratization in the Arab World,' in Augustus Richard Norton (ed), *Civil Society in the Middle East*, Leiden, New York, and Köln, E.J. Brill (1995).

Khalifa, A. M. *The United Arab Emirates: Unity in Fragmentation*, Boulder, Colorado, Westview Press and London, Croom Helm (1979).

Al Musfir, A. *The United Arab Emirates: An Assessment of Federalism in a Developing Polity*, PhD dissertation submitted to the State University of New York at Binghamton (1984).

Peck, M. C. *The United Arab Emirates: A Venture in Unity*, Boulder, Colorado, Westview Press and London and Sydney, Croom Helm (1986).

Peck, M.C. 'Rashid bin Said Al Maktum,' in Bernard Reich (ed), *Political Leaders of the Contemporary Middle East and North Africa*, New York, Westport, Connecticut and London, Greenwood Press (1990), pp 448-52.

Peck, M.C. 'Zayed bin Sultan Al Nuhayyan,' in *ibid.*, pp 515-22.

Peterson, J.E. *The Arab Gulf States: Steps Toward Political Participation*, New York, Westport, Connecticut and London, Published with the Center for Strategic and International Studies, Washington, DC (1988).

Prados, A. B. with the assistance of Ross Kaplan, *United Arab Emirates: Background and U.S. Relations,* CRS Report for Congress, Washington, DC, Congressional Research Service, The Library of Congress (19 June 1995).

Al Suweidi, J. 'Arab and Western Conception of Democracy: Evidence from a UAE Opinion Survey,' in David Garnham and Mark Tessler (eds), *Democracy, War, and Peace in the Middle East*, Bloomington and Indianapolis, Indiana University Press (1995), pp 82-115.

Taryam, A.O. *The Establishment of the United Arab Emirates 1950-85*, London, New York, and Sydney, Croom Helm (1987).

Vine, P. J., P. Hellyer, and I. Al Abed, *Yearbook of the United Arab Emirates 1995*, London, Planet Publishing Ltd (1995).

Zahlan, R.S.*The Making of the Modern Gulf States*, London, Boston, Sydney, and Wellington, Unwin Hyman (1989).

Historical and Legal Dimensions of the United Arab Emirates-Iran Dispute over Three Gulf Islands

Mohamed Abdullah Al Roken

Introduction

The current dispute between the United Arab Emirates (UAE) and Iran over the three islands of Greater and Lesser Tunb and Abu Musa is a classic example of the perpetuity of historical disputes. Time may solve many problems, but not those related to the difficult issue of sovereignty and title between states. Legal rights that have been wholly or partly usurped do not disappear with the mere passage of time.

The crisis concerning the three disputed islands is multidimensional. Politically, it reflects the hegemonic attitude of major regional powers (major in terms of population, area and wealth). Economically it highlights the strategic importance of the islands' location as a toll booth to the Straits of Hormuz, controlling the passage of a vital regional commodity, oil, and even jeopardizing the very source of that commodity in a smaller state. Furthermore, the crisis has a historical-legal dimension. Unfortunately, however, this third dimension has not been adequately probed by those concerned with, or interested in, the crisis. This is probably due to the difficulty of research into the quagmire of history and international law, and to the scarcity of references and literature dealing with the dispute.

In this chapter I shall deal with different axes indicating the historical dimension of the dispute which support the UAE's rightful title to the three islands and refute Iranian claims thereto. However, I must stress that I am wholeheartedly in favour of a peaceful solution, as strongly advocated by the UAE. The region should be spared the horrors of a further war, and should avoid anything that may unnecessarily drain its human and material resources and upset the regional balance of peace.

Historical Roots of the Dispute

The Arabian Gulf, with all its waters, islands and coasts, had become a purely Arab 'lake' since the Islamic conquests in the seventh century AD. Even in the eras that witnessed a weaker and declining Islamic Caliphate state, local powers, especially in Oman, maintained control and sovereignty over the region as a whole. The legal status of the islands was closely linked to the legal status of the southern coast area until the beginning of European imperialism early in the sixteenth century.

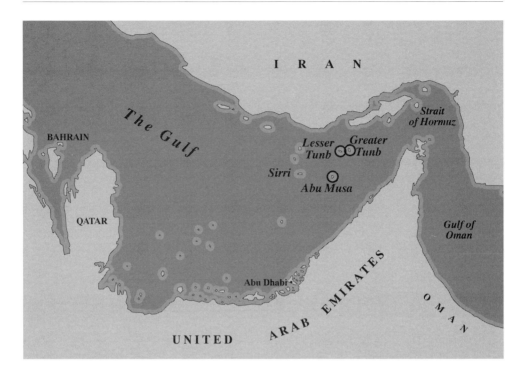

The rise of the Qawasim state and apportionment of the Gulf islands

On the fall of the Yarubi state in Oman (1624-1741), a new Arab maritime power rose to fill
the vacuum. The new power was the Qawasim state based in Ras al-Khaimah. By the middle
of the eighteenth century, the Qawasim fleet was the principal naval power in the Gulf. The
Qawasim eventually extended their influence to several states and regions in the Indian
subcontinent and the East African coast. However, their power was concentrated in the southern
coast of the Gulf, Ras al-Khaimah and Sharjah being their most outstanding cities. In 1750,
however, a faction of the Qawasim moved northward where, upon an invitation from the Arab
Ruler of Hormuz, they settled down in the area of Lingeh. The settlers eventually established
their independent state in that region and sought to extend their influence to the islands and
coastal areas of the Gulf.[1]

Historical references point to a sharing of the Gulf islands by the two Qawasim factions:
the islands of Sirri and Hengam became the property of the Lingeh Qawasim, while Abu
Musa, Greater and Lesser Tunbs, and Seer Abu Neair came under the Qawasim of the Omani
Coast (Ras al-Khaimah and Sharjah). Such arrangements were already in being by 1835.[2]

Thus, the Qawasim of the coastal areas established and maintained unopposed legal and actual
sovereignty over the islands. In 1864 their ruler sent an official message to the British Resident
informing him that the islands of Abu Musa, Greater and Lesser Tunbs, and Abu Neair had been
ruled by his early ancestors, and would therefore remain under his rule. This message was the
first document ascertaining the UAE's legal title to the islands. Sovereignty was further
demonstrated in various forms of protest against any intervention in the islands or violation of
the agreement by the Lingeh Qawasim or neighbouring emirates. As early as the 1870s, Abu
Musa island had become an agricultural seat and a resort for the Qawasim rulers of Sharjah.[3]

This division of the two Qawasim factions is further confirmed by the fact that in 1873 the ruler of the Sharjah Qawasim, Sheikh Salem Bin Sultan, dispatched 50 armed men to Abu Musa to drive away ships belonging to Lingeh Qawasim. Even earlier, in 1871, the Sheikh of Ras al-Khaimah Qawasim had denied Lingeh Qawasim entry into the Tunbs. He sent a message to the Lingeh Sheikh protesting against unauthorized visits to the islands by his subjects. The Lingeh ruler replied confirming that the islands actually belonged to the Qawasim of the Omani coast.[4]

The attitude of the then dominating colonial power (Britain, through the British Government of India) was to consider the title to the islands and division thereof between the two Qawasim factions to be a purely local issue in which it had no desire to interfere. However, the British Political Agent, Haji Abdulrahman, who had broad commercial interests with the Lingeh Qawasim, tried to demonstrate, in his correspondence with the British Government of India, that the islands belonged to the Lingeh Qawasim. He even ordered the Ruler of Ras al-Khaimah's Qawasim[5] to quit them. However, the Ruler of Ras al-Khaimah confirmed, in a message sent in February 1873, that the three islands were under his jurisdiction, and indicated that the Sirri island belonged to the Lingeh Qawasim. In a message from their ruler in 1877, the Lingeh Qawasim admitted that the title over the Tunbs belonged to Ras al-Khaimah Qawasim.[6]

A further proof that the Qawasim of the Omani Coast had title to these islands is that they exercised all aspects of sovereignty over them. In 1879, for example, the Ruler of Sharjah Qawasim, Sheikh Salem bin Sultan, exiled his political opponents to the Abu Musa island. When he himself was overthrown by his nephew, Sheikh Saqr bin Khaled in 1883, he chose to live on Abu Musa himself.[7]

The Persian Empire grew more ambitious late in the nineteenth century and in 1887, Persian armies invaded Lingeh and expelled the Qawasim governors who had ruled it for over 125 years. The Persians continued their offensive, ultimately occupying the island of Sirri. It is worth noting that in one of his reports, the Commander of the Persian campaign stated that the Qawasim had settled down in Abu Musa, which he regarded as their base.[8]

When Iran occupied the island of Sirri, the Qawasim of the southern coast began to have fears vis-a-vis the territorial ambitions of the Persian Empire. Their fears proved well-grounded when Iran set forth a series of claims to the other islands. The British Government protested mildly against Iran's occupation of the island of Sirri, while the Qawasim continued to affirm their title to it.[9]

In 1898, the Ruler of Sharjah, by virtue of his sovereignty over the island,[10] granted three Arab nationals the first concession to prospect for red oxide in Abu Musa.

Iran claims Abu Musa

Territorial and political ambitions, combined with the economic interests of influential elements within the Persian Government, helped strengthen the first Iranian claim to the island of Abu Musa in 1904. Iran began to challenge Sharjah's sovereignty over the island, with its eyes on the island's resources, particularly the red oxide. It thus dispatched a mission, headed by a Belgian officer, to hoist the Iranian flag on the island. The Ruler of Sharjah protested against this action, and his reaction was supported by the British Resident. The latter called upon Iran to submit evidence supporting its title to the island. Three months later, Iran quietly withdrew from the conflict, having failed to produce any evidence supporting its claim.[11]

Throughout the British presence in the Gulf, the British Resident kept sending messages to the Rulers of Sharjah and Ras al-Khaimah stressing his country's recognition of their title to the three islands. Moreover, the Political Agent to the Trucial States (as the UAE was called before independence), Sir Donald Hawley, states in his book *Trucial States* that from the dawn of its presence in the Gulf, 'the British Government has regarded the two islands as belonging to the states of Sharjah and RAK (Ras al-Khaimah) respectively'.[12]

In 1912, Britain and the Ruler of Sharjah agreed to establish a lighthouse in Tunb, with the assurance that this would not entail any encroachment on the ruler's sovereignty over the island.[13] In 1923, the Ruler of Sharjah granted a five-year red oxide exploration concession to a British national named Strick. Iran protested against the granting by the Ruler of Sharjah of prospecting concessions in Abu Musa. This was followed by a lull in the dispute

Anglo-Persian negotiations

On 24 August 1928 the British administration issued a memorandum on the status of the three islands. In that memorandum it was stated that the islands of Greater and Lesser Tunbs had belonged to Ras al-Khaimah since its emergence as a separate entity independent of Sharjah, while Abu Musa belonged to Sharjah, whose Ruler was entitled to the proceeds of exploiting the red oxide and had been for a long period of time.[14] This memorandum was issued following a verbal understanding between the British and Persian Governments in which it was concluded that the three islands were Arab territories.[15]

The period 1929-1930 witnessed negotiations between Britain and Persia aimed at reaching an Anglo-Persian treaty. During these negotiations, several signs emerged supporting the Qawasim's title to the three islands, and hence highlighting the weakness of the Iranian claims. In the draft of the treaty it was decided to recognize Iran's title to the island of Sirri, while the three other islands (the Tunbs and Abu Musa) would remain Arab.

The negotiations were almost a tug-of-war exercise between the two parties. The Iranian Minister of Court, Mr Taimurtash, expressed in August 1929 his country's readiness to withdraw its claim to Abu Musa, in return for recognition of its title to the Tunbs. Iran then offered to buy the Greater and Lesser Tunbs. In May 1930, Britain referred the Iranian offer to the Ruler of Ras al-Khaimah, in the presence of the Ruler of Sharjah. The two rulers, however, strongly rejected the offer, and informed the British Political Resident, Mr Barret, that the two islands were not for sale, whatever the price.[16]

The attempt was repeated in October of the same year when Mr Taimurtash set forth a fresh idea, namely that Iran might lease the two islands for a period of 50 years. This was but a bid to save Persia's face in the wake of its bitter failure to claim Bahrain. Britain welcomed the new idea, as it would have enabled it to lease the then Iranian islands from Iran at the entrance to the Gulf. For several months, British officials exerted pressure on the Ruler of Ras al-Khaimah to persuade him to accept the new offer. The ruler eventually agreed, on the strict conditions that the Qawasim flag should continue to be hoisted on the two islands; and that Iran should refrain from inspecting Arab ships and boats, or even from issuing orders to them.[17] In the end no agreement was reached and the islands were not leased to Iran. Thus, all Iranian attempts at expropriating the three islands failed, and Sharjah and Ras al-Khaimah continued to exercise sovereignty over them.

In 1935, the Ruler of Sharjah signed an agreement with Golden Valley Ochre and Oxide Co. Ltd, to exploit red oxide in Abu Musa. That company continued to function until 1968.[18] On 6 February 1953, the same company was granted exploration concessions in the Tunbs.

The exercise of sovereignty is further evidenced by the fact that on 3 March 1964, the Ruler of Ras al-Khaimah granted oil exploration concessions in the Tunbs to two companies: Union Oil Exploration and Production Company and The Southern Natural Gas Company. Meanwhile, Sharjah granted similar concessions in Abu Musa and its territorial waters extending 12 nautical miles to Buttes Gas and Oil Company.[19]

Iran raises the stakes and occupies the islands

However, the situation was not calm throughout that period. Having entirely failed to annex the island of Bahrain, following a United Nations resolution which endorsed Bahrain's independence on the basis of a referendum that was conducted in 1970, asserting the island's independence and its Arabism, Iran began to claim the three islands again, even more emphatically. The Iranian writer Pirouz Zadeh said: 'The Iranians openly and vigorously asserted their claims of Tunbs and Abu Musa islands immediately after the settlement of Bahrain issue'.[20]

The British entered intensive talks with Iran and the emirates of Sharjah and Ras al-Khaimah in 1970-1971, through its representative, Sir William Luce. To tone down Iran's threats to occupy the three islands by force, Sir William Luce set forth several compromise proposals aimed at finding acceptable negotiation terms.[21] The negotiations were overshadowed by aggressive statements by the Shah of Iran, whose prestige had been harshly bruised by the Bahrain issue. In an interview with *The Guardian* published on 28 September 1971 he said, 'We need them (the islands); we shall have them; no power on earth shall stop us. If Abu Musa and the Tunbs fell into the wrong hands, they could be of a great nuisance value'.[22]

British endeavours ultimately resulted in a Memorandum of Understanding which was signed by Iran and Sharjah on 30 November 1971. Under this agreement, Iranian troops could land on the northern edge of Abu Musa. Ras al-Khaimah, however, maintained its position of rejecting any concessions with regard to its title to the Tunbs. Iran responded to this outright rejection and refutation of its claims by forcibly occupying the two islands in an offensive that claimed two servicemen and five citizens from Greater Tunb. The offensive also resulted in the demolition of a police station and a primary school on that island, and the eviction of its citizens who sought refuge in Ras al-Khaimah.

Basis of Iranian Claims and their Refutation

Initially it may be useful to refer to certain secondary claims cited by Iran. The first is that 'Tunb' is a word of Persian origin meaning 'hill' and that it is derived from a local Persian dialect known as 'Tangistani Persian'.[23] Apart from the legal invalidity of this evidence because linguistic derivation is not a criterion for territorial title or sovereignty, it is also linguistically incorrect. 'Tunb' is a purely Arab word meaning 'a long rope used to erect a tent',[24] while 'Abu Musa 'leaves no doubt as to its being Arabic.

Secondly, Iran claims that the three islands had for some time before the eighteenth century been under Persian occupation. Such a claim is shattered by the historical facts referred to earlier. Moreover, the Persian occupation of the three islands lasted for a short while, and occurred as a result of internal conflicts and a subsequent period of weakness in the region. The Persians were soon driven out of the islands. The claim is also illogical in light of contemporary international relations. If such a short occupation period were to be taken as the basis of proving a state's title to any particular territory, it would result in the undermining of international peace and security.[25]

A third claim cited by Iran is based on geographical proximity. There is no factual basis for this claim, especially with regard to Abu Musa and, in any case, international law (to avoid repercussions in the realm of international relations) does not recognize geographical proximity as valid evidence supporting territorial claims.[26]

The fourth claim is that the Qawasim had ruled Lingeh in their capacity as 'Persian officials', and hence the islands belonged to Iran.[27] Historical facts refute this claim; the three islands had never been under the rule of Lingeh Qawasim. Throughout the years they had always been ruled by Sharjah and Ras al-Khaimah Qawasim. Unfortunately, however, many British legal advisers had laboured under such a misunderstanding, drafting legal memoranda for the British Government in which it was wrongly stated that the Lingeh Qawasim had exercised control over the Greater and Lesser Tunbs and Abu Musa. In fact they only ruled the island of Sirri.

Iran's claim to the three islands is based on three major arguments. The first argument is that under international law Iran alleges to have evidence supporting its claim of title to the islands. The second is that British maps refer to the islands as being under the sovereignty of Iran. The third is that Iran's strategic interests dictate possession of the three islands, so that Iran may be able to safeguard its security in the Gulf.

Let us now consider each of the three arguments and refute them on historical and legal grounds:

Evidence supporting Iran's claim to the islands

International law scholars are at one as to the existence of five conventional methods for the acquisition of, or claim to, sovereignty over a given territory. These are: occupation, accretion, conquest, acquisitive prescription, and cession.[28] It should be noted, however, that these methods came into being as justification for imperial European ambitions in the eighteenth and nineteenth centuries. I shall attempt briefly to explain them, and to pinpoint the extent to which each applies to the Iranian claims.

Occupation

By occupation is meant the capturing of no-man's territory by a state, with a view to extending its sovereignty over it. For occupation to be effected in this way, three conditions must be met:

- The territory to be thus occupied must be a *res nullius*.
- Occupation should culminate in imposing sovereignty over the occupied territory.
- A continuous and peaceful display of territorial sovereignty.

The basis for occupation has changed in European legal thought with the historical development of colonial expansion. Initially, it was based on a fifteenth century Papal decree; later, it was based on geographical explorations. Eventually, the basis of occupation became the actual acquisition of a territory, provided that other European powers were notified of this acquisition, in accordance with the 1885 Berlin Convention.[29]

Let us now apply this concept to the three islands. Never have they been *res nullius* territory. They have been ruled by the Qawasim for over two and half centuries, as has been recognized by Britain and by Iran itself. Moreover, the acquisition of territory through the occupation method has declined in the twentieth century due to the absence of no-man's land that may be occupied.

Accretion

Accretion means the acquisition by a state of new areas by virtue of natural factors or through human efforts, as when new islands emerge in the state's territorial waters as a result of volcanic activity, or when a state converts part (or parts) of its territorial waters into land, to be added to its land territory by placing marine blocks on the shore.

The geographic reality of the three islands does not qualify either party to claim them on that basis. The three islands have existed in the Gulf since time immemorial, and have never been within Iran's maritime zone.

Conquest

A common practice before the emergence of the new world order, conquest meant the use of force to eliminate the legal existence of a state, or the annexation of a part of it to the invading state. Under contemporary international law, this method has become illegitimate, and therefore cannot be used as a valid evidence supporting any claim to any territory. Paragraph 4 of Article 2 of the Charter of the United Nations explicitly states that:

> *All Members shall refrain in their international relations from the threat or use of force against the territorial integrity or political independence of any state, or from acting in any other manner inconsistent with the purposes of the United Nations.*

Rejection of this method was practically demonstrated by the international community through international decrees condemning conquest,[30] such as Security Council resolution No. 242 (1967) which rendered illegal the acquisition of territories through war and invasion, and various Security Council resolutions on the Iraqi occupation of Kuwait.

Iran, therefore, cannot establish its claim to the three islands on the basis of a conquest that occurred in 1971. It cannot legally justify its occupation of Greater and Lesser Tunbs and Abu Musa under international law as conquest, since such a claim to sovereignty will be deemed null and void ab initio.

Acquisitive Prescription[31]

By acquisitive prescription is meant the laying of hands by a state upon a territory under the sovereignty of another, or the exercising of actual sovereignty over it publicly and uninterruptedly for a period of time without opposition or protest on the part of the latter.[32] Iran, which has been occupying the three islands for over 25 years, may thus base its claim to them on acquisitive prescription. However, acquisitive prescription as defined by international law sets forth certain conditions for a claim to a territory in this way. These conditions are:

- Laying hands upon a territory should be effected through the sovereign party by way of exercising its authority over it. Thus, the leasing of a territory, or administration thereof by a party that recognizes the sovereignty of another over it should not be regarded as a situation granting acquisitive prescription, whatever the duration of the lease or the administration. While administering part of Abu Musa, Iran admits that the issue of sovereignty over the island has not been settled in any way.

• Peaceful acquisition is another condition for acquisitive prescription. Thus, acquisition by force, as is the case with the Tunbs, does not support Iran's claim to the two islands on the basis of acquisitive prescription.

• Acquisition should be public, and uninterrupted over a long period of time. Legal scholars differ as to the specific period needed for acquisitive prescription to occur. Some have suggested 100 years, while others opt for 50. In the case of the Tunbs, longer historically-proven acquisition lies with the UAE, rather than with Iran.

• Submission by the party to which the territory belongs: i.e. lack of protest or opposition to laying hands by another state on the territory. Diplomatic protests and legal action thus undermine acquisitive prescription. Iran cannot, therefore, claim that the UAE has succumbed to a *de facto* rule over the islands, or relinquished its established title to the three islands. From the first day of the Iranian occupation of the islands, the UAE sought to prove their legal title to them. A message was sent to the United Nations by the emirate of Ras al-Khaimah on 30 November 1971. Meanwhile, there was armed resistance on the Tunbs and the conflict resulted in some casualties. The UAE continued to defend its rights in United Nations lobbies whenever the issue of the three islands was raised.[33]

Cession

By cession is meant the relinquishing by a state of its sovereignty over a territory belonging to it, to another state through an agreement between both. The basis or mechanism of cession differs on a case-by-case basis. Cession may take place through barter, as in an exchange of territory or part of a territory. Cession may also occur in return for financial compensation, as happened with the acquisition by the US of Alaska from Russia in return for seven million dollars. Finally, cession may occur coercively as when a victor state exercises pressure on a defeated one, eventually forcing it to cede a particular territory or territories.

For cession to hold, or be regarded as a sovereignty-granting act, the following conditions must be met:

• The ceding state must have actual legal sovereignty over the territory to be ceded. On such a basis, Iran cannot claim that Britain had ceded the three islands to it before the termination of its treaties with the UAE and subsequent withdrawal from the Gulf. Britain was unqualified to do so, simply because it did not enjoy sovereignty over the islands. Meanwhile, the emirates of Sharjah and Ras al-Khaimah have never ceded their sovereignty over them, notwithstanding the agreement concluded with Sharjah.

• Cession must occur peacefully and willingly. If effected under the threat of force, it shall have no sound legal consequences and the ceding state shall not be bound by it.

• The object of cession must be sovereignty over the territory in question, not simply the administering thereof.

British maps and their validity

The second consideration on which Iran bases its claim to the three islands is the presence of a British military map presented by the Foreign Office to the Shah of Iran in 1886. This map figures the Greater and Lesser Tunbs and Abu Musa in the same colour as that given to Persian territories. Thus, Iran claims, the three islands have been under its sovereignty since that time.

Initially, it is necessary to highlight the status of geographical maps under Public International Law, and the extent of their validity as evidence supporting sovereignty rights over territories. Maps are of two kinds: official and private. Official maps are those annexed to international treaties or international arbitration verdicts. These have supplementary value, but do not by themselves create legal consequences. Private maps are those issued by geographical and scientific associations, or by specialized companies, or even by individuals. These lack the testimonial value of official maps.[34]

Iran has pointed out that all the maps then issued by British authorities show the three islands to be part of its territories and that this is shown particularly clearly in the 1886 military map presented to the Shah by the British representative. Iran therefore argues that this map is a valid proof of its title to the islands.[35]

In fact, the said map had first appeared in 1870, in *Persian Gulf Pilot*. It connects the three islands with Lingeh. However, it was but a private map that was not attached to any border treaty or agreement between Iran and rulers of the Qawasim. It should be noted that this type of map is not binding on the state in which it is issued, let alone on the states concerned. Moreover, this error was later corrected by British officials.[36]

On the other hand, an earlier map published in 1864 by a German cartographer indicates that the three islands belonged to the southern coast Qawasim.[37] Meanwhile, international maps produced until 1870 referred to the Arab character of the islands. Many subsequent maps gave clear indications that they belonged to the Emirates. Recent maps, including some produced in Iran, also indicate that the Tunbs and Abu Musa are under the sovereignty of the Emirates. The most glaring example is the map produced in 1955 by a specialized Iranian company indicating that the three islands are not part of Iran, and that they are Arab territories.[38]

The said British map cannot be taken as evidence supporting Iran's claim to the three islands. Firstly, that map might at best be interpreted as an implicit recognition of Iran's claim to the islands; but it is a recognition by a third party with neither right nor sovereignty over the islands, *nemo dat quod non habet*. Secondly, Britain itself had, as indicated in our introduction, repeatedly and explicitly recognized in official correspondences the sovereignty of Sharjah and Ras al-Khaimah over the islands. An implicit recognition whose validity and legal strength is doubtful cannot and should not supercede an explicit one to the contrary.

Iranian strategic interests

Iran recognizes the strategic importance of the three islands in the Gulf. They dominate its entrance and the lanes through which the bulk of Iran's oil exports and its vital imports pass. Therefore, maintaining control over the islands would safeguard Iran strategically and maintain its national security.

This view poses an important question: Does a state's strategic interests justify violation of international rules of law and define its territorial sovereignty? The answer must be in the negative. Whatever the importance of strategic interests, they cannot constitute a valid support for sovereignty over a territory.

Moreover, some scholars see a contradiction between the alleged strategic importance of the three islands and geographical reality; the location of the three islands cannot in any way be compared with the locations of the Iranian port of Bandar Abbas and the island of Qishm, both at the very entrance to the Straits of Hormuz. Furthermore, the island of Sirri is only a few miles away from the three islands, especially from Abu Musa, and could thus provide the same strategic protection which Iran holds as a pretext for maintaining its occupation of the three islands.[39]

The presence of Iranian strategic interests is a political rather than legal pretext. It reflects the hegemonic mentality that has been governing the Iranian political regime since the Shah's era and up to the present. Some observers go so far as to suggest that the strategic claims are simply a cover for the Iranian leadership's economic and ideological ambitions. They argue that Iran is seeking sovereignty over the three islands because its proven oil reserves are about to be exhausted; and that by exercising sovereignty over the three islands it can extend its territorial waters by an extra 12 miles. Such an act poses a threat to the Emirates' offshore oil wells in the Gulf.[40]

Irrespective of details of the Iranian strategy, it is important to stress that Gulf security is the responsibility of all Gulf states; it cannot and should not therefore be handled by a single state. Moreover, Gulf security can only be achieved through cooperation and neighbourliness, not by occupation of others' lands, nor by military hegemony.

UAE's Rightful Title to the Islands

The preceding analysis indicates that Iran cannot support its claim to the three islands by any of the conventional methods referred to in Public International Law. Let us now consider the ways and means whereby the UAE may establish title to the islands.

Initially it should be noted that sovereignty rights and their negotiation, have been transferred from the emirates of Sharjah and Ras al-Khaimah to the new union state which was proclaimed on 2 December 1971. In accordance with the Constitution of the UAE, the Union exercises sovereignty over all the lands and waters encompassed by the international borders of the member emirates.[41]

International law scholars assert that border treaties provide for succession, i.e. rights and obligations pass from the predecessor state to the successor state, in accordance with Article 4 of the 1969 Vienna Convention on the Law of Treaties.[42] Moreover, the Supreme Council of the United Arab Emirates, which is the highest federal authority in the state, comprising as it does rulers of the seven member emirates, itself declared that agreements concluded by individual emirates with neighbouring states shall be deemed as agreements between the UAE and the said states.[43]

Acquisitive prescription
In his book entitled *The Issue of Gulf Islands and International Law* Mohammed Aziz Shukri endorses the method of acquisitive prescription to support the Emirates' title to the islands.[44]

However, I disagree with this point of view. While the majority of the conditions required for acquisitive prescription to hold exist, the last one raises doubts as to the very source and base of the UAE's title to the three islands. If applied in favour of the UAE, this condition may be seen as an implicit recognition of Iran's original claim to them. Impressively, this is not so, and therefore, the Emirates should not use this method due to the danger it involves.

Immemorial possession

However, the UAE may establish their title on the basis of immemorial possession of the islands. In such a case, the origin of the status quo remains unknown or doubtful. And since it is impossible to establish whether this status quo is legitimate or otherwise, evidence emerges supporting its legitimacy.[45] The UAE has been holding the three islands for over two and half centuries and it is therefore impossible to prove whether or not this possession was legitimate at the time it occurred, namely the middle of the eighteenth century.

Historical consolidation of title

The UAE may also establish their title to the islands on the basis of the 'Historical Consolidation of Title', a recent concept by Charles de Visscher, a judge and former President of the International Court of Justice. The essence of this concept is that it attempts to combine all sovereignty-conferring elements in a single process. It also concentrates on lengthy utilization of a territory as a claim-proving factor. The concept thus reflects a blend of inseparable connections and interests and is normally employed to settle conflicting claims to territories where there is no clear former possessor state.

Some British legal experts (Bathurst, Ely & Chance) suggest that the basis of the UAE's sovereignty over the three islands stems from the above rule. They argue that the islands had not been steadily ruled by any particular state until they came under the control of the Qawasim who actually ruled them and in a peaceful manner. During their rule, the Qawasim exercised all aspects of sovereignty. Such an exercise was never accompanied by any change of intent on the part of the ruling authority; nor was it met by any significant opposition by neighbouring parties.[46]

Sharjah and Ras al-Khaimah had exercised all aspects of sovereignty over the three islands before the Iranian occupation. In addition to those aspects stated in the introduction to this study, the following may be listed:

- The governments of the two emirates exercised the right to levy and collect taxes and duties from pearl fishers and shepherds using the islands.
- Inhabitants of the islands carried the nationality of the two emirates respectively.
- Rulers of the two emirates were respectively represented on the three islands by governors.
- Public utilities on the islands, such as security, education, customs, health and mosques were under the control of the two emirates.
- The governments of the two emirates hoisted their respective flags on the three islands, and applied their laws and regulations to their inhabitants.
- The governments of the two emirates maintained the right to grant concessions and licences to the companies operating in the islands.[47]

The exercise of all such aspects of sovereignty is the 'root of title' supporting the UAE's title to the three islands. Iran, on the other hand, has never exercised any aspect of sovereignty over them. Professor Jamsheed Mumtaz, an Iranian academic, admitted in an article that Persia had at no time any tangible control over these islands; and was merely content to exercise remote and relaxed control over them, refraining from installing any official agency on any of the islands.[48]

Moreover, in one of the legal memoranda prepared by British experts, the legal adviser Mr Lacelle stated that for 184 years at least, Iran had never exercised any real authority on the islands.[49] Significantly, that memorandum is dated 4 September 1934. Given the period that then elapsed prior to the Iranian occupation of the three islands, we may correctly conclude that the total period amounts to more than 220 years.

Recognition and acquiescence[50]

Other significant evidences supporting the UAE's sovereignty over the islands are recognition and acquiescence. The UAE has been in possession of the islands for a long period and this has been recognized by a third state, Britain. In its correspondence with the rulers of Qawasim, Britain has repeatedly made a unilateral, express declaration recognizing the Qawasim's title to the islands. Moreover, there was an absence of Iranian protest to the UAE's possession of the islands over a long period of time.

Legal Characterization of the Status of the Three Islands, and the Memorandum of Understanding

What, then, is the legal status of the three islands at present? And what are the legal relationships resulting from the Iranian presence in them?

To begin with, it must be quite clear that the situation in the Greater and Lesser Tunbs is one of occupation by force as of 30 November 1971. The Ruler of Ras al-Khaimah had refused to sign a British mediated Memorandum of Understanding with Iran. Consequently, the Shah ordered troops to land on the two islands and to occupy them by force. Thus, the current status of the two islands cannot be legally recognized, in accordance with an accepted legal principle which requires countries to refrain from the threat or use of force to gain acquisition of a territory or territories. Occupation dictates upon the occupier certain legal commitments which have to be observed while administering the occupied territory.

Moreover, Iran's occupation of the Tunbs constitutes the violation of an accepted principle in international law related to border issues, namely the principle of finality and stability of boundaries. It also violates the principle of inviolability of territorial integrity of states, a cornerstone in international relations.

The status of the island of Abu Musa is governed by a Memorandum of Understanding which does not, however, amount to a final agreement determining the status of the island. Following mediation by William Luce, a special British Envoy, Iran and Sharjah agreed upon the six article memorandum. It is evident from the text of the memorandum that Sharjah has not ceded its sovereignty over Abu Musa, and has maintained its right to demand restoration of the island in full.

In the preamble of the Memorandum, it is stated that: 'neither Iran nor Sharjah shall give up their claims to the island, and neither shall heed the other's demands.'[51] Further scrutiny of the articles of the Memorandum would reveal a dual approach dealing with the presence of the two parties, i.e. Iran and Sharjah, on the island. The Memorandum refers to 'areas occupied by Iranian troops' and that Iran 'will occupy areas.' Meanwhile, it refers to the emirate's peaceful presence saying, 'Sharjah will have full jurisdiction over the remainder of the island'. It is thus clear that the island originally belongs to Sharjah, while Iranian presence is but an occupation of the northern part of the island, a situation that came into being only recently.

It should be noted that Iran still recognizes the continuity and validity of the Memorandum of Understanding, as has been stated by its Foreign Minister during a visit to Kuwait on 19 April 1992, and by the head of its negotiating team, Ambassador Mustafa Haeri, in September the same year. Meanwhile, Sharjah has continued to exercise all aspects of sovereignty over the island, including the hoisting of its own as well as the federal flags and the administering of health and education utilities for Emirates' citizens and Arab expatriates living on the island.

Quite apart from the political considerations that prevailed at the time of its signing, a purely legal examination of the Memorandum of Understanding shows it to be null and void. This nullification stems from a defect of substance relating to a signatory party (Sharjah), which signed the Memorandum under duress, as will be indicated later.

Duress and its invalidating consequences are considered differently by conventional and contemporary theories.[52] The conventional theory in international law distinguishes between two situations: duress exercised upon the representative of the state, and duress exercised on the state itself, upon signing an international treaty. Duress, material or moral, exercised on a state representative (head of state, foreign minister, ambassador or negotiator) annuls the treaty, and the state on whose representative duress was exercised is not bound by it. A very good example of this situation is the summoning by Nazi leader Adolf Hitler of the President of Czechoslovakia in 1939, whom he forced to sign a treaty under which the latter relinquished territories belonging to his country. Duress exercised upon the state itself, however, does not affect the validity of the treaty. Advocates of this theory argue that the threat to use force against a state is only a catalyst employed to urge it to sign a treaty. Legally speaking, the motive for contracting does not affect the validity of the contract. They also cite several examples of international treaties that have been concluded in the wake of wars, in which the victors imposed their will upon the defeated. They argue that any attempt to declare such treaties null and void would destabilize the world.

Under the new world order that emerged after the Second World War, and rejection of the principle of the use of force to settle disputes between states, a new theory came into being. This theory holds that duress, whether on the representative of the state or on the state itself, nullifies a treaty. Thus a treaty, concluded under duress or threat of force, shall not result in legal consequences to be complied with. An advocate of this theory, Hafez Ghanem, argues that the maintenance of unfair conditions resulting from treaties concluded under duress would not help stabilize international relations. On the contrary, such conditions would be a source of tension and instability, as the affected states would, sooner or later, seek to restore their rights through untiring efforts to null such treaties.[53] The stability cited by advocates of the conventional theory is based on unjust conditions, and as such cannot be regarded as real stability.

On the Memorandum of Understanding that was signed under duress, rendering the Ruler of Sharjah's will defective, the late Sheikh Khaled bin Muhammad Al Qassimi, then Ruler of Sharjah, explained his circumstances saying:

I had spent about two years collecting documents proving that the island is Arab territory, and that it belongs to Sharjah. I had asked a team of jurists to prepare legal documents and papers. These were presented to the Iranian Government. However, the logic of force and threat allowed no room for reason and legitimate proofs.... Several factors contributed to the delicacy of the situation, combining to form significant pressure: Britain had threatened not to maintain the status quo on the island; Iran insisted that the island was Iranian, and that they would seize it by force; unfavourable economic conditions placed Sharjah in an awkward situation and weakened its position, severely affecting its manoeuvrability; other powers came to support Iran.... Thus, after consultations with brothers, I deemed it appropriate to seek a formula that would freeze the problem politically, while dealing with it economically. Hence came the said agreement.[54]

From the above statement, it can be seen that the ruler was not acting of his own free will, and that he signed the Memorandum under an Iranian threat to use force, and for lack of support by Britain and neighbouring forces. Under such threats, the Memorandum of Understanding may be deemed abrogated as a contradiction of international law, on the basis of Article 52 of the Vienna Convention on the Law of Treaties (1969). As the Memorandum of Understanding is utterly null and void ab initio, military occupation can therefore be deemed the legal characterization of the status of the island of Abu Musa, the same status as prevails in the Greater and Lesser Tunbs.

Stances of the United Arab Emirates and Iran after 1971

Following Iran's occupation of the Tunbs, and the landing of its troops in Abu Musa in accordance with the Memorandum of Understanding, the newly emerging state, i.e. the United Arab Emirates, asked her sisterly Arab states to assist it in bringing the dispute before the United Nations. The Security Council convened on 9 December 1971. The Council President, citing Article 36 of the Charter of the United Nations, called for a resolution of the dispute by diplomatic means. It was thus decided to defer debate on the issue to give an opportunity to a third party to consider it and find an appropriate solution.

As of 30 November 1971, the UAE began a persistent drive to confirm two issues: its title to the three islands and its desire to resolve the dispute in accordance with international customs and laws.

Regarding the first question, the UAE, on 17 July 1972, sent a note to the President of the Security Council in which it affirmed that the three islands were Arab territories. On 5 October 1972, a statement was read out before the twenty-seventh session of the General Assembly, in which the UAE reaffirmed its sovereignty over them. A similar statement was read out before the Security Council on 20 February 1974. A third statement was read out before the UN Special Political Committee on 19 November 1974. Other notes were sent to the UN Secretary General on 6 August 1980 and 1 December 1980, in which the UAE reaffirmed its fixed stance and adherence to its sovereignty over the islands.

On the other side, Iran under the Shah, and later under the Islamic Republic, continued to ignore its international commitments with regard to the Tunbs, and continually violated the

Memorandum of Understanding governing the situation in Abu Musa. It looked upon the dispute as mere territorial misunderstanding between the two parties.

During the Shah's reign, Iran maintained its imperial arrogance, paying no attention to several periodical appeals by the UAE. This attitude continued, and took an even more emphatic tone after the Shah's downfall. Since the early 1980s, Iran has been acting in ways constituting flagrant violation of the Memorandum of Understanding and open intervention in the internal affairs of the UAE. Iranian actions have included the following:

- Encroachment upon territories belonging to the UAE, lying outside the assigned Iranian presence in Abu Musa, by constructing roads and an airport as well as other civilian and military installations.[55]
- Moving troops in 1987 to the southern edge of Abu Musa, and occupation thereof following an abortive coup in Sharjah.[56]
- The imposition, late in 1991, of restrictions on third party citizens wishing to enter the UAE zone of Abu Musa by requiring entry permits from Iranian authorities. As the UAE rejected this measure, Iran ordered all foreigners out of the island in April 1992.[57]
- Preventing, late in August 1992, teachers working in Abu Musa, as well as some UAE nationals, from entering the island, and returning them to Sharjah harbours after keeping them for three nights aboard the ship carrying them.
- The launching, on 29 December 1994, of an air route linking Bandar Abbas and Abu Musa, an action that violates the UAE sovereignty over the island.

On 15 April 1996, Iran opened a power station on Greater Tunb. Official circles in the UAE regard this as a further violation of its sovereignty over the island.

Iran even went so far as to promulgate a law on 12 May 1993 entitled 'Act on the Marine Areas of Iran in the Persian Gulf and Oman Sea'. Articles 1 and 2 of the said law define its scope. Article 1 states that 'sovereignty extends beyond its land territory, internal waters and its islands in the Persian Gulf'. Article 2 confirms that the islands belong to Iran. The two Articles refer to the islands even more emphatically than Article 5 of a previous law promulgated in 1959 amending the law of 15 July 1934 on territorial sea. These two Articles together constitute a grave encroachment upon the sovereignty of the UAE over the three islands.[58]

The second issue concerns the UAE's desire to solve the dispute peacefully. In spite of being the party affected by occupation, the UAE strongly advocates a peaceful solution. In an interview, the President of the UAE, Sheikh Zayed bin Sultan Al Nahyan, stressed the need to refer the dispute to the International Court of Justice.[59] Likewise, in his address on the occasion of the twenty-third anniversary of the proclamation of the United Arab Emirates, he urged Iran to enter into an objective and constructive dialogue, or otherwise to resort to international arbitration to resolve the dispute over the islands.[60] Along the same lines, the UAE Foreign Minister has, in all his speeches at successive sessions of the UN General Assembly, expressed the UAE readiness to start immediate, direct and unconditional negotiations with Iran to terminate the latter's military occupation of the three islands.[61] When Iran did not respond, he demanded that the dispute be referred to the International Court of Justice, this being the international agency entrusted with resolving border disputes.

In contrast to this moderate stance, the Iranian Government continues to be vehemently opposed to the idea of referring the dispute to the International Court of Justice. It insists on bilateral negotiations. It should be noted that Iran had, in 1929, proposed that the dispute over the three islands be referred to international arbitration. This occurred during negotiations with Britain on the conclusion of an Anglo-Persian treaty.[62] It should also be recalled that Iran itself has resorted to the International Court of Justice with regard to several issues. However, since the Shah's era, Iran has been adamantly against referring the dispute either to international arbitration, or to the International Court of Justice. Iranian President Hashimi Rafsanjani, for example, stated that 'referring the issue to an international court would not be viable'.[63]

Bilateral negotiations, however, have failed. They were started following the escalation of Iranian measures on the three islands in 1992. In the first round of negotiations, which was held in Abu Dhabi on 27-28 September 1992, the UAE delegation set forth several demands, the most important of which were: termination of the Iranian occupation of the Tunbs, reaffirmed commitment to the Memorandum of Understanding with regard to Abu Musa, non-intervention by Iran in any way in the UAE's exercise of its complete jurisdiction over the zone assigned to it in Abu Musa, and the finding of a decisive solution to the question of sovereignty over the island of Abu Musa. Iran, however, refused to debate the status of the Tunbs. Nor would it agree to refer the case to the International Court of Justice.

Following mediation by Qatar, a second round of talks was held in the period from 18 to 23 November 1995. The UAE delegation reiterated its previous demands. Unfortunately, however, no agreement was reached, even upon the agenda of the negotiations round, due to Iran's refusal to debate the status of the Tunbs, and its rejection of a proposal to refer the issue to the International Court of Justice should negotiations fail to reach a solution within a specific period of time.

It is thus evident that the stance of the UAE regarding the dispute over the three islands is based on the fact that although the Iranian occupation is de facto, the UAE cannot and would not relinquish its sovereignty over the three islands. In this connection, Hassan Al Alkim says:[64]

> The UAE sees the Iranian's occupation as a de facto and cannot do anything about it; however, it has not ceded its sovereignty over them. The UAE, as a small state, aware of the imbalance of power with Iran, and the absence of a deterring force, whether regional or international, has preferred to keep a low profile on the issue. It has pursued a policy of peaceful co-existence with Iran hoping that the development of good relations will inevitably lead to the settlement of the contentious problems.

Ways and Means of Settling the Dispute

In our contemporary world, states are required to resolve their border disputes by peaceful means. It is no longer acceptable that such disputes be resolved by force. Refraining from the use of force has become a binding legal rule in international law. It is more effective than resorting to force, which only deepens differences and further kindles conflicts between neighbouring countries from generation to generation.[65]

International law provides several ways and means of settling disputes between states peacefully. These include diplomatic ways, such as negotiations, good offices, conciliation and mediation; political ways, such as resorting to regional and international organization; and legal ways, such as referring the dispute to international arbitration or to the International Court of Justice.[66] Judicial settlement is normally effected through a neutral panel on the basis of the law, and the resulting verdict is thus legally binding.

In dealing with the dispute over the three islands, the UAE has adopted a peaceful approach compatible with its own capabilities, and with due respect for international law. Initially, it dispatched its Foreign Minister to Iran in April 1992 to discuss Iran's arbitrary measures. In September of the same year, it called for negotiations in Abu Dhabi to consider a diplomatic settlement. The attitude of the UAE delegation to these negotiations was prudent and balanced. It did not set forth prior conditions, such as the abrogation of the Memorandum of Understanding. On the contrary, it demanded full respect for the Memorandum of Understanding while calling for a framework to settle the sovereignty issue within a specific time limit.

As diplomatic ways failed, the UAE resorted to political means by referring the issue to the General Assembly of the United Nations. The UAE indicated that it adheres to its right to exercise sovereignty over the three islands, stressing its title to them. Meanwhile, the UAE has offered to resolve the issue legally through the International Court of Justice in the Hague, in accordance with Article 33 of the Charter of the United Nations and Article 36 of the Statute of the International Court of Justice. However Iran, perhaps because of the weakness of its legal position and the difficulty of supporting its claim to the three islands, has rejected such an approach. Thus, the only remaining way is to submit the issue to the UN Security Council, which would pass a recommendation referring the dispute to the International Court of Justice, this being the appropriate channel for resolving it peacefully.

On 2 January 1994, the United Nations Secretary General stated that the world organization was ready to play any role in resolving the dispute over the three islands within the context of diplomacy, mediation and arbitration, should the two parties seek its mediation.[67]

[1] *Arabian Gulf Intelligence*, Selections from the Records of the Bombay Government, Oleander Press, p 300. Also see for the early history of the Arab people of this region, based on sources of the Dutch East India Company, B.J. Slot, *The Arabs of the Gulf 1602-1784*, (Arabic Translation) Abu Dhabi, The Cultural Foundation (1993) Especially chapters seven and nine.

[2] M.E. Bathurst, E. Northcutt, and C. Chance, *Sharjah's Title to the Island of Abu Musa*, unpublished report (September 1971) pp 2-4.

[3] *bid.*, pp 4-5.

[4] Mohammed Mursi Abdullah, *The United Arab Emirates and Its Neighbours*, (Arabic) Kuwait, Darul Qalam (1981) pp 323-4.

[5] The Qawasim of Ras al-Khaimah had separated themselves from Sharjah's Qawasim and established an independent emirate in the period from 1869 to 1900. They re-united in 1900 only to separate again in 1920 and remain so until today

[6] *Ibid.,* pp 324-5.

[7] *Ibid.,* p 132.

[8] Mohammed Hassan Al Aydaroos, *Arab-Iranian Relations (1921-1971)* (Arabic) Kuwait, Zatul Salasel (1985) pp 254-6. Also see Ibrahim, Abdulaziz Abdulghani, *Pax Britannica in the Arabian Gulf: 1899-1974* (Arabic) Riyadh, Darul Marrikh (1981) pp 305-7.

[9] See R. S. Zahlan, *The Origins of the United Arab Emirates*, London, Macmillan (1978) p 80.

[10] *Ibid.*, p 129. This contradicts a claim by Pirouz Mojtahed Zadeh, Secretary of the London-based Society for Contemporary Iranian Studies, that Lingeh rulers were the first to grant exploration concessions. This was stated in his article entitled 'The Issue of Abu Musa Island From An Iranian Point of View' in *The Dispute Over the Gulf Islands*, London, Arab Research Centre (1993) p 22.

[11] See Waleed Hamdi Al Adhami, *The Dispute Between the United Arab Emirates and Iran over the Islands of Abu Musa, Greater and Lesser Tunbs in British Documents 1764-1971*, (Arabic) London, Darul Hekma (1993) p 31.

In their correspondences, British circles stress that the main reason behind this move by the Persian Customs Director, Mr. Dambrain, was Russian instigation for Iran to rival British presence in the Gulf. See D. Hawley, *The Trucial States*, London, George Allen & Unwin Ltd (1970) p 162.

[12] *Ibid.,* p 162.

[13] Telegrams from The Political Resident to Sheikh of Sharjah, 28 September 1912, and 22 October 1912. See Al Adhami, *op. cit.,* p 32.

[14] FO 371/13010, India Office, Status of Islands of Tunb, Little Tunb, Abu Musa and Sirri, 24 August, 1928. See Al Adhami, *op. cit.,* pp 22-4

[15] See Zahlan, *op. cit.,* p 90.

[16] See Al Adhami, *op. cit.,* pp 61-5

[17] Zahlan, *op. cit.,* pp 126-7. Also see Ahmed Jalal Al Tadmori, *The Three Arab Islands, A Documentary Study*, (Arabic) Ras al-Khaimah National Printing Press (1994) pp 79-80.

[18] Abdulwahhab Abdoul, *The Three Arab Islands in the Gulf: Extent of the Validity of Regional Changes Resulting from the Use of Force*, (Arabic) Ras al-Khaimah, Centre for Studies and Documents (1993) p 170.

[19] *Ibid.,* pp 279-80

[20] Zahlan, *op. cit.,* p 24. Also see F. Heard-Bey, *From Trucial States to United Arab Emirates* (2nd ed) Longman (1984) p 364.

[21] *Ibid.,* p 365. For minutes of the meetings between the British Envoy and the Ruler of Ras al-Khaimah , see Al Tadmori, *op. cit.,* pp 127-55.

[22] Heard-Bey, *op. cit.,* note 105, p 479

[23] Zadeh, *op. cit.,* p 56.

[24] Abdulwahhab Abdoul, 'Crisis of the Three Arab Islands Between a Clear UAE Attitude and a Contradicting Iranian Stance' (Arabic), a paper submitted to *Islands of Peace Seminar*, Ras al-Khaimah, November 30 to December 1, 1994, pp. 9-11.

[25] Abdoul, (1993), *op. cit., pp* 118-9

[26] *Ibid.,* p 175.

[27] Zahlan, *op. cit.,* p 80.

[28] For further details on these conventional methods see C. Rousseau, *Public International Law* (translated into Arabic) Beirut, Al Ahliyah for Publishing and Distributing (1987) pp 147-51; et al.; Hamed Sultan *Public International Law*, (4th ed) (Arabic) Cairo, Darul Nahda Al Arabia (1987) pp 380-93 ; and Ahmed Sarhal, *Law of International Relations* (Arabic), Beirut, Al Jamiyah for Studies, Publishing and Distributing (1990) pp 147- 60.

[29] Faisal Abdulrahman Taha, *International Law and Border Disputes*, (Arabic) Abu Dhabi Printing and Publishing Co., (1982) pp 21-2

[30] Sarhal, *op. cit.,* p 148.

[31] For forms and conditions of acquisitive prescription see I. Brownlie, *Principles of Public Law*, (4th ed) Oxford, Clarendon Press (1990) pp 153-9.

[32] Taha, *op. cit.,* p 26

[33] This conduct was explained by Ali Humaidan, the first UAE envoy to the UN, in a lecture entitled, 'Emirates' Islands: Legal and Security Rights', given at the UAE University in Al-Ain, 26 October 1992.

[34] Taha, *op. cit.,* pp 135-42.

[35] Mumtaz, *op. cit.,* p 59.

[36] Bathurst, Northcutt & Chance, *op. cit.,* p 13. See also Abdoul (1993) *op. cit.,* pp 131-2

[37] Bathurst, Northcutt & Chance, *op. cit.,* p 13

[38] *Ibid.,* pp 11-4.

[39] Abdoul (1993) *op. cit.,* pp 144-75

[40] Hassan Al Alkim, 'The United Arab Emirates Perspective On the Islands' Question,' in *The Dispute Over the Gulf Islands*, London, Arab Research Centre (1993) p 31. He has noted that the Iranian oil reserve will not last more than three decades.

[41] Article 20 of the *Constitution of the United Arab Emirates*.

[42] Ahmed Mohammed Rifaat, 'Dispute over the Arabian Gulf Islands and the prerequisites for a settlement in accordance to the rules of International Law', (Arabic), a paper submitted to Ras al-Khaimah, *Islands of Peace Seminar*, 30 November-1 December 1994 p 22.

[43] The declaration was published in the *Official Gazette*, Issue no. 240, Year 22, July 1992

[44] This was quoted by Al Aydaroos, *op. cit.,* pp 437-8

[45] Taha, *op. cit.,* p 26.

[46] Bathurst, Northcutt & Chance, *op. cit.,* pp 15-18

[47] For further details, see Abdoul (1993), *op. cit.,* pp 263-80

[48] Mumtaz, Jamsheed 'Legal Status of Some Gulf Islands: Abu Musa, and Greater and Lesser Tunbs' in *Shu'un al-Awsat Journal* (Arabic), Issue no. 47, December 1995 p 59.

[49] Abdullah, *op. cit.,* p 366.

[50] See Brownlie, *op.cit.,* pp 159-62.

[51] *Al Khaleej* newspaper, Sharjah, published text of the Memorandum of Understanding in its issue No. 4865, 4 September 1992.

[52] For further details, see Esam Sadeq Ramadan, *Unequal Treaties in the International Law*, (Arabic) Cairo, Darul Nahda Al Arabia (1978)

[53] This was quoted in *ibid.*, p 350.

[54] Al Aydaroos, *op. cit.*, pp 427-428. Also see Jamal Zakaria Qasem, 'Old Emirates and a New State' in *United Arab Emirates: A Comprehensive Survey*, (Arabic) The Arab League Educational, Cultural and Scientific Organization (1978) pp 68-71.

[55] Al Tadmori, *op. cit.*, p 290

[56] R. Schofield, 'Abu Musa and the Tunbs: the historical background' in *The Dispute Over the Gulf Islands*, London, Arab Research Centre (1993) p 15

[57] J. Moberly, 'Renewed Tension in the Gulf over Abu Musa and the Tunbs' in *The Dispute Over the Gulf Islands*, London, Arab Research Centre (1993) p 16

[58] For full text of the law, see: United States Department of State, Bureau of Oceans and International Environmental and Scientific Affairs; *Limits in the seas: Iran's Maritime Claims*, No. 114, 16 March 1994.

[59] An interview with the London-based *Al Hayat* newspaper, 20 March 1994.

[60] Address by the President of the UAE, 2 December 1994.

[61] See for example, address by the UAE Foreign Minister before the 49th session, 5 October 1994 and his address before the 50th session, October 4 1995. Also see an interview with Sheikh Hamdan bin Zayed, Minister of State for Foreign Affairs, in *Al Ahram* newspaper, Cairo, 3 June 1996.

[62] Zadeh, *op. cit.*, p 24.

[63] Abdoul (1994) *op. cit.*, p 47, quoting the London-based *Al Sharq Al Awsat* newspaper, Issue No. 5671, 8 June 1994.

[64] Al Alkim, *op. cit.*, pp 30-1.

[65] Rifaat, *op. cit.*, p 17.

[66] On ways and means of resolving international disputes, see J.G. Merrills, *International Dispute Settlement*, London, Sweet & Maxwell (1984); Mohammed Basheer Al Shafei,*Public International Law in War and Peace*, (Arabic) (4th ed) Cairo, Darul Fikr Al Arabi (1979) pp 603-40; Ahmed Abdulhamid Ashoushi & Omar Abubakr Bakhashab, *Concise in Public International Law* (Arabic) Alexandria, Shabab Al Jamiaa Establishment, (1990) pp 557-99; Mohammed Aziz Shukri, *An Introduction to Public International Law in Peace Time*, (Arabic) (4th ed) Damascus, Darul Fikr (1983) pp 423- 38.

[67] *Al Khaleej* newspaper, Sharjah, Issue no. 5349, 3 January 1994.

Bibliography

Abdoul, Abdulwahhab, 'Crisis of the Three Arab Islands Between a Clear UAE Attitude and a Contradicting Iranian Stance' (Arabic) a paper submitted to *Islands of Peace Seminar*, Ras al-Khaimah, 30 November-1 December 1994.

Abdoul, Abdulwahhab, *The Three Arab Islands in the Gulf: Extent of the Validity of Regional Changes Resulting from the Use of Force*, (Arabic) Ras al-Khaimah, Centre for Studies and Documents (1993).

Abdullah, Mohammed Mursi, *The United Arab Emirates and Its Neighbors* (Arabic) Kuwait, Darul Qalam (1981).

Al Adhami, Waleed Hamdi, *The Dispute Between the United Arab Emirates and Iran over the Islands of Abu Musa, Greater and Lesser Tunbs in British Documents 1764-1971* (Arabic) London, Darul Hekma (1993).

Al Alkim, Hassan, 'The United Arab Emirates Perspective On the Islands' Question' in *The Dispute Over the Gulf Islands*, London, Arab Research Centre (1993) pp 28-38.

Al Aydaroos, Mohammed Hassan, *Arab-Iranian Relations (1921-1971)* (Arabic) Kuwait, Zatul Salasel (1985).

Al Tadmori, Ahmed Jalal, *The Three Arab Islands, A Documentary Study*, (Arabic) Ras al-Khaimah, Ras al-Khaimah National Printing Press (1994).

Arabian Gulf Intelligence, Selections from the Records of the Bombay Government, Oleander Press.

Ashoushi, Ahmed Abdulhamid & Omar Abubakr Bakhashab, *Concise in Public International Law*, (Arabic) Alexandria, Shabab Al Jamiaa Establishment (1990).

Basheer, Dr Al Shafei Mohammed, *Public International Law in War and Peace*, (4th ed) (Arabic) Cairo, Darul Fikr Al Arabi (1979).

Bathurst, M. E., Ely Northcutt, and Howard Chance, *Sharjah's Title to the Island of Abu Musa*, unpublished report (September 1971).

Brownlie, Ian, *Principles of Public Law*, (4th ed) Oxford, Clarendon Press (1990).

Constitution of the United Arab Emirates.

Hawley, Donald, *The Trucial States*, London, George Allen & Unwin Ltd (1970) p 162.

Heard-Bey, Frauke,*From Trucial States to United Arab Emirates*, (2nd ed) London, Longman (1984).

Ibrahim, Abdulaziz Abdulghani, *Pax Britannica in the Arabian Gulf: 1899-1974* (Arabic) Riyadh, Darul Marrikh (1981).

Limits in the seas: Iran's Maritime Claims, United States Department of State, Bureau of Oceans and International Environmental and Scientific Affairs, No. 114 (16 March 1994).

Merrills, J.G., *International Dispute Settlement*, London, Sweet & Maxwell (1984).

Moberly, John, 'Renewed Tension in the Gulf over Abu Musa and the Tunbs' in *The Dispute Over the Gulf Islands*, London, Arab Research Centre (1993) pp 16-20.

Mumtaz, Jamsheed, 'Legal Status of Some Gulf Islands: Abu Musa, and Greater and Lesser Tunbs' *Shu'un al-Awsat Journal* (Arabic) 47, December (1995) pp. 55-74.

Qasem, Jamal Zakaria, 'Old Emirates and a New State' in *United Arab Emirates: A Comprehensive Survey,* (Arabic) The Arab League Educational, Cultural and Scientific Organization (1978).

Ramadan, Esam Sadeq, *Unequal Treaties in the International Law*, (Arabic) Cairo, Darul Nahda Al Arabia (1978).

Rifaat, Ahmed Mohammed, ' Dispute over the Arabian Gulf Islands and the prerequisites for a settlement in accordance to the rules of International Law', (Arabic) a paper submitted to *Islands of Peace Seminar*, Ras al-Khaimah, 30 November -1 December 1994.

Rousseau, Charles,*Public International Law* (Arabic translation) Beirut, Al Ahliyah for Publishing and Distributing (1987).

Sarhal, Ahmed, *Law of International Relations* (Arabic) Beirut, Al Jamiyah for Studies, Publishing and Distributing (1990).

Schofield, Richard, 'Abu Musa and the Tunbs: the historical background' in *The Dispute Over the Gulf Islands*, London, Arab Research Centre (1993) pp 6-15.

Shukri, Mohammed Aziz, *An Introduction to Public International Law in Peace Time*, (4th ed) (Arabic) Damascus, Darul Fikr, (1983).

Slot, B.J. *The Arabs of the Gulf 1602-1784*, (Arabic Translation) Abu Dhabi, The Cultural Foundation (1993).

Sultan, Hamed (et al.), *Public International Law*, (4th ed) (Arabic) Cairo, Darul Nahda Al Arabia (1987).

Taha, Faisal Abdulrahman *International Law and Border Disputes*, (Arabic) Abu Dhabi, Abu Dhabi Printing and Publishing Co. (1982).

Zadeh, Pirouz Mojtahed,'The Issue of Abu Musa Island From An Iranian Point of View' in *The Dispute Over the Gulf Islands*, London, Arab Research Centre (1993) pp 21-7.

Zahlan, Rosemarie Said, *The Origins of the United Arab Emirates*, London, Macmillan (1978).

Newspapers

Al Hayat newspaper, London.
Al Ahram newspaper, Cairo.
Al Khaleej newspaper, Sharjah.

UAE Foreign Policy

William A. Rugh

Introduction

The foreign policy of the United Arab Emirates (UAE) is similar to the foreign policy of most other countries in that it has one fundamental goal, which can be simply stated: that dealings with foreign governments, individuals and organizations should enhance the prosperity, stability, power and independence of the UAE and its citizens.

But the UAE is distinctive in two ways. First, it faces a unique set of objective conditions in its population size and composition, natural resources and wealth, and physical location, which restrict and affect its foreign policy. Secondly, it has a leader who has been UAE President for all of the country's 25 years and who has acquired enormous respect in his own country and considerable prestige abroad. His dominating role in foreign policy has given the UAE a clear characteristic style reflecting its leader's priorities and choices (for example, between more military strength and more prosperity, or between confrontation and conciliation) based on his own particular perceptions of the world and of the best interests of his own country.

This chapter will look at the objective conditions that the UAE leadership faces and the choices it has made, in order to show the fundamental characteristics of the UAE's foreign policy.

Objective Conditions

There are several objective conditions which make the United Arab Emirates unique, and these affect its foreign policy, restricting its options.

First, the UAE has extraordinary wealth in natural hydrocarbons. It is located on the Arabian Gulf, which has the world's most abundant supplies of oil and natural gas. After Saudi Arabia, which has one quarter of the world's petroleum reserves, four Gulf countries have approximately 10 per cent each of the world's reserves, and the UAE is one of them. (The others are Iran, Iraq, and Kuwait). The nearly 100 billion barrels of recoverable petroleum reserves in the UAE, amount to four times the reserves of all of North America. The sale of more than two million barrels of crude oil every day on the world markets makes the UAE one of the world's leading exporters of crude. Moreover, the total number of UAE citizens is relatively very small, so the billions of dollars which the export of petroleum generates each year, gives the UAE one of the world's highest per capita incomes.[1] It is a wealthy country, and this wealth gives it potential to have influence abroad, because other countries need its petroleum and want access to its petrodollars.

Secondly, the UAE geographically occupies an important location, with its northern border on the Gulf adjacent to the Strait of Hormuz, and its eastern border on the Indian Ocean. From a strategic point of view, UAE territory is significant because it could be the base from which to threaten or close Hormuz, through which the bulk of the world's exported oil passes every day. By the same token, if Hormuz were closed by forces outside the UAE, UAE territory could be used to provide entry to and exit from the Gulf from the Indian Ocean. From an economic point of view, the UAE's location offers a central transit point for the re-export of goods from the rest of the world, and in recent years the UAE emirate of Dubai has become the leading entrepôt of the region and the commercial centre of the Gulf. Thus geography gives the UAE potential influence beyond its borders.

Thirdly, however, while the UAE is rich in oil it has few other natural resources. This creates potential foreign policy problems by making its prosperity heavily dependent on the international oil market. And since many of the countries of the Gulf also depend heavily on petroleum exports, the UAE must look to Europe, Asia and elsewhere for petroleum markets and places to invest its petrodollars. In addition, because it has few native citizens, the UAE must import most of its labour force, and as a result, foreigners make up 70 per cent of the resident population. Thus the fact that it is a small and wealthy country in a tough neighbourhood is an important part of the framework for its foreign policy.

UAE Interests and Priorities

The interests and priorities of the UAE in foreign policy derive from these conditions, but they also show the stamp and imprint of the country's leadership.

First, it is natural that, as a small country, the UAE's foremost foreign policy priority is security and stability in the area immediately adjacent to its borders, i.e. in the Gulf. Unlike a huge country such as the United States, which has important concerns about security issues around the globe, most of the UAE's attention is focused on a shorter horizon.

Secondly, as an Arab nation, the UAE feels a close political affinity with the other Arab countries of the Middle East and North Africa. The common language, culture and history which the UAE shares with the rest of the Arab world, and which is reinforced in UAE school curricula, makes solidarity with other Arab states an important goal for the leadership. In addition, the special tribal and family affinities and interrelationships between the people of the UAE and their neighbours on the Arabian Peninsula makes the Arab states of the Peninsula especially important.

It is true that tribalism is still an important factor in the UAE, and political and social rivalries exist among tribal groups on the Peninsula, but these are - at least in public - usually subordinated to solidarity among Arabs of the Gulf.

Thirdly, economic interests, including the sale of petroleum, the investment of petrodollars, and the re-export trade, tend to focus the UAE's attention on Europe, America and Asia. Moreover, especially since the crisis created by the Iraqi invasion of Kuwait in 1990, the UAE has also looked to America and Europe to help provide security from major foreign threats, both by selling the UAE modern weapons and by potentially providing emergency assistance as was done in 1990.

Finally, the UAE in the determination of its foreign policy is concerned about the fate of Muslims throughout the world. As a Muslim nation, the UAE feels kinship with Muslims everywhere, and this concern is especially manifested when it appears that Muslims elsewhere are being badly mistreated by others, as in Bosnia in the 1990s or Afghanistan in the 1980s.

Priorities and Style of the Leadership

The particular style of the leader is important for any country's foreign policy, because within the constraints imposed by objective factors, there is still some room for choice of options and for setting of priorities among goals.

Some countries change leaders frequently but the leadership of the United Arab Emirates, and therefore its foreign policy style, has been remarkably consistent and stable since the founding of the country 25 years ago.

In December 1971, when the UAE was formed, a Provisional Constitution was promulgated, stipulating that the highest authority in the country would be the Supreme Council of Rulers, which would be ultimately responsible for foreign policy. Composed of the rulers of the seven constituent emirates, this Supreme Council elects a chairman, who is the UAE head of state or president, for a five-year term. In 1971 the Supreme Council elected Sheikh Zayed bin Sultan Al Nahyan as President. Sheikh Zayed, the leader of the Al Nahyan family of Abu Dhabi, had been the representative in the Al-Ain district of his brother the Ruler since 1946, and he had been Ruler of Abu Dhabi since 1966, when he had replaced Shakhbut in that position. After electing him in 1971, the Supreme Council subsequently re-elected Sheikh Zayed to that position every time his five-year term expired, in 1976, 1981, 1986, 1991 and 1996. The Constitution, which was formally made permanent in May 1996,[2] stipulated that Abu Dhabi would be the capital of the UAE, further reinforcing Sheikh Zayed's pre-eminence as the country's leader in the determination of national policies including foreign affairs.

The 25 year tenure of Sheikh Zayed as President reflects his prominent stature throughout the country. Over this period, by the force of his personality and leadership skills, he increasingly earned the respect of the entire population, so that by 1996 he stood clearly above all others as the most admired figure in the nation. He demonstrated that he was able to use the new-found petroleum wealth to their benefit. He showed that he could articulate the desires of his people. At the same time, he gained a reputation throughout the region and the world as a distinguished international leader, whose prestige exceeded the size of his country.

Sheikh Zayed has been the key decision maker in UAE foreign policy throughout the first quarter of a century of the country's existence. His authority derives not only from his position as leader of the major tribe in the largest of the seven emirates. It also derives from the considerable force of his personality, and from his effective leadership style. In foreign as in domestic matters, he has repeatedly demonstrated his skill at leadership, reinforcing his position and perpetuating his rule.

Sheikh Zayed's style of leadership has several basic characteristics. First, he is essentially a conservative and cautious person. He does not act compulsively or precipitously in making decisions, but prefers to take his time, and think through the options carefully. He is certainly capable of taking prompt and decisive action when necessary, for example during the Gulf crisis of 1990, as we shall see below. But generally he prefers to make decisions in a deliberate and carefully considered fashion.

Secondly, it is characteristic of Sheikh Zayed that he favours conciliation, good neighbourliness, amicable relations with other countries and the peaceful settlement of disputes, whenever possible. As in domestic matters, a prominent characteristic of his foreign policy has been his ability to reconcile differing views, and he has preferred diplomacy over the use of force. On occasion, when the national interest required it, he has been firm as recently seen in his handling of the dispute with Iran over three small islands in the Gulf (see below). But his preference generally is to find compromises which satisfy the other party's interests as well as the UAE's, and to settle differences quietly.

Thirdly, Sheikh Zayed, in line with his generally conciliatory approach, tends to be tolerant of different approaches and life styles, as long as others do not threaten the basic values of his own people. The fact that as many as 70 per cent of the people living there today are not UAE citizens, but are temporary residents working in the country for a limited period of time, presents a potential foreign policy problem. These foreign workers come from a wide variety of countries, with very different social, political and economic backgrounds. How much should they be made to conform to the very conservative UAE social customs? Would interference affect relations with their home countries? The UAE approach, under Sheikh Zayed, has made it possible for them to maintain their identities even while living in the UAE. They dress and behave much as they would do at home, practice religions other than Islam, speak their own languages, attend their own schools established freely in the UAE, and the UAE Government interferes very little in their lives. This spirit of live and let live is remarkable in that it is not found to the same degree in many other countries of the region, and it has been successful because the different national groups live harmoniously side by side. The approximately 400,000 Pakistanis and 650,000 Indians who live in the UAE side by side do so essentially without conflict, despite the fact that in their respective home countries, animosities between these two groups are deep and relations often result in violence there. Not so in the UAE because of the prevailing attitude that communal relations must be peaceful.

This does not mean that the UAE Government allows all foreigners free rein to do anything they want. There are limits on public and private behaviour by foreigners. In 1992, for example, a UAE court tried, convicted and jailed a group of Indian nationals for putting on a play in an Indian social club which the judge declared to be blasphemous against both Islam and Christianity. Also in 1992, Pakistani Muslims, many of them illegal workers, who rioted in the UAE whilst demonstrating against the destruction of a mosque in India were promptly deported. But these were unusual incidents and, generally speaking, foreigners enjoy considerable freedom in the country. At the same time, UAE society remains socially quite conservative; for example, although UAE women can drive their own cars, join the police and the army, and occupy important positions in the private and public sector, educational institutions are segregated by gender, and they follow other rules reflecting local traditions. Nevertheless, foreign women are not required to conform to local customs, as they are in some conservative states. Only in a few ways do conservative local customs affect foreigners; for example alcohol use is restricted, and Ramadan fasting generally is applied to public places. By and large, foreigners are generally left alone as long as they do not interfere with the citizenry in its observance of basic local customs. Foreigners are generally not permitted to acquire UAE citizenship, no matter how long they live there, but while they are working in the country they are treated well.

Fourthly, Sheikh Zayed gives weight in his foreign policy to tribal affiliations, cultural affinity and personal relations. As the successor to a continuous line of rulers of Abu Dhabi from the Al Nahyan family which stretches back more than two centuries, Sheikh Zayed has always been mindful of the importance of tribe, and his destiny as part of a long tradition. He is aware of the family ties with other countries in the region, such as with Yemen, where the Al Nahyan apparently originated. And he was aware of the affinity between the tribal society of the UAE and similar societies in the Gulf region, especially in the five other neighbouring Arab monarchies. Moreover, related to the prominence of family and tribe in social and political relations, is the high value placed on personal relations, another characteristic of the UAE's foreign policy.

Fifthly, the UAE is a federal state, created out of seven emirates that were separate until 1971, and these seven have retained some autonomy from the central government, particularly in financial and local security matters. As a result, Sheikh Zayed must take the views of the rulers of the other six emirates into account even in foreign policy formulation, to ensure that they are fully supportive of what he wants to do. He keeps in close touch with them on a regular basis and is fully aware of their views. In the last analysis, he as President is responsible for making foreign policy, and he is not required to go along with the majority or with any strongly held individual ruler's opinion, but he does consult.

Sixthly, and finally, Sheikh Zayed, as the President of a small but wealthy country, makes use of the financial means of Abu Dhabi and the UAE to advance the interests of the country abroad. The funds may come out of the budget of the UAE, or of Abu Dhabi, or out of his own pocket. But in line with his generally cautious approach, his 'dirham diplomacy' is not profligate or excessive, but rather has clear limits and is deliberately thought out. For example, he gave generously to PLO Chairman Yasir Arafat during the 1970s and 1980s, then suspended those payments after the Gulf crisis of 1990 when Arafat supported Saddam Hussein. Later again, after the Palestinian-Israeli agreement of 1992, he contributed to the Palestinian people. But although very many foreign organizations and individuals ask him for money every year, he is selective in his donations.

UAE Policies

Let us examine some of the specific foreign policies that the United Arab Emirates has developed over the quarter century of its existence, under the leadership of Sheikh Zayed.

As indicated above, because the UAE is a small nation with a sparse population, it tends to be most concerned about its immediate neighbourhood, and sees its foreign policy interests diminishing with distance. We will therefore look first at its policies toward its Gulf Arab neighbours, and then towards Iran, then towards the Arab world as a whole, and then to the wider world, in effect in concentric circles.

The Gulf Cooperation Council States

UAE foreign policy gives priority to its immediate Arab neighbours. The UAE seeks, above all, to ensure that the Arab states which border on or are very close to its territory are friendly, or at least non-threatening to its security, not only because they are Arab monarchies but also because they have the most potential opportunity to do harm to UAE national interests. An unfriendly neighbour could claim some of the UAE's sovereign territory, or allow hostile persons to cross their border into the UAE. The UAE's borders are long and its ability to close them is limited. It is important to the UAE that even non-contiguous Arab states close by, such as Iraq, Kuwait, Bahrain and Yemen, remain friendly and stable, because as Arab states and societies, what happens there tends to have a greater impact on the UAE than what happens in dissimilar societies (like the Persian or the Turkish, for example).

This UAE good neighbour policy has been clear only for the past 25 years since it has only been responsible for its external relations that long. During the nineteenth century the British had signed a series of treaties with Arab leaders in the Gulf region, so that by 1920 Britain controlled the foreign relations of all of the Arab territories between Oman and Iraq, including the Trucial States, now known as the UAE. Under the 'Exclusive Agreement' of 1892, for example, the ancestors of today's UAE rulers promised that they would not make any international agreements or host any foreign agents without British consent. The British, in turn, protected these rulers, and in treaties recognized the sovereignty of the existing rulers within the borders of their emirates. When Saudi Arabia made claims in the 1950s on territory in the Al-Ain/Buraimi area held by Sheikh Zayed, the British assisted him in defending his claim and expelling the Saudi force.

By 1966, Sheikh Zayed was Ruler of Abu Dhabi and firmly in control of its territory, which extended from Al-Ain to the Qatari border. Then two years later, in 1968, the British Government announced that it would withdraw from the Gulf by the end of 1971. This signalled the end of the era of British control of Zayed's foreign and defence policy, and he turned at once to the task of consolidating relations with his immediate neighbours. He sought agreement with the other six Trucial States rulers that they would form a union as a new federal state. That effort was successful, and although Ras al-Khaimah delayed its membership for a few months, the other six joined together to form the United Arab Emirates in December 1971. Sheikh Zayed also sought to include neighbouring Qatar and Bahrain in this new federal state, because he believed it would serve the UAE's interest to include all of these small emirates when the British had left. Bahrain and Qatar, however, declined to join, and became independent in August and September 1971, respectively.

During the first three years of its existence, 1971-74, UAE foreign policy faced continuing uncertainties about the country's immediate neighbours, Saudi Arabia and Oman. The UAE had old territorial and border issues with these two countries, and no longer had British guarantees to rely upon, because the British had departed. Thus Sheikh Zayed gave priority attention to resolving remaining differences with Saudi Arabia and Oman. In neighbouring Oman, the situation was somewhat unstable and worrisome because Sultan Qaboos, who had come to power through a palace coup d'etat in 1970, was then challenged by a rebellion in Dhofar which lasted until 1975.

The other immediate neighbour, Saudi Arabia, was also worrisome because it withheld official recognition of UAE sovereignty pending resolution of old territorial issues. But by 1974,

Sheikh Zayed had reached a resolution with the Saudis, through an agreement in August of that year, which gave Saudi Arabia additional territory on the UAE's southern and western borders, including a new corridor to the sea between the UAE and Qatar.[3] At that point the Saudi Government officially recognized the UAE and an era of friendlier relations with the UAE began. In subsequent years, Sheikh Zayed has continued to give special personal attention to cultivating good personal relations with the leaders of Saudi Arabia and Oman in particular, as the first prerequisite of his foreign policy.

Sheikh Zayed also continued to give special attention to good relations with Qatar and Bahrain, even though they had not joined the UAE federation, and to Kuwait. By May 1981, all four, plus Saudi Arabia and Oman, had joined together in an agreement to establish the Gulf Cooperation Council (GCC). The immediate impetus to this agreement was the Iranian revolution of 1979 and the outbreak of the Iran-Iraq war in 1980. The UAE and the other five GCC states did not want to get drawn into the conflict but they sympathized with Iraq as an Arab state. They began to support Iraq politically through the Arab League, and then in 1981 through loans to help Iraq's war effort (see more on Iraq below).

Sheikh Zayed has seen good relations among the GCC members as important to the UAE and he gives attention to that. He frequently consults with the other five GCC leaders, and encourages regular meetings between UAE ministers and their GCC counterparts, in order to coordinate foreign policy as much as he can with them. He has agreed to some joint economic measures with the rest of the GCC, and helped to reduce barriers to travel to the UAE for citizens of GCC states, on a reciprocal basis. Moreover, he has helped to reconcile differences among GCC members as they arose.[4]

At the same time, it is clear that the UAE will not surrender its essential sovereign rights to any other country, including a GCC member state. Although the UAE Government gives considerable importance to GCC solidarity, it does not hesitate to take a course independent of the GCC when the UAE leadership determines that such a course is required by the national interest. At the December 1996 GCC summit meeting. for example, the UAE held firm to its policy of free trade and low tariffs, despite pressure from other GCC members to join in on a common tariff policy which would have meant an increase in UAE tariffs.[5] The UAE took this position because its leadership believed that free trade is a vital element in UAE economic prosperity. The Dubai merchants and political leaders, incidentally, strongly believe in that philosophy because Dubai depends so heavily for its well-being on re-export business, and thus UAE national policy was very much in line with the Dubai emirate's interests.

Policy toward Iraq is another example where the UAE shows some independence from GCC conformity. Sheikh Zayed has expressed, publicly and privately, his great concern that international sanctions against Iraq are hurting the Iraqi people. The UAE defence minister has been even more explicit in public statements in early 1995 about his dismay that the sanctions are causing suffering by innocent Iraqi citizens. These expressions of concern have gone farther than official statements from other GCC states such as Kuwait, Saudi Arabia and Bahrain, which tend to take a harder line on Iraq and fix all blame on Saddam Hussein. The UAE's focus on the harm being done to Iraqi citizens has helped to fuel a discussion about the effectiveness of sanctions on Iraq, although the UAE has not gone so far as to recommend that sanctions be lifted. These examples illustrate, however, that the UAE does have its own foreign policy, separate and distinct even from other GCC states.

Iraq

Since the establishment of the UAE in 1971, its policy toward Iraq has gone through some significant changes. The UAE at the outset sought to establish cordial relations with Iraq because it is an Arab country and the most powerful one on the Gulf . Relations were never especially close because Iraq's revolutionary Baathist regime had a different outlook on governance and foreign policy from the view that prevailed in the UAE and the other Gulf monarchies. But Arab solidarity, and the UAE's desire to have a strong Iraq as a counter-weight to Iran, provided a common base which helped reinforce ties between the two countries. When the Iran-Iraq war began in 1980, the UAE remained formally neutral but sought to help Iraq politically and then also economically. The Iran-Iraq 'tanker war' which flared up in 1984 alarmed the UAE because it threatened to harm UAE oil interests directly and in fact did spill over into some damage on UAE offshore oil installations by Iranian forces. The UAE nevertheless continued its financial support for Iraq, and managed to avoid any greater involvement in the conflict. Sheikh Zayed, however, was the only head of state in the Gulf who branded the war from the start as 'unwanted, harmful and destructive'.

After that conflict ended in 1988, the UAE's relations with Iraq remained cordial until the spring of 1990, when Iraqi President Saddam Hussein began a campaign of public criticism of the UAE and Kuwait over oil policy. Sheikh Zayed took Saddam's harsh words seriously. While other Arab leaders in the region assumed that Saddam's rhetorical attacks were just empty words designed to bully others into accepting his views, Sheikh Zayed saw them as dangerous threats. As Saddam alternatively negotiated with Kuwait and threatened the region, the UAE watched with growing concern. In July 1990, Sheikh Zayed, concluding that it was time to send a signal to Saddam not to intimidate the smaller states of the region, asked the United States to undertake a joint military exercise with UAE and American air force units as a warning to Saddam not to go too far. The United States agreed, and together the two countries planned an exercise they called 'Ivory Justice'. Saddam was not deterred, because he went ahead with an invasion and occupation of Kuwait on 3 August, but in retrospect it is clear that Sheikh Zayed had read the situation better than most.

As a result of the Iraqi invasion of Kuwait, the UAE shut down the Iraqi Embassy in Abu Dhabi and publicly denounced the Iraqi regime's behaviour. More importantly, the UAE joined the international coalition against Saddam, welcoming coalition forces into its territory for staging against Iraq during the buildup (Desert Shield). When the war (Desert Storm) started in early 1991, it not only allowed coalition forces to launch from UAE territory but it also sent contingents of UAE military personnel into battle against Iraq.

After Saddam was expelled from Kuwait, the UAE, like the other coalition partners, expected that he would fall from power. But when he showed that he was able to stay on, the UAE continued to support coalition efforts against him in several ways. The UAE publicly endorsed the maintenance of the UN-sanctioned embargo against Iraq. It allowed United States Air Force tanker planes to be based at UAE airfields from which they flew refuelling missions in support of the 'Southern Watch' monitoring flights by American fighter planes over southern Iraq. It also helped enforce the embargo against Iraq by accepting into its ports a number of ships caught in 1994-95 by the US Navy trying to ship goods out of Iraq illegally. And in October 1994, when Iraqi troops moved menacingly again toward the Kuwaiti border, the

UAE sent ground troops into Kuwait as a tangible gesture of support for this threatened GCC state. This multi-national exercise, called 'Vigilant Warrior', demonstrated that the UAE was prepared to make a real contribution to the coalition effort against the Iraqi regime.

As time passed following the conclusion of Desert Storm and Saddam Hussein failed to leave power or change his behaviour, the UAE became increasingly frustrated that the embargo was not working. UAE officials were distressed that the Iraqi people - fellow Arabs - were suffering material deprivations that were only getting worse as time went on. They also feared that Iraq, by far the strongest Arab nation on the Gulf, was being severely weakened so that it would be less able to play a balancing role against Iran in the future. The situation also offended the UAE leaders' sense of Arab solidarity. They knew that Saddam Hussein was responsible for the misery of his people and the decline of his country, because the UN-imposed embargo could have been eased or lifted if he had complied fully with the terms of the UN resolutions passed during and after Desert Storm. But Saddam continued to defy the international community and his propaganda repeatedly told his people that the West and the GCC states were at fault. The UAE leaders and people wished there was a way out of this situation which was dragging on too long. They were disquieted that they could find no easy alternative and the leadership continued to support the coalition against Saddam, hoping it would bring him down soon, but it became increasingly dissatisfied with the failure to achieve that result.

The UAE's participation in the coalition confronting Iraq therefore has everything to do with the behaviour of the Iraqi leadership rather than with Iraq as a nation. When Saddam falls, and the Iraqi regime changes its policies, it would be consistent for the UAE to seek a prompt reconciliation with the new leaders in Baghdad and to restore the amicable relations that existed prior to August 1990.

Iran

The policy of the UAE towards Iran has been one of concern arising out of several factors. Iran is a large and powerful neighbour, whose leaders have in modern times seen themselves as the naturally dominant state in the Gulf. It is true that UAE merchants have in recent decades done considerable trade with Iran, that there are personal and even family ties between the two countries, and that many Iranians live in the UAE. But the UAE political leadership has tended to regard Iran, its closest neighbour after Saudi Arabia and Oman, with some apprehension and fear. This attitude is reinforced by the fact that Iran is not only non-Arab, but its Muslim population, unlike that of the UAE, is predominantly Shia.

Iran's leader for most of the first decade after the formation of the UAE was the Shah, who was not unfriendly to the UAE but who tended to regard Iran as the naturally dominant power in the Gulf. In fact, however, the birth of the UAE in 1971 coincided with Iranian actions and words which appeared in the UAE to be menacing and dangerous. The issue appeared on the surface to be a minor one, namely control of three small islands in the middle of the Gulf. But these islands were symbolically important for the countries on both sides of the water.

In November 1971, the Iranian Government unilaterally seized the Greater and Lesser Tunb islands, tiny places only about ten and two square miles, respectively, and having no known natural resources. These two islands had been inhabited and controlled by Arabs for centuries and they were at the time part of Ras al-Khaimah, one of the emirates which was about to join the UAE. During the decades prior to this event, when Ras al-Khaimah and the other Trucial

States were under British protection, Iran had tried several times to take over the two Tunbs and to raise the Persian flag, but the British had helped the Arabs reject these attempts.

Then just as the British departed, and were no longer willing to take that responsibility, Iran moved again, and this time succeeded in invading the two islands, resulting in the loss of a few Arab lives. At the same time, Iran asserted a claim to Abu Musa, another island in the Gulf only slightly larger than the Tunbs, and controlled by Sharjah, another emirate about to join the UAE. In negotiations with the Ruler of Sharjah, supported by the British, Iran managed to gain access to half of Abu Musa, by means of a written Memorandum of Understanding (MOU) that explicitly avoided resolving the competing sovereignty claims. Abu Musa had several hundred Arab inhabitants, and a small amount of petroleum; the MOU stipulated that the oil revenues would be split between Iran and Sharjah.

Sharjah and Ras al-Khaimah became constituent parts of the UAE, which in turn protested the Iranian actions, denying the Iranian claims of sovereignty over Abu Musa and the two Tunbs. The UAE was far too weak to recover control of these islands by force. But Arab UN members took the issue to the Security Council where it was debated on 9 December 1971. This was an occasion for strong criticism of Iran, and also of Britain for allowing Iran access to the islands.[6] Iran ignored the criticism.

Then in 1979, when the revolutionary Islamic fundamentalist regime under Khomeini took over in Iran and adopted an even more hegemonic policy, the UAE Government saw this as a heightening of the Iranian threat to its national interests. From then on, the regime in Tehran was more inclined to criticize the Arab monarchies of the Gulf including the UAE, alleging backwardness, corruption and too close an association with the West. The criticism was somewhat muted during the 1980-1988 Iran-Iraq war. But Iran continued to control the Tunbs and half of Abu Musa during those hostilities, fortifying all three islands as part of its military effort. In the process Iran gradually encroached on Abu Musa territory, beyond the half allocated in the 1971 MOU, where several hundred UAE citizens were living. The UAE did not abandon its claim to sovereignty over these islands, and watched Iran's military build up on them with some concern. But apparently the UAE decided it would be prudent not to challenge Iran too provocatively while Iran was at war with Iraq, which the UAE was supporting financially.

During the 1990-91 Gulf crisis, Iran criticized the GCC states, including the UAE, for welcoming Western troops into the region to deal with the Iraqi invasion of Kuwait. Then, after Desert Storm, Iran began to demand that the wealthy Arab states of the Gulf, such as the UAE, help it rebuild its economy which had been devastated by the Iran-Iraq war. Also, with Iraq defeated, Iran began to build up its military capabilities, including the development of weapons of mass destruction and the ordering of three Russian submarines. Since Iraq was tied down by UN-sanctioned measures and unable to provide a counterweight to Iran, the UAE and other GCC states became more concerned about Iran's intentions in the Gulf.

Then in early 1992, Iran took a step on Abu Musa which caused the UAE to become alarmed. The Iranian authorities, who controlled the island's only useable port, suddenly demanded that anyone disembarking on the island, even Arabs en route to the UAE side, had to have Iranian visas. This was presented as a routine requirement, but it was in fact a new rule which was intended to extend Iran's control to the Arab inhabitants. The UAE Government immediately regarded it as a sign of creeping Iranian annexation of the island, and refused to allow the Arabs working there to comply. The UAE denounced the new visa rule as an illegal act, violating the MOU, and demanded the rule be revoked. The UAE sought and received support in its position from the GCC and the Arab League, and the Iranians eventually backed down.[7]

This marked a tactical change for the UAE in dealing with Iran. Starting with this incident, and continuing on a regular basis through the following years, the UAE Government has publicly made an issue out of its claim to sovereignty over Abu Musa. Also, in raising its voice on the matter, the UAE added its claim to sovereignty over the two Tunbs, and argued that it had a legal right to all three islands.

The UAE Government became more pro-active in trying to deal with the problem, and it used a variety of means toward that end. First, the UAE tried direct negotiation with the Iranian regime. In 1992, there were several ministerial meetings between the two governments, but the issues were barely discussed, and no progress was made. Then the UAE sought and received support from the GCC and the Arab League, adding political weight to its case. After securing that endorsement, the UAE took the matter to the United Nations, asking the UN Secretary General to use his good offices to mediate the dispute. Iran refused to receive the Secretary General on the issue. The UAE then suggested that the matter be turned over to the International Court of Justice, and expressed its readiness to abide by the ICJ's decision, whatever that was. Again, Iran refused to cooperate.

The UAE did not let the matter drop there. It continued to employ every non violent means at its disposal to keep the pressure on Iran to settle the dispute. It used every opportunity, including the annual UN General Assembly debate, the annual GCC summit and the periodic GCC ministerial meetings, as well as Arab League and Arab summit meetings, to continue to reiterate its position. In doing so, the UAE made clear that it was not escalating the issue towards war. But it was also afraid that if the issue were ignored, Iran might be tempted increasingly to tighten its grip on the islands and the chance would be lost forever for the UAE to realize its claim to them.

Iran however, remained intransigent, and Iranian public statements reiterated Iranian claims to sovereignty over the islands and indicated that the matter was not negotiable. These statements also denounced the UAE for repeatedly raising the issue. On one occasion, for example, after the December 1992 GCC summit conference publicly supported the UAE on this issue, Iranian media warned that if the UAE wanted to recover them it would have to cross 'a sea of blood' to do so.

Quite apart from the islands issue, the UAE also supports other GCC states against Iran, as the occasion arises. After violent incidents began to occur in Bahrain in the fall of 1994, the Bahraini Government accused Iran of fomenting them, and the UAE sided with Bahrain. For example, in July 1996 the UAE media reported that UAE President Sheikh Zayed had sent a message to the Emir of Bahrain, Sheikh Isa bin Salman, rejecting foreign interference in Bahrain's internal affairs - a thinly veiled criticism of Iran.[8]

The Arab world and the Islamic world

Beyond the Gulf, solidarity with the Arab world as a whole is an important tenet of UAE foreign policy. The UAE Government seeks to take Arab concerns into account in the formulation of its policy. The UAE leadership consults often with Arab leaders, especially on issues which Arabs consider important, seeking to coordinate policy as much as possible.

One special association that was formed at the time of the 1990-91 Gulf crisis was that between the six GCC states on the one hand, and Egypt and Syria on the other. In the Damascus Declaration of 1991, these eight countries, which had been the core of the Arab effort to oust Saddam Hussein from Kuwait, pledged to work together in the future for their mutual security, and thus perpetuate their wartime cooperation. This so-called 'GCC Plus Two' group developed no tangible institutional framework, and the members gave up none of their sovereignty to it, but they did consult and their representatives met together from time to time. The UAE found these meetings politically useful. For example, their foreign ministers met in Muscat in mid-July 1996, and issued a declaration that (among other things) fully endorsed the UAE's claim to sovereignty over Abu Musa and the two Tunb islands, denouncing Iran's continued occupation of them.[9]

Gulf issues are vitally important to the UAE, but there is much more to its foreign policy. One central issue for the Arab states and people is the Arab-Israeli conflict. Over the past half century, the most emotional and persistently anguishing question for the Arab world has been how to deal with Israel. The UAE has been very much involved in this discussion and has regarded the issue as a central one in its foreign policy. Since the UAE's establishment in 1971, it has consistently and vocally joined the Arab chorus of criticism of Israel, and has supported the Palestinian people. This policy has undergone some modification over the years, but only in details, with characteristic caution, and in step with changes undertaken by the majority of Arab states.

Throughout the 1970s and 1980s, the UAE consistently endorsed the majority Arab position of hostility to Israel and applied the primary, secondary and tertiary boycotts against Israeli goods. The Chairman of the Palestine Liberation Organization (PLO), Yasir Arafat, was a frequent visitor to Abu Dhabi, and the UAE regularly gave him generous financial assistance, both from official sources and from a tax imposed on resident Palestinian workers. Egypt's peace agreement with Israel in 1979 did nothing to change that, because most of the rest of the Arab world continued to boycott Israel and the UAE followed that majority.

When Iraq invaded Kuwait in 1990, however, and Arafat declared his support for Iraq, the UAE abruptly stopped all financial assistance going to him from the UAE, and also made clear that he was not welcome in Abu Dhabi. In October 1991, when the Arab states met with Israeli representatives in Madrid and launched a peace process, the UAE endorsed it as the majority of Arab states had done, and the following year the UAE Government joined others in pledging money to help the Palestinians. But at that time PLO Chairman Arafat was still persona non grata in the UAE. Later, the UAE joined a pledging conference in Washington convened to show support to the Palestinians, and the UAE Government promised 25 million dollars over a five year period to the Palestinians, but on condition that the money be managed by the World Bank (through the Holst Fund) and not given directly to Arafat. The UAE still did not trust him, because he had not completely backed away from his support for Saddam Hussein. By the end of 1994, however, he had done so, and the UAE restored amicable relations (and some direct funding) to the PLO Chairman.

Even though the UAE's relations with Chairman Arafat were very poor between 1990 and 1994 because of an important Gulf issue, the UAE sought to follow a cautious middle line on the Palestinian question itself. During the 1991-95 period, the peace process was moving forward, as both the PLO and Jordan had made direct agreements with Israel. The United

States was urging the other Arab states to give the process impetus by dropping the boycott, and to normalize relations with Israel as Jordan, the PLO and, earlier, Egypt had done. Syria refused, but at their meeting in September 1994 the GCC states, including the UAE, chose a middle way and agreed to drop the secondary and tertiary boycott but not the primary one. But when the UAE's two immediate Arab neighbours, Oman and Qatar, agreed to host conferences between Arab and Israeli officials and the latter visited these countries for the first time ever, the UAE refused to follow suit, despite American urgings.

Thus as the peace process moved forward and different Arab countries followed somewhat different approaches to it, the UAE followed a middle course. It sought to stay as close as possible to a posture taken by the majority of Arab states, neither taking a lead nor lagging too far behind. The UAE authorities were comfortable in this cautious position. They wanted the peace process to succeed, and recognized the benefits that would flow from its successful conclusion. But there was no certainty that it would succeed, and the UAE did not want to go too far as it was still unfolding.

The UAE also was not going to get out in front in the peace process because it was not a direct party to the Arab-Israeli conflict and did not want to arouse the enmity of those Arab states that were closer to it. Of special importance was the maintenance of good relations with Syria, which was continuing to take a hard line on Israel. Syria could be influential in Gulf affairs, where the UAE's primary interests lay. Syria had a long-standing confrontation with Iraq, and it had cultivated good relations with Iran, so it had potential to be an outside player in the Gulf, and the UAE had to keep that in mind. As usual, the UAE saw the peace process through the optic of vital matters closer to home.

By the same token, although the UAE sought to maintain amicable relations with all Arab states, the Gulf crisis of 1990-91 caused severe friction with Yemen and Jordan because they supported Saddam Hussein rather than Kuwait. Tensions remained with these two countries even after Desert Storm had liberated Kuwait. Eventually, Yemen made an effort at reconciliation with the UAE and the breach was healed. But Jordan took a longer time to seek to restore good relations, so the cool atmosphere remained for several years. By 1996, however, meetings between the UAE President and the Jordanian King, suspended during this cool period, had recommenced.[10] Relations between the UAE and these two countries have subsequently reverted to normal.

Sheikh Zayed has a special personal interest in Yemen, since his ancestors came from there. In the 1980s the UAE financed the construction of a major new dam at Marib in Yemen, and the country also granted a number of Yemenis UAE citizenship, on an exceptional basis. In the spring of 1994, however, when a civil war broke out between the northern and southern parts of Yemen, he faced a policy dilemma. In line with his traditional policy, he sought a peaceful reconciliation and a prompt end to the fighting. Senior UAE officials urged both sides to stop hostilities immediately, but fighting continued. Saudi Arabia, which was inclined to recognize southern secession and to assist the south against the north, wanted the UAE to do the same, but Sheikh Zayed refused. Despite his desire to accommodate neighbouring Saudi Arabia, the GCC's largest and most influential member, he showed his preference for non-intervention. The civil war ended in a month and the UAE managed to stay out of it.

The United Arab Emirates in its foreign policy also takes very much into account the policies of other Islamic states, and seeks to coordinate with them to the extent possible. This priority overlaps somewhat with the UAE's support for Arab causes, for example in the way it looks at the Arab-Israel conflict. But there are other important issues for the UAE which are Muslim and non-Arab.

One such issue is the conflict in the former Yugoslavia. The UAE very clearly sides with Bosnia and has made known its deep concern for the Bosnian Muslims. For example, Sheikh Zayed in one statement said:

> All capable UAE citizens should assist the Bosnian people with cash and kind as the tragedy increases and the tragedy against the human conscience grows and becomes a disgraceful blot on the human face....As for the super powers, they should assume their historic responsibility to stop the Bosnian tragedy.[11]

South Asia

South Asia has a special place in UAE foreign policy which is often overlooked by Westerners.[12] It has a special place for several reasons. First, as mentioned above, the presence of more than one million South Asians residing in the UAE indicates the extent to which the UAE economy is dependent on South Asian skilled and unskilled labour. Secondly, trade with South Asia has been important to the emirates since long before they joined together in a union in 1971. Trade with India and Pakistan has therefore been more important to the merchants and people of the UAE for a longer time than trade with other regions of the world, and it is still vital to them. Thirdly, the UAE Government has cultivated special relations with Pakistan as an important Muslim nation in the region, which can help counterbalance Iran, a neighbour to both countries. Sheikh Zayed has a long-standing personal interest in Pakistan, which he has visited officially quite often. It is important to him to maintain good relations with South Asian countries which send so many workers to the UAE. He also regards it as important to help India and Pakistan maintain good relations with each other, and he has undertaken some quiet diplomatic efforts to that end. This effort parallels the care he has taken to see that South Asians living in the UAE are treated well and live harmoniously together.

Beyond the Middle East

Britain has always had a special place in UAE foreign policy because Britain determined it from the early part of the nineteenth century until 1971. The British controlled the coastal waters in the Gulf in order to dominate international trade, and they essentially left the interior alone until the discovery of oil in Abu Dhabi in the 1960s. British policy tended to be more of a problem for the Qawasim tribes which ruled Ras al-Khaimah and Sharjah because they depended on regular sea trade, which the British interrupted, while the Al Nahyan in Abu Dhabi were more tied to the desert and the British left them alone. Then when oil was discovered most of it was in the Abu Dhabi emirate, so it benefited further from the British presence. Sheikh Zayed remembers the British as friends of the UAE in the early days of the federation, right after its establishment in 1971 when the new nation had few friends. Some of Abu Dhabi's youth went to school and university in Britain before the UAE had its own modern educational institutions.

Sheikh Zayed knew when the UAE was formed that he would need to find friends beyond Britain, so he began to cultivate his neighbours, and others further beyond the horizon. At the same time, British power was waning, and the UAE's petroleum wealth growing. Other countries, including France, Japan and the United States, became commercially important and Britain lost its special place.

France, in particular, has developed an important role in the UAE in recent years. French manufacturers sold fighter aircraft and battle tanks to the UAE military, and the UAE became France's second trading partner in the Gulf. In January 1995 the UAE signed a joint defence agreement with the French Government. A year later the UAE signed another defence agreement with the United Kingdom.

The direct role of the United States in the UAE was at the beginning a very modest one. The US moved promptly in 1971, to become the third country to recognize the UAE, and it assigned a resident ambassador to Abu Dhabi in early 1974. The US Navy had had a long-term presence in Gulf waters since the 1940s, but it was practically invisible in the UAE. Also, American private companies had not yet discovered the UAE. In those early days, the UAE leadership saw the United States as a somewhat remote country, which was heavily involved in neighbouring Saudi Arabia and Iran but not paying much attention to the smaller countries of the Gulf. The UAE did speak out, regularly and sometimes harshly, about what it perceived as America's persistent bias in favour of Israel and against the Palestinian Arabs.[13] And the UAE's generous donations to the PLO did not please Washington. When the Shah of Iran was deposed in 1979 as America, his ally, stood by, many in the UAE saw this as a sign of American weakness. The US showed more interest in the Gulf during the Iran-Iraq war (1980-88), and US ship visits to UAE ports and diplomatic consultations with the UAE authorities became more regular. Also, American companies by the 1980s began to make connections in the UAE and to sell a few goods and services, especially in oil field equipment and air defence.

When Saddam Hussein invaded Kuwait in 1990 and President Bush responded by sending half a million troops to the Gulf, the UAE welcomed the intervention and the US image improved. The two countries shared a common perception of the threat, and worked together to counter it. American forces were allowed to make use of UAE facilities for staging, and military to military cooperation was excellent. After Desert Storm, the US Navy continued its high level of ship visits to UAE ports - sometimes averaging as many as 30 per month, the highest in the region - because the service to ships was so good and, for sailors, the UAE's quiet and pleasant atmosphere made it the preferred shore leave stopover. The UAE bought some military equipment from US firms, although America was by no means the only source for that.[14] The two countries initiated joint military exercises, and in July 1994 the United States and the UAE signed a defence cooperation agreement, symbolizing an unprecedented level of military cooperation between the two countries. In October of that same year, when Saddam Hussein sent his troops menacingly toward the Kuwaiti border, the UAE and the United States cooperated in the 'Vigilant Warrior' show of force which persuaded Saddam to back down.

The United States did not have any bases in the UAE, and the UAE was careful to preserve its sovereignty intact. It was clear from its actions and words that the United States intended to maintain a military presence in the Gulf region, and this helped to serve UAE security purposes. This presence was primarily a naval one, with sometimes 20 ships in the Gulf at one time, vastly overshadowing any other country in that respect (Britain and France normally only devoted one or two ships, at most, to the Gulf). For example, in the year 1994, 253 US Navy ships visited UAE ports, and US naval personnel registered 453,627 person-days ashore in the UAE on liberty.[15] In cooperating with the US, the UAE leadership showed that it wanted a relationship with a friendly country which had power to help defend it in case of another emergency.

After Desert Storm, American companies increased their activity in the UAE. They were not given any special treatment over non-American companies, but the UAE economy had developed facilities and conditions attractive to large companies, including very low tariffs and taxes, free trade zones, modern ports and hotels and, most of all, large government contracts. American company managers saw that the UAE had become the country in the Gulf where it was easiest to base a regional business headquarters, replacing Bahrain in that role. As a result, American firms moved there in large numbers.

By 1996, the Arab-Israeli dispute had moved a long way towards resolution. Resolution, however, is not comprehensive, and many in the region believed the peace process was stalled. Thus the seeds of renewed friction remain between the United States and the UAE (as well as with other countries supporting Israel). But as always, the UAE leadership sees that other issues closer to home, in the Gulf region, are more vital to the UAE national interest and thus deserve a higher priority and more attention.

Conclusions

We have seen that there are certain objective conditions which affect UAE foreign policy which any UAE leader would have to take into account. One of these is the importance to the country of the production and export of hydrocarbons, and secondarily (especially for Dubai) the importance of trade. Its petroleum wealth and trading skills are a distinct advantage over less fortunate third world nations, but they also make it dependent on foreign markets and imply a free trade policy. Another fact of life for the UAE is its strategic geographic location which gives it some leverage in international affairs but also makes it the object of interest by powerful nations. A third fundamental condition, its small size and sparse population, forces the country to look to cooperative relations with friends and allies to bolster its security against those who might covet its wealth or territory. Finally, the fact that the UAE was created out of seven separate emirates and remains a federation in which those emirates retain some autonomy, means that the central government, which is ultimately responsible for foreign policy, must take the interests and desires of the leaders of the constituent components into account.

Within the constraints that these factors impose on the country, UAE President Sheikh Zayed has developed a distinct foreign policy that reflects his choices and shows a certain degree of independence of action. As the country's leader since the establishment of the federation in 1971, and as its most distinguished national figure at home and abroad, he has put his stamp on policies for over a quarter of a century. His style is conservative and cautious, and he supports local traditions. At the same time he prefers conciliation to confrontation, follows a good neighbour policy, and encourages tolerance of others, as manifested in the harmonious relations that prevail among the many different foreign workers who reside in the UAE side by side.

Nevertheless, he stands for certain principles that he advocates clearly and without hesitation. He supports Arab solidarity and tends to endorse positions adopted by the Arab consensus, such as its stand on Israel and the Palestinians. Yet he was quick to oppose and help act against

Iraq's occupation of Kuwait and he has continued to oppose the behaviour of Saddam Hussein. He broke with the Palestinian leader Yasir Arafat over the Iraq issue and remained distant from him for several years. Likewise he stood up to Iran - despite the fact that it is an immediate neighbour and much more powerful than the UAE - because of his concern for Iranian encroachment on territory claimed by the UAE. His approach to many foreign policy issues is similar to that of the other members of the Gulf Cooperation Council, but not identical, as he has carved out a position independent even of his closest Arab neighbours.

By the same token, UAE cooperation with the West, including the United States, has grown in recent years, especially after the 1990-91 crisis over Iraq's occupation of Kuwait, yet the UAE retains its independence and freedom of action there too. UAE has not accepted all aspects of American policy toward Israel, for example, nor does it decide for purely political reasons to buy American goods and services.

As is true for any country formulating its policy to achieve multiple objectives in a changing world, the UAE modifies its tactics while basic goals and even a characteristic style remain the same. Iraq's unexpected invasion of Kuwait in 1990, and the beginning of the comprehensive peace process between the Arabs and Israelis starting in 1991, were changes in the international environment which brought about such shifts, because UAE policies had to be modified to take those changes into account. Nevertheless, the country's basic foreign policy principles, including a preference for good neighbourly relations, tolerance, peaceful settlement and reconciliation - except where a line had to be drawn, as with Iraq in 1990, and Iran since 1992 - remained intact. This style has now been established as a precedent in the first 25 years of the nation's existence, and it probably will persist.

[1] According to official UAE Government sources, in 1996 the number of UAE citizens was 580,000, and the country's gross domestic product was 152 billion dirhams. UAE Ministry of Information and Culture, *The Emirates: A Daily Digest of News and Features on the UAE,* 7 July 1996, no.15396, and 17 July 1996, no.16296.

[2] *Al Khalij,* 21 May 1996, p 1.

[3] A.O. Taryam, *The Establishment of the United Arab Emirates, 1950-85,* London, Croom Helm (1987) pp 216, 219-220.

[4] Some of the information and analysis here and following have appeared, in another form, in W.A. Rugh, 'The Foreign Policy of the United Arab Emirates', *The Middle East Journal,* Vol.50 no.1 (1996) pp 57-70.

[5] For a discussion of the December 1995 GCC summit, see John Duke Anthony's monograph, 'The 16th GCC Heads of State Summit', Washington DC, National Council on US-Arab Relations, 1995.

[6] Taryam, *op.cit.,* p 183-85.

[7] The foreign ministers of the GCC, Egypt and Syria, on 11 September 1992, issued a declaration supporting the UAE, *Manama Wakh News Agency,* 11 September 1992, 0500. The Arab League supported the UAE in a statement two days later, *MENA News Agency, Cairo,* 13 September 1992, no.1224.

[8] *The Emirates,* 4 July 1996, no.15196.

[9] *The Emirates, op.cit.,* 14 July 1996, no. 15996 and 15 July 1996, no.16096.

[10] *The Emirates, op.cit.,* 18 July 1996, no. 16396 .

[11] Statement by Sheikh Zayed, 28 July 1995, *Emirates News,* 6 August 1995.

[12] The author is grateful to Dr Jamal S. Suweidi for helping to focus attention on this important aspect of UAE foreign policy.

[13] S. Zunes, 'The US-GCC Relationship', *Middle East Policy,* Vol.3, no.1, p 105.

[14] In the 1980s the UAE had bought air defence missiles from the US, but planes from France and other equipment from Britain. In the 1990s, the UAE bought helicopters and communication equipment from the US, but tanks from France, armoured personnel carriers from Russia and other equipment from South Africa and elsewhere.

[15] Unclassified information from the US embassy in Abu Dhabi, 1994.

The United Arab Emirates and International Organizations

Muhammad Jenab Tutunji

Introduction

This chapter deals with the United Arab Emirates' ties with international organizations; specifically the United Nations, the World Trade Organization, the Arab League, the Gulf Cooperation Council and OPEC. During the last three decades, the salience of these organizations for the United Arab Emirates (UAE) has evolved in keeping with the changes in the primacy of security and economic problems facing the Middle East and the Gulf region. As the Arab-Israeli conflict ceded pride of place to the Iran-Iraq war and then to Iraq's invasion of Kuwait, the UAE's primary reference group changed from the Arab League to the Gulf Cooperation Council. The analysis in this chapter will focus on the structure of interests embodied in the organizations under discussion, and the resulting incentives or obstacles to collective action. The members of the GCC are united by long-term common political, economic and security interests, the members of OPEC are united by medium to long-term common economic interests but have divergent security interests, while members of the Arab League are united by long-term ideological concerns but short-term practical political interests and tend to form rival blocs around political and security issues.

While the above is not of course an exhaustive list of the international organizations to which the UAE is linked, space limitations forbid a more ambitious approach. The four most salient political issues emanating from the UAE's institutional links will be examined in some detail. At the United Nations, the UAE made a significant contribution to Security Council resolution 598 of 1987, demanding an immediate cease-fire in the Gulf war between Iran and Iraq. The dispute between the UAE and Iran over the Abu Musa and Greater and Lesser Tunb islands will be discussed in some detail in the section on the Arab League, while also demonstrating the involvement of the United Nations and the Gulf Cooperation Council in the problem of the three islands. UN sanctions against Iraq will be dealt with under the heading of the GCC, while emphasizing relations with the Security Council. The UAE's accession to the Nuclear Non-Proliferation Treaty (NPT) will also be discussed because the NPT is an important international treaty organization and the UAE's accession to the treaty was inextricably tied up with events at the UN. Two general criteria determine under which organization an issue is to be discussed: either which institution is the forum for the UAE's direct involvement, or which organization has the longest or most eventful history of direct involvement with the issue. The UN will serve as a cross reference point for the UAE's other institutional ties. The World Trade Organization will be dealt with in a separate section at the end.

The United Nations

Collective action at the UN

The UAE became a member of the United Nations on 9 December 1971. Out of the six principal organs of the United Nations, the UAE has been a member of three: it is a member of the General Assembly; it was elected a member of the Security Council for the two year period 1986-87; and it became a member of the Economic and Social Council for a standard three-year term from 1977 to 1980 (the other three principal organs of the UN are the Trusteeship Council, the International Court of Justice and the Secretariat).

Effective action in the United Nations has to be of a collective nature (with notable exceptions, such as the exercise of the power of veto in the Security Council). Here, as in society at large, politics is about the socialization of conflict: the outcome depends on the scope of the conflict and on where the lines of cleavage are drawn. In order to pass resolutions and successfully complete the arduous process leading to action on the part of the United Nations, its organs or agencies, nations find it necessary to act as members of groups. The UAE tends to act (in descending order of importance) as a member of the Gulf Cooperation Council, the Arab League, the Organization of the Islamic Conference, the Non-Aligned movement (or its successor, the Group of 77 and China) or the group of Asian countries.

To a certain extent since the mid-1980s, and particularly since 1990, the UAE has demonstrated a preference for acting as a member of the Gulf Cooperation Council (GCC), which can be said to serve as its primary reference group. The situation today is that there is a ministerial level GCC committee which represents the first level of consultation for the UAE and other GCC members before the issue goes on to the level of the Arab League, OPEC, the Organization of the Islamic Conference or the United Nations; for instance, the committee of oil ministers of the GCC states consults beforehand on all issues scheduled on the agenda of OPEC conferences.

Perhaps the taste for collective action is a manifestation of the political culture of the UAE or a reflection of the fact that it is a federation. There is no consistency within the GCC in this regard. Saudi Arabia, the most influential member of the GCC, is not keen on collective action within the UN, refusing to become a member of the Security Council and get deeply involved in UN affairs; Qatar and Kuwait, however, are more like the UAE in this respect. That is not to say, however, that Saudi Arabia does not act collectively within the GCC or does not support GCC initiatives at the UN.

Next in rank as a reference group is the Arab League. Iraq's occupation of Kuwait drew the UAE all that much further into the embrace of the GCC; and the subsequent divisions in the Arab world made the Arab League ineffective. Still, the Arab League represents a group of 21 states as opposed to the GCC's six, and the League can muster support among its members on certain issues which command relative unanimity, such as standing up for Palestinian human and civil rights, and trying to shield Lebanon against Israel's dramatic incursions.

The Organization of the Islamic Conference (OIC) represents a large group from which the UAE can draw support for issues relating to Islam or other common values, such as the situation in Afghanistan or opposition to Serbian atrocities in Bosnia and Hercegovina. The UAE, with the backing of other Muslim countries, encouraged the US to bring about a peaceful resolution of the conflict in the former Yugoslavia, which could have led to another Afghanistan (Shaali

1996). Yet the commonality of interests in the case of the OIC is too diffuse; by contrast, the interests shared by GCC countries are concentrated. One also notes that the demand for international action on Bosnia has consistently been an item in the decisions of GCC Supreme Council or Ministerial Council regular meetings submitted to the Secretary General of the UN. The GCC appears to mediate the UAE's relations with virtually all other organizations. What used to be the Non-Aligned group constitutes a large reservoir of support by over a hundred states that are by and large sympathetic to many of the interests of the UAE and other Arab countries which are still, after all, part of the South. Since the demise of the Soviet Union, however, it has become much more difficult to mobilize support among the members of the former Non-Aligned group or the Group of 77 and China for Arab causes. The United States now dominates the UN as never before.

Resolutions on the Iran-Iraq war

The most significant period for the UAE at the United Nations was during the UAE's two-year membership in the Security Council (1986-87), when the UAE was able to make a contribution to resolutions to end the Iran-Iraq war.

Various Arab countries undertook to mediate the conflict between Iraq and Iran. Algerian Foreign Minister Muhammad Benyahia and the entire negotiating team accompanying him were killed when their plane was shot down in 1982 while flying from Baghdad to Tehran. Starting in 1983, the foreign ministers of the UAE and Kuwait, at the behest of GCC member states, engaged in several rounds of shuttle diplomacy to convince Iran and Iraq to accept a cease-fire and to ward off the probable intervention by outside forces in the Gulf region. At considerable personal risk, the envoys of the GCC flew to Tehran and Baghdad as shells were landing around them. The Iranians were particularly disturbed by Iraqi attacks on oil wells and storage, refining and shipping installations. At one point they took members of the visiting UAE and Kuwaiti delegation to one such site that had been set on fire and told them that if they could bring a halt to that type of attack, their mediation mission might be successful (Saad 1996). During 1983-84 that conflict spilled over into a 'tanker war' which endangered shipping in the Gulf, a vital area to the members of the GCC and the West. Mediation missions continued until 1984-5, when the entire effort was aborted due to Iran's rejection (Shaali 1996). Some attribute the failure to untimely disclosure in the press (Peck 1986: p 144). The UAE then shifted its focus to helping forge a series of Security Council cease-fire resolutions, including Resolution 582 (adopted on 24 February 1986), and 588 (adopted on 8 October 1986), as well as Resolution 598 (adopted on 20 July 1987). The credibility of members of the GCC was instrumental in securing passage of these resolutions (Saad 1996).

Resolution 582 called for a cease-fire, the immediate cessation of hostilities and the withdrawal of forces. It 'deplored the initial act which gave rise to the conflict' without pointing the finger of blame at either of the parties, and it also deplored 'the escalation of the conflict,... attacks on neutral shipping or civilian aircraft, the violation of international humanitarian law ... and, in particular, the use of chemical weapons contrary to obligations under the 1925 Geneva protocol' (S/RES/582 (1986)).

There was an intense debate among Council members as to what the proper role of the Council should be in the conflict. In a sense, the passage of Resolution 598 represented Security Council history in the making, as it was the first time that the five permanent members of the Council worked together on a significant issue as a team, and it was the first time that they took the initiative as a group to resolve a conflict (Shaali 1996).

A particular difficulty was that Iran did not trust the Security Council. The Iranians felt that the Council had tilted towards Iraq in the earliest resolutions passed after the outbreak of hostilities, while it had also passed several resolutions condemning Iran for the taking of American hostages. The entire history of animosity between the US and Iran was therefore reflected in Iran's attitude towards the Council. Various formulas were tried which included working through a committee of Non-Aligned nations (Iran in effect rejected this in its typical round-about way) and through a committee of the Organization of the Islamic Conference (which was also unsuccessful). On the other hand, the Iranians did trust Secretary General Javier Perez De Cuellar and consequently his initiatives tended to get results (Shaali 1996).

De Cuellar had begun preparations for a major cease-fire initiative by the Security Council in 1985; Resolution 582 of February 1986 requested the Secretary General to continue his efforts to induce the belligerent parties to accept the resolution. Iran refused to sign a peace treaty with the Ba'ath regime in Iraq under the leadership of Saddam Hussein which it felt was dedicated to the overthrow of the Islamic republic (S/18480, p 5).

At the UN, the UAE had become an integral part of the Security Council effort to deal with the Iran-Iraq war. In October 1986, the UAE permanent representative at the United Nations was serving as president of the Security Council for that month. As was customary, he hosted the representatives of the members of the Security Council and Secretary General Perez De Cuellar to a dinner at his home. The five permanent members, the Secretary General and Ambassador Shaali were seated at the same table. Mr Perez De Cuellar proposed that all members of the Security Council should agree to prevent the export of arms to both Iran and Iraq. Ambassador Vernon Walters of the US remarked that the US had no objection. The representatives of the United Kingdom and France adopted the same position. The representative of the USSR said that it was a good idea, but it needed to be explored further. The representative of the People's Republic of China said he had to consult his government (Shaali 1996).

That initiated a new political process at the Security Council. A month later, the Secretary General called all five permanent members into his office to discuss what could be done. This led to the idea that the five permanent members should adopt a unified cease-fire resolution and put pressure on both sides to stop the fighting. Three principal issues had alarmed members of the Council a great deal: the prolonged nature of the war, the attacks on neutral shipping in the Gulf, and the use of chemical and other unconventional weapons (Shaali 1996).

The five permanent members started holding meetings in January 1987 with the sole purpose of drafting a cease-fire resolution. The British took the initiative among the five in early 1987, and in May the US assumed the leadership in marshalling support among the permanent members, following a visit by Assistant Secretary of State for Near Eastern Affairs, Richard Murphy, to Baghdad (Sick 1989: p 240). Meanwhile discussions continued into April, when the draft was presented to the five members of the Non-Aligned group in the Security Council (the five permanent members and the five Non-Aligned members constituted the two basic blocs in the Council). The Non-Aligned group met and decided to invite the remaining five non-permanent members to join the discussions towards the end of April. They went to work, the five permanent members meeting regularly in one room and the ten non-permanent members meeting in another, with drafts and amendments being passed back and forth between them. This exercise lasted through June (Shaali 1996). The UAE assumed the chairmanship of the Non-Aligned caucus in July. Due to this, and to the fact that it was the only Muslim and Arab member of the Council, the UAE was able to play an influential role.

The UAE's basic position was that a cease-fire draft resolution should be fair to both parties. It should be clear and unambiguous; it should be based on the inadmissibility of the acquisition of territory by force; and it should explicitly lay down the steps leading to a cease-fire and the withdrawal of forces. It was important to avoid another Resolution 242 (for ending the Arab-Israeli conflict) which had proven so difficult to implement (Shaali 1996).

The UAE was known and trusted by both Iran and Iraq. It insisted on what it felt to be a firm and fair position. It made a point of avoiding taking sides, except in case of gross violations of international law, such as the use of chemical weapons, first by Iraq and later by both sides. It served as a conduit for negotiations between members of the Security Council and Iraq; it did the same with Iran. The UAE saw as its role to communicate, mediate and refine the resolution until it became acceptable to both sides. From the beginning, Iran had asked for a kind of judiciary panel to assign responsibility for the outbreak of the war and for a UN team to assess the damages it had suffered from the war. The non-permanent members of the Council were able to secure Iran's consent in principle to the cease-fire by including provisions for the Secretary General to set up an impartial body to 'inquire into responsibility for the conflict', to dispatch teams to assess the damages caused by the war and to offer international assistance to help with the reconstruction effort. These conditions were worked into Resolution 598 as operative paragraphs 6 and 7 respectively. The UAE sought to insert a paragraph requesting both sides to refrain from attacking the littoral states in the Gulf, so as to prevent a spillover of the war (Shaali 1996). An OIC mission was active in efforts to negotiate a cease-fire.

The resolution was adopted on 20 July. Provisions for a judiciary panel had been inserted in the resolution as a carrot for Iran, but Tehran wanted to reverse the order of implementation of the operative paragraphs in the resolution as it wanted to start, not with the cease-fire (which is in the first operative paragraph), but with the formation of the panel which was in paragraph six (Shaali 1996).

Resolution 598 was far more significant than its predecessor in that, invoking Articles 39 and 40 of the UN Charter, it ordered a cessation of hostilities and a halt to all attacks on shipping. The aforementioned articles, which constitute part of Chapter VII, empower the Council initially to resort to measures 'not involving the use of armed force' (under Article 41); but then, if such measures prove inadequate, the Council is empowered to 'take such action by air, sea, or land forces as may be necessary to maintain or restore international peace and security' under Article 42 of the Charter.

Resolution 598 states that the Security Council:

Demands that, as a first step towards a negotiated settlement, Iran and Iraq observe an immediate cease-fire, discontinue all military actions on land, at sea and in the air, and withdraw all forces to the internationally recognized boundaries without delay. (S/RES/598)

The importance that members of the Council attached to this resolution, which was adopted unanimously by the Council members, is evident from the fact that US Secretary of State George Shultz, the Foreign Minister of the United Kingdom, Sir Geoffrey Howe, Vice-

Chancellor and Foreign Minister Hans-Dietrich Genscher of the Federal Republic of Germany, Italy's Minister for Foreign Affairs, Giulio Andreotti, and Japan's Vice-Minister for Foreign Affairs, Ryohei Murata represented their countries in person at the Security Council meeting in which the resolution was adopted. The United Arab Emirates was represented by Minister of State for Foreign Affairs, Rashid Abdullah. All emphasized the extraordinary nature of the resolution which was the culmination of months of consultation. Sir Geoffrey noted that the Security Council was ordering a mandatory cease-fire (p 16), Mr Shultz said that the US supports 'the decisive application of enforcement measures should either or both parties reject the call of this body' (p 22) and Mr. Genscher noted that 'This resolution is only the third in the life of the United Nations to exhaust all the means envisaged in the charter' (p 27). Mr Aleksander Belonogov of the Soviet Union, while supporting the resolution, noted that his government 'envisaged that, *inter alia,* all warships that did not belong to the area should be withdrawn from the Gulf as soon as possible' (p 72).

In its official reply to the Security Council on 11 August 1987 Iran adopted a tough position, maintaining that 'Resolution 598 (1987) has been formulated and adopted by the United States with the explicit intention of intervention in the Arabian Gulf and the region, mustering support for Iraq and its supporters in the war' ((S/19031, p 2). It charged the US with being 'the first violator of the resolution' (p 3) and emphasized the centrality of operative paragraphs 5 and 8 which called on third parties not to engage in acts that might lead to escalation. It called on the Secretary General to consult with Iran and Iraq and other states of the region on 'measures to enhance the security and stability of the region'. Emphasis was put on freeing the Gulf zone from intervention by foreign powers, a goal to which, in principle, the GCC members were sympathetic at the time, despite their dependence on US protection of shipping. Despite this seemingly defiant position, according to a report by the Secretary General to the Security Council on 16 September 1987 regarding his consultations in Tehran and Baghdad from 12-15 September (which was published by the Kuwait News Agency on 19 September), 'there was no reference on the part of the Iranian authorities to a rejection of any part of the resolution' and Iran was prepared to accept 'an integrated approach that would include a cease-fire as a first step' (FBIS-NES-87-183, 22 September 1987, p 46).

Nevertheless, Iran insisted that the process of setting up a panel of inquiry must be started before an official cease-fire could be declared, but allowed that 'an undeclared cessation of hostilities could come into effect during the process of identification of the responsibility for the conflict'. Iraqi officials told the Secretary General that Baghdad would 'under no circum-stances accept an undeclared cease-fire' and stressed that 'a cease-fire should be followed without delay by the withdrawal of all forces' (FBIS-NES-87-183, p 47).

Iraq took advantage of Tehran's position to regain territory lost to Iran. The US proceeded to reflag Kuwaiti tankers and to punish Iran's navy for its attacks on neutral shipping. The final blow to Iran came when a ship-launched missile fired by the *USS Vincennes* brought down an Iranian civilian aircraft carrying 290 passengers bound for Dubai as a result of misiden-tification by the ship's crew of the radar image. Iran failed to secure enough support for a resolution in the UN condemning the incident, although the Islamic Conference Organization did issue a press statement expressing outrage at the US action (S/20002).

Tehran finally accepted the cease-fire officially on 17 July 1988 (S/20020) after Iran's position had eroded considerably; Khomeini later described the act as 'more deadly than taking poison'. Iraq issued a statement on 19 July saying that Resolution 598 must be approached 'in accordance with the sequence of its operative paragraphs' - which gave lower priority to the assignment of responsibility for the war and assessment of the damages suffered by Iran - and 'be crowned with a lasting peace accord' (S/20031).

Other notable resolutions adopted by the Security Council during the UAE's period on the Council are Resolution 605 (adopted on 22 December 1987) strongly deploring the violation of the human rights of Palestinians under Israeli occupation, notably the shooting of defenceless civilians by the Israeli army, and calling on Israel to desist from violations of the Geneva Convention of 12 August 1949 relative to the Protection of Civilian Persons in Time of War in its treatment of the Palestinians (S/RES/605). Resolution 592 (adopted on 8 December 1986) also strongly deplores 'the opening of fire by the Israeli army resulting in the death and the wounding of defenceless students' and calls on Israel to observe the Geneva Convention scrupulously (S/RES/592). In addition, the Council adopted three resolutions strongly condemning South Africa: in Resolution 601 of 30 October 1987 'for its continued illegal occupation of Namibia' (S/RES/601), in Resolution 602 of 25 November 1987 for South Africa's aggression against the People's Republic of Angola (S/RES/602) and in Resolution 606 of 23 December 1987 for its continued occupation of parts of Angola (S/RES/606).

Arab issues at the United Nations

The UAE's position is that an Arab representative on the Security Council can have a considerable impact, specially when the issue is a regional one. Success by Arab and other envoys requires group action; it depends on rallying support and regional issues evoke commitments and allegiances that facilitate the formation of consensus among a solid core of nations. The more supporters one has, the stronger one's position is. 'A unified Arab position was very important. One can also gain strong support from Islamic countries, then African and Asian ones.' (Shaali 1996). But one needs to start with a solid core. Lack of unity among a solid core group spells defeat.

Arab nationalism and an Arab identity are strong driving forces for the UAE. 'The UAE became a member of the United Nations as a country with Arab convictions, seeking to defend Arab causes in international organizations.' (Shaali 1996). The question of Palestine and the Arab-Israeli conflict have topped the list of UAE concerns at the UN. The UAE mission has been active in defending the right of the Palestinian people to self-determination and supporting efforts of 'frontline' Arab states to liberate the territories they had lost to Israel. The UAE was one of the countries that helped the PLO to achieve observer status at the UN.

Some of the most important issues during the UAE's two years on the Security Council were the question of Jerusalem, the US attack on Libya, the hijacking of civilian aircraft by Israeli fighters and Israeli attacks on Lebanon, particularly after the intifada started.

On 30 November 1987, in celebration of the International Day of Solidarity with the Palestine People, UAE President, Sheikh Zayed bin Sultan Al Nahyan, (along with other heads of state) addressed a message to the Committee on the Exercise of the Inalienable rights of the Palestinian People, in which he recalled that 1987 marked the seventieth anniversary of the Balfour declaration, the fortieth anniversary of the UN resolution for the partition of Palestine, and the twentieth anniversary of the occupation of the West Bank and other Arab territories by Israel. Regretting the 'domination-oriented policies' of certain major powers who opposed an international conference to find a settlement for the Palestinian issue under UN auspices, Sheikh Zayed went on to say:

Until such a settlement is achieved and the Palestinian people regain their rights, the Government and people of the United Arab Emirates remain pledged to support the struggle of the Palestinian people and to render all possible assistance to them. (A/AC.183/PV.148, p 113)

This protest against the attempt by the United States and other Western powers to impose their will on the Arab world is characteristic of the UAE and is a recurrent theme in its unapologetic insistence on an evenhanded approach at United Nations fora. The United States has accepted this approach because it realizes that the UAE's position is based on principle; it has not forgotten that the UAE is a moderate country that maintains good relations with the West, and is not posturing or seeking political gains for itself (Shaali 1996).

The UAE played a role in the Security Council as a representative of the Middle East region and the Arabs in general, regardless of inter-Arab disputes; it acted as a voice for Syria, Libya and the Palestinians irrespective of the state of their relations with the UAE. This was made possible by the UAE's refusal to engage in factional politics in the Arab world. 'When the US attacked Libya, we were very hurt by the US; we do not agree with this policy of tyranny.' (Shaali 1996). In fact, following the Gulf of Sidra incident, the UAE issued a statement on 26 March 1986, which its representative read to the Security Council:

The United Arab Emirates is greatly concerned at the dangerous military escalation in the Gulf of Sidra stemming from the United States aggression against the Libyan Arab Jamahiriya. The United Arab Emirates condemns that aggression in flagrant violation of Libya's independence, sovereignty and territorial integrity. We affirm our solidarity with the Jamahiriya and express the hope that an end will be put to this escalation, which is threatening the security of Arab states, their territorial integrity, and the security of the eastern Mediterranean, not to mention the security of the international community as a whole. (S/PV.2671, p 17)

The UAE was shocked by the United States' 'flagrant violation of the provisions of Article 2 of the United Nations Charter,' pointing out that 'One cannot choose the parts of international law that one likes and ignore the rest'(S/PV.2671, pp 13-15), particularly in the case of a state that has special responsibilities vis-a-vis the international community. When the US launched another serious attack on Libya in mid-April, the UAE's envoy told the Council:

As I have said, arrogant power needs no legal, logical or even ethical justification. The United States of America possesses military force sufficient to annihilate Libya and all the countries of the third world. We had hoped it would demonstrate enough reason and wisdom to control that force. (S/PV.2674, p 5)

The UAE has consistently served as an Arab voice at the United Nations. Following the massacre of dozens of Palestinian worshippers at Al-Haram Al-Ibrahimi near Hebron by an Israeli settler on 25 February 1994, the UAE protested to the Security Council about the shooting of Palestinian demonstrators by Israeli troops, the arming of settlers, the confiscation of Palestinian land and the establishment of settlements on those lands in 'flagrant violation of

United Nations resolutions declaring the settlements illegal'. The UAE Government called on the Council to adopt 'an unambiguous resolution to protect the Palestinian people in the occupied Palestinian territories', and to 'appoint an international commission to investigate the circumstances under which the carnage was perpetrated'. (S/PV.3341, pp 5-6)

Of course there are issues over which permanent members of the Council may choose to exercise a veto, and no amount of support can prevail against that. The first four draft resolutions sponsored by the UAE during its term on the Council (one relating to Lebanon, two to the occupied West Bank) drew a US veto. Days of negotiating support for these draft resolutions were wiped out in an instant, due to domestic pressures in the United States.

The United Arab Emirates seems to thrive in multilateral contexts, and the General Assembly is just such a forum; but the Security Council is not. If multilateralism is understood to entail the principles of non-discrimination and indivisibility among members of the collectivity (for example, peace is indivisible in the sense that an attack on one is an attack on all), then the Security Council cannot be said to embody multilateralism either in its make-up or in its operations. Instead the Council is based on the leadership of the small group of its five permanent members which is effective only when there is a consensus among them or when none of them exercises the power of veto. This has frequently opened the way for discrimination in favour of clients of the permanent members, notably the United States and the former Soviet Union. Persistent US vetoes of resolutions critical of Israel have been a source of recurrent frustration for Arab sponsors of such resolutions, including, of course, the UAE.

The UAE's former permanent representative to the UN, Muhammad Shaali, complains that the UN of the 1990s is quite different from the UN of the 1970s. Following the collapse of the Soviet Union, the Non-Aligned movement, which used to be a third moral power, also collapsed. This has opened the door to dominance by the West, and by the US, especially since the Gulf War. Countries of the Third World are no longer free to vote as they like; they are being pressured.

Both the UN and the Security Council have changed. The role of the Security Council used to be to initiate peaceful and diplomatic resolutions to any problem. Peaceful and democratic initiatives are not there any more; Chapter VII sanctions (against Iraq) were used for the first time with such force. The Security Council has become a 'sanctions council'. During the eight years of the Iran-Iraq war, the Security Council did not issue a single sanction; nor did it do so in the 45-year history of the Arab-Israeli conflict. During my membership, the US and the UK refused even the mention of the term 'sanctions' against the apartheid regime in South Africa. There is a tendency now to go straight to Chapter VII and adopt sanctions. We have a different UN now, one that is designed to serve the interests of the victorious powers of the Second World War.

The Gulf Cooperation Council

On 25 May 1981 the heads of state of Saudi Arabia, the UAE, Kuwait, Bahrain, Qatar and Oman met in Abu Dhabi and signed the charter of the Gulf Cooperation Council. The agreement went into force immediately. The Council therefore includes all countries in the Arabian

Peninsula other than Yemen. Yemen in fact had applied, but was excluded because it was divided into two: the Yemen Arab Republic and the Yemen People's Democratic Republic. It was felt that the GCC grouped together countries that were similar in culture, political structure and legal frameworks. They are all conservative states that tend to have common security and economic problems. If the recently united Yemen were to apply for membership, it might well be accepted (Saad 1996).

The most important organs of the GCC are the Supreme Council (composed of the heads of state of the six member nations), the Ministerial Council, which comprises the foreign ministers of the member states, and the General Secretariat. The Ministerial Council coordinates the positions of the member states in relation to, among others, the United Nations and the Arab League. The members of the GCC are united by long-term common political, economic and security interests. That is not to say that all disputes within the GCC have been settled - despite the impressive progress made towards resolving most disagreements over territorial limits, a few issues remain to be settled (Schofield 1996).

The primacy of the GCC in coordinating the UAE's relations with the outside world is due to the political, economic and security interests which the UAE shares with its Gulf neighbours and the sense of a common threat emanating from Iran and Iraq, particularly after Iraq's invasion of Kuwait. In fact, since the 1980s one notices a decline of collective action at the UN by members of the Arab League (except where Palestinian rights and Israeli attacks on Lebanon are concerned) under the name of the League, and a shift to reliance on the Gulf Cooperation Council for the major issues concerning the security, politics and economic relations of the Gulf states.

Political processes within the UAE depend on consensus. As a federal country, as an Arab country, the UAE is aware of the Arab and regional dimensions of stability. The UAE believes the GCC provides the kind of formula for cooperation that will allow the countries of the region to deal most efficiently with developments, such as the economic and security challenges of the future, which no small country can handle on its own (Shaali 1996).

The Gulf Cooperation Council is a multifaceted alliance: political, economic and military. The fact that the GCC came into being in the wake of the revolution in Iran and the outbreak of the Iran-Iraq war has led many analysts to see it as primarily a regional security organization. From this perspective, the GCC was born in response to the security threat emanating from the new regime in Tehran or the danger of radical Arab nationalism or Ba'thism emanating from Baghdad. The Iran-Iraq war itself was a seminal event that threatened the territorial integrity and the safety of navigation in the Gulf. Although not incorrect, this perspective is one-sided however, in that it cannot explain the absence of a mutual defence treaty among the GCC states from the outset, nor can it explain the existence of economic and political cooperation prior to the formation of the GCC.

The key to understanding the GCC is to conceive of it as a political alliance that seeks to capitalize on and enhance the source of strength of its members (their economic capabilities) but is deeply conscious of the demographic shortcomings that make self-reliance for defence or deterrence unfeasible. The preferred approach of the GCC states is political mediation, crisis management and balance of power politics. Thus the GCC became involved in mediation in the Iran-Iraq war from fairly early on (in 1982-3), and its members, including the UAE, are particularly proud of their contribution to bringing about a cease-fire in that conflict.

When the Iran-Iraq war spilled over into Iranian attacks on commercial shipping to and from Kuwaiti and Saudi Arabian ports, the UAE joined the other GCC members in taking the matter to the Security Council (S/16574). The Council passed Resolution 552 on 1 June 1984 calling on all states to respect the right of free navigation and to respect the territorial integrity of states that were not a party to the hostilities. The Council also decided to 'consider effective measures' in the event of non-compliance (S/RES/552). This led to further resolutions, culminating in Resolution 598. It should not be forgotten however, as explained above, that the UAE helped mediate that resolution.

The conclusion to be drawn is that collective action by the GCC states in security related issues tends to rely on political and diplomatic action, and conflict resolution techniques. When mediation attempts failed to lead to a cessation of hostilities between their two powerful neighbours, the next logical step for the GCC was to try a balance of power approach, giving financial aid to Iraq until it was able to counterbalance Iran's superior manpower with sophisticated weaponry. When Iran countered by threatening to widen the conflict and began to attack shipping, military action was required. At that point the GCC was forced to rely on the United States. When the dispute between Iraq and Kuwait led to the invasion of Kuwait, the GCC was again forced to rely on the United States and to a lesser extent the UK and other members of the coalition, and on sanctions by the Security Council.

When Iraq invaded Kuwait, the other members of the GCC did not have the capabilities to come to the aid of Kuwait; they relied instead on a multi-nation alliance led by the United States. In March 1991, an attempt was made to put together a regional alliance grouping the GCC, Egypt and Syria which came to be referred to as (GCC+2), but which the GCC preferred to call the countries of the Damascus Declaration. It was announced on 6 March in Damascus that Egypt and Syria were to maintain troops in the Gulf which would constitute the nucleus for a regional peace-keeping force. Four days later, the foreign ministers of the eight countries met in Riyadh and endorsed a security arrangement for the Gulf proposed by US Secretary of State James Baker which entailed cooperation between their armed forces and those of the United States. The cooperation envisaged in the Damascus Declaration did not endure.

Following the December 1994 Supreme Council meeting, a GCC decision 'to develop a deterrent force to arm the Peninsula' which could serve as a rapid deployment force (an idea which originated at the 1993 Supreme Council meeting), was submitted as a document of the Security Council as well as the General Assembly. Of course, regional organizations are required to work with the Security Council and not independently in the service of area security and to promote peace. It is doubtful, however, that a force put together by members of the GCC without US assistance would be up to the task of dealing with Iran and Iraq. In the face of such opponents, the GCC's contribution to regional security seems to be primarily to lend moral and political support to the actions of the Security Council in the Gulf, whereas enforcement relies heavily on the deployment of US and other western forces to the region.

During the last five years five topics have tended to dominate GCC Supreme Council and Ministerial Council meetings: ensuring compliance by Iraq with all relevant Security Council resolutions and the sanctions imposed in the wake of its invasion of Kuwait (discussed below); supporting the UAE in its dispute with Iran over the Abu Musa and Tunb islands (discussed in the following section); supporting the Middle East peace process; demanding a halt to Serbian atrocities in Bosnia-Hercegovina; and dealing with economic issues. Economic ties with the European Union are frequently mentioned and, since the latter half of 1994, support is voiced for the WTO, and for increasing economic integration between GCC members. Reports of annual meetings of the GCC Supreme Council and the Ministerial Council have been submitted to the UN and circulated as official documents of the General Assembly or the Security Council under the relevant agenda items.

Since Iraq's invasion of Kuwait, members of the GCC have demonstrated consistent solidarity with Kuwait and maintained a solid front against Iraq. On 8 August 1990 representatives of GCC member states in the UN requested a Security Council meeting to consider the situation resulting from Iraq's annexation of Kuwait. On 24 August of the same year, the permanent representatives of the six GCC states called on the Security Council to convene so as to adopt measures to implement previous resolutions (660, 661 and 662) regarding Iraq's occupation of Kuwait. Since 1991, successive GCC Supreme and Ministerial Council meetings have repeatedly condemned Iraq for not complying fully with Security Council cease-fire Resolution 687 of 8 April 1991 - and later with Resolution 833 of 1993, establishing the boundary between Iraq and Kuwait - through its 'persistent repetition of its expansionist claims against Kuwait', and for its failure to release Kuwaiti prisoners, return Kuwaiti property or pay compensation to Kuwait. In the communiqué which was issued by the fourteenth session of the Supreme Council in December 1993, submitted to the Secretary General and circulated as an official document of the General Assembly and the Security Council, the GCC affirmed 'the need to maintain international pressure until such time as the [Iraqi] regime desists from its aggression and complies with all its international obligations' (A/49/56, p 4). The following year, the Supreme Council noted with satisfaction Iraq's recognition of its border with Kuwait as drawn by the Security Council, 'and considered that to be an important step towards Iraqi compliance with all relevant Security Council resolutions.' (A/49/815, p 3). However, in September 1995, the Ministerial Council blasted Iraq's 'lack of credibility and seriousness in addressing its international obligations' in the light of revelations by Iraqi defectors, including Saddam Hussein's sons-in-law (A/50/466, p 3). The GCC has repeatedly reaffirmed its commitment to Iraq's territorial integrity, and it has consistently blamed the Iraqi regime for not taking up Security Council offers to allow it to sell very limited amounts of oil to pay for badly needed food and medicinal imports.

It is estimated that 567,000 Iraqi children may have died since the imposition of the sanctions, and that 28 per cent of the children under ten years of age are stunted in growth (*The Lancet*, 2.12.1995: pp1485, 1439). This has led to misgivings concerning the sanctions on the part of the UAE, which believes the sanctions need to be rationalized because, as currently constituted, they are hurting the wrong people.

Dominance of the Council by the United States and the other Western powers has led to a proclivity to apply sanctions without regard for their unintended consequences for non-Western populations. The sanctions against Iraq imposed by the Security Council under US leadership are unprecedented. While the UAE supports the arms embargo and trade sanctions against Iraq, as do all members of the GCC, the UAE feels the trade sanctions need to be directed against the regime rather than the people of Iraq. The UAE believes that the sanctions on Iraq, which have been in effect for five years, have proven ineffective in bringing about the changes that GCC members and the Security Council are seeking. Sanctions alone are powerless to do that, according to the UAE's ambassador to Washington:

That is not to say we want to lift the sanctions, but to rationalize them so that they do not hurt innocent people. We do not believe that it is in the interest of the countries of the Gulf Cooperation Council to create animosity with the people of Iraq. Sanctions should be re-evaluated and rationalized, which is different from saying that they should be reconsidered. When diplomacy and political initiative are bankrupt, one uses sanctions. Major powers are behaving like small, insecure states. (Shaali 1996)

The Secretary General of the United Nations, Boutros Boutros Ghali, is of the same mind. He has himself been critical of the application of sanctions under Article 41 of the Charter, noting that 'the purpose of sanctions is to modify the behavior of a party that is threatening international peace and security and not to punish or otherwise exact retribution' (A/50/60, p 16). He adds that:

Sanctions, as is generally recognized, are a blunt instrument. They raise the ethical question of whether suffering inflicted on vulnerable groups in the target country is a legitimate means of exerting pressure on political leaders whose behavior is unlikely to be affected by the plight of their subjects. (A/50/60, p 16)

The Arab League

The relationship between the Arab League and the Trucial States predates the formation of the UAE. When Abu Dhabi began exporting crude oil in 1962, Sheikh Shakhbut was wary of modernization and British assistance was meagre (amounting to only one million pounds from 1955 to 1965). Some of the rulers of the Trucial States therefore found themselves compelled to request aid from the Arab League in 1964. When the Arab League delegation toured the emirates it was warmly welcomed in an outpouring of nationalist sentiment. Britain was apprehensive of losing its control and put pressure on Saudi Arabia not to honour its aid commitments. Britain then deposed the ruler of Sharjah and prompted the rulers to insist that all aid had to be channelled through the Development Bureau which Britain controlled. The rulers acquiesced, and the project was aborted (Taryam 1987: pp 48-51). When the UAE later became wealthy from the export of oil, it proved generous in its aid to projects administered by the Arab League.

The islands occupied by Iran

The UAE became the eighteenth member of the Arab League on 6 December 1971 despite opposition from the Democratic People's Republic of Yemen (Taryam 1987: p 190). On the very day that the UAE joined the League of Arab States, the League met in emergency session to consider the occupation of Abu Musa and the Tunb islands by Iran. Britain had apparently permitted the Shah to occupy the islands in exchange for Tehran's dropping its claim to Bahrain, and in the hope that Iran could replace the UK as the protector of Western interests in the Gulf. The reaction by the Arab League was muted, perhaps stemming from a desire not to alienate Iran. Resolution 2865 was passed charging the Secretary General of the League with responsibility for pursuing the matter with Iran and countries of the region. An Arab

League delegation reported, after visiting the Gulf, that the rulers of the member emirates in the union were in favour of an amicable settlement with Iran and wanted the League to undertake negotiations with that objective in mind, declaring themselves to be prepared to commit themselves to the result. However, the efforts of the League with Tehran in this matter proved futile (Taryam 1987: p 189).

On 3 December 1971, six days before the UAE became a member of the UN, four Arab states - Algeria, Iraq, Libya and South Yemen - put the issue before the UN Security Council, arguing that Iran's occupation of the Greater and Lesser Tunbs constituted a violation of the UN Charter, that the understanding between Iran and Sharjah over Abu Musa was invalid and that Sharjah did not have the right to enter into an agreement concerning any part of its territory without British approval, which had not been secured (Taryam 1987: pp 187-88). The agreement, which the ruler of Sharjah accepted under duress, provided for the inhabitants of Abu Musa to remain under the legal jurisdiction of Sharjah, for Iran to occupy part of the island without thereby prejudicing Sharjah's rights of sovereignty over it, and for oil revenues from off-shore oil wells to be shared equally between Iran and Sharjah (Taryam 1987: p 183). Ras al-Khaimah refused to sign a similar agreement (Zahlan 1978: p 195).

In the wake of the overthrow of the Shah, the Islamic Republic of Iran opted to reaffirm Iran's determination to continue the occupation of the islands (S/13987), as laid out in a letter circulated by Foreign Minister Sadeq Ghotbzadeh as a document of the Security Council. The UAE's Minister of State for Foreign Affairs, Rashid Abdullah, replied on 18 August 1980 with a letter to the Secretary General in which he regretted Iran's intention of continuing the expansionist policies of the Shah, saying that 'the Government of the United Arab Emirates finds itself obliged to re-emphasize its firm attachment to those islands, which form an integral part of the territory of the State', and inviting Iran to open a dialogue leading to the restoration of the islands to the UAE (A/35/399). The UAE had occasion to submit yet another letter to the Secretary General of the UN on 1 December, protesting a statement by Iranian President, Bani Sadr, to the *Nouvelle Observateur* on 13 October 1980 which claimed that Iran had paid 'certain sheikhs' to keep silent about Tehran's takeover of the islands. In April 1992, Iran took full control of Abu Musa after expelling the staff of the school administered by the UAE on the island (Caldwell 1996: p 53), thus violating the 1971 agreement with Sharjah. On 13 September 1992 the Council of Ministers of Foreign Affairs of the League of Arab States decided:

1. *To stand by the United Arab Emirates in its adherence to full sovereignty over the islands of Abu Musa, Greater Tunb and Lesser Tunb, and to denounce Iran's illegal occupation of these islands;*
2. *To state the Council's unqualified support for all measures taken by the United Arab Emirates to assert its sovereignty over the islands and to place the issue of the Iranian violations - which most seriously endanger the security and stability of the region - before the United Nations;*
3. *To call upon the Islamic Republic of Iran to respect the pacts and covenants it has concluded with the United Arab Emirates, as well as that country's sovereignty over the Abu Musa, Greater Tunb and Lesser Tunb islands;*
4. *To request the Secretary General to pursue this matter.* (A/47/516)

The above Arab League resolution (5223/98/3) was circulated as an official document of the General Assembly. At the end of September 1992, Iran announced that it had full rights of sovereignty over the island. The UAE brought the issue of the three islands before the GCC as well as the Arab League and won support for its position. The GCC has consistently backed the right of the UAE to sovereignty over the islands while endorsing peaceful means to resolve the dispute. The final communiqué issued by the Supreme Council of the GCC at the end of its December 1993 meeting (submitted as a document of the Security Council and General Assembly) expressed full support for the UAE's position and issued a warning to Iran that future relations with the GCC depended on its 'respect for the sovereignty and territorial integrity of States of the region' (A/49/56, p 5). The final report of the Supreme Council's meeting in December of the following year called on Iran to refer the issue of Abu Musa and the Tunbs to the International Court of Justice (A/49/815, p 4), a position already outlined in the GCC Ministerial Council's communique at the end of the session of September 1994 (A/49/412, p 3) and reiterated in September 1995 (A/50/466, p 4).

Of course, there are instances when unilateral action by the UAE is sufficient. For example, it has been 25 years since Algeria, Iraq, Libya and Yemen requested - as mentioned above - that the issue of the islands occupied by Iran be listed as an item on the agenda of the Security Council. The Council is about to delete a number of agenda items unless there is a request for their renewal; consequently, the UAE, at the time of writing, is on the verge of submitting a formal request that the occupation of the three islands should continue to be listed under Security Council agenda, item 16.

The Arab League was never an ideal regional arrangement or agency either for promoting inter-Arab cooperation or for collaboration with the Security Council in the maintenance of international peace and security. To begin with, the political and security interests of the members of the League did not converge; in fact the League was founded by Egypt to grant it better leverage in its competition with Iraq and to foil attempts at Arab unity under the banner of the Hashemites. Nor did the Arab League represent a security alliance - the pact drafted for that purpose by Egypt in 1950 was directed against Jordan, another member of the League, and initially only five of the seven members of the League were signatories (Iraq did join in 1951 but only after securing revisions which guaranteed that the pact would not automatically come into force). The issue of who was to control Palestine after British withdrawal and the question of the Baghdad Pact deeply divided the League. In Lenczowski's sardonic account:

> *In the 1950s and the early 1960s the Arab League followed a seemingly paradoxical course of Pan-Arab solidarity and deep inner conflict. The paradox, however, was more apparent than real because the policies of solidarity and internecine conflict were not mutually exclusive. Solidarity existed on most of the issues where the Arab struggle for emancipation from imperialism was involved.* (1980: p 746)

The Arab League's fortunes waned following the division in Arab ranks caused by Egypt's separate peace agreement with Israel in 1979. Egypt was ostracized by the other Arab states, including the UAE, and the League's headquarters were moved to Tunis. Regular meetings of the Arab League were not held for three years, from 1982 to 1985, when an emergency meeting in Morocco revealed divisions between one camp, led by Syria, that opposed attempts by Jordan and PLO to initiate peace talks with Israel, and another camp, led by Jordan, favouring the talks. At the November 1987 Arab summit in Amman, many Arab countries renewed relations with Egypt and the conferees condemned Iran and came out in support of Iraq, Kuwait and Saudi Arabia. Egypt was later readmitted to the fold and the headquarters were moved back to Cairo. But the League's impotence was very soon thereafter unveiled by the Iraqi invasion of Kuwait, which split the Arab world and threatened the continued existence of the League.

One reason for the Arab League's weakness is that only unanimous League decisions are binding. 'Unfortunately, the Arab League is a mirror of its members. Political tensions have not helped the League play its role.' (Shaali 1996)

The influence of the Arab League has been in severe decline since the Gulf war and the Arab states have not been voting as a single bloc. At the end of December, the heads of state of Egypt, Saudi Arabia and Syria met in Alexandria and asked the Secretary General of the Arab League to undertake measures to energize or reactivate the League. In January 1995, the leaders of Egypt, Jordan, the PLO and Prime Minister Yitzhak Rabin of Israel held their own summit in Cairo.

Arab states decided that the UN resolutions were to be superseded by the Camp David accords and their offspring, the Declaration of Principles (DOP) between Israel and the PLO (signed in September 1993) and the Israeli-Jordanian peace treaty (signed in October 1994). This in turn led to the removal of the Palestine question and the Middle East conflict, for all practical purposes, from UN jurisdiction, and became the prelude to attempts to replace the Arab state system with a Middle East regional construct. (Maksoud 1995: p 587)

This has led the Palestinian National Authority to take its complaints about Israel's non-compliance with the terms of its agreement with the PLO to Egypt, and, to a lesser extent, to Jordan. This responsibility, coupled with Egypt's reluctance to allow Israel to assume the leadership of a Middle Eastern system of states, in turn prompted Cairo to make an issue of US willingness to overlook Israel's refusal to accede to the Nuclear Non-Proliferation Treaty (NPT). On 29 March 1995, the League passed Resolution no. 5455 in favour of ridding the Middle East of weapons of mass destruction (Maksoud 1995: p 588). Fourteen Arab states, including Egypt, Jordan and the four members of the GCC that were signatories to the NPT (and therefore participants in the conference) put a draft resolution (L.7) before the 1995 Review and Extension Conference of the Parties to the NPT, embodying an unadulterated Arab position, in which they expressed 'deep concern at the continued existence in the Middle East of unsafeguarded Israeli nuclear facilities'. They called for a nuclear-weapon-free zone in the Middle East and urged those states possessing nuclear weapons to provide security assurances to the states of the region not possessing such weapons. Significantly, the draft resolution:

Calls upon Israel to accede without delay to the Treaty on the Non-Proliferation of Nuclear Weapons and to place all its nuclear activities under [International Atomic Energy] Agency full-scope safeguards . (NPT/CONF.1995/L.7, p 2)

The exercise backfired, however, with unexpected repercussions for the UAE (see the discussion on the NPT below).

The United States vetoed an Arab League-sponsored resolution at the Security Council in May 1995 that would have condemned Israel for confiscating Arab property in East Jerusalem, highlighting the powerlessness of the League and US control over the UN. Nevertheless, the election of Benjamin Netanyahu as Prime Minister of Israel has united the Arab world as nothing else could have. The June 1996 Arab summit in Cairo was the first of its kind since August 1990. If Arab cooperation endures, particularly in response to the new Likud prime minister in Israel, the UAE may well find itself sponsoring resolutions on behalf of the League once again, not least because Sheikh Zayed of Abu Dhabi harbours genuine Arab nationalist sympathies.

The Non-proliferation Treaty

UN General Assembly Resolution 50/73 (of 10 January 1996) 'Welcomes the accession of the United Arab Emirates on 26 September 1995 to the Treaty on the Non-Proliferation of Nuclear Weapons.' (A/RES/50/73) This unintendedly belated accession by the UAE to the treaty was the result of a tug of war, between the group of Non-Aligned countries led by Indonesia and Arab countries (with Egypt and Jordan leading) on the one side and the United States backed by Western nations on the other, concerning the universality of the treaty, notably whether Israel should be made to accede to the NPT.

Paragraph 2 of article X of the NPT states that 25 years after the treaty comes into force, the signatories shall decide whether to extend it indefinitely or for a fixed period of time. President Clinton, in his State of the Union Address in January 1995 declared the indefinite and unconditional extension of the Nuclear Non-Proliferation Treaty to be a priority for US foreign policy. The US Arms Control and Disarmament Agency described it as 'the centerpiece of all of [the Agency's] post-Cold War arms control efforts.' (USDoS,95/04/13 briefing: p 1) Since the treaty was up for renewal, the US wanted to seize the opportunity to make it permanent while this could be done without having to go back to national legislatures for ratification (USDoS: p 4).

Deliberations by the 1995 Review and Extension Conference of the Parties to the Treaty on the Non-Proliferation of Nuclear Weapons began on 17 April. Egypt and Jordan engaged in a series of consultations with African, Latin American and Asian countries on this issue. It was felt that the Middle East presented an anomalous situation in that there was neither a rough balance among states possessing nuclear arms, as is the case in South Asia with India and Pakistan, nor was there a mutual agreement among countries of the region to forgo the acquisition of nuclear weapons, as in Central America (Abu Odeh 1996). Egypt and Jordan were in favour of extension, but objected to the fact that an indefinite extension allowing Israel to remain outside the Treaty would perpetuate the nuclear imbalance in the Middle East with no opportunity for review. Egypt worked to insert wording in a draft resolution calling on Israel to sign the treaty.

In the words of the representative of Egypt, recapping his country's position during the seventeenth meeting of the NPT Extension Conference on 11 May:

The option of the indefinite extension of the Treaty before the realization of its univer-
sality ignores the important fact that it represents a request to states, in particular those
in the Middle East region, to fulfill indefinite obligations in respect of the non-prolif-
eration of nuclear weapons, without similar obligations being placed on Israel. That
perpetuates a structural imbalance in rights and duties and endangers national, regional
and international peace. (NPT/CONF.1995/PV.17, p 20)

The Jordanian representative argued that, in addition, the Israeli nuclear facility at Dimona in the Negev needed to be brought under international inspection and the control of the International Atomic Energy Agency as it was in fact closer to four Jordanian provinces than it was to Tel Aviv (Abu Odeh, and NPT/CONF.1995/PV.17, p 6).

The Western powers, led by the United States, did their best to head off the move to compel Israel to join, and instead called on all countries of the Middle East, including Arab countries which were not signatories to the Treaty, to accede to it. The UAE was one of these countries. Oman and the UAE were the only two members of the GCC which had not acceded to the Treaty. Not being engaged in a programme to develop a nuclear capability, neither had been overly concerned with this issue. The UAE now found that this lapse on its part was causing embarrassment to its Arab friends. The United States started applying pressure on Arab and other capitals not to insist on Israel's accession at that time. Some delegates interpreted the proceedings as a prophetic albeit undesirable example of the New World Order in the making.

At the crucial session on 11 May, three proposals were before the 1995 Review and Extension Conference of the Parties to the NPT. One was a draft resolution sponsored by Mexico which accepted indefinite extension of the treaty (but would have instituted review and evaluation proceedings every five years) (NPT/CONF.1995/L.1/REV.1, p 3). A second proposal, a draft decision sponsored by Canada and supported by 103 out of 175 countries, was a one-paragraph affair in favour of indefinite extension of the Treaty (NPT/CONF 1995/L.2). The third proposal, a draft decision supported by 11 countries, including Jordan - Egypt having dropped out - was submitted by Indonesia as president of the Non-Aligned group at the time. It proposed that 'the Treaty shall continue in force for rolling fixed periods of twenty-five years', with a review and extension conference at the end of each period. It requested a 'legally binding international instrument to provide comprehensive assurances to the non-nuclear-weapon States against the use or threat of use of nuclear weapons', and called for the establishment of nuclear-weapon-free zones and 'the commitment of States parties to achieve universality of the Treaty' (NPT/CONF.1995/L.3). Egypt had succumbed to US pressure, Jordan and the few remaining holdouts among the Non-Aligned group had modified their position, accepting a 25-year extension rather than an indefinite one. This would have constituted a legal basis to continue the review of compliance of the states possessing nuclear weapons (NPT/CONF.1995/PV.17, p 7).

The French president of the conference managed to negotiate three new draft decisions, the first of which provided for review conferences to be held every five years (NPT/CONF.1995/L.4). The second endorsed universal adherence to the Treaty, calling on 'All States not yet party to the Treaty ... to accede to the Treaty at the earliest date, particularly those States that operate unsafeguarded nuclear facilities.' (NPT/CONF.1995/L.5) This language, of course, put the UAE and Oman on the spot (Oman not being a signatory either), alongside Israel, although the reference to unsafeguarded nuclear facilities could not apply to them. The third draft decision simply provided for the Treaty to remain in force indefinitely (NPT/CONF.1995/L.6).

In the end, in an absence of any objections, draft decisions L.4, L.5 and L.6, which enjoyed majority support and had been negotiated by the president of the conference, were adopted without a vote, effectively renewing the Treaty indefinitely. In addition, a draft resolution (NPT/CONF.1995/L.8), sponsored by the US, UK and the Russian Federation, was adopted without a vote on 11 May after the first paragraph was orally amended to read that the Conference:

Endorses the aims and objectives of the Middle East peace process and recognizes that efforts in this regard, as well as other efforts, contribute to, inter alia, a Middle East zone free of nuclear weapons as well as other weapons of mass destruction. (NPT/CONF.1995/PV.17, p 4)

The resolution, having endorsed the idea of a nuclear free zone in the Middle East, tied that issue to the progress in securing a Middle East peace agreement. It also called upon 'all States of the Middle East that have not yet done so, without exception, to accede to the Treaty as soon as possible' (NPT/CONF.1995/L.8, p 2). The same resolution:

Notes with concern the continued existence in the Middle East of unsafeguarded nuclear facilities, and reaffirms in this connection the recommendation contained in paragraph IV/3 of the report of the Main Committee III urging those non-parties to the Treaty which operate unsafeguarded nuclear facilities to accept full scope International Atomic Energy Agency safeguards (NPT/CONF.1995/L.8, p 2).

The UAE, which had not intentionally avoided acceding to the treaty, hastened to do so. Israel did not. It is interesting, however, that on 10 January 1996, in the same resolution welcoming the accession of the UAE to the NPT, the General Assembly:

Calls upon Israel and all other states of the region that are not yet party to the Treaty on the Non-Proliferation of Nuclear Weapons not to develop, produce, test or otherwise acquire nuclear weapons, to renounce possession of Nuclear weapons and to accede to the Treaty at the earliest date: (A/RES/50/73)

Of course, General Assembly resolutions are not binding. The resolution, in calling on Middle Eastern countries to accede to the NPT, took note of 'positive developments in the Middle East peace process, which could be further strengthened by States of the region undertaking practical confidence building measures in order to consolidate the non-proliferation regime'.

The Organization Of Petroleum Exporting Countries

The Organization of Petroleum Exporting Countries (OPEC) was founded in Baghdad in September 1960. Abu Dhabi became a member of the organization in November 1967. The UAE belongs both to OPEC and the Organization of Arab Petroleum Exporting Countries (OAPEC) which was born and acquired international prominence in the wake of the October 1973 Arab-Israeli war. The UAE still attaches a great deal of importance to its membership in OPEC, but since Iraq's invasion of Kuwait the group of oil ministers of the GCC states has essentially replaced OAPEC. The GCC's Petroleum Cooperation Committee includes the oil ministers of the GCC states who are charged with coordinating the petroleum policies of the member states and with formulating a united position in OPEC meetings.

OPEC is best understood not as a classic monopoly cartel, but as an organization of producer countries whose function is to augment market power and improve the terms of trade for its members. The oil shocks of 1973 and 1979 - when oil prices increased by 300 per cent and 170 per cent respectively, reaching a high of $34 to $40 a barrel in 1979-80 - succeeded in shifting wealth from the industrialized countries of the West to the oil-producers in the Middle East. However, world market conditions, notably the emergence of an oil glut from 1982 to 1986 led to a crisis for the producers. In 1982, OPEC assigned production quotas to its members for the first time, and Saudi Arabia took on the role of swing producer. By managing and allocating production, in conjunction with setting the price, OPEC came to resemble a cartel. Here the free rider problem, or the temptation for members to cheat on their quotas, became manifest. Furthermore, by nationalizing foreign oil companies, OPEC countries had broken the vertically integrated monopolies that the oil majors had established. The logical culmination of this was that oil was on its way to becoming 'just another commodity' when the New York Mercantile Exchange introduced a futures contract in oil in 1983 (Yergin: p 724).

In the first half of the 1980s, the UAE tended to march in step with Saudi Arabia in defence of price moderation (a policy devised by Saudi Arabia's Oil Minister Ahmad Zaki Yamani with the staunch backing of the UAE's Mana Said Al Otaiba). The two countries were arrayed against the radicals, including Libya and Algeria, who were led by Iran. But by early 1985 the UAE had begun to show resentment of its quota and at depressed world demand, and was allying itself against Saudi Arabia and Kuwait, who were producers of heavy crude, and with Algeria and Libya, who were producers, like the UAE, of lighter crude oil (Peck 1986: p 100).

At the height of the crisis in 1986, OPEC producers were furiously battling for market share. Oil prices reached a nadir of $6 a barrel, and it was a decision by Saudi Arabia, Kuwait and the UAE (at the prompting of Iran) to bear three-quarters of a 4 million barrel per day (mb/d) cutback that allowed prices to level out at $14-$16 by the end of the year (Amuzegar: p 245). In early 1990, Kuwait and the UAE exceeded their quotas and OPEC output reached its highest level in eight years. By June, Iraq (with the support of Iran and Saudi Arabia) brought pressure on Kuwait and the UAE to cut back production. Iraq described the negative spillover effects of the increased production as a form of 'economic warfare' and used it as a justification for invading Kuwait in August. Although oil prices peaked briefly due to the invasion, the OPEC crude basket price has fluctuated within a band of between $15 and $20 a barrel.

OPEC has not had an easy ride in the nineties. World demand increased by 2 mb/d between 1993 and 1995, but the increase was absorbed by non-OPEC producers. Although Iraq's oil has been off the market, Iranian production has been restored to pre-revolution levels of about 3.6 mb/d (*MEED*, 16.6.1995: pp 4-5). OPEC has been bedevilled by the power of commodity traders and institutional investors. Traders in futures and derivatives were major forces in the oil trade during the period 1993-94 (*MEED*,20.1.1995).

In this context, it is interesting that Iraq has been given permission to sell a limited supply of oil under Security Council Resolution 986 for humanitarian reasons, and has been assigned a quota of 800,000 b/d (*MEED*, 19.7.1996: pp 7-8) by OPEC. On 7 August 1996, the US finally withdrew its objection to the sale of up to $2 billion worth of oil by Iraq (*FT*, 8.8.1996: p 1).

To help put matters in perspective, it is useful to compare the structure of interests embodied in OPEC, OAPEC and the GCC, as these considerations have a strong bearing on the problems that normally beset collective action, which inevitably determines the success or failure of the organization in meeting its goals.

The GCC, for example, embodies a commonality of interests and contributes to the economic and security welfare of its members without giving rise to the relative gains problem; in this case one can treat the states concerned as rational egoists, who are out to maximize their economic and security gains. The main problem one would expect is the free rider problem; that is, the propensity of member states to take advantage of the benefits the organization offers but to cheat on their contribution to the success of the organization. The security externalities or spillover effects of economic cooperation are strictly of a positive nature; the GCC contributes to the economic welfare of its members and the resulting increase in prosperity translates in part into enhanced military capability for the GCC member states. As Gowa (1994) points out:

> *Because political-military alliances internalize the external effects of trade, it makes sense for states to trade more freely with allies than with actual or potential adversaries* . (p 121)

Similarly, cooperation in security-related issues, such as the safety of shipping in the Gulf, has positive spillover effects in terms of the enhanced economic welfare of all members.

The same cannot be said of OPEC or OAPEC. It should be remembered that Iran and Iraq are two of the five founding members of OPEC. While the free rider problem remains, in the form of the formidable temptation for members to cheat on their oil production quotas, security externalities can be either positive, as in the case of GCC members, or negative (from the GCC perspective, of course), as in the case of both Iran and Iraq. Plainly speaking, improvements in the economic prosperity of either Iran or Iraq translates into an increase in military capabilities which are threatening to the members of the GCC.

The wide array of economic sanctions on Iraq and the isolation of Iran through the economic boycott spearheaded by Washington are largely designed to contain the undesirable security externalities of enhanced prosperity resulting from trade. Clearly, in this case, GCC members, Iran and Iraq cannot be viewed simply as rational egoists who are out to maximize absolute gains; it is more appropriate to think of them as 'defensive positionalists' (see Grieco 1990) who are seeking to maximize relative advantage with respect to each other.

The problem of relative advantage does not arise in the case of a limited sale of oil by Iraq, even if renewed every six months, which will have an insignificant effect on addressing the structural problems besetting the Iraqi economy. Even if Iraq's output were to return to its prewar capacity, Iraq's oil revenues would only come to about $20 billion a year. This would make no impact on the bill for replacing the infrastructure destroyed during the Gulf war (estimated at $232 billion) and the Iran-Iraq war ($67 billion), the reparations to Kuwait ($100 billion) and Iran ($97 billion), and repaying Iraq's national debt (between $42 and $86 billion), all of which adds up to approximately $550 billion (Alnasrawi 1996: p 13).

The World Trade Organization

The World Trade Organization (WTO) was officially established on 1 January 1995, the culmination of the seven-year Uruguay Round of talks within the General Agreement on Tariffs and Trade (GATT) process. The WTO 'is a single institutional framework encompassing the GATT and all the agreements and legal instruments negotiated in the Uruguay Round' (*About the WTO*).

On 10 April 1996, the UAE became a member of the WTO, following two years of arduous negotiations (Saad 1996), involving the submission of a memorandum to the WTO on all aspects of the UAE's trade and economic policies which have relevance to WTO agreements. While a working party from the WTO examined the request, interested member nations (including the US) conducted bilateral negotiations with the UAE concerning market access. Schedules were agreed. Since over two thirds of the members approved the application, the UAE was invited to sign the protocol and accede to the WTO.

Bahrain, Qatar, Kuwait, Egypt, Tunisia and Morocco are also members, while Saudi Arabia, the Sultanate of Oman, Jordan and Sudan have applied for membership. At the time of writing, four of the six members of the GCC are members and the remaining two are prospective members. This is not surprising in view of the trade-expanding nature of the benefits of membership. Once all members of the GCC join, it will be possible for them to present unified statements to the WTO and to act through a single spokesman in negotiations. In December 1994, the Supreme Council of the GCC 'welcomed the establishment of the World Trade Organization, and looked forward to it assuming the role which it had been given of liberalizing international trade' (A/49/815, p 8).

A Unified Economic Agreement was signed by the six GCC members on 11 November 1982, which, among other things, provided for the abolition of tariffs between GCC member states, the unification of tariffs on imports from outside the GCC, the free movement of capital and labour, the adoption of a unified investment policy, coordination of fiscal, monetary and banking policies, industrial activities and the coordination of oil policies. Tariffs have not been unified yet. For example, Saudi Arabia applies a rate of 7 per cent on many goods where the UAE applies the lower rate of 4 per cent. Higher tariffs are undesirable for the UAE because of its flourishing re-export and transit trade. One demand that has come up repeatedly in negotiations between the GCC and the EU is for the unification of GCC tariffs (Saad 1996). If GCC members achieve a high level of economic integration, then the GCC could itself become a member; the EU, for example, is a member of the WTO in its own right.

According to IMF estimates, the Gulf region is expected to realize real income effects amounting to a 0.5 per cent increase in GDP, while the rest of the Middle East and the Maghreb are expected to experience negative gains equal to 0.5 per cent and 0.4 per cent of GDP respectively (Salvatore 1996: p 43). The biggest winners will be high-income Asian countries (2.6 per cent), China (2.5 per cent, but it is not yet a member), the European Union and the European Free Trade Association (1.4 per cent each) and Japan (0.9 per cent). It is expected that as a result of the reduction in import tariffs in their export markets, the Arab countries, Turkey and Iran will benefit from a expansion of between $800 million and $1.4 billion annually; in return, however, they will lose some of the preferential treatment from which they are benefiting (*MEED*, 10.3.1995) under the Generalized System of Preferences and the Lome Convention, or in the form of regional or country-specific quotas set by importing countries. Fortunately, developing countries are allowed ten years to make the necessary adjustments, double the time allotted to industrialized nations.

The 'core principle' of the World Trade Organization is multilateralism, which is embodied in the Most-Favoured-Nation (MFN) clause. The MFN principle signifies that a benefit extended to one trading partner that is a member of GATT or the WTO must be extended to all trading partners that are members of the GATT or the WTO. Discrimination and favouritism are disallowed; discrimination against one member is discrimination against all. Multilateralism therefore entails the principles of non-discrimination and indivisibility among members of the collectivity, as well as the principle of diffuse reciprocity -- roughly, that the benefits of collective action shared among members even out in the long run, they are not extended on a *quid pro quo* basis (Ruggie 1993). Of course this works better in theory than in practice. Another point that needs to be emphasized is that the principle of multilateralism is operative only among members of the group; in that sense the benefits of membership in the WTO are not a public good since non-members can be excluded from enjoyment of those benefits. Consequently, the benefits of membership are privatizable, and if a nation delays in becoming a member while other countries join, it becomes more difficult or more costly to join at a later date because of the logic of the situation (Oye 1992).

Yet another operative principle for the WTO is 'national treatment', meaning non-discrimination against foreign firms or individuals: nationals of other members of the WTO must be given treatment no less favourable than that extended to nationals of the host country.

Trade in goods is governed by GATT 1994, an 'updated version of GATT 1947' (*About the WTO*). Significantly, the Uruguay Round applies to trade in goods and services, and includes a General Agreement on Tariffs, Trade and Services (GATS). National treatment would mean that the UAE would have to allow foreign firms to compete on an equal footing with domestic companies in providing financial or telecommunications services (once the latter are privatized).

The distinctive aspects of the Uruguay Round and the WTO are, for our purposes: a) its more advanced dispute settlement procedure; b) the Agreement on Trade-Related Aspects of Intellectual Property Rights (TRIPs); c) Services; d) Trade-Related Investment Measures (TRIMs).

Dispute settlement

Prior to the establishment of the WTO, consensus was required in rulings on trade disputes, so that an offending country could, by dissenting, derail a judgement against it. Under the new rules, a judgement, once the appeal process has been exhausted, is binding unless there is a consensus against it (Jackson 1994). This is particularly useful to small or developing countries since they do not have the capability to employ sanctions unilaterally as a tool to obtain satisfaction in the course of bilateral bargaining with the offending party. For example, the UAE and other GCC members are concerned about the possibility that the European Union may apply a carbon tax to their oil exports, which would have the effect of restricting free trade. Developing countries are resorting to the WTO's dispute settlement procedures with much greater frequency than they did with GATT. As WTO deputy director general Warren Lavorel puts it: 'We are a negotiating forum and a dispute resolution forum,' but he adds that the WTO is most appropriately seen as a catalyst promoting the settlement of disputes, not as an enforcement agency (Stokes 1996: p 719). The organization may be able to use moral persuasion to induce the US or the EU to abide by its decisions in the case of disputes, but it cannot force them to do so.

A prominent principle that guided the Uruguay Round was the desire to combat the 'new protectionism', or the growing tendency of nations to resort to non-tariff barriers such as voluntary export restraints (for example in the export of textiles from developing countries to industrialized ones), orderly marketing agreements, quotas, subsidies, regulatory barriers, and arbitrary technical standards. These practices had become widespread among industrialized nations as a hedge against GATT, and are to be replaced in the case of WTO members with visible tariffs so that the extent of protection will not be concealed. 'Transparency' is required in regulations governing trade; WTO members agreed to make available to their trading partners lists of their laws and practices which may hamper free trade. Doing away with quotas will help some countries, but may hurt others. The removal of US quotas on cheap textiles from China and India could make UAE garment exports to the US less competitive. India has made use of the WTO's dispute settlement mechanism to get the US to rescind its quotas on women's wool coats, and a WTO panel investigation is under way into US import quotas on wool shirts and blouses as the result of another complaint lodged by India in April 1996 (*FT*, 8.8.1996: p 6). Still, tariffs on textiles will be reduced by 25 per cent overall. In addition, the removal of subsidies on agricultural production will result in higher prices for food importers.

TRIPs

The Uruguay Round resulted in an agreement governing Trade Related Aspects of Intellectual Property rights. The agreement requires a commitment to national treatment, and includes a most-favoured-nation clause which extends the benefits granted to the nationals of one member to the nationals of all other members of the organization.

The TRIPs agreement adopts the conventions of the World Intellectual Property Organization: the Paris Convention for the Protection of Industrial Property and copyright laws embodied in the Berne Convention for the Protection of Literary and Artistic Works. The UAE acceded to the Paris Convention on 18 March 1996 through Federal Decree No. 20 of 1996. The Paris Convention states that any trademark duly registered in the holders' country of origin can be filed and receive protection in any other WTO nation. Under the TRIPs agreement, industrial designs are protected for ten years, and patents for inventions in products or processes are covered for 20 years in nearly all areas of technology. The Paris Convention also stipulates a 'right of priority': once a national of a WTO member country files a trademark or industrial design patent application in one country, he may later file within 12 months in any other member country, or within six months in his own country, and receive protection retroactive to the date of filing in the first country. However, it is not clear how the UAE's accession to the Paris Convention will affect the fact that UAE patent law does not provide protection for pharmaceutical products, or how compulsory licensing regulations will change (*MEER* 6.1996: p 4). The WTO allows developing countries ten years to introduce patent protection for techno-logical products and processes. However, pharmaceutical patents must be accepted from the beginning of the ten-year transitional period, even if they are granted at the end of the period.

The agreement on TRIPs protects computer programmes as it does literary works in the Berne Convention. One innovation concerns rental rights for computer programmes, sound recordings and films, which are protected for 50 years. Designs of integrated circuits are protected under the terms of the Washington Treaty on Intellectual Property in Respect of Integrated Circuits with the additional conditions that protection will last for ten years. Strict limitations are placed on government use and compulsory licensing.

Copyright legislation is relatively new in the entire Gulf area. The UAE had a serious problem in that it was being used as a base for the distribution of pirated copies, to be sold particularly in Iran. To remedy this and other intellectual property infringements, Law No. 37 for the Protection of Trade Marks (see *MEED*, 17. 5 1996) and Federal Law No. 40 On the Protection of Intellectual Works and Copyright (Ministry of Information and Culture, April 1993) were passed in 1992. The UAE has received international acclaim for the implementation of these laws.

Federal Law No. 40 (section 2) provides protection for books, pamphlets, lectures, addresses, sermons, dramatic and musical works, choreographic, television and radiophonic works, pantomimes, photographic works, 'cinematographic, television and radiophonic works, as well as original audiovisual works and computer programmes', handicrafts and applied art produced through industrial processes, 'works of drawing, painting, architecture, sculpture, decorative art, etchings, plans, sketches and three-dimensional works relating to geography and topography' as well as encyclopedias and anthologies or other compilations that are considered intellectual creations (p 4).

Section 3 extends protection to works of nationals of the UAE or foreigners published for the first time in the UAE and to works of nationals of foreign countries which provide reciprocal treatment to citizens of the UAE (p 5). The 'publication, exhibition or circulation of any work' must be accompanied by a 'certificate of origin indicating the name of the author or the beneficiary of a right of exploitation that has been assigned', according to section 8 (p 7).

The author's rights include direct communication of the work to the public 'in any form' including 'musical arrangement ,theatrical performance, public exhibition' or sound or visual broadcast, as well as indirect communication of the work to the public virtually by any 'means of graphic or three-dimensional arts, or by photographic or cinematographic publication'. (section 10, p 8). Authorized translations, adaptations, or reproductions of the work in a new form are protected and do not prejudice the rights of the author. Regarding translations in particular, section 5 states:

Protection of the author's right and the right of the person who translated his work to translate that work into Arabic shall lapse if the author or translator fails to exercise that right himself or through a third person within a period of three years from the date of the first publication of the original or translated work (p 6).

Interestingly, section 13 of the law states that although the author has the right to prevent 'any suppression, addition or modification' of his work, he 'shall not have the right to prevent such acts ' if the said modifications occur in the course of translation, unless the translator fails to indicate where such modifications were made or in the event that such changes 'entail prejudice to the author's reputation and artistic prestige.' (p 9).

The author's rights are protected 'for his lifetime and for 25 years after his death', however, section 20 states:

> 2) *The author's rights regarding the following works shall be protected for 25 years from the date of publication:*
> a) *cinematographic films and works of applied art;*
> b) *works made by any legal entities;*
> c) *works published under a pseudonym or anonymously, until the author reveals his identity;*
> d) *works published for the first time after the death of the author.* (p 13)

Section 13 also states that photographic works shall enjoy protection for 10 years from the date of publication and, in the case of a work of several volumes, 'each volume shall be considered as an independent work for the purpose of calculating the term of protection.' (p13)

Establishments authorized to produce, distribute or sell copyrighted works, including those produced abroad, are obliged to possess written documentation of the rights granted by the author (p 22).

The UAE issued new internal guidelines for licensing media-related activities in the state, including special rules for computer programmes, cinema and theatre, films broadcasts, printing presses, press services and advertising and promotion (see *MEER* , 6. 1996: p 18).

A registration system has been set up. The Copyright Law provides for penalties of not less than DH 50,000 for publishing a work without proper authorization, imprisonment, or both. Persons not operating through licensed establishments who publish, copy or print protected works are subject to fines of up to DH 10,000, imprisonment or both. The proprietors of establishments that publish, print or copy works in infringement of the law are liable to fines of not less than DH 50,000, imprisonment or both. Unauthorized copies are subject to seizure and establishments in violation of the law may be closed. Ministerial Decree no. 41 of 1993 promulgated by the Minister of Information and Culture enacted enforcement regulations for the Copyright Law. Police and inspectors from the ministry conducted regular inspection visits to retail outlets for audio and video tapes, computer software and books. In practice, this had little effect on piracy during 1993 because some administrative measures had yet to be put in place. The Censorship department issued Circular No.1 of 1994 to regulate the import and distribution of software and strong action was promised against violators of copyright on recordings and software; shopkeepers were given a five-month period of grace (up to 15 September 1994) to clear their stocks of pirated copies of video and audio tapes, films and computer discs. Copyright owners are advised to use trademark alongside copyright registration. Trademark laws are being strictly enforced. The next logical step is to target corporate users of pirated software (*Webster*, 6. 1995).

The GCC countries are well aware of their need for advanced technology to diversify their economies. In 1993, Gulf businessmen came to Washington, DC to meet with American businessmen and company executives. They presented feasibility studies for petrochemical projects that required technologies possessed by a very short list of firms. US companies, on the other hand, were worried about lack of protection for industrial secrets, trademarks and copyrights. The legislation being passed in the UAE to protect such rights should be instrumental in attracting the needed investment.

GATS

The Uruguay Round was the first to establish a set of rules governing trade in services such as financial services, insurance, tourism, telecommunications, construction and air transport which now account for about 20 per cent of world trade. The resulting GATS agreement stipulates that the principles of Most Favoured Nation, national treatment, market access and the unhindered flow of transfers and payments are to be observed. Bilateral agreements may complement GATS rules on national treatment, market access and the movement of labour. Meetings are to be held every five years in quest of further liberalization. A working party has been established to consider ways to eliminate discrimination in professional services, such as accounting. The UAE has passed recent legislation governing the profession.

In the case of services, trade restraints are less obvious than in the case of goods. A knowledge of the rules governing tariffs, subsidies and dumping may be sufficient to reach a determination about commodities, but when it comes to services, one needs to be knowledgeable about the industry itself (Stokes 1996: p 710). Trade in services, such as telecommunications, which are heavily regulated, often state-owned monopolies, has not been significantly liberalized as a result of the WTO (Stokes 1996: p 711). Tourism and transport industries are expected to benefit, however, and Dubai may benefit here.

TRIMs

Trade-Related Investment Measures are important because of the possible trade distorting effects of investment regulations or other measures. TRIMs are required to be consistent with the principles of national treatment and the prohibition on quantitative restrictions (Articles III and XI of GATT). Such measures as 'local content requirements' or 'trade balancing requirements' are good examples of TRIMs. Developing countries will be allowed a five-year grace period to phase out such TRIMs. Further progress in negotiations on competition policy or investment policy could bring in additional requirements by the turn of the century if the members so decide.

Looking to the future, the International Energy Agency (IEA) estimates that world energy consumption is expected to rise to between 85 and 105 mb/d by 2010, as compared to 68 mb/d in 1994. The Middle East will have an opportunity to expand production by as much as 20 mb/d. Middle East producers, including Iran and Iraq, now have a 6 mb/d excess capacity, but the investment needed to satisfy the remainder of the projected demand could be as high as $100 billion by the turn of the century for the UAE, Kuwait, Saudi Arabia, Iran, Iraq and Qatar. Under this scenario, the Gulf countries will have to invite foreign oil companies back in and offer them production sharing agreements. The UAE in fact has maintained production sharing arrangements with international oil companies. These companies will be all that much more needed because of their command of advanced technology and managerial skills as well as capital (IEA/OECD 1995: pp 21-3).

Bibliography

Alnasrawi, A. 'What Economic Future for Iraq?' *Middle East Executive Reports*, March 1996, pp 8, 13-19.
Amuzegar, J. *Iran's Economy under the Islamic Republic*, London and New York, IB Taurus (1993).
Caldwell, D. 'Flashpoints in the Gulf: Abu Musa and the Tunb Islands', *Middle East Policy*, Vol.4, no.3 (March 1996) pp 50-57.
Gowa, J. *Allies, Adversaries and International Trade*, Princeton, New Jersey, Princeton University Press (1994).
Grieco, J.M. *Cooperation among Nations: Europe, America and Non-Tariff Barriers to Trade*, Ithaca and London, Cornell University Press (1990).
International Energy Agency. *Middle East Oil and Gas*, Paris, OECD, 1995.
Jackson, J. 'Dispute Settlement Procedures', in *The New World Trading System: Readings*, Paris, OECD, 1994, pp 117-123.
Laubach, C.S. and Khan, A.A. 'New Rules for Licensing Media-Related Activities' *Middle East Executive Reports*, June 1996, p 18.
Lenczowski, G. *The Middle East in World Affairs* (4th ed), Ithaca and London, Cornell University Press (1980).
Maksoud, C. 'Diminished Sovereignty, Enhanced Sovereignty: United Nations-Arab League Relations at 50', *Middle East Journal*, Vol. 49, no.4 (1995) pp 582-594.
Oye, K.A. *Economic Discrimination and Political Exchange: World Political Economy in the 1930s and 1890s*, Princeton, New Jersey, Princeton University Press (1992).
Peck, M.C. *The United Arab Emirates*, Boulder, Colorado, Westview Press and London, Croom Helm (1986).
Reiterer, M. 'Trade-Related Intellectual Property Rights', *The New World Trading system: Readings*, Paris, OECD, 1994, pp199-203.
Ruggie, J.G. 'Multilateralism: The Anatomy of an Institution' in Ruggie J.G. (ed) *Multilateralism Matters: The Theory and Praxis of an Institutional Form*, New York, Columbia University Press (1993) pp 3-50.
Said Zahlan, R. *The Origins of the United Arab Emirates: A Political and Social History of the Trucial States*, New York, St. Martin's Press (1978).
Salvatore, D. 'International Trade Policies, Industrialization, and Economic Development', *The International Trade Journal*, Vol. 10, No.1 (Spring 1996) pp 21-47.

Schofield, R. 'Mending Gulf Fences', *Middle East Insight*, March/April 1996, pp 36-41.

Sick, G. 'Trial by Error: Reflections on the Iran-Iraq War', *Middle East Journal*, Vol.43, No.2, Spring 1989, pp 230-245.

Stokes, B. 'Up and Crawling', *National Journal* 3/30/96, pp 709-712.

Taryam, A.O. *The Establishment of the United Arab Emirates 1950-85*, London, Croom Helm (1987).

Webster, G. 'IPR in Multimedia Technology: License Terms and Enforcement from a UAE Perspective -- Part I - IPR in Multimedia and the Multimedia Challenge', *Middle East Executive Reports*, May 1995, pp 9, 26-7.

'IPR in Multimedia Technology: License Terms and Enforcement from a UAE Perspective -- Part II- Licensing in Multimedia Products and Enforcement of Copyright Protection', *Middle East Executive Reports*, June 1995, pp 8, 24-7.

Wong, J.W.P. 'Overview of TRIPs, Services and TRIMs', *The New World Trading System: Readings*, Paris, OECD, 1994, pp173-6.

UAE legislation

Federal Law No. 40 of 1992, On the Protection of Intellectual Works and Copyright, Ministry of Information and Culture, the United Arab Emirates [translation prepared for MIC by the World Intellectual Property Organization (WIPO)], April 1993.

Interviews

Interview with Muhammad Hussein Al Shaali, Permanent Representative of the United Arab Emirates at the United Nations (1985-92), currently UAE Ambassador to the United States, on 29 July and 21 August 1996.

Interview with Saif Saeed Saad, Acting Under-Secretary, Ministry of Foreign Affairs of the United Arab Emirates, on 5 August 1996.

Interview with Adnan Abu Odeh, former Permanent Representative of Jordan to the United Nations, on 1 August 1996.

Selected UN Documents

Iran-Iraq War

Security Council.*Resolution 598 (1987). Adopted By The Security Council At Its 2750th Meeting, On 20 July 1987* (S/RES/598) (Mimeo).

Security Council. *Provisional Verbatim Record Of The Two Thousand Seven Hundred And Fiftieth Meeting Held At Headquarters, New York, On 20 July 1987, At 3 p.m.* [Original text of speeches on occasion of adoption of SC Resolution 598] (S/PV.2750).

Security Council. *Letter dated 11 August 1987 From the Permanent Representative Of The Islamic Republic Of Iran To The United Nations Addressed To The Secretary General Annex. Detailed And Official Position Of The Islamic Republic Of Iran On The Security Council Resolution 598 (1987)* (S/19031) (Mimeo).

Security Council. *Letter Dated 17 July From The Acting Permanent Representative Of The Islamic Republic Of Iran To The United Nations Addressed To The Secretary General. Annex: Letter dated 17 July 1988 from the President of the Islamic Republic of Iran addressed to the Secretary-General* [accepting Resolution 598] (S/20020) (Mimeo).

Security Council. *Resolution 582 (1986). Adopted By The Security Council At Its 2666th Meeting, On 24 February 1986* (S/RES/582) (Mimeo).

Security Council. *Resolution 552 (1984). Adopted By The Security Council At Its 2546th Meeting on 1 June 1984* [in response to letter from representatives of GCC states complaining against Iranian attacks on commercial ships] (S/RES/552) (Mimeo).

Non-Proliferation Treaty

General Assembly. *Resolution Adopted By The General Assembly. 50/73/ The Risk of Nuclear Proliferation In The Middle East* (A/RES/50/73) (Mimeo).

Treaty on the Nonproliferation of Nuclear Weapons. *Verbatim Record Of The 17th Meeting. Held At The United Nations Headquarters, New York, 11 May 1995, At 10 a.m.* [1995 Review and Extension Conference of the Parties to the Treaty on the Non-Proliferation of Nuclear Weapons at which the NPT was extended indefinitely] (NPT/CONF.1995/PV.17) (Mimeo).

Iraq and the GCC

Security Council. *Resolution 687 (1991) Adopted By The Security Council On Its 2981st Meeting On 3 April 1991* (S/RES/687) (Mimeo).

General Assembly and Security Council. *Letter dated 21 September 1995 from the Permanent Representative of Bahrain to the United Nations addressed to the Secretary-General. Annex: Press communique issued in Riyadh on 19 September 1995 by the Ministerial Council of the Gulf Cooperation Council following its fifty-sixth session* (A/50/466) and (S/1995/817) (Mimeo).

General Assembly and Security Council. *Letter dated 22 December 1994 from the Permanent Representative of Bahrain to the United Nations addressed to the Secretary General. Annex: Final Report of the Fifteenth Session of the Supreme Council*(A/49/815) and (S/1994/1446) (Mimeo).

General Assembly. Fiftieth Session. Report of the Secretary-General on the Work of the Organization. *Supplement To An Agenda For Peace: Position Paper Of The Secretary-General On The Occasion Of The Fiftieth Anniversary Of The United Nations* (A/50/60) (Mimeo).

Security Council. *Resolution 986. (1995) Adopted By The Security Council At Its 3519th Meeting, On 14 April 1995* (S/RES/986) (Mimeo).

Other Arab Issues

Security Council. *Provisional Verbatim Record Of The Two Thousand Six Hundred And Seventy-Fourth Meeting Held at Headquarters, New York, on Tuesday, 15 April 1986, at 12.20 p.m.* [Concerning the UAE reaction to the US attack on Libya] (S/PV.2674) (Mimeo).

General Assembly. Committee On The Exercise Of The Inalienable Rights Of The Palestinian People (A/AC.183/PV.148) (Mimeo).

Weekly and Monthly Publications, Journalistic Sources

Middle East Economic Digest for January 1995-July 1996.
Middle East Executive Reports for January 1995-June 1996.
Financial Times.
FBIS/NES/87-183, 22 September 1987 *'Text' of Perez de Cuellar Statement*, pp.45-47.
US Department of State, 95/04/13 Briefing: John Holum, Director, US Arms Control and Disarmament Agency on Non-Proliferation Issues. April 13, 1995.

Electronic Sources

'About the WTO' <URL:http://www.unicc.org/wto/about_wpf.html>

Evolution and Performance of the United Arab Emirates Economy 1972 - 1995

Ali Tawfik Al Sadik

Introduction

The United Arab Emirates' (UAE) economy has been transformed from a precarious base of fishing and pearling together with some local agriculture to an oil based high-income economy with a high concentration of expatriate labour force driving the different sectors. The transformation of the economy brought with it challenges and opportunities that induced discussions on how best to confront the challenges and utilize the opportunities in an optimal manner.

The analysis of the evolution of the economy that will be presented indicates that the UAE Government has succeeded, to a great extent, on both counts. In section two, an overview of the economy in 1995 is presented, utilizing a production and demand structure. Section three traces, discusses and analyses the evolution of the economy over the period 1972-1995, highlighting the oil boom challenges and opportunities, the sources of growth and instability in incomes and prices. In section four the evolution of the consolidated budget, an effective policy tool for economic and social development, is outlined and the achievements in the social sphere are highlighted. Section five presents a brief discussion of the evolution of the trade and current account balances in the balance of payments. Section six indicates briefly the monetary and credit policy in the UAE and this is followed by a short concluding section.

Overview of the Economy

The UAE, which was established on 2 December 1971, is a federation of the seven emirates: Abu Dhabi, Dubai, Sharjah, Ajman, Umm al-Qaiwain, Ras al-Khaimah and Fujairah. It has a total area of approximately 84,000 square kilometres (sq. km) with an estimated population of 2,377,453 inhabitants in 1995, of which about 72 per cent are expatriates.[1] The UAE per capita income on the basis of the gross domestic product (GDP) amounted to $16,500 in 1995 and is considered relatively high compared to the average per capita income of developing countries.[2]

Three emirates - Abu Dhabi, Dubai and Sharjah - account for more than 93 per cent and 84 per cent of the UAE GDP and population respectively. The distribution of GDP and population between the emirates in 1995 was as in Table 1 below.

Table 1. Distribution of GDP and population between the Emirates in 1995

	GDP	Population	GDP PER	CAPITA
	%	%	DH	US$
Abu Dhabi	61.09	39.05	94737	25807
Dubai	24.03	28.35	51328	13982
Sharjah	8.36	16.84	30077	8193
Ras al-Khaimah	2.98	6.07	29702	8091
Ajman	1.28	5.00	15572	4242
Fujairah	1.58	3.21	29834	8127
Umm al-Qaiwain	0.68	1.48	27448	7477

Memorandum :1995 UAE GDP = 143,970 mn Dirhams; US$ 39,218 mn; population = 2,377,453
Source: On the basis of Ministry of Planning. *Annual Economic Report 1995,* Tables 1 and 5.

The income distribution between the emirates is skewed in favour of Abu Dhabi as its income share of 61.09 per cent is 156.44 per cent of its population share. In fact, this is reflected in the differences between the per capita incomes of the emirates presented in Table 1. Abu Dhabi's 1995 per capita income at $25,807 is the highest for the emirates and is six times the lowest per capita income, that of Ajman, which did not exceed $4250. In fact, the per capita incomes of all the emirates except Abu Dhabi are lower than the UAE average per capita income of $16,500.

The cited income differences between the emirates are generated mainly by the variations in their natural resource endowments. The most important resource the UAE possesses is petroleum (oil and gas). UAE proven oil reserves are estimated at 98.10 billion barrels (bbl) and gas reserves were 5777 billion cubic metres (bcm) at the end of 1995. UAE crude oil production was 2.18 million barrels per day (mb/d) in 1995 and gas production was 34,370 million cubic metres (mcm) per year in 1995. These UAE petroleum-related amounts are split between the emirates as shown in Table 2 below.

Table 2. Production and reserves of oil and gas in 1995

(Oil: production in mb/d & reserves in bbl)

(Gas: production in mcm per year & reserves in bcm)

	Production	Reserves	*Production	Reserves
	Oil	Oil	Gas	Gas
Abu Dhabi	1.815	92.20	14.30	5324
Dubai	0.316	5.90	1.70	121
Sharjah	.049	-	0.20	303
Ras al-Khaimah	-	-	0.04	31
Total	2.180	98.10	34,370	5779
World	66.602	1045.73	2,693,480	150,379

*1994

Sources: 1) *Petroleum Economist,* September 1994: p 37.
2) OAPEC. *Secretary General Annual Report* 1995
Tables 2-6 to 2-9, pp 116 -123.
3) EIU. *Country Profile United Arab Emirates* 1995-1996: p 43

The impact on their income shares of the distribution of the petroleum resource between the emirates is reflected in its contribution to their GDPs. The shares of value added of the oil sector in the emirates' GDPs are shown in Table 3 below.

Table 3. Contributions of the oil sector to Emirates' GDPs in 1995

(per cent of the Emirate's GDP)

Abu Dhabi	Dubai	Sharjah	Ras al-Khaimah	UAE
47	18.8	8.06	2.3	33.4

Source : Calculated on the basis of Ministry of Planning. *Annual Economic Report 1995*, Table 6.

Structure of gdp: the demand side

Crude oil production contributed about 33 per cent to UAE GDP in 1995. However, the oil sector's impact on UAE economic activities and evolution is more extensive. Oil exports are the main source for foreign exchange earnings and government revenues, accounting for more than 75 per cent of their totals in 1995 (total exports and re-exports = DH 63.4 billion of which DH 50 billion from oil and gas).[3]

The impact and importance of such shares on the overall economic activity may be analysed and gauged through the structure of expenditure on GDP utilizing the income determination equality, namely.

GDP = Cp + Ip + G + X - Z (1)

where: Cp = private consumption expenditure

Ip = private investment expenditure

G = government consumption and investment expenditure

X = exports of goods and non-factor services

Z = imports of goods and non-factor services

It is appropriate to mention that available national accounts data do not split investment expenditures between the private sector and the government. However, government financial statistics contain data on government investment expenditures (Ig) which may be used to obtain private investment expenditure (Ip) from the relation:

Ip = I - Ig

where I= total gross investment and Ig = government investment expenditure.

The shares of the variables on the right-hand side of the income determination equality were, in 1995, as follows:

Cp/GDP = 49.48%

Ip/GDP = 19.85%

G/GDP = (Cg + Ig)/GDP = (17.5 + 8.3)=25.8%

X/GDP = 75.57%

Z/GDP = (71.02)%

(net indirect taxes) /GDP = 0.3%

Source: Based on Tables 2 and 3 in the annex.

These shares reveal significant information about the UAE economy: that it is highly dependent on the external sector, as reflected by the trade ratio (export plus import shares) which exceeded 145 per cent. Both export and import shares are relatively high and consequently the external sector plays a major role in the performance and evolution of the UAE economy. In addition, the government sector, as reflected by its expenditure share (G/GDP), plays an important role in the economy. Private sector expenditures accounted for 69 per cent of GDP in 1995. Thus, domestic absorption (A) (equal to the sum of private and government expenditures on consumption and investment) accounted for 95 per cent of GDP, indicating a positive net exports of goods and non-factor services (X-Z). However, imports of goods and non-factor services (Z) accounted for 76 per cent of A. This is another measure of the dependence of the UAE economy on the policies of and developments in economies of its international trade partners

Structure of gdp: the production side

The production side of the UAE economy is heavily dependent on expatriate labour. A production theory framework may be utilized to understand the economic impact of expatriate labour on the economy. At the aggregate level labour and capital, the traditional factors of production, technology and organization (management) are combined to produce aggregate output Q. In mathematical terms, this relation takes the form:

Q = F(K, L, O) (2)

> where: Q = Output
> K = Capital input
> L = Labour input
> O = Organization, Management
> F = Technology

The UAE has had no capital constraint, thanks to the foreign exchange earnings from oil exports, because it could purchase from international markets the capital goods and services needed for its production processes. But indigenous population (nationals) and consequently indigenous labour force was, and still is, a constraint, from quantitative and qualitative aspects. For example, labour force employment in the UAE numbered 955,100 workers in 1995 (about 40.2 per cent of the population) of which 90 per cent were expatriates. This labour force, together with the capital services, management and available technologies in the different sectors of the economy, produced the equivalent of DH 143,970 million (US$ 39,218 million) of final goods and services (GDP at factor cost) in 1995.

Compensation of employees (wages and salaries) accounted for only 26.4 per cent of the GDP, a share less than half of the two thirds' share estimated from Cobb-Douglas production functions for other economies (Table 4 in the annex). The balance in the 1995 GDP is allocated to depreciation of fixed capital stock and operating surplus (stock owners). This large divergence between labour share in the UAE GDP and in other economies may be comprehended by analysing the distribution of the labour force between the economic sectors and their contribution to GDP. Table 5 in the annex presents the labour force distribution and the structure of GDP by origin.

The information content in Table 5 is important for understanding the low share in GDP and for labour policy discussions on the issue of national versus foreign labour involvement in the economy. It is clear that there are large differences between the productivities of labour employed in the different sectors. The average labour productivity (GDP divided by number of workers) is about DH 151,000 in 1995 prices. The maximum labour productivity is in crude oil (DH 5,072,170) and the minimum is in domestic services of households (DH 11,350) with a standard deviation of DH 1,372,435.

Table 4. Some statistics on labour productivity in the UAE economy in 1995 (dirhams)

Average	150,740
Maximum	5, 072,170
Minimum	11,350
Standard Deviation (St. d.)	1,372,435

Source: Based on Table 5 in the annex.

The crude oil subsector employed roughly 1 per cent of the labour force, but contributed about 34 per cent of GDP. The next best labour productivities are in finance and insurance (DH 406,250) and real estate (DH 404,840). These two sectors (crude oil, finance, insurance and real estate) employed less than 6 per cent of the labour force yet they contributed about 47 per cent of GDP. In contrast, the three sectors, wholesale and retail trade, government and domestic services of households, employed a percentage exceeding 43 per cent of the labour force, but contributed about 25 per cent of GDP. If the construction and agriculture sectors are added, then the employment percentage increases to about 67 per cent, but their contribution to GDP increases only to about 36 per cent.

The analysis of the employment shares and sectoral shares in the UAE GDP leads to the issue of optimal allocation of the labour resource. In theory, the allocation of a resource between different uses should be in accordance with the principle of equality of the marginal productivities of the resource in the different uses, if one is to achieve optimal results. In the case under analysis, marginal productivities of labour in the different sectors are not available. However, as a proxy, the average labour productivities are presented in Table 5 in the annex.

These average productivities show wide variations and the oil sector is ahead of all sectors by a very large margin. The wide and extensive variation between the labour productivities in the different sectors is to be expected on the basis of differences in the quality of labour and the nature of the sector.

The special nature of the oil sector

The oil sector is not like any other sector, because oil reserves are non-financial assets and these are part and parcel of national wealth.[4] Given this concept, then the contribution of the crude oil subsector of DH 49,200 million in 1995 is not value added. That is, it is not income generated from an asset. It is rather transforming an asset from one form (oil) to another (foreign exchange or financial asset). This way of looking at the oil sector shows that the confusion between the concepts of wealth and income leads to income illusion about the proceeds of petroleum exports. The income illusion manifests itself in several economic variables, namely;[5]

- overestimation in national income level
- overestimation in national saving
- distortion in the current account position
- underestimation in the domestic absorption
- overestimation in the accumulation of national wealth
- distortions of the contributions of the different sectors to the national income
- underestimation of foreign aid

These are important issues that have been raised in the literature and have been addressed in the framework of the 1993 United Nations System of National Accounts.

The adjusted gdp (agdp) and labour productivity

To remove some of the distortions of the contributions of the different sectors to GDP, the contribution of crude oil is removed and an adjusted GDP is considered for 1995:

AGDP = GDP - crude oil = 143,970 - 49,200= 94,770

Table 6 in the annex presents sectoral employment and contributions to adjusted GDP (AGDP) in 1995.

Average labour productivity relative to AGDP is about DH 100,000, with a maximum of DH 406,000 in the finance and insurance subsector and a minimum of about DH 11,000 in the domestic services of households and a standard deviation of (DH 129,092).

It is important to note that the domestic services sector employs more than 11 per cent of the labour force (excluding employment in the crude oil sub sector) but contributes less than 1.5 per cent of AGDP. Low contribution to value added, an outcome of low productivity, is a good and practical starting point for discussion on labour policy in the UAE. If this is granted, then a criterion to identify low labour productivity would be to compare the variable indicator **prod** with one, **prod** being defined as:

$$\textbf{prod} = \frac{\text{Sector's share in GDP}}{\text{Sector's employment share}}$$

If **prod** for a sector is less than one, the sector should be a target for study, analysis and reform aiming to raise its labour productivity.

According to this indicator the five sectors, agriculture, construction, transport, storage and communication, other services and domestic services of households, are low productivity sectors. Agriculture and the last two sectors are especially low productivity and should be targeted for study and reform. These sectors employ about 50 per cent of the labour force, excluding the oil sector, yet their contribution was less than 30 per cent of AGDP in 1995 (Table 6 in the annex).

To conclude this section, it is appropriate to mention that the UAE economy is market based, open with a relatively high trade ratio, has a liberal trade policy and exchange rate convertibility for current and capital transactions. The lifeline of the economy is petroleum and it is heavily dependent on expatriate labour. The UAE economy has made important strides in its development despite the violent fluctuations of its income during the last 25 years, thanks to the sincere and persistent efforts of the UAE President, His Highness Sheikh Zayed bin Sultan Al Nahyan, and the rulers of the emirates.

In the following sections, the evolution of the economy during the period 1972-1995 is presented, analysed and evaluated.

Evolution of the Economy

The UAE economy has witnessed several phases of growth and development. Up to the end of the 1950s, the economy was characterized by limited natural and human resources. Economic activities were centred mainly on agriculture (date cultivation, locally consumed vegetables and fruits), fishing, the raising of livestock, mostly camels, traditional manufacturing (tents, rugs and carpets, gowns, daggers and swords and some dried foods) and pearling.[6] The UAE population is estimated at 72,000 and 86,000 inhabitants in 1950 and 1958 respectively.[7]

Oil boom challenges and opportunities

Foreign trade activity entered a new phase with the production and export of oil in the Emirates: Abu Dhabi in 1962, Dubai in 1969 and Sharjah in 1970.[8] The oil activity started to shape the evolution and development of the UAE economy in the seventies as a result of the huge increase in oil production and exports and government revenues. Oil production increased from 253 mn.b in 1970 to about 619 mn.b in 1975; exports increased from 253 mn.b to about 606 mn.b and oil revenues jumped from $233 million to $6000 million. The huge growth in oil revenues during the period 1970-1975 (about 24/5 per cent) is an outcome of the increase in production and the adjustment in government take.[9]

The unprecedented affluence the UAE started experiencing from the early 1970s, thanks to the structural changes in the international oil industry, brought challenges and opportunities to its leadership. The challenges were tri-dimensional: political, social and economic. As mentioned earlier, the UAE was established in December 1971 as a federation of seven emirates with limited natural resources in addition to petroleum which was mainly concentrated in Abu Dhabi. Thus, Abu Dhabi and, to a lesser degree, Dubai received the oil revenues. Given this situation, the first challenge facing the government was how to utilize the revenues for strengthening and cementing the federation, improving and expanding the social services to improve the standard of living and developing the non-oil productive base of the economy. In the event, the UAE President, H.H Sheikh Zayed bin Sultan Al Nahyan, supported and promoted development through planning and action as a single unified country. His paradigm was a trade off between Abu Dhabi's oil wealth and the rulers' release of personal authority to the Federal Government. This paradigm helped to cement and strengthen the federation politically, socially and economically. One of the early achievements of the UAE Government was the monetary integration of the emirates, which culminated in May 1973 by establishing the UAE Monetary Agency and issuing the UAE national currency, the Dirham, which replaced both the Qatari/Dubai Riyal circulating in the northern emirates and the Bahraini Dinar circulating in Abu Dhabi.[10] In 1980 the Monetary Agency was replaced by the UAE Central Bank, which was charged with the responsibilities usually assigned to a central bank.

In June 1974 the UAE Council of Ministers defined and outlined the main themes and directions for development.[11] Thus, in the economic sphere, development should aim to:

• Change the productive structure of the economy, optimize its capacity, diversify its activities and maximize export revenues.
• Concentrate on the expansion and exploitation of natural resources, promote and support

manufacturing and lower the pressure on the growth of imports.
* Adopt capital intensive projects so as to lower the demand for labour.
* Develop the infrastructure in a compatible way with the requirements of production of goods
  and services without barriers or bottlenecks.

Development in the social sphere should proceed on the following basis:

* The ultimate objective of any development plan is the human being. The different social
  services are therefore a basic right for him/her. These services include health care, education
  (with a view to supplying the country's labour demand for the different skills and special-
  izations, along with its cultural and information aspects), the care of the environment,
  achieving the country's security and safeguarding the foundations of society, its morale,
  holy beliefs and shrines.
* With this foundation, the aim should be to supply the country with a trained and skilled
  national labour force to manage the economy and prepare and implement development plans.

Given these economic and social development objectives, it is appropriate to mention that
the UAE Government in general, and the UAE President in particular, has always stressed
that the fundamental objective of development is the welfare of society and ensuring its
continuity for the present and future generations. The human being has always been at the
centre of development in the UAE, which indicates the importance the government placed
on human development long before the publication of the first report: Human Development
1990, by the United Nations Development Program (UNDP).[12]
The opportunities and challenges brought with affluence could be outlined as follows:

* no budget constraint as a result of high saving rate.[13]
* regulations and institutions for the public and private sectors need to be provided.
* build data banks and research centres to support decision making.
* rationalize the answers to the basic economic questions of what, how and for whom to produce.

In light of the said challenges and opportunities it is appropriate to study and evaluate the
evolution of the main economic indicators.

Fig. 1. UAE real GDP in mn dirhams

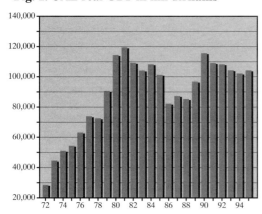

Fig. 2. UAE real GDP growth rates (per cent per annum)

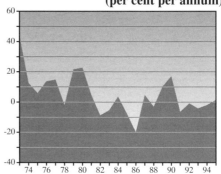

Evolution of income and prices

The size of the UAE economy, measured by the nominal GDP, has grown by more than 22 fold during the period 1972-1995: nominal GDP increased from DH 6450 million in 1972 ($1471 million) to DH 143, 970 mnb ($39,218 million). However, the UAE real GDP in 1995 was only about 3.81 times its level in 1972, due to the erosion of purchasing power as a result of the increase in inflation index by about 5.86 times (Table 1 in the annex).

The expansion of the economy was not smooth. In fact, it witnessed violent instabilities as reflected in the large expansions and contractions during the period (Figs. 1 and 2). Using the sign of GDP growth rate as a criterion, four phases can be distinguished: 1972-1981, 1982-1986, 1987-1991 and 1992-1995. Average, maximum, minimum and standard deviations of the growth rates over these sub-periods are presented in Table 5 below.

During the period the maximum growth rate was 44 per cent in 1979 and the minimum was -20 per cent in 1986, with an average growth rate of 5.6 per cent and 13.80 per cent standard deviation.

Table 5. Growth rates of real GDP :1972-1995 (per cent per annum)

Period	Average	Max	Min	St.d.
1972-1981	15.90	44.49	-1.86	13.50
1982-1986	-7.46	4.03	-20.82	8.94
1987-1991	5.65	17.84	-5.83	9.92
1992-1995	-1.16	2.04	-3.85	2.48
1972-1995	5.63	44.49	-20.83	13.79

Source : Based on Table 1 in the annex.

The volatility of GDP during the period under study imparted volatility to per capita income (Fig. 3). The overall trend of per capita GDP has been downwards since the early eighties despite the rebounds in the oil market . This may be explained by the continued increase in the UAE population, coupled with the slowdown in the economy (Fig. 4).

Fig. 3. UAE per capita real GDP (dirhams)

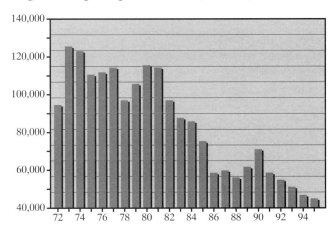

Fig. 4. UAE real GDP (mn.dh) and population (number)

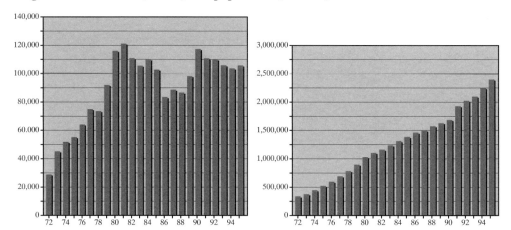

Sources of growth and instability

The sources of growth and instability in the evolution of the UAE economy might be traced to the development of the crude oil subsector. In fact, it turns out that it is the lifeline of the UAE because economic activities, directly or indirectly, are linked with it. The direct impact of the oil subsector may be investigated through the evolution of its value added.

A. Crude Oil Value Added

The value added of the crude oil subsector fluctuated violently between 1972 and 1995. The average value added is estimated at DH 40,820 million. During these years its maximum and minimum reached DH 70,532 million and DH 4099 million respectively, with a standard deviation of DH 16,570 million. These variation levels are reflected in some statistics for the annual growth rates of the value added of crude oil from 1972 to 1995:

- Maximum rate = 115.86 %
- Average rate = 10.80 %
- Minimum rate = -53.55 %
- Standard deviation = 34.00 %

Figures 5 and 6 clearly show that the value added of crude oil passed through four phases similar, if not congruent, to those of GDP. The trend of value added was increasing in the sub-periods 1972-1980 and 1987-1990, while it was decreasing during the periods 1981-1986 and 1991-1995. Fluctuations in the value added of crude oil are exogenous to the economic policy-making of the UAE. They are an outcome of international oil market development.

The international oil market experienced major, sometimes violent, changes during the period 1971-1995. Crude oil prices fluctuated between $2 and $33 per barrel and the oil market shifted from a seller's market up to 1981 to a buyer's market for the rest of the period.[14]

Fig. 5. UAE value added in the crude oil sub sector (mn.dh)

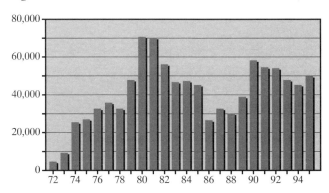

Fig. 6. UAE growth rates of value added of crude oil sub sector (per cent per annum)

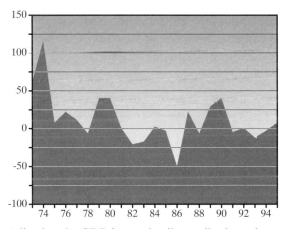

Adjusting the GDP for crude oil contributions shows less volatility in the non-oil GDP, as will be seen in the next section.

B. Non-oil GDP

Non-oil GDP, christened adjusted gross domestic product (AGDP) and defined as: **AGDP = GDP- Crude Oil Value Added** has grown more than 40 fold during the period 1972-1995: from DH 2351 million to DH 94,770 million (Table 9 in the annex). AGDP experienced less volatility than GDP. Only during the period 1984-86 did it experience negative growth rates (Fig. 7).The average, maximum and minimum growth rates and standard deviations for AGDP and NGDP (nominal GDP) are presented in Table 6 below.

Table 6. Growth rates and standard deviations:

for AGDP and NGDP(1972 1995) (per cent)

	Average	Max	Min	St.d.
AGDP	16.07	77.18	-2.72	20.49
NGDP	13.50	100.50	-22.27	25.40

Source : On the basis of Table 10 in the annex.

These variables indicate clearly that AGDP achieved a higher average growth rate with less volatility, as measured by the standard deviations, than nominal GDP (Fig. 7).

The AGDP also experienced an increasing share of GDP while that of crude oil declined from 1972 to 1995. The paths of the two shares crossed each other in 1982 (Fig. 8).

Thus, the share of non-oil GDP increased from less than 37 per cent in 1972 to more than 65 per cent in 1995 with a peak of about 67 per cent in 1986.[15] In fact the volatility of the two shares are similar as reflected by their standard deviations:

Table 7. Some statistics for the shares of AGDP and crude oil (per cent)

	Average	Max	Min	St.d.
AGDP share	50.17	67.11	19.45	13.42
Crude Oil share	49.83	80.55	32.89	13.42

Source : On the basis of Table 10 in the annex.

Fig. 7. UAE GDP, crude oil value added and AGDP (mn.dh)

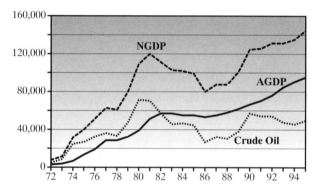

Fig. 8. UAE shares of AGDP and crude oil value added in GDP (per cent)

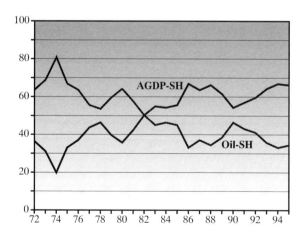

C. Evolution of Aggregate Demand

Another source of growth and volatility in the UAE economic activity is the evolution of aggregate demand. Aggregate demand is expenditure on GDP and may be represented as (see equation 1 and the subsequent discussion):

GDP = Cp + Cg + I + X - Z (3)

It is made up of two parts: domestic absorption A and net exports (X-Z).

a. Shares of components of aggregate demand

Figure 9 presents the paths for the shares of private consumption (Cp), government consumption (Cg), investment (I), exports (X) and imports (Z) in GDP from 1972 to 1995. Private consumption turns out to have experienced the largest volatility compared to the other components of aggregate demand.

Fig. 9. UAE - shares of aggregate demand components in GDP (per cent)

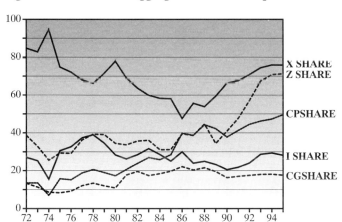

In contrast, the share of government consumption in GDP experienced the least volatility. Both exports and imports showed relatively high volatility. Table 8 presents some statistics for the evolution of the different shares in GDP.

Table 8. Some statistics for the shares of aggregate demand (per cent)

	Average	Maximum	Minimum	Standard Deviation
Cp	29.1	49.64	6.91	13.19
Z	41.38	71.24	37.90	12.84
X	68.71	94.64	47.63	10.79
I	27.75	39.03	15.50	5.25
Cg	15.82	22.10	8.26	4.19

Source: on the basis of Table 2 in the annex.

All the shares of the components except that of exports were higher in 1995 than in 1972. The Cp share was less than 15 per cent in 1972 and reached about 50 per cent in 1995. This increase in the share of private consumption is to be expected on the basis of the increase in population from 309,243 persons in 1972 to 2,377,453 in 1995 and in per capita income (on the basis of nominal GDP) from DH 20,857 to DH 60,556 in the same years.[16] Also, the Cg share was about 13 per cent in 1972 and reached a minimum of about 8 per cent in 1975 and increased to 18 per cent in 1995 with a maximum of about 22 per cent in 1986. This surge in the government share in 1986 was not policy induced, but rather a result of the decline in GDP as a consequence of the turmoil in the international oil market which resulted in the crash of oil prices to below $13 per barrel.

In contrast, the X share declined in 1986 to reach a minimum of about 48 per cent because of the negative impact of the oil market on the UAE exports which are mainly oil-related.

b. Growth rates of aggregate demand

On the basis of growth rates, exports experienced the highest volatility, followed by investments, private consumption, government consumption and imports (Fig. 10). Table 9 presents some statistics for the growth rates of the different components of aggregate demand.

Table 9. Some statistics for growth rates of the components of aggregate demand and GDP (per cent)

	Average	Maximum	Minimum	Standard Deviation
X	13.01	113.80	-41.88	30.34
I	13.67	91.61	-16.81	24.30
Cp	19.15	106.13	-21.77	23.36
Cg	14.69	73.22	-21.77	22.28
Z	16.15	75.56	-13.29	19.34
A	15.97	80.30	-40.49	21.05
GDP	13.49	100.50	-22.27	25.26

Source: on the basis of Table 2 in the annex.

The contributions of the components of aggregate demand to the growth rates of GDP may be estimated from the relation:

Growth rate of GDP =(growth rate of Cp)(share of Cp) + (growth of Cg)(share of Cg) + (growth of I)(share of I) + (growth of X)(share of X)(Growth of Z)(share of Z).

Thus, the contributions to the average growth rate of GDP from 1972 to 1995 may be calculated as follows;[17]

(grth Cp)(share Cp) = (19.15)(29.1) - 5.57%
(grth Cg)(share Cg) = (14.69)(15.82) - 2.32%
(grth I)(share I) = (27.75) (13.67) - 3.79%
(grth X)(share X) - (68.71)(13.01) - 8.94%
(grth Z)(share Z) = (16.15)(-41.38) = -6.68%

The contributions of the components to the average growth rate of GDP are:

Cp: 39.98%
Cg: 16.64%
I: 27.19%
X: 64.13%
Z: -47.92%

Fig. 10. UAE-growth rates of GDP and Cp, Cg, I, X and Z (per cent per annum)

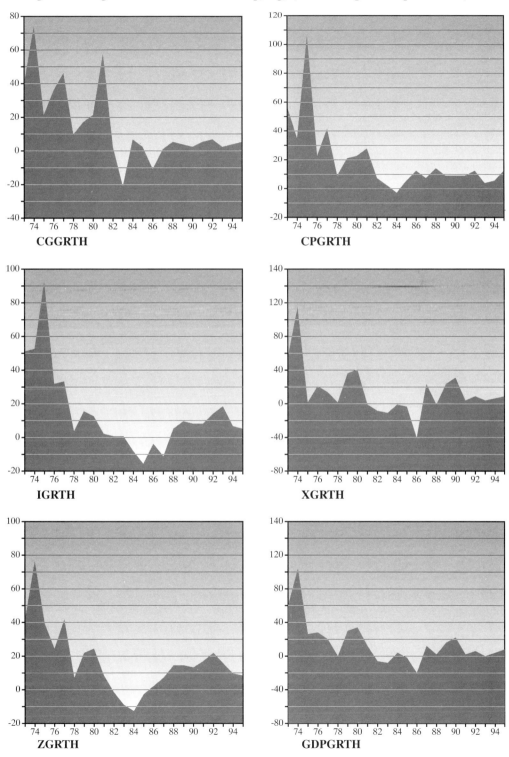

Exports turn out to have contributed about 64 per cent to the average growth rate of GDP from 1972 to 1995. Such a high contribution renders exports the most effective factor in shaping GDP. However, the export concentration index for the UAE economy is relatively high at 0.691 in 1992, though it has declined from 0.801 in 1984.[18]

Given the high contribution of X, the high export concentration index makes GDP highly sensitive to international developments in general and to the oil market in particular. Next in importance is the import contribution to GDP growth which averaged about -47 per cent. Thus, the external sector is the mover of the economy of the UAE.[19]

Private consumption contributed about 40 per cent to average GDP growth while government consumption contributed about 17 per cent. This relatively low government contribution to the growth of GDP should not be interpreted as limited or implying a small government impact on the overall economic activity in the UAE. In fact, the government receives the oil revenues and spends on investments, transfers and subsidies, all activities which influence the behaviour of the private sector in its consumption and investment activities. Investment, both private and government, contributed about 27.49 per cent to the average growth of GDP. But the incremental capital output ratio (ICOR) (investment divided by the increase in GDP between two dates) on the basis of real GDP is about 4.92 (ICOR=(I/GDP)(1/grthGDP)=(27.75)(1/5.63)= 4.92). This is a rough measure of the productivity of investments; the lower the number the better is the productivity.

The ICORs for some groups are:

• Low-income economies: 4.84
• Middle-income economies: 130.0
• Upper-income economies: 7.35
• High-income economies: 13.53

D. Structure of the UAE Economy: Production

The UAE economy, as mentioned earlier, has expanded in size by more than 264 per cent between 1972 and 1995 (Table 1 in the annex). At the beginning of the period, value added in the crude oil subsector dominated production with more than 63 per cent of total GDP. However, the UAE Government aimed, through its economic policy, to lower the country's dependence on the oil sector. Thus, when oil prices were adjusted upward in 1979/1980 for the second time, and oil revenues surged by more than 100 per cent (from DH 24,018 million in 1978 to DH 52,727 million in 1980), the Ministry of Planning prepared a five year plan for the period 1981-1985. The plan centred on three major issues, namely:[21]

• Optimal size and structure of population
• Improvement in the standard of living in all regions of the UAE and development of the skills and capabilities of the citizens.
• Expansion of the productive base by increasing growth in the non-oil sectors in order to lower the dependence on the oil sector and development of non-oil sources of income.

The funding of the plan assumed constant oil revenues and about 70 per cent of the funds were to be provided by the Federal Government. However, oil revenues were down to less than DH 35,000 million in 1982 and DH 27,000 million in 1983. Oil market developments in the first half of the 1980s discouraged the adoption of the development plan and it was shelved. This resulted in uncoordinated investments in the emirates that produced overcapacity and duplication in several activities in the economy. So, the non-oil economy did not improve as much as was expected, though the share of non-oil GDP improved from about 50 per cent in 1982 to about 55 per cent in 1985.[22]

The agricultural sector expanded, but because of the climate situation of the UAE, it contributed less than 3 per cent in 1995 (Table 5 in the annex).

The manufacturing sector has expanded from 2.7 per cent of GDP in 1972 to about 9 per cent in 1995. Government services also increased its share of GDP from 4.48 per cent in 1972 to 11.34 per cent in 1995. The increase in government share is associated with the population increase (from 309,243 to 2,377,453) and the improvement in living standards. Also associated with the growth of population is the expansion in construction activity, the distributive sectors and the other service sectors.

The tremendous evolution and development that has taken place from 1972 to 1995 may not be easily quantified, evaluated and recorded. However, it may be appreciated and comprehended through the simple, but clear and deep understanding of what the priorities of development were to the UAE President, H.H. Sheikh Zayed bin Sultan Al Nahyan:[23]

> *The first fundamental change, and the most important, is the availability of drinking water. In the past, we had no drinking water here in Abu Dhabi, and we had to bring brackish water by tanker. The bringing of water was the most important. I remember telling my brother (then ruler) that had we not got water, we would all of us have had to have moved somewhere, and to look for a place with sweet water. After that, everything started changing. Housing became available when there was none before, then infrastructure and everything else. Our policy was first to concentrate all our efforts to develop this country, and to develop its citizens. When I look around at what has been achieved, I realize I could not have imagined before that it could all have happened. It is like a dream. I had dreams, but would never have believed that it would all have been possible in such a short space of time.*

The realization of what H.H. was talking about may be seen and experienced through the modern cities that have been built with modern facilities, the highways, the airports and ports, the schools and colleges, the hospitals and clinics and the forestation of the desert, in addition to other infrastructures that support further expansion and development in the future. A quantitative assessment of this growth may be made by studying the evolution of the consolidated budget of the UAE, which is the subject of the next section.

Evolution of the Consolidated Budget

Revenues increased from DH 2424 million in 1972 to DH 43,654 million in 1995, an increase of more than 17 fold (1700 per cent), while total expenditures increased from DH 1257 million to DH 61,857 million, an increase of about 48 fold. Revenues have been shaped to a great extent by oil revenues (Table 7 annex) and Fig. 11. The share of total expenditure in GDP increased from less than 20 per cent in 1972 to more than 40 per cent in 1995. The average share over the period is about 36 per cent with a maximum share of 48 per cent and a minimum share of 16 per cent with a standard deviation of 7.75 per cent.

Fig. 11. UAE- total and oil revenues in consolidated budget (mn.dh)

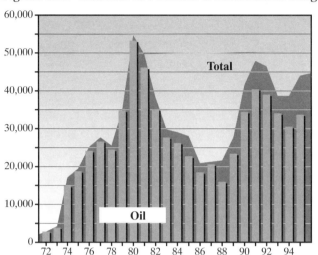

The expansion of the government role in overall economic activities has been the result of the huge increase in government revenues and population during the period, given the government's commitment to improving the standard of living for all residents, nationals and non-nationals.

Expenditure on social services (education, health, social security, welfare, housing and community amenities) increased from 20.5 per cent in 1980 to nearly 30 per cent of total expenditure in 1994.[24] The counterpart of the financial expenditure may be appreciated through the expansion in the services of education, health and housing presented in the following Tables.

Table 10. Evolution of education in the UAE

		1974/1975	1984/1985	1992/1993
1.	Students	60,254	229,759	418,881
	Govt.(G)	52,790	167,320	269,404
	Privt.(P)	7,464	62,439	149,477
	Male	33,233	121,813	213,503
	Female	27,021	107,946	204,901
2.	Teachers	3,681	14,088	26,892
	G.	3,380	10,597	18,485
	P.	301	3,491	8,407
3.	Schools	198	551	861
	G	171	394	540
	P	27	157	321
4.	University Ed.			
	Faculty	76	469	634*
	Students	520	5,374	11,388

* 1989/1990

Sources: Ministry of Planning (1987) Tables (11-15), p 314. (11-17) p 316. (11-18) p 317.
Gulf Cooperation Council Secretariat. *Economic Bulletin,* No.10 (1995), Tables 2/4 p 224. 10/4 p 232.

Table 11. Percentage of the age group enrolled in education (per cent)

	Primary: 1980 1993	Secondary: 1980 1993	Tertiary: 1980 1993
Female	88 108	49 94	
Male	90 112	55 84	
Total			3 11
Adult illiteracy rate (%) in 1995		Female 20	Male 21

Source: World Bank. *World Development Report 1996*, Table 7, p 200.

Table 12. Health services in the UAE

		1975	1985	1990	1993
Hospitals		19	40	42	45
G		15	31	33	
P		4	9	9	
Beds		1745	5812	6397	6461
G		1525	4528	6010	
P		220	384	387	
Doctors		751	2361	2991	
G		671	1699		
P		80	662		
Dentists		65	259	383	
G		58	119	141	
P		7	140	242	
No. of people per	Doctor	617	584	743	
	Bed	320	237	288	
	Nurse	258	226		

Source: Ministry of Planning (1987) Table 11-20 p 319; (1993) Table 62 p 137.

Table 13. Percentage of total UAE population with access to

	Health Care	Safe Water	Sanitation
1980	96	100	75
1993	90	100	95

Infant mortality rate (per 1000 live births)	1980	1994
UAE	55	16
Low income	87	58
Middle income	63	40
High income	12	7
World	81	53

Source: World Bank. *World Development Report 1996*, Table 6, p 198.

Table 14. Evolution of housing services in the UAE (housing units)

	1975	1980	1985	1990
	94,380	209,077	272,791	305,920

Source : Ministry of Planning (1987) and (1990)

The indicators on education and health services presented in the preceding Tables reflect the implication of the proverb 'action speaks louder than words' and translate the President's motto 'education is like a lantern which lights your way in a dark alley'.[25] The improvement in the status of women in the UAE is highly commendable and owes much to Her Highness Sheikha Fatima bint Mubarak, wife of the President, who emphasizes the importance of education to girls: ' education is the real wealth which we should preserve and care for. A girl has the legal right to a proper education'.[26]

The continued expansion in the budget, despite the fall in oil revenues in the early 1980s, has resulted in an overall deficit position since 1982. The continued budget deficit has brought the issue of dependence on the oil sector to the forefront once again. The issue of charging for government services on the basis of cost recovery is being applied partially, while privatization of some utilities, water and electricity, is under discussion. The private sector has been encouraged to shoulder more and more economic activities. From 1975 to 1995, total investment is estimated at DH 575,769 million, of which DH 168,226 million is accounted for by the government and the balance is the private sector's share. The budgetary expansion coupled with the fall in the oil revenues had a negative impact on the external sector, as can be seen from its evolution during the period 1972-1995.

The External Sector

It has been mentioned before that the UAE economy has a high trade ratio and adopts a liberal trade policy. In fact, the UAE economy experienced substantial trade surplus based on oil exports and prices. But the dependence of the economy, and especially the external sector, on development in the international oil market means that the balance fluctuates with its evolution. The peak of the trade surplus was realized in 1980 as a result of the increase in oil exports and prices. Similarly the current account surplus reached its peak in 1980 at DH 37.33 billion.

The 1980s witnessed a decline in the surplus of both the trade and current account balances. However, from 1990 to 1995, trade surplus declined from DH 37 billion to about DH 17 billion, while the current account surplus of DH 20 billion went into a deficit of about DH 11 billion in 1995. Transfers, private and public, continued to realize deficits throughout the period. This result is due to two factors: one is the development assistance the UAE Government extends to the Arab and other developing countries through the Abu Dhabi Fund for Development,[27] and the other is the presence of expatriates to the extent of 90 per cent of the labour force. Despite the decline and later change from current account surplus to deficit, the UAE foreign reserves are estimated at nearly $6.7 billion in 1994 and $7.7 billion at the end of 1995. Other assets are managed by Abu Dhabi Investment Authority.[28]

Despite these foreign assets, the UAE foreign debt is estimated at $12.65 billion at the end of 1995. Most of the debt is short-term trade and development-related debt. Less than 3 per cent of the debt is owed to official creditors and the balance is to commercial creditors. The debt service ratio is less than seven per cent.[29]

Despite the fall in the current account in the balance of payments, the monetary authorities have continued to provide the economy with the liquidity it needs as reflected in the evolution of monetary and credit policy in the UAE.

Monetary and Credit Policy

The UAE Central Bank was established in 1980 to succeed the UAE Currency Board (set up in 1973) in managing the country's monetary and credit policy. It issues currency, advises the government on monetary and financial matters, manages the country's foreign reserves and supervises the banking sector. The Central Bank overcame numerous problems to apply uniform federal laws throughout the emirates. The oil boom attracted many commercial banks to the UAE. At the end of 1995 there were 47 commercial banks, 19 of them locally incorporated with 204 branches and 28 foreign banks with 119 branches. In addition, there are specialized banks and investment institutions and foreign exchange offices.[30] Since 1993 all banks have had to conform to a risk weighted capital adequacy ratio of 10 per cent (two points higher than the minimum ratio of 8 per cent recommended by the Basle Committee). The Central Bank has maintained the Dirham's exchange rate fixed at DH 3.671 equal to 1 US dollar since 1981. From 1972 to 1980, the exchange rate appreciated from DH 4.386 to the US dollar to DH 3.707 to the US dollar (Table 15 in the annex). The UAE Monetary Authorities (the Board and the Central Bank) have provided the economy with the liquidity it needed. In fact, if the velocity equation paradigm is utilized:

$MV = PxRGDP = GDP$, where M = money supply, V = velocity of the circulation, P = price level, and RGDP = real gross domestic product, then growth rate of M + growth rate of V = growth rate of GDP. The following growth rates are calculated over the period 1973-1995:

Annual growth rates (per cent)	GDP	M1	M2
Average	13.50	13.90	16.30
Maximum	100.50	59.60	98.38
Minimum	-22.30	-6.50	-8.55
Standard Deviation	25.30	17.50	24.20

Source: on the basis of Tables 1 and 16.

Growth rate of narrow money (M1 = Currency outside the banks and demand deposits) is close to the nominal growth rate of GDP, which implies that V was stable. In fact, since 1986 it was almost constant. This was associated with low or no inflation. In conclusion, one could infer that monetary policy was accommodating to economic activity.

Conclusion

Prior to December 1971, the United Arab Emirates was characterized politically as seven separate emirates under colonial British rule, economically as separate and underdeveloped entities and socially as backward and lacking essential and basic needs in the areas of education, health and housing services. In 1996, by contrast, having made major strides politically, economically and socially, it can boast of being in the company of high income countries on both the Human Development Index and by GDP Index criteria.[31]

Notwithstanding these achievements, the UAE continues to face at least two challenges. First is the issue of economic diversification and the development of non-oil income sources. Although the share of non-oil income (AGDP) has continued to increase and has, since 1982, surpassed the oil share, the linkage and dependence of the former on the latter is large. Thus the recession in the oil sector has had a negative impact on the overall performance of the non-oil GDP.

The other challenge is the high percentage share of expatriates in the size of the population and consequently in the labour force. Careful and prudent considerations are essential elements for any intelligent discussion on the issue. Concepts need to be defined and understood and historical and present experiences of other countries (USA, Canada, Australia and others) should be studied before taking decisions on this issue as it is not a social one only, but is first and foremost an economic problem.

[1] The Economist Intelligence Unit estimates non-nationals at 80 per cent, see EIU *Country Profile*, United Arab Emirates (1995-1996) p 16.

[2] In 1994 the weighted average of gross national product (GNP) per capita for the middle - income economies was US$ 2520 and that of the upper -middle income was US$4640. However, the weighted average of GNP per capita for the high -income economies was US$23,420. The highest GNP per capita was that of Switzerland at US$37,930. Although the UAE is a member of the high income economies according to the World Bank classification, its per capita GNP is less than 70 per cent of the group average and only about 44 per cent of that of Switzerland. See World Bank. *World Development Report 1996*, Oxford, Oxford University Press (1996) Table 1, p 188.

[3] UAE Central Bank, *Annual Report* (1996) pp 28-9.

[4] See John Kendrick, *Economic Accounts and Their Uses*, New York, McGraw Hill (1972); Irving Fisher, *The Nature of Capital and Income*, New York, Augustus (1965); and John Hicks, *Value and Capital*, (2nd ed) Oxford, Oxford University Press (1978).

[5] Ali Tawfik Al Sadik, 'National Accounting and Income Illusion of Petroleum Exports: The Case of the Arab Gulf Cooperation Council (AGCC)', in Tim Niblock and Richard Lawless (eds), *Prospects in the World Oil Industry*, London, Croom Helm (1985) p 86-7.

[6] Najeeb Abdallah Al Shamsi, *The Economies of the Emirates Before 1971* (1995) chapters 1-5; Malcolm C. Peck, *The United Arab Emirates: A Venture in Unity*, Westview, Boulder, Colorado (1986) p 92.

[7] Al Shamsi, *op.cit.*, p 55 and p 60.

[8] *Ibid.*, Table 17, p 187.

[9] Average government take increased from US$0.89 in late 1970 to about $9.79 in October 1975. See Ali Tawfik Al Sadik, 'Managing The Petrodollar Bonanza: Avenues and Implications of Recycling Arab Capital', *Arab Studies Quarterly*, Vol 6, nos. 1 & 2 (1984) Table 2, p 20.

[10] UAE Monetary Agency, *Annual Report*, 31 December (1979) p 231.

[11] UAE Ministry of Planning, *Main Aspects of Economic and Social Development in the United Arab Emirates during 1972-1977*, May (1978) pp 3-2.

[12] The President, Sheikh Zayed is quoted as saying, 'The federation has embodied the hopes and aspirations of the UAE people for a good life, and represents the start of a great leap forward that will permit us to catch up with civilization in the rest of the world.' see *UAE Yearbook 1995*, p 19.

[13] In the development literature, two gaps are identified as constraints on development in the developing countries: the foreign exchange gap (insufficient foreign earnings) and the saving-investment gap (saving less than investment).

[14] For a review of the changes in the international oil market see Ian Seymour, *OPEC Instrument of Change*, London, Macmillan (1980).

[15] In 1986 the oil market witnessed the lowest prices since their adjustments in 1973/1974. The nominal average oil price declined to less than $13 per barrel, Table 14 in the annex.

[16] In theory real income should be considered assuming no income illusion. In fact per capita income (real GDP) declined from DH92,332 in 1972 to DH43,830 in 1995 (Table 12 in the annex). On the real income basis the income effect on the share of consumption is negative. However, the positive effect of the increase in population on Cp exceeded the negative effect of the decline in income on Cp.

[17] Numbers are taken from Tables 8 and 9 in the text. The sum of these contributions is not exactly equal to the growth rate of GDP reported in Table 9 due to rounding and not allowing for net indirect taxes.

[18] Export concentration index measures the degree to which a country's exports are concentrated in, or diversified among SITIC (revision 2) three-digit level commodities. The index is calculated using Hirschman methodology: $Ix = (Xi/X)^2$, Xi/X is share of exports of commodity Xi in total exports X with a maximum concentration index equal one. See World Bank, *op. cit.* (1996) p 192 and p 226.

[19] The high degree of openness of the UAE economy to the international economies as measured by the trade ratio is a very good reason for the UAE Government to continue its favourable oil policy aiming at stability in the international oil market.

[20] On the basis of average growth rates of GDP over the period 1990 - 1994 and investment/GDP ratio in 1994, World Bank, *op. cit.* (1996) Table 11 p 208 and Table 13 p 212.

[21] Ministry of Planning (1987) p 175.

[22] Between 1981-1988, GDP was trending downward and in 1989 its level was less than in 1981, see Table 1 in the annex.

[23] *UAE Yearbook 1995*, London, Planet Publishing Ltd (1995) p 19.

[24] World Bank, *op. cit.,* p 215.

[25] *UAE Yearbook, op. cit.,* p 99.

[26] *Ibid.,* p 99.

[27] The Fund was established in July 1971, under the name: The Abu Dhabi Fund for Arab Economic Development, and in 1993 changed the name to Abu Dhabi Fund for Development to reflect the actual emphasis on extending aid throughout the developing countries.

[28] The cumulative surpluses of the current account from 1980 to 1993 amounted to about DH 263 bn (approximately $72 bn). Taking account of the DH 19.78 bn current deficits during 1994 and 1995 would leave more than $66 bn in foreign assets before adding any derived interest or other income.

[29] E.I.U. *United Arab Emirates: Country Profile 1995 -1996,* p 36.

[30] UAE Central Bank. *Annual Report 1996,.*

[31] *United Nation Development Program* (UNDP) (1995) p 155.

Table 1. UAE nominal GDP in mn. dirhams and GDP DEF (1987 = 100)

	Nominal GDP	GDP DEF	REAL GDP
1972	6,450	22.59	28,553
1973	11,392	25.57	44,553
1974	31,123	60.93	51,079
1975	39,460	72.5	54,428
1976	51,033	80.75	63,199
1977	63,419	85.78	73,932
1978	60,699	83.6	72,571
1979	79,972	88.2	90,671
1980	109,833	95.98	114,443
1981	121,100	101.35	119,487
1982	112,433	102.85	109,317
1983	102,909	98.87	104,085
1984	101,843	93.98	108,367
1985	99,416	98.11	101,331
1986	79,566	96.7	82,281
1987	87,366	100	87,366
1988	87,106	102.09	85,323
1989	100,781	104.12	96,793
1900	125,266	108.26	115,708
1991	126,264	115.67	109,159
1992	131,676	121.49	108,384
1993	132,116	126.65	104,316
1994	135,065	132.28	105,105
1995	143.970	138.16	104,205

Sources: For GDP UAE Ministry of Planning.
1) Main Features of Economic and Social Development in the United Arab Emirates During 1972 - 1977, May ??
2) Economic and Social Development in the United Arab Emirates During 1975 - ??
3) Economic and Social Development in the United Arab Emirates During 1985 - ??
4) Annual Economic Report 1994 & 1995

Table 2. Components of aggregate demand

	Cp	Cg	I	X	Z	GDP
1972	871.6	859.2	1747.7	5464.8	-2,493	6,450
1973	1535.5	1284.8	2880.6	9438.5	-3,747	11,392
1974	2150.04	2671.9	4824.7	29,453.5	-7,979	31,123
1975	6215	3261	12059	29522	-11,597	39,460
1976	7695	4648	16585	36559	-14,802	50,683
1977	11557	7413	22966	41779	-22,296	61,419
1978	12501	8163	23679	40200	-23,874	60,669
1979	15245	9600	27643	57201	-29,717	79,972
1980	18968	11992	31155	85592	-37,874	109,833
1981	24946	21475	31801	83662	-40,784	121,100
1982	26846	22000	32063	71576	-40,152	112,333
1983	27467	17696	32193	60874	-36,665	101,565
1984	26744	19030	29496	60008	-32,101	103,177
1985	28317	19554	24933	57672	-31,060	99,416
1986	31640	11581	23872	37901	-31,428	79,566
1987	33852	17762	20956	48562	-33,766	87,366
1988	38605	18722	21770	46879	-33,870	87,106
1989	42510	19603	23526	59853	-44,711	100,781
1990	46717	20120	25314	81978	-50,590	123,539
1991	51376	21131	27210	84246	-59,444	124,519
1992	57921	22792	31435	92000	-74,148	130,000
1993	59849	23377	37259	96380	-87,298	129,567
1994	63314	24197	39324	101574	-94,656	133,753
1995	71240	25200	40530	108800	-102,250	143,520

Sources: Ministry of Planning.
1) Main Aspects of Development in the United Arab Emirates: 1972-1977, May 1978
2) Economic and Social Development in the United Arab Emirates: 1975-1985, 1987
3) Economic and Social Development in the United Arab Emirates: 1985-1900, 1993
4) Annual Economic Report, 1994 & 1995

Table 3. UAE consolidated government fiscal accounts (mn.dh.)

	REVENUES	CUR.EXP	CAP.EXP	Capital Participation and Aid	Total Expenditure	Surp. or Deficit(-)	OIL REVENUE
1972	2423.9	934.7		322.1	1256.8	1167.1	2194
1973	3699.1	1327.6		1226.6	2554.2	1144.9	3166
1974	16466.3	2841.2		2188.4	5029.6	11436.7	14041
1975	19033	4044	4075		13364	6287	18025
1976	24766	5703	6761		18562	7362	23484
1977	27347	7713	10332	1678	24476	4542	26116
1978	25489	8895	11391	1853	26250	1087	24018
1979	34653	10693	10154	5193	29617	6431	34265
1980	54550	16763	9593	5749	39811	16211	52727
1981	49617	24604	9207	9412	46082	5275	45480
1982	37729	25818	9756	7188	42723	-3344	34643
1983	29539	24384	8096	6957	38119	-6781	27005
1984	28800	24075	6817	5023	33997	-4015	25631
1985	27762	24535	6534	6941	34389	-5802	22247
1986	20397.8	23706.7	7400.8	3788	34896.2	-14498.4	17855
1987	20683.4	31723.1	4492.6	3438	37517	-16833.6	20042
1988	20793.5	31048.4	3596.2	1532	36176.5	-15383	15425
1989	27367.5	32459.5	4229.7	1414	38105.6	-10738.1	22934
1990	41277.9	34475.4	4758.1	12587	53461.8	-12183.9	34034
1991	47833	33051	7171	19234	59456	-11623	39915
1992	46154.9	39098.2	9269.6	3800	52132.9	-5978	38412
1993	38517.2	38468.7	10910.4	2973	54616.1	-16098.9	33243
1994	38664	38103	11737	4859	54792	-16128	29894
1995	43654	43593	11945		61857	-18023	33233
			168226.4				

Sources: UAE Central Bank   1) Annual Reports (1993, 1994, 1995)
2) Bulletin (1991) Ministry of Planning.
3) Main Aspects of Economic and Social Development during 1972 - 1977, (1978)

Table 4. Number of employees and their compensation

	Employees (Number)	Compensation (Mn. DH)	Average Compens. Dirhams per year
1972	144770	1256.7	8,681
1973	182850	2524.2	13,805
1974	234380	5103.9	21,776
1975	288414	5633	19,531
1976	383983	8138	21,194
1977	477301	11442	23,972
1978	494485	12617	25,515
1979	523240	14166	27,074
1980	541033	16011	29,593
1981	578810	21123	36,494
1982	592300	23300	39,323
1983	600418	24297	40,467
1964	607682	24573	40,467
1985	619429	24997	40,355
1986	531822	24007	38.608
1987	624746	24426	39,097
1988	643669	25226	39,191
1989	667246	26784	40,141
1990	694201	28019	40,362
1991	737690	29883	40,509
1992	799427	31904	39,909
1993	859717	34484	40,111
1994	912929	36242	39,699
1995	955100	38000	39,786

Source: Ministry of Planning.
Main Features of Economic and Social Development in the United Arab Emirates 1972-1977, May 1978
Economic and Social Development in the UAE: 1975-1985, 1987 and during 1985-1990, 1993
Annula Economic Report 1995

Table 5. UAE labour force distribution between the sectors and GDP by origin in 1995

Sectors	Labour Number	GDP Mn.Dh.	Labour Share % of total	Sector's Share in % of total	Labour Productivity (GDP/Labour)
Agriculture	67500	3550	7.07	2.47	52590
Mining					
Crude Oil	9700	49200	1.02	34.17	5072170
Others	3100	450	0.32	0.31	145160
Manufacture	99400	12500	10.4	8.68	125750
Elect&Water	22800	3210	2.39	2.23	140790
Construction	156300	13300	16.36	9.24	85090
Wholesale	173700	17800	18.19	12.36	102480
Transport???	88500	8500	9.27	5.9	96050
Finance, Insurance & Real Estate					
Finance & Ins.	17600	7150	1.84	4.97	406250
Real Estate	28900	11700	3.03	8.13	404840
Other Services	49400	1640	5.17	1.14	33200
Government	132500	16320	13.87	11.34	123160
Domestic Services	105700	1200	11.07	.83	11350
Less Imputed Bank Services		2550			
Total	**955100**	**143970**	**100**	**100**	**150740**
Average			6.25	6.78	496400
Max			18.19	34.17	5072170
Min			0.32	0.83	11350
St.D			6.21	8.69	1322340

Source: Ministry of Planning. Annual Economic Report 1995, tables 7 & 8.

Table 6. UAE oil revenues (mn.US $)

1970	212
1971	410
1972	551
1973	900
1974	5536
1975	6000
1976	7000
1977	9030
1978	8000
1979	12400
1980	19200
1981	18306
1982	14465
1983	11441
1984	12400
1985	12500
1986	6100
1987	5460
1988	4141
1989	11300
1990	15600
1991	14765
1992	14490
1993	12086
1994	12300
1995	13350

Sources: 1970 1978 Bryan Cooper, (ed), Opec Oil Report London, Petroleum Economist, 2nd Edition, 1978
1978 1982, Petroleum Economist, June 1981 and 1983
1983-1995, OAPEC. Secretary General Annual Report, Various Numbers.

Table 7. UAE oil production (mn. barrels)

1972	440.2
1973	555.6
1974	611.6
1975	619.077
1976	708.88
1977	729.51
1978	667.77
1979	667.5
1980	626.39
1981	548.8
1982	460.79
1983	451.58
1984	468.78
1985	477.8
1986	500.05
1987	542.025
1988	571.23
1989	706.64
1990	774.89
1991	883.3
1992	835.85
1993	792.05
1994	810.3
1995	799.35

Sources: Petroleum Economist, February 1995. p64
Ministry of Planning. Aspects of Economic and Social Development in the UAE 1972-1977, 1978

Table 8. UAE value added in crude oil sub sector (mn dh)

1972	4,099
1973	7,870
1974	25,070
1975	26,364
1976	32,275
1977	35,575
1978	32,618
1979	47,884
1980	70,532
1981	69,814
1982	55,982
1983	46,145
1984	46,604
1985	44,707
1986	26,171
1987	32,423
1988	29,643
1989	38,792
1990	57,632
1991	54,260
1992	53,753
1993	47,341
1994	45,154
1995	49,220

Sources: Minstry of Planning.
Main Features of Economic and Social Development in the United Arab Emirates 1972-1977, 1978.
Economic and Social Development in the UAE 1975-1985, 1987 and during 1985-1990, 1993.
Annual Economic Report 1995.

Table 9. UAE GDP, oil GDP and AGDP (mndh)

	AGDP	Oil GDP	NGDP
1972	2351.200	4099.00	6450.200
1973	3521.700	7870.4	11392.1
1974	6053.00	25069.00	31122.7
1975	13096.00	26364.00	39460.00
1976	18758.00	32275.00	51033.00
1977	27844.00	35575.00	63419.00
1978	28051.00	32618.00	60699.00
1979	32088.00	47884.00	79972.00
1980	39301.00	70532.00	109833.00
1981	51286.00	69814.00	121100.00
1982	56451.00	55982.00	112433.00
1983	56764.00	46145.00	102909.00
1984	55239.00	46604.00	101843.00
1985	54709.00	44707.00	99416.00
1986	53395.00	26171.00	79566.00
1987	54943.00	32423.00	87366.00
1988	57463.00	29643.00	81706.00
1989	61989.00	37892.00	100781.00
1990	67634.00	57632.00	125266.00
1991	72004.00	54260.00	126264.00
1992	77923.00	53753.00	131676.00
1993	84775.00	47341.00	132116.00
1994	89911.00	45154.00	135065.00
1995	94700.00	49200.00	143970.00

Source: on the basis of tables 1 & 8 in the Annex

Table 10. UAE population (number)

1970	223000
1971	262605
1972	309243
1973	364164
1974	428839
1975	505000
1976	580669
1977	667669
1978	667708
1979	882736
1980	1015000
1981	1079159
1982	1147375
1983	1219902
1984	1297014
1985	1379000
1986	1433001
1987	1489118
1988	1547432
1989	1608029
1990	1671000
1991	1908800
1992	2011400
1993	2083100
1994	2230000
1995	2377453

Ministry of Planning. Annual Economic Reports
Aspects of Economic and Social Development in the UAE during 1972-1977 (1978).
Economic and Social Development in the UAE during 1975-1985, (1987)

Table 11. UAE Per capita real GDP (dirhams per year)

1972	92,333
1973	122,342
1974	119,111
1975	107,111
1976	108,838
1977	110,732
1978	94,529
1979	102,716
1980	112,742
1981	110,722
1982	95,276
1983	85,323
1984	83,551
1985	73,482
1986	57,419
1987	58,670
1988	55,138
1989	60,194
1990	69,245
1991	57,187
1992	53,885
1993	50,077
1994	45,787
1995	43,831

Source: On the basis of tables 1 and 10

Table 12. Structure of the UAE GDP by origin (percent)

	1972	1975	1980	1985	1990	1995
Agriculture, Livestock & Fishing	1.8	0.008	0.007	1.14	1.64	2.47
Mining & Quarrying						
a. Crude Oil	63.49	66.52	63.27	43.83	46.01	34.17
b. Others	0.001	0.002	0.002	0.003	0.002	0.003
Manufacturing	2.73	0.009	3.76	9.07	7.74	8.68
Electricity & Water	1.3	0.005	1.16	2.1	1.96	2.23
Construction	6.33	10.87	8.82	8.71	7.73	9.24
Whole, Retail Trade, Restaurants	7.6	8.19	8.16	8.54	8.97	12.36
Transport, Storage & Comm.	7.38	3.17	3.35	4.14	4.95	5.9
Finance & Insurance	0.007	1.58	1.9	5.05	4.09	4.96
Real Estate	3.72	4.02	3.59	5.08	5.48	8.13
Other Services	0.005	0.009	0.007	1.61	1.97	1.14
Less Imputed Bank Services	0	-1.39	-1.26	-1.01	-1.57	-1.77
Domestic Services of Households	0	0.001	0.002	0.004	0.004	0.008
Government Services	4.48	3.44	5.37	10.78	10.35	11.34
Total (Million Dirhams)	**6450**	**39635**	**111470**	**101990**	**125266**	**143970**
Non-oil Sectors	2355	13271	40938	57283	67634	94770
Percentage of Total	36.51	44.57	36.24	56.17	53.99	65.83

Sources: For 1972, Ministry of Information and Culture
Economic and Social Development in the UAE: 1972-1994, Facts and Figures, December, 1995, Table 1, p35
For 1975-1990, UAE Central Bank Reports, Tables 3-2 & 3-3, P 64 & 67
For 1995, Ministry of Planning, Annual Economic Report, 1995, Table 3

Table 13. Nominal and real oil prices ($ per barrel)

	Index 72	Index 95	Nominal	Real 72	Real 95
1970	85.19	23	2.1	2.47	9.13
1971	92.59	25	2.57	2.78	10.28
1972	100.00	27	2.8	2.80	10.37
1973	122.22	33	3.14	2.57	9.52
1974	148.15	40	10.41	7.03	26.03
1975	166.67	45	10.43	6.26	23.18
1976	166.67	45	11.63	6.98	25.84
1977	181.48	49	12.6	6.94	25.71
1978	203.70	55	12.91	6.34	23.47
1979	233.33	63	29.19	12.51	46.33
1980	266.67	72	36.01	13.50	50.01
1981	255.56	69	34.17	13.37	49.52
1982	244.44	66	31.71	12.97	48.05
1983	240.74	65	30.05	12.48	46.23
1984	233.33	63	28.06	12.03	44.54
1985	229.63	62	27.52	11.98	44.39
1986	266.67	72	12.97	4.86	18.01
1987	296.30	80	17.73	5.98	22.16
1988	318.52	86	14.24	4.47	16.56
1989	318.52	86	17.31	5.43	20.13
1990	344.44	93	22.26	6.46	23.94
1991	344.44	93	18.62	5.41	20.02
1992	351.85	95	18.44	5.24	19.41
1993	333.33	90	16.33	4.90	18.14
1994	344.44	93	15.54	4.51	16.17
1995	370.37	100	16.86	4.55	16.86

Source: OAPEC. Secretary General Annual Report 1995, table 1-18, p.7

Table 14. Dirham exchange rate
(dirhams per US$)

1972	4,386
1973	3,996
1974	3,959
1975	3,961
1976	3,953
1977	3,903
1978	3,871
1979	3,816
1980	3,707
1981	3,671
1982	3,671
1983	3,671
1984	3,671
1985	3,671
1986	3,671
1987	3,671
1988	3,671
1989	3,671
1990	3,671
1991	3,671
1992	3,671
1993	3,671
1994	3,671
1995	3,671

Source: World Bank. World Bank Tables, Baltimore, The John
Hopkins University Press (1995) p 696-99

Table 15. Narrow and broad money (mn dh and growth rates in per cent)

	GRTHM 1	GRTHM 2	MONEY M1	MONEY M2
1972	NA	NA	NA	NA
1973	NA	NA	970	2,260
1974	45.99	98.38	1,540	6,040
1975	52.74	37.94	2,600	8,820
1976	59.62	64.16	4,730	16,800
1977	9.86	-7.52	5,210	15,500
1978	10.22	12.31	5,780	17,600
1979	8.18	3.61	6,270	18,200
1980	15.98	25.55	7.350	23,500
1981	19.85	21.24	8,970	29,100
1982	8.23	14.54	9,740	33,600
1983	-6.52	7.71	9,120	36,330
1984	-2.58	25.44	8,890	46,900
1985	6.67	6.24	9,510	49,900
1986	-3.25	4.3	9,200	52,100
1987	9.28	5.35	10,100	54,900
1988	6.30	5.69	10,800	58,200
1989	2.78	8.3	11,100	63,200
1990	-2.70	-8.55	10,800	58,000
1991	18.99	13.58	13,000	66,400
1992	14.09	4.51	15,000	69,500
1993	19.30	-1.60	18,200	68,400
1994	5.41	7.60	19,200	73,800
1995	8.20	9.79	20,800	81,400

Sources: UAE Central Bank. Annual Reports, various issues

Oil and Gas in the UAE:
the Foundation for Growth and Stability

Philip M.Barnes

The Early Days

The spectacular development of the United Arab Emirates (UAE) from a collection of obscure desert sheikhdoms to a modern and sophisticated state has been based almost entirely on the wealth it derives from oil and gas. At its peak in the mid 1970s, oil accounted for as much as 96 per cent of export earnings and over 60 per cent of Gross Domestic Product (GDP). Although it now contributes less than 35 per cent to GDP, the oil and gas industry remains the main and crucial source of funding for the further development and economic well-being of the country.

Oil in commercial quantities was only discovered in the Emirates in the late 1950s, long after the pre-War discoveries in Kuwait, for example. Scarcely any active exploration for oil occurred between the two World Wars in what were then the Trucial States. There was, however, always an awareness of the potential oil resources that might be in place. During the inter-War period and despite the rise of independent nationalistic powers in the Gulf area, the Trucial States remained largely undisturbed under British control. Nonetheless, a series of agreements made in 1922 had obligated the rulers of the Trucial States to grant oil concessions exclusively to companies approved by the UK Government. Subsequently, this was made even more restrictive by an ultimatum from the British Political Resident that all the rulers should deal with only one company, Petroleum Concessions Ltd. At the time, this ultimatum on exclusivity probably had much more to do with the British wish to keep other parties out of the economic and political affairs of the Trucial States than with an immediate interest in the oil potential of the region. There were, after all, plenty of other sources of oil already being exploited in other Middle Eastern countries (Peck 1986). Petroleum Concessions Ltd was a wholly owned subsidiary of the Iraq Petroleum Company (IPC) based in London. IPC itself was deeply involved in the machinations of oil politics in the Middle East and was to remain so well into the 1950s. The UK had conceded shares in IPC to its allies after the First World War. But Anglo Persian, later to be renamed BP, and the Royal Dutch Shell Group each retained a 23.75 per cent share.

In the late 1930s another IPC subsidiary, Petroleum Development (Trucial Coast) Ltd (PDTC) contacted individual rulers to offer arrangements for concessions to explore for oil in parts of what was to become the UAE. As a result, in 1938 the Rulers of Dubai and Ras al-Khaimah signed agreements which gave concessions to IPC in return for rental payments.

These payments were to commence immediately on signature (El Mallakh 1981). Subsequently in January 1939, PDTC was given the right to explore for oil in the whole of the Abu Dhabi Emirate's onshore territories and in part of its offshore territories. Other rulers signed agreements in the 1940s and 1950s. These agreements were concessions of the type then standard in the Middle East and elsewhere. They covered long periods, 75 years in the case of Abu Dhabi, and generally embraced the whole territory of the country concerned. Payment to the host country was based on royalties before and after discovery of oil.

The signing of these concession agreements marked a significant step in the wider recognition of the eventual components of the UAE as modern political entities. It was, at the least, a token of their independence that presaged their establishment as a modern nation state. The main direct benefit to them at the time was that, although no oil was discovered in commercial quantities until much later, the payment for exploration rights became a significant source of new wealth and strength for the rulers. The growing interest in the oil potential of the region also revealed a need to establish precise political borders where before often only a rather vague sense of territory may have existed. As a result a number of disputes were generated between neighbouring states.

During the Second World War the oil companies were unable to continue their exploration activities in the Gulf area; but they were quickly resumed on a limited scale once the war had ended. Much of the investment by IPC and its subsidiary companies in the Gulf was initially concentrated in Qatar and elsewhere rather than in the Trucial States. In the light of its preliminary exploration findings, IPC relinquished concession rights in the emirates of Dubai, Sharjah, Ras al-Khaimah, Ajman, Umm al-Qaiwain and Fujairah. (Al Otaiba 1977). Subsequently, the rulers granted concession rights to other companies not necessarily directly owned by the IPC partners. During the 1940s and 1950s the new concept of marking a country's continental shelf as its territorial boundary meant that more concessions could be granted. As it turned out, the most important of the new concessions was that granted in 1954 by Abu Dhabi to Abu Dhabi Marine Areas Ltd, whose ownership was largely in the hands of the old IPC partners. It was the discovery of oil by this company in commercial quantities offshore at Umm Shaif in 1958 that started the UAE on the road to becoming a leading oil-producing state. As a result of this discovery the processing centre and export terminal at Das Island was established, with the first crude oil being exported in 1962. Subsequently, substantial reserves of oil were also discovered offshore at Zakum in 1963 and put into production in 1967. The Abu Dhabi Petroleum Company (ADPC), the renamed old PDTC which operated on land, also made the first significant oil discovery on land of the Murban field at Bab in 1958. There have been other major discoveries in Abu Dhabi both onshore and offshore, notably of the giant Bu Hasa field in 1962, but there has not been a significant major commercial oil discovery since Arzanah in 1973. It now seems unlikely, although not impossible, that there are any giant fields remaining to be discovered.

The withdrawal of the British from the Gulf at the end of 1971 led to the formation of the UAE and, in line with trends in other oil-producing states, a stronger national role in oil development. At the time of the Umm Shaif discovery, Abu Dhabi Marine Areas (ADMA), one of the two main concessionaires, was wholly owned by a group of international companies which included CFP/Total and BP who were members of the old IPC companies. Later a 45 per cent interest in the company was sold to a Japanese consortium, JODCO. The other main concessionaire, Abu Dhabi Petroleum Company (ADPC), which now owns a 40 per cent share in the Abu Dhabi Company for Onshore Operations (ADCO), was also jointly owned by the international companies, BP, Shell, CFP/Total, Exxon and Mobil. The present structure of the oil industry in Abu Dhabi dates from 28 November 1971 when the government established a national oil company, the Abu Dhabi National Oil Company (ADNOC). Law No. 7 of 1971 stipulated that ADNOC should operate in all areas of the oil and gas industry. This was the move that was eventually to lead to the state taking a controlling interest in all oil and gas fields. Initially, the government acquired a 25 per cent stake in the two concessionary companies but later, under the terms of the participation agreement of 2 September 1974, this share was raised to 60 per cent.

The discoveries of hydrocarbons made during the decades between the end of the Second World War and the 1970s established Abu Dhabi as the main producer in the UAE and also as one of the world's foremost sources of oil. This is a position which it has never lost. In 1995 it possessed well over 90 per cent of the UAE's proven reserves of oil and gas and produced around 84 per cent of its oil.

In Dubai the first commercial discovery, the Fateh offshore field, was made by a subsidiary of the US company Conoco in 1966. Conoco had taken over concessions relinquished by ADPC in 1963. This was followed by a few other discoveries in the early 1970s and a major discovery of gas and condensate at Margham in 1981. Little of significance has been found since.

In Sharjah, the offshore Mubarak oilfield was discovered by Crescent Petroleum Co. in 1972 but since then no further commercial reserves of crude oil have been found. However, substantial reserves of natural gas were found onshore in 1980 and later in 1992 and Sharjah is now regarded as a major gas province. The results of exploration by a variety of companies over many decades in the other states of the UAE have been disappointing. The only other member of the UAE to have found hydrocarbons in commercial quantities so far is Ras al-Khaimah where a small gas and condensate field, Saleh, was discovered in 1983. Minor accumulations of oil and gas have been discovered in Umm al-Qaiwain and Ajman, but they have yet to be exploited.

Based largely on the discoveries in Abu Dhabi of the late 1950s and 1960s, oil production in the UAE had reached the 1 million barrels per day (mn b/d) mark by 1971 and by 1977 had been doubled to 2 mn b/d. An apparent peak of 2.6 mn b/d was reached in 1991, since when production of crude oil and natural gas liquids has hovered around the 2.5 mn b/d mark. The UAE is currently the world's fourth largest oil producer amongst the members of OPEC, after Saudi Arabia, Iran and Venezuela, and the tenth largest in the world. Exports of crude oil from the UAE reached 2.2 mn b/d in 1991 and, although there is the capacity to produce and export considerably more, they are still running at a little over 2 mn b/d.

The use of natural gas associated with crude oil production started in the early 1970s and Abu Dhabi began exporting liquefied natural gas (LNG) in 1977. This was a pioneering project, planned and built at a time when few states in the Middle East were even contemplating gas exports. Overall, natural gas production has been increasing steadily since the early 1980s. Associated and non-associated natural gas is now produced in Dubai and Sharjah as well as Abu Dhabi and is widely utilized for domestic consumption in most of the emirates.

With the rise in oil and gas production came investment in all the infrastructure necessary for a modern oil state. The effect of the discovery of oil and gas on the overall prosperity of

Fig. 1. Crude oil and natural gas liquids production in the UAE: 1962 to 1995

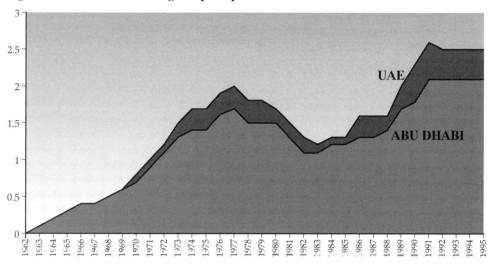

Source: BP Stats & DeGolyer & MacNaughton

the UAE's inhabitants can be roughly gauged by the corresponding increase in oil revenue. This increased from just $6 million in 1963 to nearly $16 billion in 1990, with high oil prices and with production at a peak. With weaker oil prices, revenue is now a little lower at around $14 billion. Nonetheless, largely on the basis of its oil and gas resources, the UAE's income per capita remains one of the highest in the world *(OPEC Stats.* 1995; WDR 1996).

The Structure of the Oil and Gas Industry

Under the Federal Constitution of the UAE, each emirate has total responsibility and authority for its oil and gas affairs. In general, the right to explore for and to develop oil and gas resources in each emirate has to be negotiated with the ruler. The actual structure of the oil industry and the extent and manner in which the government's role is exercised varies considerably between the emirates. In Abu Dhabi, for example, the state has a controlling interest in all significant activities relating to oil and gas, whereas, in some of the other emirates, similar activities remain largely in the hands of foreign and often relatively small companies.

All of Abu Dhabi's oil and gas business is run by a Supreme Petroleum Council (SPC) which directly manages the affairs of ADNOC, the national oil company. The company has no separate governing body and the posts of both Secretary General of the SPC and Chairman of ADNOC are held by one man, currently H.E. Yousef Omair bin Yousef. The Chairman of the SPC is Sheikh Khalifa bin Zayed Al Nahyan, the Crown Prince and Chairman of the Abu Dhabi Executive Council.

ADNOC's share in the two main concessionary companies, ADMA-OPCO and ADCO, has remained at 60 per cent. This gives the state effective control over production whilst keeping the original international companies as partners to help finance development and operate the fields. The other private shareholders in ADMA are now BP with 14.7 per cent, Total with

13.3 per cent and the Japanese consortium, JODCO, with 12 per cent. Shell, BP and Total each have a 9.5 per cent share in ADCO; another 9.5 per cent is split between Exxon and Mobil with the remaining 2 per cent held by Partex .

The operations of the companies that are active in Abu Dhabi are largely governed by Law 8 of 12 July 1978, the 'Law on the Conservation of Petroleum Resources'. This is not a petroleum law in the general sense of the word as it does not include taxation and fiscal arrangements, but it does provide detailed regulation of exploration and production operations. In format it closely resembles the standard OPEC law on conservation. The original concession agreements for exploration and development, as amended, continue to apply to the 40 per cent share in ADMA and ADCO retained by the international companies. In addition, by a separate agreement, the companies have been given 'buy back' rights entitling them to purchase the government's 60 per cent entitlement at defined prices. Apart from Nigeria, the UAE is the only OPEC member country where foreign companies can still hold concessions. Taxes and royalties are paid to the government by participants, mainly at standard OPEC rates of 85 per cent and 20 per cent respectively. The need for additional encouragement for companies to invest in finding and developing smaller, high cost oil fields and particularly those offshore have been recognized by giving incentives on the fiscal conditions. The operators of the offshore Mubarraz field, for example, pay tax at 55 per cent and royalty at 12.5 per cent (Barrows 1996). The national oil company itself pays tax to the government at 55 per cent and royalty at 20 per cent on its 60 per cent share of production.

ADNOC also has an 88 per cent interest in ZADCO, which is a combination of two joint ventures set up with Total to develop and operate five offshore fields. ADNOC also has the exclusive rights to explore for and develop hydrocarbons in a number of other areas in Abu Dhabi. In addition, there are two independent operating consortia in Abu Dhabi, ADOC and MOCO, controlled by Japanese interests, and two joint ventures set up to operate specific fields. Since it was formed in 1971, ADNOC has steadily broadened its activities in the oil and gas business and has established a large number of subsidiary companies. Mainly through its two main operating subsidiaries, ADNOC accounts for the bulk of exploration and production activity in Abu Dhabi.

ADNOC, as the holding company for all oil and gas related companies in Abu Dhabi, is now a broadly based and widely experienced organization covering almost all aspects of the hydrocarbon business from oil and gas production through refining and transportation to retail marketing. A separate state agency, International Petroleum Investment Corporation (IPIC), also has minority shareholdings in a number of overseas oil and gas related companies including the Spanish refining company, CEPSA and the Austrian state oil company, OeMV.

In Dubai there is no single organization directing the oil and gas industry and no general petroleum law. Direct government interest in the main activities of production and marketing is somewhat less than in Abu Dhabi although, in July 1975, the Ruler of Dubai announced the transfer of ownership of all hydrocarbon rights to the government. However, the private and foreign companies have remained. The four main oilfields are operated by Dubai Petroleum Company (DPC), which also has the major share of licensed acreage in the emirate. DPC is a wholly owned subsidiary of the US company Conoco, which operates on behalf of a licensee group. This consists of Conoco 32.5 per cent, Total 27.5 per cent, Repsol 25 per cent and two German companies with the remaining 15 per cent. Arco, a subsidiary of Atlantic Richfield, is the sole licence holder of an onshore tract in the south-west of Dubai. It was Arco who made the major onshore discovery of gas and condensate at Margham in 1981. The offshore concessions were originally granted to Superior Oil in 1954 and later taken over by a company owned jointly by Total and Hispanoil. Two other small US companies also hold a licence on an onshore and partly offshore tract although there are no active operations taking place at present.

In 1993, the Dubai Government set up a new company called the Emirates National Oil Company (ENOC). This operates as a holding company for downstream projects inside and outside the country and as the parent company for the government's interests in existing companies. ENOC took over the government's 60 per cent holding in a joint venture between the state and Caltex which had entered the retail oil product market in the late 1980s. The introduction of this joint venture, EPPCO, was in competition with the Abu Dhabi-based Emirates General Petroleum Corporation (EGPC) which had been set up by the Federal Government of the UAE to distribute oil products in Dubai and the northern emirates.

In Sharjah there is no legislation regulating hydrocarbon operations as such. The three producing fields are operated by the Sharjah-based Crescent Petroleum Company (CPC) and by the US independent, Amoco. Crescent was originally owned mainly by various US independents but is now largely owned by its former managing director. The Sharjah Government owns a majority holding in the country's single gas processing plant.

In the two other emirates where oil or gas has been found, Umm al-Qaiwain and Ras al Khaimah, exploration and production is generally in the hands of a range of rather small foreign companies. Exploration in Fujairah and Ajman, as well as other oil and gas related activities such as bunkering and fertilizer production, is also mainly in the hands of minor and largely independent companies.

The latest available indication of the parent companies' ownership of crude oil production in the UAE as a whole is given below:

Table 1. Ownership of crude oil production in the UAE in 1994

	thousands b/d	%
BP	308	14
Total/CFP	272	13
Exxon	44	2
Mobil	44	2
Shell	86	4
National oil coys.	1059	49
Others	353	16
Total	2166	100

Source: OPEC Stats/IEA

Oil Production and its Potential

By any standards, the UAE possesses one of the world's largest resources of hydrocarbons. As a result of a major revision in the late 1980s, the then current estimate of oil reserves was trebled from 33 billion barrels. Proven reserves of oil and condensates have remained at around 98 billion barrels ever since. This estimate represents a high rate of recovery of 50 per cent, but not one that is necessarily unrealistic with sophisticated technology. At current rates of production such substantial proven reserves would last well over 100 years. In the rest of the world, only Iraq and Saudi Arabia are reported as having larger reserves than the UAE (BP Stats. 1996).

The overwhelming bulk of the UAE's oil reserves, as well as its gas reserves, are located in Abu Dhabi which has at least five 'super giant' fields, each with reserves of over 5 billion barrels (Nehring 1978).

Table 2. UAE oil reserves and production

	Proven reserves @ 1.1.96		Oil production in 1995	
	billion bbls	%	million b/d	%
Total UAE	98.1	100.0	2.486	100.0
Abu Dhabi	92.1	93.9	2.078	83.6
Dubai	4.3	4.4	0.343	13.8
Sharjah	1.5	1.6	0.064	2.6
Ras al-Khaimah	0.1	0.1	0.001	n

Note: Oil includes ngls. Source: Production: Energy Data Associates. 7.1996.
Reserves: Oil and Gas Journal. 12.1995

As the earlier chart shows, crude oil and natural gas liquids (ngls) production in the UAE as a whole reached a peak of 2.6 mn b/d in 1991 and has been running at around 2.5 mn b/d ever since.

Active drilling has continued in the Emirates since oil was first discovered. The peak of exploration activity and well completion was reached early in the 1980s. The number of active rigs was 51 in 1982 but has been running at between 15 and 20 per annum in recent years. Overall well completions have been fairly stable since 1991 but completions for oil have fallen in relation to those for natural gas (OPEC Stats.1995).

Abu Dhabi is clearly the dominant producer of oil and gas in the federation. This is a position which seems likely to be further reinforced in the coming years. Dubai is the second largest oil producer, but its reserves are low in relation to its production and production has been falling in recent years. Indeed, some estimates put Dubai's actual proven reserves at around half the volume quoted above (AOGD, 1995). Sharjah and Ras al-Khaimah have remained minor oil producers, mainly of condensate. There is no commercial production elsewhere amongst the emirates.

In late 1990 and the first half of 1991, Abu Dhabi increased its crude oil output to a peak level of 2.1 mn b/d but subsequently had to cut production to ensure overall compliance with the UAE's OPEC quota. Subsequently, in 1993 it was able to take up the slack when Dubai's output fell and its production increased to about 1.8 mn b/d of crude oil, together with an additional 0.3 mn b/d of ngls. It has remained at around this level in subsequent years.

Between 1989 and 1994, production capacity in Abu Dhabi was increased very substantially by 650,000 b/d, largely through the enhancement of existing and mainly offshore fields. Onshore capacity is in the process of being raised further, to around 1.35 mn b/d, and offshore capacity to 1.25 mn b/d. These increases are planned to be completed by the beginning of 1997 at which time total crude oil production capacity should be around 2.6 mn b/d. Against the present OPEC quota this appears to mean that, even with taking up the fall in Dubai's production, over 0.5 mn b/d of capacity will have to be shut in. Additional investment of some $10 billion (*OGJ*, 5.96) is planned to bring total crude capacity to 3 mn b/d by 2003 and to 4 mn b/d by 2020 (*IEA, IPE,* 1996). Production of ngls from both associated and non-associated gas has been increasing roughly in line with gas production. It is expected that production of ngls will at least have trebled by the turn of the century.

Table 3. Main oil-producing fields in the UAE

Field	Discovered	Producing wells	API gravity
Abu Dhabi			
Abu al Bukhush	1969	42	32.0
Arzanah	1973	14	42.0
Asab	1965	106	41.0
Bab	1958	100	44.0
Bu Hasa	1962	201	39.0
Bunduq	1964	23	40.0
Mubarraz	1969	28	37.0
Sahil	1967	22	39.7
Satah	1975	10	39.8
Umm Ad-dalkh	1969	32	32.5
Umm Shaif	1958	142	37.0
Lower Zakum	1963	131	39.0
Upper Zakum	1963	142	35.0
Total		**993**	
Dubai			
Falah	1972		25.5
Fateh	1966		31.8
Rashid	1973	141	38.0
Margham	1981	10	43.5
Total		**151**	
Ras al-Khaimah			
Saleh	1983	7	50.0
Sharjah			
Kahaif	1992	4	50.0
Saja'a/Moyeyid	1980	30	50.0
Mubarak	1972	14	47.0
Total		**48**	

Source: IPE 1996

The biggest increase in onshore crude oil capacity in recent years came from the full completion of the 'super giant' Bab field in December 1993. This increased the field's sustainable capacity to 250,000 b/d and its peak capacity to 350,000 b/d. The other major onshore producing fields in Abu Dhabi are Bu Hasa, with a capacity of 750,000 b/d, and Asab with 250,000 b/d. Offshore, capacity is dominated by the two fields operated by ADMA-OPCO, Umm Shaif and Lower Zakum, with some 600,000 b/d of production capacity between them and by the Upper Zakum field operated by ZADCO. A few years ago, this latter field had its production capacity increased from between 300 to 350,000 b/d to nearly 500,000 b/d. Upper Zakum which is also classed as a 'super giant' is estimated to have some 50 billion barrels in place. Unfortunately it has a tight reservoir formation and has proved extremely expensive to develop. However, even at a low recovery factor of 20 per cent proven recoverable reserves should be around 10 billion barrels (*MEES*, 24.10.1994.). This should enable capacity to be at least doubled given the mobilization of the necessary investment, if and when such a decision is thought to be economically feasible.

The major onshore and offshore fields in Abu Dhabi were all discovered in the late 1950s or early 1960s. Given the age of its fields and the lack of new major prospects, the national oil company's long range strategy is to maximize oil recovery from the existing fields and its investment projects are guided accordingly. The main efforts are directed towards increasing sustainable production and maintaining sound reservoir management policies. Water and gas injection has been used for some years to improve production. At the end of 1994, ADNOC had 715 wells injecting 3.33 mn b/d of water and was also injecting 94 mn cubic feet per day (cfd) of gas into its crude reservoirs (*AODG*, 1995). In order to further improve recovery rates and productivity, more advanced and expensive processes are now being used. For example, the offshore Mubarraz field is sustained by electric submersible pumps and high pressure miscible gas injection. Horizontal drilling has also been used for some years and considerable expertise in deflected drilling has been developed. There is also a highly sophisticated in-house reservoir modelling capability in place.

Partly as a result of the recovery methods that have had to be used, the full cycle production costs of Abu Dhabi's crude oils are rather higher than those of the other major Gulf producers (Barnes 1991). Onshore they are said to range from $2.50 to $ 3.75 and offshore from $6.00 to $10.00 per barrel of crude oil. The cost of adding new capacity is estimated at an average of around $6000 per barrel daily of capacity, although offshore investment costs are rather higher (*IEA*, 1996).

In Dubai, the combination of mature oilfields and the absence of any new structures to develop has led to falling production. The offshore fields, Rashid and the Fatehs, are suffering from severe reservoir depressurization. As a result, crude oil production peaked in the first half of 1991 at 420,000 b/d and then fell rather more rapidly than had been expected. By 1993 production was only 330,000 b/d. During 1996 it has been running at around 275,000 b/d (*Energy Compass*, 31.5.1996.). The only other significant oil production is of condensates at the Margham field.

DPC have hopes of stabilizing Dubai's overall production at around the 300,000 b/d level through gas injection. However, unless substantial investment is forthcoming, production seems set to continue to decline, possibly to below 200,000 b/d in two or three years. Sophisticated enhanced recovery techniques are already being used in the offshore fields in addition to the water and gas injection systems that have been operating since the mid 1970s. As a result, recovery rates are believed to have been increased from 30 per cent to 60 per cent and it is hoped that horizontal drilling and miscible gas injection could push recovery even higher, perhaps to 80 per cent. However, miscible gas injection is a costly process and seems likely to increase production costs to perhaps $10 or so per barrel. All associated gas produced in Dubai is now being used for reinjection and increasing volumes of non-associated gas are also having to be used. This has led to the need to import increasing volumes of gas from outside the emirate.

Sharjah's hydrocarbon production consists mainly of gas and condensates, with only about 5000 b/d of crude oil being produced from the offshore Mubarak field. Since the discovery of Mubarak in 1972, no further commercial reserves of crude oil have been found. This field is relatively expensive to produce and is also in decline. Exploration in Sharjah continues on a limited scale, concentrated around existing structures with some further accumulations of gas and condensate having been found. Despite the lack of real success and the deteriorating production in existing fields, Sharjah's stated proven reserves of oil have remained at the same level for some years.

The only hydrocarbon structure to be developed within Ras al-Khaimah itself is the Saleh gas and condensate field. This was discovered in 1983 but is now almost depleted and producing less than 750 b/d of condensate. The government at one time considered the possibility of redeveloping this field despite the substantial investment required. Elsewhere in the emirate there is virtually no exploration taking place at present, although an agreement was signed in 1996 between the government and a consortium of US companies for exploration offshore.

In the late 1970s, it looked as if Umm al-Qaiwain might become a hydrocarbon producer following the discovery of an offshore gas field. This appears to have come to nothing. There is no exploration at present and the emirate's sole interest in hydrocarbon production remains its 20 per cent share in the revenues from the Mubarak field, part of which lies in its territorial waters.

In the other emirates a little exploration has taken place but only a few very small accumulations have been discovered in the past, none of which have proved commercial. Prospects for commercial discoveries are not seen as good.

Total sustainable crude oil production capacity for the whole of the UAE is likely to be at least 2.650 mn b/d at the end of 1996. This compares with the current OPEC allowable production of 2.161 mn b/d.

The Expansion of Natural Gas Use

In addition to its oil, the UAE has very substantial resources of natural gas. At the beginning of 1996, proven reserves of gas were reported to be 5.8 tcm or 205 trillion cubic feet (*OGJ*, 12.95), which is equivalent to some 36 billion barrels of oil reserves. This latest reserve estimate is well over 60 times the volume of reserves that was estimated in 1985, which is an indication of the way in which the understanding of the value of natural gas to the country has grown in recent years. The UAE now has the fourth largest gas reserve in the world, after Russia, Iran and Qatar. At present rates of production their gas reserves would last for more than 200 years.

Table 4. Proven reserves of natural gas in the UAE at 1.1.1996.

	tcm
Abu Dhabi	5.34
Dubai	0.12
RAK	0.03
Sharjah	0.30
Total	5.79

Source. OGJ. 12.9195

Over 90 per cent of proven reserves of gas are currently shown as being within Abu Dhabi, although some government estimates put the emirate's recoverable reserves at half as much again as those shown above.

Production from these reserves and the consumption of natural gas in the UAE has made dramatic strides since the mid 1980s. In 1983, gross production of natural gas was just over 14 bcm, of which only 65 per cent was actually used for domestic consumption or for exports. Most of the remaining 35 per cent was flared. By 1995, gross production of natural gas had reached 36 bcm and the proportion of gas flared or otherwise 'lost' had been reduced to 12 per cent. As the table below illustrates, the bulk of gas production in the UAE comes from fields in Abu Dhabi. At present this is still mainly associated gas, with some 70 per cent coming from onshore fields.

Table 5. Natural gas production in the UAE 1994 Unit bcm

	Abu Dhabi	Dubai	RaK	Sharjah	UAE
Gross production	20.78	5.33	0.09	8.17	34.37
Reinjected	1.98	3.00	-	-	4.98
Flared/vented	0.20	-	0.04	0.10	0.34
Other losses	2.73	0.50	0.01	0.40	3.64
Exports of LNG	4.25	=	=	=	4.25
Domestic consumption	11.62	5.43	1.04	3.07	21.16
Internal imports/exports	-	+3.60	+1.00	-4.60	-

Source: Cedigaz 1995

In common with a number of other countries in the Middle East, the Government of Abu Dhabi is looking to the development of its enormous reserves of natural gas to increase its revenues and to support further economic growth. The government's gas development strategy is designed to provide Abu Dhabi with sufficient gas for domestic use as a fuel or feedstock, in conjunction with greatly increased capacity to supply gas to the other emirates. Elsewhere in the UAE gas has also become an increasingly important basis for industrial and overall development, although only Sharjah has sufficient reserves to support its own needs or to export. Gas injection is also used extensively to sustain crude oil production.

In Abu Dhabi, the early 1990s have seen a flurry of major projects being initiated to expand dramatically the entire gas chain from production and processing to export facilities. Offshore, output of natural gas was boosted in the last quarter of 1994 when the massive Khuff gas reservoir, which lies under the Umm Shaif oil field, was brought into production at an initial rate of 600 mn cfd (6.1 bcm). This supplemented the associated gas that had been extracted from the field since 1988 and doubled the total volume of gas being sent from Umm Shaif. Subsequently, output was increased to 1.04 bn cfd (11.4 bcm) to supply the new third liquefied natural gas (LNG) train on Das Island (*Gas World,* 4. 1996). All the emirate's offshore gas is sent to the Das Island gas plant for processing.

On shore, substantial accumulations of both associated and non-associated gas were discovered in the late 1980s in the Thamama formations underlying the oil layers in the Habshan area of the Bab field. These formations are now being developed as part of a major onshore gas development programme called Project 545, which is designed to quadruple total onshore gas production to nearly 25 bcm, from 5.7 bcm per annum in 1992 (IEA). Two of the three Thamama formations involved, Thamama C and F, are of non-associated gas and one, Thamama B, is of associated gas. As a part of this project, condensate recovery at the ADNOC gas processing plant at Bab has been doubled to 130,000 b/d. The bulk of the processed gas from Thamama is currently being supplied to the water and electricity companies, the Umm al-Nar refinery and various industries in the Ruwais industrial zone.

After gathering, gas from the onshore fields is piped to three processing plants at Bu Hasa, Bab and Asab. Abu Dhabi Gas Industries (GASCO), a joint venture between ADNOC, Total, Shell and Partex, operates the separation and gathering stations and the three processing plants. At these plants the natural gas liquids are extracted and piped to a fractionation plant at Ruwais, also operated by GASCO. The Ruwais plant is currently being debottlenecked to expand its capacity from 4.75 million tonnes per annum (t/y) to 6 million t/y to meet increased production from the Bab field. The individual GASCO shareholders are responsible for lifting their pro rata share and marketing the finished gas products.

Additional gas reserves located in the Asab oil field are also to be developed for the late 1990s. This $500 million project will be one of the biggest gas ventures yet undertaken by ADNOC and will include the construction of a gas treatment plant with a capacity of 826 mn cfd and a pipeline network to Ruwais. The plant will also have the ability to produce 100,000 b/d of condensates (*Gas Matters,* 5.1996). After extraction of ngls, it is anticipated that gas from Asab will initially be reinjected into the field until markets can be found. There would appear to be considerable scope for additional volumes of gas to be recovered from associated and non-associated fields in Abu Dhabi and there is a target to double gas production between 1998 and 2003.

The LNG plant on Das Island is operated by the Abu Dhabi Gas Liquefaction Company (ADGAS). This is a company set up in 1973 and owned 51 per cent by ADNOC, with the Mitsui Group, BP and Total as the other shareholders. Initial negotiations with the Tokyo Electric Company were concluded as long ago as 1972 and the plant was in production by 1977. Tokyo Electric remains the main customer. A new offtake agreement, made in 1990 in connection with plans to expand the plant, provides for Tokyo Electric to lift 5 mn t/y of LNG over a 25 year period starting in 1994. A final contract for these liftings was signed in 1993. The Das Island plant was originally built with two liquefaction trains with a total nominal capacity of 2.3 million tonnes. The addition of another liquefaction train in 1994 brought total nominal capacity to 4.6 million tonnes of LNG per annum. Eight new methane carriers were ordered by ADGAS in 1994 to cope with this new production and as replacements for the existing fleet. This order for carriers was the most costly part of the whole expansion project, costing over $2 billion in comparison with the third train which cost $1.3 billion.

Due to the success of its sales policy, ADGAS is considering methods to increase capacity even further through debottlenecking. In 1995, production of LNG was running considerably higher than the plant's design capacity. Sales to Japan, largely to Tokyo Electric, totalled 5.4 million tonnes of LNG. Seven hundred and fifty thousand tonnes of liquefied petroleum gases (LPG) were also exported from Das Island to Tokyo Electric, while an additional 450,000 tonnes or so of LPG is being sold to European customers. At the end of 1994, ADGAS also began selling cargoes of LNG into the European spot market. Spot sales of LNG have continued through 1995 and 1996 with cargoes going to Enagas of Spain, Gaz de France and Distrigaz of Belgium.

Dubai consumes more natural gas than it can produce. Its marketed natural gas production consists entirely of non-associated gas from the Margham field, since all the other gas produced at the main oil fields is now being reinjected into the oil formations. The gas from Margham has been treated at the Jebel Ali industrial zone since 1980, in a plant operated by Dubai Natural Gas (DUGAS). This is a joint venture between the Dubai Government (80 per cent) and a Canadian company, Sunningdale Oils. The Jebel Ali plant has a production capacity of around 1700 tonnes per day of butane and propane and 9000 b/d of condensates. The whole of the plant's output of LPG is currently being taken by two Japanese companies with the bulk of the dry gas being supplied to the Dubai aluminium smelter at Jebel Ali and to power stations. Before 1993, some associated gas was also being supplied to the Jebel Ali plant. However at the beginning of 1993, DUGAS started to import dry gas from Crescent's Mubarak field in Sharjah and the whole of Dubai's associated natural gas is now used for reinjection into the Fateh oilfield. Dubai has also, since 1986, been importing gas from Sharjah under an agreement with Amoco for supplies from their Saja'a field.

As part of its successful efforts to diversify its economy away from oil and gas, Dubai needs increasing volumes of gas to power industrial and commercial projects at the Jebel Ali 'Free Trade Zone'. It also needs more gas to inject into its offshore oil fields to try to maintain production levels. With only modest and falling gas reserves, Dubai has little choice but to import additional volumes of gas from neighbouring countries in the Gulf. It has considered Iran, Qatar and Oman amongst others as potential sources for additional supplies. However, it now seems likely that it will be purchasing natural gas from Abu Dhabi's Khuff field both for injection into oil reservoirs and for domestic consumption (*Energy Compass*, 31.5.1996.).

Sharjah possesses the second largest reserves of gas in the UAE and is a significant exporter of gas to its fellow emirates. The start-up of the Kahaif natural gas field in Sharjah in the second half of 1994 boosted the emirate's production by some 30 per cent. Production has also been increased at the Saja'a and Mubarak fields through further development work, while gas condensate recovery facilities have been installed at Mubarak. As a result, Sharjah has been able to step up its gas exports, particularly to Dubai. Most of its marketable production is now absorbed by Dubai, although some gas is piped directly to Sharjah City and to the other northern emirates. The capacity of the only LPG plant in the emirate has also recently been expanded to handle additional volumes of gas from the Kahaif field and to produce some 500,000 b/d of LPG and 300,000 t/y of condensate. This plant is operated by the Sharjah LPG company (SHALCO), which is owned 60 per cent by the government and 25 per cent by Amoco. The latter company handles the sales of condensate and two Japanese companies, also with shareholdings in the plant, handle the sales of LPG.

In Ras al-Khaimah, a small LPG plant was built at Khor Khwair to process gas from the Saleh field. Unfortunately, this field is almost depleted and the plant now receives its feedstock from the the offshore Bukha field. Apart from the LPG plant, it is also hoped to use gas from the Bukha field in a fertilizer plant. The local cement works were originally being supplied with indigenous gas by the Ras al-Khaimah Gas Commission (RAKGAS). As this is no longer possible, gas is being purchased from the Emirates General Petroleum Corporation.

An offshore natural gas discovery was made in 1976 in Umm al-Qaiwan and it was planned to use the gas from this field for a proposed aluminium smelter. The project was abandoned in 1988 and with it disappeared the main reason for developing the field. Small accumulations of gas have also been found in Ajman, but these do not appear to be commercial and have never been developed. Even so, a fertilizer plant was built in Ajman which came into operation in 1994. It has, of necessity, to use imported gas.

Domestic Oil Use and Supply

Total energy consumption in the UAE, including international aviation and marine bunkers, has been fairly stable over the last year or so and is currently put at some 700,000 b/d or 35 million toe per annum. Internal domestic consumption is around 500,000 b/d. Per capita consumption of energy, at around 19,000 kg, is over double that of the USA and one of the highest in the world. This is a reflection of the combination of very low prices with very high incomes as well as a relatively large bunker trade. Natural gas supplies just over half of the UAE's domestic energy needs, with all the rest being met by oil (*BP Stats.*1996).

Domestic consumption of oil products has doubled over the last ten years, although most of the growth occurred in the late 1980s. Consumption has grown only slowly in more recent years as gas has become more widely used and overall economic growth has slowed.
Total consumption of oil products of all kinds within the UAE in 1995 was around 320,000 b/d, which was little changed from the previous two years. These volumes include substantial sales of international aviation fuel and marine bunkers, as well as some losses in refineries; actual consumption of refined products by domestic consumers is only about half this amount. A breakdown of consumption for 1993 by products is shown below.

Table 6. Oil product consumption in the UAE in 1993

	Thousands b/d
LPGs etc	11
Mogas	26
Aviation fuels	5
Kerosene	1
Gas/Diesel	55
Residual	47
Bunkers	177
Total	322

Source: OECD 1995

At one time the marketing of products in the UAE was either through ADNOC, who held a monopoly on oil distribution within Abu Dhabi, or through EGPC, who had a monopoly in the five northern emirates. This monopoly was broken in 1988 when a third company, EPPCO, based in Dubai, set up a number of service stations. EPPCO imports most of its products, but also has supply contracts with ADNOC for gasoline and other products. ADNOC also markets in the other emirates, except Dubai, so that there is now some competition in the market place.

At present there are only two refineries in the UAE, both of which are situated in Abu Dhabi and operated by ADNOC. Their combined capacity is nearly 213,000 b/d. The first refinery in Abu Dhabi started up at Umm al-Nar in 1976, but has since been replaced, in the same location, by a larger and more sophisticated unit with a continuous regeneration catalytic reforming unit. A second refinery, at Ruwais, came onstream in mid 1981 with a distillation capacity of 120,000 b/d. The Ruwais refinery is a highly flexible unit, able to vary refinery output considerably to meet changes in market demand and operating conditions. Under an expansion and upgrading project started in 1995, its hydrocracking capacity is to be increased to 73,000 b/d from 27,000 b/d and its crude distillation capacity by 135,000 b/d. There will also be a 200,000 b/d condensate distillation unit. Both refineries produce lubricating oils and there is also a 30,000 tonne per annum lube blending plant and a grease plant.

Elsewhere in the UAE, the only refinery operating at present is a small private one in Fujairah which is designed to supply bunker fuel for ships using the country's ports. In Dubai, a refinery company was established by decree in 1971 and there has been a feasibility study on the possibility of installing a 150,000 b/d refinery. However, the lack of sufficient supplies of indigenous crude oil must be hampering a final decision on its construction. Dubai already has a lube oil blending plant and a plant producing gasoline additives and conditioning products. In Sharjah, it is planned to put a new, privately-owned oil refinery in place during 1997. This is being prefabricated in Canada and should be able to produce a full range of products.

Table 7. Refinery capacity in the UAE		Thousand b/d
	1996	Planned future capacity
Umm al-Nar	80750	80750
Ruwais	132050	ca.267000
Total Abu Dhabi	212800	ca.347750
Dubai	-	-
Fujairah	35000	35000
Sharjah	-	40000
Total UAE	247800	ca.422750

Source: Oil and Gas Journal. 28.12.95.

This very substantial increase in refining capacity is partly in response to rising domestic demand, but is also a reflection of the potential for increasing product exports, especially into Asian markets. At present, the UAE as a whole is a net importer of oil products. Exports of oil products from the UAE were running at around 160,000 b/d in 1995, considerably lower than the volumes imported.

Oil Exports and Pricing

The export of oil is the foundation of the UAE's prosperity and is unlikely to be displaced as its main source of export earnings for many years to come. Exports of crude oil and ngls are now nearly double the level of ten years ago and are currently running at just over 2 mn b/d. The bulk of these oil exports are sold into Asian markets and particularly to Japan where the main export grades are highly favoured. Over 25 per cent of Japan's crude oil imports are now obtained from the UAE. The increasing importance of the Japanese market and the decline of sales to the USA and Western Europe is clear from the table below.

Table 8. Exports of crude oil from the UAE				Thousand b/d	
Destination	1990	1991	1992	1993	1994
North America	84.0	65.0	86.9	94.4	23.6
Latin America	40.0	20.0	10.0	10.0	10.0
Europe	210.0	200.0	192.8	85.8	61.7
Middle East and Africa	45.0	45.0	35.0	35.0	30.0
Japan	815.0	1057.0	1041.2	1083.5	1212.9
Rest of Far East and Oceania	701.0	808.0	694.1	661.3	616.8
Total	**1895.0**	**2195.0**	**2060.0**	**1970.0**	**1955.0**

Source: OPEC Stats. 1995

While Abu Dhabi also uses some of its crude oil for processing in its own refineries for domestic use and for export as products, it still has some production capacity shut in. In contrast, Dubai exports all the crude oil it is able to produce. This leaves Abu Dhabi to adjust its production to the overall OPEC allocation for the UAE.

Dubai's main export crude is Fatah of 31 to 32 degrees API. Small volumes of Dubai crude are sold under term contracts but most is sold on the spot market and it is the most freely traded crude in the region. Despite the limited supplies available, Dubai crude is still used as a benchmark to price sales into eastern markets by other Gulf producers who export very much larger volumes. Platts quotes three 'paper Dubai' assessments in recognition of the forward Dubai market, frequently traded each day either on an outright basis or in arbitrage with paper Brent crude oil. However, it seems likely that further falls in the availability of Dubai will make it increasingly difficult for its role as a marker crude to continue.

Most of the Abu Dhabi export crudes, with their high middle distillate yields, are very suitable for Japanese refineries and patterns of product demand and are usually in steady demand. Both ADNOC and the equity producers sell much of their crude oil under term contracts. Abu Dhabi once had an official export price structure, but this was abandoned in 1988 and their selling prices now follow the international market. Originally, export crude prices were set in terms of premia over the spot price for Oman crude, but now ADNOC announces a monthly retroactive assessment price for its four main crudes. The price differentials between the main export crudes, Murban, Umm Shaif, Lower Zakum (with APIs ranging from 37 to 40 degrees) and Upper Zakum (32 to 34 degrees) are fairly stable with the lighter crudes usually trading at a premium of between $1 to $2 per barrel over the heavier ones. Actual prices for UAE crude oils have improved in recent years after the low prices of the late 1980s. In March 1994, Murban was priced at $13.75 per barrel. During 1995 it reached between $16 and $18 per barrel and, by the middle of 1996, was running at $19 per barrel.

In addition to the crude oil volumes shown in the table above, substantial amounts of ngls and condensates are exported as well as being spiked into crude oil. During 1996, a major new export stream of condensates from the Thamama field started up, initially with some 90,000 b/d (*MEES,* 24.6.1996.). Apart from their ready marketability, a major advantage of these exports is that they do not count against OPEC allowables.

Diversification

Overall export earnings of all goods from the UAE reached a peak of over $24 billion in 1991, of which 61 per cent was from oil. It is a measure of the major diversification that has taken place in a relatively short time that, back in 1975, oil made up 94 per cent of total exports by value. It is, of course, partly a reflection of the substantial fall in oil prices that has taken place over that period. In 1994, oil exports were 57 per cent of total exports in terms of value.

Table 9. Oil Exports from the UAE

	Value FOB in millions US$	As a % of total exports
1975	6762	94
1980	19558	89
1985	12978	88
1986	7453	74
1990	15600	66
1991	14765	61
1992	14490	69
1993	12086	58
1994	12200	57

Source: OPEC Stats. (ex IMF)

The growth of the non-oil sector in the UAE is also reflected in terms of its contribution to GDP. From representing less than 40 per cent of GDP in the early 1980s, it now provides some 66 per cent. The value of UAE oil production has actually fallen or remained fairly static in every year in nominal terms, since a sharp improvement in 1989/1990. GDP as a whole has, in contrast, continued to grow steadily. In general, the enormous wealth accruing from the oil sector has been wisely used in diversifying the economy onto a more balanced footing. The economy is reported to have grown by 6.5 per cent in 1995, mainly as a result of continued buoyancy in the non-oil sector although the strengthening of oil prices played a major role.

Dubai in particular, with its limited reserves of oil and declining production, has for many years had a policy of using its oil revenues and foreign investment funds to diversify its economy. It has undertaken widespread development of non-oil industries, actively encourages direct foreign investment and promotes itself as a regional manufacturing and re-exporting centre. It is one of the Gulf's leading commercial and trading centres and has been especially successful in developing a broad based service sector, which includes tourism as well as banking and other financial services. Most industrial activities in Dubai are located in the 'Jebel Ali Free Zone', where full foreign ownership of enterprises is allowed. This Zone was originally established in 1980 and has become the leading centre for entrepôt trade throughout the Gulf. Jebel Ali also claims to be the world's largest man made port and its activities include the world's largest dry dock and extensive ship repair facilities. It has an aluminium smelter and various chemical plants.

Sharjah has also succeeded in developing industrial and commercial activities, capitalizing on its strategic location at the mouth of the Gulf. This gives it the advantage of being the only member of the UAE to have ports on either side of the Straits of Hormuz, both of which incorporate container terminals. Sharjah operates an open door foreign investment policy and has become a centre for manufacturing in the UAE. Although (to some extent from necessity) Dubai and Sharjah have taken the lead in terms of economic diversification, Abu Dhabi is now setting up a new industrial and trading zone as well.

The Relationship with OPEC

Abu Dhabi joined the Organization of the Petroleum Exporting Countries (OPEC) in 1967, some seven years after that organization had been formed in September 1960. This was before the federation came into being, but membership was transferred to the UAE in January 1974. The UAE is also a member of the Organization of Arab Petroleum Exporting Countries (OAPEC) and the Gulf Cooperation Council (GCC). In March 1994 it joined the General Agreement on Tariffs and Trade (GATT)

The UAE has traditionally taken a moderate position at OPEC meetings and, in the past, has usually cooperated with other GCC countries to ensure a conservative approach to prices. As a fellow 'low absorber' and neighbour, Abu Dhabi is a natural ally of other GCC states and its moderate line is understandable, although there are subtle differences that arise every once in a while.

In late 1984, the production quota allocated to the UAE was 0.95 mn b/d. After the low price period between 1986 to 1988, the UAE refused in OPEC to support any increase in price until its long-term grievance against the low level of its allocated quota was settled. By July 1990, the allocation was 1.5 mn b/d. However, Abu Dhabi still had to cut its production between 1991 and 1993, in order to comply with the quota, because Dubai was producing at maximum, regardless of OPEC. In October 1993, the allowable was increased to 2.161 mn b/d and it has remained at this level ever since. Abu Dhabi was able to raise its production in 1994, even though the allowable remained pegged, because of the decline in Dubai's production capability.

Abu Dhabi's production is carefully calculated month by month to fit in with the volumes left to it from the OPEC quota after Dubai's production has been taken into account. Separate production allowables are set by the government for the various fields. In 1994 and 1995, Abu Dhabi reduced its allowables for the ADCO and ADMA-OPCO fields in favour of ZADCO's Upper Zakum crude oil. This was said to be because of the higher fixed costs of this field and the need to recover the substantial investment made in a field in which ADNOC itself holds a 88 per cent share. It was clearly not a move that found favour with the international shareholders in ADCO and ADMA.

As Dubai's production may well continue to fall over the next year or so, Abu Dhabi should have some leeway for further increases in its production even within an unchanged quota. However, there is still substantial spare capacity available, perhaps of the order of 500,000 b/d, and capacity is currently being expanded considerably further.

Forward with Confidence

As part of its energy related policies, the UAE has followed a consistent pattern of determining and exploiting the full measure of its oil and gas reserves and maximizing their value on the international market. The new refinery expansion project in Abu Dhabi will provide the additional capacity needed to meet growing domestic demand for products for some years to come, as well as providing the flexibility needed to add more value to oil exports. Crude oil production capacity has already nearly doubled over the last ten years, and further expansion is underway to bring it up to well over 3 mn b/d within a few years. The expansion of the oil and gas business has been, and continues to be, successfully achieved, despite the need for gas injection and other relatively expensive measures. The long term nature of the UAE's relationship with the international oil companies on concession and fiscal arrangements has played a major part in ensuring that the necessary investment and expertise has been adequately deployed.

In the past the UAE, in the form of Abu Dhabi, has faced up to its responsibilities within OPEC to restrain its crude oil production. The strains resulting from such constraint will undoubtedly be even stronger in future as production capacity grows. It will require considerable political and commercial expertise, both internally and externally, to manage the situation.

The potential of the UAE's enormous gas reserves is already being exploited in a determined fashion as an additional basis for developing the economy. The competition with other suppliers for international gas markets is likely to remain severe, with new rival schemes being built or planned in the Middle East and elsewhere. Nonetheless, the UAE should be able to continue to build successfully on the strengths of its pioneering, and recently expanded, LNG plant at Das Island. Further expansion is planned and gas from the UAE has already entered new markets in Europe. The use of gas within the emirates themselves, to support domestic industry and to release more oil for export, is another major plank in the UAE's policy of maximizing its hydrocarbon resources. The construction of new gas treatment plants, the expansion of existing ones and the growth in the pipeline network in recent years has been particularly impressive. It is also resulting in additional supplies of valuable natural gas liquids for export.

Oil and gas is set to continue to provide the main source of funding for the development and support of a modern, broadly based UAE economy. Abu Dhabi, with the overwhelming bulk of reserves, will continue to dominate the hydrocarbon business. However, Sharjah should be able to build on its relatively strong gas position and strengthen its role as a supplier to the other emirates. Dubai has a difficult and costly task to prevent further decline in its oil and gas production but, fortunately, has had the foresight to prepare its economy accordingly. The other emirates have little to show for years of exploration, but their economies can only benefit from their close association in the UAE and from the general dynamism of the area.

The overall approach to future oil and gas markets has been generally innovative and forward looking and this is unlikely to change. At the same time, in contrast to some other less successful oil-producing countries, the UAE has managed to maintain a stable and relatively amicable relationship with the international companies. This dual approach of innovation and stability has provided the confidence needed to attract investment. The coming years should prove exciting and rewarding ones for all those involved with the UAE, not least in the oil and gas business.

The federation has already gone a long way along the road away from over reliance on hydrocarbons but its key strength still rests on what are, by any measure, some of the largest reserves of oil and gas in the world. Certainly, these reserves are more than adequate to sustain further development and to continue to make a major contribution to satisfying the world's demand for oil. The development plans for oil and gas already in place give the UAE a sound basis to build on and it can look forward to the future with confidence.

Bibliography

ABECOR Country Report, London, Barclays Bank (1994).
ADCO Annual Report, Abu Dhabi, ADCO (1994).
ADNOC Annual Report, Abu Dhabi, ADNOC (1994).
Arab Oil and Gas Directory, (AOGD) Paris, Arab Petroleum Research Center (1995).
Barnes, P. *OIES Review of Energy Costs*, Oxford, OIES (1991).
Barnes, P. *The Oil Supply Mountain: is the Summit in Sight?* Oxford, OIES (1993).
Barnes, P. 'Oil Reserves: Concepts, Sources and Interpretation' *The Journal of Energy Literature,* Oxford, OIES (1995).
Barrows Petroleum Legislation, USA, Barrows Inc. (1996).
BP Statistical Review of World Energy:1996, (BP Stats) London, BP. (1996).
DeGolyer and MacNaughton, *Twentieth Century Petroleum Statistics,* Dallas, Texas (1994).
Energy Compass, London, Petro Publishing (31.5.1996).
Energy Statistics and Balances of Non-OECD Countries, (IEA) Paris, IEA/OECD (1995).
Gas Matters, London, Econo Matters Ltd. (various editions).
'Guide to Petroleum Specifications', (June 1996) Standard and Poor's
'*International Petroleum Encyclopedia*' (IPE) USA, Pennwell (1996).
Khalifa', Ali Mohammed, *The United Arab Emirates. Unity in Fragmentation*, London, Croom Helm (1979).
El Mallakh, Ragaei *The Economic Development of the UAE,* London, Croom Helm (1981).
Middle East Economic Survey, (MEES) Cyprus, Middle East Petroleum and Economic Publications (various editions).
Middle East Oil and Gas, (MEOG) IEA (1995).
Natural Gas in the World: 1995 Survey, Paris, Cedigaz (July 1995).
Nehring, R. *Giant Oil Fields and World Oil Resources,* Santa Monica, USA, Rand (June 1978).
Oil and Gas Journal, (OGJ) Pennwell, USA (various editions).
OPEC Annual Statistical Bulletin, (OPEC Stats) OPEC Secretariat (1994).
OPEC Bulletin, OPEC Secretariat (various editions).
Al-Otaiba, Mana Saeed, *Petroleum and the Economy of the UAE* London, Croom Helm (1977).
Al Otaiba, Mana Saeed, *The Petroleum Concession Agreements of the UAE,* London, Croom Helm (1982).
Peck, M.C. *The United Arab Emirates: a Venture in Unity,* Colorado, Westview Press (1986).
Petroleum Economist, London, The Petroleum Economist Ltd (December 1995).
Petroleum Intelligence Weekly, New York, Petroleum Energy and Intelligence Weekly (various editions).
Sluglett, P. and M. Farouk-Sluglett, *The Times Guide to the Middle East,* London (1996).
World Development Report, World Bank OUP (1995).
World Oil, USA, Gulf Publishing Company (August 1995).

The Tribal Society of the UAE and its Traditional Economy

Frauke Heard-Bey

Introduction

Hundreds of millions of years ago a source of wealth was trapped several thousand metres under the territory of the UAE. Before this oil and gas were discovered and exploited, there was precious little to be found on the surface which could be called 'natural wealth'. Yet, the scant resources were sufficient to sustain the inhabitants of this area throughout the centuries. They had developed the means to make all aspects of their seemingly inhospitable environment work for them. Management of these economic resources was harmonized with an age-old social structure producing unique socio-economic responses to the rigours of life in the eastern corner of the Arabian Peninsula.

The local population of the present day UAE is tribal in origin. Does that mean that every person in the UAE who wears a white *thob* is descended from the bedouin of the Arabian desert and would once have lived as a nomad? What does the word 'tribal' encompass? To shed some light on such questions and to be able to understand why these concepts are central to the structure of the traditional society of the UAE, it is necessary to know how this society supported itself economically in the past.

The Tribe as Society's Genealogical Building Block

Most national householders can quote a tribal name, which forms rightfully part of his own name. This name could be a generic name *(nisbah)* such as 'Ameri (plural 'Awamir) used as the last part of a name after his father's name and possibly his paternal grandfather's (e.g. Muhammad bin [=son of] Khalifah bin Muhammad Al 'Ameri). It could also be the name of a forebear of countless generations back, who is considered the 'patron' or eponym of the many groups of families, which see themselves as his offspring.[1] Such a tribal name is Al Rashidi or Bani Yas or Ahl 'Ali (family of 'Ali). A link can be established with the two famous ancestors of all the tribes of Arabia, Qahtan or Adnan[2] through this *jadd*, whose historical existence need not always be verifiable with chronological precision. Thus, a person's individual existence is embedded in his group *(qabilah)*, which is committed to him because of their common descent. The members of this group of common descent have a corporate responsibility to provide support and protection. In practical terms a tribe is often too widely dispersed to be able to rally around one individual except in cases of general warfare, which might in earlier times even have been the result of one man's action leading to a blood feud.

Within the fold of the tribe, the individual head of the family (himself, wife and children) is traditionally bound by inescapable obligations of mutual assistance and a concept of joined honour to his immediate blood relatives - father, brothers, paternal uncles, cousins. Part of this particular relationship is the strong preference for marriages between the son and his paternal uncle's daughter (*bint 'amm*). If this arrangement cannot be made because of age difference or for other reasons, marriage with a first cousin on the mother's side, or with a more distant cousin, is the norm in this society. Marriage outside the extended family is the exception, but does also occur, such as between families who are neighbours, or as a political move, as when a sheikh marries the daughter of another tribal leader.

A woman's place is clearly defined in this society. On marriage she keeps her father's name and remains emotionally most closely attached to her own family, to which she can return in case of a divorce. The bride moves into the house of her husband's family, where separate accommodation is prepared for the young couple and, if at all possible, for the families of all the other sons. Because her own family is losing a worker, the groom must give compensation to that family in money or kind. At the time of the marriage contract he also has to give the bride the means to support herself in case he were to divorce her later. This *mahr* remains her own property and is managed separately from the rest of the household.

The woman's role in the traditional economy was pivotal because, as will be seen later, the need to alternate between various economic activities placed great responsibilities on the women during the long periods of time that men were obliged to be away from home. Her contribution earned her a high status in society, and a husband's reputation and honour rested on the conduct of his wife and daughters. Although it was permissible to have more than one wife, in practice few men could afford more than the one household; but because many women died in childbirth, it was not uncommon for a man to have several wives in succession.

It may be noticed that not every man uses the name of his tribe *(nisbah)* as the last part of his name (e.g. Al Mansuri, Al Dhahiri, Al Za'abi). Considering the size of some of the tribes, this could lead to confusion, even if everyone were to include his grandfather's name. Many of the last names of local families in the UAE today are derived from one of the several possible sub-divisions of the tribe *(qabilah)*. These horizontal divisions are kinship groups (*'ayal* [3]) and the sub-tribes *(fakhdh* pl. *afkhadh)*, which are likewise perceived in genealogical terms. In the graphical rendering of the tree-like relationship between a man and his tribal eponym, these divisions figure as the extension of the extended family.[4] Thus, many members of the Bani Yas tribe of Abu Dhabi and Dubai have family names like Al Mazrui, Al Qubaisi or Al Hamili, referring to the sub-tribe to which they belong.

The Political Aspect of Tribal Cohesion

The boundaries between tribe and sub-tribe are not clear cut for several reasons. A tribe could be a confederation of tribes which have decided, for political or economic reasons, to follow the leadership of one of the constituent tribes' sheikhs, as is the case with the Bani Yas, where Yas figures as a common eponym to signify the tribal cohesion. There could also be an alliance between two tribes to form one. In other cases a sub-tribe may assert itself over time or become remote from the main tribe, and its members may eventually adopt the name of the subdivision as their tribal name - as is now the case with the Al Bu Shamis, whose relationship with the Na'im[5] is well known in local understanding, but who were nevertheless listed separately in the population census of Abu Dhabi of 1968. Whether a group deems it more useful to be identified as the smallest unit (*fakhdh*) which often also lives together in one and the same locality, or as part of of a bigger unit, may also vary from one community to another, and from one political situation to another.[6] Individuals may have different views on the matter, depending on their current status and, if questioned, on the view of the inquirer. The relationship of tribes and their constituent parts is not static - it has always been the result of regional politics and remains a matter of tribal dynamics.

The Population of the Trucial States

Therefore neither the names and numbers of the tribes which make up the local society, nor their sizes, can be stated with precision. Considering the above mentioned tribal dynamics, assessments of numbers are bound to vary over time. The first such statements with regard to the whole country, which was then called the Trucial States,[7] were possible after a concerted effort was made by J.G. Lorimer, the author of an official publication on behalf of the Government of India. During a visit to Sharjah in 1904 he collected detailed information and also enlisted the help of other government officials, who undertook several journeys to supplement these findings.[8] At this time 44 tribes were listed, with some having main subdivisions and a number of further subsections. Lorimer remarks that 'indeed, the country is tribally one of the most composite and perplexing'. [9] The word 'country' is used here as a geographical term; the Government of India considered each emirate as a separate political entity, headed by a ruler, who attracted or commanded the loyalty of some or many of these tribes or tribal sections.

   The political affiliations of these 44 tribes were listed by Lorimer as being divided between only five 'principalities', whose territorial extent is, however, approximately that of the UAE of today. The tribes comprised an estimated 80,000 people.[10] One tenth of them were then considered bedouin and would not necessarily have spent all the year within the territory of the Trucial States. The Bani Qitab and the Bani Yas had the largest bedouin contingent; their way of life will be discussed later. In 1968 the Trucial States Council organized the first population census for Dubai and the five northern emirates, and in Abu Dhabi the Department of Planning carried out a census simultaneously. The population of Dubai had reached 58,971, the five northern emirates were together 74,880, and that of Abu Dhabi was 46,375.[11] The number of people who gave the information that they belonged to one of the local tribes was 44,668 for the five northern emirates and 17,750 for Abu Dhabi.[12] In Abu Dhabi a further 2600 were listed as nationals, but were not reported to belong to any particular tribe; they are most likely the descendants of people who came into the Trucial States at the height of the pearling industry's boom. There seemed to have developed a fragmentation among the tribes as well as a greater awareness of a tribesman's own place in his society, because by 1968 the number of separately listed tribes reached 67. Compared to the first decade of this century all the additional names are, however, not new names, but those which figured as names of sub-tribes in the past. For the people of this region - settled or bedouin - the tribe is the principal building block for the structure of their society. For the individual, this tribal 'belonging' is far more reassuring than the comforts of 'home' and the sense of security, which is paramount for people whose social structures are associated with the land they live on.

Origins of the Arab Tribes and their Dispersal throughout the Region

The ancestors of this tribal population have not always lived in the region. They took possession of this land during successive waves of population movement, which brought Arab tribes from Yemen by way of Oman as well as by way of Central and Northern Arabia. They would have found people already settled in the economically viable locations[13] and there were probably some nomadic groups here as well, combining herding, hunting and fishing. The descendants of this original population were probably absorbed, although some were for a long time identifiable as separate communities, particularly in the mountains of Oman. Coming from the tribally structured, highly organized culture, where a sophisticated edifice such as the Marib dam was built and maintained, the new arrivals retained their tribal structures and their community-building genealogies and legends. Thus they also retained their strong kinship ties with the people elsewhere on the Arabian Peninsula, and their sense of belonging to the Arab *ummah*. That sense of nationhood could be maintained throughout such a vast and inhospitable region because they all shared Arabic as their common language - a language which was to become the language of their common religion.

Although there is evidence of linguistic links between northern Oman and the Old South Arabian culture going back at least to the middle of the first millennium BC, larger numbers of Arab tribal groups started to arrive here in successive waves only since the second century AD. They moved to areas such as Taw'am, the old name for the twin oasis of Al-Ain and Buraimi, and to other areas in the mountains, the mountain foreland and Inner Oman, where people had cultivated the land since time immemorial.[14] Those who came later had to find other opportunities to make their living in the less well-watered parts of the country, which required them to adapt to a more rigorous environment. Over time there developed a great diversity of economic pursuits, while the unity in the social structure was retained, both of which were the hallmark of the traditional society of the UAE. The result of a long process of adaptation to the rigours of a land with limited resources can be seen in the traditional economy of the country, an economy which entered a new phase only 30 years ago.

Life in the Sandy Desert

A tribe's quest for water

The general climatic conditions of the UAE are much the same throughout, with summer temperatures reaching close to 50°C and unpredictable, localized rains mostly in winter. But the landscape of the UAE varies considerably and so, therefore, does the usage which people have learnt to make of what the land can offer them. The availability of water dictates this usage and has been the key to the economic life and to much of the social structure of this country's past. The country can be broadly divided into three geographically and therefore

Aerial view of the Ruler of Abu Dhabi's Palace (March 1962).

economically different regions: firstly, the coasts and islands, secondly, the Hajar mountain range with its valleys (wadis) and adjacent gravel plains and, thirdly, the sandy desert.

On the face of it, the desert seems to offer the least resources. How could people live there throughout the year, finding enough water to drink during the summer months? Yet the largest tribe of the UAE, the Bani Yas, has for several centuries inhabited the vast spaces of aeolian sands which cover most of the country's territory, and almost all of the emirates of Abu Dhabi and Dubai.[15] Other tribes, too, such as the Awamir, Manasir and others, have shared this challenging habitat for countless generations. The sandy desert begins behind a stretch of coastal salt marsh, called *sabkha*, with little white dune ripples rising as one goes south - eventually forming large orange-red dunes. Within this vast desert, which stretches to beyond Abu Dhabi's southern border, some of the highest dunes in all of the Empty Quarter are found about 100 km distant from the coast. Some tower up to 200 m above the desert floor, catching some of the precipitation, fog and dew, which, although often heavy at the coast, diminishes considerably further inland in the desert.

In the distant past the ancestors of the bedouin, who made this region their home, discovered that they could find water in the dunes, which was adequately plentiful and often also relatively sweet. In many of the hollows between the dunes they created date gardens and built themselves houses using the branches of the date palms, eventually forming about 40 settlements,[16] some of which were inhabited all the year round. This half moon arc of villages called Liwa, spanning about 70 km from east to west, has been the centre for the economic and social life of the Bani Yas at least since the sixteenth century.[17] A changing number of subsections[18] have acknowledged the leadership of the sheikh of one particular subtribe - the Al Bu Falah - for at least ten recorded generations. Under their leadership their undisputed grazing area, their *dar,* included the Liwa, the intervening territory between it and the coast, called Al Dhafrah, the area called Khatam stretching eastwards as far as the foreland of the Hajar mountains and, in the west, the land known as Bainunah and the Sabkha Matti and the area up to the Qatar peninsula.[19] Other tribes' participation in the grazing was usually acceptable on the basis of mutuality.

During the summer months many tribes retreated from the sandy desert to the savannah-like outwash plains at the foot of the mountains, whereas, on the other hand, the Bani Yas and their associates adapted to the rigorous desert environment and made it their home. The patterns of their economic exploitation varied over time, but all the subtribes and clans were accustomed to wander great distances over long periods of time with their camels in search of grazing, moving as entire family units, seeking the precious gifts which the desert had to offer for those who knew how to make use of them. Almost all Bani Yas families returned to a home in one of the Liwa settlements at certain times of the year.

The thicker the sand cover or the higher the dunes, the better the chance there is of finding a good source of water. The seasonal rainfall and quite frequent heavy dew rapidly sinks into the absorbing sand, which also acts as insulation against evaporation. The water which is thus trapped in the dunes frequently does not escape downwards, because there is a fairly level, impermeable rock formation below the dunes and the intervening depressions. However, the water which rains down on the sand and is collected in shallow wells at the bottom of high dunes is not potable everywhere in this desert. Depending on the composition of the sand, the water may dissolve chemicals during its passage through the dune and then be too brackish for human consumption. It may even be unusable for animals or plants.[20] The inhabitants of the Liwa developed the knowledge of where best to dig for good water and often did not have to go down much more than 3 m to find some. Out in the sands some wells have been established for centuries, and the right to draw water from one of those has been of the greatest significance in tribal politics.

The date palm - a wonder of the desert

Wherever it is found and whatever its quality, the water in the sandy desert never flows and extensive agriculture could not be developed there. But one tree, which combines many wonderful properties, is ideally suited to grow even at the foot of a huge sand dune in the middle of the desert: *Phoenix dactylifera,* the date palm. It can tolerate very high salinity and thrives even in intense heat.[21] As a cultivated fruit tree, the date palm is not propagated from the date stone, but from side shoots which grow at the foot of a mature tree. These are separated and planted when they are already 100-150 cm high and have a good nest of roots. The newly-planted saplings need to be watered regularly. In the desert the water is carried from the well - one leather bagful at a time. After months, or even years, the young bushy plant's roots will reach the water table and be self-sufficient. However, its rate of growth and eventual yield of dates is significantly influenced by the amount and quality of the water available.[22] Care for the date tree does not end when watering by hand ceases. The bushy plant grows branches at ground level and thereby increases its volume; eventually the outer branches are trimmed and every year as it grows these branches are cut higher up, and thus eventually the trunk is formed. The stumpy ends of the cut-off branches serve as footholds for the cultivator when he needs to climb into the crown of the tree. After three or more years, depending on the amount of available water, the tree begins to flower in spring; then the caretaker must be there to pollinate with the panicles from a male tree, of which only very few are planted. He has to climb every tree and carefully distribute the pollen to all the little waxen flowers. The harvest of the dates takes place during the hottest period of the year, between late June and early October, depending on the type of date tree. The harvest involves climbing the tree and cutting the heavy bunches, which are either carried down or thrown to helpers below.

In this country people like to eat dates fresh when only half the fruit is soft and brown. The harvested dates were essential for the survival of the inhabitants in the desert. The ripe dates are lightly boiled and compressed into a congealed substance called *tamr* which can be kept almost indefinitely, because the high sugar content kills germs which might settle on it. The dried palm fronds are plaited into containers, in which the nourishing, vitamin-rich staple diet can be taken on journeys through the desert, into the mountains, or out to sea. The date tree, which grows so well in the desert where water is available, is like an anchor for the existence of the Arabs in this environment. But the yield from the small palm groves which were established in the sandy desert was insufficient for entire families to live off throughout the year.

The camel - God's gift to the bedouin

The bedouin like to say that God has been fair because He gave them the ideal tree for their desert, but that He has shown His bounty by giving them the camel as well. This animal is not only as superbly suited to the desert environment as the date palm, but it also provides for almost all the further needs of its owner. The camel gives the local tribesman his mobility. The camel is his mount as well as his beast of burden. He can ride it to war, to his date garden, to a distant market, to a port - or for fun, such as in the traditional races. He can load his camels and take them in a caravan across terrain where no other transport could pass. Often camel milk and the products derived from it were almost the only source of protein for the entire family for months on end; then one day there would be a feast to celebrate a wedding or the arrival of a guest and a he-camel would be slaughtered to provide the meat. Camel hide was used to make bags and other useful utensils, while some of the finest mens' outer garments (*bisht*) were woven from the hair.

The camels bred in the desert of Eastern Arabia were renowned for their endurance and speed. Throughout generations, to sell or barter them was the principal means of obtaining goods, which could not otherwise be obtained from within the extended clan. The possession of camels constituted great wealth and caring for them had a high priority. In the winter their owners or caretakers would wander for weeks in an area where sufficient rain had made the dormant vegetation of the desert sprout. If there was no water well nearby, the milk from the camels was enough for the people to drink. When the camels have good grazing, they do not need any water themselves in the winter.[23] But in the heat of the summer, when the grazing is dry, the camels are kept close to a well and they return daily by themselves. Each camel

Hunting falcon outside the Ruler of Abu Dhabi's palace, 1957.

requires about 40-50 litres of water, which meant hauling maybe more than ten leather bags of water up from the well and emptying them into the *hawd,* a leather trough slung over a wooden frame. The camel owners were fortunate if there was enough summer grazing close to where they owned date trees, because in this way they could participate in the harvest and make use of the water wells which supplied the communities occupying their palm frond homes (known as *'arishah* or *khaimh)* in the Liwa.

Life on the Coast of the Gulf

Fishing

The territory which had over time become the exclusive *dar* of the Bani Yas tribes is bordered by 600 km of coast. As can be expected, the inhabitants of the hinterland made every possible use of the resources which this area of beaches, sand banks, creeks and inshore islands offered. They also colonized the many more distant islands. The extensive tidal shallows, which are characteristic of most of this coast, are ideal for fishing with traps. These were intricately constructed fences, placed to shape a letter V, where the fish were caught when the water receded. Another method involved stretching two nets at right angles to the tidal creek from a central pole; the use of a small dugout and working in a team of two or three fishermen was essential in some locations. But there were also methods by which one man alone could secure a good catch as, for instance, by stalking a shoal of small fish in the shallow water and casting over it a circular net weighted with stones.[24] Fish which was not consumed fresh was hung up in the sun to dry, or treated with salt, and taken to the inland settlements where this additional protein was very welcome. Some of the small fish was dried and used as camel fodder or as fertilizer for the gardens, but, as for the fresh fish, the fishermen on the coast of Abu Dhabi were a long way from markets. There is archaeological evidence that on most of Abu Dhabi's numerous islands, tribes people came to fish in the winter and even brought their camels over in boats. They used rainwater, stored in cisterns, or caught in horizontally placed sails. But the coast between Dubai and Khaur al-Odaid, at the foot of the Qatar Peninsula, was not suitable for the establishment of larger, permanent settlements, because of the lack of reliable supplies of drinking water.

This was to change dramatically after the end of the eighteenth century, when it was discovered that a dune belt at the northern end of Abu Dhabi island yielded some fresh water, (which, being lighter, floats in lenses above the salty water table). The water was drawn from shallow wells, which, when brackish water intruded, were abandoned and new ones were dug. In 1760, several of the Bani Yas tribal groups built themselves palm frond houses on the island near its northern shore. By the early 1790s, the town of Abu Dhabi had already become so important a centre of activity that the political leader of all the Bani Yas groups transferred his residence there from the Liwa. After 1793, Sheikh Shakhbut constructed the fort, which still stands today near the centre of the city. Soon, the supply of such limited amounts of sweet water did not suffice for the rapidly growing population; additional drinking water was brought in bitumen-lined containers by boat from Dubai, Ras al-Khaimah or even Delma Island.

Pearling

The reason for this increase in the population of Abu Dhabi was a resource which had played a role for the Arabs of this area since antiquity: the *lulu* (locally called *qamashah*), the pearl. These timeless items of adornment, which grow inside some of the local oysters,[25] have probably always been collected by wading fishermen, who would have kept their finds until an opportunity arose to barter them. The oysters accumulate in larger quantities on oyster beds (*fasht*) in water about 30-40 m deep, off the Arab shores of the Gulf. To bring enough of them up to make a living from selling the pearls and mother-of-pearl required a big communal effort, as well as sea-going vessels and people who could dive that deep. When, during the eighteenth and nineteenth centuries, the market for pearls grew rapidly in prospering India, pearling became an ever more important industry for the inhabitants of the Arabian coast and the hinterland.

By the turn of the twentieth century about 1200 boats were based in ports on the Trucial Coast, manned by some 22,000 men, mostly tribesmen, but with extra hands brought in from Baluchistan and elsewhere to augment the work force. The pearling industry had transformed the traditional economy of the tribal population. Many families moved to live permanently in one of the coastal settlements, increasing, in particular, the size and importance of Abu Dhabi and Dubai.[26] Sharjah, Ras al-Khaimah and the intervening coastal villages were already long-established as ports of the tribal Arabs and they, too, participated in this industry.

During its modest beginnings, pearling constituted just another means of exploiting all the resources available to the tribal people. They cared for their camels and tended the date palms - often in locations which were many days' travelling apart - and then, as pearling flourished, an increasing number of the able-bodied men participated in the dive *(ghaus)* during four months in the summer. Many of the Liwa-based sub-tribes of the Bani Yas formed co-operatives, which jointly owned a boat[27] and shared the proceeds of the sale of the pearls according to an established arrangement, giving the biggest share to the captain, a larger share to the divers than the haulers and leaving some money aside to finance preparations for the following year. It was due to pearling that, over several generations, some tribes became more specialized in one economic activity or another and became tied to particular locations. Thus, the Rumaithat and the Qubaisat favoured maritime activities and became attached to the coastal settlements and the islands, eventually giving up many of the date gardens they had in the Liwa. Other tribal groups such as the Mazari' remained dedicated to the desert. The Manasir went pearling, but did not own any boats.

Social changes due to the pearling boom

Towards the end of the nineteenth century, the pearling industry became increasingly the domain of individual entrepreneurs in the now flourishing ports throughout the Gulf. Some of the merchants, who were involved in the trade in pearls or imported consumer goods from India, accumulated enough capital to buy a boat, for which the wood had to be imported too, and to equip it with provisions for the 120 days of the diving season. In good years, the owner of a boat made a handsome profit by selling the pearls directly or through a local merchant *(tajir)* to one of the Hindus, who came seasonally from Bombay chiefly to Bahrain or Dubai. But storms, epidemics or other adversities could mean that the season's proceeds were insufficient to finance the next season and the owner would, in such circumstances, be forced to take an advance on the next year's catch. Because neither the captain *(nakhudah)* nor the rest of the crew were paid a salary, but instead obtained an agreed share of the profit, a bad year could spell disaster for years to come for all those who were locked into a system of financial interde-pendence. The divers were particularly vulnerable. They were no longer part of the multi-faceted tribal economy, but had settled in ports and lived from the money they earned during the third of the year they worked on a pearling boat. They needed advances from the captain to pay for their families' upkeep during their absence at sea. If the season's income was not as much as the advance, the debt was carried over into the next year and thus the diver became compelled to work for a particular captain year after year. [28]

Life in the Oases

The cash (resulting almost exclusively from the pearling industry) which flowed ever more freely into the Trucial States, had a great impact on the entire society, and also brought important changes to the hinterland. For the bedouin family, who had managed to wrest from the sandy desert the means to survive, a date garden watered by a flowing stream was the height of luxury. Thus, when individual families had accumulated surplus wealth, they turned their attention to the villages in the Al-Ain area, the nearest oasis, where several age-

Water running through the irrigation channels of an experimental garden in Buraimi Oasis, where a few luxuriant acres grow trees, shrubs, bananas, mangoes, and other plants, 1963.

old *aflaj*[29] brought underground water from springs near the mountains to the fertile soil in the plain. This oasis is already mentioned by the name of Taw'am in the early days of Islam, and prehistoric finds from the area point to it having been a centre of settled civilization for several thousand years.

In the nineteenth century many of the Bani Yas bought date gardens in this area, and members of the ruling family also established new date gardens and associated settlements there. There was a resident labour force of descendants of earlier inhabitants which did not belong to the tribal society, the *bidar*; they were accustomed to look after the gardens of absentee landlords and bedouin owners for reward in kind. The tribal population, which had lived in and around the oasis for generations, resisted the inroads of the Bani Yas. But eventually the dominant tribe of Dhawahir and some of the Shawamis preferred an amicable coexistence with, and the benefits of political protection by, the powerful Al Bu Falah leaders of the Bani Yas, who were much closer to home as compared to the distant overlordship of the Sultan of Muscat and Oman.

The availability of water made the nine villages of the Al-Ain and Buraimi area a very desirable place. The economy of all such oases in the region differs a great deal from that of the sandy desert. The Hajar mountains, which run from the Musandam Peninsula in the north at the entrance to the Gulf through the UAE and Oman, form the spine of the land dividing the eastern coast areas from the desert region in the west. These mountains rise to just over 1000 m in the UAE, but reach 2000 m near the Straits of Hormuz and 3000 m in the Jabal Akhdar region of Oman. Although the mountains consist of barren, friable rock devoid of topsoil, in the valleys (wadis) and the outwash plains on either side, fertile soil can be found in many places. The unpredictable, in some years prolific, winter rains run off the rocks quickly, but much of the water collects in the thick layers of gravel in the wadi beds and the plains. The communal effort which is required to put these aquifers to good use is the hallmark of the tribes which live in and near the mountains.[30]

The most efficient system is the *falaj* (pl. *aflaj*), initially a tunnel reaching for several miles to where the ground water table is higher than the gardens to be watered. Between the source and the gardens there are vertical shafts at regular intervals, which were needed during the time of construction and still now serve during maintenance for bringing out the spoil and admitting air to the people working in the tunnel. There is usually a village near where the *falaj* comes out of the tunnel to form an open stream. This is where the drinking water is collected by the women; downstream is the off-take for watering the camels and, below that, the communal bathing houses - one for the men and one for the women with steps down into the running water. Further down the stream again, there is a set of sluices to divert the water into various channels leading to the different gardens. Thus every date garden can get a meticulously measured time of water delivered by rivulets. A supervisor or *arif* is paid by the community to give every garden owner his allotted or acquired share; he keeps time by the stars at night and by a sundial on the ground by day. In these favourable conditions other trees besides palms can grow, such as figs, mangoes, oranges, pomegranates, grapes, bananas and, in particular, limes. Lucerne for animal fodder and a limited variety of vegetables, mostly sweet potatoes and onions, are grown inside these walled palm groves. Wheat, barley and millet are grown outside on land watered by the winter rains. Usually there are also wells in these oases to facilitate the drawing of drinking water near the houses, or to supplement the *falaj* waters in the gardens.

A *falaj* always serves many date gardens and is the focal utility for an entire village or tribal settlement area. The *aflaj* of this region are probably of great antiquity; and possessing a *falaj* signifies a dominant role for a tribe in the social web. However, most *falaj*-irrigated oases are a melting pot for different sedentary tribal communities, of which some have older rights or more property and therefore keep the upper hand in local politics. In addition to the tribal sections each having their sheikh, the administration of such an economically important place was often entrusted to a *wali,* the representative of the distant ruler. The bedouin of the region, often being absentee landlords, also greatly influenced life in an oasis, because they could provide the fighting force in the event of a conflict.

Life in the Mountains

The important oases, such as Masafi, or Manamah, are situated away from the confining wadi walls, where good soil on level ground lends itself to agriculture. While they were usually shared between more than one tribe, there are countless small villages and hamlets in the wadis, which belong most frequently to just one clan or even a single family. There are *falaj*-like watercourses in use, which serve these smaller communities tucked away in the wadis. Some are even constructed by just one family for a terraced garden in the mountains: the wadi is dammed where surface water can be expected to run at least occasionally. The water is channelled into an open runnel called *ghayl*, which follows the wadi at a gentle gradient - in places forming a gallery above the valley floor - until it arrives at the terraced field or date garden. Terracing was known in these mountains since prehistoric times and this technique of increasing the potential for agriculture played an important role for these small tribal communities. They built retaining stone walls and levelled the ground above with topsoil to form small fields, which could be sown before the rains, or when the *ghayl* was prolific enough. The owners did not necessarily always live nearby, but visited several such favourable locations to see to whatever needed to be done, hoping for a reasonable crop from at least some of these terraces. A home - or, in times of strife, a hideout - could be constructed fairly easily with walls of wadi stones and a roof of palm fronds or brushwood. Choosing which of these temporary abodes to use at any one time depended largely on the additional economic activity which played a role for a tribe of the mountain regions: the herding of sheep and goats. The wadi beds and plains, and even the hills themselves, offer plenty of forage for these animals during the cooler part of the year.

Domestic animals, sheep, goats and some cows, were kept by the villagers mostly for their milk; donkeys were their preferred beast of burden, but camels and bulls were also kept nearby to help with drawing water. These animals did not need to be taken out for grazing, but were hand-fed with fodder grown in the gardens or, after rains had brought the vegetation to life again, with grass and herbs which the women collected daily. Some of the mountain tribal people, called *shawawi*, were semi-nomadic pastoralists, forming part of a village community, but wandering in the mountain region with their herds of sheep and goats. They also offered their services to transport goods on their donkeys or, more rarely, on camels through the mountains.

Life on the East Coast

On the eastern flank of the Hajar mountains the plain along the Indian Ocean is only a few kilometres wide and, in its northern part near the oasis of Dibba, some mountain spurs reach all the way to the sea. The communities which live on this coast have the opportunity to combine, within easy distance from their settlements, all the different resources of their environment: fishing, oasis agriculture and husbandry. The most profitable type of fish was traditionally the anchovy *(bariya)*. Side by side with modern craft, wooden boats with a straight stern manned by about 20 people, are still used to place a weighted net of about 100 m length parallel to the beach. After several hours the ends of the net are pulled to the shore and the contents spread on the beach. The dried catch is sold locally and abroad as fertilizer. For large fish such as tuna or shark heavier tangle nets are now used, as well as handlines.[31] The meat is either eaten fresh or salted and dried on wooden racks. Sharks' fins are sold to merchants, who export them to China. Individual fishermen used (and still use today) the local craft, which is typical for the entire eastern coast including the Batinah in Oman. This boat, the *shashah*, is made entirely of palm sticks and filled with the buoyant cut-off lower ends of the palm branches. The boatman is partly submerged, but he paddles the boat skilfully through the surf to lay out his net or line.

The villages along this coast, which until the middle of this century were under the distant rule of Sharjah, and many of which now belong to the Emirate of Fujairah, have always been able to water their extensive date gardens from wells. The run off water from the mountains sinks into deep layers of gravel before it reaches the sea. Once underground, this extensive wedge of ground water meets the saltwater, but does not mix. Sweet water is thus forced near to the surface at the beach, making it possible to plant date trees close to the sea. When they are mature they reach the brackish water table. Further back from the beach more date gardens were established with the help of many neighbouring water wells, some of which were operated by bulls lifting the waterbags with the help of a scaffold-mounted wheel. As in the *falaj*-irrigated oases, other fruit trees and some vegetables were also produced under these favourable conditions.

The Advantageous Combination of Resources in Ras al-Khaimah

The hydrological conditions which obtain on the East Coast, are also found on the Ras al-Khaimah coast between the western slopes of the mountains and the Gulf. There, too, extensive date cultivation and agriculture were traditionally combined with fishing; but while only a few people from the East Coast journeyed to Sharjah or Dubai to join the pearling season in the summer, the pearling industry played a bigger role for people in and near Ras al-Khaimah, even though the main pearl banks are located off-shore from Abu Dhabi and Dubai.[32]

Ras al-Khaimah in particular, but also some other settlements along the coast to the south-west, have been favourably located for trade with distant countries. The ports of medieval Julfar (near modern Ras al-Khaimah), Jazirah al-Hamrah, Umm al-Qaiwain, Hamriyah, 'Ajman, Sharjah as well as Dubai all benefit from being situated on a peninsula or a sand spit near a lagoon (*khaur*), where the local ships could shelter behind a barrage of difficult to navigate shallows and sand banks. Because the hinterland was sparsely populated and its subsistence economy supported little in the way of export or import trade before the pearling industry flourished, shipping from these ports specialized in the carrying trade. Their ships sailed up and down the Gulf, to India, East Africa and most probably at some stage to the Far East and China. Trade on that scale was much influenced by changes in the political climate of the region and beyond. During the eighteenth century the Qawasim, the leading clan in the tribal grouping of the northern and eastern part of the country, dominated the maritime transportation and trade at the head of the Gulf. But, due to the vicissitudes of history, they later lost this position to overseas competitors, not least to the steamships of British India.

Life in the Musandam Peninsula

A survey of the influence of geography on the economy and, consequently, on the social structures of the population of this area is not complete without a description of the habitat of the Shihuh and their neighbours the Dhahuriyin - even though the land of most members of this and associated tribes belongs to Oman. Many of these people now live in the UAE or depend economically on her northern ports. The Musandam Peninsula (locally called Ru'us al-Jibal) north and east of Ras al-Khaimah consists of precipitous limestone mountains reaching the height of 2000 m within a distance of barely 20 km from the sea. In most places the wadi walls are vertical cliffs, making communication between them and across the peninsula extremely difficult, particularly since access from the fjord-like openings in the mountains at sea level is equally forbidding. Only a few of the wadis have filled up the ancient bay to form an inshore delta, where the run-off water collects in the gravel. In such locations sizable settlements could be established - the biggest one being Khasab in the north of the Sultanate of Oman. The inhabitants of Musandam developed methods with which they could exploit the resources of the sea and the wadis to the full, and grow essential staple food in the mountains.

The economy of one of the two groups found in Musandam is based on the combination of agriculture and husbandry. They refer to themselves as *badu*.[33] Another group has fishing added as a third economic activity and is called *sayyadin*. This occupational differentiation cuts across the tribal divides. The agriculture consists of building, tending and sowing terraced fields in various locations, on the very top of the mountain, on a high slope, or just above the wadi bed. The crop is wheat *(burr)* or barley *(sha'ir),* which is sown after the winter rains and harvested in March or April. Fig trees are also grown on such terraces high up in the mountains. The rain which falls within the small area of the terrace would not be sufficient to sustain the crops. A network of dams and stone-lined canals has long been in place, to collect water and make it run through channels and openings in the field walls, or to cascade gently over the terraces. Thus a vast area of the rocky surrounding countryside contributes its rainwater.

Nearby are the houses of the owners. They have either a small stone-built house with a flat roof made from beams of the *sidr* tree and covered with brushwood and earth, or a *bayt al qufl*, a 'house of the key'. This type of small house is often built against a rock, with walls made from very large fashioned stones and a floor no more than one metre below ground level. Inside will be some earthenware storage vessels, which - being bigger than the low door - will have been placed there before the house was completed. The large and intricately carved lock on the heavy door gives this type of house its name. This is where the mountain bedouin store their seed grains and any surplus which they harvested in readiness for a lean year of drought.

Besides crop-farming, the raising of small animals is of equal importance to the economy of the *badu* of Musandam. A family might have a herd *(hawsh)* of between 80-130 goats and sheep, along with some donkeys.[34] These animals are taken to locations (which may be some distance from the fields), but where the family has another house and a pen in which to keep the animals at night. The same family may also own a date garden in a coastal oasis, such as Dibba on the East Coast or Khasab in the north, and move there for the date harvest in a group of about one to six families with their animals and few household goods. A house made of palm fronds, situated on the fringe of the oasis, awaits the family in this location. Between visits, one member of the family may walk from the winter home in the mountains to their date garden in order to pollinate or water the trees. Depending on the geography, the different locations of their economic activities may only be half an hour's walk apart, or they may be separated by as much as a day's climbing or hiking.

The *sayyadin* constitute the larger group of inhabitants of the Musandam Peninsula. Fishing is their primary source of income and they live in palm frond houses in settlements by the sea. They own nets and other fishing gear and have at least a share in a *batil*, a local type of seagoing boat. They spend between half and two thirds of the year fishing, but also move up into the mountains to sow grain and tend their fields. In yet another location they own date gardens. Their sheep and goats move with them from place to place.[35] Ras al-Khaimah and Dibba were the nearest markets where the tribes of Musandam could sell surplus animals, dried fish, and occasionally rent out their donkeys or boats for the transport requirements of the local inhabitants. Therefore, some of the individual tribal groups became quite dependent on a good relationship with the rulers of neighbouring areas, particularly Ras al-Khaimah, and eventually put themselves under their leadership.

Nomadic Versus Settled Life

In the sandy desert, as well as in the mountains or in the coastal villages, people adapted in different ways to the geographical conditions and to the availability of some resources and the lack of others. In some instances a sedentary existence in one place was not at all possible because the small amount of available water was enough only for a short stay by a small group of people and for the survival of a limited number of date palms. Faced with these conditions, it was essential to adopt a nomadic lifestyle in order to take maximum advantage of the meagre resources spread over a wide area. In other cases, as, for instance, with the fishing communities of Musandam or the owners of the marginal mini-oases in the wadis, mobility has always been required to supplement the otherwise insufficient resources available at the principal abode. In yet other situations, such as obtained for the population in the villages on the East Coast, in the Ras al-Khaimah area and in the up-and-coming ports of the country, the possibilities to pursue a variety of occupations were all close at hand, and such people could lead a settled life.

In the original areas of population concentration, the large oases, various tribes often lived side by side and in many issues of economic or political importance this neighbourhood became the guiding factor in the society's political life. In most villages they also mixed and mingled because one instance of inter-tribal marriage was usually the beginning of further marriages between two groups. But there were also some long-established social differences relating to the ownership of land in these oases - a kind of class distinction, where often the bedouin absentee landlords were at the top of the social structure.

The Impact of Urbanization

The urbanization which set in with the accelerating pearling boom also brought a great mix of tribes into the coastal towns, where they lived in their separate areas forming tribally distinct quarters, as was already the custom in the large oases. In the nineteenth century it was palm frond houses for every family - except for the rulers' forts. During the first decades of the twentieth century an ever increasing number of families could afford to build themselves houses made of coral stone, add an upper floor and even an ornate wind tower for comfort during the hot summer months. The few Hindu traders and some Persian-speakers who visited seasonally, or moved to the coastal towns during the pearling boom, remained on the fringes of local society. Some local merchants, who made good money from pearls and from the big increase in general trade, began to seek political influence on the running of their city states. The bedouin in the hinterland were still considered to hold the balance of power by providing the fighting force to the ruler of their choice. There was growing social differentiation reflected in the wealth of the individual families. When the pearling industry went into a steep decline during the 1930s, due to the world economic recession and the introduction of cultured pearls in Japan, the economic hardship hit many families so hard that they eventually decided to emigrate to seek employment in the neighbouring oil-producing countries.

Yet, whether people lived in the coastal towns, the oases, the mountains or in the desert, the families and groups were welded together by their tribal background, their common religious practices and their Arabic language; they wore the same clothes - even if some had more than one set - they ate the same food - though some had more of it than others - and they all endured the rigours of the forbidding climate. Thus, before the advent of oil the entire population formed one homogenous society.

In the 1990s, after three decades of immigration by foreign experts and labourers have swelled the population figures, the UAE's society as a whole is anything but homogenous. However, for nationals, the basic structure of their tribal society has remained intact, even though for some families their changed economic circumstances have dramatically revolutionized many aspects of their lives. For others, access to modern housing, education and healthcare have made a great difference, but the basic pattern of their lives has not yet changed. Belonging to a well respected local tribe or an influential family is still of prime importance in today's local society. In spite of the overwhelming majority of expatriates around them, local families socialize almost exclusively amongst themselves. Thus it is not surprising that the traditional local customs are still very much part of daily life. The local people greet one another with the traditional nose kiss. They are instantly recognizable by their traditional clothes, which have remained the same in style even if the materials are more varied and refined than in the past. The women in the family still have a special position and are not expected to share the routine of the men, who have always congregated in the *majlis,* the publicly accessible part of any household. In the *majlis* of the sheikh as well as of the business man or of the fisherman on the coast, matters of state and matters of general interest are discussed, while the tiny cups of unsweetened light coffee with cardamom make the round. Since the days of widespread illiteracy people have kept the memory of legends, stories and the beloved local poetry called *nabati,* because the spoken word has always been the superior art form of the tribal people, who lacked the raw materials used elsewhere for more tangible forms of artistic expression.

For the benefit of the generations who have not grown up with them, some traditions are upheld with official backing and encouragement, such as camel racing, traditional boating and poetry competitions, while a variety of heritage villages and museums with ethnological collections are being established. Hunting the migratory bustard *(hubara)* with falcons, which were caught in early winter and released after the season, was practised by many bedouin in the past. Now, this is a sport practised mostly by the members of the ruling families and others who can keep these rare falcons and travel abroad for the hunt. The local tribesman would not begrudge their continuing this 'sport of the kings' as it was known in medieval Europe, because his tribal leader's position should be manifestly different and be recognized as such by the outsider. Among the tribal population an individual's honour and pride is his selfless hospitality. It is an essential aspect of the egalitarian society of the Arab tribes that the hospitality afforded on behalf of the tribe in the sheikh's tent or house should be impressive and reflect the tribe's standing in the eyes of the visitor. The nationals of the UAE of today can have great pride in their country.

[1] See also for the following J.C. Wilkinson, *Water and Tribal Settlement in South-East Arabia. A Study of the Aflaj of Oman*, Oxford, Clarendon Press (1977) pp156ff.

[2] See S.B. Miles, *The Countries and Tribes of the Persian Gulf*, (2nd ed) London, Frank Cass (1966),(1st ed 1919) p 2: 'The tribes that now dispersed and took possession of Arabia were composed of two main stocks, derived from the fourth and fifth generation from Shem. One of the stocks was Kahtan, who identified with Joktan, son of Eber, colonized the Yemen, or the southern half of the peninsula, while the other, Adnan, who descended from Ishmael, occupied the northern part...Under the one or the other of these great progenitors, Kahtan and Adnan, the whole Arabian race is comprised.'

[3] See Wilkinson, *op. cit.,* p 158. With the tribes of the Musandam Peninsula the words *batinah, ahliyah* or *usrah* are also in use; see W. Zimmermann, *Tradition und Integration mobiler Lebensformgruppen. Eine empirische Studie über Beduinen und Fischer in Musandam/ Sultanat Oman*, Göttingen (Dissertation 1981) p 36.

[4] See the example of the tribe of Ma'awil in Fig.28 in Wilkinson, *op. cit.,* p 163.

[5] The Na'im are spread between Oman, the UAE, Qatar and Bahrain. All members of this tribe belong to one or the other of its big divisions, Al Bu Khuraiban or Al Bu Shamis, which have even adopted separate eponyms *(jadd)* called Khazraj and 'Aus. These divisions are further divided into sections, one of which, the Khawatir living mostly in Ras al-Khaimah territory, is itself now often considered as a tribe in its own right; see also J.G. Lorimer, *Gazetteer of the Persian Gulf, 'Oman and Central Arabia,* 2 vols., Vol.I Historical, Vol.II Geographical and Statistical, Calcutta, Superintendent Government Printing (1908-15) pp 1301-6.

[6] The members of the Za'ab tribe, half of which lived in Jazirah al-Hamrah in Ras al-Khaimah territory, but moved to Abu Dhabi in 1970, do not use sectional names, all preferring to be known as Al Za'abi.

[7] The word 'trucial' refers to the fact that the rulers of the states on the southern coast of the Gulf had since 1820 signed several treaties with the Government of India. In British documents the area is also referred to as 'Trucial Oman'. Its extent is approximately that of the UAE today.

[8] See Lorimer, *op. cit.,* pp 1425ff, where a detailed account is given of the written sources and the special investigations concerning the population and the geography of what he calls 'Trucial Oman'.

[9] *Ibid.*, p 1431.

[10] The most populated 'principality' was Sharjah (at the time including Ras al-Khaimah and Fujairah) with 45,000, then came Abu Dhabi with 11,000, Dubai with 10,000, Umm al-Qaiwain with 5000 and 'Ajman with 750 settled people; see *ibid.,* p 1437.

[11] See K.G.Fenelon, *The United Arab Emirates. An Economic and Social Survey*, London, Longman (1973) p 126.

[12] See Trucial States Council, Development Office, *Census 1968,* mimeograph. For details of the way in which tribal distribution and numbers developed between the first decade of the century and the 1968 census see Heard-Bey, F. *From Trucial States to United Arab Emirates. A Society in Transition*, London, Longman (1982) pp 72ff.

[13] For the ample archaeological evidence of diverse economic activities including copper smelting see D.T. Potts, *The Arabian Gulf in Antiquity* 2 vols., Oxford, Clarendon Press (1990) Vol.I particularly pp 119ff.

[14] See Wilkinson, *op. cit.,* pp 126ff and footnote 6.

[15] The size of the UAE is 83,600 sq.km, of which 86.7 per cent are Abu Dhabi territory, 5 per cent are Dubai; see UAE Ministry of Planning, *Annual Statistical Abstract*, (7th ed) (1992) p 3ff.

[16] The number given varies over time and in the different sources; see also Wilkinson, *op. cit.,* p 54.

[17] The Bani Yas tribe is mentioned living in Al-Dhafrah, of which the Liwa is a part, in the seventeenth century Omani source by ibn Razik, Salil *History of the Imams and Seyyids of 'Oman from A.D. 661-1856*, ed. and trans. into Eng. by G.B. Badger (1871) repr. London, Darf Publishers (1986) p70f. The island Sir Bani Yas figures in Balbi's list of 1580.

[18] See Heard-Bey, *op. cit.,* pp 501f and 507-510.

[19] See Heard-Bey, *ibid.,* map. 4a p 30.

20 The WHO recommends that people should not drink water which has more than 750ppm dissolved minerals over a long period of time. While date palms can tolerate salinity of over 6000 ppm, camels can drink water with 10,000 ppm. Wilkinson, *op. cit.,* p 58 ff and Heard-Bey, *op. cit.,* p 408. Seawater has 35-40,000 ppm.

21 See F. Heard-Bey, 'Development Anomalies in the Bedouin Oases of Al Liwa', *Asian Affairs*, Vol. 61, Part III, 1974, pp 272-286.

22 See Wilkinson, *op. cit.* p 59 and pp 71f.

23 Therefore they do not return by themselves to the well and to their minders, as they do in the summer; they have to be hobbled to prevent them from wandering away too far.

24 See for more detail Heard-Bey, *op. cit.,* pp 172-175.

25 Pearls and mother-of pearl are found in three types of molluscs; they are layers of nacre, which are formed around an intrusion, such as a sandcorn.

26 Dubai being more favourably placed for water, which comes from the precipitation in the mountains, has been used by maritime communities for longer; a settlement in Jumairah dates back to the Umayyad period.

27 Boats were made of imported wood; to pay for this and the season's provisions required a big community effort. See for further details Heard-Bey, *op. cit.,* pp 182-190 and pp 200ff.

28 Instances have been recorded where a captain exploited the fact that a particularly good diver could not read and check the season's financial records. See also M.G. Rumaihi, 'The Mode of Production in the Arab Gulf Before the Discovery of Oil' in T. Niblock (ed), *Social and Economic Development in the Arab Gulf,* London, Croom Helm (1980) pp 49 - 60.

29 See below p 17

30 In this case they are too numerous to list here; the reader is referred to a map of the tribal distribution in the northern area in Heard-Bey, *op. cit.,* p 71.

31 The Arabic, English and Latin names and valuable information about 200 fishes of the region are given in A. W. White, and M.A. Barwani, *Common Sea Fishes of the Arabian Gulf and the Gulf of Oman*, Dubai, Trucial States Council (1971).

32 See the sketch map in Wilkinson, *op. cit.,* p 21.

33 See also for the following Zimmermann, *op. cit.,* pp 46ff; here in particular p 51f.

34 See *ibid., p 57.*

35 For the period of the date harvest in the summer both groups leave their animals unattended in the wadi where they own land and a house.

Social Development in the United Arab Emirates

Mouza Ghubash

Introduction

Development[1] is a multi-faceted concept in terms of its meaning, its aims, its methods and its results. While the emphasis on what development should entail will differ depending on whether it is considered from an economic or a social point of view, development in either area will be impeded by deficiencies in the other. Ali Khalifa defines development as a direct process creating essential changes to the majority of the population, providing a decent standard of living and the gradual removal of inequality. Such a process cannot occur in the absence of economic power; but development in terms of an increased GDP does not necessarily translate into an improvement in the conditions of the individuals living in that society. In order to fulfil the social contract that exists between the governing and the governed, methods must be devised which will ensure that the benefits of wealth reach those who have no direct access to its source.

This chapter attempts to describe how the Government of the United Arab Emirates (UAE) has approached the task, looking particularly at the areas of health, education and the voluntary services. It will also outline the historical roots of the process of social development with regards to society in the UAE, and consider how social programmes in the UAE have led to changes in other aspects of life.

The UAE has a vast source of wealth which exists irrespective of the efforts of its population. This wealth has appeared in a region which, up to the time of that wealth's appearance, demanded of its people a high level of organization and ingenuity merely to survive. It required a society which was both mobile and possessing the ability to adapt to abrupt changes within its environment. It also required a society in which each member was aware of the necessity to curb his own desires in order for the needs of the society as a whole to be fulfilled in times of stress. UAE society was developed highly and precisely to cope with the conditions which pertained at the time. It might, therefore, be more correct to talk of re-development rather than development when one looks at the changes which have taken place since the discovery of oil and the subsequent establishment of the UAE in 1971.

The Historical Roots of Modern Development

An objective assessment of Emirati society in the pre-oil era reveals a foundation upon which, in the era of subsequent wealth, development policy was able to build. The kernel of this development policy can be seen in those characteristic structures of organization upon which Emirati society was based before the advent of oil. Fundamental to those structures were:

- The blood relationships on both maternal and paternal sides (consanguinity).
- Social and political alliance.
- The concept of *al-teraz* or tax and social insurance.
- The concept of *al-weliya*, or protection and authority.
- Social welfare systems.
- *al-azwa* and *al-shofa* (systems of cooperation).

Intrinsic principles of social welfare existed between individuals within UAE society because that society was based on a tribal structure with strong bonds of consanguinity. These bonds were fundamental to the development of UAE society, enhancing and strengthening the social relationship amongst any group of people belonging to the same family or the same tribe, their strength ensuring that group's survival through periods of economic or environmental stress. The 'Affinity Relationship', which was based on marriage, determined the role of an individual in the tribe. All traditions and rules in the society were based on this type of relationship, in which the chief of the tribe issued directives and laws to his fellow men who would then obey those orders. Decisions were usually taken by a tribe's assembly, in which were represented members of the strongest and richest families. All members of the tribe were obliged to obey the assembly's decisions.[2]

The first set of relationships determined an individual's place within a tribe. The second set of relationships in tribal society, the 'Alliance Relationship', provided the fundamental base for the creation of links between the tribes. As different tribes united to form an alliance, this was called a 'union' and it was understood that all fighting or other forms of aggression between members of the united tribes was banned. Further, the union could agree to have a joint army. Such an army or political union was responsible for decisions regarding, and the subsequent organizing of, individual relationships within a single tribe or within the union. The Alliance Relationship was thus used to strengthen the ties stemming from the Affinity Relationship.[3] In addition to the political advantages gained through the above mechanisms, this inter-bonding within and between tribes gave rise to social advantages by which those in need were cared for by the tribe or by the union of tribes to which they belonged.

These 'Affinity' and 'Alliance' relationships could be described as the first exposure to social politics for the UAE's tribal society. But there were elements other than these purely tribal elements contributing to social politics; there were the relationships which existed between the urban and the non-urban sectors.

Many tribes had settled on the western (Arabian Gulf) coast and their settlements eventually expanded to become major cities such as Dubai, Sharjah, Ras al-Khaimah and Abu Dhabi. As time passed, new settlers came from different areas of the country and managed to gain the protection of the rulers within these townships. These migrations, together with commercial factors, created a new social structure for which social development based on economic and social policies was required; and so a policy of taxation was introduced.

The third base within Emirati society was, therefore, represented by a tax known to the tribes as *al-teraz,* meaning a type of indemnity paid to the ruler by the pearl divers in exchange for the ruler's protection. After the establishment of the towns, members of the tribes were asked to fulfil certain compulsory duties, in return for which the rulers would take responsibility for the provision of various social services.

Within this system of *al-teraz,* we notice that a dialogue has effectively taken place between members of a tribe — who became the builders and developers of the new towns - on the one hand, and the ruler — representing the political system - on the other. Services such as protection, payment to those who worked in the mosques and compensation to those who faced hardships were all offered by the ruler as part of traditional Arab and Islamic values. This led to a redistribution of wealth amongst citizens in the form of awards, donations and so forth. In today's parlance, they are presented in the form of the budget.

The second half of the foregoing list is best dealt with as a web of concepts, interlocking amongst one another and with the system of *al-teraz* itself.

The concept of *al-weliya* (guardianship, custodianship) as a social system has special values which played an active role in encouraging poorer members of a tribe to remain loyal to the sheikh or chief of their tribe. The *al-weliya* was thus an essential root of the social policies in Emirati society in the past as well as in the present, because if the ruler did not fulfil his responsibilities in serving the members of his tribe, he would not enjoy their loyalty. *Al-weliya,* as a social system creating a social contract between ruler and ruled, stems from Islamic religion as well as from the bedouin culture which has dominated UAE society in the past as it continues to do in the present.

Patronage and *al-weliya*[4] together represent one of the foundations of the social system and social policies upon which all types of social services and projects related to modern social development are based. It is interesting to note that excessive use of these concepts in certain applications has led to social problems amongst members of UAE society.

However, the next task is to examine the various forms of social welfare, which existed in this pre-oil era.

Firstly, there was voluntary assistance, offered when individuals faced unexpected hardships or difficulties. In such circumstances, the aggrieved family would receive services and support from other members of the family or tribe. A family's difficulties might stem from external problems, or they might come from within the family itself. In either situation, help would be forthcoming. For example, where a woman had been unfairly divorced and badly treated, the settled or nomadic community would offer her their assistance and support to obtain all her rights from her ex-husband, to raise her children and to ensure her a respectable and dignified life. (This type of solidarity continues to this day in certain areas and desert groups, whereby the people of a village will still take appropriate initiatives to help and support any women aggrieved by her husband and family.) Other types of cooperative services existed within the same tribe, further reflecting the social solidarity amongst families within the tribal system.

In situations where the ruler or sheikh faced some political or social problem (an inter-tribal battle, for example, or the arrangement of a son's wedding festival), he would call for the help and support of the members of his tribe and this system of cooperation was called *al-shofah* (the sixth mentioned base of tribal society), a system of which the Emirati people were familiar practitioners. There are many examples to corroborate this type of effective cooperation between members of the tribes and their chiefs.

Secondly, there were those services which the ruler traditionally provided in return for the previously-mentioned tax (*al-teraz*) which he collected from certain sectors of the population, in particular from the pearl divers. For example, salaries were paid to employees of the mosques and compensation was awarded to those who became disabled. While diving itself was the most important commercial activity for the population of the emirates, it was also one of the most risky. Divers frequently faced serious financial difficulties arising from natural catastrophes such as storms, or failure of the pearl harvest. During difficult times, the sheikhs of all the emirates would help those who were seeking help and support. (Such assistance was also received from generous and well-known families such as, earlier in this century, those of Khalaf bin Otaiba and Abdullah bin Sultan[5]). This type of service might be considered as similar to the insurance and social welfare funds in modern societies. In addition, the money could be spent on gatherings reflecting the traditional Arab and Islamic values of hospitality.

Thirdly, one of the main features of the people of the emirates has long been their strong interest in education and their desire that it should not be confined only to the sheikhs and the families of the wealthy but that it should extend to all sectors of society. Cultural and educational services existed in the emirates before the oil boom, despite the limitation of financial resources and the small population. They were usually restricted, however, to the houses of the wealthy and were regarded as cultural clubs for entertainment.[6] In the absence of proper educational services and policies, the people of the emirates participated in the activities of these houses or clubs because they were motivated to learn more about religion and to further their understanding of Islamic legislation, known as *al-shariya*. Women came there to learn to read and write. Occasionally, more than a hundred people would attend one of these educational sessions.

These clubs could be seen as proof of a kind of solidarity between the people of the emirates because they represented equality, consideration and communication amongst the people. Certain well-established families throughout the country would also hold social gatherings on both public and private occasions where food was served to each person in the community. (In addition to these educational and cultural clubs, there were some houses which became specialized in offering counselling services on other aspects of life. The people used to visit these houses or centres to seek advice, help and counsel for problems which could not be tackled or solved by ordinary or unqualified persons.)

The education process was further developed by an influx of Arab teachers from Naheid and Faris (Iran), in particular from the island of Qishm. Examples of such teachers were Al Yamani and Al Thalbi, each of whom taught both male and female pupils. These educational missions were used to strengthen knowledge regarding Islamic studies. This was apparent from such missions to the emirates of Ras al-Khaimah, Ajman, Sharjah and Umm al-Qaiwain. Teachers such as Muhammad bin Abd al Salam Al Magraby and Muhammad Al Shanqity came to Dubai from Morocco. While some of these teachers offered their services free of charge, merchants and wealthy families continued to pay salaries to other teachers because they were so highly valued for their contribution to the education process.

Besides expatriate teachers, there were teachers from the local community who contributed to the teaching of Islamic culture. The local teachers either studied directly under the supervision of the expatriate teachers or they received their education and training by going abroad and studying in institutions overseas. Two examples are Muhammad bin Ghobash and Sheikh Saqr of Ras al-Khaimah. Besides the teaching of Qur'anic and Islamic studies other subjects, including mathematics and natural science, were also taught.

Higher education for local residents was arranged through overseas missions but it was done on a very small scale and was limited to the wealthy since they were the only ones who could afford such education.[7]

It should be stressed that the Islamic religion was deeply influential in making the people of the emirates seriously interested in education since Islamic subjects dominated Arab society and those libraries that existed were dominated by religious works. It is no surprise, then, to find that the rulers played an active role in encouraging the spread of education by offering grants for students as well as for teachers. In the emirate of Ajman, for example, the first school was opened and managed by Muhammad bin Salem Al Suweidi and Said bin Bader despite financial difficulties and limited facilities, and food was given free of charge to their students. That initiative was one of the pioneering attempts in the field of education.

Initiatives have come from the people themselves too. This can be seen from campaigns to raise donations in order to establish new schools, one instance of which included the efforts of several of the sheikhs and public-spirited individuals.

Fourthly, there was what might be termed a commercial service, to encourage commercial work by those capable of it, through loan schemes. The idea was that some type of commodity was purchased by the investor on behalf of those taking advantage of the scheme and, when sold by the latter, the profits would enable any loans incurred to be repaid. These loans showed the considerable amount of cooperation, as well as trust, amongst the people of the emirates.

The sheikhs and tribal chiefs were concerned about, and wished to be kept informed of, the conditions and well-being of their fellow tribesmen through regular or seasonal visits. These occasions enabled the leaders to hear at first-hand the requests and requirements of the people. They cemented the strong bonds which existed between the sheikhs and the individual members of their society and demonstrated the genuine responsibility felt on the part of the sheikhs to ensure that everything possible was provided to the members of the tribe or emirate.

Finally, health services were extremely poor and of a very low standard because until recently the area was unfamiliar with modern medicine. Patients were treated through local and traditional medical treatments. Some of the local families were specialized in traditional medicine[8] and had been for several generations. However, despite their best efforts, the death rate was very high, especially amongst children. Local medical treatments such as cupping and cauterization were widely used in the emirates, together with some herbal remedies. In parallel with local medicine, there were some religious families who offered succour to needy patients through the use of special religious prayers and incantation.[9]

The Establishment of the Modern State and its Role in Social Development

The discovery of oil and the establishment of the new state known as the United Arab Emirates (UAE) led to a completely different form of development compared to that of the pre-oil period. The main reasons for this are:

- The change in economic conditions due to the availability of huge financial resources.
- The sound policies and values adopted and implemented by His Highness President Sheikh Zayed bin Sultan Al Nahyan.

Nevertheless, that development came about because the basis for it already existed. A social contract between ruler and ruled had long been acknowledged. When Sheikh Zayed first came to power in 1966, before the birth of the federation, he was already aware of the importance of the social contract between himself and his people and was determined that it should be extended to cover all those emirates who chose to join the federation. He was aware of his own obligations as ruler of the richest of those emirates. He must also have known the importance of distributing wealth in such a way as to bind a loosely-federated society together and the dangers of failing to do so. He was therefore the driving force behind the policies of social development initiated by the UAE. These policies have contributed positively to the modern state, which has taken on the responsibility of directing and controlling the means of achieving the desired degree of development. The UAE population has, in the process, been exposed to many influences which have led irresistibly to social change and modernization.

To explain the extent of development and modernization in the UAE, we shall refer to the main aims adopted by the state in order to achieve them. Briefly, these goals were:

- To issue the appropriate legislative laws to ensure equality among all citizens, to confirm existing legislation and to extend citizens' rights.
- To increase all educational and social services in order to improve levels of health and culture.
- To create and spread telecommunications and media services and to monitor developments in the modern world.
- To improve transportation to facilitate the movement of different products internally or with other countries.
- To organize the process of urbanization.
- To improve agricultural production in order to ensure the achievement of food security.
- To increase the cooperation movement and develop small groups.
- To encourage modern industry to develop human resources.
- To ensure cultural independence, provide every opportunity for an educated elite and extend modern culture to all, particularly those formerly deprived of exposure to culture.[10] The state realized that these aims could not be achieved without proper planning and active participation on the part of the population. As a result, the Ministry of Planning was formed, with instructions to:
- Plan all projects requiring implementation by the state.
- Observe and monitor the course of their implementation.
- Cooperate with specialized international organizations on technical matters and prepare relevant economic projects and studies.

Federal Law No. 3/1973 considered that planning was essential for success. Comprehensive long-term development plans were decided upon. These were then broken down into yearly and medium-term goals.

The main aims of development in relation to human resources were:

- The provision of all social, cultural, media, environmental, educational and health services as the basic right of every citizen on the grounds that the human being is the developmental priority.
- The achievement of high levels of well-being based on justice and the need to ensure such benefits for future generations.
- The development of the work force together with proper training programmes in different fields to improve and increase productivity levels.

Development strategy in the UAE has thus attempted to create a balance between free market principles and the modern role of the state. It has put in place a modern infrastructure of public utilities, evident from the many different services available to the citizens of the UAE in the areas of education, health, culture, housing and the improvement of women's conditions.

Educational services

Within the UAE, education is seen as the key factor in the long-term success of any development strategy adopted by the state. When it was realized, in 1990-1991, that there existed a large number of people who had missed out on educational opportunities, the allocation for education was increased from 10 per cent to 14.9 per cent of the total budget. As a result, a dual education system was established, comprising both the state education sector and a private education sector. At the same time, more educational centres were established to teach adults.

In 1972, the proportion of schools in private ownership was not more than 10 per cent. This had risen to 34 per cent by 1991, with the majority of those private schools being at primary level. However, the private school sector has expanded during the last few years to cover intermediate and secondary schools. The combined number of schools in both the state and private sectors is now 978, while the number of Adult Education Centres increased from 54 in 1972 to 135 in 1991. The educational sector in the UAE made major advances with the establishment, in 1977, of the Emirates University, and, subsequently, of the Higher Colleges of Technology.

Teaching staff in the UAE have made a crucial input to the educational process, with huge increases in their numbers over the last 30 years. Teachers in the combined state and private sectors rose from 2319 in 1972, to 28,922 in 1992. By 1995, there were 37,000 teachers, of which 25,000 were in state schools. The number of lecturers at the Emirates University rose from 447 in 1977 to 772 in 1991.

Student numbers rose equally impressively. In 1972, there were 43,428 students in state and private schools. By 1977, this number had risen dramatically to 388,115. By 1995-96, a further increase, to approximately 500,000 had taken place. At Adult Educational Centres, the number rose from 4912 in 1972 to 8496 in 1991. Finally, the number of university students graduating in 1981 was 472. Ten years later, in 1991, that number had risen to 1176.

One important feature of these statistics is the increasing number of female students at all levels. One explanation for this is that males are either engaged in commercial business from an early age or they are employed in government positions and so do not continue with their higher education. The females, on the other hand, are in a position to continue. This argument is given weight by the figures. At secondary level, for instance, 59.4 per cent of those graduating in the academic year 1992-1993 were female. Looking at university figures, it can be seen that while the number of males who registered at the University in 1977 was 60.5 per cent of the total, this figure had dropped to 22.4 per cent by the year 1991-1992. Female graduate numbers, on the other hand, have been increasing remarkably since the first graduation ceremony in 1981. In 1981, the balance was 58.8 per cent and 41.2 per cent for males and females respectively, but by 1992 those proportions had been dramatically reversed to 32.5 per cent and 67.5 per cent respectively, although it should be noted that more males than females pursue higher education abroad.

By far the majority of university graduates are from the indigenous population of the UAE. In 1992, for example, the percentage of non-local graduates was 7.6 per cent, or a total of 95 students. Of these 95 students, 29 were from the other Arab Gulf Cooperation Council (AGCC) states - namely, Bahrain, Qatar, Saudi Arabia, Oman and Kuwait.

The level of adult literacy was lower amongst females than amongst males. It has, however, been gradually increasing. In 1975 the level was around 44 per cent for females, but had increased to 82 per cent by 1993. Male adult literacy levels increased during the same period from 60 per cent to 82 per cent.

In 1975, the average number of years of studies for males was 4.40, compared with only 2.10 for females. By 1993, the average number of years spent in study for males and females was virtually equal at 7.15 years for males compared with 7.10 for females. This is one of the greatest achievements in women's education.

Health services

The available information shows that there have been tremendous developments in this sector over the past 30 years. This relates not only to the increased number of doctors and hospitals but also to the wide range of health care services which are planned and offered by the state to the people. As an example, the number of government hospitals has approximately doubled since the foundation of the state. The number of doctors has also risen, though at a lower rate, from approximately 827 in 1977 to 1159 in 1990.

One of the important aspects of the health service in the UAE is the existence of two complementary types of health care options: the hospitals and the primary care centres. The number of primary health care centres (which often provide urgent health care services to the population) increased from 63 in 1973 to 93 in 1990. The total number of doctors who work in these centres was 238 in 1977 and 396 in 1990. In addition to the above types of services, there are others such as special centres for women and children. There were 10 such centres in 1990, with a total number of 24 doctors employed in them. Further, there are special health centres to treat pupils and students: in 1990 there were 11 such centres. In addition, there are a large number of clinics based in different schools throughout the country. These clinics are usually staffed by a nurse who can offer primary health care and immunization services to students. The UAE also offers financial support to its citizens requiring medical treatment outside the country.

However, despite the excellent developments in the Health Service, the ratio of doctors to patients in the UAE has actually dropped since the establishment of the federation. Thus, in 1977, there was one doctor for every 809 patients; in 1990, there was one doctor for each 1186 patients. This may be due, firstly, to the increase of private medical health care services (for which no accurate information is available) and secondly, to the preference of local citizens for foreign medical treatment, as well as to the dramatic growth of the population.

Social care services

The available information concerning social care services reflects two important factors relating to the level of development in the UAE. The first is that there has been virtually no change in the number of applications from individuals seeking help and support from the state. The number of aid applications in 1977 was 29,060 whereas, in 1990, the number was 28,990. The second is that the state has increased the financial resources available to aid applicants so that while the number of applications has stayed roughly the same, the financial resources distributed increased from Dh 127.2 million (US$ 34.6 million) in 1977 to Dh 529.6 million (US$ 144.1 million) in 1992.

Unpublished information provided for this study by the Ministry of Labour reveals that the expenditure on social help between 1983 and 1992 was around Dh 4.46 billion. This money was spent on 11 legally-defined groups:

- the elderly
- spinsters
- divorcées
- the abandoned
- non-citizen wives
- widows
- orphans
- invalids
- bankrupts
- married students
- families of prisoners.

The state also considers special cases which do not fit into any of these categories.

Improvement of women's conditions

One of the most important challenges for social development in the UAE has been how to create new opportunities for the involvement of women in general activities and for their integration into the workforce. As has already been shown in a previous section, the UAE, with its policy of human development, has managed to create opportunities for women to succeed within the formal educational system. This can be seen as a continuation of the traditional respect for education. However, although the traditional culture encouraged the education of women, it was based on a concept of segregation between males and females; this cultural concept creates conflict in the handling of certain women's issues. Women, for example, are not entirely free to pursue their chosen career should it fall outside the actively encouraged areas of teaching and medicine. As a result, a large number of females obtain university degrees but, technically, they are unable to use their educational achievements to serve their society. This is a major obstacle to future human development.

Conditions for women within the UAE have nevertheless been improved due to the hard work of many women's organizations. These organizations serve women's interests and also positively contribute to the women's movement, which in turn plays a vital role in the development policy. Details related to the activity of these organizations are given below.

The UAE Women's Federation states quite simply that the condition of women in various aspects of life must be improved. Not until improvement is achieved in both the personal and social status of women, can they actively participate in the national boom of the country.

Women's Associations play a major role in the attempt to achieve this goal. The concept behind these associations is to promote the role of women in serving their society in many fields. By uniting the efforts of women in public life more effectively through their programmes of social and voluntary work, they can be regarded as an apparatus for the development and organization of society. They are strongly involved in:

Educational and cultural activities
These include:

- Offering specific help to members and non-members who are illiterate.
- Participation in seminars and cultural meetings.
- Contributing and preparing articles required by magazines published in the state.
- Visiting public libraries and encouraging members to make use of those libraries.

Training and educational activities
These cover educational centres and adult education as well as training campaigns outside the country. Nurseries and child care services are also covered by these activities.

Religious and cultural activities
These cover different arrangements such as seminars and symposia at national or AGCC levels in order to encourage the youth to seek knowledge. They also cover religious presentations at all educational levels in the country.

Social activities
These include:

- Participation in national and Pan-Arab occasions.
- Visits to villages and rural areas in order to explore their problems.
- Cooperation with other establishments in relation to environmental projects.
- Offering supervision for such projects.
- Directing, implementing and promoting social projects in rural areas.

Health activities
These include:

- Cooperation with women's and children's centres in order to supervise and to present health promotion programmes.
- The organization of visits and trips to rural areas for education and health promotion purposes.
- Participation in official committees for the social health of the state.
- The organization of First Aid courses.
- The organization of training and seminars to cover First Aid and primary health care subjects.

Despite the efforts of Women's Associations to promote an active role for women in UAE society, it is frequently said that the role of women in the past was more effective and more positive. While it is difficult to prove such generalized claims, it is certainly true that women in the past provided help and support for their families in severe and difficult conditions, often while suffering serious financial hardship and in the absence of their husbands. Despite these difficulties, they nevertheless did not hesitate to offer their help and support to needier members in their society. A balance existed between the limitation of resources and religious, human and voluntary needs. Even with all the progress made in women's conditions, their achievements in education, social care, health and the availability of modern technology, the role of women is much more insignificant than it should be in our present society.

Youth services

Sheikh Zayed has said that 'The youth of any nation are its backbone in the present and in the future'. Therefore, the question arises: What have the youth in the UAE gained from the social development projects? In fact the state has, since its establishment, treated this sector as one of the most important, offering every possible opportunity in education, housing, health, information and the freedom to enjoy sporting hobbies.

One of the aims of the state has been to ensure that the youth should have an important status in society (for example, the UAE actively participated in the celebrations marking the International Year of Youth). Any future plans should also pay special attention to improving all services available to the youth of the country. A brief account is given below to demonstrate how the youth have been treated by the state:

The number of young people between 15 and 23 years of age in the UAE is 183,659 or 17.62 per cent of the total population, while the number of young Emiratis is 50,020, equivalent to 27.23 per cent of the total young citizens in the country. Of this, there are 23,968 young female and 26,052 young male UAE nationals.

The state offers them many services, including:

Free education
This is offered for citizens at every level within the UAE, while grants for education outside the country are also made available.

The Ministry of Youth and Sports *(part of the Ministry of Education and Youth since March 1997)*
This plans appropriate programmes to ensure improvement in the quality of life for youth in all aspects, including culture, sports and social status.

Sports Clubs and Federations
These include:

- The Football Association
- The Handball Federation
- The Basketball Federation
- The Volleyball Federation
- Swimming
- The Cycling Federation
- The Chess Federation
- The Bowling Association
- The Emirates Tennis Association
- Yacht Clubs
- The General Union of Popular Sports, such as camel racing and horse riding.

Youth centres in summer vacations (summer camps)

There are seven of these centres in the UAE, one in each emirate, with a total membership of 1101. Their aim is to run special programmes for youth and to educate people in general to participate in, and become involved in, the affairs of their society, including decision-making and the implementation of programmes for economic and social development. Activities at these centres range from amateur dramatics, craft and workshop training, photography, scientific activity, to gardening and food manufacture.

Youth associations

The Association of Youth Hostels comes under this heading. Youth hostels accommodate youth delegations and UAE youth campaigners. The homes are modern, comfortable and well-equipped. Membership of these hostels is open to UAE, Arab and foreign youth. and the social and psychological services play an important role in their social activities.

Women's clubs in Sharjah

Based in Sharjah and its surrounding areas, these clubs play an active role in the field of social development for child and youth groups, as well as providing cultural advancement for young females, women and families.

Private associations

There are many private associations, including women's associations, associations for religious counselling, associations for arts and cultural activities and science associations for both male and female students at the Emirates University.[11]

Community associations

These associations play a cultural and social role for both Arab and foreign communities, acting as social safety nets and helping to foster cooperation amongst different social segments and sectors in the UAE.

Maintaining the structure and stability of Emirati society is a major goal in the development policy of the UAE. As a result, the UAE created, in 1992, what has become known as 'The Marriage Fund' to help and encourage young Emirati males to marry their female compatriots, thereby reducing the trend of marrying foreign women.

Cooperative and voluntary services

These services are offered through professional associations which the state has allowed to be established and which it financially supports. The voluntary associations are trying to help in the development of modern society by discovering its requirements and attempting to fulfil them in order to ensure that society can become self-sufficient.[12] The most important roles that such societies undertake within this frame work are:

Mobilization

This can be seen as a framework in which people can have an opportunity to participate in organized activity and is very useful when the state has difficulty in absorbing people's potential to offer their work and help.

Participation

The aim being to develop and improve people's conditions so that their active participation in development programmes is ensured; participation can be achieved by enabling them either to help themselves or to help others.

Specialization

This allows voluntary organizations to determine the areas in which they can best achieve good results and a high degree of efficiency. In general, these have been those areas demanding a high personal input from volunteers, as in the care of the elderly, the sick and the young.

As well as women's associations and charitable organizations, many other non-governmental associations have sprung up to meet the needs of a changing society within the UAE[13]. In 1993, 91 associations were registered with the Ministry of Labour and Social Services embracing the following spheres of activity:

Table 1.	Scope of activity	Number
	Folkloric arts	27
	Communities	17
	Professional	10
	Theatrical	10
	Women's services	7
	Humanitarian services	6
	Religious services	5
	Cultural services	4

The highest number of these associations exists in Abu Dhabi city (28), followed by Dubai Emirate (19), Ras al-Khaimah (12), Sharjah Emirate (11), with the rest distributed over the other emirates. Out of the total number of associations registered, 57 percent responded to a questionnaire circulated by Ousha Bint Hussein Cultural REWAQ. The highest percentage response was from associations based in Abu Dhabi city (96 per cent), followed by Sharjah (64 per cent), then Ras al-Khaimah (42 per cent). From the above figures, it can be seen that the responses will reflect (more vocal) city interests and those generally of the larger, more concentrated populations. With this reservation in mind, the questionnaire showed that of those organizations which responded, 44 per cent regarded their most important objective to be the promulgation of cultural awareness. The main objective of 23 per cent was the strengthening of solidarity, brotherhood and collaborative ties. Fifteen per cent stated as their objective the preservation of heritage and its promulgation. The provision of humanitarian services and aid was the objective listed by 13 per cent, while a further 13 per cent listed their main objective to be the upgrading of health, social and educational standards of women.

Table 2. Association programme principal fields	Number	%
Pure technology	1	2
Community development	30	58
Credit	2	4
Culture	31	60
Literacy programmes for adults	13	25
Emergencies/disasters	4	8
Recruitment	1	2
Environment	1	2
Handcrafts	4	8
Health	1	2
Human rights	1	2
Infrastructure	1	2
Establishing institutes	1	2
Legal assistance	1	2
Management of natural resources	1	2
Refugees	4	8
Rural development	1	2
Women's affairs	11	21
Youth	9	17
Others	8	15

It can be seen from the above table that the principal fields of programme vary considerably, with culture and community development, at 60 and 58 percent respectively, being by far the most important areas of activity. Literacy programmes for adults and women's affairs were next at 25 and 21 per cent respectively. Rural development, on the other hand, is the principal field of programme for only two per cent of those associations which responded. Given that the highest response came from the more urbanized areas, this may be an inaccurate picture of activity on the ground. There is, however, an overall rural deficiency in the distribution of associations which would indicate the accuracy of the general thrust of the findings.

The workforce

Regarding the labour force in the UAE, certain characteristics can be highlighted. Firstly, the work force in the UAE is high compared to the total population. The 1980 census showed it to be 53 per cent, though by 1992 this figure had been reduced to 47.8 per cent. This differs from the characteristics of the work force in the developing countries and other Arab countries where the percentage of work force to the total population ranges from 22 per cent to 40 per cent. Secondly, while male inhabitants do outnumber female inhabitants, the participation of females in the workforce compared to that of males is very low, though gradually increasing. Also, as mentioned in an earlier section, women's participation is concentrated in certain areas, namely health and education. Thirdly, because of the high rate of illiteracy in the foreign non-Arab labour force, and the non-technical level of labour, the standard of skills is low within the workforce. The fourth characteristic of the UAE labour force lies in the concentration of labour in the public services sector. UAE nationals are concentrated in government positions and in the services and administrative sector. They tend not to work in skilled trades. In the absence of a comprehensive overall plan for the development of the work force, we expect that the UAE labour force will continue to suffer from its turbulent characteristics. The state will probably face a major problem if it tries to replace the foreign work force by its local citizens.

In relation to local citizens and ex-patriates, available figures show the participation of local citizens in the workforce to be considerably less than that of ex-patriates. This can be seen clearly from the comparison of the rate of crude activity for both groups, as given in the following table.

Table 3. Crude activity rate for local and non-local citizens for 1975 and 1992.

Year	Local Citizens	Foreign Ex-patriates
1975	22.1	69.9
1992	16.7	660.1

The unemployment rate for local citizens is higher than that for ex-patriates. For example, in 1992, it was 3.2 and 1.1 for local and ex-patriates respectively. This is not surprising, in that the majority of ex-patriates will have come to the UAE specifically to work.

However, the available information indicates (as stated above) that the majority of local citizens work in the services sector. It has also been shown that their percentage there is increasing. For example, it has increased from 54 per cent of the sector's total workforce in 1975 to 71.8 per cent in 1990.

Housing services

The UAE's population has managed to adapt to the difficult environment over the years, through a major housing and infrastructural building programme. As far as housing is concerned, we can only present general information since it is very difficult to differentiate between citizens and non-citizens and, likewise, between rural and urban areas. There is also an absence of data regarding the number of houses built by the state and given or sold, at nominal prices, to UAE citizens. Regarding other services, such as electricity, water and sewerage utilities, the infrastructural framework can be determined through the length of roads (both inside and outside the main population centres) and also the number of vehicles as given in the following table:

Table 4. Social development indicators	1975	1993
Completed houses for Emiratis	1,074	14,820
Access to safe water	—	100%
Access to electricity	—	100%
Access to sanitation	—	82%
Individual average consumption of energy	223	(1995 fig.) 947
Individual average share of water (in gallons)	—	17225,085
Public gardens	—	—
Length of roads inside cities (km)	—	(1990) 346
Length of roads between cities (km)	—	(1990) 65,308
Number of cars and other vehicles	—	(1990) 303,284

Conclusion

From the above survey of development in the UAE, it can be clearly seen that the state, under the leadership of Sheikh Zayed, is fulfilling its social contract with the people. Within the Human Development Index (HDI), the measure of development (based on income, education and life expectancy) adopted by the UN, the UAE performs very well. The HDI can be used to evaluate and criticize development policy and its achievements. Further, it can be an effective apparatus in the planning of the development process, helping, where necessary, to transfer its aims to new and better targets. However, what the HDI does not measure clearly in a country such as the UAE is the involvement of the people themselves in that process of development, and one of the most serious challenges faced by human and social development in the UAE is the imbalance between economic growth and development as a comprehensive concept with the development of people at its core. Despite the appearance of financial and economic affluence everywhere (in housing, in infrastructural development and in the workplace), the population's interest in participation is still weak, because the people of the UAE depend upon the state in almost every instance. While economic growth and the rate of development is increasing, participation by the human element of the UAE — the main target of development — is decreasing because there has been no creation of an appropriate development programme by the people themselves. (There have also been decreases in the rate of productivity and the re-investment of income in line with those achievements offered by the state, despite the fact that the UAE managed to reach very high levels on the HDI, whether judged by global, Arab or Gulf standards.)

Some Arab sociologists have questioned whether progress based on a westernized concept of modernization is an appropriate goal for Arab countries to strive for. Al Kaweri,[14] for instance, thinks that the system of material incentives which has characterized this society since the flow of oil revenues in the Gulf area has subverted the system of values which was the bedouin legacy to the Emirates. Bedouin values such as courageousness, self-reliance, generosity, faithfulness, aiding the weak and a love of freedom, while still viewed as the best framework for social relationships, have been undermined by an undesirable trend towards such economically-based values as conspicuous consumption, self-promotion, speculation and the pursuit of personal interests at the expense of community needs. Al Alem also criticizes the present culture in 'modernized' Arab countries as arising from subjective and pragmatic actions which lack any objective basis. Like Al Kaweri, he sees Arab society as growing increasingly hedonistic, superficial and individualistic. While acknowledging that such trends are being resisted by that domestic Arab culture which is characterized by strict religious attitudes, he does not see that particular form of resistance, sometimes dominated by value judgements, moral, emotional and irrational, as offering the solution for Arab society. He says that:

> *a comprehensive modernization of our Arab culture cannot be achieved without particulation of this culture in the process of modernization. This process should be based on a critical understanding and a comprehensive vision and responsibility.*[15]

From the beginning of the process of modernization and development tribal society in the UAE was receptive to the process and did not reject it, at least from the economic point of view, particularly the rise in the standard of living, and the improvement in education and health services. But when modernization projects were extended to include the family, especially those relating to women, particularly unmarried women, tribal society objected, even though it accepted change in general. The tribal society was not a participant in development, it was largely a consumer.

Given the perceived need, as part of the process of development, for people to be involved in determining the direction and future of their country,[16] then the next stage of development may be for the state to encourage its citizens to participate more deeply in the creation of their own development programmes. However, through the state's strong commitment to education, it has already set up the means by which this next stage will come about, whether of its own accord, or through continued state involvement.

Development in the UAE still requires a great deal of work and effort to create individuals whose production and participation is based on rationalism, science and a capacity to ensure effectiveness within society.

---

[1] For further discussion of the concept of development and its application to the UAE, see Ahmed Al Sherbas, *Asking You In Religion And Life* , Byrouth, Dar-al-Jalil (1981) pp 403-424; Maha Suhail Al Mokadam, *Social Developments Basis And Challenges*, Arab Development Institute (1978), Mohammed Jawad Reda, *The State and its Roles in Social Engineering*, Al Mustakbal al Arabi No. 189, pp 76-79, based on *The World Situation,* New York, United Nations, Department of International Economic and Social Affairs (1985).

[2] Mohammed Al Moutawa, *Development And Social Changes In The Emirates,* al farabi (1991) p12; based on *Dynamics Of Culture Change,* by B. Malinowaski, (Wallerstein) and *Social Change: The Colonial Situation,* New York, Sydney, John Wiley and Sons, Ltd (1966).

[3] According to Al Moutawa, this kind of marriage is for the purpose of strengthening the union and it represents socio-political policy as the structure for the bedouin, based on affinity whether genuine or assumed. This was true equally for small as well as large tribal groups.

[4] One of the clear examples of privilege in the *al-weliya* and *al-reaia* system is the fact that the British justified their presence in the emirates on the same concept, managing to establish some sort of acceptance for their presence because they claimed to be protecting the people of the emirates from outside interference. It is possible that the concept of 'independence' is in sharp contrast to the concept of *al-weliya*. Thus, comprehensive changes in human relationships within a society open the doors to a demand for independence from colonialism.

[5] The house of Khalifa bin Kutima used to be called a hotel since he offered all manner of assistance from food to money to all visitors, the homeless, refugees or those who faced times of hardship or catastrophe. It should be noted that at that time, the concept of the modern hotel did not exist in this area. Thus, the Arabs and the people of the tribes are proud that this form of hospitality is intrinsic to their natural and noble values.

[6] For example, the house of Saliha Al Madfa in Sharjah and a prominent figure in this field.

[7] For example, Saif bin Ghobash studied in Iraq. He was sponsored by his family and relatives.

[8] Some of the families renowned for offering their popular (local, traditional) medical services included the family of Ibn Al Mazroui, the family of Ahmed bin Nasser Lootah and Hussain bin Nasser Lootah. It is interesting to note that the latter managed to treat some dangerous diseases, such as tumours, through cauterization. Also, he managed to treat a tumour in his own neck, using this technique, and subsequently lived a further 60 years. For further information about popular medicine, the reader is advised to refer to a book by the name of *Popular Medicine* by Ibrahim bin Suliman al Ashkar, publ. UAE Higher Committee of Heritage and History. (The book was checked for accuracy by Hamad bin Ahmed al Khazraji.)

[9] The late Rashid Ahmed bin Lootah gave his personal account of many historical events. The author of this study interviewed him many times and he offered valuable contributions to the present study in relation to the culture which was associated with the past social services of the UAE.

[10] Mohammed Jawad Reda, *op. cit.,* p 89.

[11] Taha Hussein, *The Youth In The United Arab Emirates*, Social Affairs No 8, (1985).

[12] *Ibid.*, pp 89-93.

[13] Information for non-governmental associations comes from Ousha Bint Hussein Cultural REWAQ.

[14] Ali Khalifa Al Kaweri, *The Reality of Oil Development*, Al Mustakbal al Arabi, No. 7.

[15] Al Alem, 1993, p 16.

[16] Al Kaweri, *op. cit.,* p 22.

Social and Economic Changes in the United Arab Emirates 1975-1995

Mohamed Shihab

Introduction

Twenty years ago the UAE was one of the least developed countries of the world. Today, it has achieved an income level comparable to that of the industrialized nations. The UAE did not pass through the hypothetical development 'stages' that most developed countries seem to have experienced. Rather, its large oil revenues have enabled the UAE to leap these phases to the stage of high mass consumption. Large oil revenues have enabled the UAE to short cut the usually difficult and lengthy process of saving and capital accumulation necessary for economic development.

Given an abundance of natural resource endowments (oil and gas), the UAE has embraced resource-based industries (RBI) as a development strategy, i.e an industrial strategy that is based on utilization of natural resources. There has been a deployment of windfall income, largely directed at a 'once-for-all' boost to the social and economic infrastructure, which enabled the UAE to achieve economic development in a very short time from 1973 to 1982, a period of relatively high oil prices.

This chapter takes account of the fact that development economics cannot be separated from the institutional, social, cultural, economic and political context. It also takes into account the all-important human factor both as a goal and a source of economic development.

Economic and Institutional Constraints

Before the discovery and exportation of oil, the economy of the Trucial States (which today form the UAE) depended mainly on subsistence agriculture, nomadic animal husbandry, the extracting of pearls and the trade in pearls, fishing, and seafaring. The period before the discovery of oil, therefore, reflected limited natural resources, and resulted in a simple nomad economy.

The epoch of economic development in the UAE (or the UAE's First Development Decade) began in the early 1970s, coinciding with:

- its formation on 2 December 1971;
- the establishment of its formal institutions (economic, social, and political);
- a massive increase in both oil production and oil exports;
- an explosive rise in oil prices in 1973.

Political and Social Stability

Since the formation of the UAE in 1971 the UAE has enjoyed a stable political regime. Political structures appear to suit the tribal society of the UAE, and the distribution of huge oil revenues in the form of social and economic infrastructure, high salaries, and a high standard of social services, such as health and education, have raised the standard of living for UAE citizens and reduced the potential for internal political and social unrest.

It is worth mentioning that the UAE Government has maintained a relatively good record on human rights since the formation of the UAE in 1971. This in turn has promoted political and social stability.

The UAE is an active member of many regional and international associations such as the Arab League, the United Nations, the Non-aligned Movement, the Arab Gulf Cooperation Council, and the Organization of the Islamic Conference. Relations with many countries of the world, particularly the Western democratic countries, have been traditionally warm.

Political and social stability has gone hand in hand with liberal trade policies and has paved the way for investment (domestic and international) in the industrial sector.

Oil and Mineral Resources

The UAE is endowed with vast resources of oil, explored and produced on the mainland and offshore. Associated gas from crude production and non-associated gas is also produced on the mainland and offshore.

Since the early 1970s the UAE's phenomenal growth has depended entirely on the discovery and exploitation of oil. The oil and gas industries are well managed and technology is continuously harnessed to increase productive efficiency.

According to the UAE Ministry of Petroleum and Mineral Resources, the UAE maximum sustainable daily capacity of oil production (maximum production rate that can be sustained daily for one year in present conditions of exploitation) is nearly 2.5 million barrels a day. Its installed production capacity is over 3 million barrels per day. In 1992, proven oil reserves in the UAE were 98,100 million barrels, the second largest oil reserves after Saudi Arabia, (260,340 million barrels). The UAE's proven oil reserves were estimated to be 9.82 per cent of the proven world oil reserves on 1 January 1994 (EIU 1994). On the basis of current daily oil production of 2.1 million barrels per day, it is estimated that oil reserves in the UAE will last for more than 134 years.

Proven gas reserves were estimated to be 5794 billion cubic feet (in 1992). The UAE was estimated to have natural gas reserves equivalent to 4.6 per cent of the known world gas reserves at the beginning of 1992. The UAE holds the third largest reserves of natural gas in the world. Daily gas production was estimated in 1992 to be 1806 million cubic feet, 1067 million cubic feet from inshore fields and 739 million cubic feet from offshore fields. Gas reserves are estimated to last for more than 60 years. The UAE possesses, therefore, huge reserves of oil and gas, capable of sustaining long term economic growth.

Other mineral resources in the UAE are divided into three categories: rocks, sands and soils, and metals. The exploitation of minerals is restricted to rocks and sands. Rocks and gravel are used for construction. Limestone, sand, marl and gypsum are used to manufacture cement. None of the metals or other minerals of interest is exploited.

Agricultural Resources

The total area of land under agriculture and forestry constitutes under 1.5 per cent of the total land area of the UAE. Agriculture has made only a small contribution to GDP (2 per cent in 1995). There has, however, been a consistent and substantial increase in the amount of land devoted to agriculture and forestry over the past 20 years as the result of sustained efforts by the UAE Government to promote agricultural development using the following incentives:

- Agricultural plots are granted free to any UAE citizen.
- Land is levelled and prepared mechanically for free.
- Production inputs such as seeds, fertilizers and insecticides are provided at half cost.
- Water wells are drilled for free.
- There is provision of free technical services such as installation of water pumps.
- An agricultural credit line was established in 1978 to grant farmers loans for water pumps, fence wires, fishing boat engines, green houses, and drip irrigation systems. This agricultural credit attracts no interest.
- A market is secured by government intervention. Small farmers are protected from foreign competition by buying the farmers' products at favourable prices.

The very limited agricultural potential of the UAE, with unsuitable land, water scarcity, and harsh climate, has not been an obstacle to its economic development. Clark (1984) argues that although improvement in agricultural productivity is normally a necessary condition for successful development, there are exceptions when a developing country (particularly richly endowed with minerals) produces what he terms 'food substitutes' - mineral or forest products, which can be exported to world markets, purchasing food imports which can partially substitute for the productivity of the country's own agriculture.

Population and Labour Force

The UAE population is essentially small in number. However, after the discovery of oil and its exportation in the last two decades, the UAE population has experienced very rapid growth, the result of a combination of high natural rates of increase of population among the UAE indigenous citizenry, and massive inward migration of expatriates who now comprise more than three quarters of the population. Thus, a small indigenous population, a large expatriate population and immense wealth generated by oil are the dominant socio-economic features of the UAE.

In addition to population size and age composition, social factors in the UAE have a great impact in determining the size of the UAE labour force. Female participation in the UAE labour force remains small (16.3 per cent in 1990). However, incentives and legislation have aimed to rectify this situation. Greater female participation is seen as a way of increasing the UAE indigenous labour force and lessening the country's dependence on foreign labour.

A two-tier labour market has emerged in the UAE. At the top is the indigenous labour force, which constitutes about 10 per cent of the total workforce. Below this is an unlimited supply of foreign labour. The UAE has reaped benefits from foreign skilled and unskilled workers, who initiated its economic development in the early 1970's and subsequently have come to sustain it.

The employment pattern in the UAE does not reflect the structure of output. The oil sector employs only 1.4 per cent of the UAE labour force, reflecting the capital-intensive nature of the industry. Nearly 39 per cent of the labour force is engaged in community, social and personal services. The unemployment rate in the UAE (0.5 per cent) is remarkably low (3938 unemployed in 1990), which means that the UAE economy is effectively at full employment.

The UAE is highly urbanized. This has been attributed to the cluster of the public services, transportation and communications, financial markets and service-based industries in the cities.

Table 1. UAE's main economic indicators 1990-1995

Economic Indicators	1990	1991	1992	1993	1994	1995
GDP at current prices (DH billion)	125.3	126.0	128.4	131.7	135.0	143.9
Real GDP growth (%)	11.9	-2.4	-0.9	-0.6	-2.4	-0.8
Population (million)	1.84	1.91	2.01	2.09	2.23	2.37
Total Exports (fob), $ billion	21.25	22.15	23.37	23.31	21.78	23.44
Imports (fob) ($ billion)	11.69	13.92	15.83	17.75	18.25	18.98
Current account ($ billion)	5.09	1.53	3.00	0.18	-0.72	0.36
Reserves excl. gold ($ billion)	4.58	5.37	5.71	6.10	---	---
Total external debt ($ billion)	11.05	10.20	10.80	11.07	---	---
Oil production mnb/d	2.12	2.42	2.29	2.22	2.17	2.22
Oil price (average) $/barrel	---	---	18.5	16.4	14.3	15.5
Crude oil exports ($ billion)	---	---	14.10	12.10	10.28	11.44
Exchange rate DH: $ (average)	3.671	3.671	3.671	3.671	3.671	3.671
Inflation (%)	---	---	5.5	3.2	5.0	5.5

Sources: EIU (1994), Country Report: United Arab Emirates, 3rd Quarter 1994, (June), p 3 and p 5.
MoP (Ministry of Planning, UAE), (1995), Annual Economic Report, 1995.
--- not provided.

Structural Changes in the UAE's Economy

Economic development can be perceived as change in the structure of the economy. Structural change refers to terms such as agricultural transformation, industrialization, demographic transition, urbanization, transformation of domestic demand and production, foreign trade, finance, and employment.

In considering structural changes in the UAE's economy, this chapter intends to discern the pattern of the UAE's economic growth and to determine its achieved level of development. The distinct sectors of economic activity will be examined and how these sectors respond to changes in demand to which the development process subjects them. This partition of the economy into sectors permits greater understanding of the problems of development.

One clear pattern of changing economic structure in the course of economic development is that the share of industry increases as gross output per capita rises. Following the Second World War, rapid industrialization was viewed as a prerequisite for modernization and structural change. The difference in the output and the contribution to GDP of the industrial sector in developing countries as opposed to its place in developed countries was seen as the main manifestation of economic backwardness and dependence.

While value added growth rate in the oil sector was fluctuating during the period 1975-1995, the manufacturing sector value added growth rate was steadily increasing. The manufacturing value added increased considerably from DH 472 million in 1975 to DH 9443 million in 1985, and to DH 9770 million in 1991 (at constant prices). Its contribution to GDP increased significantly from 0.9 per cent in 1975 to 3.8 per cent in 1980, and to 9.2 per cent in 1985, but dropped to 8.7 per cent in 1995. Nonetheless, it is obvious that the substantial increase in the manufacturing value added has made a modest contribution to the UAE's total output growth.

Agricultural production increased more than fourfold from 1975 to 1995 at an average annual growth rate of 12.6 per cent. This consistent increase in the agricultural output is attributed to the sustained efforts of the UAE's Government to promote agricultural development with generous agricultural incentives and subsidies. Changes in the contribution to GDP of the non-oil sector (agriculture), however, increased at moderate rate. In 1995, the agricultural sector comprised about 2 per cent of GDP.

The conspicuous sectoral shift and contribution to GDP is evident in the service sector: commerce (wholesale and retail trade), restaurants, hotels, transport, storage, communications, finance, insurance, real estates and government services. The service sector contribution to GDP increased from 22.3 per cent in 1975 to 37.4 per cent in 1995, the second important sector (after the oil sector) that comprises GDP.

Table 2. Relative importance of UAE's main economic sectors 1975-1995
(percentage of GDP)

Sector	1975	1980	1985	1995
Agriculture	0.7	0.9	1.5	2.0
Crude oil	67.7	56.4	44.0	41.1
Manufacturing	0.9	6.9	9.2	8.7
Electricity and water	0.5	1.3	2.2	2.1
Construction	9.0	8.3	8.8	8.4
Commerce, restaurants and hotels	9.3	9.0	8.8	10.1
Transport, storage and communications	3.0	3.4	3.8	5.5
Financing & insurance	1.6	3.5	5.1	4.3
Real estate	2.5	3.8	4.9	6.2
Government services	4.8	7.0	10.5	10.9

Source: MoP (Ministry of Planning, UAE), (1987), Economic and Social Indicators in the UAE, 1975-1985.
MoP (Ministry of Planning, UAE),(1993), Economic and Social Indicators in the UAE, 1985-1990.
MoP (Ministry of Planning, UAE), (1995), Annual Economic Report 1995.

Structural Change in the UAE's Employment Pattern

The service sector which includes trade, restaurants, hotels, transport, storage, communications, finance, insurance, real estate, business services, transport, storage, communication, and community, social and personal services ranks first in size of employment (62.4 per cent of the labour force), which reflects the powerful dominance of the service sector in the UAE. The share of employment in the service sector increased from 51.91 per cent in 1975, to 56.97 per cent in 1980, to 63.8 per cent in 1985, and to 62.4 per cent in 1995, corresponding to the increase in the sector's real output over the same period 1975-1995. The service sector value added comprised the second largest value added (after the oil sector) in the UAE's GDP in 1995.

The agricultural sector employed 7.1 per cent of the UAE labour force in 1995, fourth ranking sector in labour force distribution. Its employment share increased from 4.55 per cent in 1975 to 7.58 per cent in 1985, and to 7.7 per cent in 1995, corresponding to its steady increase of real output over the period (1975-1995).

Although the manufacturing sector accounts for a low proportion of employment (10.4 per cent of the labour force), its share of employment increased from 5.83 per cent in 1975 to 7.41 per cent in 1985, and to 10.4 per cent in 1995, matching its increase in real output for the same period (1975-1995).

In employing 1.4 per cent of the labour force, quarrying, petroleum extraction and mining sector was ranked last in share of employment despite its paramount importance in the UAE economy, reflecting the fact that the oil sector is highly capital-intensive.

Industrialization

In the process of economic development, industrialization has been considered as crucial to the transition. Industrialization is linked to the idea of stimulating forward and backward linkages with the rest of the economy. In addition, industrialization creates new employment opportunities. In common with other developing countries, the UAE, whose economy has been significantly dependent on the export of one primary product, namely oil, pursued the industrialization strategy to diversify the sources of its national income and reduce its dependence on oil.

The main factors which have acted as a constraint on the UAE industrial development are limited raw materials, and the size of the domestic market. On the other hand, the abundance of natural mineral resources, the ready availability of financial capital, a well-established infrastructure, a flexible labour and employment policy, the availability of cheap energy, industrial zones and various incentives in legislation, plus political and social stability have been the main resource and incentives for UAE industrialization.

From the UAE Industrial Survey of 1988 and 1992 (MoFI 1988, 1992), the pattern of industrial establishments can be summarized as follows:

- the first industrial establishment in the UAE, in the Emirate of Dubai, was a small workshop for steel boxes and containers, established in 1950.

- the period from 1951 to 1958 did not witness the establishment of any industrial firm.
- the increase in industrial establishments began in 1959, the period which coincides with the discovery of oil in the emirate of Abu Dhabi.
- the year 1977 was the golden year in UAE industrial development, in which 84 industrial establishments were recorded, the highest number of industrial establishments in a single year during the period 1950-1992.
- the number of industrial establishments grew at an increasing rate during the period 1959-1977;
- however, the growth in industrial establishments slowed down during the period 1978-1995.

To some extent industrialization in the UAE has broadened the base of the economy, increased industrial productivity, diversified exports to more than 184 exportable industrial products, increased the value of industrial exports from DH 11 million in 1975 to DH 539 million in 1980, DH 4825 million in 1985, and to DH 8070 million in 1990 (in constant prices). Nevertheless, industrialization in the UAE has not significantly reduced the economy's reliance on oil.

Human Development Indicators

The main human development indicators in the UAE can be analysed at two levels: a) nationally over time and b) internationally (or cross-sectionally), comparing performance with both developing and industrial countries. The first level, nationally over time, enables us to explore the rate, structure, and character of human development in the UAE. The latter, internationally, enables us to examine the degree of human development in the UAE compared to both developing and developed countries.

At the national level, the UAE has achieved impressive improvements in many human development indicators during the past two decades. At the international level, the UAE has recorded high levels of development bearing comparison with the average of the developing countries, and even with some individual industrial countries.

Educational Institutions

A positive relationship between education and economic growth is well-established. Education and training are viewed as major determinants of increasing productivity, and as a factor diffusing growth.

Education is considered a key element in developing the necessary skill levels for growth and modernization in the UAE. The UAE Government offers free education to all UAE citizens, and Arabic-speaking children of expatriates employed in the public sector.

Educational institutions in the UAE consist of public and private sector schools, military schools, and higher education and vocational training establishments. The existing educational structure was established in the early 1970s and consists of a four-tier system covering 14 years of education, as follows: kindergarten (for 4 to 5 years old); primary (6 to 11 years); intermediate (12-14 years); and secondary (15-17 years). For higher education (i.e. university,

Master, and Ph.D programmes) UAE citizens are entitled to choose between study in the Emirates University or abroad through a generous scholarship system. Primary school education is compulsory for all UAE citizens. Government policy is to provide staff/student ratios of 1:20 at kindergarten and primary levels and 1:15 at intermediate and secondary levels. The existing staff/student ratios are well within this proposed range. (The staff/student ratio of kindergarten and primary levels is 1:17; intermediate and secondary levels is 1:10.)

The Higher Colleges of Technology, located in several Emirates, were established in 1988 and are aimed at offering courses of three years' technical training in skills such as business administration, accounting, banking, information systems, computers, engineering, aviation technology, and health sciences.

Encouraged by financial incentives, government civil servants are required to attend yearly at least one seminar (at local or international level) within their respective fields as a condition for future promotion.

In his influential article, Schultz (1961) stressed the role of education in development. He maintained that education could be considered as a process of accumulating capital, which could increase a worker's productivity and income. He referred to this investment in education as an investment in 'human capital'. Human capital is defined as a productive investment embodied in human resources. Improved skills and health result from expenditures on education, training programmes, and medical care. As indicated by Chatterji (1994), the skill level of the workforce in any economy is a factor which has an important bearing on economic performance.

Carnoy (1967) concluded that education and income are highly correlated at both individual and social levels. People intuitively recognize this fact and consequently bid to grasp the largest possible amount of education. The more schooling and certificates people can accumulate, the better will be their chances of obtaining secure and better-paid jobs. This desire for well-paid jobs has created demand for education as a means of economic improvement.
On the supply side, a country's political institutions determine:

- the quantity of schools and classrooms at the primary, secondary, and university levels;
- who is admitted to these schools; and
- the kind of education and instructions (values, attitudes, ideas and aspiration) students acquire.

Current concern, however, centres upon how to improve the quality of education (teaching, facilities and curricula) and how to provide basic education to the vast majority of the population. Behrman and Birdsall (1983) indicate that it is the quality of education and not its quantity alone (years of schooling) that best explains differential earnings and productivity.

Health Services

Many developing countries struggle against malnutrition, disease and poor health. Expenditures on health have been regarded as investments in human capital (Mushkin 1962). Anand and Ravallion (1993) conclude that the quantitative effect of public expenditure in the area of health appears to be sizeable.

The relationship between health and economic development is reciprocal. Economic development policies tend to improve the health status of the population. Better health contributes to economic development. Better health is an important goal in its own right, and is a basic human need. Health increases human potential and improves the quality of human resources. Health programmes, therefore, aim to cut morbidity and mortality and to provide adequate nutrition, health care and sanitation.

The UNDP's (1995) Report has estimated that 99 per cent of the UAE overall population has access to health services (the percentage of the population that can reach appropriate local health services on foot or by the local means of transport in no more than one hour), 95 per cent of the population has access to safe water, and 77 per cent per cent of the population has access to sanitation (for the period 1985-1993).

The UAE Government's health policies aim at providing a range of facilities and at implementing programmes to advance the level of service and health education throughout the UAE. There are also preventative medical programmes such as 'mother and child health care', vaccination and inoculations for children, monitoring and notification of infectious diseases, and health education programmes.

In addition, the UAE Ministry of Health (MoH) provides special medical centres for school children, and health units in every school throughout the UAE. These health units are provided with qualified nurses as well as first-aid equipment. Hospitals, beds, doctors and nurses are located throughout the UAE mainly in accordance with the distribution of the population. Health facilities are in general evenly distributed.

There are also a large number of private health facilities. The private health sector makes a significant contribution to the provision of health facilities in all parts of the UAE. Its main contribution lies in the supply of materials, drugs and equipment to the Ministry of Health and private retail outlets. In addition there is a large number of private clinics, medical complexes, hospitals and pharmacies. The main noticeable growth in private sector health services has been in the number of general clinics. As is shown in Table 3, the number of private clinics not only has exceeded the number of public clinics, but has been increasing from 50 in 1975 to 174 in 1980, to 456 in 1985, to 675 in 1990, and to 752 in 1994.

The number of hospitals (public and private) increased from 19 in 1975 to 42 in 1990, and to 50 in 1994. This increase in hospitals has been associated with increases in hospital beds. In 1975, for example, there were 1745 hospital beds; by 1994 hospital bed numbers had increased to more than 6365 beds.

Numbers of doctors (general physicians) increased from 751 in 1975 to 3469 in 1994. Dentists increased from 65 in 1975 to 569 in 1994. Nurses increased from 1555 in 1975 to 7547 in 1994. According to the Human Development Report 1995, there is one doctor per 1042 persons and a nurse per 568 persons (1988-1991).

In short, advanced health care has done much to lower mortality levels in the UAE and as a result mortality rates have declined substantially. The crude death rate, deaths per thousand of the population, decreased from 7.3 per 1000 in 1975 to 4 per 1000 in 1992, and to 2.06 per 1000 in 1994. Infant mortality rate (i.e. the number of children who die before their first birthday out of every 1000 live births) has fallen in the UAE from 145 per 1000 in 1960 to 65 per 1000 in 1975, to 54 per 1000 in 1980, to 19 per 1000 in 1992, and to 9.44 per 1000 in 1994. On the other hand, life expectancy at birth, the average number of years members of a given population are expected to live, has risen in the UAE from 53 years in 1960 to 65 years in 1975, and to 73.8 years in 1992.

Table 3. Health services in the UAE (1975-1994).

Indicators	1975	1980	1985	1990	1994
Hospitals	19	27	40	42	50
Beds (hospital)	1745	3872	5817	6297	6365
General physicians	751	1484	2361	2991	3469
Dentists	65	141	259	383	569
Nurses	1555	4346	6327	7130	7547
Pharmacists (public)	60	117	190	237	351
Public clinics	38	69	107	118	126
Private clinics	50	174	456	675	752
Population/bed	320	269	237	288	513
Population/doctor	743	702	1004	1236	1212
Population/nurse	359	240	339	438	451

Sources: MoP (Ministry of Planning, UAE), (1987), Economic and Social Indicators in the UAE, 1975-1985.
MoP (Ministry of Planning, UAE), (1993), Economic and Social Indicators in the UAE, 1985-1990.
MoH (Ministry of Health, UAE), (1994), Statistical Yearbook
UNDP (United Nations Development Program), (1995), Human Development Report 1995.

It can be argued that the UAE has high health standards compared with other developing countries and even with some developed countries (see Table 4). Measures of malnutrition, mortality and morbidity show impressive improvement in the last two decades. Epidemics have been eliminated and diseases have declined as a cause of death. Both crude and infant death rates have fallen, and life expectancy has risen to 73.8 years in 1992. Credit for continued improvement since the formation of the UAE in 1971 belongs primarily to the UAE Federal Government, which has consistently accorded a high priority to improving the health of its population.

Table 4. International human development comparisons 1992

Indicator	UAE	All Dev. Countries	All Indust. Countries
		(average)	(average)
Real GDP per capita ($)	21,830	2,591	15,291
Human Development Index (HDI)	0.861	0.570	0.916
Life Expectancy (years)	73.8	61.5	76.1
Maternal mortality rate (per 100,000 live births)	130	351	10
Infant mortality rate (per 1,000 live births)	19	70	13
Adult Literacy (%)	77.7	68.3	98.3
Population with access to health services (%)	99	79	---
Daily calorie supply (as % of requirements)	151	109	---

Source: UNDP, Human Development Report, 1995.
---not provided.

Conclusion

The UAE is a very wealthy country, due to the modest population base and its huge oil resources. The major surpluses achieved have enabled the UAE to accumulate a sizeable current account balance, held mainly by the governments of the individual emirates and partly by other private establishments.

Progress in social and economic development has been favourable to date. The successful implementation of human development policy in the UAE, hand in hand with industrialization, urbanization, and modernization, is one of the rare examples of a country which has been harnessing income from its huge natural resources for long-term development within a very short period (from the early 1970s to mid-1990s).

In conclusion, the UAE has achieved impressive improvements in many social and economic development indicators during the past two decades. Furthermore, this chapter emphasizes the high levels of human development in UAE, together with a relatively good record on human rights. But these are goals which must still be borne in mind in attempts to sustain development.

Bibliography

Anand, S. and Ravallion, M. 'Human Development in Poor Countries: On the Role of Private Incomes and Public Services', *Journal of Economic Perspectives*, Vol.7, No.1,(Winter 1993) pp133-150.

Behrman, J. and Birdsall, S. 'The Quality of Schooling: Quantity Alone is Misleading', *American Economic Review*, Vol.73 (1983).

Carnoy, M. 'Rate of Return to Schooling in Latin America', *Journal of Human Resources* (1967).

Chatterji, M. Training Subsidies, Technical Progress and Economic Growth, Paper Presented to the ESRC Development Economics Workshop on Endogenous Growth, University of Leicester, 25-26 March, 1994.

Clark, C. 'Development Economics: The Early Years', in G.M. Meier and Dudley Seers (eds), *Pioneers in Development*, (1984) New York: Oxford University Press.

EIU (1994), *Country Report: United Arab Emirates*, 3rd Quarter, London: The Economist Intelligence Unit.

MoFI (Ministry of Finance and Industry, UAE), Industrial Directory 1988.

MoFI (Ministry of Finance and Industry, UAE), Industrial Directory 1992.

MoP (Ministry of Planning, UAE), Economic and Social Indicators in the UAE, 1975-1985 (1987).

MoP (Ministry of Planning, UAE), Economic and Social Indicators in the UAE, 1985-1990 (1993).

Mushkin, S. 'Health as an Investment', *Journal of Political Economy*, Vol. 70, pp.129-157 (1962).

Schultz, T.W. 'Investment in Human Capital', American Economic Review, Vol.51 (1961), pp 1-17.

UNDP (United Nations Development Program), (1995), Human Development Report 1995, Oxford University Press.

Author Profiles

Clovis Maksoud is Professor of International Law and Organization and Founder-Director of the Center for the Global South at the American University in Washington DC. He served as the Arab League Ambassador to India, to the US and to the UN from 1979 to 1990. Dr Maksoud is the author of several books and articles on the Middle East, the United Nations, and International Law.

Edmund Ghareeb is an adjunct professor of Middle Eastern history at George Washington University. A specialist on Media Issues and Middle Eastern affairs, he received a Ph.D in modern Middle Eastern and North African history from Georgetown University. Dr Ghareeb has taught Middle Eastern history, politics and international relations at a number of universities, including the University of Virginia, American University, and McGill University. The author of a number of books including *Split Vision: The Portrayal of Arabs in the US. Media,* Dr Ghareeb is a leading expert on the Kurds, Iraq and the Gulf region. His works in the area include *The Kurdish Question; The Kurdish Nationalist Movement,* and the forthcoming *Iraq: A Historical Dictionary.* He has also lectured on US policy towards the Middle East and US-Gulf relations in the US, Europe and the Middle East. He is a former journalist and he has been widely interviewed by Arab, American and European TV, radio and newspapers including NPR, ABC, CNN, BBC World Service TV and Radio, BBC Arab TV and Radio, and CBC. He has published over a hundred articles, interviews and book reviews. Dr Ghareeb is an information advisor to the UAE embassy in Washington, DC.

K. W. Glennie was educated at Edinburgh University (B. Sc, 1953; D. Sc, 1984) and spent over 32 years working as an exploration geologist for Shell in New Zealand, Canada, Nepal, India, the Middle East, London and The Hague. His main research interests comprise desert geology (present and past), geology of the Oman Mountains, and geology of the North Sea. Since his 'retirement' in 1987, he has continued to be active in these areas, including organizing an annual course in London on the Petroleum Geology of the North Sea. He was co-convener of an international conference held in Al-Ain, UAE, in December 1995 on Quaternary Deserts and Climatic Change, and also led pre- and post-conference field trips in the Emirates and Oman. He is an honorary professor in geology at the University of Aberdeen, and member of the geological societies of London, Edinburgh, Aberdeen, The Netherlands, and American Assoc. Petroleum Geologists. Glennie is on the editorial board of Sedimentary Geology, Journal of Petroleum Geology & First Break and is author of over 30 scientific papers and sole author or contributor and editor of five books, including *Desert Sedimentary Environments* (1970), *Geology of the Oman Mountains* (1970; simple updated version 1995) and *Introduction to the Petroleum Geology of the North Sea* (3 editions: 1984, 1986, 1990).

D.T. Potts is Edwin Cuthbert Hall Professor of Middle Eastern Archaeology (1991-) at the University of Sydney, Sydney, Australia. Born in New York in 1953, he was educated at Harvard (A.B. 1975, Ph. D 1980). A Fellow of the Society of Antiquaries (London) and of the Australian Academy of the Humanities (Canberra), he taught previously at the Free University of Berlin, Germany (1981-86) and the University of Copenhagen, Denmark (1980-81, 1986-91). His fieldwork experience in the Near East includes excavations in Iran, Saudi Arabia, Turkey and the United Arab Emirates, where he has excavated at ed-Dur, Tell Abraq, Jabal al-Emalah, Al Sufouh and most recently Awhala. He is the founder-editor of the international journal *Arabian Archaeology & Epigraphy*. In addition to writing many articles and several monographs on his excavations at Tell Abraq in the UAE, he is the author of *The Arabian Gulf in Antiquity* and *Mesopotamian Civilization*: *The Material Foundations*. He is currently working on a book on Elam, the ancient state which occupied much of what is today southwestern Iran.

G.R.D. King is presently Senior Lecturer at the Department of Art and Archaeology, School of Oriental and African Studies (SOAS), University of London. He was previously Assistant Lecturer in Islamic Art at the Centre for Arabic Studies, American University in Cairo (1977-80); Associate Professor in Islamic Archaeology, Department of Archaeology and Museology, King Saud University, Riyadh (1980-87); Research Fellow, Classics Department, King's College London (1988-89). King has carried out archaeological surveys and other field work in Jordan, Syria, Saudi Arabia and Yemen and was Director of the British team engaged in the international excavation at the Islamic port site of Julfar, Ras al-Khaimah, UAE (1989-1992). He is presently Director of the Abu Dhabi Islands Archaeological Survey (ADIAS) (1992-1997, continuing). ADIAS was appointed by H.H. President Sheikh Zayed bin Sultan Al Nahyan to survey and excavate archaeological sites on the western coasts and offshore islands of Abu Dhabi emirate. ADIAS is based at Abu Dhabi under the patronage of H.H. Lieut. General Sheikh Muhammad bin Zayed Al Nahyan.

Frauke Heard-Bey studied History and Political Science in Heidelberg and Berlin, obtaining her Ph.D from the *'Frei Universitat'* in Berlin in 1967. Her thesis on the political changes in the capital Berlin between 1912 and 1920 was published in Stuttgart. She married her British husband in 1967 and followed him to Abu Dhabi, where he pursued a career with an oil company. In 1969 the author joined the recently established Centre for Documentation and Research in Abu Dhabi, which is dedicated to the collection of archive material from all over the world pertaining to the Gulf and the adjacent regions. Frauke Heard-Bey has published in English, German, French and Arabic in leading journals and handbooks for historical, sociological and Middle Eastern studies, participated in conferences and seminars; and she has been a member of the IISS since 1973. A second edition of her book *From Trucial States to United Arab Emirates. A Society in Transition*, which was first published in 1982 was issued in autumn 1996.

Ibrahim Al Abed has served as an Adviser at the Ministry of Information and Culture of the United Arab Emirates since 1975 and has been the Director of that Ministry's External Affairs Department since 1990. A holder of two degrees from the American University of Beirut, he is an expert on UAE government administration, and international affairs. Well versed in the history of the region's development he has been a member of the UAE team at all Conferences of the

Gulf Ministers of Information since 1976 and of all Conferences of the GCC Ministers of Information. A Board Member of the Gulf News Agency he has considerable experience of media development, both in the UAE and within the region as a whole. In this regard he has served as Chairman of the Group of Experts on Information in the OPEC Countries and has lectured on Media Affairs at the UAE University. He is author of 12 books on the Arab-Israeli conflict and of a number of papers and articles dealing with the political development of the United Arab Emirates.

Malcolm C. Peck is a programme officer at Meridian International Centre in Washington, DC where he arranges professional study tours for international visitors sponsored by the US Information Agency. Previously he was director of programmes at the Middle East Institute in Washington and Arabian Peninsula Affairs analyst at the US Department of State. He is the author of *The United Arab Emirates: A Venture in Unity* (1986) and *A Historical Dictionary of the Gulf Arab States* (to be published in autumn 1996). He has written chapters for several books on Middle Eastern subjects and has contributed entries to *The World Book Encyclopedia*, *Microsoft Encarta Encyclopedia*, and *The Encyclopedia of the Modern Middle East* . Peck holds A. B and A. M degrees, the latter in Middle Eastern studies, from Harvard University. At the Fletcher School of Law and Diplomacy he earned M. A, MALD, and Ph. D degrees in international affairs.

Mohamed Abdulla Al Roken, a UAE national and graduate of Al-Ain University, received his LL.M and Ph.D in Constitutional Law from the University of Warwick, Coventry, England in 1992. Al Roken is a lecturer of law at UAE University, Al-Ain, and has been appointed as Assistant Dean of the Faculty of Sharia Law. He is admitted as advocate and legal consultant at all levels of local and federal courts in the UAE and is also the Vice-Chairman of the UAE Jurist Association.

William A. Rugh holds a Ph.D in political science from Columbia University, and he has taught as an adjunct professor at the Fletcher School of Law and Diplomacy of Tufts University (1987-89). He is the author of the book *The Arab Press: News Media and Political Process in the Arab World (1979 and 1987)*, and several journal articles on Middle Eastern subjects. He was a United States foreign service officer for 30 years, serving tours in Washington and in Beirut, Cairo, Jidda, Riyadh, Damascus, Sanaa and Abu Dhabi. In Sanaa he was the American ambassador to Yemen (1984-87) and in Abu Dhabi he was the American ambassador to the United Arab Emirates (1992-95). Since 1995 he has been President and CEO of America-Mideast Educational and Training Services, Inc. (AMIDEAST), a non-profit organization with headquarters in Washington DC and offices in 11 Arab countries, which promotes understanding between Americans and peoples of the Middle East and North Africa through education and training

Muhammad Jenab Tutunji was born in Amman, Jordan in 1942. He received a B.A in 1965 from Franklin & Marshall College in Pennsylvania, an M.A in philosophy from the American University in Beirut in 1968, and a Ph.D in political science from George Washington University in January 1995. He was Assistant Editor of the Journal of Palestine Studies from 1975-76, Managing Editor of the Jordan Times 1977-80, and is currently an adjunct professor of political science at George Washington University.

Ali Tawfik Al Sadik, joined the Arab Monetary Fund as Senior Economist in 1979 and since June 1989 has been Chief of the Analysis and Economic Policies Division of its Economic Policy Institute in Abu Dhabi. Al Sadik has also held the post of Chief Economist of the Organization of Arab Petroleum and Exporting Countries (OAPEC) and Visiting Assistant Professor, Economics Department, North Carolina State University, Raleigh, USA. He holds B.Sc. and M.Sc. degrees from the American University of Beirut and a Ph.D from North Carolina State University, Raleigh. He is the author of over 25 papers on energy, economic development, finance and economic management, as well as *Arab Economic Integration*, (1995) and *Privatization in the Arab Countries*, (co-editor) (1995).

P. M.L. Barnes has had extensive practical experience in the international energy business. After a long and varied career with a major international oil company, he is now a Research Fellow at the Oxford Institute for Energy Studies. He also acts as a consultant to a number of organizations and governments on a variety of energy planning, investment and organizational matters. His recent publications include: 'Indonesia: The Political Economy of Oil', 'The Review of Long Term Energy Supplies', 'Energy Demand in Developing Countries' and 'The Oil Mountain', as well as articles on a range of energy related matters.

Mouza Ghubash is a UAE national who received her education in the UAE, Kuwait (B.A 1977) and Cairo (M.A 1983; Ph.D 1987). She has been Assistant Professor at the Department of Sociology, UAE University since 1987 and is Head of Ousha Bint Hussain Cultural Rewaq, a charitable organization which was founded in 1993. Ghubash was chairperson and founding member of the Sociological Association Sharjah, a founding member of the consultative board of the Social Affairs journal issued by the Sociological Association, and headed the committee for hosting Kuwaiti families who fled to the UAE in the wake of the Iraqi invasion in 1990. She is also a member of the Arab Sociologists Board and a member of the International Society of Sociologists. Dr Ghubash has published a number of papers, reports and books on social affairs in the UAE, including a series of reports on the UAE for the United Nations Development Programme (UNDP).

Mohamed Abdulsalam Shihab, a UAE national, is Economic Consultant at the Department of Planning, Abu Dhabi. He was educated at Cairo University, Egypt (B.Sc), University of Arizona, USA (M.Sc) and University of Salford, England (Ph. D.) and was awarded the Rashid Prize for Academic Excellence, the highest academic prize for academic excellence in the UAE for his research 'Industrial Development in the United Arab Emirates'. Dr Shihab was a tutor in the Department of Economics at the University of Salford, a Project Coordinator for the Abu Dhabi Comprehensive Development Plan, and has been enrolled in the Roster of Experts for short time assignments, United Nations Industrial Development Organization, Vienna, Austria since February 1990.

Index

A

'arish, 59, 79, 87

Abbasid, 75, 80, 82, 87-89

Abd , 77-78, 83-87

Abd Al Malik, 86

Abd Al Qays, 77, 85

Abdul Aziz Al Saud, 104

Abi'el, 65

Abu Bakr, 67, 83-85, 88

Abu Dhabi, 4, 9-10, 12 13, 15, 18-19, 25, 27-30, 33-34, 40, 43, 48, 67-68, 70-71, 73-77, 79-81, 86, 91-94, 97-99, 101-102, 104-106, 108-111, 113-115, 121, 123-136, 140, 154-156, 158, 161, 163-164, 166, 170, 172-173, 175, 184, 188, 192, 194, 205-207, 211, 221, 224, 235-238, 240-242, 244-246, 248-249, 251-253, 255-256, 258, 261-262, 267, 271, 274, 285, 296, 302-304

Abu Dhabi Company for Onshore Operations (ADCO), 236-238, 251, 243

Abu Dhabi Development Fund (also Abu Dhabi Fund for Arab Economic Development), 124, 127

Abu Dhabi Gas Industries(GASCO), 245

Abu Dhabi Gas Liquefaction Company (ADGAS), 245-246

Abu Dhabi Investment Authority, 224

Abu Dhabi Marine Areas Operating Company (ADMA-OPCO), 235, 237-238, 242, 251

Abu Dhabi National Oil Company (ADNOC), 236-238, 242, 245, 248-249, 251, 253

Abu Dhabi Petroleum Company (ADPC), 235-236

Abu'l-Faraj Qudama, 76

Abu Musa, 13, 16, 111, 125, 133, 135, 139-148, 150, 152-158, 168-170, 176, 186, 188-190, 202

Abu Odeh, 192-193, 203

Abu Tahir, 89

Abu Zayd Al Ansari, 67, 83

Achaemenid, 57-58, 68

Aden, 12, 125-127

Adjusted Gross Domestic Product (AGDP, see also GDP), 210, 215-216, 226, 230

Adnan Abu Odeh, 203

Adud Al Dawla, 89

Adult Education Centres, 279

Affinity Relationship, 274

Afghanistan, 21, 51, 95, 161, 177

aflaj, 57, 265, 271

Arab Gulf Cooperation Council (see also GCC), 233, 280, 282

agriculture, 12, 16, 36-37, 69, 105, 205, 209-211, 229, 231, 259, 266-268, 290, 292, 294

Ahl 'Ali, 254

Ahmed bin Lootah, 289

Ajman, 12, 48, 70-71, 76-77, 80, 91, 99, 102, 104, 110, 115, 122, 127, 131, 205-206, 235-236, 239, 247, 267, 271, 276-277

Ajman Television, 122

Akkadian, 48, 50, 68

Al Baladhuri, 84, 93

Al Bu Falah, 259, 265

Al Bu Falasah, 129

Al Bu Shamis, 256, 271

Al Dhafrah, 259

Al Dhahiri, 255

Al Hajjaj b. Yusuf Al Thaqifi, 86-87

Al Hamdani, 87, 89, 94

Al Hamili, 255

Al-Hasa, 96

Al Idrisi, 76-77, 86, 90, 94

Al Julanda (see alsoJulanda), 67, 78, 83-86

Al Kalbi, 78, 94

Al Maktoum, 100-101, 106, 124, 128

Al Maqdisi, 75-76, 94

B

Berlin Convention, 144

Berne Convention for the Protection of Literary and Artistic Works, 199

Bet Mazunaye, 82

Bet Qatraye, 82

Beydoun, 18, 21, 35

bidar, 264

Bidya (see also al-Biddya), 47-48, 52, 55, 68

bisht, 260

Bithna, 53

Black Stone, 88

Bombay, 103, 155, 157, 263

Bosnia, 161, 172, 177-178

Bosnia-Hercegovina (see also Hercegovina), 186

Boutros Boutros Ghali, 188

Bowling Association, 283

Brent crude oil, 249

Britain, 12, 95-106, 110-111, 124, 126, 141-142, 145-147, 150, 152, 154, 164, 168, 172-173, 175, 188

British Petroleum (BP) 18-19, 21, 24, 26-27, 29, 31-32, 98, 234-240, 245, 247, 253

British Political Resident, 95, 98, 142, 234

bronze, 54, 57, 59, 65, 71

Bu Hasa, 43, 235, 241-242, 245

buffalo, 26

buffware, 50

Buhays, 43-44, 53, 57-58, 60

Bukha, 247

bulls, 75, 266-267

Buraimi (see also al-Buraimi), 67, 69, 86, 164, 257, 264-265

burr, 268

Bush, George 173

Bushir, 86

Bushire, 95-98

bustard, 271

Buttes Gas and Oil Company, 143

Buwayhid, 89

Byzantine, 77-78

C

Cairo, 137, 156-158, 175, 191-192, 302-304

Caliphate, 86-89, 139

Caliphs, 15, 82-89, 86-87

Caltex, 239

camel racing, 270, 283

camels, 29, 86, 211, 259-260, 262-263, 265-266, 272

Camelus dromedarius, 38, 52

Canada, 193, 226, 248, 301

Carmania, 62

carnelian, 51

cattle, 38, 44, 47, 52, 56, 75, 266

Cedigaz, 244, 253

cement, 13, 106, 211, 247, 292

Cenozoic, 24-25

Central America, 192

Central Bank (UAE), 211, 225, 228, 232

CEPSA (of Spain), 238

ceramics, 46, 48, 52, 56-57, 59, 62, 66, 69-70, 72, 79-80, 90, 92-93

cereals, 47

Characene, 62, 64, 72

Chelb (Kalba), 77

Cherizan (Khawr Qirqishan), 77

Chess Federation, 283

China, 67, 78, 90, 93, 177-179, 197, 199, 267

Chorf (Khor Fakkan), 77

Christianity, 66-68, 78, 81-82, 162

cinematographic, 200

Climate, 10, 17, 26, 30-32, 35-36, 40, 59, 66, 221, 267, 270, 292

Climatic Optimum, 27, 32, 43-44

Clinton, Bill 192

Committee on the Exercise of the Inalienable Rights of the Palestinian People, 182, 204

communications, 10-13, 84, 88, 96-98 119, 121, 123-124, 134, 175, 200, 210, 268, 276, 293-295

community associations, 284

Conoco, 236, 238

Constantinople, 77

Constitution, 13, 15, 102, 109-122, 127, 129-134, 148, 156-157, 161, 237

copper, 37, 46, 55, 61, 71, 271

Copyright Law, 200-203

Council of Ministers, 113-117, 119, 130, 133, 189, 211

Courts of First Instance, 131

Crescent Petroleum Company (CPC), 236, 239

Cretaceous, 19-20, 22-24, 33, 35

crocodile, 26

Crush Zone, 25

fasht, 262

Fateh, 236, 241-242, 246

Federal Assembly, 102

Federal Government, 14, 110, 116, 118, 129, 131-133, 136, 211, 220, 239, 299

Federal National Counci (FNC), 110, 113-117, 122, 129, 131, 133-134

Federal Supreme Council (FSC), Supreme Council, 107-110, 112-118, 120-122, 124, 129-131, 133, 148, 161, 178, 185-187, 190, 197, 204

figs, 28, 45, 57, 64-66, 213, 265

First World War, 15, 95-96, 234

fishing, 12, 28, 37, 44, 70, 83, 95, 205, 211, 231, 257, 261, 266-269, 290, 292

Flandrian Transgression, 40

Foreign Office, 97, 126, 147

foreign trade, 16, 211, 293

forestry, 292

France, 12, 45, 59, 69, 79-80, 90, 94, 105, 173, 175, 179, 193, 246, 302

Free Trade Zone, 246

Fujairah, 12, 46, 53, 57, 66-69, 71, 74-75, 79, 91-92, 94, 96, 99, 102, 104, 110, 115, 127, 131-134, 205-206, 235, 239, 248, 267, 271

Fujairah Museum, 53, 57

G

Gaz de France, 246

gazelle, 37-38, 56

General Agreement on Tariffs, Trade and Services (GATS), 198, 201

General Agreement on Tariffs and Trade (GATT), 196-199, 202, 251

General Union of Popular Sports, 283

Generalized System of Preferences and the Lome Convention, 197

Geneva Convention for the Protection of Civilian Persons in Time of War, 182

Germany, 73, 95, 128, 147, 181, 238, 302

Ghagha', 76, 80, 93

Ghalilah, 52

Ghallah, 66

Ghanadha, 48, 68

ghaus, 263

ghayl, 266

glaciation, 15, 30-31, 33, 43

Goa, 90

goats, 29, 38, 44, 52, 56, 266, 268-269

Godin Tepe, 57

Golden Valley Ochre and Oxide Company, 143

Gondwana, 19, 21, 23, 33

grapes, 265

Greek, 58-59, 65, 71

Greenland, 26

Gross Domestic Product (GDP), 16, 197, 175, 205-210, 212-221, 225-227, 229-231, 233-234, 250, 273, 292-295, 299

Gulf Cooperation Council (GCC, see also Arab Gulf Cooperation Council AGCC), 14, 16, 164-165, 167-171, 175-178, 181, 184-187, 188, 190,-191, 193-198, 201, 203, 222, 251, 280, 291, 303

Gulf crisis, 162-163, 168, 170-171

Gulf of Oman, 17, 134, 140, 272

Gulf of Sidra, 183

gypsum, 19, 28-29, 32-34, 48, 64, 292

H

Hadramawt, 84

Hafez Ghanem, 151

Hafit, 25, 30, 45-46, 49, 53, 71

Hagil Window, 25, 34

Hague (The), 155, 301

Hajar, 20-21, 75-76, 84, 258-259, 265-266

Haji Abdulrahman, 141

halite, 18, 27-28, 32-33

Hameem, 30

Handball Federation, 283

handicrafts, 200

Harappan, 48, 51

Harter, 80, 94

Hasaitic, 60

Hashemites, 190

Hashimi Rafsanjani, 154

Hassan Al Alkim, 154, 156

Hatta, 48

Hawasina, 20, 22-25, 32-34

hawd, 261

hawsh, 268

Hebron, 183

I

J

N

R

S

application of the duty of loyalty — the corporate opportunity doctrine. Thus, while courts will require a director or officer to automatically account to the corporation for diversion of a corporate opportunity to personal use, they will first inquire to see whether there was a possibility of a loss to the corporation — *i.e.*, whether the corporation was in a position to potentially avail itself of the opportunity — before deciding that a corporate opportunity in fact existed. Similarly, when scrutinizing transactions between a director or officer and the corporation under the light of the duty of loyalty, most courts now inquire as to whether there was any injury to the corporation, *i.e.*, whether the transaction was fair and in good faith, before permitting the latter to avoid the transaction. An analogous question might be posed with respect to the *Diamond* court's unjust enrichment analysis: is it proper to conclude that an insider has been unjustly enriched *vis-á-vis* the corporation (as compared to other traders in the market) when there is no way that the corporation could have used the information to its own profit, just because the insider's trading was made possible by virtue of his corporate position?

Not all information generated in the course of carrying on a business fits snugly into the corporate asset mold. Information in the form of trade secrets, customer lists, etc., can easily be categorized as a valuable or potentially valuable corporate "possession," in that it can be directly used by the corporation to its own economic advantage. However, most information involved in insider trading is not of this ilk, *e.g.*, knowledge of an impending merger, a decline in earnings, etc. If the corporation were to attempt to exploit such non-public information by dealing in its own securities, it would open itself up to potential liability under federal and state securities laws, just as do the insiders when they engage in insider trading. This is not to say that the corporation does not have any interests with regard to such information. It may have an interest in either preventing the information from becoming public or in regulating the timing of disclosure. However, insider trading does not entail the disclosure of inside information, but rather its use in a manner in which the corporation itself is prohibited from exploiting it.

... It must be conceded that the unfairness that is the basis of the widespread disapproval of insider trading is borne primarily by participants in the securities markets, rather than by the corporation itself. By comparison, the harm to corporate goodwill posited by the *Diamond* court pales in significance. At this point, the existence of such an indirect injury must be considered speculative, as there is no actual evidence of such a reaction. Furthermore, it is less than clear to us that the nature of this harm would form an adequate basis for an action for an accounting based on a breach of the insiders' duty of loyalty, as opposed to an action for damages based on a breach of the duty of care. The injury hypothesized by the *Diamond* court seems little different from the harm to the corporation that might be inferred whenever a responsible corporate official commits an illegal or unethical act using a corporate asset. Absent is the element of loss of opportunity or potential susceptibility to outside influence that generally is present when a corporate fiduciary is required to account to the corporation....

A second problem presented by the recognition of a cause of action in favor of the corporation is that of potential double liability. The *Diamond* court thought that this problem would seldom arise, since it thought it unlikely that a damage suit would be brought by investors where the insiders traded on impersonal exchanges. The court further reasoned that:

> ... A defendant's course, if he wishes to protect himself against double liability, is to interplead any and all possible claimants and bind them to the judgment (CPLR 1006, subd. [b])....

Since the *Diamond* court's action was motivated in large part by its perception of the inadequacy of existing remedies for insider trading, it is noteworthy that over the decade since *Diamond* was decided, the 10b-5 class action has made substantial advances toward becoming the kind of effective remedy for insider trading that the court of appeals hoped that it might become. Most importantly, recovery of damages from insiders has been allowed by, or on the behalf of, market investors even when the insiders dealt only through impersonal stock exchanges, although this is not yet a well-settled area of the law. In spite of other recent developments indicating that such class actions will not become as easy to maintain as some plaintiffs had perhaps hoped, it is clear that the remedies for insider trading under the federal securities laws now constitute a more effective deterrent than they did when *Diamond* was decided.

[H]aving carefully examined the decision of the New York Court of Appeals in *Diamond*, we are of the opinion that although the court sought to ground its ruling in accepted principles of corporate common law, that decision can best be understood as an example of judicial securities regulation. Although the question is a close one, we believe that were the issue to be presented to the Indiana courts at the present time, they would most likely join the Florida Supreme Court in refusing to adopt the New York court's innovative ruling....

Section II
General Federal Securities Fraud Law

Rule 10b-5 was passed in the early 1940s in response to an enforcement need of the Securities and Exchange Commission. Section 17(a) of the Securities Act of 1933 prohibited a variety of fraudulent conduct in connection with the sale of securities, but neither this nor any other provision prohibited fraudulent acts in connection with the purchase of securities. The SEC plugged this hole by rewriting § 17(a) and adopting it as a rule under § 10(b) of the Securities Exchange Act of 1934. Here is the text of the rule:

> It shall be unlawful for any person, directly or indirectly, by the use of any means or instrumentality of interstate commerce, or of the mails, or of any facility of any national securities exchange,
>
> (a) to employ any device, scheme, or artifice to defraud,

(b) to make any untrue statement of a material fact or to omit to state a material fact necessary in order to make the statements made, in the light of the circumstances under which they were made, not misleading, or

(c) to engage in any act, practice, or course of business which operates or would operate as a fraud or deceit upon any person, in connection with the purchase or sale of any security.

The enforcement need that triggered the passage of Rule 10b-5 was one involving insider trading, and the regulation of insider trading has been the main thrust of the rule all along. But not its only thrust. The rule has been pressed into service to cover various kinds of "fraud" somehow connected to the buying or selling of securities. Most, but not all, of the uses of the rule will show up in the cases that follow. Left for a course in securities regulation are examples of its use against market manipulation (basically artificially influencing the market price of a security) and various misdeeds by securities professionals, such as "churning" (buying and selling securities for a customer's account, over which a securities firm has discretionary authority, for the purpose of generating commissions).

As is apparent from its language ("It shall be unlawful...."), Rule 10b-5 is a criminal provision. Section 32 of the Exchange Act provides that a willful violation of such a rule is a felony. Criminal actions may be brought only by the Justice Department, not by the SEC. Under authority of §§ 21 and 21A of the Exchange Act, however, the SEC does have power to bring actions in court seeking injunctions against violations of the Act and its rules and requesting the court to impose civil penalties. Exchange Act §§ 21B and 21C give the SEC power to impose civil penalties in administrative actions heard in its quasi-judicial capacity and to issue its own cease-and-desist orders. In addition, Exchange Act §§ 20, 20A, and 20D cover the liability of controlling persons, of aiders and abettors, and of certain inside traders, and also provide for limitations on damages and proportionate liability. Also, courts have long held that an implied private right of action exists under Rule 10b-5, though the exact scope of that right remains contested.

This section presents Criminal Federal Securities fraud case, emphasizing basic issues in these cases. The next section illustrates how those principles apply to federal insider trading cases.

A. Materiality; Reliance

Halliburton Co. v. Erica P. John Fund, Inc.

United States Supreme Court
134 S. Ct. 2398 (2014)

CHIEF JUSTICE ROBERTS delivered the opinion of the Court.

Investors can recover damages in a private securities fraud action only if they prove that they relied on the defendant's misrepresentation in deciding to buy or sell a company's stock. In *Basic Inc. v. Levinson*, 485 U.S. 224 (1988), we held that investors could satisfy this reliance requirement by invoking a presumption that the price of stock traded in an efficient market reflects all public, material information — including material misstatements. In such a case, we concluded, anyone who buys or sells the stock at the market price may be considered to have relied on those misstatements.

We also held, however, that a defendant could rebut this presumption in a number of ways, including by showing that the alleged misrepresentation did not actually affect the stock's price — that is, that the misrepresentation had no "price impact." The questions presented are whether we should overrule or modify *Basic*'s presumption of reliance and, if not, whether defendants should nonetheless be afforded an opportunity in securities class action cases to rebut the presumption at the class certification stage, by showing a lack of price impact.

I

Respondent Erica P. John Fund, Inc. (EPJ Fund) is the lead plaintiff in a putative class action against Halliburton alleging violations of section 10(b) of the Securities Exchange Act of 1934, and Rule 10b-5. According to EPJ Fund, between June 3, 1999, and December 7, 2001, Halliburton made a series of misrepresentations regarding its potential liability in asbestos litigation, its expected revenue from certain construction contracts, and the anticipated benefits of its merger with another company — all in an attempt to inflate the price of its stock. Halliburton subsequently made a number of corrective disclosures, which, EPJ Fund contends, caused the company's stock price to drop and investors to lose money. EPJ Fund moved to certify a class comprising all investors who purchased Halliburton common stock during the class period. The District Court found that the proposed class satisfied all the threshold requirements of Federal Rule of Civil Procedure 23(a): It was sufficiently numerous, there were common questions of law or fact, the representative parties' claims were typical of the class claims, and the representatives could fairly and adequately protect the interests of the class. And except for one difficulty, the court would have also concluded that the class satisfied the requirement of Rule 23(b)(3) that "the questions of law or fact common to class members predominate over any questions affecting only individual members." The difficulty was that Circuit precedent required securities fraud plaintiffs to prove "loss causation" — a causal connection between the defendants' alleged misrepresentations and the plaintiffs' economic losses — in order to invoke *Basic*'s presumption of reliance and obtain class certification. EPJ Fund had not demonstrated such a connection for any of Halliburton's alleged misrepresentations, the District Court refused to certify the proposed class. The United States Court of Appeals for the Fifth Circuit affirmed the denial of class certification on the same ground.

We granted certiorari and vacated the judgment, finding nothing in "*Basic* or its logic" to justify the Fifth Circuit's requirement that securities fraud plaintiffs prove loss causation at the class certification stage in order to invoke *Basic*'s presumption of reliance. "Loss causation," we explained, "addresses a matter different from whether an investor relied on a misrepresentation, presumptively or otherwise, when buying or selling a stock." We remanded the case for the lower courts to consider "any further arguments against class certification" that Halliburton had preserved.

On remand, Halliburton argued that class certification was inappropriate because the evidence it had earlier introduced to disprove loss causation also showed that none of its alleged misrepresentations had actually affected its stock price. By demonstrating the absence of any "price impact," Halliburton contended, it had rebutted *Basic's* presumption that the members of the proposed class had relied on its alleged misrepresentations simply by buying or selling its stock at the market price. And without the benefit of the *Basic* presumption, investors would have to prove reliance on an individual basis, meaning that individual issues would predominate over common ones. The District Court declined to consider Halliburton's argument.

The Fifth Circuit affirmed.... We once again granted certiorari, this time to resolve a conflict among the Circuits over whether securities fraud defendants may attempt to rebut the *Basic* presumption at the class certification stage with evidence of a lack of price impact. We also accepted Halliburton's invitation to reconsider the presumption of reliance for securities fraud claims that we adopted in *Basic*.

II

Halliburton urges us to overrule *Basic's* presumption of reliance and to instead require every securities fraud plaintiff to prove that he actually relied on the defendant's misrepresentation in deciding to buy or sell a company's stock. Before overturning a long-settled precedent, however, we require "special justification," not just an argument that the precedent was wrongly decided. Halliburton has failed to make that showing.

A

Section 10(b) of the Securities Exchange Act of 1934 and the Securities and Exchange Commission's Rule 10b-5 prohibit making any material misstatement or omission in connection with the purchase or sale of any security. Although section 10(b) does not create an express private cause of action, we have long recognized an implied private cause of action to enforce the provision and its implementing regulation. To recover damages for violations of section 10(b) and Rule 10b-5, a plaintiff must prove " '(1) a material misrepresentation or omission by the defendant; (2) scienter; (3) a connection between the misrepresentation or omission and the purchase or sale of a security; (4) reliance upon the misrepresentation or omission; (5) economic loss; and (6) loss causation.' "

The reliance element " 'ensures that there is a proper connection between a defendant's misrepresentation and a plaintiff's injury.' The traditional (and most direct) way a plaintiff can demonstrate reliance is by showing that he was aware of a company's statement and engaged in a relevant transaction—e.g., purchasing common stock—based on that specific misrepresentation." In *Basic*, however, we recognized that requiring such direct proof of reliance "would place an unnecessarily unrealistic evidentiary burden on the Rule 10b-5 plaintiff who has traded on an impersonal market." That is because, even assuming an investor could prove that he was aware of the misrepresentation, he would still have to "show a speculative state of facts, i.e., how he would have acted ... if the misrepresentation had not been made." ...

We also noted that "[r]equiring proof of individualized reliance" from every securities fraud plaintiff "effectively would ... prevent[ ] [plaintiffs] from proceeding with a class action" in Rule 10b-5 suits. If every plaintiff had to prove direct reliance on the defendant's misrepresentation, "individual issues then would ... overwhelm[ ] the common ones," making certification under Rule 23(b)(3) inappropriate.

To address these concerns, *Basic* held that securities fraud plaintiffs can in certain circumstances satisfy the reliance element of a Rule 10b-5 action by invoking a rebuttable presumption of reliance, rather than proving direct reliance on a misrepresentation. The Court based that presumption on what is known as the "fraud-on-the-market" theory, which holds that "the market price of shares traded on well-developed markets reflects all publicly available information, and, hence, any material misrepresentations." The Court also noted that, rather than scrutinize every piece of public information about a company for himself, the typical "investor who buys or sells stock at the price set by the market does so in reliance on the integrity of that price"—the belief that it reflects all public, material information. As a result, whenever the investor buys or sells stock at the market price, his "reliance on any public material misrepresentations ... may be presumed for purposes of a Rule 10b-5 action."

Based on this theory, a plaintiff must make the following showings to demonstrate that the presumption of reliance applies in a given case: (1) that the alleged misrepresentations were publicly known, (2) that they were material, (3) that the stock traded in an efficient market, and (4) that the plaintiff traded the stock between the time the misrepresentations were made and when the truth was revealed.

At the same time, *Basic* emphasized that the presumption of reliance was rebuttable rather than conclusive. Specifically, "[a]ny showing that severs the link between the alleged misrepresentation and either the price received (or paid) by the plaintiff, or his decision to trade at a fair market price, will be sufficient to rebut the presumption of reliance." So for example, if a defendant could show that the alleged misrepresentation did not, for whatever reason, actually affect the market price, or that a plaintiff would have bought or sold the stock even had he been aware that the stock's price was tainted by fraud, then the presumption of reliance would not apply. In either of those cases, a plaintiff would have to prove that he directly relied on the defendant's misrepresentation in buying or selling the stock.

B

Halliburton contends that securities fraud plaintiffs should *always* have to prove direct reliance and that the *Basic* Court erred in allowing them to invoke a presumption of reliance instead. According to Halliburton, the *Basic* presumption contravenes congressional intent and has been undermined by subsequent developments in economic theory. Neither argument, however, so discredits Basic as to constitute "special justification" for overruling the decision....

Halliburton's primary argument for overruling *Basic* is that the decision rested on two premises that can no longer withstand scrutiny. The first premise concerns what is known as the "efficient capital markets hypothesis." *Basic* stated that "the market price of shares traded on well-developed markets reflects all publicly available information, and, hence, any material misrepresentations." From that statement, Halliburton concludes that the *Basic* Court espoused "a robust view of market efficiency" that is no longer tenable, for "'overwhelming empirical evidence' now suggests that capital markets are not fundamentally efficient.'" To support this contention, Halliburton cites studies purporting to show that "public information is often not incorporated immediately (much less rationally) into market prices."

Halliburton does not, of course, maintain that capital markets are always inefficient. Rather, in its view, *Basic's* fundamental error was to ignore the fact that "'efficiency is not a binary, yes or no question.'" The markets for some securities are more efficient than the markets for others, and even a single market can process different kinds of information more or less efficiently, depending on how widely the information is disseminated and how easily it is understood. Yet *Basic*, Halliburton asserts, glossed over these nuances, assuming a false dichotomy that renders the presumption of reliance both underinclusive and overinclusive: A misrepresentation can distort a stock's market price even in a generally inefficient market, and a misrepresentation can leave a stock's market price unaffected even in a generally efficient one.

Halliburton's criticisms fail to take *Basic* on its own terms. Halliburton focuses on the debate among economists about the degree to which the market price of a company's stock reflects public information about the company — and thus the degree to which an investor can earn an abnormal, above-market return by trading on such information. That debate is not new. Indeed, the *Basic* Court acknowledged it and declined to enter the fray, declaring that "[w]e need not determine by adjudication what economists and social scientists have debated through the use of sophisticated statistical analysis and the application of economic theory." To recognize the presumption of reliance, the Court explained, was not "conclusively to adopt any particular theory of how quickly and completely publicly available information is reflected in market price." The Court instead based the presumption on the fairly modest premise that "market professionals generally consider most publicly announced material statements about companies, thereby affecting stock market prices." *Basic's* presumption of reliance thus does not rest on a "binary" view of market efficiency. Indeed, in making the presumption rebuttable, *Basic* recognized that market efficiency is a matter of degree and accordingly made it a matter of proof.

The academic debates discussed by Halliburton have not refuted the modest premise underlying the presumption of reliance. Even the foremost critics of the efficient capital-markets hypothesis acknowledge that public information generally affects stock prices. Halliburton also conceded as much in its reply brief and at oral argument. Debates about the precise degree to which stock prices accurately reflect public information are thus largely beside the point. "That the ... price [of a stock] may be inaccurate does not detract from the fact that false statements affect it, and cause loss," which is "all that *Basic* requires." Even though the efficient capital markets hypothesis may have "garnered substantial criticism since *Basic*," Halliburton has not identified the kind of fundamental shift in economic theory that could justify overruling a precedent on the ground that it misunderstood, or has since been overtaken by, economic realities.

Halliburton also contests a second premise underlying the *Basic* presumption: the notion that investors "invest 'in reliance on the integrity of [the market] price.'" Hal-

liburton identifies a number of classes of investors for whom "price integrity" is sup-
posedly "marginal or irrelevant." The primary example is the value investor, who believes that certain stocks are undervalued or overvalued and attempts to "beat the
market" by buying the undervalued stocks and selling the overvalued ones. If many
investors "are indifferent to prices," Halliburton contends, then courts should not
presume that investors rely on the integrity of those prices and any misrepresentations
incorporated into them.

But *Basic* never denied the existence of such investors. As we recently explained,
Basic concluded only that "it is reasonable to presume that *most* investors—knowing
that they have little hope of outperforming the market in the long run based solely
on their analysis of publicly available information—will rely on the security's market
price as an unbiased assessment of the security's value in light of all public information." ... (emphasis added).

In any event, there is no reason to suppose that even Halliburton's main coun-
terexample—the value investor—is as indifferent to the integrity of market prices
as Halliburton suggests. Such an investor implicitly relies on the fact that a stock's
market price will eventually reflect material information—how else could the market
correction on which his profit depends occur? To be sure, the value investor "does
not believe that the market price accurately reflects public information *at the time he
transacts*." But to indirectly rely on a misstatement in the sense relevant for the *Basic*
presumption, he need only trade stock based on the belief that the market price will
incorporate public information within a reasonable period. The value investor also
presumably tries to estimate *how* undervalued or overvalued a particular stock is,
and such estimates can be skewed by a market price tainted by fraud.

C

The principle of *stare decisis* has " 'special force' " "in respect to statutory interpretation" because " 'Congress remains free to alter what we have done.' " So too with
Basic's presumption of reliance. Although the presumption is a judicially created doctrine designed to implement a judicially created cause of action, we have described
the presumption as "a substantive doctrine of federal securities-fraud law." That is
because it provides a way of satisfying the reliance element of the Rule 10b-5 cause
of action. As with any other element of that cause of action, Congress may overturn
or modify any aspect of our interpretations of the reliance requirement, including
the Basic presumption itself. Given that possibility, we see no reason to exempt the
Basic presumption from ordinary principles of *stare decisis*.

To buttress its case for overruling *Basic*, Halliburton contends that, in addition to
being wrongly decided, the decision is inconsistent with our more recent decisions
construing the Rule 10b-5 cause of action. As Halliburton notes, we have held that
"we must give 'narrow dimensions ... to a right of action Congress did not authorize
when it first enacted the statute and did not expand when it revisited the law.' " Yet
the *Basic* presumption, Halliburton asserts, does just the opposite, *expanding* the
Rule 10b-5 cause of action.

Not so. In *Central Bank* and *Stoneridge* [Eds.: excerpted below.] we declined to extend Rule 10b-5 liability to entirely new categories of defendants who themselves had not made any material, public misrepresentation. Such an extension, we explained, would have eviscerated the requirement that a plaintiff prove that he relied on a misrepresentation made *by the defendant*. The *Basic* presumption does not eliminate that requirement but rather provides an alternative means of satisfying it. While the presumption makes it easier for plaintiffs to prove reliance, it does not alter the elements of the Rule 10b-5 cause of action and thus maintains the action's original legal scope....

Finally, Halliburton and its *amici* contend that, by facilitating securities class actions, the *Basic* presumption produces a number of serious and harmful consequences. Such class actions, they say, allow plaintiffs to extort large settlements from defendants for meritless claims; punish innocent shareholders, who end up having to pay settlements and judgments; impose excessive costs on businesses; and consume a disproportionately large share of judicial resources.

These concerns are more appropriately addressed to Congress, which has in fact responded, to some extent, to many of the issues raised by Halliburton and its *amici*. Congress has, for example, enacted the Private Securities Litigation Reform Act of 1995 (PSLRA), which sought to combat perceived abuses in securities litigation with heightened pleading requirements, limits on damages and attorney's fees, a "safe harbor" for certain kinds of statements, restrictions on the selection of lead plaintiffs in securities class actions, sanctions for frivolous litigation, and stays of discovery pending motions to dismiss. And to prevent plaintiffs from circumventing these restrictions by bringing securities class actions under state law in state court, Congress also enacted the Securities Litigation Uniform Standards Act of 1998, which precludes many state law class actions alleging securities fraud. Such legislation demonstrates Congress's willingness to consider policy concerns of the sort that Halliburton says should lead us to overrule *Basic*.

III

Halliburton proposes two alternatives to overruling *Basic* that would alleviate what it regards as the decision's most serious flaws. The first alternative would require plaintiffs to prove that a defendant's misrepresentation actually affected the stock price — so-called "price impact" — in order to invoke the *Basic* presumption. It should not be enough, Halliburton contends, for plaintiffs to demonstrate the general efficiency of the market in which the stock traded. Halliburton's second proposed alternative would allow defendants to rebut the presumption of reliance with evidence of a *lack* of price impact, not only at the merits stage — which all agree defendants may already do — but also before class certification.

A

As noted, to invoke the *Basic* presumption, a plaintiff must prove that: (1) the alleged misrepresentations were publicly known, (2) they were material, (3) the stock traded in an efficient market, and (4) the plaintiff traded the stock between when the misrepresentations were made and when the truth was revealed. Each of these requirements follows from the fraud-on-the-market theory underlying the presumption. If the misrepresentation was not publicly known, then it could not have distorted the stock's market price. So too if the misrepresentation was immaterial—that is, if it would not have " 'been viewed by the reasonable investor as having significantly altered the "total mix" of information made available,' "—or if the market in which the stock traded was inefficient. And if the plaintiff did not buy or sell the stock after the misrepresentation was made but before the truth was revealed, then he could not be said to have acted in reliance on a fraud-tainted price.

The first three prerequisites are directed at price impact—"whether the alleged misrepresentations affected the market price in the first place." ... Halliburton argues that since the *Basic* presumption hinges on price impact, plaintiffs should be required to prove it directly in order to invoke the presumption. Proving the presumption's prerequisites, which are at best an imperfect proxy for price impact, should not suffice.

Far from a modest refinement of the *Basic* presumption, this proposal would radically alter the required showing for the reliance element of the Rule 10b-5 cause of action. What is called the *Basic* presumption actually incorporates two constituent presumptions: First, if a plaintiff shows that the defendant's misrepresentation was public and material and that the stock traded in a generally efficient market, he is entitled to a presumption that the misrepresentation affected the stock price. Second, if the plaintiff also shows that he purchased the stock at the market price during the relevant period, he is entitled to a further presumption that he purchased the stock in reliance on the defendant's misrepresentation.

By requiring plaintiffs to prove price impact directly, Halliburton's proposal would take away the first constituent presumption. Halliburton's argument for doing so is the same as its primary argument for overruling the *Basic* presumption altogether: Because market efficiency is not a yes-or-no proposition, a public, material misrepresentation might not affect a stock's price even in a generally efficient market. But as explained, *Basic* never suggested otherwise; that is why it affords defendants an opportunity to rebut the presumption by showing, among other things, that the particular misrepresentation at issue did not affect the stock's market price. For the same reasons we declined to completely jettison the *Basic* presumption, we decline to effectively jettison half of it by revising the prerequisites for invoking it.

B

Even if plaintiffs need not directly prove price impact to invoke the *Basic* presumption, Halliburton contends that defendants should at least be allowed to defeat the presumption at the class certification stage through evidence that the misrepresentation did not in fact affect the stock price. We agree.

1

There is no dispute that defendants may introduce such evidence at the merits stage to rebut the *Basic* presumption. *Basic* itself "made clear that the presumption was just that, and could be rebutted by appropriate evidence," including evidence that the asserted misrepresentation (or its correction) did not affect the market price of the defendant's stock.

Nor is there any dispute that defendants may introduce price impact evidence at the class certification stage, so long as it is for the purpose of countering a plaintiff's showing of market efficiency, rather than directly rebutting the presumption. As EPJ Fund acknowledges, "[o]f course ... defendants can introduce evidence at class certification of lack of price impact as some evidence that the market is not efficient."

After all, plaintiffs themselves can and do introduce evidence of the *existence* of price impact in connection with "event studies"—regression analyses that seek to show that the market price of the defendant's stock tends to respond to pertinent publicly reported events. In this case, for example, EPJ Fund submitted an event study of various episodes that might have been expected to affect the price of Halliburton's stock, in order to demonstrate that the market for that stock takes account of material, public information about the company. The episodes examined by EPJ Fund's event study included one of the alleged misrepresentations that form the basis of the Fund's suit.

Defendants—like plaintiffs—may accordingly submit price impact evidence prior to class certification. What defendants may not do, EPJ Fund insists and the Court of Appeals held, is rely on that same evidence prior to class certification for the particular purpose of rebutting the presumption altogether.

This restriction makes no sense, and can readily lead to bizarre results. Suppose a defendant at the certification stage submits an event study looking at the impact on the price of its stock from six discrete events, in an effort to refute the plaintiffs' claim of general market efficiency. All agree the defendant may do this. Suppose one of the six events is the specific misrepresentation asserted by the plaintiffs. All agree that this too is perfectly acceptable. Now suppose the district court determines that, despite the defendant's study, the plaintiff has carried its burden to prove market efficiency, but that the evidence shows no price impact with respect to the specific misrepresentation challenged in the suit. The evidence at the certification stage thus shows an efficient market, on which the alleged misrepresentation had no price impact. And yet under EPJ Fund's view, the plaintiffs' action should be certified and proceed as a class action (with all that entails), even though the fraud-on-the-market theory does not apply and common reliance thus cannot be presumed.

Such a result is inconsistent with *Basic's* own logic. Under *Basic's* fraud-on-the-market theory, market efficiency and the other prerequisites for invoking the presumption constitute an indirect way of showing price impact. As explained, it is appropriate to allow plaintiffs to rely on this indirect proxy for price impact, rather than requiring them to prove price impact directly, given *Basic's* rationales for recognizing a presumption of reliance in the first place.

But an indirect proxy should not preclude direct evidence when such evidence is available. As we explained in *Basic*, "[a]ny showing that severs the link between the alleged misrepresentation and ... the price received (or paid) by the plaintiff ... will be sufficient to rebut the presumption of reliance" because "the basis for finding that the fraud had been transmitted through market price would be gone." And without the presumption of reliance, a Rule 10b-5 suit cannot proceed as a class action: Each plaintiff would have to prove reliance individually, so common issues would not "predominate" over individual ones, as required by Rule 23(b)(3). Price impact is thus an essential precondition for any Rule 10b-5 class action. While *Basic* allows plaintiffs to establish that precondition indirectly, it does not require courts to ignore a defendant's direct, more salient evidence showing that the alleged misrepresentation did not actually affect the stock's market price and, consequently, that the *Basic* presumption does not apply.

2

The Court of Appeals relied on our decision in *Amgen* in holding that Halliburton could not introduce evidence of lack of price impact at the class certification stage. The question in Amgen was whether plaintiffs could be required to prove (or defendants be permitted to disprove) materiality before class certification. Even though materiality is a prerequisite for invoking the *Basic* presumption, we held that it should be left to the merits stage, because it does not bear on the predominance requirement of Rule 23(b)(3). We reasoned that materiality is an objective issue susceptible to common, classwide proof. We also noted that a failure to prove materiality would necessarily defeat every plaintiff's claim on the merits; it would not simply preclude invocation of the presumption and thereby cause individual questions of reliance to predominate over common ones. In this latter respect, we explained, materiality differs from the publicity and market efficiency prerequisites, neither of which is necessary to prove a Rule 10b-5 claim on the merits.

EPJ Fund argues that much of the foregoing could be said of price impact as well. Fair enough. But price impact differs from materiality in a crucial respect. Given that the other Basic prerequisites must still be proved at the class certification stage, the common issue of materiality can be left to the merits stage without risking the certification of classes in which individual issues will end up overwhelming common ones. And because materiality is a discrete issue that can be resolved in isolation from the other prerequisites, it can be wholly confined to the merits stage.

Price impact is different. The fact that a misrepresentation "was reflected in the market price at the time of [the] transaction"—that it had price impact—is "*Basic's* fundamental premise." It thus has everything to do with the issue of predominance at the class certification stage. That is why, if reliance is to be shown through the *Basic* presumption, the publicity and market efficiency prerequisites must be proved before class certification. Without proof of those prerequisites, the fraud-on-the-market theory underlying the presumption completely collapses, rendering class certification inappropriate.

But as explained, publicity and market efficiency are nothing more than prerequisites for an indirect showing of price impact. There is no dispute that at least such indirect proof of price impact "is needed to ensure that the questions of law or fact common to the class will 'predominate.'" That is so even though such proof is also highly relevant at the merits stage.

Our choice in this case, then, is not between allowing price impact evidence at the class certification stage or relegating it to the merits. Evidence of price impact will be before the court at the certification stage in any event. The choice, rather, is between limiting the price impact inquiry before class certification to indirect evidence, or allowing consideration of direct evidence as well. As explained, we see no reason to artificially limit the inquiry at the certification stage to indirect evidence of price impact. Defendants may seek to defeat the *Basic* presumption at that stage through direct as well as indirect price impact evidence.

More than 25 years ago, we held that plaintiffs could satisfy the reliance element of the Rule 10b-5 cause of action by invoking a presumption that a public, material misrepresentation will distort the price of stock traded in an efficient market, and that anyone who purchases the stock at the market price may be considered to have done so in reliance on the misrepresentation. We adhere to that decision and decline to modify the prerequisites for invoking the presumption of reliance. But to maintain the consistency of the presumption with the class certification requirements of Federal Rule of Civil Procedure 23, defendants must be afforded an opportunity before class certification to defeat the presumption through evidence that an alleged misrepresentation did not actually affect the market price of the stock....

Justice GINSBURG, with whom Justice BREYER and Justice SOTOMAYOR join, concurring.

Advancing price impact consideration from the merits stage to the certification stage may broaden the scope of discovery available at certification. But the Court recognizes that it is incumbent upon the defendant to show the absence of price impact. The Court's judgment, therefore, should impose no heavy toll on securities-fraud plaintiffs with tenable claims. On that understanding, I join the Court's opinion.

Justice THOMAS, with whom Justice SCALIA and Justice ALITO join, concurring in the judgment.

The implied Rule 10b-5 private cause of action is "a relic of the heady days in which this Court assumed common-law powers to create causes of action." We have since ended that practice because the authority to fashion private remedies to enforce federal law belongs to Congress alone. Absent statutory authorization for a cause of action, "courts may not create one, no matter how desirable that might be as a policy matter."

Basic Inc. v. Levinson, demonstrates the wisdom of this rule. *Basic* presented the question how investors must prove the reliance element of the implied Rule 10b-5 cause of action—the requirement that the plaintiff buy or sell stock in reliance on the defendant's misstatement—when they transact on modern, impersonal securities exchanges. Were the Rule 10b-5 action statutory, the Court could have resolved this question by interpreting the statutory language. Without a statute to interpret for guidance, however, the Court began instead with a particular policy "problem": for investors in impersonal markets, the traditional reliance requirement was hard to prove and impossible to prove as common among plaintiffs bringing 10b-5 class-action suits.

With the task thus framed as "resol[ving]"that "'problem'" rather than interpreting statutory text, the Court turned to nascent economic theory and naked intuitions about investment behavior in its efforts to fashion a new, easier way to meet the reliance requirement. The result was an evidentiary presumption, based on a "fraud on the market" theory, that paved the way for class actions under Rule 10b-5.

Today we are asked to determine whether *Basic* was correctly decided. The Court suggests that it was, and that *stare decisis* demands that we preserve it. I disagree. Logic, economic realities, and our subsequent jurisprudence have undermined the foundations of the *Basic* presumption, and *stare decisis* cannot prop up the façade that remains. *Basic* should be overruled.

B. "In Connection With" Requirement

Superintendent of Insurance of New York v. Bankers Life & Casualty Co.

United States Supreme Court
404 U.S. 6 (1971)

JUSTICE DOUGLAS delivered the opinion of the Court.

Manhattan Casualty Co., now represented by petitioner, New York's Superintendent of Insurance, was, it is alleged, defrauded in the sale of certain securities in violation of § 17(a) of the Securities Act of 1933 and of § 10(b) of the Securities Exchange Act of 1934. The District Court dismissed the complaint, and the Court of Appeals affirmed, by a divided bench. The case is here on a petition for a writ of certiorari which we granted.

It seems that Bankers Life & Casualty Co., one of the respondents, agreed to sell all of Manhattan's stock to one Begole for $5,000,000. It is alleged that Begole conspired with one Bourne and others to pay for this stock, not out of their own funds, but with Manhattan's assets. They were alleged to have arranged, through Garvin, Bantel & Co. — a note brokerage firm — to obtain a $5,000,000 check from respondent Irving Trust Co., although they had no funds on deposit there at the time. On the same day they purchased all the stock of Manhattan from Bankers Life for $5,000,000 and as stockholders and directors, installed one Sweeny as president of Manhattan.

Manhattan then sold its United States Treasury bonds for $4,854,552.67.[4] That amount, plus enough cash to bring the total to $5,000,000, was credited to an account of Manhattan at Irving Trust and the $5,000,000 Irving Trust check was charged against it. As a result, Begole owned all the stock of Manhattan, having used $5,000,000 of Manhattan's assets to purchase it.

To complete the fraudulent scheme, Irving Trust issued a second $5,000,000 check to Manhattan which Sweeny, Manhattan's new president, tendered to Belgian-American Bank & Trust Co. which issued a $5,000,000 certificate of deposit in the name of Manhattan. Sweeny endorsed the certificate of deposit over to New England

---

4. [1] Manhattan's Board of Directors was allegedly deceived into authorizing this sale by the misrepresentation that the proceeds would be exchanged for a certificate of deposit of equal value.

Note Corp., a company alleged to be controlled by Bourne. Bourne endorsed the certificate over to Belgian-American Banking Corp.[5] as collateral for a $5,000,000 loan from Belgian-American Banking to New England. Its proceeds were paid to Irving Trust to cover the latter's second $5,000,000 check.

Though Manhattan's assets had been depleted, its books reflected only the sale of its Government bonds and the purchase of the certificate of deposit and did not show that its assets had been used by Begole to pay for his purchase of Manhattan's shares or that the certificate of deposit had been assigned to New England and then pledged to Belgian-American Banking.

Manhattan was the seller of Treasury bonds and, it seems to us, clearly protected by § 10(b) of the Securities Exchange Act, which makes it unlawful to use "in connection with the purchase or sale" of any security "any manipulative or deceptive device or contrivance" in contravention of the rules and regulations of the Securities and Exchange Commission.

There certainly was an "act" or "practice" within the meaning of Rule 10b-5 which operated as "a fraud or deceit" on Manhattan, the seller of the Government bonds. To be sure, the full market price was paid for those bonds; but the seller was duped into believing that it, the seller, would receive the proceeds. We cannot agree with the Court of Appeals that "no investor [was] injured" and that the "purity of the security transaction and the purity of the trading process were unsullied."

Section 10(b) outlaws the use "in connection with the purchase or sale" of any security of "any manipulative or deceptive device or contrivance." The Act protects corporations as well as individuals who are sellers of a security. Manhattan was injured as an investor through a deceptive device which deprived it of any compensation for the sale of its valuable block of securities.

The fact that the fraud was perpetrated by an officer of Manhattan and his outside collaborators is irrelevant to our problem. For § 10(b) bans the use of any deceptive device in the "sale" of any security by "any person." And the fact that the transaction is not conducted through a securities exchange or an organized over-the-counter market is irrelevant to the coverage of § 10(b). *Hooper v. Mountain States Securities Corp.*, 282 F.2d 195, 201. Likewise irrelevant is the fact that the proceeds of the sale that were due the seller were misappropriated. As the Court of Appeals for the Fifth Circuit said in the *Hooper* case, "Considering the purpose of this legislation, it would be unrealistic to say that a corporation having the capacity to acquire $700,000 worth of assets for its 700,000 shares of stock has suffered no loss if what it gave up was $700,000 but what it got was zero."

The Congress made clear that "disregard of trust relationships by those whom the law should regard as fiduciaries, are all a single seamless web" along with manipulation, investor's ignorance, and the like. H. R. Rep. No. 1383, 73d Cong., 2d Sess., 6. Since

---

5. [2] Belgian-American Banking at the same time made a loan to New England Note in the amount of $250,000 which was distributed in part as follows: Belgian-American Banking $100,000, Bourne $50,000, Begole $50,000, and Garvin, Bantel $25,000.

practices "constantly vary and where practices legitimate for some purposes may be turned to illegitimate and fraudulent means, broad discretionary powers" in the regulatory agency "have been found practically essential." *Id.*, at 7. Hence we do not read § 10(b) as narrowly as the Court of Appeals; it is not "limited to preserving the integrity of the securities markets," though that purpose is included. Section 10(b) must be read flexibly, not technically and restrictively. Since there was a "sale" of a security and since fraud was used "in connection with" it, there is redress under § 10(b), whatever might be available as a remedy under state law.

We agree that Congress by § 10(b) did not seek to regulate transactions which constitute no more than internal corporate mismanagement. But we read § 10(b) to mean that Congress meant to bar deceptive devices and contrivances in the purchase or sale of securities whether conducted in the organized markets or face to face. And the fact that creditors of the defrauded corporate buyer or seller of securities may be the ultimate victims does not warrant disregard of the corporate entity. The controlling stockholder owes the corporation a fiduciary obligation — one "designed for the protection of the entire community of interests in the corporation — creditors as well as stockholders." *Pepper v. Litton*, 308 U.S. 295, 307.

The crux of the present case is that Manhattan suffered an injury as a result of deceptive practices touching its sale of securities as an investor. As stated in *Shell v. Hensley*, 430 F.2d 819, 827:

> When a person who is dealing with a corporation in a securities transaction denies the corporation's directors access to material information known to him, the corporation is disabled from availing itself of an informed judgment on the part of its board regarding the merits of the transaction. In this situation the private right of action recognized under Rule 10b-5 is available as a remedy for the corporate disability.

The case was before the lower courts on a motion to dismiss.

Bankers Life urges that the complaint did not allege, and discovery failed to disclose, any connection between it and the fraud and that therefore, the dismissal of the complaint as to it was correct and should be affirmed. We make no ruling on this point.

The case must be remanded for trial. We intimate no opinion on the merits, as we have dealt only with allegations and with the question of law whether a cause of action as respects the sale by Manhattan of its Treasury bonds has been charged under § 10(b). We think it has been so charged and accordingly we reverse and remand for proceedings consistent with this opinion.

All defenses except our ruling on § 10(b) will be open on remand.

Reversed.

C. Standing

Blue Chip Stamps v. Manor Drug Stores
United States Supreme Court
421 U.S. 723 (1975)

JUSTICE REHNQUIST delivered the opinion of the Court.

This case requires us to consider whether the offerees of a stock offering, made pursuant to an antitrust consent decree and registered under the Securities Act of 1933 (1933 Act), may maintain a private cause of action for money damages where they allege that the offeror has violated the provisions of Rule 10b-5 of the Securities and Exchange Commission, but where they have neither purchased nor sold any of the offered shares. *See Birnbaum v. Newport Steel Corp.*, 193 F.2d 461 (CA2), *cert. denied*, 343 U.S. 956 (1952).

I

In 1963 the United States filed a civil antitrust action against Blue Chip Stamp Co. (Old Blue Chip), a company in the business of providing trading stamps to retailers, and nine retailers who owned 90% of its shares. In 1967 the action was terminated by the entry of a consent decree. The decree contemplated a plan of reorganization whereby Old Blue Chip was to be merged into a newly formed corporation, Blue Chip Stamps (New Blue Chip). The holdings of the majority shareholders of Old Blue Chip were to be reduced, and New Blue Chip, one of the petitioners here, was required under the plan to offer a substantial number of its shares of common stock to retailers who had used the stamp service in the past but who were not shareholders in the old company. Under the terms of the plan, the offering to nonshareholder users was to be proportional to past stamp usage and the shares were to be offered in units consisting of common stock and debentures.

The reorganization plan was carried out, the offering was registered with the SEC as required by the 1933 Act, and a prospectus was distributed to all offerees as required by § 5 of that Act. Somewhat more than 50% of the offered units were actually purchased. In 1970, two years after the offering, respondent, a former user of the stamp service and therefore an offeree of the 1968 offering, filed this suit in the United States District Court for the Central District of California. Defendants below and petitioners here are Old and New Blue Chip, eight of the nine majority shareholders of Old Blue Chip, and the directors of New Blue Chip (collectively called Blue Chip).

Respondent's complaint alleged, *inter alia*, that the prospectus prepared and distributed by Blue Chip in connection with the offering was materially misleading in its overly pessimistic appraisal of Blue Chip's status and future prospects. It alleged that Blue Chip intentionally made the prospectus overly pessimistic in order to discourage respondent and other members of the allegedly large class whom it represents from accepting what was intended to be a bargain offer, so that the rejected shares might later be offered to the public at a higher price. The complaint alleged that class members because of and in reliance on the false and misleading prospectus failed to purchase the offered units. Respondent therefore sought on behalf of the alleged class some $21,400,000 in damages representing the lost opportunity to purchase the units; the right to purchase the previously rejected units at the 1968 price; and in addition, it sought some $25,000,000 in exemplary damages.

The only portion of the litigation thus initiated which is before us is whether respondent may base its action on Rule 10b-5 of the Securities and Exchange Commission without having either bought or sold the securities described in the allegedly misleading prospectus. The District Court dismissed respondent's complaint for failure to state a claim upon which relief might be granted. On appeal to the United States Court of Appeals for the Ninth Circuit, respondent pressed only its asserted claim under Rule 10b-5, and a divided panel of the Court of Appeals sustained its position and reversed the District Court. After the Ninth Circuit denied rehearing en banc, we granted Blue Chip's petition for certiorari. Our consideration of the correctness of the determination of the Court of Appeals requires us to consider what limitations there are on the class of plaintiffs who may maintain a private cause of action for money damages for violation of Rule 10b-5, and whether respondent was within that class.

II

[In 1952] the Court of Appeals for the Second Circuit concluded that the plaintiff class for purposes of a private damages action under § 10(b) and Rule 10b-5 was limited to actual purchasers and sellers of securities. *Birnbaum v. Newport Steel Corp., supra.*

The Court of Appeals in this case did not repudiate *Birnbaum*.... But in this case a majority of the Court of Appeals found that the facts warranted an exception to the *Birnbaum* rule. For the reasons hereinafter stated, we are of the opinion that *Birnbaum* was rightly decided, and that it bars respondent from maintaining this suit under Rule 10b-5.

III

The panel which decided *Birnbaum* consisted of Chief Judge Swan and Judges Learned Hand and Augustus Hand: the opinion was written by the last named. Since both § 10(b) and Rule 10b-5 proscribed only fraud "in connection with the purchase or sale" of securities, and since the history of § 10(b) revealed no congressional intention to extend a private civil remedy for money damages to other than defrauded purchasers or sellers of securities, ... the court concluded that the plaintiff class in a Rule 10b-5 action was limited to actual purchasers and sellers.

[V]irtually all lower federal courts facing the issue in the hundreds of reported cases presenting this question over the past quarter century have reaffirmed *Birnbaum*'s conclusion that the plaintiff class for purposes of § 10(b) and Rule 10b-5 private damage actions is limited to purchasers and sellers of securities.

In 1957 and again in 1959, the Securities and Exchange Commission sought from Congress amendment of § 10(b) to change its wording from "in connection with the purchase or sale of any security" to "in connection with the purchase or sale of, *or any attempt to purchase or sell,* any security." In the words of a memorandum submitted by the Commission to a congressional committee, the purpose of the proposed change was "to make section 10(b) also applicable to manipulative activities in connection with any attempt to purchase or sell any security." Opposition to the amendment was based on fears of the extension of civil liability under § 10(b) that it would cause. Neither change was adopted by Congress.

The longstanding acceptance by the courts, coupled with Congress' failure to reject *Birnbaum's* reasonable interpretation of the wording of § 10(b), wording which is directed toward injury suffered "in connection with the purchase or sale" of securities, argues significantly in favor of acceptance of the *Birnbaum* rule by this Court.

Available evidence from the texts of the 1933 and 1934 Acts as to the congressional scheme in this regard, though not conclusive, supports the result reached by the *Birnbaum* court....

Having said all this, we would by no means be understood as suggesting that we are able to divine from the language of § 10(b) the express "intent of Congress" as to the contours of a private cause of action under Rule 10b-5. When we deal with private actions under Rule 10b-5, we deal with a judicial oak which has grown from little more than a legislative acorn.... It is therefore proper that we consider, in addition to the factors already discussed, what may be described as policy considerations when we come to flesh out the portions of the law with respect to which neither the congressional enactment nor the administrative regulations offer conclusive guidance.

Three principal classes of potential plaintiffs are presently barred by the *Birnbaum* rule. First are potential purchasers of shares, either in a new offering or on the Nation's post-distribution trading markets, who allege that they decided not to purchase because of an unduly gloomy representation or the omission of favorable material which made the issuer appear to be a less favorable investment vehicle than it actually was. Second are actual shareholders in the issuer who allege that they decided not to sell their shares because of an unduly rosy representation or a failure to disclose unfavorable material. Third are shareholders, creditors, and perhaps others related to an issuer who suffered loss in the value of their investment due to corporate or insider activities in connection with the purchase or sale of securities which violate Rule 10b-5. It has been held that shareholder members of the second and third of these classes may frequently be able to circumvent the *Birnbaum* limitation through bringing a derivative action on behalf of the corporate issuer if the latter is itself a purchaser or seller of securities. But the first of these classes, of which respondent is a member, cannot claim the benefit of such a rule.

A great majority of the many commentators on the issue before us have taken the view that the *Birnbaum* limitation on the plaintiff class in a Rule 10b-5 action for damages is an arbitrary restriction which unreasonably prevents some deserving plaintiffs from recovering damages which have in fact been caused by violations of Rule 10b-5. The Securities and Exchange Commission has filed an *amicus* brief in this case espousing that same view. We have no doubt that this is indeed a disadvantage of the *Birnbaum* rule, and if it had no countervailing advantages it would be undesirable as a matter of policy, however much it might be supported by precedent and legislative history. But we are of the opinion that there are countervailing advantages to the *Birnbaum* rule, purely as a matter of policy, although those advantages are more difficult to articulate than is the disadvantage.

There has been widespread recognition that litigation under Rule 10b-5 presents a danger of vexatiousness different in degree and in kind from that which accompanies litigation in general. This fact was recognized by Judge Browning in his opinion for the majority of the Court of Appeals in this case and by Judge Hufstedler in her dissenting opinion when she said:

> The purchaser-seller rule has maintained the balances built into the congressional scheme by permitting damage actions to be brought only by those persons whose active participation in the marketing transaction promises enforcement of the statute without undue risk of abuse of the litigation process and without distorting the securities market.

Judge Friendly in commenting on another aspect of Rule 10b-5 litigation has referred to the possibility that unduly expansive imposition of civil liability "will lead to large judgments, payable in the last analysis by innocent investors, for the benefit of speculators and their lawyers...." *SEC v. Texas Gulf Sulphur Co.*, 401 F.2d 833, 867 (CA2 1968) (concurring opinion).

We believe that the concern expressed for the danger of vexatious litigation which could result from a widely expanded class of plaintiffs under Rule 10b-5 is founded in something more substantial than the common complaint of the many defendants who would prefer avoiding lawsuits entirely to either settling them or trying them. These concerns have two largely separate grounds.

The first of these concerns is that in the field of federal securities laws governing disclosure of information even a complaint which by objective standards may have very little chance of success at trial has a settlement value to the plaintiff out of any proportion to its prospect of success at trial so long as he may prevent the suit from being resolved against him by dismissal or summary judgment. The very pendency of the lawsuit may frustrate or delay normal business activity of the defendant which is totally unrelated to the lawsuit.

Congress itself recognized the potential for nuisance or "strike" suits in this type of litigation, and in Title II of the 1934 Act amended § 11 of the 1933 Act to provide that:

> In any suit under this or any other section of this title the court may, in its discretion, require an undertaking for the payment of the costs of such suit, including reasonable attorney's fees....

The potential for possible abuse of the liberal discovery provisions of the Federal Rules of Civil Procedure may likewise exist in this type of case to a greater extent than they do in other litigation. The prospect of extensive deposition of the defendant's officers and associates and the concomitant opportunity for extensive discovery of business documents, is a common occurrence in this and similar types of litigation.... [T]o broadly expand the class of plaintiffs who may sue under Rule 10b-5 would appear to encourage the least appealing aspect of the use of the discovery rules.

Without the *Birnbaum* rule, an action under Rule 10b-5 will turn largely on which oral version of a series of occurrences the jury may decide to credit, and therefore no matter how improbable the allegations of the plaintiff, the case will be virtually impossible to dispose of prior to trial other than by settlement....

The *Birnbaum* rule, on the other hand, permits exclusion prior to trial of those plaintiffs who were not themselves purchasers or sellers of the stock in question. The fact of purchase of stock and the fact of sale of stock are generally matters which are verifiable by documentation, and do not depend upon oral recollection, so that failure to qualify under the *Birnbaum* rule is a matter that can normally be established by the defendant either on a motion to dismiss or on a motion for summary judgment.

... The *Birnbaum* rule undoubtedly excludes plaintiffs who have in fact been damaged by violations of Rule 10b-5, and to that extent it is undesirable. But it also separates in a readily demonstrable manner the group of plaintiffs who actually purchased or actually sold, and whose version of the facts is therefore more likely to be believed by the trier of fact, from the vastly larger world of potential plaintiffs who might successfully allege a claim but could seldom succeed in proving it. And this fact is one of its advantages.

The second ground for fear of vexatious litigation is based on the concern that, given the generalized contours of liability, the abolition of the *Birnbaum* rule would throw open to the trier of fact many rather hazy issues of historical fact the proof of which depended almost entirely on oral testimony.... The Commission suggests that in particular cases additional requirements of corroboration of testimony and more limited measure of damages would correct the dangers of an expanded class of plaintiffs.

But the very necessity, or at least the desirability, of fashioning unique rules of corroboration and damages as a correlative to the abolition of the *Birnbaum* rule suggests that the rule itself may have something to be said for it....

In today's universe of transactions governed by the 1934 Act, privity of dealing or even personal contact between potential defendant and potential plaintiff is the exception and not the rule. The stock of issuers is listed on financial exchanges utilized by tens of millions of investors, and corporate representations reach a potential audience, encompassing not only the diligent few who peruse filed corporate reports or the sizable number of subscribers to financial journals, but the readership of the Nation's daily newspapers....

[I]n the absence of the *Birnbaum* rule, it would be sufficient for a plaintiff to prove that he had failed to purchase or sell stock by reason of a defendant's violation of Rule 10b-5. The manner in which the defendant's violation caused the plaintiff to fail to act could be as a result of the reading of a prospectus, as respondent claims here, but it could just as easily come as a result of a claimed reading of information contained in the financial pages of a local newspaper. Plaintiff's proof would not be that he purchased or sold stock, a fact which would be capable of documentary verification in most situations, but instead that he decided *not* to purchase or sell stock. Plaintiff's entire testimony could be dependent upon uncorroborated oral evidence of many of the crucial elements of his claim, and still be sufficient to go to the jury.

The jury would not even have the benefit of weighing the plaintiff's version against the defendant's version, since the elements to which the plaintiff would testify would be in many cases totally unknown and unknowable to the defendant. The very real risk in permitting those in respondent's position to sue under Rule 10b-5 is that the door will be open to recovery of substantial damages on the part of one who offers only his own testimony to prove that he ever consulted a prospectus of the issuer, that he paid any attention to it, or that the representations contained in it damaged him. The virtue of the *Birnbaum* rule, simply stated, in this situation, is that it limits the class of plaintiffs to those who have at least dealt in the security to which the prospectus, representation, or omission relates. And their dealing in the security, whether by way of purchase or sale, will generally be an objectively demonstrable fact in an area of the law otherwise very much dependent upon oral testimony....

Thus we conclude that what may be called considerations of policy, which we are free to weigh in deciding this case, are by no means entirely on one side of the scale. Taken together with the precedential support for the *Birnbaum* rule over a period of more than 20 years, and the consistency of that rule with what we can glean from the intent of Congress, they lead us to conclude that it is a sound rule and should be followed.

IV

The majority of the Court of Appeals in this case expressed no disagreement with the general proposition that one asserting a claim for damages based on the violation of Rule 10b-5 must be either a purchaser or seller of securities. However, it noted that prior cases have held that persons owning contractual rights to buy or sell securities are not excluded by the *Birnbaum* rule. Relying on these cases, it concluded that respondent's status as an offeree pursuant to the terms of the consent decree served the same function, for purposes of delimiting the class of plaintiffs, as is normally performed by the requirement of a contractual relationship.

... While the *Birnbaum* rule has been flexibly interpreted by lower federal courts, we have been unable to locate a single decided case from any court in the 20-odd years of litigation since the *Birnbaum* decision which would support the right of persons who were in the position of respondent here to bring a private suit under Rule 10b-5. Respondent was not only not a buyer or seller of any security but it was not even a shareholder of the corporate petitioners....

Beyond the difficulties evident in an extension of standing to this respondent, we do not believe that the *Birnbaum* rule is merely a shorthand judgment on the nature of a particular plaintiff's proof. As a purely practical matter, it is doubtless true that respondent and the members of its class, as offerees and recipients of the prospectus of New Blue Chip, are a smaller class of potential plaintiffs than would be all those who might conceivably assert that they obtained information violative of Rule 10b-5 and attributable to the issuer in the financial pages of their local newspaper. And since respondent likewise had a prior connection with some of petitioners as a result of using the trading stamps marketed by Old Blue Chip, and was intended to benefit from the provisions of the consent decree, there is doubtless more likelihood that its managers read and were damaged by the allegedly misleading statements in the prospectus than there would be in a case filed by a complete stranger to the corporation.

But respondent and the members of its class are neither "purchasers" nor "sellers," as those terms are defined in the 1934 Act, and therefore to the extent that their claim of standing to sue were recognized, it would mean that the lesser practical difficulties of corroborating at least some elements of their proof would be regarded as sufficient to avoid the *Birnbaum* rule. While we have noted that these practical difficulties, particularly in the case of a complete stranger to the corporation, support the retention of that rule, they are by no means the only factor which does so. The general adoption of the rule by other federal courts in the 20-odd years since it was announced, and the consistency of the rule with the statutes involved and their legislative history, are likewise bases for retaining the rule. Were we to agree with the Court of Appeals in this case, we would leave the *Birnbaum* rule open to endless case-by-case erosion depending on whether a particular group of plaintiffs was thought by the court in which the issue was being litigated to be sufficiently more discrete than the world of potential purchasers at large to justify an exception. We do not believe that such a shifting and highly fact-oriented disposition of the issue of who may bring a damages claim for violation of Rule 10b-5 is a satisfactory basis for a rule of liability imposed on the conduct of business transactions. Nor is it as consistent as a straightforward application of the *Birnbaum* rule with the other factors which support the retention of that rule. We therefore hold that respondent was not entitled to sue for violation of Rule 10b-5, and the judgment of the Court of Appeals is

Reversed.

D. Scienter

Ernst & Ernst v. Hochfelder

United States Supreme Court
425 U.S. 185 (1976)

Justice Powell delivered the opinion of the Court.

The issue in this case is whether an action for civil damages may lie under § 10(b) of the Securities Exchange Act of 1934 (1934 Act), and Securities and Exchange Commission Rule 10b-5, in the absence of an allegation of intent to deceive, manipulate, or defraud on the part of the defendant.

I

Petitioner, Ernst & Ernst, is an accounting firm. From 1946 through 1967 it was retained by First Securities Company of Chicago (First Securities), a small brokerage firm and member of the Midwest Stock Exchange and of the National Association of Securities Dealers, to perform periodic audits of the firm's books and records. In connection with these audits Ernst & Ernst prepared for filing with the Securities and Exchange Commission (the Commission) the annual reports required of First Securities under § 17(a) of the 1934 Act. It also prepared for First Securities responses to the financial questionnaires of the Midwest Stock Exchange (the Exchange).

Respondents were customers of First Securities who invested in a fraudulent securities scheme perpetrated by Leston B. Nay, president of the firm and owner of 92% of its stock. Nay induced the respondents to invest funds in "escrow" accounts that he represented would yield a high rate of return. Respondents did so from 1942 through 1966, with the majority of the transactions occurring in the 1950's. In fact, there were no escrow accounts as Nay converted respondents' funds to his own use immediately upon receipt. These transactions were not in the customary form of dealings between First Securities and its customers. The respondents drew their personal checks payable to Nay or a designated bank for his account. No such escrow accounts were reflected on the books and records of First Securities, and none was shown on its periodic accounting to respondents in connection with their other investments. Nor were they included in First Securities' filings with the Commission or the Exchange.

This fraud came to light in 1968 when Nay committed suicide, leaving a note that described First Securities as bankrupt and the escrow accounts as "spurious." Respondents subsequently filed this action for damages against Ernst & Ernst in the United States District Court for the Northern District of Illinois under § 10(b) of the 1934 Act. The complaint charged that Nay's escrow scheme violated § 10(b) and Commission Rule 10b-5, and that Ernst & Ernst had "aided and abetted" Nay's violations by its "failure" to conduct proper audits of First Securities. As revealed through discovery, respondents' cause of action rested on a theory of negligent nonfeasance. The premise was that Ernst & Ernst had failed to utilize "appropriate auditing procedures" in its audits of First Securities, thereby failing to discover internal practices of the firm said to prevent an effective audit. The practice principally relied on was Nay's rule that only he could open mail addressed to him at First Securities or addressed to First Securities to his attention, even if it arrived in his absence. Respondents contended that if Ernst & Ernst had conducted a proper audit, it would have discovered this "mail rule." The existence of the rule then would have been disclosed in reports to the Exchange and to the Commission by Ernst & Ernst as an irregular procedure that prevented an effective audit. This would have led to an investigation of Nay that would have revealed the fraudulent scheme. Respondents specifically disclaimed the existence of fraud or intentional misconduct on the part of Ernst & Ernst.

After extensive discovery the District Court granted Ernst & Ernst's motion for summary judgment and dismissed the action [and the Court of Appeals reversed]. . . . We granted certiorari to resolve the question whether a private cause of action for damages will lie under § 10(b) and Rule 10b-5 in the absence of any allegation of "scienter" intent to deceive, manipulate, or defraud.[6] We conclude that it will not and therefore we reverse.

---

6. [12] ... In this opinion the term "scienter" refers to a mental state embracing intent to deceive, manipulate, or defraud. In certain areas of the law recklessness is considered to be a form of intentional conduct for purposes of imposing liability for some act. We need not address here the question whether, in some circumstances, reckless behavior is sufficient for civil liability under § 10(b) and

II

... During the 30-year period since a private cause of action was first implied under § 10(b) and Rule 10b-5, a substantial body of case law and commentary has developed as to its elements. Courts and commentators long have differed with regard to whether scienter is a necessary element of such a cause of action, or whether negligent conduct alone is sufficient. In addressing this question, we turn first to the language of § 10(b), for "[t]he starting point in every case involving construction of a statute is the language itself." *Blue Chip Stamps, supra*, at 756 (Powell, J., concurring).

A

Section 10(b) makes unlawful the use or employment of "any manipulative or deceptive device or contrivance" in contravention of Commission rules. The words "manipulative or deceptive" used in conjunction with "device or contrivance" strongly suggest that § 10(b) was intended to proscribe knowing or intentional misconduct.

In its *amicus curiae* brief, however, the Commission contends that nothing in the language "manipulative or deceptive device or contrivance" limits its operation to knowing or intentional practices. In support of its view, the Commission cites the overall congressional purpose in the 1933 and 1934 Acts to protect investors against false and deceptive practices that might injure them. The Commission then reasons that since the "effect" upon investors of given conduct is the same regardless of whether the conduct is negligent or intentional, Congress must have intended to bar all such practices and not just those done knowingly or intentionally. The logic of this effect-oriented approach would impose liability for wholly faultless conduct where such conduct results in harm to investors, a result the Commission would be unlikely to support. But apart from where its logic might lead, the Commission would add a gloss to the operative language of the statute quite different from its commonly accepted meaning. The argument simply ignores the use of the words "manipulative," "device," and "contrivance," terms that make unmistakable a congressional intent to proscribe a type of conduct quite different from negligence. Use of the word "manipulative" is especially significant. It is and was virtually a term of art when used in connection with securities markets. It connotes intentional or willful conduct designed to deceive or defraud investors by controlling or artificially affecting the price of securities.

In addition to relying upon the Commission's argument with respect to the operative language of the statute, respondents contend that since we are dealing with "remedial legislation," *Tcherepnin v. Knight*, 389 U.S. 332, 336 (1967), it must be construed "'not technically and restrictively, but flexibly to effectuate its remedial purposes.'" *Affiliated Ute Citizens v. United States, supra*, 406 U.S. at 151, quoting *SEC v. Capital Gains Research Bureau, supra*, 375 U.S., at 186. They argue that the "remedial purposes" of the Acts demand a construction of § 10(b) that embraces negligence as a standard of liability. But in seeking to accomplish its broad remedial

---

Rule 10b-5.
  Since this case concerns an action for damages we also need not consider the question whether scienter is a necessary element in an action for injunctive relief under § 10(b) and Rule 10b-5.

goals, Congress did not adopt uniformly a negligence standard even as to express civil remedies. In some circumstances and with respect to certain classes of defendants, Congress did create express liability predicated upon a failure to exercise reasonable care. *E.g.*, 1933 Act § 11(b)(3)(B) (liability of "experts," such as accountants for misleading statements in portions of registration statements for which they are responsible). But in other situations good faith is an absolute defense. 1934 Act § 18 (misleading statements in any document filed pursuant to the 1934 Act). And in still other circumstances Congress created express liability regardless of the defendant's fault, 1933 Act § 11(a) (issuer liability for misleading statements in the registration statement).

It is thus evident that Congress fashioned standards of fault in the express civil remedies in the 1933 and 1934 Acts on a particularized basis.... In view of the language of § 10(b) which so clearly connotes intentional misconduct, and mindful that the language of a statute controls when sufficiently clear in its context, further inquiry may be unnecessary. We turn now, nevertheless, to the legislative history of the 1934 Act to ascertain whether there is support for the meaning attributed to § 10(b) by the Commission and respondents.

B

Although the extensive legislative history of the 1934 Act is bereft of any explicit explanation of Congress' intent, we think the relevant portions of that history support our conclusion that § 10(b) was addressed to practices that involve some element of scienter and cannot be read to impose liability for negligent conduct alone....

[T]he intended scope of § 10(b) [is not] revealed explicitly in the legislative history of the 1934 Act, which deals primarily with other aspects of the legislation. There is no indication, however, that § 10(b) was intended to proscribe conduct not involving scienter. The extensive hearings that preceded passage of the 1934 Act touched only briefly on § 10, and most of the discussion was devoted to the enumerated devices that the Commission is empowered to proscribe under § 10(a). The most relevant exposition of the provision that was to become § 10(b) was by Thomas G. Corcoran, a spokesman for the drafters. Corcoran indicated:

> Subsection (c) [§ 9(c) of H.R. 7852—later § 10(b)] says, "Thou shalt not devise any other cunning devices."

... Of course subsection (c) is a catch-all clause to prevent manipulative devices. I do not think there is any objection to that kind of clause. The Commission should have the authority to deal with new manipulative devices.

Hearings on H.R. 7852 and H.R. 8720 before the House Comm. on Interstate and Foreign Commerce, 73d Cong., 2d Sess., 115 (1934). This brief explanation of § 10(b) by a spokesman for its drafters is significant. The section was described rightly as a "catch-all" clause to enable the Commission "to deal with new manipulative [or cunning] devices." It is difficult to believe that any lawyer, legislative draftsman, or legislator would use these words if the intent was to create liability for merely negligent acts or omissions....

The legislative reports do not address the scope of § 10(b) or its catch-all function directly. In considering specific manipulative practices left to Commission regulation, however, the reports indicate that liability would not attach absent scienter, supporting the conclusion that Congress intended no lesser standard under § 10(b)....

In the portion of the general analysis section of the Report entitled "Manipulative Practices," however, there is a discussion of specific practices that were considered so inimical to the public interest as to require express prohibition such as "wash" sales and "matched" orders,[7] and of other practices that might in some cases serve legitimate purposes, such as stabilization of security prices and grants of options. These latter practices were left to regulation by the Commission. 1934 Act §§ 9(a)(6), (c). Significantly, we think, in the discussion of the need to regulate even the latter category of practices when they are manipulative, there is no indication that any type of criminal or civil liability is to attach in the absence of scienter. Furthermore, in commenting on the express civil liabilities provided in the 1934 Act, the Report explains:

> ... [I]f an investor has suffered loss by reason of illicit practices, it is equitable that he should be allowed to recover damages from the guilty party.... The bill provides that any person who unlawfully manipulates the price of a security, or who induces transactions in a security by means of false or misleading statements, or who makes a false or misleading statement in the report of a corporation, shall be liable in damages to those who have bought or sold the security at prices affected by such violation or statement. In such case the burden is on the plaintiff to show the violation or the fact that the statement was false or misleading, and that he relied thereon to his damage. The defendant may escape liability by showing that the statement was made in *good faith. Id.*, at 12–13 (emphasis supplied)....

C

The 1933 and 1934 Acts constitute interrelated components of the federal regulatory scheme governing transactions in securities.... Recognizing this, respondents and the Commission contrast § 10(b) to other sections of the Acts to support their contention that civil liability may be imposed upon proof of negligent conduct. We think they misconceive the significance of the other provisions of the Acts.

The Commission argues that Congress has been explicit in requiring willful conduct when that was the standard of fault intended, citing § 9 of the 1934 Act, which generally proscribes manipulation of securities prices.... From this the Commission concludes that since § 10(b) is not by its terms explicitly restricted to willful, knowing, or purposeful conduct, it should not be construed in all cases to require more than negligent action or inaction as a precondition for civil liability.

---

7. [25] "Wash" sales are transactions involving no change in beneficial ownership. "Matched" orders are orders for the purchase sale of a security that are entered with the knowledge that orders of substantially the same size, at substantially the same time and price, have been or will be entered by the same or different persons for the sale/purchase of such security....

The structure of the Acts does not support the Commission's argument. In each instance that Congress created express civil liability in favor of purchasers or sellers of securities it clearly specified whether recovery was to be premised on knowing or intentional conduct, negligence, or entirely innocent mistake....

We also consider it significant that each of the express civil remedies in the 1933 Act allowing recovery for negligent conduct, see §§ 11, 12(2), 15, is subject to significant procedural restrictions not applicable under § 10(b).... We think these procedural limitations indicate that the judicially created private damage remedy under § 10(b) — which has no comparable restrictions — cannot be extended, consistently with the intent of Congress, to actions premised on negligent wrongdoing. Such extension would allow causes of action covered by § 11, § 12(2), and § 15 to be brought instead under § 10(b) and thereby nullify the effectiveness of the carefully drawn procedural restrictions on these express actions....

D

We have addressed, to this point, primarily the language and history of § 10(b). The Commission contends, however, that subsections (2) and (3) of Rule 10b-5 are cast in language which if standing alone — could encompass both intentional and negligent behavior. These subsections respectively provide that it is unlawful "[t]o make any untrue statement of a material fact or to omit to state a material fact necessary in order to make the statements made, in light of the circumstances under which they were made, not misleading ..." and "to engage in any act, practice, or course of business which operates or would operate as a fraud or deceit upon any person...." Viewed in isolation the language of subsection (2), and arguably that of subsection (3), could be read as proscribing, respectively, any type of material misstatement or omission, and any course of conduct, that has the effect of defrauding investors, whether the wrongdoing was intentional or not.

We note first that such a reading cannot be harmonized with the administrative history of the rule, a history making clear that when the Commission adopted the rule it was intended to apply only to activities that involved scienter. More importantly, Rule 10b-5 was adopted pursuant to authority granted the Commission under § 10(b). The rulemaking power granted to an administrative agency charged with the administration of a federal statute is not the power to make law. Rather, it is "'the power to adopt regulations to carry into effect the will of Congress as expressed by the statute.'" *Dixon v. United States*, 381 U.S. 68, 74 (1965), quoting *Manhattan General Equipment Co. v. Commissioner*, 297 U.S. 129, 134 (1936). Thus, despite the broad view of the Rule advanced by the Commission in this case, its scope cannot exceed the power granted the Commission by Congress under § 10(b). For the reasons stated above, we think the Commission's original interpretation of Rule 10b-5 was compelled by the language and history of § 10(b) and related sections of the Acts.... [Reversed.]

Mr. Justice Blackmun, with whom Mr. Justice Brennan joins, dissenting.

Once again — *see Blue Chip Stamps v. Manor Drug Stores*, 421 U.S. 723, 730 (1975) — the Court interprets § 10(b) of the Securities Exchange Act of 1934 and the Securities and Exchange Commission's Rule 10b-5, restrictively and narrowly and thereby stultifies recovery for the victim. This time the Court does so by confining the statute and the Rule to situations where the defendant has "scienter," that is, the "intent to deceive, manipulate, or defraud." Sheer negligence, the Court says, is not within the reach of the statute and the Rule, and was not contemplated when the great reforms of 1933, 1934, and 1942 were effectuated by Congress and the Commission.

Perhaps the Court is right, but I doubt it. The Government and the Commission doubt it too, as is evidenced by the thrust of the brief filed by the Solicitor General on behalf of the Commission, as *amicus curiae*. The Court's opinion, *ante*, to be sure, has a certain technical consistency about it. It seems to me, however, that an investor can be victimized just as much by negligent conduct as by positive deception, and that it is not logical to drive a wedge between the two, saying that Congress clearly intended the one but certainly not the other.

No one questions the fact that the respondents here were the victims of an intentional securities fraud practiced by Leston B. Nay. What is at issue, of course, is the petitioner-accountant firm's involvement and that firm's responsibility under Rule 10b-5. The language of the Rule, making it unlawful for any person "in connection with the purchase or sale of any security"

> (b) To make any untrue statement of a material fact or to omit to state a material fact necessary in order to make the statements made, in the light of the circumstances under which they were made, not misleading, or

> (b) To engage in any act, practice, or course of business which operates or would operate as a fraud or deceit upon any person,

seems to me, clearly and succinctly, to prohibit negligent as well as intentional conduct of the kind proscribed, to extend beyond common law fraud, and to apply to negligent omission and commission. This is consistent with Congress' intent, repeatedly recognized by the Court, that securities legislation enacted for the purpose of avoiding frauds be construed "not technically and restrictively, but flexibly to effectuate its remedial purposes."

On motion for summary judgment, therefore, the respondents' allegations, in my view, were sufficient, and the District Court's dismissal of the action was improper to the extent that the dismissal rested on the proposition that suit could not be maintained under §10(b) and Rule 10b-5 for mere negligence. The opposite appears to be true, at least in the Second Circuit, with respect to suits by the SEC to enjoin a violation of the Rule....

The critical importance of the auditing accountant's role in insuring full disclosure cannot be overestimated. The SEC has emphasized that in certifying statements the accountant's duty "is to safeguard the public interest, not that of his client." *In re Touche, Niven, Bailey & Smart*, 37 S.E.C. 629, 670–671 (1957). "In our complex society the accountant's certificate and the lawyer's opinion can be instruments for inflicting pecuniary loss more potent than the chisel or the crowbar." *United States v. Benjamin*, 328 F.2d 854, 863 (CA2), *cert. denied sub nom. Howard v. United States*,

377 U.S. 953 (1964). In this light, the initial inquiry into whether Ernst & Ernst's preparation and certification of the financial statements of First Securities Company of Chicago were negligent, because of the failure to perceive Nay's extraordinary mail rule and in other alleged respects, and thus whether Rule 10b-5 was violated, should not be thwarted.

But the Court today decides that it is to be thwarted; and so once again it rests with Congress to rephrase and to re-enact, if investor victims, such as these, are ever to have relief under the federal securities laws that I thought had been enacted for their broad, needed, and deserving benefit.

From a technical standpoint, one of the more interesting things about *Ernst & Ernst v. Hochfelder* is what it left undecided. First, it left for another time the question of whether scienter is required in a Rule 10b-5 injunction action brought by the Securities and Exchange Commission. Second, it left open whether in a Rule 10b-5 case recklessness is enough by itself to constitute scienter. The Supreme Court answered the first of these questions in *Aaron v. SEC.*, 446 U.S. 680 (1980). Using essentially the same reasoning presented in *Hochfelder*, the Court said scienter is required in an SEC injunction action brought under Rule 10b-5. The second question has not reached the Supreme Court, but other courts agree that recklessness meets the Rule 10b-5 scienter requirement (though they differ on significant issues relating to scienter and to what must be alleged as to scienter in a complaint in order to avoid summary judgment for the defendant).

E. Loss; Loss Causation

Dura Pharmaceuticals, Inc. v. Broudo

United States Supreme Court
544 U.S. 336 (2005)

JUSTICE BREYER delivered the opinion of the Court:

A private plaintiff who claims securities fraud must prove that the defendant's fraud caused an economic loss. We consider a Ninth Circuit holding that a plaintiff can satisfy this requirement—a requirement that courts call "loss causation"—simply by alleging in the complaint and subsequently establishing that "the price" of the security "*on the date of purchase* was inflated because of the misrepresentation." In our view, the Ninth Circuit is wrong, both in respect to what a plaintiff must prove and in respect to what the plaintiffs' complaint here must allege.

Respondents are individuals who bought stock in Dura Pharmaceuticals, Inc., on the public securities market between April 15, 1997, and February 24, 1998. They have brought this securities fraud class action Daniel S. Sommers, and Paul R. Hoeber, for respondents against Dura and some of its managers and directors (hereinafter Dura) in federal court. In respect to the question before us, their ... complaint makes substantially the following allegations:

(1) Before and during the purchase period, Dura (or its officials) made false statements concerning both Dura's drug profits and future Food and Drug Administration (FDA) approval of a new asthmatic spray device.

(2) In respect to drug profits, Dura falsely claimed that it expected that its drug sales would prove profitable.

(3) In respect to the asthmatic spray device, Dura falsely claimed that it expected the FDA would soon grant its approval.

(4) On the last day of the purchase period, February 24, 1998, Dura announced that its earnings would be lower than expected, principally due to slow drug sales.

(5) The next day Dura's shares lost almost half their value (falling from about $39 per share to about $21).

(6) About eight months later (in November 1998), Dura announced that the FDA would not approve Dura's new asthmatic spray device.

(7) The next day Dura's share price temporarily fell but almost fully recovered within one week.

Most importantly, the complaint says the following (and nothing significantly more than the following) about economic losses attributable to the spray device misstatement: *"In reliance on the integrity of the market, [the plaintiffs] ... paid artificially inflated prices for Dura securities"* and the plaintiffs suffered *"damage[s]"* thereby.

The District Court dismissed the complaint. In respect to the plaintiffs' drug-profitability claim, it held that the complaint failed adequately to allege an appropriate state of mind, *i.e.,* that defendants had acted knowingly, or the like. In respect to the plaintiffs' spray device claim, it held that the complaint failed adequately to allege "loss causation."

The Court of Appeals for the Ninth Circuit reversed. In the portion of the court's decision now before us—the portion that concerns the spray device claim—the Circuit held that the complaint adequately alleged "loss causation." The Circuit wrote that "plaintiffs establish loss causation if they have shown that the price *on the date of purchase* was inflated because of the misrepresentation." It added that "the injury occurs at the time of the transaction." Since the complaint pleaded "that the price at the time of purchase was overstated," and it sufficiently identified the cause, its allegations were legally sufficient.

Because the Ninth Circuit's views about loss causation differ from those of other Circuits that have considered this issue, we granted Dura's petition for certiorari. We now reverse.

Private federal securities fraud actions are based upon federal securities statutes and their implementing regulations. Section 10(b) of the Securities Exchange Act of 1934 forbids (1) the "use or employ[ment] ... of any ... deceptive device," (2) "in connection with the purchase or sale of any security," and (3) "in contravention of" Securities and Exchange Commission "rules and regulations." 15 U.S.C. § 78j(b).

Commission Rule 10b-5 forbids, among other things, the making of any "untrue statement of a material fact" or the omission of any material fact "necessary in order to make the statements made ... not misleading."

The courts have implied from these statutes and Rule a private damages action, which resembles, but is not identical to, common-law tort actions for deceit and misrepresentation. See, *e.g., Blue Chip Stamps v. Manor Drug Stores*, 421 U.S. 723, 730, 744 (1975); *Ernst & Ernst v. Hochfelder*, 425 U.S. 185, 196 (1976). And Congress has imposed statutory requirements on that private action. *E.g.*, 15 U.S.C. §78u-4(b)(4).

In cases involving publicly traded securities and purchases or sales in public securities markets, the action's basic elements include: (1) *a material misrepresentation (or omission)*, see *Basic Inc. v. Levinson*, 485 U.S. 224, 231–232 (1988); (2) *scienter, i.e.*, a wrongful state of mind, see *Ernst & Ernst, supra*, at 197, 199; (3) *a connection with the purchase or sale of a security*, see *Blue Chip Stamps, supra*, at 730–731; (4) *reliance*, often referred to in cases involving public securities markets (fraud-on-the-market cases) as "transaction causation," see *Basic, supra*, at 248–249 (nonconclusively presuming that the price of a publicly traded share reflects a material misrepresentation and that plaintiffs have relied upon that misrepresentation as long as they would not have bought the share in its absence); (5) *economic loss*, 15 U.S.C. §78u-4(b)(4); and (6) *"loss causation," i.e.*, a causal connection between the material misrepresentation and the loss, *ibid.; cf.* T. Hazen, Law of Securities Regulation §§12.11[1], [3] (5th ed.2005).

Dura argues that the complaint's allegations are inadequate in respect to these last two elements.

We begin with the Ninth Circuit's basic reason for finding the complaint adequate, namely, that at the end of the day plaintiffs need only "establish," *i.e.*, prove, that "the price *on the date of purchase* was inflated because of the misrepresentation." In our view, this statement of the law is wrong. Normally, in cases such as this one (*i.e.*, fraud-on-the-market cases), an inflated purchase price will not itself constitute or proximately cause the relevant economic loss.

For one thing, as a matter of pure logic, at the moment the transaction takes place, the plaintiff has suffered no loss; the inflated purchase payment is offset by ownership of a share that *at that instant* possesses equivalent value. Moreover, the logical link between the inflated share purchase price and any later economic loss is not invariably strong. Shares are normally purchased with an eye toward a later sale. But if, say, the purchaser sells the shares quickly before the relevant truth begins to leak out, the misrepresentation will not have led to any loss. If the purchaser sells later after the truth makes its way into the marketplace, an initially inflated purchase price *might* mean a later loss. But that is far from inevitably so. When the purchaser subsequently resells such shares, even at a lower price, that lower price may reflect, not the earlier misrepresentation, but changed economic circumstances, changed investor expectations, new industry-specific or firm-specific facts, conditions, or other events, which taken separately or together account for some or all of that lower price. (The same is true in respect to a claim that a share's higher price is lower than it would otherwise have been — a claim we do not consider here.) Other things being equal, the longer the time between purchase and sale, the more likely that this is so, *i.e.*, the more likely that other factors caused the loss.

Given the tangle of factors affecting price, the most logic alone permits us to say is that the higher purchase price will *sometimes* play a role in bringing about a future loss. It may prove to be a necessary condition of any such loss, and in that sense one might say that the inflated purchase price suggests that the misrepresentation (using language the Ninth Circuit used) "touches upon" a later economic loss. But, even if that is so, it is insufficient. To "touch upon" a loss is not to *cause* a loss, and it is the latter that the law requires. 15 U.S.C. § 78u-4(b)(4).

For another thing, the Ninth Circuit's holding lacks support in precedent. Judicially implied private securities fraud actions resemble in many (but not all) respects common-law deceit and misrepresentation actions. The common law of deceit subjects a person who "fraudulently" makes a "misrepresentation" to liability "for pecuniary loss caused" to one who justifiably relies upon that misrepresentation. And the common law has long insisted that a plaintiff in such a case show not only that had he known the truth he would not have acted but also that he suffered actual economic loss.

Given the common-law roots of the securities fraud action (and the common-law requirement that a plaintiff show actual damages), it is not surprising that other Courts of Appeals have rejected the Ninth Circuit's "inflated purchase price" approach to proving causation and loss. Indeed, the Restatement of Torts, in setting forth the judicial consensus, says that a person who "misrepresents the financial condition of a corporation in order to sell its stock" becomes liable to a relying purchaser "for the loss" the purchaser sustains "when the facts ... become generally known" and "as a result" share value "depreciate[s]." § 548A, Comment *b*, at 107. Treatise writers, too, have emphasized the need to prove proximate causation. Prosser and Keeton § 110, at 767 (losses do "not afford any basis for recovery" if "brought about by business conditions or other factors").

We cannot reconcile the Ninth Circuit's "inflated purchase price" approach with these views of other courts. And the uniqueness of its perspective argues against the validity of its approach in a case like this one where we consider the contours of a judicially implied cause of action with roots in the common law.

Finally, the Ninth Circuit's approach overlooks an important securities law objective. The securities statutes seek to maintain public confidence in the marketplace. They do so by deterring fraud, in part, through the availability of private securities fraud actions. But the statutes make these latter actions available, not to provide investors with broad insurance against market losses, but to protect them against those economic losses that misrepresentations actually cause.

The statutory provision at issue here and the paragraphs that precede it emphasize this last mentioned objective. Private Securities Litigation Reform Act of 1995, 109 Stat. 737. The statute insists that securities fraud complaints "specify" each misleading statement; that they set forth the facts "on which [a] belief" that a statement is misleading was "formed"; and that they "state with particularity facts giving rise to a strong inference that the defendant acted with the required state of mind." 15 U.S.C. §§ 78u-4(b)(1), (2). And the statute expressly imposes on plaintiffs "the burden of proving" that the defendant's misrepresentations "caused the loss for which the plaintiff seeks to recover." § 78u-4(b)(4).

The statute thereby makes clear Congress' intent to permit private securities fraud actions for recovery where, but only where, plaintiffs adequately allege and prove the traditional elements of causation and loss. By way of contrast, the Ninth Circuit's approach would allow recovery where a misrepresentation leads to an inflated purchase price but nonetheless does not proximately cause any economic loss. That is to say, it would permit recovery where these two traditional elements in fact are missing.

In sum, we find the Ninth Circuit's approach inconsistent with the law's requirement that a plaintiff prove that the defendant's misrepresentation (or other fraudulent conduct) proximately caused the plaintiff's economic loss. We need not, and do not, consider other proximate cause or loss-related questions....

Section III
Insider Trading under Federal Law

Chiarella v. United States
United States Supreme Court
445 U.S. 222 (1980)

Justice Powell delivered the opinion of the Court.

The question in this case is whether a person who learns from the confidential documents of one corporation that it is planning an attempt to secure control of a second corporation violates § 10(b) of the Securities Exchange Act of 1934 if he fails to disclose the impending takeover before trading in the target company's securities.

I

Petitioner is a printer by trade. In 1975 and 1976, he worked as a "markup man" in the New York composing room of Pandick Press, a financial printer. Among documents that petitioner handled were five announcements of corporate takeover bids. When these documents were delivered to the printer, the identities of the acquiring and target corporations were concealed by blank spaces or false names. The true names were sent to the printer on the night of the final printing.

The petitioner, however, was able to deduce the names of the target companies before the final printing from other information contained in the documents. Without disclosing his knowledge, petitioner purchased stock in the target companies and sold the shares immediately after the takeover attempts were made public. By this method, petitioner realized a gain of slightly more than $30,000 in the course of 14 months. Subsequently, the Securities and Exchange Commission (Commission or SEC) began an investigation of his trading activities. In May 1977, petitioner entered into a consent decree with the Commission in which he agreed to return his profits to the sellers of the shares. On the same day, he was discharged by Pandick Press.

In January 1978, petitioner was indicted on 17 counts of violating § 10(b) of the Securities Exchange Act of 1934 (1934 Act) and SEC Rule 10b-5. After petitioner unsuccessfully moved to dismiss the indictment, he was brought to trial and convicted on all counts.

The Court of Appeals for the Second Circuit affirmed petitioner's conviction. We granted certiorari, and we now reverse.

II

... This case concerns the legal effect of the petitioner's silence. The District Court's charge permitted the jury to convict the petitioner if it found that he willfully failed to inform sellers of target company securities that he knew of a forthcoming takeover bid that would make their shares more valuable. In order to decide whether silence in such circumstances violates § 10(b), it is necessary to review the language and legislative history of that statute as well as its interpretation by the Commission and the federal courts.

Although the starting point of our inquiry is the language of the statute, § 10(b) does not state whether silence may constitute a manipulative or deceptive device. Section 10(b) was designed as a catchall clause to prevent fraudulent practices. But neither the legislative history nor the statute itself afford specific guidance for the resolution of this case. When Rule 10b-5 was promulgated in 1942, the SEC did not discuss the possibility that failure to provide information might run afoul of § 10(b).

The SEC took an important step in the development of § 10(b) when it held that a broker-dealer and his firm violated that section by selling securities on the basis of undisclosed information obtained from a director of the issuer corporation who was also a registered representative of the brokerage firm. In *Cady, Roberts & Co.*, 40 S.E.C. 907 (1961), the Commission decided that a corporate insider must abstain from trading in the shares of his corporation unless he has first disclosed all material inside information known to him.... The Commission emphasized that the duty arose from (i) the existence of a relationship affording access to inside information intended to be available only for a corporate purpose, and (ii) the unfairness of allowing a corporate insider to take advantage of that information by trading without disclosure.

That the relationship between a corporate insider and the stockholders of his corporation gives rise to a disclosure obligation is not a novel twist of the law. At common law, misrepresentation made for the purpose of inducing reliance upon the false statement is fraudulent. But one who fails to disclose material information prior to the consummation of a transaction commits fraud only when he is under a duty to do so. And the duty to disclose arises when one party has information "that the other [party] is entitled to know because of a fiduciary or other similar relation of trust and confidence between them."[8] In its *Cady, Roberts* decision, the Commission rec-

---

8. [9] Restatement (Second) of Torts § 551 (2)(a) (1976)....

ognized a relationship of trust and confidence between the shareholders of a corporation and those insiders who have obtained confidential information by reason of their position with that corporation.[9] This relationship gives rise to a duty to disclose because of the "necessity of preventing a corporate insider from ... tak[ing] unfair advantage of the uninformed minority stockholders." *Speed v. Transamerica Corp.*, 99 F. Supp. 808, 829 (Del. 1951).

The federal courts have found violations of § 10(b) where corporate insiders used undisclosed information for their own benefit. *E.g., SEC v. Texas Gulf Sulphur Co.*, 401 F.2d 883 (CA2 1968). The cases also have emphasized, in accordance with the common-law rule, that "[t]he party charged with failing to disclosed market information must be under a duty to disclose it." *Frigitemp Corp. v. Financial Dynamics Fund, Inc.*, 524 F.2d 275, 282 (CA2 1975). Accordingly, a purchaser of stock who has no duty to a prospective seller because he is neither an insider nor a fiduciary has been held to have no obligation to reveal material facts. *See General Time Corp. v. Talley Industries, Inc.*, 403 F.2d 159, 164 (CA2 1968).

This Court followed the same approach in *Affiliated Ute Citizens v. United States*, 406 U.S. 128 (1972). A group of American Indians formed a corporation to manage joint assets derived from tribal holdings. The corporation issued stock to its Indian shareholders and designated a local bank as its transfer agent. Because of the speculative nature of the corporate assets and the difficulty of ascertaining the true value of a share, the corporation requested the bank to stress to its stockholders the importance of retaining the stock. Two of the bank's assistant managers aided the shareholders in disposing of stock which the managers knew was traded in two separate markets — a primary market of Indians selling to non-Indians through the bank and a resale market consisting entirely of non-Indians. Indian sellers charged that the assistant managers had violated § 10(b) and Rule 10b-5 by failing to inform them of the higher prices prevailing in the resale market. The Court recognized that no duty of disclosure would exist if the bank merely had acted as a transfer agent. But the bank also had assumed a duty to act on behalf of the shareholders, and the Indian sellers had relied upon its personnel when they sold their stock. Because these officers of the bank were charged with a responsibility to the shareholders, they could not act as market makers inducing the Indians to sell their stock without disclosing the existence of the more favorable non-Indian market.

Thus, administrative and judicial interpretations have established that silence in connection with the purchase or sale of securities may operate as a fraud actionable under § 10(b) despite the absence of statutory language or legislative history specifically

---

9. [10] ... The dissent of MR. JUSTICE BLACKMUN suggests that the "special facts" doctrine may be applied to find that silence constitutes fraud where one party has superior information to another. This Court has never so held. In *Strong v. Repide*, 213 U.S. 419, 431–434 (1909), this Court applied the special-facts doctrine to conclude that a corporate insider had a duty to disclose to a shareholder. In that case, the majority shareholder of a corporation secretly purchased the stock of another shareholder without revealing that the corporation, under the insider's direction, was about to sell corporate assets at a price that would greatly enhance the value of the stock. The decision in *Strong v. Repide* was premised upon the fiduciary duty between the corporate insider and the shareholder.

addressing the legality of nondisclosure. But such liability is premised upon a duty to disclose arising from a relationship of trust and confidence between parties to a transaction. Application of a duty to disclose prior to trading guarantees that corporate insiders, who have an obligation to place the shareholder's welfare before their own, will not benefit personally through fraudulent use of material, nonpublic information.

III

In this case, the petitioner was convicted of violating § 10(b) although he was not a corporate insider and he received no confidential information from the target company. Moreover, the "market information" upon which he relied did not concern the earning power or operations of the target company, but only the plans of the acquiring company. Petitioner's use of that information was not a fraud under § 10(b) unless he was subject to an affirmative duty to disclose it before trading. In this case, the jury instructions failed to specify any such duty. In effect, the trial court instructed the jury that petitioner owed a duty to everyone; to all sellers, indeed, to the market as a whole. The jury simply was told to decide whether petitioner used material, nonpublic information at a time when "he knew other people trading in the securities market did not have access to the same information."

The Court of Appeals affirmed the conviction by holding that "[a]nyone—corporate insider or not—who regularly receives material nonpublic information may not use that information to trade in securities without incurring an affirmative duty to disclose." Although the court said that its test would include only persons who regularly receive material, nonpublic information, its rationale for that limitation is unrelated to the existence of a duty to disclose. The Court of Appeals, like the trial court, failed to identify a relationship between petitioner and the sellers that could give rise to a duty. Its decision thus rested solely upon its belief that the federal securities laws have "created a system providing equal access to information necessary for reasoned and intelligent investment decisions." The use by anyone of material information not generally available is fraudulent, this theory suggests, because such information gives certain buyers or sellers an unfair advantage over less informed buyers and sellers.

This reasoning suffers from two defects. First, not every instance of financial unfairness constitutes fraudulent activity under § 10(b). *See Santa Fe Industries, Inc. v. Green,* 430 U.S. 462, 474–477 (1977). Second, the element required to make silence fraudulent—a duty to disclose—is absent in this case. No duty could arise from petitioner's relationship with the sellers of the target company's securities, for petitioner had no prior dealings with them. He was not their agent, he was not a fiduciary, he was not a person in whom the sellers had placed their trust and confidence. He was, in fact, a complete stranger who dealt with the sellers only through impersonal market transactions.

We cannot affirm petitioner's conviction without recognizing a general duty between all participants in market transactions to forgo actions based on material, nonpublic information. Formulation of such a broad duty, which departs radically from the established doctrine that duty arises from a specific relationship between two parties, should not be undertaken absent some explicit evidence of congressional intent.

As we have seen, no such evidence emerges from the language or legislative history of § 10(b). Moreover, neither the Congress nor the Commission ever has adopted a parity-of-information rule. Instead the problems caused by misuse of market information have been addressed by detailed and sophisticated regulation that recognizes when use of market information may not harm operation of the securities markets. For example, the Williams Act limits but does not completely prohibit a tender offeror's purchases of target corporation stock before public announcement of the offer. Congress' careful action in this and other areas contrasts, and is in some tension, with the broad rule of liability we are asked to adopt in this case.

Indeed, the theory upon which the petitioner was convicted is at odds with the Commission's view of § 10(b) as applied to activity that has the same effect on sellers as the petitioner's purchases. "Warehousing" takes place when a corporation gives advance notice of its intention to launch a tender offer to institutional investors who then are able to purchase stock in the target company before the tender offer is made public and the price of shares rises. In this case, as in warehousing, a buyer of securities purchases stock in a target corporation on the basis of market information which is unknown to the seller. In both of these situations, the seller's behavior presumably would be altered if he had the nonpublic information. Significantly, however, the Commission has acted to bar warehousing under its authority to regulate tender offers after recognizing that action under § 10(b) would rest on a "somewhat different theory" than that previously used to regulate insider trading as fraudulent activity.

We see no basis for applying such a new and different theory of liability in this case. As we have emphasized before, the 1934 Act cannot be read "'more broadly than its language and the statutory scheme reasonably permit.'" *Touche Ross & Co. v. Redington*, 442 U.S. 560, 578 (1979), quoting *SEC v. Sloan*, 436 U.S. 103, 116 (1978). Section 10(b) is aptly described as a catchall provision, but what it catches must be fraud. When an allegation of fraud is based upon nondisclosure, there can be no fraud absent a duty to speak. We hold that a duty to disclose under § 10(b) does not arise from the mere possession of nonpublic market information. The contrary result is without support in the legislative history of § 10(b) and would be inconsistent with the careful plan that Congress has enacted for regulation of the securities markets.

IV

In its brief to this Court, the United States offers an alternative theory to support petitioner's conviction. It argues that petitioner breached a duty to the acquiring corporation when he acted upon information that he obtained by virtue of his position as an employee of a printer employed by the corporation. The breach of this duty is said to support a conviction under § 10(b) for fraud perpetrated upon both the acquiring corporation and the sellers.

We need not decide whether this theory has merit for it was not submitted to the jury. The jury was told, in the language of Rule 10b-5, that it could convict the petitioner if it concluded that he either (i) employed a device, scheme, or artifice to defraud or (ii) engaged in an act, practice, or course of business which operated or would operate as a fraud or deceit upon any person. The trial judge stated that a "scheme to defraud" is a plan to obtain money by trick or deceit and that "a failure by Chiarella to disclose material, non-public information in connection with his purchase of stock would constitute deceit." Accordingly, the jury was instructed that the petitioner employed a scheme to defraud if he "did not disclose ... material non-public information in connection with the purchases of the stock."

Alternatively, the jury was instructed that it could convict if "Chiarella's alleged conduct of having purchased securities without disclosing material, non-public information would have or did have the effect of operating as a fraud upon a seller." The judge earlier had stated that fraud "embraces all the means which human ingenuity can devise and which are resorted to by one individual to gain an advantage over another by false misrepresentation, suggestions or by suppression of the truth."

The jury instructions demonstrate that petitioner was convicted merely because of his failure to disclose material, non-public information to sellers from whom he bought the stock of target corporations. The jury was not instructed on the nature or elements of a duty owed by petitioner to anyone other than the sellers. Because we cannot affirm a criminal conviction on the basis of a theory not presented to the jury, we will not speculate upon whether such a duty exists, whether it has been breached, or whether such a breach constitutes a violation of § 10(b).[10] [Reversed.]

Dirks v. SEC

United States Supreme Court
463 U.S. 646 (1983)

JUSTICE POWELL delivered the opinion of the Court.

... [Raymond] Dirks was an officer of a New York broker-dealer firm who specialized in providing investment analysis of insurance company securities to institutional investors.... Dirks received information from Ronald Secrist, a former officer of Equity Funding of America. Secrist alleged that the assets of Equity Funding, a diversified corporation primarily engaged in selling life insurance and mutual funds, were vastly overstated as the result of fraudulent corporate practices.... He urged Dirks to verify the fraud and disclose it publicly.

---

10. [21] The dissent of THE CHIEF JUSTICE relies upon a single phrase from the jury instructions, which states that the petitioner held a "confidential position" at Pandick Press, to argue that the jury was properly instructed on the theory "that a person who has misappropriated nonpublic information has an absolute duty to disclose that information or to refrain from trading." The few words upon which this thesis is based do not explain to the jury the nature and scope of the petitioner's duty to his employer, the nature and scope of petitioner's duty, if any, to the acquiring corporation, or the elements of the tort of misappropriation. Nor do the jury instructions suggest that a "confidential position" is a necessary element of the offense for which petitioner was charged. Thus, we do not believe that a "misappropriation" theory was included in the jury instructions.

The conviction would have to be reversed even if the jury had been instructed that it could convict the petitioner either (1) because of his failure to disclose material, nonpublic information to sellers or (2) because of a breach of a duty to the acquiring corporation. We may not uphold a criminal conviction if it is impossible to ascertain whether the defendant has been punished for noncriminal conduct.

[Dirks investigated, and as he did so "he openly discussed the information he had obtained with a number of clients and investors," some of whom sold Equity Funding securities. After the Equity Funding fraud came to light publicly, the Securities and Exchange Commission censured Dirks after determining that he had aided and abetted violations of Rule 10b-5 "by repeating the allegations of fraud to members of the investment community." The court of appeals affirmed the decision of the SEC, and the Supreme Court granted certiorari.]

We were explicit in *Chiarella* in saying that there can be no duty to disclose where the person who has traded on inside information "was not [the corporation's] agent, ... was not a fiduciary, [or] was not a person in whom the sellers [of the securities] had placed their trust and confidence." Not to require such a fiduciary relationship, we recognized, would "depar[t] radically from the established doctrine that duty arises from a specific relationship between two parties" and would amount to "recognizing a general duty between all participants in market transactions to forgo actions based on material, nonpublic information." This requirement of a specific relationship between the shareholders and the individual trading on inside information has created analytical difficulties for the SEC and courts in policing tippees who trade on inside information. Unlike insiders who have independent fiduciary duties to both the corporation and its shareholders, the typical tippee has no such relationships.[13] In view of this absence, it has been unclear how a tippee acquires the ... duty to refrain from trading on inside information....

In determining whether a tippee is under an obligation to disclose or abstain, it ... is necessary to determine whether the insider's "tip" constituted a breach of the insider's fiduciary duty [, and the test for this] is whether the insider personally will benefit ... from his disclosure....

... This requires courts to focus on objective criteria, *i.e.*, whether the insider receives a direct or indirect personal benefit from the disclosure, such as a pecuniary gain or a reputational benefit that will translate into future earnings.... The elements of fiduciary duty and exploitation of nonpublic information also exist when an insider makes a gift of confidential information to a trading relative or friend....

Under the insider-trading and tipping rules set forth above, we find that there was no actionable violation by Dirks.... Unless the insiders breached their ... duty to shareholders in disclosing the nonpublic information to Dirks, he breached no duty when he passed it on to investors....

---

13. [14] Under certain circumstances, such as where corporate information is revealed legitimately to an underwriter, accountant, lawyer, or consultant working for the corporation, these outsiders may become fiduciaries of the shareholders. The basis for recognizing this fiduciary duty is not simply that such persons acquired nonpublic corporate information, but rather that they have entered into a special confidential relationship in the conduct of the business of the enterprise and are given access to information solely for corporate purposes. When such a person breaches his fiduciary relationship, he may be treated more properly as a tipper than a tippee. For such a duty to be imposed, however, the corporation must expect the outsider to keep the disclosed nonpublic information confidential, and the relationship at least must imply such a duty.

It is clear that neither Secrist nor the other Equity Funding employees violated their ... duty to the corporation's shareholders by providing information to Dirks.... As the facts of this case clearly indicate, the tippers were motivated by a desire to expose the fraud. In the absence of a breach of duty to shareholders by the insiders, there was no derivative breach by Dirks....

United States v. O'Hagan

United States Supreme Court
521 U.S. 642 (1997)

JUSTICE GINSBERG delivered the opinion of the Court.

[We address this issue, among others:] Is a person who trades in securities for personal profit, using confidential information misappropriated in breach of a fiduciary duty to the source of the information, guilty of violating § 10(b) [of the Securities Exchange Act of 1934] and Rule 10b-5 [thereunder]?

I

Respondent James Herman O'Hagan was a partner in the law firm of Dorsey & Whitney in Minneapolis, Minnesota. In July 1988, Grand Metropolitan PLC (Grand Met), a company based in London, England, retained Dorsey & Whitney as local counsel to represent Grand Met regarding a potential tender offer for the common stock of the Pillsbury Company, headquartered in Minneapolis.... O'Hagan did no work on the Grand Met representation....

On August 18, 1988, O'Hagan began purchasing call options for Pillsbury stock. Each option gave him the right to purchase 100 shares of Pillsbury stock.... By the end of September, he owned 2,500 unexpired Pillsbury options, apparently more than any other individual investor. O'Hagan also purchased, in September 1988, some 5,000 shares of Pillsbury common stock, at a price just under $39 per share. When Grand Met announced its tender offer in October, the price of Pillsbury stock rose to nearly $60 per share. O'Hagan then sold his Pillsbury call options and common stock, making a profit of more than $4.3 million.

[O'Hagan was convicted of violating rule 10b-5 under the misappropriation theory, but the Eighth Circuit reversed, rejecting that theory.]

II

... We hold, in accord with several other Courts of Appeals, that criminal liability under § 10(b) may be predicated on the misappropriation theory....

We agree with the Government that misappropriation ... satisfies § 10(b)'s requirement that chargeable conduct involve a "deceptive device or contrivance" used "in connection with" the purchase or sale of securities. We observe, first, that misappropriators, as the Government describes them, deal in deception. A fiduciary who "[pretends] loyalty to the principal while secretly converting the principal's information for personal gain," Brief for United States, "dupes" or defrauds the principal.

We turn next to the § 10(b) requirement that the misappropriator's deceptive use of information be "in connection with the purchase or sale of [a] security." This element is satisfied because the fiduciary's fraud is consummated, not when the fiduciary gains the confidential information, but when, without disclosure to his principal, he uses the information to purchase or sell securities. The securities transaction and the breach of duty thus coincide....

Section IV
Scope of Liability

Central Bank of Denver v. First Interstate Bank
United States Supreme Court
511 U.S. 164 (1994)

JUSTICE KENNEDY delivered the opinion of the Court.

As we have interpreted it, § 10(b) of the Securities Exchange Act of 1934 imposes private civil liability on those who commit a manipulative or deceptive act in connection with the purchase or sale of securities. In this case, we must answer a question reserved in two earlier decisions: whether private civil liability under § 10(b) extends as well to those who do not engage in the manipulative or deceptive practice but who aid and abet the violation....

II

... With respect ... to ... the scope of conduct prohibited by § 10(b), the text of the statute controls our decision. In § 10(b), Congress prohibited manipulative or deceptive acts in connection with the purchase or sale of securities. It envisioned that the SEC would enforce the statutory prohibition through administrative and injunctive actions. Of course, a private plaintiff now may bring suit against violators of § 10(b). But the private plaintiff may not bring a 10b-5 suit against a defendant for acts not prohibited by the text of § 10(b)....

Our consideration of statutory duties, especially in cases interpreting § 10(b), establishes that the statutory text controls the definition of conduct covered by § 10(b). That bodes ill for respondents, for "the language of Section 10(b) does not in terms mention aiding and abetting." Brief for SEC as *Amicus Curiae* 8....

Congress knew how to impose aiding and abetting liability when it chose to do so. If, as respondents seem to say, Congress intended to impose aiding and abetting liability, we presume it would have used the words "aid" and "abet" in the statutory text. But it did not.

We reach the uncontroversial conclusion, accepted even by those courts recognizing a § 10(b) aiding and abetting cause of action, that the text of the 1934 Act does not itself reach those who aid and abet a § 10(b) violation. Unlike those courts, however, we think that conclusion resolves the case. It is inconsistent with settled methodology in § 10(b) cases to extend liability beyond the scope of conduct prohibited by the statutory text. To be sure, aiding and abetting a wrongdoer ought to be actionable in certain instances. The issue, however, is not whether imposing private civil liability on aiders and abettors is good policy but whether aiding and abetting is covered by the statute.

As in earlier cases considering conduct prohibited by § 10(b), we again conclude that the statute prohibits only the making of a material misstatement (or omission) or the commission of a manipulative act. The proscription does not include giving aid to a person who commits a manipulative or deceptive act. We cannot amend the statute to create liability for acts that are not themselves manipulative or deceptive within the meaning of the statute....

As a result of the *Central Bank* case, it was uncertain whether the SEC had authority to bring aiding and abetting actions for Rule 10b-5 violations (and, indeed, for other violations). This uncertainty was cleared up when Congress amended Exchange Act Section 20 to give the SEC such power in the case of any violation of an Exchange Act section or rule. (There never has been a question about the Justice Department's ability to bring criminal aiding and abetting actions for Exchange Act violations, because 18 U.S.C. § 2 creates aiding and abetting liability in the case of all federal crimes.)

Stoneridge Investment Partners v. Scientific-Atlanta, Inc.

United States Supreme Court
552 U.S. 148 (2008)

JUSTICE KENNEDY delivered the opinion of the Court.

We consider the reach of the private right of action the Court has found implied in § 10(b) of the Securities Exchange Act of 1934.... [I]nvestors alleged losses after purchasing common stock. They sought to impose liability on entities who, acting both as customers and suppliers, agreed to arrangements that allowed the investors' company to mislead its auditor and issue a misleading financial statement affecting the stock price. We conclude the implied right of action does not reach the customer/supplier companies because the investors did not rely upon their statements or representations....

I ...

For purposes of this proceeding, we take these facts, alleged by petitioner, to be true. Charter, a cable operator, engaged in a variety of fraudulent practices so its quarterly reports would meet Wall Street expectations for cable subscriber growth and operating cash flow. The fraud included misclassification of its customer base; delayed reporting of terminated customers; improper capitalization of costs that should have been shown as expenses; and manipulation of the company's billing cutoff dates to inflate reported revenues. In late 2000, Charter executives realized that, despite these efforts, the company would miss projected operating cash flow numbers by $15 to $20 million. To help meet the shortfall, Charter decided to alter its existing arrangements with respondents, Scientific-Atlanta and Motorola. Petitioner's theory as to whether Arthur Andersen [Charter's outside auditor] was altogether misled ... is not clear at this stage of the case. The point, however, is neither controlling nor significant for our present disposition, and in our decision we assume it was misled.

Respondents supplied Charter with the digital cable converter (set top) boxes that Charter furnished to its customers. Charter arranged to overpay respondents $20 for each set top box it purchased until the end of the year, with the understanding that respondents would return the overpayment by purchasing advertising from Charter. The transactions, it is alleged, had no economic substance; but, because Charter would then record the advertising purchases as revenue and capitalize its purchase of the set top boxes, in violation of generally accepted accounting principles, the transactions would enable Charter to fool its auditor into approving a financial statement showing it met projected revenue and operating cash flow numbers. Respondents agreed to the arrangement.

So that Arthur Andersen would not discover the link between Charter's increased payments for the boxes and the advertising purchases, the companies drafted documents to make it appear the transactions were unrelated and conducted in the ordinary course of business. Following a request from Charter, Scientific-Atlanta sent documents to Charter stating—falsely—that it had increased production costs. It raised the price for set top boxes for the rest of 2000 by $20 per box. As for Motorola, in a written contract Charter agreed to purchase from Motorola a specific number of set top boxes and pay liquidated damages of $20 for each unit it did not take. The contract was made with the expectation Charter would fail to purchase all the units and pay Motorola the liquidated damages.

To return the additional money from the set top box sales, Scientific-Atlanta and Motorola signed contracts with Charter to purchase advertising time for a price higher than fair value. The new set top box agreements were backdated to make it appear that they were negotiated a month before the advertising agreements. The backdating was important to convey the impression that the negotiations were unconnected, a point Arthur Andersen considered necessary for separate treatment of the transactions. Charter recorded the advertising payments to inflate revenue and operating cash flow by approximately $17 million. The inflated number was shown on financial statements filed with the Securities and Exchange Commission (SEC) and reported to the public.

Respondents had no role in preparing or disseminating Charter's financial statements. And their own financial statements booked the transactions as a wash, under generally accepted accounting principles. It is alleged respondents knew or were in reckless disregard of Charter's intention to use the transactions to inflate its revenues and knew the resulting financial statements issued by Charter would be relied upon by research analysts and investors.

Petitioner filed a securities fraud class action on behalf of purchasers of Charter stock alleging that, by participating in the transactions, respondents violated § 10(b) of the Securities Exchange Act of 1934 and SEC Rule 10b-5....

II. ...

In *Central Bank*, the Court determined that § 10(b) liability did not extend to aiders and abettors. The Court found the scope of § 10(b) to be delimited by the text, which makes no mention of aiding and abetting liability. The Court doubted the implied § 10(b) action should extend to aiders and abettors when none of the express causes of action in the securities Acts included that liability. It added the following:

> "Were we to allow the aiding and abetting action proposed in this case, the defendant could be liable without any showing that the plaintiff relied upon the aider and abettor's statements or actions. *See also Chiarella* [*v. United States*]. Allowing plaintiffs to circumvent the reliance requirement would disregard the careful limits on 10b-5 recovery mandated by our earlier cases."

III. . . .

A

Reliance by the plaintiff upon the defendant's deceptive acts is an essential element of the § 10(b) private cause of action. It ensures that, for liability to arise, the "requisite causal connection between a defendant's misrepresentation and a plaintiff's injury" exists as a predicate for liability. *Basic Inc. v. Levinson.* We have found a rebuttable presumption of reliance in two different circumstances. First, if there is an omission of a material fact by one with a duty to disclose, the investor to whom the duty was owed need not provide specific proof of reliance. Second, under the fraud-on-the-market doctrine, reliance is presumed when the statements at issue become public. The public information is reflected in the market price of the security. Then it can be assumed that an investor who buys or sells stock at the market price relies upon the statement. *Basic, supra,* at 247.

Neither presumption applies here. Respondents had no duty to disclose; and their deceptive acts were not communicated to the public. No member of the investing public had knowledge, either actual or presumed, of respondents' deceptive acts during the relevant times. Petitioner, as a result, cannot show reliance upon any of respondents' actions except in an indirect chain that we find too remote for liability.

B

Invoking what some courts call "scheme liability," *see, e.g., In re Enron Corp. Securities, Derivative & "ERISA" Litigation,* 439 F.Supp.2d 692, 723 (S.D.Tex.2006), petitioner nonetheless seeks to impose liability on respondents even absent a public statement. In our view this approach does not answer the objection that petitioner did not in fact rely upon respondents' own deceptive conduct.

Liability is appropriate, petitioner contends, because respondents engaged in conduct with the purpose and effect of creating a false appearance of material fact to further a scheme to misrepresent Charter's revenue. The argument is that the financial statement Charter released to the public was a natural and expected consequence of respondents' deceptive acts; had respondents not assisted Charter, Charter's auditor would not have been fooled, and the financial statement would have been a more accurate reflection of Charter's financial condition. That causal link is sufficient, petitioner argues, to apply Basic's presumption of reliance to respondents' acts.

In effect petitioner contends that in an efficient market investors rely not only upon the public statements relating to a security but also upon the transactions those statements reflect. Were this concept of reliance to be adopted, the implied cause of action would reach the whole marketplace in which the issuing company does business; and there is no authority for this rule.

As stated above, reliance is tied to causation, leading to the inquiry whether respondents' acts were immediate or remote to the injury. In considering petitioner's arguments, we note § 10(b) provides that the deceptive act must be "in connection with the purchase or sale of any security." 15 U.S.C. § 78j(b).

Though this phrase in part defines the statute's coverage rather than causation (and so we do not evaluate the "in connection with" requirement of § 10(b) in this case), the emphasis on a purchase or sale of securities does provide some insight into the deceptive acts that concerned the enacting Congress.... [W]e conclude respondents' deceptive acts, which were not disclosed to the investing public, are too remote to satisfy the requirement of reliance. It was Charter, not respondents, that misled its auditor and filed fraudulent financial statements; nothing respondents did made it necessary or inevitable for Charter to record the transactions as it did.

The petitioner invokes the private cause of action under § 10(b) and seeks to apply it beyond the securities markets—the realm of financing business—to purchase and supply contracts—the realm of ordinary business operations. The latter realm is governed, for the most part, by state law. It is true that if business operations are used, as alleged here, to affect securities markets, the SEC enforcement power may reach the culpable actors. It is true as well that a dynamic, free economy presupposes a high degree of integrity in all of its parts, an integrity that must be underwritten by rules enforceable in fair, independent, accessible courts. Were the implied cause of action to be extended to the practices described here, however, there would be a risk that the federal power would be used to invite litigation beyond the immediate sphere of securities litigation and in areas already governed by functioning and effective state-law guarantees. Our precedents counsel against this extension.... [Section 10(b)] does not reach all commercial transactions that are fraudulent and affect the price of a security in some attenuated way.

These considerations answer as well the argument that if this were a common-law action for fraud there could be a finding of reliance. Even if the assumption is correct, it is not controlling. Section 10(b) does not incorporate common-law fraud into federal law. [Section 10(b)] should not be interpreted to provide a private cause of action against the entire marketplace in which the issuing company operates.

Petitioner's theory, moreover, would put an unsupportable interpretation on Congress' specific response to *Central Bank* in § 104 of the [Private Securities Litigation Reform Act (PSLRA)]. Congress amended the securities laws to provide for limited coverage of aiders and abettors. Aiding and abetting liability is authorized in actions brought by the SEC but not by private parties. See 15 U.S.C. § 78t(e). Petitioner's view of primary liability makes any aider and abettor liable under § 10(b) if he or she committed a deceptive act in the process of providing assistance Were we to adopt this construction of § 10(b), it would revive in substance the implied cause of action against all aiders and abettors except those who committed no deceptive act in the process of facilitating the fraud; and we would undermine Congress' determination that this class of defendants should be pursued by the SEC and not by private litigants ...

The practical consequences of an expansion, which the Court has considered appropriate to examine in circumstances like these, *see Virginia Bankshares, Inc. v. Sandberg*, provide a further reason to reject petitioner's approach. In *Blue Chip*, the Court noted that extensive discovery and the potential for uncertainty and disruption in a lawsuit allow plaintiffs with weak claims to extort settlements from innocent companies. Adoption of petitioner's approach would expose a new class of defendants to these risks. As noted in *Central Bank*, contracting parties might find it necessary to protect against these threats, raising the costs of doing business. Overseas firms with no other exposure to our securities laws could be deterred from doing business here. This, in turn, may raise the cost of being a publicly traded company under our law and shift securities offerings away from domestic capital markets.

C

The history of the § 10(b) private right and the careful approach the Court has taken before proceeding without congressional direction provide further reasons to find no liability here. The § 10(b) private cause of action is a judicial construct that Congress did not enact in the text of the relevant statutes....

Concerns with the judicial creation of a private cause of action caution against its expansion. The decision to extend the cause of action is for Congress, not for us. Though it remains the law, the § 10(b) private right should not be extended beyond its present boundaries....

IV

Secondary actors are subject to criminal penalties, see, e.g., 15 U.S.C. § 78ff, and civil enforcement by the SEC, see, e.g., § 78t(e). The enforcement power is not toothless. Since September 30, 2002, SEC enforcement actions have collected over $10 billion in disgorgement and penalties, much of it for distribution to injured investors. And in this case both parties agree that criminal penalties are a strong deterrent. In addition some state securities laws permit state authorities to seek fines and restitution from aiders and abettors. All secondary actors, furthermore, are not necessarily immune from private suit. The securities statutes provide an express private right of action against accountants and underwriters in certain circumstances, and the implied right of action in § 10(b) continues to cover secondary actors who commit primary violations. *Central Bank, supra*, at 191.

Here respondents were acting in concert with Charter in the ordinary course as suppliers and, as matters then evolved in the not so ordinary course, as customers. Unconventional as the arrangement was, it took place in the marketplace for goods and services, not in the investment sphere. Charter was free to do as it chose in preparing its books, conferring with its auditor, and preparing and then issuing its financial statements. In these circumstances the investors cannot be said to have relied upon any of respondents' deceptive acts in the decision to purchase or sell securities; and as the requisite reliance cannot be shown, respondents have no liability to petitioner under the implied right of action. This conclusion is consistent with the narrow dimensions we must give to a right of action Congress did not authorize when it first enacted the statute and did not expand when it revisited the law....

JUSTICE BREYER took no part in the consideration or decision of this case.

JUSTICE STEVENS, with whom Justice SOUTER and Justice GINSBURG join, dissenting.

Charter Communications, Inc., inflated its revenues by $17 million in order to cover up a $15 to $20 million expected cash flow shortfall. It could not have done so absent the knowingly fraudulent actions of Scientific-Atlanta, Inc., and Motorola, Inc. Investors relied on Charter's revenue statements in deciding whether to invest in Charter and in doing so relied on respondents' fraud, which was itself a "deceptive device" prohibited by § 10(b) of the Securities Exchange Act of 1934. This is enough to satisfy the requirements of § 10(b) and enough to distinguish this case from *Central Bank of Denver*.

I

The allegations in this case—that respondents produced documents falsely claiming costs had risen and signed contracts they knew to be backdated in order to disguise the connection between the increase in costs and the purchase of advertising—plainly describe "deceptive devices" under any standard reading of the phrase.

What the Court fails to recognize is that this case is critically different from Central Bank because the bank in that case did not engage in any deceptive act and, therefore, did not itself violate § 10(b). The Court sweeps aside any distinction, remarking that holding respondents liable would "reviv[e] the implied cause of action against all aiders and abettors except those who committed no deceptive act in the process of facilitating the fraud." But the fact that Central Bank engaged in no deceptive conduct whatsoever—in other words, that it was at most an aider and abettor—sharply distinguishes *Central Bank* from cases that do involve allegations of such conduct.

The Central Bank of Denver was the indenture trustee for bonds issued by a public authority and secured by liens on property in Colorado Springs. After default, purchasers of $2.1 million of those bonds sued the underwriters, alleging violations of § 10(b); they also named Central Bank as a defendant, contending that the bank's delay in reviewing a suspicious appraisal of the value of the security made it liable as an aider and abettor. The facts of this case would parallel those of *Central Bank* if respondents had, for example, merely delayed sending invoices for set-top boxes to Charter. Conversely, the facts in *Central Bank* would mirror those in the case before us today if the bank had knowingly purchased real estate in wash transactions at above-market prices in order to facilitate the appraiser's overvaluation of the security. *Central Bank*, thus, poses no obstacle to petitioner's argument that it has alleged a cause of action under § 10(b).

II

… The Court's view of the causation required to demonstrate reliance is unwarranted and without precedent. In *Basic Inc.*, we held that the "fraud-on-the-market" theory provides adequate support for a presumption in private securities actions that shareholders (or former shareholders) in publicly traded companies rely on public material misstatements that affect the price of the company's stock. The holding in *Basic* is surely a sufficient response to the argument that a complaint alleging that deceptive acts which had a material effect on the price of a listed stock should be dismissed because the plaintiffs were not subjectively aware of the deception at the time of the securities' purchase or sale. This Court as not held that investors must be aware of the specific deceptive act which violates § 10b to demonstrate reliance.

The Court is right that a fraud-on-the-market presumption coupled with its view on causation would not support petitioner's view of reliance. The fraud-on-the-market presumption helps investors who cannot demonstrate that they, themselves, relied on fraud that reached the market. But that presumption says nothing about causation from the other side: what an individual or corporation must do in order to have "caused" the misleading information that reached the market. The Court thus has it backwards when it first addresses the fraud-on-the-market presumption, rather than the causation required. The argument is not that the fraud-on-the-market presumption is enough standing alone, but that a correct view of causation coupled with the presumption would allow petitioner to plead reliance.…

Even if but-for causation, standing alone, is too weak to establish reliance, petitioner has also alleged that respondents proximately caused Charter's misstatement of income; petitioner has alleged that respondents knew their deceptive acts would be the basis for statements that would influence the market price of Charter stock on which shareholders would rely. Thus, respondents' acts had the foreseeable effect of causing petitioner to engage in the relevant securities transactions.…

The Court's view of reliance is unduly stringent and unmoored from authority. The Court first says that if the petitioner's concept of reliance is adopted the implied cause of action "would reach the whole marketplace in which the issuing company does business." The answer to that objection is, of course, that liability only attaches when the company doing business with the issuing company has itself violated § 10(b). The Court next relies on what it views as a strict division between the "realm of financing business" and the "ordinary business operations." But petitioner's position does not merge the two: A corporation engaging in a business transaction with a partner who transmits false information to the market is only liable where the corporation itself violates § 10(b). Such a rule does not invade the province of "ordinary" business transactions.

The majority states that "[s]ection 10(b) does not incorporate common-law fraud into federal law," … Of course, not every common-law fraud action that happens to touch upon securities is an action under [but this Court's opinions do] not purport to jettison all reference to common-law fraud doctrines from § 10(b) cases. In fact, our prior cases explained that to the extent that "the antifraud provisions of the securities laws are not coextensive with common-law doctrines of fraud," it is because common-law fraud doctrines might be too restrictive. *Herman MacLean v. Huddleston*, [459 U.S. 375, 388–389 (1983)]. "Indeed, an important purpose of the federal securities statutes was to rectify perceived deficiencies in the available common-law protections by establishing higher standards of conduct in the securities industry." *Id*. I, thus, see no reason to abandon common-law approaches to causation in § 10(b) cases.

Finally, the Court relies on the course of action Congress adopted after our decision in *Central Bank* to argue that siding with petitioner on reliance would run contrary to congressional intent. Senate hearings on *Central Bank* were held within one month of our decision. [But] Congress stopped short of undoing *Central Bank* entirely, instead adopting a compromise which restored the authority of the SEC to enforce aiding and abetting liability. A private right of action based on aiding and abetting violations of § 10(b) was not, however, included in the PSLRA.... This compromise surely provides no support for extending *Central Bank* in order to immunize an undefined class of actual violators of § 10(b) from liability in private litigation. [P]rivate litigation under § 10(b) continues to play a vital role in protecting the integrity of our securities markets. That Congress chose not to restore the aiding and abetting liability removed by *Central Bank* does not mean that Congress wanted to exempt from liability the broader range of conduct that today's opinion excludes.

The Court is concerned that such liability would deter overseas firms from doing business in the United States or "shift securities offerings away from domestic capital markets." But liability for those who violate § 10(b) [will not harm American competitiveness, and investor faith in US markets is a strength].

Accordingly, while I recognize that the *Central Bank* opinion provides a precedent for judicial policymaking decisions in this area of the law, I respectfully dissent from the Court's continuing campaign to render the private cause of action under § 10(b) toothless....

Chapter 20

Short-Swing Trading: Section 16 of the Securities Exchange Act of 1934

Situation

In the course of working on questions relating to purchases of Daytron stock by Anderson and Baker, you learn that in the past year both Anderson and Baker have sold Daytron stock on the stock exchange. Baker sold shares both before and after she became a Daytron director, and Anderson sold at three points spread fairly evenly over the year. The shares they sold were ones purchased on the stock exchange since the Daytron-Biologistics acquisition.

Anderson and Baker assure you that they had no negative inside information at the times of their sales, and that they sold shares simply to take care of immediate cash needs. Because there has not been any announcement of negative information by Daytron, because the price of its stock has risen rather than declined, and because Anderson and Baker each purchased more Daytron shares within a few weeks of the sales, the facts seem to support them.

Rule 10b-5 is now a fairly refined legal device for policing insider trading. During all of the life of this rule, § 16 of the Securities Exchange Act of 1934 has existed alongside of it. Section 16 was also designed to regulate insider trading, but, compared to Rule 10b-5, it is a spring gun that can hit the innocent as easily as the guilty. The method by which this section gets at the abuse of inside information is the regulation of so-called "short-swing trading." Its most basic provisions are these:

1. Section 16(a) requires that each beneficial owner of more than 10% of any equity security registered under the Exchange Act (except an exempt security), and each director and officer of an issuer of such a security, file reports with the Securities and Exchange Commission and relevant stock exchanges concerning their holdings of all equity securities of such issuer and changes in such holdings.

2. Section 16(b) provides that any profit realized by any of the above persons on any purchase and sale, or sale and purchase, of any non-exempt equity security of such an issuer, within any period of less than six months, "shall

inure to and be recoverable by the issuer" (unless the security was acquired in good faith in connection with a debt previously contracted).

3. Section 16(c) makes it unlawful for any of the above persons to sell any non-exempt equity security of such an issuer if (a) the person does not own the security (*i.e.*, a "short sale") or (b) if owning the security, does not deliver the security against the sale within prescribed periods.

The most interesting and troublesome of these provisions is § 16(b), as will be seen in the cases that follow. Its interpretations contain many quirks that probably are not expected. Interpretations aside, § 16(b) is on its face unusual in that it does not prohibit short-swing trading. In a statute filled with provisions making this or that conduct unlawful, Congress chose not to do so here. Instead, it simply provided that any profits on short-swing trading are to go to the issuer. It should be noted that many of the trickiest questions involving § 16 are answered in the rules the SEC has passed under the section.

Section I
Profit Realized

Smolowe v. Delendo Corp.
United States Court of Appeals, Second Circuit
136 F.2d 231 (1943)

CLARK, CIRCUIT JUDGE.

The issue on appeal is ... the construction ... of § 16(b) of the Securities Exchange Act of 1934, rendering directors, officers, and principal stockholders liable to their corporation for profits realized from security tradings within any six months' period. Plaintiffs, Smolowe and Levy, stockholders of the Delendo Corporation, brought separate actions under this statute on behalf of themselves and other stockholders for recovery by the Corporation — joined as defendant — against defendants Seskis and Kaplan, both directors and president and vice-president respectively of the Corporation.... After trial at which the facts were stipulated, the district court in a careful opinion held the named defendants liable for the maximum profit shown by matching their purchases and sales of corporate stock, some transacted privately and some upon a national securities exchange, between December 1, 1939, and May 30, 1940, in conceded good faith and without any "unfair" use of inside information.

The named defendants had been connected with the Corporation (whose name was Oldetyme Distillers Corporation until after the transactions here involved) since 1933, and each owned around 12 per cent (approximately 100,000 shares) of the 800,000 shares of $1 par value stock issued by the Corporation and listed on the New York Curb Exchange. The Corporation had negotiated for a sale of all its assets to Schenley Distillers Corporation in 1935–1936; but the negotiations were then terminated because of Delendo's contingent liability for a tax claim of the United States against a corporation acquired by it, then in litigation. This claim, originally in the amount of $3,600,000, had been reduced by agreement to $487,265, with the condition that trial was to be postponed (to await the trial of other cases) until, but not later than, December 31, 1939. The Corporation was, therefore, pressing for trial when on February 29, 1940, the present attorney for the defendants submitted to the Attorney General a formal offer of settlement of $65,000, which was accepted April 2 and publicly announced April 5, 1940. Negotiations with Schenley's were reopened on April 11 and were consummated by sale on April 30, 1940, for $4,000,000, plus the assumption of certain of the Corporation's liabilities. Proceedings for dissolution of the Corporation were thereupon initiated and on July 16, 1940, an initial liquidating dividend of $4.35 was paid.

During the six months here in question from December 1, 1939, to May 30, 1940, Seskis purchased 15,504 shares for $25,150.20 and sold 15,800 shares for $35,550, while Kaplan purchased 22,900 shares for $48,172 and sold 21,700 shares for $53,405.16. Seskis purchased 584 shares on the Curb Exchange and the rest from a corporation; he made the sale at one time thereafter to Kaplan at $2.25 per share — 15,583 shares in purported satisfaction of a loan made him by Kaplan in 1936 and 217 shares for cash. Kaplan's purchases, in addition to the stock received from Seskis, were made on the Curb Exchange at various times prior to April 11, 1940; he sold 200 shares on February 15, and the remaining shares between April 16 and May 14, 1940 (both to private individuals and through brokers on the Curb). Except as to 1,700 shares, the certificates delivered by each of them upon selling were not the same certificates received by them on purchases during the period. The district court held the transactions within the statute and by matching purchases and sales to show the highest profits held Seskis for $9,733.80 and Kaplan for $9,161.05 to be paid to the Corporation. Both the named defendants and the Corporation have appealed.

. . .

The controversy as to the construction of the statute involves both the matter of substantive liability and the method of computing "such profit." The first turns primarily upon the preamble, viz., "For the purpose of preventing the unfair use of information which may have been obtained by such beneficial owner, director, or officer by reason of his relationship to the issuer." Defendants would make it the controlling grant and limitation of authority of the entire section, and liability would result only for profits from a proved unfair use of inside information. We cannot agree with this interpretation.

. . .

The primary purpose of the Securities Exchange Act — as the declaration of policy in § 2 makes plain — was to insure a fair and honest market, that is, one which would reflect an evaluation of securities in the light of all available and pertinent data. Furthermore, the Congressional hearings indicate that § 16(b), specifically, was designed to protect the "outside" stockholders against at least short-swing speculation by insiders with advance information. It is apparent too, from the language of § 16(b) itself, as well as from the Congressional hearings, that the only remedy which its framers deemed effective for this reform was the imposition of a liability based upon an objective measure of proof....

A subjective standard of proof, requiring a showing of an actual unfair use of inside information, would render senseless the provisions of the legislation limiting the liability period to six months, making an intention to profit during that period immaterial, and exempting transactions wherein there is a bona fide acquisition of stock in connection with a previously contracted debt. It would also torture the conditional "may" in the preamble into a conclusive "shall have" or "has." And its total effect would be to render the statute little more of an incentive to insiders to refrain from profiteering at the expense of the outside stockholder than are the common-law rules of liability; it would impose a more stringent statute of limitation upon the party aggrieved at the same time that it allowed the wrongdoer to share in the spoils of recovery.

Had Congress intended that only profits from an actual misuse of inside information should be recoverable, it would have been simple enough to say so. Significantly, however, it makes recoverable the profit from any purchase and sale, or sale and purchase, within the period. The failure to limit the recovery to profits gained from misuse of information justifies the conclusion that the preamble was inserted for other purposes than as a restriction on the scope of the Act. The legislative custom to insert declarations of purpose as an aid to constitutionality is well known. Moreover, the preamble here serves the desirable purpose of guide to the Commission in the latter's exercise of its rule-making authority....

The present case would seem to be of the type which the statute was designed to include. Here it is conceded that the defendants did not make unfair use of information they possessed as officers at the time of the transactions. When these began they had no offer from Schenley's. But they knew they were pressing the tax suit; and they, of course, knew of the corporate offer to settle it which re-established the offer to purchase and led to the favorable sale. It is naive to suppose that their knowledge of their own plans as officers did not give them most valuable inside knowledge as to what would probably happen to the stock in which they were dealing. It is difficult to find this use "unfair" in the sense of illegal; it is certainly an advantage and a temptation within the general scope of the legislature's intended prohibition.

The legislative history of the statute is perhaps more significant upon a determination of the method of computing profits—defendants' second line of attack upon the district court's construction of the statute. They urge that even if the statute be not construed to impose liability only for unfair use of inside information, in any event profits should be computed according to the established income tax rule which first looks to the identification of the stock certificate, and if that is not established, then applies the presumption which is hardly more than a rule of administrative convenience of "first in, first out." Defendants rely on the deletion from early drafts of the statute, H.R. 7852, H.R. 8720, and S. 2693, of a provision that profit should be calculated irrespective of certificates received or delivered. H.R. 9323, which was finally passed by the House, failed even to penalize short-swing speculations, other than to prohibit short sales. But H.R. 8720 was never discussed by a House Committee of the Whole, and the omission of the penalty provision in H.R. 9323 suggests at most only an opinion of the Committee on Interstate and Foreign Commerce which drafted it, and one which concerns merely the advisability of any penalty, not the method for its computation.

Actually the Act as passed is a combination of H.R. 9323 and S. 3420. In the process § 16(b) was taken bodily from S. 3420 and written into H.R. 9323. S. 3420 was introduced into the Senate after elaborate hearings on S. 2693 were closed. And its failure to specify a method of computation may well be thought more of a sanction of the formula devised in S. 2693 than an expression of hostility towards it.

Such a conclusion can be reached upon the face of the Act. "Purchase" is defined in § 3(a)(13) to include "any contract to buy," and "sale," in § 3(a)(14), to include "any contract to sell." "Equity security" is defined in § 3(a)(11) as "any stock or similar security." Section 16(b) then appears simply as a statement that any profit from any contract to purchase and any contract to sell — or vice versa — any stock or similar security shall be recoverable by the corporate issuer. There is no express limitation in this language; its generality permits and points to the matching of purchases and sales followed below. The fact that purchases and sales may be thus coupled, regardless of the intent of the insider with respect to a particular purchase or a particular sale and without limitation to a specific stock certificate, points to an arbitrary matching to achieve the showing of a maximum profit. Thus, where an insider purchases one certificate and sells another, the purchase and sale may be connected, even though the insider contends that he is holding the purchased security for sale after six months....

The statute is broadly remedial. Recovery runs not to the stockholder, but to the corporation. We must suppose that the statute was intended to be thorough-going, to squeeze all possible profits out of stock transactions, and thus to establish a standard so high as to prevent any conflict between the selfish interest of a fiduciary officer, director, or stockholder and the faithful performance of his duty. The only rule whereby all possible profits can be surely recovered is that of lowest price in, highest price out — within six months — as applied by the district court. We affirm it here, defendants having failed to suggest another more reasonable rule....

While it is well settled that in a stockholder's or creditor's representative action to recover money belonging to the class the moving party is entitled to lawyer's fees from the sum recovered, this was not strictly an action for money belonging to either class, but for a penalty payable to the corporation. Ordinarily the corporate issuer must bring the action; and only upon its refusal or delay to do so, as here, may a security holder act for it in its name and on its behalf. But this in effect creates a derivative right of action in every stockholder, regardless of the fact that he has no holdings from the class of security subjected to a short-swing operation or that he can receive no tangible benefits, directly or indirectly, from an action because of his position in the security hierarchy. And a stockholder who is successful in maintaining such an action is entitled to reimbursement for reasonable attorney's fees on the theory that the corporation which has received the benefit of the attorney's services should pay the reasonable value thereof....

While the allowance made here was quite substantial, we are not disposed to interfere with the district court's well-considered determination. Since in many cases such as this the possibility of recovering attorney's fees will provide the sole stimulus for the enforcement of § 16(b), the allowance must not be too niggardly.

Affirmed.

The "lowest price in, highest price out" method of calculating profits sometimes results in confusion on three points. First, to find a match for any particular purchase or sale, one looks at transactions within six months before and after the purchase or sale. That is, the total period involved in possible matching is just short of one year, not six months. Second, a multi-share transaction may be split as needed for purposes of matching. That is, a 100 share purchase on July 1 could be matched with a 50 share sale on February 1 and another 50 share sale on December 1. Third, any losses during the period are ignored. It is entirely possible to have profits for purposes of § 16(b) when, in fact, one has suffered a loss when all transactions during a period are taken into account.

Perhaps a comprehensive example will be helpful. Assume the following transactions:

February 1: sold 50 shares at $75

March 1: purchased 100 shares at $75

July 1: purchased 100 shares at $50

August 1: sold 200 shares at $50

November 1: purchased 100 shares at $75

December 1: sold 50 shares at $75

Profits for purposes of § 16(b) were $2,500. This is calculated by matching the 50 shares sold at $75 on each of February 1 and December 1 ($7,500) against the 100 shares purchased on July 1 at $50 ($5,000). The fact that matching the other transactions results in a loss of $5,000 (a total of 200 shares purchased at $75 matched against 200 shares sold at $50) is irrelevant under § 16(b).

Section II
Who Is a Director?

Blau v. Lehman

United States Supreme Court
368 U.S. 403 (1962)

Mr. Justice Black delivered the opinion of the Court.

The petitioner Blau, a stockholder in Tide Water Associated Oil Company, brought this action in a United States District Court on behalf of the company under § 16(b) of the Securities Exchange Act of 1934 to recover with interest "short swing" profits, that is, profits earned within a six months' period by the purchase and sale of securities, alleged to have been "realized" by respondents in Tide Water securities dealings. Respondents are Lehman Brothers, a partnership engaged in investment banking, securities brokerage and in securities trading for its own account, and Joseph A. Thomas, a member of Lehman Brothers and a director of Tide Water. The complaint alleged that Lehman Brothers "deputed ... Thomas, to represent its interests as a director on the Tide Water Board of Directors," and that within a period of six months in 1954 and 1955 Thomas, while representing the interests of Lehman Brothers as a director of Tide Water and "by reason of his special and inside knowledge of the affairs of Tide Water advised and caused the defendants, Lehman Brothers, to purchase and sell 50,000 shares of ... stock of Tide Water, realizing profits thereon which did not inure to and [were] not recovered by Tide Water."

The case was tried before a district judge without a jury. The evidence showed that Lehman Brothers had in fact earned profits out of short-swing transactions in Tide Water securities while Thomas was a director of that company. But as to the charges of deputization and wrongful use of "inside" information by Lehman Brothers, the evidence was in conflict.

First, there was testimony that respondent Thomas had succeeded Hertz, another Lehman partner, on the board of Tide Water; that Hertz had "joined Tidewater Company thinking it was going to be in the interests of Lehman Brothers"; and that he had suggested Thomas as his successor partly because it was in the interest of Lehman. There was also testimony, however, that Thomas, aside from having mentioned from time to time to some of his partners and other people that he thought Tide Water was "an attractive investment" and under "good" management, had never discussed the operating details of Tide Water affairs with any member of Lehman Brothers; that Lehman had bought the Tide Water securities without consulting Thomas and wholly on the basis of public announcements by Tide Water that common shareholders could thereafter convert their shares to a new cumulative preferred issue; that Thomas did not know of Lehman's intent to buy Tide Water stock until after the initial purchases had been made; that upon learning about the purchases he immediately notified Lehman that he must be excluded from "any risk of the purchase or any profit or loss from the subsequent sale"; and that this disclaimer was accepted by the firm.

From the foregoing and other testimony the District Court found that "there was no evidence that the firm of Lehman Brothers deputed Thomas to represent its interests as director on the board of Tide Water" and that there had been no actual use of inside information, Lehman Brothers having bought its Tide Water stock "solely on the basis of Tide Water's public announcements and without consulting Thomas."

On the basis of these findings the District Court refused to render a judgment, either against the partnership or against Thomas individually, for the $98,686.77 profits which it determined that Lehman Brothers had realized holding:

> The law is now well settled that the mere fact that a partner in Lehman Brothers was a director of Tide Water, at the time that Lehman Brothers had this short swing transaction in the stock of Tide Water, is not sufficient to make the partnership liable for the profits thereon, and that Thomas could not be held liable for the profits realized by the other partners from the firm's short swing transactions. *Rattner v. Lehman*, 2d Cir., 1952, 193 F.2d 564, 565, 567. This precise question was passed upon in the *Rattner* decision.

Despite its recognition that Thomas had specifically waived his share of the Tide Water transaction profits, the trial court nevertheless held that within the meaning of §16(b) Thomas had "realized" $3,893.41, his proportionate share of the profits of Lehman Brothers. The court consequently entered judgment against Thomas for that amount but refused to allow interest against him. On appeal, taken by both sides, the Court of Appeals for the Second Circuit adhered to the view it had taken in *Rattner v. Lehman*, 193 F.2d 564, and affirmed the District Court's judgment in all respects, Judge Clark dissenting. The Securities and Exchange Commission then sought leave from the Court of Appeals *en banc* to file an *amicus curiae* petition for rehearing urging the overruling of the *Rattner* case. The Commission's motion was denied, Judges Clark and Smith dissenting. We granted certiorari on the petition of Blau, filed on behalf of himself, other stockholders and Tide Water, and supported by the Commission. The questions presented by the petition are whether the courts below erred: (1) in refusing to render a judgment against the Lehman partnership for the $98,686.77 profits they were found to have "realized" from their "short-swing" transactions in Tide Water stock, (2) in refusing to render judgment against Thomas for the full $98,686.77 profits, and (3) in refusing to allow interest on the $3,893.41 recovery allowed against Thomas.

Petitioner apparently seeks to have us decide the questions presented as though he had proven the allegations of his complaint that Lehman Brothers actually deputized Thomas to represent its interests as a director of Tide Water, and that it was his advice and counsel based on his special and inside knowledge of Tide Water's affairs that caused Lehman Brothers to buy and sell Tide Water's stock. But the trial court found otherwise and the Court of Appeals affirmed these findings. Inferences could perhaps have been drawn from the evidence to support petitioner's charges, but examination of the record makes it clear to us that the findings of the two courts below were not clearly erroneous. Moreover, we cannot agree with the Commission that the courts' determinations of the disputed factual issues were conclusions of law rather than findings of fact. We must therefore decide whether Lehman Brothers, Thomas or both have an absolute liability under § 16(b) to pay over all profits made on Lehman's Tide Water stock dealings even though Thomas was not sitting on Tide Water's board to represent Lehman and even though the profits made by the partnership were on its own initiative, independently of any advice or "inside" knowledge given it by director Thomas.

First. The language of § 16 does not purport to impose its extraordinary liability on any "person," "fiduciary" or not, unless he or it is a "director," "officer" or "beneficial owner of more than 10 per centum of any class of any equity security ... which is registered on a national securities exchange." Lehman Brothers was neither an officer nor a 10% stockholder of Tide Water, but petitioner and the Commission contend that the Lehman partnership is or should be treated as a director under § 16(b).

(a) Although admittedly not "literally designated" as one, it is contended that Lehman is a director. No doubt Lehman Brothers, though a partnership, could for purposes of § 16 be a "director" of Tide Water and function through a deputy, since § 3(a)(9) of the Act provides that "'person' means ... partnership" and § 3(a)(7) that "'director' means any director of a corporation or any person performing similar functions with respect to any organization, whether incorporated or unincorporated." Consequently, Lehman Brothers would be a "director" of Tide Water, if as petitioner's complaint charged Lehman actually functioned as a director through Thomas, who had been deputized by Lehman to perform a director's duties not for himself but for Lehman. But the findings of the two courts below, which we have accepted, preclude such a holding. It was Thomas, not Lehman Brothers as an entity, that was the director of Tide Water.

(b) It is next argued that the intent of § 3(a)(9) in defining "person" as including a partnership is to treat a partnership as an inseparable entity. Because Thomas, one member of this inseparable entity, is an "insider," it is contended that the whole partnership should be considered the "insider." But the obvious intent of § 3(a)(9), as the Commission apparently realizes, is merely to make it clear that a partnership can be treated as an entity under the statute, not that it must be. This affords no reason at all for construing the word "director" in § 16(b) as though it read "partnership of which the director is a member." And the fact that Congress provided in § 3(a)(9) for a partnership to be treated as an entity in its own right likewise offers no support for the argument that Congress wanted a partnership to be subject to all the responsibilities and financial burdens of its members in carrying on their other individual business activities.

(c) Both the petitioner and the Commission contend on policy grounds that the Lehman partnership should be held liable even though it is neither a director, officer, nor a 10% stockholder. Conceding that such an interpretation is not justified by the literal language of § 16(b) which plainly limits liability to directors, officers, and 10% stockholders, it is argued that we should expand § 16(b) to cover partnerships of which a director is a member in order to carry out the congressionally declared purpose "of preventing the unfair use of information which may have been obtained by such beneficial owner, director, or officer by reason of his relationship to the issuer...." Failure to do so, it is argued, will leave a large and unintended loophole in the statute — one "substantially eliminating the great Wall Street trading firms from the statute's operation." 286 F.2d, at 799. These firms it is claimed will be able to evade the Act and take advantage of the "inside" information available to their members as insiders of countless corporations merely by trading "inside" information among the various partners.

The argument of petitioner and the Commission seems to go so far as to suggest that §16(b)'s forfeiture of profits should be extended to include all persons realizing "short swing" profits who either act on the basis of "inside" information or have the possibility of "inside" information. One may agree that petitioner and the Commission present persuasive policy arguments that the Act should be broadened in this way to prevent "the unfair use of information" more effectively than can be accomplished by leaving the Act so as to require forfeiture of profits only by those specifically designated by Congress to suffer those losses. But this very broadening of the categories of persons on whom these liabilities are imposed by the language of §16(b) was considered and rejected by Congress when it passed the Act. Drafts of provisions that eventually became §16(b) not only would have made it unlawful for any director, officer or 10% stockholder to disclose any confidential information regarding registered securities, but also would have made all profits received by *anyone*, "insider" or not, "to whom such unlawful disclosure" had been made recoverable by the company.

Not only did Congress refuse to give §16(b) the content we are now urged to put into it by interpretation, but with knowledge that in 1952 the Second Circuit Court of Appeals refused, in the Rattner case, to apply §16(b) to Lehman Brothers in circumstances substantially like those here, Congress has left the Act as it was. And so far as the record shows this interpretation of §16(b) was the view of the Commission until it intervened last year in this case.... Congress can and might amend §16(b) if the Commission would present to it the policy arguments it has presented to us, but we think that Congress is the proper agency to change an interpretation of the Act unbroken since its passage, if the change is to be made.

Second. The petitioner and the Commission contend that Thomas should be required individually to pay to Tide Water the entire $98,686.77 profit Lehman Brothers realized on the ground that under partnership law he is co-owner of the entire undivided amount and has therefore "realized" it all. "[O]nly by holding the partner-director liable for the *entire* short-swing profits realized by his firm," it is urged, can "an effective prophylactic to the stated statutory policy ... be fully enforced." But liability under §16(b) is to be determined neither by general partnership law nor by adding to the "prophylactic" effect Congress itself clearly prescribed in §16(b). That section leaves no room for judicial doubt that a director is to pay to his company only "any profit realized *by him*" from short-swing transactions. (Emphasis added.) It would be nothing but a fiction to say that "Thomas realized" all the profits earned by the partnership of which he was a member. It was not error to refuse to hold Thomas liable for profits he did not make.

Third. It is contended that both courts below erred in failing to allow interest on the recovery of Thomas' share of the partnership profits. Section 16(b) says nothing about interest one way or the other. This Court has said in a kindred situation that "interest is not recovered according to a rigid theory of compensation for money withheld, but is given in response to considerations of fairness. It is denied when its exaction would be inequitable." *Board of Commissioners v. United States*, 308 U.S. 343, 352. Both courts below denied interest here and we cannot say that the denial was either so unfair or so inequitable as to require us to upset it.

Affirmed.

MR. JUSTICE DOUGLAS, with whom THE CHIEF JUSTICE concurs, dissenting.

What the Court does today is substantially to eliminate "the great Wall Street trading firms" from the operation of § 16(b), as Judge Clark stated in his dissent in the Court of Appeals. This result follows because of the wide dispersion of partners of investment banking firms among our major corporations. Lehman Bros. has partners on 100 boards. Under today's ruling that firm can make a rich harvest on the "inside information" which § 16 of the Act covers because each partner need account only for his distributive share of the firm's profits on "inside information," the other partners keeping the balance. This is a mutilation of the Act....

We forget much history when we give § 16 a strict and narrow construction. Brandeis in *Other People's Money* spoke of the office of "director" as "a happy hunting ground" for investment bankers. He said that "The goose that lays golden eggs has been considered a most valuable possession. But even more profitable is the privilege of taking the golden eggs laid by somebody else's goose. The investment bankers and their associates now enjoy that privilege."

The hearings that led to the Securities Exchange Act of 1934 are replete with episodes showing how insiders exploited for their personal gain "inside information" which came to them as fiduciaries and was therefore an asset of the entire body of security holders. The Senate Report labeled those practices as "predatory operations." S. Rep. No. 1455, 73d Cong., 2d Sess., p. 68. It said:

> Among the most vicious practices unearthed at the hearings before the subcommittee was the flagrant betrayal of their fiduciary duties by directors and officers of corporations who used their positions of trust and the confidential information which came to them in such positions, to aid them in their market activities. Closely allied to this type of abuse was the unscrupulous employment of inside information by large stockholders who, while not directors and officers, exercised sufficient control over the destinies of their companies to enable them to acquire and profit by information not available to others. *Id.*, at 55. *See also* S. Rep. No. 792, 73d Cong., 2d Sess., p. 9.

The theory embodied in § 16 was the one Brandeis espoused. It was stated by Sam Rayburn as follows: "Men charged with the administration of other people's money must not use inside information for their own advantage." H.R. Rep. No. 1383, 73d Cong., 2d Sess. 13.

What we do today allows all but one partner to share in the feast which the one places on the partnership table. They in turn can offer feasts to him in the 99 other companies of which they are directors. This result is a dilution of the fiduciary principle that Congress wrote into § 16 of the Act. It is, with all respect, a dilution that is possible only by a strained reading of the law. Until now, the courts have given this fiduciary principle a cordial reception. We should not leave to Congress the task of restoring the edifice that it erected and that we tear down.

Section III
What Is a Sale?

Kern County Land Co. v. Occidental Petroleum Corp.

United States Supreme Court
411 U.S. 582 (1973)

Mr. Justice White delivered the opinion of the Court.

Section 16(b) of the Securities Exchange Act of 1934 provides that officers, directors, and holders of more than 10% of the listed stock of any company shall be liable to the company for any profits realized from any purchase and sale or sale and purchase of such stock occurring within a period of six months. Unquestionably, one or more statutory purchases occur when one company, seeking to gain control of another, acquires more than 10% of the stock of the latter through a tender offer made to its shareholders. But is it a § 16(b) "sale" when the target of the tender offer defends itself by merging into a third company and the tender offeror then exchanges his stock for the stock of the surviving company and also grants an option to purchase the latter stock that is not exercisable within the statutory six-month period? This is the question before us in this case.

I

On May 8, 1967, after unsuccessfully seeking to merge with Kern County Land Co. (Old Kern), Occidental Petroleum Corp. (Occidental) announced an offer, to expire on June 8, 1967, to purchase on a first-come, first-served basis 500,000 shares of Old Kern common stock at a price of $83.50 per share plus a brokerage commission of $1.50 per share. By May 10, 1967, 500,000 shares, more than 10% of the outstanding shares of Old Kern, had been tendered. On May 11, Occidental extended its offer to encompass an additional 500,000 shares. At the close of the tender offer, on June 8, 1967, Occidental owned 887,549 shares of Old Kern.

Immediately upon the announcement of Occidental's tender offer, the Old Kern management undertook to frustrate Occidental's takeover attempt. A management letter to all stockholders cautioned against tender and indicated that Occidental's offer might not be the best available, since the management was engaged in merger discussions with several companies. When Occidental extended its tender offer, the president of Old Kern sent a telegram to all stockholders again advising against tender. In addition, Old Kern undertook merger discussions with Tenneco, Inc. (Tenneco), and, on May 19, 1967, the Board of Directors of Old Kern announced that it had approved a merger proposal advanced by Tenneco. Under the terms of the merger, Tenneco would acquire the assets, property, and goodwill of Old Kern, subject to its liabilities, through "Kern County Land Co." (New Kern), a new corporation to be formed by Tenneco to receive the assets and carry on the business of Old Kern. The shareholders of Old Kern would receive a share of Tenneco cumulative convertible preference stock in exchange for each share of Old Kern common stock which they owned. On the same day, May 19, Occidental, in a quarterly report to stockholders, appraised the value of the new Tenneco stock at $105 per share.

... Realizing that, if the Old Kern-Tenneco merger were approved and successfully closed, Occidental would have to exchange its Old Kern shares for Tenneco stock and would be locked into a minority position in Tenneco. Occidental took other steps to protect itself. Between May 30 and June 2, it negotiated an arrangement with Tenneco whereby Occidental granted Tenneco Corp., a subsidiary of Tenneco, an option to purchase at $105 per share all of the Tenneco preference stock to which Occidental would be entitled in exchange for its Old Kern stock when and if the Old Kern-Tenneco merger was closed. The premium to secure the option, at $10 per share, totaled $8,866,230 and was to be paid immediately upon the signing of the option agreement. If the option were exercised, the premium was to be applied to the purchase price. By the terms of the option agreement, the option could not be exercised prior to December 9, 1967, a date six months and one day after expiration of Occidental's tender offer. On June 2, 1967, within six months of the acquisition by Occidental of more than 10% ownership of Old Kern, Occidental and Tenneco Corp. executed the option. Soon thereafter, Occidental announced that it would not oppose the Old Kern-Tenneco merger and dismissed its state court suits against Old Kern.

The Old Kern-Tenneco merger plan was presented to and approved by Old Kern shareholders at their meeting on July 17, 1967. Occidental refrained from voting its Old Kern shares, but in a letter read at the meeting Occidental stated that it had determined prior to June 2 not to oppose the merger and that it did not consider the plan unfair or inequitable. Indeed, Occidental indicated that, had it been voting, it would have voted in favor of the merger.

Meanwhile, the Securities and Exchange Commission had refused Occidental's request to exempt from possible § 16(b) liability Occidental's exchange of its Old Kern stock for the Tenneco preference shares that would take place when and if the merger transaction were closed....

The Old Kern-Tenneco merger transaction was closed on August 30. Old Kern shareholders thereupon became irrevocably entitled to receive Tenneco preference stock, share for share in exchange for their Old Kern stock. Old Kern was dissolved and all of its assets, including "all claims, demands, rights and choses in action accrued or to accrue under and by virtue of the Securities Exchange Act of 1934...," were transferred to New Kern.

The option granted by Occidental on June 2, 1967, was exercised on December 11, 1967....

On October 17, 1967, New Kern instituted a suit under § 16(b) against Occidental to recover the profits which Occidental had realized as a result of its dealings in Old Kern stock. The complaint alleged that the execution of the Occidental-Tenneco option on June 2, 1967, and the exchange of Old Kern shares for shares of Tenneco to which Occidental became entitled pursuant to the merger closed on August 30, 1967, were both "sales" within the coverage of § 16(b). Since both acts took place within six months of the date on which Occidental became the owner of more than 10% of the stock of Old Kern, New Kern asserted that § 16(b) required surrender of the profits realized by Occidental. New Kern eventually moved for summary judgment, and, on December 27, 1970, the District Court granted summary judgment in favor of New Kern. The District Court held that the execution of the option on June 2, 1967, and the exchange of Old Kern shares for shares of Tenneco on August 30, 1967, were "sales" under § 16(b). The Court ordered Occidental to disgorge its profits plus interest. In a supplemental opinion, Occidental was also ordered to refund the dividends which it had received plus interest.

On appeal, the Court of Appeals reversed and ordered summary judgment entered in favor of Occidental. The Court held that neither the option nor the exchange constituted a "sale" within the purview of § 16(b). We granted certiorari. We affirm.

II

... As specified in its introductory clause, § 16(b) was enacted "[f]or the purpose of preventing the unfair use of information which may have been obtained by [a statutory insider] ... by reason of his relationship to the issuer." Congress recognized that short-swing speculation by stockholders with advance, inside information would threaten the goal of the Securities Exchange Act to "insure the maintenance of fair and honest markets." Insiders could exploit information not generally available to others to secure quick profits. As we have noted, "the only method Congress deemed effective to curb the evils of insider trading was a flat rule taking the profits out of a class of transactions in which the possibility of abuse was believed to be intolerably great." *Reliance Electric Co. v. Emerson Electric Co.*, 404 U.S. 418, 422 (1972). As stated in the report of the Senate Committee, the bill aimed at protecting the public "by preventing directors, officers, and principal stockholders of a corporation ... from speculating in the stock on the basis of information not available to others." S. Rep. No. 792, 73d Cong., 2d Sess., 9 (1934).

Although traditional cash-for-stock transactions that result in a purchase and sale or a sale and purchase within the six-month statutory period are clearly within the purview of § 16(b), the courts have wrestled with the question of inclusion or exclusion of certain "unorthodox" transactions. The statutory definitions of "purchase" and "sale" are broad and, at least arguably, reach many transactions not ordinarily deemed a sale or purchase. In deciding whether borderline transactions are within the reach of the statute, the courts have come to inquire whether the transaction may serve as a vehicle for the evil which Congress sought to prevent—the realization of short-swing profits based upon access to inside information—thereby endeavoring to implement congressional objectives without extending the reach of the statute beyond its intended limits. The statute requires the inside, short-swing trader to disgorge all profits realized on all "purchases" and "sales" within the specified time period, without proof of actual abuse of insider information, and without proof of intent to profit on the basis of such information. Under these strict terms, the prevailing view is to apply the statute only when its application would serve its goals. "[W]here alternative constructions of the terms of § 16(b) are possible, those terms are to be given the construction that best serves the congressional purpose of curbing short-swing speculation by corporate insiders." *Reliance Electric Co. v. Emerson Electric Co.*, 404 U.S., at 424. Thus, "[i]n interpreting the terms 'purchase' and 'sale,' courts have properly asked whether the particular type of transaction involved is one that gives rise to speculative abuse." *Reliance Electric Co. v. Emerson Electric Co.*, *supra*, at 424, n. 4.

In the present case, it is undisputed that Occidental became a "beneficial owner" within the terms of § 16(b) when, pursuant to its tender offer, it "purchased" more than 10% of the outstanding shares of Old Kern. We must decide, however, whether a "sale" within the ambit of the statute took place either when Occidental became irrevocably bound to exchange its shares of Old Kern for shares of Tenneco pursuant to the terms of the merger agreement between Old Kern and Tenneco or when Occidental gave an option to Tenneco to purchase from Occidental the Tenneco shares so acquired.

III

On August 30, 1967, the Old Kern-Tenneco merger agreement was signed, and Occidental became irrevocably entitled to exchange its shares of Old Kern stock for shares of Tenneco preference stock. Concededly, the transaction must be viewed as though Occidental had made the exchange on that day. But, even so, did the exchange involve a "sale" of Old Kern shares within the meaning of § 16(b)? We agree with the Court of Appeals that it did not, for we think it totally unrealistic to assume or infer from the facts before us that Occidental either had or was likely to have access to inside information, by reason of its ownership of more than 10% of the outstanding shares of Old Kern, so as to afford it an opportunity to reap speculative, short-swing profits from its disposition within six months of its tender-offer purchases.

It cannot be contended that Occidental was an insider when, on May 8, 1967, it made an irrevocable offer to purchase 500,000 shares of Old Kern stock at a price substantially above market. At that time, it owned only 1,900 shares of Old Kern stock, far fewer than the 432,000 shares needed to constitute the 10% ownership required by the statute....

It is also wide of the mark to assert that Occidental, as a sophisticated corporation knowledgeable in matters of corporate affairs and finance, knew that its tender offer would either succeed or would be met with a "defensive merger." If its takeover efforts failed, it is argued, Occidental knew it could sell its stock to the target company's merger partner at a substantial profit. Calculations of this sort, however, whether speculative or not and whether fair or unfair to other stockholders or to Old Kern, do not represent the kind of speculative abuse at which the statute is aimed, for they could not have been based on inside information obtained from substantial stockholdings that did not yet exist....

By May 10, 1967, Occidental had acquired more than 10% of the outstanding shares of Old Kern. It was thus a statutory insider when, on May 11, it extended its tender offer to include another 500,000 shares. We are quite unconvinced, however, that the situation had changed materially with respect to the possibilities of speculative abuse of inside information by Occidental. Perhaps Occidental anticipated that extending its offer would increase the likelihood of the ultimate success of its takeover attempt or the occurrence of a defensive merger. But, again, the expectation of such benefits was unrelated to the use of information unavailable to other stockholders or members of the public with sufficient funds and the intention to make the purchases Occidental had offered to make before June 8, 1967.

The possibility that Occidental had, or had the opportunity to have, any confidential information about Old Kern before or after May 11, 1967, seems extremely remote....

There is, therefore, nothing in connection with Occidental's acquisition of Old Kern stock pursuant to its tender offer to indicate either the possibility of inside information being available to Occidental by virtue of its stock ownership or the potential for speculative abuse of such inside information by Occidental. Much the same can be said of the events leading to the exchange of Occidental's Old Kern stock for Tenneco preferred, which is one of the transactions that is sought to be classified a "sale" under § 16(b). The critical fact is that the exchange took place and was required pursuant to a merger between Old Kern and Tenneco. That merger was not engineered by Occidental but was sought by Old Kern to frustrate the attempts of Occidental to gain control of Old Kern. Occidental obviously did not participate in or control the negotiations or the agreement between Old Kern and Tenneco....

Once the merger and exchange were approved, Occidental was left with no real choice with respect to the future of its shares of Old Kern. Occidental was in no position to prevent the issuance of a ruling by the Internal Revenue Service that the exchange of Old Kern stock for Tenneco preferred would be tax free; and, although various lawsuits were begun in state and federal courts seeking to postpone the merger closing beyond the statutory six-month period, those efforts were futile. The California Corporation Commissioner issued the necessary permits for the closing that took place on August 30, 1967. The merger left no right in dissenters to secure appraisal of their stock. Occidental could, of course, have disposed of its shares of Old Kern for cash before the merger was closed. Such an act would have been a § 16(b) sale and would have left Occidental with a prima facie § 16(b) liability. It was not, therefore, a realistic alternative for Occidental as long as it felt that it could successfully defend a suit like the present one. We do not suggest that an exchange of stock pursuant to a merger may never result in § 16(b) liability. But the involuntary nature of Occidental's exchange, when coupled with the absence of the possibility of speculative abuse of inside information, convinces us that § 16(b) should not apply to transactions such as this one.

IV

Petitioner also claims that the Occidental-Tenneco option agreement should itself be considered a sale, either because it was the kind of transaction the statute was designed to prevent or because the agreement was an option in form but a sale in fact. But the mere execution of an option to sell is not generally regarded as a "sale." ... And we do not find in the execution of the Occidental-Tenneco option agreement a sufficient possibility for the speculative abuse of inside information with respect to Old Kern's affairs to warrant holding that the option agreement was itself a "sale" within the meaning of § 16(b)....

Neither does it appear that the option agreement, as drafted and executed by the parties, offered measurable possibilities for speculative abuse. What Occidental granted was a "call" option. Tenneco had the right to buy after six months, but Occidental could not force Tenneco to buy. The price was fixed at $105 for each share of Tenneco preferred. Occidental could not share in a rising market for the Tenneco stock. If the stock fell more than $10 per share, the option might not be exercised, and Occidental might suffer a loss if the market further deteriorated to a point where Occidental was forced to sell....

The option, therefore, does not appear to have been an instrument with potential for speculative abuse, whether or not Occidental possessed inside information about the affairs of Old Kern. In addition the option covered Tenneco preference stock, a stock as yet unissued, unregistered, and untraded.... If Occidental had inside information when it negotiated and signed the option agreement, it was inside information with respect to Old Kern. Whatever it may have known or expected as to the future value of Old Kern stock, Occidental had no ownership position in Tenneco giving it any actual or presumed insights into the future value of Tenneco stock. That was the critical item of intelligence if Occidental was to use the option for purposes of speculation....

Nor can we agree that we must reverse the Court of Appeals on the ground that the option agreement was in fact a sale because the premium paid was so large as to make the exercise of the option almost inevitable, particularly when coupled with Tenneco's desire to rid itself of a potentially troublesome stockholder.... We see no satisfactory basis or reason for disagreeing with the judgment of the Court of Appeals in this respect.

The judgment of the Court of Appeals is affirmed.

Section IV
Timing Issues

Reliance Electric Co. v. Emerson Electric Co.

United States Supreme Court
404 U.S. 418 (1972)

MR. JUSTICE STEWART delivered the opinion of the Court.

Section 16(b) of the Securities Exchange Act of 1934 provides, among other things, that a corporation may recover for itself the profits realized by an owner of more than 10% of its shares from a purchase and sale of its stock within any six-month period, provided that the owner held more than 10% "both at the time of the purchase and sale." In this case, the respondent, the owner of 13.2% of a corporation's shares, disposed of its entire holdings in two sales, both of them within six months of purchase. The first sale reduced the respondent's holdings to 9.96%, and the second disposed of the remainder. The question presented is whether the profits derived from the second sale are recoverable by the corporation under § 16(b). We hold that they are not.

I

On June 16, 1967, the respondent, Emerson Electric Co., acquired 13.2% of the outstanding common stock of Dodge Manufacturing Co., pursuant to a tender offer made in an unsuccessful attempt to take over Dodge. The purchase price for this stock was $63 per share. Shortly thereafter, the shareholders of Dodge approved a merger with the petitioner, Reliance Electric Co. Faced with the certain failure of any further attempt to take over Dodge, and with the prospect of being forced to exchange its Dodge shares for stock in the merged corporation in the near future, Emerson, following a plan outlined by its general counsel, decided to dispose of enough shares to bring its holdings below 10%, in order to immunize the disposal of the remainder of its shares from liability under § 16(b). Pursuant to counsel's recommendation, Emerson on August 28 sold 37,000 shares of Dodge common stock to a brokerage house at $68 per share. This sale reduced Emerson's holdings in Dodge to 9.96% of the outstanding common stock. The remaining shares were then sold to Dodge at $69 per share on September 11.

After a demand on it by Reliance for the profits realized on both sales, Emerson filed this action seeking a declaratory judgment as to its liability under § 16(b). Emerson first claimed that it was not liable at all, because it was not a 10% owner at the time of the *purchase* of the Dodge shares. The District Court disagreed, holding that a purchase of stock falls within § 16(b) where the purchaser becomes a 10% owner by virtue of the purchase. The Court of Appeals affirmed this holding, and Emerson did not cross-petition for certiorari. Thus that question is not before us....

Among the "objective standards" contained in § 16(b) is the requirement that a 10% owner be such "both at the time of the purchase and sale ... of the security involved." Read literally, this language clearly contemplates that a statutory insider might sell enough shares to bring his holdings below 10%, and later—but still within six months—sell additional shares free from liability under the statute. Indeed, commentators on the securities laws have recommended this exact procedure for a 10% owner who, like Emerson, wishes to dispose of his holdings within six months of their purchase.

Under the approach urged by Reliance, and adopted by the District Court, the apparent immunity of profits derived from Emerson's second sale is lost where the two sales, though independent in every other respect, are "interrelated parts of a single plan." But a "plan" to sell that is conceived within six months of purchase clearly would not fall within § 16(b) if the sale were made after the six months had expired, and we see no basis in the statute for a different result where the 10% requirement is involved rather than the six-month limitation....

To be sure, where alternative constructions of the terms of § 16(b) are possible, those terms are to be given the construction that best serves the congressional purpose of curbing short-swing speculation by corporate insiders. But a construction of the term "at the time of . . . sale" that treats two sales as one upon proof of a pre-existing intent by the seller is scarcely in harmony with the congressional design of predicating liability upon an "objective measure of proof." *Smolowe v. Delendo Corp.*, [136 F.2d 231, 235 (2d Cir. 1943)]. Were we to adopt the approach urged by Reliance, we could be sure that investors would not in the future provide such convenient proof of their intent as Emerson did in this case. If a "two-step" sale of a 10% owner's holdings within six months of purchase is thought to give rise to the kind of evil that Congress sought to correct through § 16(b), those transactions can be more effectively deterred by an amendment to the statute that preserves its mechanical quality than by a judicial search for the will-o'-the-wisp of an investor's "intent" in each litigated case....

Foremost-McKesson, Inc. v. Provident Securities Co.

United States Supreme Court
423 U.S. 232 (1976)

Mr. Justice Powell delivered the opinion of the Court.

This case presents an unresolved issue under § 16(b) of the Securities Exchange Act of 1934 (Act).... Section 16(b)'s last sentence ... provides that it "shall not be construed to cover any transaction where such beneficial owner was not such both at the time of the purchase and sale, or the sale and purchase, of the security involved...." The question presented here is whether a person purchasing securities that put his holdings above the 10% level is a beneficial owner "at the time of the purchase" so that he must account for profits realized on a sale of those securities within six months. The United States Court of Appeals for the Ninth Circuit answered this question in the negative. We affirm....

The meaning of the exemptive provision has been disputed since § 16(b) was first enacted. The discussion has focused on the application of the provision to a purchase-sale sequence, the principal disagreement being whether "at the time of the purchase" means "before the purchase" or "immediately after the purchase." The difference in construction is determinative of a beneficial owner's liability in cases such as Provident's where such owner sells within six months of purchase the securities the acquisition of which made him a beneficial owner. The commentators divided immediately over which construction Congress intended, and they remain divided. The Courts of Appeals also are in disagreement over the issue....

The Court of Appeals considered this case against the background ... of ambiguity in the pertinent statutory language, continued disagreement among the commentators, and a perceived absence in the relatively few decided cases of a full consideration of the purpose and legislative history of § 16(b). The court found unpersuasive the rationales offered in [*Stella v. Graham-Paige Motors Corp.*, 232 F.2d 299 (1956),] and its progeny for the "immediately after the purchase" construction. It noted that construing the provision to require that beneficial-ownership status exist before the purchase in a purchase-sale sequence would not foreclose an "immediately after the purchase" construction in a sale-repurchase sequence. More significantly, the Court of Appeals challenged directly the premise of the earlier cases that a "before the purchase" construction in a purchase-sale sequence would allow abuses Congress intended to abate. The court reasoned that in § 16(b) Congress intended to reach only those beneficial owners who both bought and sold on the basis of inside information, which was presumptively available to them only after they became statutory "insiders." ...

The general purpose of Congress in enacting § 16(b) is well known. Congress recognized that insiders may have access to information about their corporations not available to the rest of the investing public. By trading on this information, these persons could reap profits at the expense of less well informed investors. In § 16(b) Congress sought to "curb the evils of insider trading [by] ... taking the profits out of a class of transactions in which the possibility of abuse was believed to be intolerably great." *Reliance Electric Co.* [*v. Emerson Electric Co.*, 404 U.S. 418, 422 (1972)]. It accomplished this by defining directors, officers, and beneficial owners as those presumed to have access to inside information and enacting a flat rule that a corporation could recover the profits these insiders made on a pair of security transactions within six months.

Foremost points to this purpose, and invokes the observation in *Reliance Electric Co.* that "where alternative constructions of the terms of § 16(b) are possible, those terms are to be given the construction that best serves the congressional purpose of curbing short-swing speculation by corporate insiders." From these premises Foremost argues that the Court of Appeals' construction of the exemptive provision must be rejected because it makes § 16(b) inapplicable to some possible abuses of inside information that the statute would reach under the *Stella* construction. We find this approach unsatisfactory in its focus on situations that § 16(b) may not reach rather than on the language and purpose of the exemptive provision itself. Foremost's approach also invites an imposition of § 16(b)'s liability without fault that is not consistent with the premises upon which Congress enacted the section. ...

The exemptive provision, which applies only to beneficial owners and not to other statutory insiders, must have been included in § 16(b) for a purpose. Although the extensive legislative history of the Act is bereft of any explicit explanation of Congress' intent, the evolution of § 16(b) from its initial proposal through passage does shed significant light on the purpose of the exemptive provision.

The original version of what would develop into the Act was S. 2693, 73d Cong., 2d Sess. (1934). It provided in § 15(b):

> It shall be unlawful for any director, officer, or owner of securities, owning as of record and/or beneficially more than 5 per centum of any class of stock of any issuer, any security of which is registered on a national securities exchange—
>
> (1) To purchase any such registered security with the intention or expectation of selling the same security within six months; and any profit made by such person on any transaction in such a registered security extending over a period of less than six months shall inure to and be recoverable by the issuer,

irrespective of any intention or expectation on his part in entering into such transaction of holding the security purchased for a period exceeding six months.

In the next version of the legislation, H.R. 8720, 73d Cong., 2d Sess. (1934), § 15(b) read almost identically to § 16(b) as it was eventually enacted:

> Any profit realized by such beneficial owner, director, or officer from any purchase and sale or sale and purchase of any such registered equity security within a period of less than six months, unless such security was acquired in good faith in connection with a debt previously contracted, shall inure to and be recoverable by the issuer, irrespective of any intention on the part of such beneficial owner, director, or officer in entering into such transaction of holding the security purchased or of not repurchasing the security sold for a period exceeding six months. . . . This subsection shall not be construed to cover any transaction where such beneficial owner was not such both at the time of the purchase and sale or sale and purchase of the security involved, nor any transaction or transactions which the Commission by rules and regulations may exempt as not comprehended within the purpose of this subsection of preventing the unfair use of information which may have been obtained by such beneficial owner, director, or officer by reason of his relationship to the issuer.

Thomas G. Corcoran, a spokesman for S. 2693's drafters, introduced § 15(b) as forbidding an insider "to carry on any short-term specu[la]tions in the stock. He cannot, with his inside information get in and out of stock within six months." Hearings on H.R. 7852 and H.R. 8720 before the House Committee on Interstate and Foreign Commerce, 73d Cong., 2d Sess., 133 (1934). The Court of Appeals concluded that § 15(b) of S. 2693 would have applied only to a beneficial owner who had that status before a purchase-sale sequence was initiated, 506 F.2d, at 609, and we agree. Foremost appears not to contest this point. The question thus becomes whether H.R. 8720's change in the language imposing liability and its addition of the exemptive provision were intended to change S. 2693's result in a purchase-sale sequence by a beneficial owner. We think the legislative history shows no such intent. . . .

The legislative record . . . reveals that the drafters focused directly on the fact that S. 2693 covered a short-term purchase-sale sequence by a beneficial owner only if his status existed before the purchase, and no concern was expressed about the wisdom of this requirement. But the explicit requirement was omitted from the operative language of the section when it was restructured to cover sale-repurchase sequences. In the same draft, however, the exemptive provision was added to the section. On this record we are persuaded that the exemptive provision was intended to preserve the requirement of beneficial ownership before the purchase. Later discussions of the present § 16(b) in the hearings are consistent with this interpretation. We hold that, in a purchase-sale sequence, a beneficial owner must account for profits only if he was a beneficial owner "before the purchase." . . .

Section V
Standing

Gollust v. Mendell

United States Supreme Court
501 U.S. 115 (1991)

JUSTICE SOUTER delivered the opinion of the Court.

… This case … requires us to address a plaintiff's standing under [1934 Act] § 16(b) and, in particular, the requirements for continued standing after the institution of an action. We hold that a plaintiff, who properly "instituted [a § 16(b) action as] the owner of [a] security of the issuer," may continue to prosecute the action after his interest in the issuer is exchanged in a merger for stock in the issuer's new corporate parent.

I

In January 1987, respondent Ira L. Mendell filed a complaint under § 16(b) against petitioners in the United States District Court for the Southern District of New York, stating that he owned common stock in Viacom International, Inc. (International) and was suing on behalf of the corporation. He alleged that petitioners, a collection of limited partnerships, general partnerships, individual partners and corporations, "operated as a single unit" and were, for purposes of this litigation, a "single … beneficial owner of more than ten per centum of the common stock" of International. Respondent claimed that petitioners were liable to International under § 16(b) for approximately $11 million in profits earned by them from trading in International's common stock between July and October 1986. The complaint recited that respondent had made a demand upon International and its Board of Directors to bring a § 16(b) action against petitioners and that more than 60 days had passed without the institution of an action.

In June 1987, less than six months after respondent had filed his § 16(b) complaint, International was acquired by Arsenal Acquiring Corp., a shell corporation formed by Arsenal Holdings, Inc. (now named Viacom, Inc.) (Viacom) for the purpose of acquiring International. By the terms of the acquisition, Viacom's shell subsidiary was merged with International, which then became Viacom's wholly owned subsidiary and only asset. The stockholders of International received a combination of cash and stock in Viacom in exchange for their International stock.

As a result of the acquisition, respondent, who was a stockholder in International when he instituted this action, acquired stock in International's new parent corporation and sole stockholder, Viacom. Respondent amended his complaint to reflect the restructuring by claiming to prosecute the § 16(b) action on behalf of Viacom as well as International.

Following the merger, petitioners moved for summary judgment, arguing that respondent had lost standing to maintain the action when the exchange of stock and cash occurred, after which respondent no longer owned any security of International, the "issuer." The District Court held that § 16(b) actions "may be prosecuted only by the issuer itself or the holders of its securities," and granted the motion because respondent no longer owned any International stock. The court concluded that only Viacom, as International's sole security holder, could continue to prosecute this action against petitioners.

A divided Court of Appeals reversed....

We granted certiorari ... to determine whether a stockholder who has properly instituted a § 16(b) action to recover profits from a corporation's insiders may continue to prosecute that action after a merger involving the issuer results in exchanging the stockholder's interest in the issuer for stock in the issuer's new corporate parent.

II

A

... The only textual restrictions on the standing of a party to bring suit under § 16(b) are that the plaintiff must be the "owner of [a] security" of the "issuer" at the time the suit is "instituted."

Although plaintiffs seeking to sue under the statute must own a "security," § 16(b) places no significant restriction on the type of security adequate to confer standing.... Nor is there any restriction in terms of either the number or percentage of shares, or the value of any other security, that must be held. In fact, the terms of the statute do not even require that the security owner have had an interest in the issuer at the time of the defendant's short-swing trading, and the courts to have addressed this issue have held that a subsequent purchaser of the issuer's securities has standing to sue for prior short-swing trading.

The second requirement for § 16(b) standing is that the plaintiff own a security of the "issuer" whose stock was traded by the insider defendant. An "issuer" of a security is defined under § 3(a)(8) of the 1934 Act as the corporation that actually issued the security and does not include parent or subsidiary corporations. While this requirement is strict on its face, it is ostensibly subject to mitigation in the final requirement for § 16(b) standing, which is merely that the plaintiff own a security of the issuer at the time the § 16(b) action is "instituted." Today, as in 1934, the word "institute" is commonly understood to mean "inaugurate or commence; as to institute an action." Black's Law Dictionary 985–986 (3d ed. 1933) (citing cases); see Black's Law Dictionary 800 (6th ed. 1990) (same definition). Congressional intent to adopt this common understanding is confirmed by Congress' use of the same word elsewhere to mean the commencement of an action. See, e.g., 8 U.S.C. § 1503(a) ("action ... may be instituted only within five years after ... final administrative denial"); 42 U.S.C. § 405(g) ("Any action instituted in accordance with this subsection shall survive notwithstanding any change in the person occupying the office of Secretary or any vacancy in such office").

The terms of § 16(b), read in context, thus provide standing of signal breadth, expressly limited only by conditions existing at the time an action is begun. Petitioners contend, however, that the statute should at least be read narrowly enough to require the plaintiff owning a "security" of the "issuer" at the time the action is "instituted" to maintain ownership of the issuer's security throughout the period of his participation in the litigation. But no such "continuous ownership requirement" is found in the text of the statute, nor does § 16(b)'s legislative history reveal any congressional intent to impose one.

This is not to say, of course, that a § 16(b) action could be maintained by someone who is subsequently divested of any interest in the outcome of the litigation. Congress clearly intended to put "a private-profit motive behind the uncovering of this kind of leakage of information, [by making] the stockholders [its] policemen." Hearings on H. R. 7852 and H. R. 8720 before the House Committee on Interstate and Foreign Commerce, 73d Cong., 2d. Sess., 136 (1934) (testimony of Thomas G. Corcoran). The sparse legislative history on this question, which consists primarily of hearing testimony by one of the 1934 Act's drafters, merely confirms this conclusion.

Congress must, indeed, have assumed any plaintiff would maintain some continuing financial stake in the litigation for a further reason as well. For if a security holder were allowed to maintain a § 16(b) action after he had lost any financial interest in its outcome, there would be serious constitutional doubt whether that plaintiff could demonstrate the standing required by Article III's case or controversy limitation on federal court jurisdiction....

Hence, we have no difficulty concluding that, in the enactment of § 16(b), Congress understood and intended that, throughout the period of his participation, a plaintiff authorized to sue insiders on behalf of an issuer would have some continuing financial interest in the outcome of the litigation, both for the sake of furthering the statute's remedial purposes by ensuring that enforcing parties maintain the incentive to litigate vigorously, and to avoid the serious constitutional question that would arise from a plaintiff's loss of all financial interest in the outcome of the litigation he had begun.

B

The conclusion that § 16(b) requires a plaintiff security holder to maintain some financial interest in the outcome of the litigation does not, however, tell us whether an adequate financial stake can be maintained when the plaintiff's interest in the issuer has been replaced by one in the issuer's new parent. We think it can be.

The modest financial stake in an issuer sufficient to bring suit is not necessarily greater than an interest in the original issuer represented by equity ownership in the issuer's parent corporation. A security holder eligible to institute suit will have no direct financial interest in the outcome of the litigation, since any recovery will inure only to the issuer's benefit. Yet the indirect interest derived through one share of stock is enough to confer standing, however slight the potential marginal increase in the value of the share. A bondholder's sufficient financial interest may be even more attenuated, since any recovery by the issuer will increase the value of the bond only because the issuer may become a slightly better credit risk.

Thus, it is difficult to see how such a bondholder plaintiff, for example, is likely to have a more significant stake in the outcome of a § 16(b) action than a stockholder in a company whose only asset is the issuer. Because such a bondholder's attenuated financial stake is nonetheless sufficient to satisfy the statute's initial standing requirements, the stake of a parent company stockholder like respondent should be enough to meet the requirements for continued standing, so long as that is consistent with the text of the statute. It is consistent, of course, and in light of the congressional policy of lenient standing, we will not read any further condition into the statute, beyond the requirement that a § 16(b) plaintiff maintain a financial interest in the outcome of the litigation sufficient to motivate its prosecution and avoid constitutional standing difficulties.

III

In this case, respondent has satisfied the statute's requirements. He owned a "security" of the "issuer" at the time he "instituted" this § 16(b) action. In the aftermath of International's restructuring, he retains a continuing financial interest in the outcome of the litigation derived from his stock in International's sole stockholder, Viacom, whose only asset is International. Through these relationships, respondent still stands to profit, albeit indirectly, if this action is successful, just as he would have done if his original shares had not been exchanged for stock in Viacom. Although a calculation of the values of the respective interests in International that respondent held as its stockholder and holds now as a Viacom stockholder is not before us, his financial interest is actually no less real than before the merger and apparently no more attenuated than the interest of a bondholder might be in a § 16(b) suit on an issuer's behalf....

Appendix

Financial Statements

Lawyers advising business clients need to know accounting fundamentals in order to be effective counselors. Accounting issues arise in connection with organizing and financing businesses, distributing company earnings to its owners, structuring business transactions, and buying, selling and investing in companies. Although accountants are available to provide expert advice on these issues, lawyers must know when an expert is needed and be able to discuss accounting issues intelligently with both the expert and the client.

The business organization law student can approach accounting as one might approach parachute jumping. To be really good at either parachute jumping or accounting requires a lot of knowledge and skill; to be good enough to survive at either requires little knowledge or skill, but what each requires, it requires absolutely. The basics of jumping can be found in four lines of verse:

Stand up, hook up, shuffle to the door. Jump right out and count to four.
If your chute don't open wide, Pull that rip cord by your side.

We cannot quite get the essentials of accounting pared down this far, but we think the next few pages will work as well for the business organization law student as these lines do for a parachute jumper. They will provide enough accounting basics to read most financial statements.

Introduction to Accounting

The first known accounting system was developed sometime in the fifteenth century to keep track of daily business transactions and, in the process, to determine if mistakes were being made or, worse, if someone was up to no good. Accounting systems provide a set of controls designed to reduce waste, prevent dishonesty and provide information about the company's financial position. More recently, accounting data has also been used as a factor in determining a company's value. Whether it should be so used is a matter of debate. Courts and lawyers often do use accounting data for valuation purposes. Economists typically focus on the control and monitoring functions of accounting.

The use of an accounting system involves two types of activities: keeping records of business transactions as they occur and producing reports that summarize the results of the transactions. The reports, called financial statements, are typically prepared according to generally accepted accounting principles (GAAP). The most basic and most frequently encountered financial statements are the balance sheet and the income statement. These are discussed below somewhat fully. Two subsidiary statements, the retained earnings statement and the statement of cash flows, are mentioned briefly. These statements are designed to provide financial information useful to persons making economic decisions about a company, including the company's owners, managers, investors, and creditors.

Financial statements are prepared based on several common principles. Each statement deals with a particular time period, such as a quarter or a year. Businesses are regarded as going concerns. They are also treated as entities separate and distinct from their owners, even when state law considers them to be one and the same. Usually, financial statement values reflect historical cost rather than current market value, and all transactions are recorded in the same currency, in our case, the U.S. dollar. Companies are expected to be consistent in the way they record transactions from year to year.

A. Balance Sheet

The balance sheet shows a company's assets (what it owns) and liabilities (what it owes), plus the owners' equity in the business (the amount left over for the owners) at a particular point in time, such as at the close of business on December 31. The simplest corporate balance sheet possible, showing only totals and leaving out all detail, might look like this:

<u>**Acme Corporation Balance Sheet**</u>
(as of year-end; amounts in dollars)

Assets		**Liabilities**	
Cash	385,000	Bank Debt	285,000
		Owners' Equity	100,000
Total Assets	385,000	**Total Liabilities and Owners' Equity**	385,000

In this example, the assets are equal to the liabilities plus the shareholders' equity (which might be called "proprietor's equity" in a proprietorship or "partners' capital" in a partnership). This is always true for a balance sheet, because what a balance sheet shows is simply how much the company owns (its assets), how much it owes (its liabilities) and how much is left over for the company's owners (equity). Another way to look at the balance sheet is to say that it states the types of assets held by the company and the persons (creditors and owners) with claims to the assets. The following two equations may be helpful in understanding balance sheets:

assets = liabilities + equity

assets − liabilities = equity

The first of these equations, called "the fundamental equation" in accounting, reflects the way information is organized on the balance sheet, with assets listed on the left and liabilities and equity on the right. The fundamental equation also shows why this financial statement is called a balance sheet. Just like the equation, the two sides of the balance sheet must equal each other. The equation also reflects the way information is recorded in the company records and on the balance sheet. Since one must keep the equation in balance, company transactions are recorded using what is called the double entry bookkeeping system. Every transaction will cause two changes on the accounting statements. A transaction affecting one side of the equation will also affect the other side, unless there are two offsetting entries on one side. For example, a $2,000 increase in assets will also require one of the following: an offsetting $2,000 decrease in assets (if, for example, a new asset worth $2,000 was purchased with $2,000 cash); a $2,000 increase in liabilities (if the company borrowed the $2,000 needed to buy the asset); or a $2,000 increase in equity (if a $2,000 increase in the equity, the amount contributed by the company's owners, provided the funds to buy the asset).

With this background, we now can turn to a balance sheet showing details. This balance sheet will show the types of assets a company has, the types of obligations it has incurred, and the types of equity (owners' investments in the company and company earnings). A more detailed version of the balance sheet shown above might look like the one on the following page:

Even without further discussion, it is now possible to "read" a good deal of this balance sheet, since much of the detail that has been added is self-explanatory. To understand this detail, however, some explanation is in order. Each item on the balance sheet is called an account. Increases and decreases in each account are recorded in the company's books and ultimately reflected on the balance sheet. The most common accounts are described below.

1. Assets

The assets accounts on the balance sheet show how the company has used the money it has obtained from lenders, investors, and company earnings. Assets can be grouped according to whether they are monetary (cash and accounts receivables), liquid (whether they can easily be converted to cash) or whether they are tangible or intangible. The assets of this corporation are shown under three headings: current assets, fixed assets and intangibles. Current assets consist of cash and those items, such as accounts receivable, that are normally expected to be converted into cash within one year. Fixed assets are the company's more or less permanent physical assets, such as its land, buildings, machinery and equipment. Intangible assets include, among other things, such items as patents and trademarks. An asset can be valued in several ways: 1) how much it cost to acquire it (historical cost); 2) its current market value; 3) its value in use; 4) its liquidation value based on its sale after use.

Acme Corporation Balance Sheet
(as of year-end; amounts in dollars)

Assets		Liabilities	
Current Assets		*Current Liabilities*	
Cash	50,000	Accounts Payable	60,000
Accounts Receivable (net)	75,000	Notes Payable	40,000
Inventory (FIFO)	125,000	Taxes Payable	25,000
Total Current	250,000	Total Current	125,000
Long-Term Assets		*Long-Term Liabilities*	
Land	50,000	Five-Year Notes Payable	160,000
Building	75,000		
Equipment	50,000	Total Liabilities	285,000
Less Accumulated Depreciation	(50,000)		
Net Fixed Assets	125,000	**Owners' Equity**	
		Common stock ($1.00 par × 1,000)	1,000
Intangibles		Paid-in capital in excess of par	49,000
Patents	10,000	Retained Earnings	50,000
		Total Owners' Equity	100,000
Total Assets	385,000	**Total Liabilities and Owners' Equity**	385,000

Assets are typically recorded on financial statements at their historical cost expressed in dollars. Current assets and fixed assets are discussed below.

i. Current Assets

Cash. — Cash includes not only currency, which a company might keep in "petty cash," but also bank deposits and other "cash equivalents."

Accounts Receivable. — If a company sells goods or services on credit, the amounts owed to the company by the purchasers are "accounts receivable." The company must, however, anticipate that some of the accounts receivable will not be received. An account, which might be called "allowance for bad debts," therefore is established in the company's books and set-off against, or subtracted from, the accounts receivable shown in the balance sheet. This is necessary in order to present a fair picture of how much the company will likely receive from its credit sales.

Inventory. — In a manufacturing company, inventory includes raw materials, work in process and finished goods. Other types of companies have other types of inventory. For example, a retail store has in inventory only the purchased goods it sells. Service companies, of course, have no inventory. In preparing a balance sheet, a company must first determine what its inventory is (preferably by physically counting it) and then place a value on that inventory. The generally accepted method of valuation is to record the inventory at its cost or market value, whichever is lower (here "market value" is not retail value, but what it would cost the company to replace the inventory). For simplicity, we will ignore the methods a manufacturing company would use in measuring the cost of goods that are in various stages of the manufacturing process and deal only with the valuation of purchased goods a company has in inventory. The following are two common ways to measure the "cost" of inventory that has been purchased at different times and at varying prices.

(a) *First-in, first-out ("FIFO").* Under the FIFO method of valuation, the items of inventory that are purchased first are deemed to be sold first. Under this method, the most recent purchase prices are deemed to represent the cost of the items remaining. For example, suppose that the purchases and sales of a particular item are as follows:

Sample Inventory Record

Item	Quantity	Cost per item	Total Cost
January Purchase	100	$ 0.60	$ 60
March Purchase	500	.70	350
June Purchase	300	.80	240
September Purchase	100	.90	90
Total purchases	1,000		$ 740
Less sales	700		
Ending inventory	300		

Under the FIFO method of valuation, the cost of the ending inventory of 300 items would be deemed to be $250 ($.90 each for 100 and $.80 each for 200). Obviously, in times of rising prices, use of the FIFO method will result in inventory being shown on the balance sheet at the highest possible amount.

(b) *Last-in, first-out ("LIFO").* Under the LIFO method of valuation, the items of inventory that are purchased last are deemed to be sold first, and so the cost of the ending inventory is deemed to be the cost of the items that were purchased first. In the situation described above, the cost of the ending inventory of 300 items would be deemed to be $200 ($.60 each for 100 items and $.70 each for 200 items).

ii. Fixed Assets

As indicated above, fixed assets include such items as land, buildings, machinery and equipment. Fixed assets are typically shown on the balance sheet at their cost, less accumulated depreciation. "Depreciation" is the term used to describe the allocation of the cost of certain fixed assets, such as buildings, machinery and equipment, over their estimated useful lives. The term "depletion" rather than "depreciation" is used in the case of "wasting assets," such as oil and gas fields. "Amortization" is the term used when intangible assets, such as patents or trademarks, are involved. Land is not depreciated, since it does not have (at least for accounting purposes) a limited useful life.

When a fixed asset is depreciated, the cost of the asset is allocated over its expected useful life, and each annual installment of depreciation is added to an account in the company's books called "accumulated depreciation." On the balance sheet, accumulated depreciation is set-off against the total fixed assets (shown at their total cost at time of purchase). Notice that appreciation in the value of assets, which is likely for certain assets in times of rising prices, is not reflected on the balance sheet.

Several methods are used to calculate depreciation. Here are two of the most frequently encountered.

Straight-line method. — The straight line depreciation method is the most common. Under this method, depreciation is calculated by dividing the cost of the asset, less its salvage value, by the estimated useful life of the asset. For example, a computer costing $50,000, with a salvage value of $10,000 and an estimated useful life of 5 years, would have annual depreciation of $8,000 ($50,000 – $10,000 = $40,000; $40,000 ÷ 5 = $8,000), or 20% per year.

Double declining balance method. — Under the double declining balance method, depreciation is calculated by taking twice the straight-line depreciation percentage rate and multiplying this percentage rate by either the initial cost of the asset, which is what is done the first year depreciation is calculated, or, in succeeding years, by each declining balance figure that results from subtracting previously calculated depreciation from the initial cost. Salvage value does not enter into the computation, but under this method an asset is not depreciated below a reasonable salvage value.

Using the example above, the depreciation percentage rate would be 40% (20% doubled). This rate multiplied by $50,000 (the initial cost of the computer) gives a result of $20,000, which would be the amount of depreciation for the first year. For the following year, depreciation would be calculated by multiplying the "declining balance" of $30,000 ($50,000 – $20,000) by 40%, to give a result of $12,000. This method of calculating annual depreciation would continue until a reasonable salvage figure is reached. The double declining balance method, and certain other methods not discussed here, are called accelerated depreciation methods because they produce a greater amount of depreciation in the initial years of an asset's life than does the straight-line method.

2. Liabilities

The second portion of the balance sheet consists of the liabilities of the company. Liabilities are usually separated into two categories: current liabilities and long-term liabilities. Current liabilities consist of those debts that are to be paid within a year. Accounts payable, short-term notes payable and income taxes payable are typical current liabilities. Long-term liabilities are often in the form of long-term notes or bonds, but include any debt that is not due within one year. In the case of a debt that is partially due within one year and partially due in future years, the portion of the debt payable within one year is shown as a current liability and the rest as a long-term liability.

3. Equity

The third and final portion of a balance sheet represents the owners' equity (also referred to as the company's net worth). In a company owned by only one person (sole proprietorship), this section would have only one entry: proprietor's equity. In a partnership, the equity section has only one account: partners' capital. In the case of a corporation, the equity portion usually is subdivided into three categories. These categories are given various names in state corporation statutes. In many they are called stated capital, capital surplus and earned surplus.

Irrespective of the names used in corporation statutes, however, accountants use their own terms on balance sheets. Thus, what a corporation statute calls stated capital is shown on the ACME balance sheet as "common stock"; capital surplus is shown as "paid-in capital in excess of par value" and earned surplus as "retained earnings." In the discussion below, we will use the "lawyers' terms" commonly found in statutes. The accountants' terms will be noted in parentheses. To explain these terms fully would take more space and time than is warranted here, particularly since these terms are discussed in Chapters 4 and 9.

Briefly, stated capital (here shown as common stock) is calculated by multiplying the number of shares of stock outstanding by the par value of each share. (In this discussion of stated capital and both categories of surplus, we will ignore stock without par value and will also ignore the possibility of transfers between these categories of shareholders' equity, which is allowed by corporation statutes in some circumstances.) In the case of the balance sheet shown above, the par value of the corporation's common stock is $1.00 per share and 1,000 shares have been issued, yielding a stated capital of $1,000. For current purposes, par value is perhaps best explained as being simply an arbitrary dollar figure assigned to the stock, the major purpose of which is to determine the amount of stated capital. The importance of this is that some corporation statutes place restrictions on what a corporation can do with its stated capital.

Capital surplus (paid in capital in excess of par) is basically the difference between what shareholders paid the corporation for their stock and the par value of the stock.

In the case of the balance sheet shown above, it appears that the 1,000 shares of common stock were sold by the corporation for $50 each, or $50,000 in total ($49,000 shown in paid-in capital in excess of par value plus $1,000 shown in common stock). Some corporation statutes also restrict what a corporation can do with its capital surplus, although the restrictions are different from those for stated capital.

Again ignoring transfers between categories of shareholders' equity, earned surplus (retained earnings) shows the total amount of profits and losses of the corporation since its formation, decreased by any dividends paid the shareholders. One might ask what happens if the corporation has had losses rather than profits. In this case, earned surplus is shown as a negative number (indicated by placing the number in parentheses).

B. Income Statement

Unlike the balance sheet, which shows a company's financial status at a particular point in time (such as on December 31), the income statement shows the results of a company's operations over a period of time (such as for the year ending December 31). Stated simply, it shows the company's revenues and expenses, and how much the company made in profits. An income statement for Acme Corporation might look like this:

Acme Corporation Income Statement
(for the fiscal year; amounts in dollars)

Net sales		500,000
Operating Expenses		
Cost of Goods Sold	304,000	
Depreciation	15,000	
Administrative	100,000	
Total Operating Expenses		419,000
Operating Income		81,000
Less Interest Expense		13,000
Earnings Before Income Taxes		68,000
Less Income Taxes		18,000
Net income		50,000
Earnings Per Share		
(1,000 shares outstanding)		50

Some explanation of specific income statement items may be helpful.

Net Sales. — Net sales is calculated by totaling all sales during the period, and then subtracting the sales price of all returned goods and all allowances made because of damaged or defective goods.

Cost of Goods Sold. — Calculating the cost of goods sold begins where calculating the cost of ending inventory for balance sheet purposes ends. In the case of goods that are sold in the form in which they are purchased, the cost of goods sold during a period (assuming there is no "operating inventory" at the beginning of the period) is calculated by subtracting the cost of ending inventory from the total cost of the purchased goods. In our example above, relating to inventory valuation, the total cost of the purchases of the item in question were $740. Under the FIFO method of valuation the cost of ending inventory was $250 and under the LIFO method $200. Under these methods, the cost of goods sold for this item would be $490 ($740 minus $250) and $540 ($740 minus $200).

Obviously, the cost of goods sold has a direct effect on the amount of income shown on a company's income statement. As can easily be seen, the amount of income shown may vary, sometimes to a great extent, depending on the method of inventory valuation used.

Depreciation. — We have already discussed depreciation as it is shown on the balance sheet. There, the total amount of depreciation over the past life of fixed assets is shown as a set-off from the total cost of these assets. On the income statement, only depreciation for the period covered by the statement is shown. In the case of the above income statement, this is one year's depreciation.

By using an accelerated depreciation method, such as the double declining balance method, the depreciation over the first few years of an asset's life will be much greater than it would be if the straight line method were used. This, of course, will result in lower income — and lower taxes — during these years. A company's decisions with respect to the estimated useful life of assets also affects the amount of depreciation, and therefore income, shown on its income statement. For example, within the limits of what are called "generally accepted accounting principles" (GAAP), a company might estimate the useful life of a particular piece of machinery as five years, or ten years, or any number of years in between, thus causing a possible variation in depreciation of as much as 100 percent.

Selling and Administrative Expenses. — Selling and administrative expenses are exactly what one would expect. This item generally encompasses all the expenses of a company not included under another heading (called "line items" on financial statements) on the income statement.

Interest on Long-term Notes. — The interest accrued on long-term debt during the period covered by an income statement is generally shown as a line item separate from other expenses. In the case of Acme Corporation, the long-term debt is in the form of notes. In the case of other corporations, it could be represented by other debt instruments, such as bonds.

Income Taxes. — Income taxes are also shown as a separate line item, allowing the reader of the income statement to see at a glance what the company's income was both before and after taxes.

Net Income Per Share. — This item is simply net income divided by the number of shares outstanding.

C. Accumulated Retained Earnings Statement

The term "earnings" refers to the amount of money a company makes as a result of conducting its business. Retained earnings is an accountant's term used to refer to earnings that have been retained by the business and have not been distributed to shareholders as dividends. (Lawyers refer to this as earned surplus.) Earnings kept in the business are accumulated from accounting period to accounting period. Accumulated retained earnings thus refers to the total amount of retained earnings a company has at the beginning of an accounting period increased by the earnings retained during the current accounting period. The amount of retained earnings at the end of an accounting period is recorded in the retained earnings (earned surplus) account on the balance sheet.

The accumulated retained earnings statement shows increases and decreases in the corporation's retained earnings (earned surplus) during the period covered by the income statement it accompanies. An accumulated retained earnings statement showing changes during a calendar year would show (i) the amount of accumulated retained earnings (earned surplus) on January 1, (ii) any additions to accumulated retained earnings arising from profits during the year, (iii) any decreases arising from dividends paid to shareholders, or from transfers to capital surplus or stated capital, and (iv) the amount of accumulated retained earnings on December 31. The amount of accumulated retained earnings on December 31 would also appear in the accumulated retained earnings (earned surplus) account on the balance sheet.

The accumulated retained earnings statement for Acme might look like the following.

Acme Corporation Statement of Retained Earnings
(amounts in dollars)

Opening Balance	5,000
Annual Net Income	50,000
Total	55,000
Less Dividends Paid	5,000
Endings Balance	50,000

D. Statement of Cash Flows

The statement of cash flows involves some concepts that are beyond the needs of students in a basic corporation law course and will not be discussed here in detail. Basically, this statement covers the same period as the income statement it accompanies and shows from what sources the company received its cash flow (which is net income plus an add-back of depreciation and other non-cash charges that were subtracted from the company's revenues when calculating its net income).

E. Financial Statement Analysis

The foregoing summary of the basic components of a set of financial statements tells you basic information about what goes into preparing them. The following summary provides some analytical tools people commonly apply to financial statements to generate useful information about them. Discussion is divided between (1) analysis concerning liquidity and activity and (2) analysis concerning profitability and performance. Discussion is adapted from Lawrence A. Cunningham, Introductory Accounting, Finance and Auditing for Lawyers (West 5th ed. 2010).

(1) **Liquidity and Activity**. The basic financial health of a business can be stated in terms of its ability to pay its debts as they come due. At any moment, an entity will have assets that will generate cash in the ordinary course and liabilities requiring payment of cash in the ordinary course. The reference to ordinary course suggests these are best characterized as short-term assets and short-term liabilities. A significant mismatch between these two categories can create short-term liquidity problems— impaired ability to pay debts as they come due. Several alternative tests can be applied to gauge relative liquidity

Working Capital. The first test focuses on the concept of *working capital*. This is a measure of the resources an entity has available to operate on a day-to-day basis. Technically, working capital is the amount by which current assets exceed current liabilities. It is a measure, in a sense, of the fuel in the business at a moment in time. Too little working capital threatens an entity's ability to operate in the ordinary course over the immediate future. On the other hand, too much working capital can mean resources are not being deployed in optimal ways. But how can one tell whether working capital is too high or too low?

One way to determine how much working capital is needed and to assess its adequacy is to compare the working capital to sales. Typically, a retailing business that generates substantial sales of low-cost items such as a supermarket needs less working capital per dollar of sales (perhaps around 10 to 15%) than does an industrial manufacturer of high-ticket items such as airplanes (perhaps around 25 to 35%). A manufacturer of consumer goods might require some level in between these sorts of entities.

Current Ratio. A more general way to evaluate the working capital position is to compare the relationship between current assets and current liabilities in relative terms. This gauge of working capital management is obtained by calculating the ratio of current assets to current liabilities. In evaluating current ratios, intuition plays a significant role. As a rule of thumb, for most entities the optimal current ratio is around 2.

A current ratio of 1 or less is a warning signal that an entity may face difficulties in paying its debts as they come due in the short term — it risks having more dollars coming due than it has dollars to pay them. At the other extreme, a current ratio substantially higher is a sign of potential problems, though not with respect to liquidity but with respect to efficiency. It implies that current assets may not be being deployed in their most productive manner but are instead sitting idle, not producing profits. As the ratio falls below 2 and approaches 1 or goes below 1, a user of financial statements should investigate the liquidity question further.

Quick Ratio. One way to refine the current ratio to get a more precise gauge of liquidity is to limit the sorts of current assets included in the calculation. In particular, current assets are all those that are expected to be realized in cash within the operating cycle, usually one year. For any entity about whom there is any question regarding liquidity, however, analysis may limit the liquidity test to those assets expected to be converted into cash more quickly than one year — say six months or so. This would exclude current assets like inventory and focus on cash and only those accounts receivable due within the next few months rather than the full year. This more demanding liquidity test is known by three synonyms: *quick ratio, liquidity ratio* or *acid test ratio.*

Inventory Turnover Ratio. Inventory is considered a current asset under the definition that it is expected to be realized in cash within a reasonably short time, usually one year. It is possible to be more precise about the expected, relative liquidity of inventory by measuring the speed at which inventory is sold over time — the speed of inventory turnover. This is done by computing the *inventory turnover ratio*. The inventory turnover for any year is the cost of goods sold (COGS) for that year divided by the average inventory over that year (in turn usually determined by adding the beginning inventory to the ending inventory and dividing by two).

Apart from liquidity, we could also use the inventory turnover ratio to assess how well the inventory levels are being managed. After all, the longer inventory sits around without being sold, the less value that inventory is adding to the business, since the cash into which it could be converted could be deployed to more productive uses. Large inventory levels can also cause other problems, such as increasing the risk of its obsolescence or spoilage, requiring large amounts of bank borrowings to finance it, absorbing large amounts of cash, or posing the risk of loss if the market price at which it can be sold declines materially. Comparisons to comparable companies can be useful.

In making comparisons, however, note the need to consider effects of inventory accounting conventions used by that particular entity and the entities with which it is being compared. For example, an entity using LIFO rather than FIFO will, all other things being equal, report inventory at lower amounts on its balance sheet and this would imply a higher apparent inventory turnover ratio.

Accounts Receivable Turnover Ratio. The same insights that motivate and make meaningful the inventory turnover ratio can also be applied to accounts receivable. The speed with which accounts receivable are collected during a period indicate their relative liquidity and give a basis for appraising the integrity of the entity's credit and collection policies. The accounts receivable turnover ratios is the dollar amount of sales made on credit during the period divided by the average accounts receivable outstanding during the period.

After computing the accounts receivable turnover ratio in this manner, it can be compared to other entities in the same way the inventory ratio is. Also, as with the inventory ratio, you can determine the speed of collection of accounts receivable. To do so, divide the number of days in a year by the accounts receivable turnover ratio. The result expresses the average number of days the receivables are outstanding (called *days sales uncollected*). A low number, say 44, implies that accounts receivable are relatively liquid. Before concluding that it is good, however, one should also compare this velocity to the terms of the accounts. If payments are due within 60 days, then this record is fine; but if payments are due within 30 days, then this raises questions about the entity's debt collection practices.

Debt-to-Equity Ratio. The debt-to-equity ratio measures the entity's borrowing capacity or, in more practical terms, the level of comfort a lender or potential lender can have in the entity's ability to repay debt. As the name *debt-to-equity ratio* may imply, the components of the calculation can vary depending on the purpose for which the calculation is made and the subject entity's capital structure. In its most general formulation, the calculation is the ratio between the entity's total debt, short-term and long-term, divided by the amount of owners' equity. Sometimes the calculation is performed using only long-term debt in the numerator.

In general, the ratio indicates how many dollars of equity (or capital, as the case may be) are invested in the entity for every dollar of indebtedness (whether long-term or both long-term and short). A comparison of the ratio across entities within an industry gives some measure of the entity's relative borrowing capacity and debt-paying over the long term. Entities with relatively high debt-to-equity ratios are characterized as "highly-leveraged," meaning that the debt level in relation to the investment level of the owners in the business (the shareholders) is very high. What levels of debt-to-equity ratios are normal has varied historically, in accordance with economic conditions and collective beliefs about credit.

(2) **Profitability and Performance.** Most liquidity/activity ratios concentrate on how an entity is managing its assets and liabilities, which can also reveal information about its prospective ability to meet its obligations as they come due. Another level of analysis concerns the entity's profitability and performance.

Profit Margin. A principal method of evaluating the performance of a business is to consider how well it is meeting its basic financial objective, which is to generate a profit in operating its business in the ordinary course. Operating income, reported as a raw dollar amount, does not reveal much in terms of business performance. In particular, it does not show what went in to generating that amount of operating income. The issue is whether the entity getting a lot or a little out of its sales effort? This can be revealed by relating operating income to sales. This relationship, called the *profit margin*, is computed by dividing operating income by total net sales for a period and expressing the result as a percentage.

The time trend of the profit margin may reveal important information about the entity's direction and how well it is being managed. Positive trends suggest that the business is constantly improving its operating and sales efficiency. But a positive trend in profit margin should not be taken at face value. It could be due to other factors that either have nothing to do with efficient operations or which may be counterproductive over the long term. Perhaps it is the consequence simply of favorable market conditions that are benefiting all businesses and reveals nothing special about the particular entity. These questions can be probed by comparing the subject entity with its peers and examining particular line items more closely, an exercise called variation analysis.

Variation Analysis. Variation analysis examines changes in items of financial data from period-to-period with a view toward determining trends in an entity's financial condition performance. Also sometimes called *line item trend analysis*, this exercise can reveal significant information about how an entity is being managed. In particular, the level of expenses in every income statement expense account over the relevant comparison years can be examined. For example, a significant reduction in expense for research and development would have the effect of significantly increasing operating income in a period. But growth in operating income due to reduction in such an expense would not mean the entity is being managed more efficiently, and could even mean that there are reasons to worry about its prospects for growth in the future. Similarly, suppose sales are increasing, but you also find that accounts receivable turnover is slowing—maybe sales increases are being driven by greater laxity in credit extension or collection.

Interest Coverage Ratio. A ratio whose function is similar to the balance sheet ratio of debt-to-equity is the *interest coverage ratio*. Sometimes also referred to as the *times interest earned ratio (TIER)*, this compares earnings to interest payment obligations. The ratio expresses the number of times interest obligations are covered by earnings. It provides a basis for gauging the entity's ability to cover its interest expense on indebtedness over time. For most industrial companies, an interest coverage ratio in the range of 3 to 4 is considered prudent and implies a relatively safe level of borrowings.

Fixed Charge Coverage Ratio. A slightly more conservative variation on the interest coverage ratio is called the *fixed charge coverage ratio*. In addition to interest coverage, this ratio also tests for earnings coverage of fixed charges such as lease obligations.

Preferred Dividend Coverage Ratio. A similar analysis can be applied to evaluate the coverage of dividends, particularly on preferred stock. Where no debt ranks higher than the preferred stock, the calculation is simply earnings divided by the number of preferred shares outstanding. If senior debt exists, however, the earnings available for payment of dividends on the preferred stock must be first be reduced by the interest obligations on that debt.

Earnings Per Share. Beyond these line item analyses that can offer an understanding of an entity's relative efficiency in a period and over time, a different sort of question can be analyzed by looking at an entity's earnings. This is the more general proposition about what results the entity is producing for its shareholders, usually expressed in terms of *earnings per share (EPS)*. EPS is the total earnings during the period (after giving effect to interest and taxes) divided by the average number of equity shares outstanding during that period. It expresses the portion of earnings mathematically allocable to each equity share and provides a useful element in valuing that share.

The first issue in calculating earnings per share is determining the number of shares outstanding. The number outstanding can vary throughout an accounting period due to stock being issued or repurchased. The total outstanding is adjusted for these changes weighted according to the length of time given numbers were outstanding. For example, suppose on January 1, a corporation has 10,000 shares outstanding and on April 1, the corporation repurchases 2,000 of these and no other changes occur. The weighted-average common stock outstanding is:

$$\left(10{,}000 \times \frac{3}{12}\right) + \left(8{,}000 \times \frac{9}{12}\right) = 8{,}500$$

A second issue in calculating and evaluating EPS is determining which shares are to be included in calculating average shares outstanding. It would obviously include at least the average number of common shares outstanding, but what about other instruments that are convertible into common shares or which provide an option to elect to purchase common shares? Those rights upon exercise will have the effect of diluting the portion of earnings mathematically allocable to each common share prior to that exercise. To address this, EPS is calculated in two ways: basic EPS and diluted EPS.

Basic EPS is computed by dividing income available for distribution to common stockholders by the weighted average number of common shares outstanding during the reporting period. For purposes of determining such shares outstanding, certain contingently issuable shares must also be counted. Such shares include those that will be issued in the future upon satisfaction of specific conditions, those that have been placed in escrow when all or part must be returned if specified conditions are not met, and those that have been issued but the holder must return if specified conditions are not met.

Diluted EPS is computed by also including in the number of shares deemed outstanding other common shares issuable upon certain other events or pursuant to other instruments or plans to the extent they would, upon issuance, affect the calculation of basic EPS. These instruments or plans include options and warrants, stock-based compensation arrangements, written put options, convertible securities, and contracts that may be settled in cash or in stock.

The Price-Earnings Ratio. A common way of making comparisons between the performances, or at least the perceived performances, of entities is drawn from the way public markets price common stocks for entities with various earnings. It compares the market price per share of common stock with the earnings per share of that common stock. Called the *price-earnings ratio* (the "*P/E Ratio*"), it is computed by dividing the market price of a share of common stock by the entity's earnings per share.

In general, higher P/E Ratios suggest that investors are more optimistic about an entity's prospects than comparable entities with lower P/E Ratios. However, the relative levels of P/E ratios also vary according to an entity's growth outlook, its industry, its relative maturation (whether it is a start-up entity or an established business), and the accounting policies used by the entity in arriving at its calculation of net income.

Return on Equity, Investment and Assets. "Returns" are a measure of what bang a business gets for its buck. The bang is invariably measured in terms of earnings. There are several bases against which to measure the bang, of which the following considers three: equity, investment, and assets. In each measure, it is smart to gauge the return over a relatively long period of time — say five to ten years — rather than over short periods. This enables a perspective that tracks an entity's ability to weather the downsides, and reap the upsides, of the ever-fluctuating economic environment in which it operates.

Return on equity what a business earned on capital owned by its shareholders (owners' equity). Owners' equity equals total assets minus total liabilities. If a business earns $10 million on equity of $100 million, its return on equity is 10%.

Return on investment is what a business earned on both capital owned by its shareholders plus capital supplied by lenders on a long term (over one year) basis. A business might borrow capital rather than issue equity if it needs funds and believes it will generate greater returns on borrowed funds than what it costs to borrow them.

Suppose a business with $100 million in owners' equity borrows $50 million from long-term lenders and then generates earnings before interest and taxes (EBIT) of $15 million on that total capital. (EBIT is used in this calculation since interest is the return on debt.) Its return on investment would be 10% (15/150). But this leveraging boosts the business's return on equity — earnings of $15 million on owners' equity of $100 million means a return on equity of 15%.

Return on assets is what a business earned on all its resources — not only owners' equity and long-term borrowing but short term resources generated by effective management of working capital. (The sum of these is of course equal to total assets under the fundamental equation, so it is customary to denominate this measure as return on assets.) A business may seek short term, low rate loans or buy goods on credit that it resells for cash, thus increasing assets available for deployment at low or no cost. Those assets contribute to incremental increases in earnings, boosting both return on equity and return on investment.

Suppose a business maintains an average amount of short term assets of $20 million over a year (by continually repaying the obligations as they come due and incurring new ones as roll-overs). That could increase incremental annual earnings by say $2 million. So a company with owners' equity of $100 million, long-term debt of $50 million, carrying that additional $20 million in short-term assets, and earning $17 million, generates a return on assets of 10% (17/170). This deployment boosts return on investment to 11.3% (17/150) and return on equity to 17% (17/100).

Return on assets is thus the toughest measure of performance based on returns, as it reveals the results of deploying all resources at management's disposal. Starting with a high return on assets should yield a high return on investment and hence on equity. Some analysts calculate a *financial leverage index* equal to the return on equity divided by the return on assets.

Think back to the fundamental equation that assets equal liabilities plus owners' equity (A = L + OE). The three measures of return can be decomposed in terms of the fundamental equation. Return measures express an income statement figure divided by one of the following balance sheet concepts: (a) owners' equity (return on equity or ROE); (b) owners' equity plus long-term liabilities (return on investment or ROI); and (c) owners' equity plus long-term liabilities plus current liabilities which, given the fundamental equation, is equivalent to total assets (so return on assets or ROA).

Summary and Integration. If return on equity is an ultimate performance measure, note that the other analytics drive it. For example, the faster a company turns over its assets, the higher its return on equity will be. So higher inventory and receivables turns drive higher returns on equity. Likewise, higher profit margins drive higher returns on equity as they express how much of every sales dollar turns into profit. Finally, the more debt compared to equity is used the higher the return on equity will be (subject of course to risks of overleveraging that prevent a company from repaying debt when due).

Other Measures. The ratios discussed above are just some of the leading methods employed to analyze financial statements. Some can be calculated or approached in slightly different ways than set forth above. For example, an entity's ratio of interest expense (or all fixed charges) to gross revenues may be helpful in evaluating its debt capacity. The amount of an entity's annual depreciation expense also may be of interest in evaluating its future needs for capital expenditures. These are all potentially helpful tools that will be more or less significant depending on the purpose for which analysis is made.

For that matter, all these income statement ratios are driven by reported earnings, and a whole set of analogous ratios can be developed and applied to learn about an entity from its statement of cash flows. A user of financial statements can learn a lot from conducting a rigorous ratio analysis of those statements along the lines suggested above. But often that analysis raises as many questions as it answers. In light of this, federal securities laws require that financial statements of public companies be accompanied by a narrative discussion and analysis of trends management sees the financial statements to reveal (or to obscure). That narrative is called the Management's Discussion and Analysis ("MD&A").

F. Exercise

1. What is the ultimate effect on the Acme Balance Sheet of each of the following transactions?[1] Consider each transaction separately.

   a. Acme buys a parcel of land for $20,000 cash.

   b. Acme borrows $20,000, payable in 3 years at 8% interest, to buy a parcel of land.

   c. Acme collects $5,000 of accounts receivables.

   d. Acme buys $10,000 of inventory on credit, with the total amount payable in 6 months.

   e. Acme pays off $5,000 of a note due in 180 days.

2. What is the amount of each of the following and what does each tell you about Acme?

   a. working capital.

   b. current ratio.

   c. quick ratio.

   d. debt/equity ratio.

   e. profit margin.

   f. interest coverage ratio.

   g. earnings per share.

   h. return on equity.

   i. return on assets.

   j. return on investment.

G. Auditing

A corporation's management prepares its financial statements in accordance with applicable accounting principles. Publicly-held corporations are required to engage an independent accounting firm to audit these financial statements (and many other corporations choose to do so). The independent accountant conducts an audit of the financial statements. This exercise is designed to provide reasonable assurance that the financial statements fairly present the corporation's financial condition and results of operations and cash flows, in conformity with generally accepted accounting principles. An audit of the corporation's internal control over financial reporting is also required for publicly-held corporations to determine whether these systems and

---

1. The balance sheet is a financial statement that periodically summarizes a company's financial condition. Individual transactions are recorded in a company's books as the transactions occur. At the end of the reporting period, the results of those transactions are summarized on the balance sheet. Nevertheless, considering the way a particular transaction will ultimately affect the balance sheet helps one understand the interrelationships among balance sheet entries.

processes are effective in assuring conformity with applicable accounting principles, the corporation's managerial policies and federal securities laws.

The audit function can be a pivotal component of corporate governance for many corporations. The Sarbanes-Oxley Act of 2002 makes this role clear in its numerous provisions addressing the relationship between independent auditors and board audit committees. For example, it requires that outside auditors provide various reports to board audit committees. First, auditors must report to the committee all critical accounting policies and practices. Second, auditors must report to the audit committee all alternative accounting treatments of financial information they discussed with management, the implication of the choices, and which the auditor prefers. Third, auditors must share with audit committees all material written communications between the auditor and management.

The audit function's effectiveness requires that auditors be independent of corporations they audit and of corporate management. The Sarbanes-Oxley Act also addresses independence requirements. First, no audit firm is independent if certain corporation executive, financial or accounting officers worked there and on that corporation's audit within the year before the start of the audit service in question. Second, corporate officers and directors or their agents are forbidden to fraudulently influence, coerce, manipulate, or mislead any accountant auditing the company's financial statements. Third, auditors must rotate lead and reviewing partners so that neither role is performed by the same accountant for the same corporation for more than five consecutive years.

Auditor independence is strongly influenced by what role auditors assume for their clients in addition to certifying financial statements. Under Sarbanes-Oxley, auditors in no event may perform any of the following services for audit clients: bookkeeping; financial information systems; appraisal, valuation or fairness opinions; actuarial; internal audit; human resources; broker/dealer, investment adviser or investment banking services; or legal and expert services. Expressly permitted are comfort letters relating to securities underwriting. Unaddressed are compliance and tax services. Audit committees must pre-approve all services, including comfort letters, performed by outside auditors and disclose them in regular periodic reports. The committee can delegate this authority to members who are independent directors.

Table of Cases

Index

[References are to sections.]

T